Illustrator® 10
Bible

Illustrator® 10
Bible

Ted Alspach and Kelly Murdock
Foreword by Pierre E. Bézier

Hungry Minds™

Best-Selling Books • Digital Downloads • e-Books • Answer Networks • e-Newsletters • Branded Web Sites • e-Learning

New York, NY✦ Cleveland, OH ✦ Indianapolis, IN

Illustrator® 10 Bible

Published by
Hungry Minds, Inc.

909 Third Avenue
New York, NY 10022
www.hungryminds.com

Library of Congress Control Number: 2001099727

ISBN: 0-7645-3658-3

Printed in the United States of America

10 9 8 7 6 5 4 3 2

1B/RR/QS/QS/IN

Distributed in the United States by Hungry Minds, Inc.

Distributed by CDG Books Canada Inc. for Canada; by Transworld Publishers Limited in the United Kingdom; by IDG Norge Books for Norway; by IDG Sweden Books for Sweden; by IDG Books Australia Publishing Corporation Pty. Ltd. for Australia and New Zealand; by TransQuest Publishers Pte Ltd. for Singapore, Malaysia, Thailand, Indonesia, and Hong Kong; by Gotop Information Inc. for Taiwan; by ICG Muse, Inc. for Japan; by Intersoft for South Africa; by Eyrolles for France; by International Thomson Publishing for Germany, Austria, and Switzerland; by Distribuidora Cuspide for Argentina; by LR International for Brazil; by Galileo Libros for Chile; by Ediciones ZETA S.C.R. Ltda. for Peru; by WS Computer Publishing Corporation, Inc., for the Philippines; by Contemporanea de Ediciones for Venezuela; by Express Computer Distributors for the Caribbean and West Indies; by Micronesia Media Distributor, Inc. for Micronesia; by Chips Computadoras S.A. de C.V. for Mexico; by Editorial Norma de Panama S.A. for Panama; by American Bookshops for Finland.

For general information on Hungry Minds' books in the U.S., please call our Consumer Customer Service department at 800-762-2974. For reseller information, including discounts and premium sales, please call our Reseller Customer Service department at 800-434-3422.

For information on where to purchase Hungry Minds' books outside the U.S., please contact our International Sales department at 317-572-3993 or fax 317-572-4002.

For consumer information on foreign language translations, please contact our Customer Service department at 800-434-3422, fax 317-572-4002, or e-mail rights@idgbooks.com.

For information on licensing foreign or domestic rights, please phone +1-650-653-7098.

For sales inquiries and special prices for bulk quantities, please contact our Order Services department at 800-434-3422 or write to the address above.

For information on using Hungry Minds' books in the classroom or for ordering examination copies, please contact our Educational Sales department at 800-434-2086 or fax 317-572-4005.

For press review copies, author interviews, or other publicity information, please contact our Public Relations department at 650-653-7000 or fax 650-653-7500.

For authorization to photocopy items for corporate, personal, or educational use, please contact Copyright Clearance Center, 222 Rosewood Drive, Danvers, MA 01923, or fax 978-750-4470.

Hungry Minds™ is a trademark of Hungry Minds, Inc.

Credits

Acquisitions Editor
Tom Heine

Project Editors
Kenyon Brown
Rev Mengle

Technical Editor
Dennis Cohen

Copy Editor
Kenyon Brown

Project Coordinator
Regina Snyder

Graphics and Production Specialists
Beth Brooks
Sean Decker
Melanie DesJardins
Joyce Haughey
LeAndra Johnson
Gabriele McCann
Betty Schulte
Ron Terry
Erin Zeltner

Quality Control Technicians
Laura Albert
John Greenough
Andy Hollandbeck
Carl Pierce
Marianne Santy

Proofreading and Indexing
TECHBOOKS Production Services

About the Author

Ted Alspach is the Illustrator Product Manager at Adobe Systems. He is the author of many books on desktop publishing and graphics, as well as hundreds of articles on related topics, including *Illustrator 7 Studio Secrets*, *Illustrator 7 Bible*, *Photoshop Complete*, *Kai's Power Tools Studio Secrets*, and *Illustrator Filter Finesse*. He is also a contributing editor to *Adobe Magazine*.

Kelly Murdock has written extensively on graphics and Web technologies. His credits include the *Adobe Atmosphere Bible*, *3ds max 4 Bible*, *3D Studio Max R3 Bible*, *Master HTML and XHTML Visually*, *JavaScript Blueprints*, and *3D Graphics and VRML 2*. He is also the creative force behind the children's education site at www.animabets.com.

Foreword

Around 1960, engineers and technicians in the European car industry were divided into two groups: those who worked on mechanical parts and those who worked on car body parts.

For the mechanical group, the surfaces that could be manufactured were clearly defined with dimensions and limits — there was no place for haggling or bargaining at inspection time, and the verdict was simple: GOOD or SCRAP.

For the body-design group, things were far from being simple. From the stylist's small-scale mock-up to the full-scale drawing of the "skin," to the clay model, to the final drawing, to the master model, to the stamping tools — each rendering was supposed to be in accordance with the preceding one. Designers used French curves, sweeps, and lathes (plastic splines), but small discrepancies could not be avoided at each step. These minor errors added up, to the detriment of the final product.

Although these problems had been experienced for decades, people were not satisfied and still looked for a solution. They believed, as Plato said, that "Number is the expression of everything" and, as Lord William Kelvin said, that "No one can claim to have mastered a phenomenon as long as he has not been able to express it with figures."

By 1960, a small number of people believed that the computer could provide an acceptable solution to the problem of discrepancies in measurements. The aircraft industry was probably the first industry in the United States to use computers, but the automotive industry rapidly followed suit.

At this time, two solutions were considered. The first solution was to keep the general process of manufacturing and, with the help of computers (CRT or numerically controlled machine tools), improve one or two steps. The second solution was to forget the existing scheme and start from scratch to take full advantage of the computer's capabilities. This step entailed greater risks but also had greater advantages.

For those who chose the latter solution, the first task was to build a list of requirements that included the following:

✦ Creating or adopting a mathematical system that could be easily understood and operated by draftsmen, designers, and methods people. The system needed to describe space curves — not only conics and surfaces — and to provide an accurate, complete, and distortion-free definition of the curves. It needed to be easily transmitted between offices, shops, and subcontractors.

✦ Providing the body- and tool-drawing offices with full-scale drawing machines, controlled completely by computers that worked in interactive mode, such as those capable of tracing curves at a speed of one foot per second.

✦ Equipping the drawing offices, not the tool shops, with rapid milling machines that could carve large portions of a car—the top, the hood, and so on—in a soft material, such as Styrofoam, urethane foam, or plaster.

✦ Devising the relevant software.

✦ Equipping the tool shops with heavy numerical control (NC) milling machines for manufacturing stamping units.

In 1960, the mathematical theory was based on the use of conics—nonrational polynomials with vector coefficients. Mathematical theory now includes B-splines and NURBS, but mathematicians still search for other solutions.

By the end of the 1960s, some simple systems were functioning, but a complete system was not fully operative until the end of the 1970s. Since that time, many basic improvements in car design have been developed, including color, reflection lines, perspective viewing, animation, finite elements, crash simulation, aerodynamics, stress and strain, vibration and noise, and so on.

No doubt, the advent of CAD/CAM has been one of the most important changes that took place in the automotive industry during the present century. Of course, it is not necessary for the lay user to master the complete theory—one can play basketball without referring to Galileo, Newton, Keppler, or Einstein—but students and engineers who take part in the development or improvement of a system will find plenty of food for thought in this book.

Pierre E. Bézier

Pierre Bézier was the creator of Bézier curves, a unique mathematical system used for defining curves. Bézier curves were adopted by Adobe when the company created the PostScript page-description language. Illustrator is very much a "front end" for PostScript, and the software would undoubtedly be quite different today were it not for Bézier's (unknown at the time) contribution. Pierre Bézier passed away recently, at the age of 89. We mourn his loss.

Preface

You are holding in your hands the biggest, most thorough, and most helpful guide to Adobe Illustrator you'll find anywhere.

Gives you a bit of a rush, doesn't it?

This is the fifth edition of the best-selling *Illustrator Bible,* the first book I had ever written, and still my favorite (well, I'm also partial to the original version of *The Stand*, but Mr. King probably won't let me take credit for that . . . especially because I was only about nine when I first read it).

The *Illustrator Bible* is the book I wrote because I couldn't find the book I wanted about Adobe Illustrator. Now I have it, and believe it or not, I'm constantly using my own book as a reference. I'd love to tell the world, "sure, I know that," without putting them on hold while I search my own index for the "Reset Tracking to 0" Mac key command (⌘+Shift+X, by the way). There's just too much about Illustrator for any one person to keep in his or her head at one time; now, this latest edition of the book gathers all the Illustrator information you can't remember and makes it more available and easier to follow than the plot twists on your favorite soap opera.

If you're at your local bookstore looking at the different Illustrator books to choose from, don't just pick this one because it weighs the most (sorry about that . . . I get more thank-you letters from chiropractors who've stayed in business because of this monstrosity . . .) or because it works great as a booster seat for your two-year-old nephew. Instead, take a look-see through these pages, which are stuffed to over-flowing with in-depth Illustrator information that you just won't find anywhere else.

What's New in This Edition

Illustrator has once again gone through a serious makeover with version 10. So has this book. I've reorganized the chapters into a leaner, meaner book. Okay, it's not any leaner, but it is meaner, in a good way.

Illustrator 10 has added many very cool new features as well as revamping some of the old standby tools. In this edition, you'll find complete coverage of the new tools and features and extensive explanations on how these new features work. Adobe has enhanced some of the drawing tools to our delight. They have paid attention to user comments and given us what we want.

There's stunning new art in the color section, as well as a handy Pantone color reference chart for process-based Pantone colors, making the color section more of a tool than you'll find in any other similar color pages.

This edition also includes another feature that hasn't appeared in any of the previous editions — a coauthor, Kelly Murdock. Adobe has considered me a valuable asset to the product and felt I could do more good for the product in-house as the Illustrator product manager. I think this move was simply to shut me up, but it won't work of course. I'm still going to push the software to its limits. Ha, ha, the power.

When I asked the Hungry Minds' editors to find an expert to help me complete this edition, they brought Kelly Murdock into the picture. Kelly has an engineering degree and has studied all the math behind Bézier curves and splines. He also has a passion for computer graphics. Perhaps most important, Kelly has extensive experience with the Web. This experience is especially helpful because many of Illustrator 10's new features are designed to help create graphics for the Web.

You may be asking — where is the CD-ROM? Well, the secret is that this book doesn't have one. Because most of the demos typically included on the CD-ROM are available as downloads off the Web, the demos included on the CD-ROM quickly become outdated. The publisher decided that you would rather have a reduction in price than a CD-ROM of outdated content that you can easily get elsewhere. If you don't like this decision, just let them know and we can probably get the CD-ROM back in future editions.

Is This the Illustrator Book for You?

We've been to bookstores. We've seen the other Illustrator books out there. Some of them are quite good. Some of them are fairly awful. But none of them can match the *Illustrator 10 Bible* for thoroughness, usefulness, or completeness. We've left no vector-based stone unturned.

Here are more reasons the *Illustrator 10 Bible* is the best overall book on Illustrator:

+ **The most complete coverage of Illustrator.** This book isn't big because we wanted to hog all of the retail book space to myself (of course, that's not a bad idea) but because we've tried to include every possible thing you'd ever want to know about Illustrator. From learning the basics of drawing to creating outstanding special effects with vectors and rasters, it's all here.

+ **Fun, original, different artwork to illustrate the techniques and capabilities of Illustrator.** When we say different, we're not talking about the type of "art" where there's a naked guy in a room sitting on a stool reciting the first few lines of the Declaration of Independence over and over and over again (that's supposedly "performance art," heh), but instead, we mean that each technique is created with a different piece of artwork. Some of it is simple and some of it is complex, with each piece showing not only a particular feature but other Illustrator capabilities as well.

✦ **Clean artwork without those annoying jaggies.** This is vector software. When you think of vectors, you probably think of smooth, flowing paths that don't look like someone filled in a bunch of squares on a sheet of graph paper. So instead of using screen shots for paths shown in this book, each path was painstakingly drawn in Illustrator. We think you'll appreciate the difference.

✦ **Top-notch technical prowess.** Once again, the *Illustrator 10 Bible* has gotten the best possible people to do a technical review of the book. Previous editions were technically reviewed by Eric Gibson, the lead technical support engineer for Illustrator, and Andrei Herasimchuk, who designed and implemented the Illustrator 7 interface and was behind such useful new features as the visible transformation origin point. This edition was tech-edited by Dennis Cohen, a long-time Illustrator user with a degree in design, a critical eye, and years of advanced design work.

✦ **Perfect for teaching.** If you know Illustrator inside and out, you'll find the *Illustrator 10 Bible* the best teaching tool available for Illustrator, with examples and explanations that complement a teaching environment perfectly. Many computer training companies teaching Illustrator use this book, as do schools and universities.

✦ **Real-world examples and advice.** Illustrator doesn't exist in a vacuum. Instead, it is often used in conjunction with other programs, in a variety of different environments and situations. Some people use Illustrator to create logos, others create full-page advertisements, and still others create entire billboards with Illustrator. Throughout this book, we present various real-world situations and examples that truly add to your understanding of each topic.

You don't need to be an artist or a computer geek to learn Illustrator with this book. No matter what your level of Illustrator experience — from the person who calls tech support for help getting the #$@&#!! shrink-wrap off the box to the person who puts the frustrated party on hold at Adobe — you'll undoubtedly find new things to try, and learn more about Illustrator along the way.

How to Get the Most Out of This Book

You may want to be aware of a few matters before you dive too deeply into the mysteries of vector-based graphics, Adobe style:

✦ **Versions.** When you see the word Illustrator, it refers to all versions of Illustrator. When we stick a number after the word Illustrator, it's relevant to that version only. Version numbers in the software industry change faster than time slots for *Frasier*, so version 10.0 may become version 10.0.1, 10.1, 10.2, or some other number before you know it. When we're talking about version 10, we'll be referring to 10.*x*, where *x* is any number at all. When Adobe releases version 11 or the next major upgrade, look for a new version of this book to help you through it.

◆ **Menu and keyboard commands.** To indicate that you need to choose a command from a menu, we write something like MenuName ➪ Command. For instance, File ➪ Save. If a command is nested in a submenu, it is presented as MenuName ➪ Submenu ➪ Command, as in Filter ➪ Distort ➪ Roughen. If a command has a keyboard command, we mention that as well for both Macintosh and Windows versions. For instance, Save uses "Command+S" on the Mac, which we'll present as ⌘+S (⌘ corresponds to the ⌘ symbol on your keyboard). The other Mac keys are spelled out — Option, Shift, Control, and so forth. Save uses "Ctrl+S" in Windows (corresponds to the Ctrl key on the Windows keyboard).

◆ **This is not a novel.** As much as we'd like you to discover plot intricacies, subtle characterizations, and moral fabric woven into the story, none of those things exist in this book (if they do, be sure to let us know about them). You can use this book in two really good ways:

1. Look up what you're interested in the Contents or the Index, and refer to that section. Rinse and repeat as necessary.

2. Slowly, calmly work your way through the entire book, trying out examples (the funky Steps that are almost everywhere) and techniques as you run across them. The book is designed to be read this way, each chapter building on the previous chapter.

◆ **Have fun.** This book is a pretty straightforward, serious tome, although we have managed to include many bad puns ("rotate the image as far as you're inclined to") and terrible jokes: How many FreeHand users does it take to draw a light bulb? Three. One at the computer, one on hold to Macromedia tech support, and the other back at the computer store, trying to exchange the software for Illustrator. Of course, we show you how to draw a realistic-looking light bulb in Chapter 11, "Using Path Blends, Compound Paths, and Masks."

What's a Computer Book Without Icons?

Nonexistent, for the most part. We've included several icons throughout this edition that may make reading this book a little more enjoyable and helpful.

These icons indicate some sort of power-user secret you absolutely need to know to be able to illustrate with the big kids.

Did you know that the third edition of this book was the best-selling book on Illustrator 7? Interesting tidbits such as this one are noted by this icon. Sort of like having Cliff from *Cheers* rambling on about something every few pages. Slightly interesting, but they won't increase your Illustrator skills. Just something we thought you might want to know.

Danger Will Robinson!!! If Robby the Robot used Illustrator, he'd be reading about all the nasty things that can happen and how to avoid them.

These icons indicate what's brand new in version 10 of Illustrator. Kind of like finding a prize in your cereal box.

 These icons point you to other places in the book where you can find more information on a given topic. If you're bored, you can play of game of jumping from one cross reference to another and see if you can make it back to where you started.

What's Inside the Book

Here's a brief rundown on what to expect in the *Illustrator 10 Bible*:

✦ **Part I: Illustrator Basics.** This section has us pointing out all the funky elements of the cool Illustrator interface (can you say palettes a plenty) and how to work with documents (you know, the open, close and save stuff). It also covers the basics of drawing, painting and working with objects. You learn how to color things, how to uncolor things, and how to delete those things when you don't like their color.

✦ **Part II: Putting Illustrator to Work.** This section puts you to work learning about type and how to fine-tune those paths and objects you drew in Part I. It also gives you a chance to bend and distort paths. Part II also contains a healthy dose of the hard stuff — such as compound paths, masks, blends, patterns, and type.

✦ **Part III: Mastering Illustrator.** This is the section that contains the nitty-gritty — and we don't mean the dirt band. Hot topics such as using Illustrator styles, effects, filters, and techniques for creating fantastic graphics are presented. This section includes several newer features such as transparency and working with raster images. We even show you how to customize Illustrator to work better and faster.

✦ **Part IV: Outputting Illustrator.** This section describes the ways to get stuff out of Illustrator. Artwork can leave to go to the print world, or go on an all-expenses paid trip to the Web.

✦ **Appendixes.** The four appendixes contain information on installing Illustrator, what's new in Illustrator 10, shortcuts, and Illustrator resources.

Help Make Illustrator Better

Okay, you know by now that we just love Illustrator. But the program can always be made more user-friendly, more functional, and just plain better. If you have such an idea, please send an e-mail to suggestions@adobe.com.

Adobe does listen to its users, and the more readers that ask for a feature, the more likely that feature will get into a future version of Illustrator. The Illustrator product managers, including me, are eager for any and all suggestions.

—Ted Alspach

Acknowledgments

Whew. As we write these acknowledgments, we're just about finished with the total revamping of this gigantic book. And while we're just plain exhausted, we know we'd be much more tired if it were not for the help and support of several key people. This list is by no means exhaustive, but the individuals named here are the ones most responsible for getting this book out the door.

Jennifer Alspach took it upon herself to make sure this book was up to date and as accurate as possible.

Angie, Eric, and Thomas Murdock were a great support and we know we couldn't get anything done without their help. We also thank Chris Murdock for his work on the Animabets characters and to Dennis Cohen for tech editing the book.

Tom Heine at Hungry Minds is always a great support to have on our side. Thanks to Kenyon Brown, who led the project to its glorious completion.

We also acknowledge all the great artists who contributed images for the color insert sections including Cole Gerst, Andreas Seidel, Joe Jones, Nicole Weedon and Jean-Paul Leonard at Angry Monkey, Joe Barsin, and Chris Spollen. An extra thanks goes out to Joe Jones for contributing an additional sidebar.

Contents at a Glance

Contents

Part II: Putting Illustrator to Work 273

Chapter 11: Using Path Blends, Compound Paths, and Masks . . . 505

Part IV: Outputting Illustrator   689

Chapter 16: Understanding Printing, Separations, and Trapping . . 691

Illustrator Basics

Where do you start with Illustrator? Part I has us pointing out all the funky elements of the cool Illustrator interface (can you say palettes a plenty) and how to work with documents (you know, the open, close and save stuff). This part also covers the basics of drawing, painting, and working with objects. You learn how to color things, how to un-color things, and how to delete those things when you don't like their color.

Learning the Illustrator Interface

Not too long ago, commercial artists and illustrators worked by hand, not on computers. It might seem hard to believe, but they spent hours and hours with T-squares, rulers, French curves, and type galleys from their local typesetters.

Now, of course, most artists and artist wannabes spend hours and hours with their computers, mouses (or should that be mice?), monitors, and onscreen type that they set themselves. Some traditional artists are still out there, of course, but more and more make the transition to the digital world every day.

Once that transition is accomplished, computer artists usually come face-to-face with Illustrator, the industry-standard, graphics-creation software for both print and the Web. The following is a typical example of how people get to know Illustrator.

Picasso Meets Illustrator: Getting Started

Illustrator arrives and the enthusiastic artist-to-be — we'll call him Picasso — opens the box, pops in the CD-ROM, and installs the product, while glancing at the quick reference card and thumbing through the manual. A few minutes later Picasso launches Illustrator and is faced with a clean, brand new, empty document. A world of possibilities awaits, only a few mouse clicks away. But Picasso is a little intimidated by all that white space, just as many budding young writers wince at a new word processing document with the lone insertion point blinking away.

So, Picasso decides he'll "play" with the software before designing anything "for real." He chooses the rectangle tool first, clicks, drags, and voilà! A rectangle appears on the screen! His confidence soars. He may try the other shape tools next, but sooner or later Picasso starts playing with some of the software's other features. Eventually, he eyes the dreaded Pen tool. And thus starts his downward spiral into terror.

Confusion ensues. Hours of staring at an Illustrator document and wondering "Why?" take up the majority of his time. Picasso doesn't really understand fills and strokes, he doesn't understand stacking order and layers, and he certainly doesn't understand Bézier curves.

Even Picasso's painting-factory boss can't help him much with Illustrator; questions result in a knowing nod and the customary tilt and swivel of his head toward the Illustrator manual. Picasso goes through the tutorial three times, but whenever he strays one iota from the set-in-stone printed steps, nothing works. Picasso becomes convinced that the Pen tool is Satan's pitchfork in disguise. Patterns make about as much sense as differential equations. Then he encounters things such as effects that can be edited later (huh?), miter limits for strokes (yeah, right), and the difference between targeting a group or all the objects in that group (huh? again). All are subjects that might as well have been written about in a third-century Chinese dialect, such as the hard-to-find *Chinese Book of Patterns*.

Picasso had never used or seen software as *different* as Illustrator.

Ah, but you have an advantage over Picasso. You have this book. The following sections in this chapter start with an overview of the user interface and all the different controls that will enable you to do great things. The remaining chapters in this part will focus on the basics of Illustrator, including topics that range from setting up a new document to understanding exactly what paths are and how Illustrator uses them.

Getting started with Illustrator

The first step in getting started is to install the software. Appendix D, "Installing Illustrator," helps you with this process, which is slightly different depending on the type of computer you are using. Once installed, you can launch Illustrator in one of the following ways:

✦ Double-click its application icon

✦ Double-click an Illustrator document

✦ In Windows, choose Start ➪ Programs ➪ Adobe Illustrator

Who's the Model on the Adobe Illustrator Box?

The woman that adorns the Adobe Illustrator box is Venus, goddess of love, from Sandro Bottecelli's *Birth of Venus* painting. A portion of the painting, shown in the following figure, appears as the program is installed, when Illustrator launches, and in the Help ⇨ About Illustrator dialog box. It is also included at the top of the Toolbox in case you get lonely.

Sandro Bottecelli's *Birth of Venus*

Venus has graced each and every Illustrator package since Illustrator 1, released back in 1987. With Illustrator 9 came the introduction of the first all-vector replication of Venus and Illustrator 10's version is even more realistic. Earlier versions of Illustrator included a raster version of Venus. She's the official Illustrator "mascot," gracing not only boxes but user guides, splash screens, and icons as well. A good-sized print of Bottecelli's painting hangs in a hallway in the middle of the Illustrator engineering team's offices at Adobe Systems headquarters in San Jose, California. Bottecelli would be proud.

Quitting Illustrator

End your Illustrator session at any time by choosing File ⇨ Quit (or Exit). This action closes the current document (you'll be prompted to save it if it hasn't been saved) and exits the application. Window users can also close Illustrator by right clicking on the program's task bar icon and choosing Close (or by pressing Alt + F4) from the pop-up menu. Mac OS X users can click and hold (or ⌘+click) on the Illustrator icon in the dock and choose quit from the menu that appears.

Note   For Mac OS X, the Quit menu is under the Illustrator menu.

If you run into a situation in which the Quit function doesn't work, or is unavailable, Mac OS 9 users can press ⌘+Option+Esc, Mac OS X users can hold down the Option key while ⌘+clicking on the dock and selecting the Quit changes to Force Quit (or users choose the Force Quit option from the Application menu and select Illustrator from the Force Quit dialog box) and Windows users can press Ctrl+Alt+Delete to "force" Illustrator to quit. However, doing so may cause you to lose your work and may make your system unstable; if you do this, you'll be better off if you take the time to restart your computer before running Illustrator again (or before opening any other software applications, for that matter). Restarting isn't necessary for Mac OS X users.

Note   One of the most likely reasons that Illustrator becomes unstable is due to a lack of memory. If the computer on which you are running Illustrator doesn't have enough memory, then working on large complex images will cause the interface to respond slowly, and if many other programs are open at the same time, Illustrator may quit responding.

Using the User Interface Elements

Before you can create amazing illustrations using Illustrator, you'll need to learn the tools and controls of Illustrator's user interface. If you've used other Adobe products such as Photoshop or InDesign, the user interface should look familiar. Adobe has made user interface elements consistent across their product line. Adobe's main products, including Illustrator, Photoshop, InDesign, PageMaker, Premiere, Dimensions, and Streamline, all have a fairly consistent interface that includes menus, palettes, and dialog boxes. Adobe listened carefully to its users and has made certain that the Illustrator environment is very similar to that of the other software products its users typically use. This gives Photoshop users a headstart into understanding and using Illustrator and vice versa.

The Illustrator user interface includes many unique elements that hold a lot of power. As you learn to use these elements, you'll discover many shortcuts to accomplish certain tasks. The Illustrator elements, shown in Figure 1-1, include the following:

✦ **Document Window:** The document window consists of the Artboard and the Pasteboard where the actual artwork will be displayed.

✦ **Toolbox:** This palette includes a set of common tools. Each tool is represented by an icon that can be selected by clicking on it.

✦ **Palettes:** These tabbed floating windows can be opened and closed as needed. They contain an assortment of controls and settings.

✦ **Menus:** At the top of the window are menus that open to submenus of options and commands.

✦ **Status Bar:** Along the lower left edge of the window is an area that displays information about the current state of the selected tool.

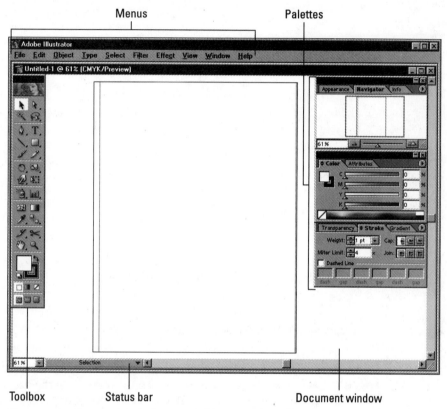

Figure 1-1: Illustrator includes many different user interface elements.

Working in the Document Window

The document window is where you perform all your work. It contains two main elements: the artboard and the page. The page (sometimes referred to as the pasteboard) is always centered in the artboard, as shown in Figure 1-2 and all the palettes have been closed in order to make the full document window visible. You can move the printable area represented by the dashed lines using the Page tool, which is explained later in this section.

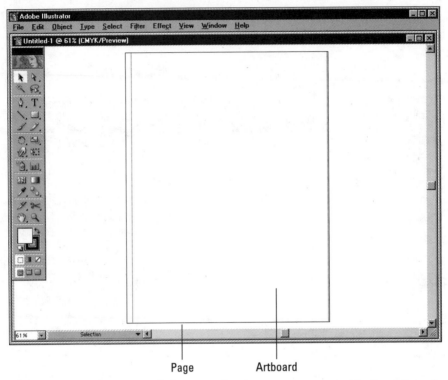

Page   Artboard

Figure 1-2: The document window contains the page, surrounded by the artboard.

Illustrator windows act like windows in most other programs. You use the title bar at the top of the window to move the window around your screen. On the title bar is the name of the document. If you have not yet saved your document, the name of the document is Untitled-1, with the number changing for each new document you create. (Hint: Save it as soon as you create it!) Next to the title of the document is the current viewing percentage relative to actual size.

The scroll bars on the right side of the window let you see what is above and below the current viewing area (see "Using the scroll bars to view your document," later in this chapter).

In Windows, the upper right corner of the document window includes three buttons — Minimize, Maximize and Close. In OS X, the Close, Minimize and Zoom buttons are on the left and in OS 9 or earlier, the Close button is on the left and the Zoom and Windowshade buttons are on the right. These buttons work exactly the same as the similar buttons on application window. In Windows, the Minimize button will display the document window as an icon along the bottom edge of the application window. Once minimized, a Restore button appears which will return the document window to its former size and position. In OS X, the document will change to an icon in the dock. In OS 9, the document will rollup until only the title bar is displayed.

The Maximize button in Windows will open the document window to the largest size that will fit in the application window. For Macs, the Zoom button will toggle the between its current size and the screen's maximum size. The Close button will close the window and offer a dialog box where you can save the current file if it hasn't been saved. Multiple document windows can be opened at the same time and the title of each open document window will be displayed at the bottom of the Window menu. A checkmark will appear in the Window menu next to the current active document window.

Although only one document window is active at a time, several document windows can be opened at a time. The Window menu includes a couple of commands that make it easy to see all the opened document windows. Window ⇨ Cascade will line up the title bars of all the opened document windows, Window ⇨ Tile will tile the opened document windows next to one another to fill the application window and Window ⇨ Arrange Icons will arrange all the minimized icons into neat rows. Figure 1-3 shows two document windows opened next to each other.

Caution The Cascade, Tile and Arrange Icons options are only available for Windows computers.

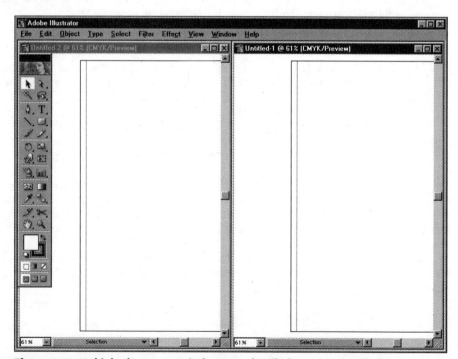

Figure 1-3: Multiple document windows can be tiled next to one another.

The artboard

The artboard is displayed in Illustrator using solid black lines and identifies the maximum printable area. This area can be different than the actual printed page, which is displayed as dotted lines. For example, you could have the page size set to letter-sized and the artboard set to a smaller section in the center of the page. When printing this document, only the art contained within the artboard will be printed.

The size, units and orientation of the artboard can be set using the Document Setup dialog box, which is opened using the File ⇨ Document Setup menu option. Conversely, the printed page size is set using the Page [Print] Setup dialog box also found in the File menu.

Tip   You'll typically want to keep the artboard and page size the same. To do this, just enable the Use Print Setup option in the Document Setup dialog box. This will change the artboard size and orientation to match the page setup.

Using the View menu, you can hide the artboard with the View ⇨ Hide Artboard menu option. Once hidden, this menu option changes to View Artboard. Double clicking on the Hand tool will quickly maximize the artboard within the Illustrator window.

If you are taking your Illustrator artwork into another application, such as Photoshop or QuarkXPress, the size of the artboard is irrelevant; your entire illustration appears in most other software applications even if that artwork is larger than the artboard.

The pasteboard

Probably the worst thing that can possibly happen when you are using Illustrator is for you to lose everything you've worked on. "Where'd it all go?" you cry, perhaps adding a few vulgarities. This can happen very easily in Illustrator. Just click a few times on the gray parts of the scroll bars at the bottom of the document window. Each time you click you're moving about half the width (or height) of your window, and three clicks later, your page and everything on it is no longer in front of you. Instead you see the pasteboard, usually a vast expanse of white nothingness.

The pasteboard measures 227.5×227.5 inches, which works out to around 360 square feet of drawing space. At actual size, you see only a very small section of the artboard. A little letter-size document looks extremely tiny on a pasteboard this big. If you get lost on the pasteboard, a quick way back is to choose View ⇨ Actual Size. This puts your page in the center of the window at 100-percent view, at which time you should be able to see at least part of your drawing. To see the whole page quickly, choose View ⇨ Fit in Window, which resizes the view down to where you can see the entire page.

This discussion assumes, of course, that you have actually drawn artwork on the defined page. We used to get frantic calls from people who would choose Fit in Window, resulting in the immediate disappearance of all their artwork. It took us a while to figure out that they had drawn their artwork way off on the side of the pasteboard.

The Page tool

The Page tool (found as a flyout to the Hand tool) changes how much of your document will print; it does this by moving the printable area of the document without moving any of the printable objects in the document. Clicking and dragging the lower-left corner of the page relocates the printable area of the page to the place where you release the mouse button.

Tip Double-clicking the Page tool slot resets the printable-area dotted line to its original position on the page.

The Page tool is useful when your document is larger than the biggest image area your printer can print. The tool enables you to tile several pages to create one large page out of several sheets of paper. *Tiling* is the process in which an image is assembled by using several pieces of paper arranged in a grid formation. A portion of the image is printed on each page, and when you fit the pages together you can view the image in its entirety. This is really only good for rough laser prints, as a quarter inch around the edge of each paper will need to be manually trimmed.

Cross-Reference Chapter 16, "Understanding Printing, Separations, and Trapping," further addresses issues related to printing and changing page sizes and printing areas.

The toolbox

The toolbox appears on top of your document window, covering up part of your document window in the upper-left corner. The toolbox (see Figure 1-4) has no close box; to close it you must choose Window ➪ Tools. If the Tools menu has a checkmark to its left, the toolbox is visible. If no checkmark exists, then the toolbox is hidden. You can also press the Tab key (which hides *all* palettes, not just the toolbox).

Tip You can show and hide all the palettes *except* the toolbox by pressing Shift+Tab.

To choose a tool, click the tool you want to use in its slot within the toolbox and release the mouse button. The background for the selected tool will be displayed white to highlight it. The selected tool will stay active until you select another tool. You can also choose tools by pressing a key on the keyboard; for instance, pressing P selects the Pen tool.

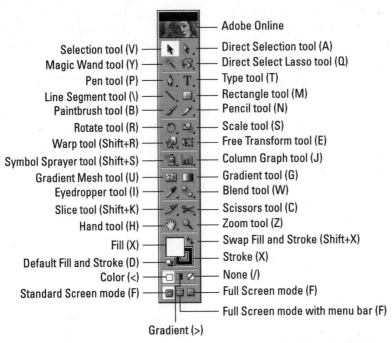

Selection tool (V) ——— Adobe Online

Selection tool (V) ——— Direct Selection tool (A)
Magic Wand tool (Y) ——— Direct Select Lasso tool (Q)
Pen tool (P) ——— Type tool (T)
Line Segment tool (\) ——— Rectangle tool (M)
Paintbrush tool (B) ——— Pencil tool (N)
Rotate tool (R) ——— Scale tool (S)
Warp tool (Shift+R) ——— Free Transform tool (E)
Symbol Sprayer tool (Shift+S) ——— Column Graph tool (J)
Gradient Mesh tool (U) ——— Gradient tool (G)
Eyedropper tool (I) ——— Blend tool (W)
Slice tool (Shift+K) ——— Scissors tool (C)
Hand tool (H) ——— Zoom tool (Z)
Fill (X) ——— Swap Fill and Stroke (Shift+X)
Default Fill and Stroke (D) ——— Stroke (X)
Color (<) ——— None (/)
Standard Screen mode (F) ——— Full Screen mode (F)
——— Full Screen mode with menu bar (F)
Gradient (>)

Figure 1-4: The toolbox in its initial (default) state, with all tools labeled. The letter that appears in parentheses after each tool is the key you can press to quickly access that tool.

Many tools have additional *pop-up tools* called flyouts, which are tools that appear only when you click and hold down the mouse on the default tool. The default tools that have pop-up tools are indicated by a little triangle in the lower-right corner of the tool. To select a pop-up tool, click and hold on a tool with a triangle until the pop-up tools appear; then drag to the pop-up tool you want. The new pop-up tool replaces the default tool in that tool slot. You can also browse through the tools by Option [Alt]+clicking a toolslot; each click displays the next tool. Figure 1-5 shows all the pop-up tools for each toolslot.

Any tool with a pop-up option also has a tearoff tab at the rightmost end of the flyout. If you click on this tearout tab, the flyout tools become a free-floating palette of tools. Figure 1-6 shows the Graph tools as a floating palette.

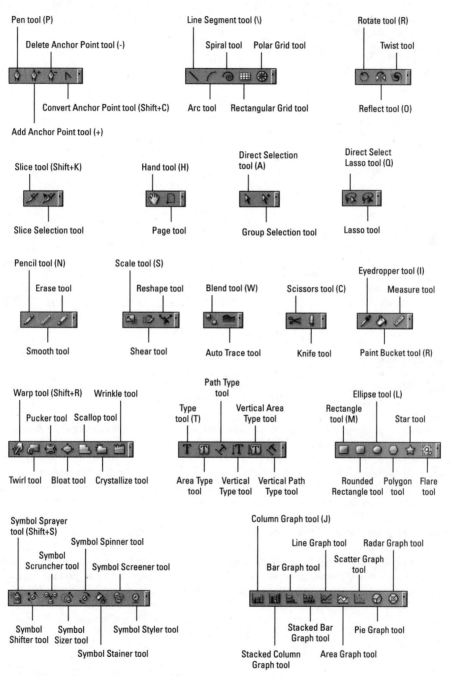

Figure 1-5: All the flyout tools in Illustrator

Figure 1-6: A free-floating palette of tearout tools

Tooltips

If you ever forget what a specific tool looks like or have trouble finding it, you simply need to stop and think about it for a second and maybe, just maybe, the answer will pop into your mind. Or it will pop onto the screen. Tooltips are pop-up text that appears next to the cursor if you leave it over the top of an interface element. For example, if you hold the mouse cursor over the Selection tool, the tip, "Selection Tool (V)" appears in a yellow box. The letter in parentheses is the keyboard shortcut for selecting this tool. Tooltips are available for all the tools in the toolbox and for all palette controls.

If you find that the tooltips are getting in the way and you are expert enough that you don't need them popping up every time you pause for a second, you can disable them with an option in the General screen of the Preferences dialog box. This dialog box can be opened using the Illustrator [Edit] ➪ Preferences ➪ General menu option.

Palettes

Illustrator has more than two dozen palettes, all of which can remain open while you work on your document (providing you can still see your document through all those palettes!). Technically speaking, a palette is a window. Everything on the Mac and in Windows is a window except the desktop. Movable modeless windows (palettes) are variations on windows.

Note   A modeless window is different than a dialog box in that it doesn't require the window to be closed before other operations can be performed. This lets you work with the settings in the palette without having to close the palette.

Palettes are like regular windows in many ways. They have a title bar that can be clicked and dragged to move the palette. Under the title bar is a tab that contains the name of the palette. A close button usually appears in the upper corner of the palette that you can use to hide the palette. The title bar also includes a button that toggles between Minimize and Maximize for Windows or a Zoom button for the Macintosh OS. This button will toggle between displaying only the palette title tab or the entire palette. You can also toggle between these two states by double-clicking the title tab. Figure 1-7 shows the Navigator palette.

Minimize/maximize toggle

Palette tab   Close

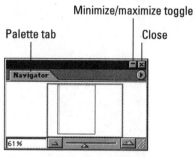

Figure 1-7: The Navigator palette

Occasionally, a manual resize box (which looks like three diagonal lines) appears in the lower-right corner for changing the palette's size. Any palette that has this resize box can be resized by dragging on the palette's edges or corners.

 For some palettes, a double arrow icon appears to the left of the title name. Clicking this icon toggles the palette size among several different sizes.

Unlike windows, palettes are never really active. Instead, the one you are working in is in the front, and if it has editable text fields, one is highlighted, or a blinking text cursor appears. To bring a palette to the forefront — that is, bring it into focus — simply click it anywhere. Palettes seldom have scroll bars, although the Layers palette is an exception.

Tabbing and docking palettes

Palettes can be linked together in different ways called *tabbing* and *docking*. Each palette (except for the toolbox) has a tab on it. Clicking the tab of a palette brings it to the front. Dragging a tab from one palette to another moves that palette into another palette. Dragging a tab out of a palette makes the palette separate from the previous palette. Figure 1-8 includes a "set" of palettes that have been tabbed together.

 The default installation of Illustrator includes many palettes that are tabbed together, but you can change them to fit your needs. For example, the Appearance, Navigator and Info palettes are tabbed together by default.

You can dock palettes together by dragging the tab of one palette to the bottom of another palette; when the bottom of the other palette darkens, releasing the mouse button "docks" the moved palette to the bottom of the other one. Then, when the other palette is moved, the docked palette moves with it. Figure 1-9 shows a "set" of palettes that have been docked together. To undock a palette, simple click on its tab and drag it away from the other palettes.

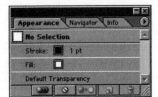

Figure 1-8: Several palettes have been tabbed together

Figure 1-9: A set of palettes that have been docked together

Showing and hiding palettes

The palettes are only helpful if you can access them and the Windows menu can be used to show or hide all the various palettes available in Illustrator. In addition to the palettes, you can use the Windows menu to show or hide the Toolbox, the library palettes, as well as any documents that are currently open. For all palette commands, the command will read "Show x palette" if the palette is hidden, and "Hide x palette" if the palette is visible. Many palettes have keyboard shortcuts that can be used to show them. These shortcuts are listed to the right of the palette option in the Windows menu.

ASK TOULOUSE: Moving Palettes

Kramer: When I start Illustrator, these tiny windows are everywhere.

Toulouse: Those are palettes.

Kramer: But I thought palettes are boards with daubs of paint of them.

Toulouse: Some Illustrator palettes hold colors, patterns and even styles.

Kramer: Oh, I've got plenty of style.

Toulouse: I'm sure you do.

Kramer: But, these palettes get in the way of my drawing space.

Toulouse: If you click and drag on the palette you can place it anywhere you want.

Kramer: Great! Now stay palette. Stay!

Toulouse: The palettes are very well behaved. They will stay where you put them even after you close and reopen Illustrator.

Kramer: Hey, that's okay.

The Windows menu will place a checkmark to the left of all the palettes that are currently open.

The various palettes

The content of the various palettes will be covered throughout the remainder of the chapters, but a summary of the available palettes is presented here and the keyboard shortcut, if available, will be listed in parentheses. They are listed as they appear in the Window menu alphabetically.

New Feature   Several of these palettes are new to Illustrator 10 including: Document Info, Flattening Preview, Magic Wand, Symbols, Type and Variables.

✦ **Actions palette:** The Actions palette can record a sequence of commands that can be replayed at any time.

✦ **Align palette (Shift + F7):** The Align palette provides functions for aligning objects in your document.

✦ **Appearance palette (Shift + F6):** The Appearance palette shows various attributes of the current object such as stroke weight and fill color.

✦ **Attributes palette (F11):** The Attributes palette contains settings such as Overprint options and a URL.

✦ **Brushes palette (F5):** The Brushes palette can be used to select a unique brush to paint with.

✦ **Color palette (F6):** The Color palette is used to apply color to objects.

✦ **Document Info palette:** The Document Info palette shows information about the current document such as its name, Color Profile and dimensions.

✦ **Gradient palette (F9):** The Gradient palette is used to modify gradient color and spacing. The Gradient palette also appears automatically when the Gradient tool is double-clicked.

✦ **Info palette (F8):** The Info palette shows information about the current selection. The Info palette appears automatically when the Measure tool is used.

✦ **Layers palette (F7):** The Layers palette can be used to organize artwork into independent layers.

✦ **Links palette:** The Links palette shows the embedded images that are linked to the current file.

✦ **Magic Wand palette:** The Magic Wand palette includes options for the Magic Wand tool.

✦ **Navigator palette:** The Navigator palette assists you in moving around your document.

✦ **Pathfinder palette (Shift + F9):** Pathfinder functions are used to control how paths interact with each other.

✦ **Stroke palette (F10):** The Strokes palette is used to apply and change strokes that are applied to paths.

✦ **Styles palette (Shift + F5):** The Styles palette organizes and applies styles to objects.

✦ **SVG Interactivity palette:** The SVG Interactivity palette lets you define interactive events that can be used with the Scalable Vector Graphics (SVG) format.

✦ **Swatches palette:** The Swatches palette contains preformatted gradients, colors, and patterns.

✦ **Symbols palette (Shift + F11):** The Symbols palette holds and organizes symbols.

✦ **Tools palette:** This is the toolbox that holds all the tools.

✦ **Transform palette (Shift + F8):** The Transform palette is used to make transformations (including move, scale, and rotate) to selected objects.

✦ **Transparency palette (Shift + F10):** The Transparency palette lets you set the opacity of the current object.

✦ **Type ⇨ Character palette (Ctrl + T):** The Type ⇨ Character palette sets the font and format for the selected characters.

✦ **Type ⇨ MM Design palette:** The Type ⇨ MM Design palette includes the setting for any Multi Master fonts installed on your system.

✦ **Type ⇨ Paragraph palette (Ctrl + M):** The Type ⇨ Paragraph palette sets the format for the selected paragraph.

✦ **Type ➪ Tab Ruler palette (Ctrl + Shift + T):** The Type ➪ Tab Ruler palette can be used to set tab breaks.

✦ **Variables palette:** The Variable palette includes an interface for defining data variables for data driven graphics.

Using Illustrator's menus

Menus are one of the most common interface elements for all software packages. Over time, Adobe has pushed a lot of their functionality to the palettes and other interface elements rather than the menus, but menus are still important and offer another way to work with the program. Some general rules apply to Illustrator menus:

✦ To select a menu item, pull down the menu, highlight the menu item you want, and release or click the mouse button (Macintosh) or click that item (Windows). If the cursor is not on that item, but it is still highlighted, the command will not take effect.

✦ Whenever an ellipsis appears (three little dots that look like this . . .), choosing that menu item brings up a dialog box where you must verify the current information by selecting an OK button, or enter more information and then select OK. If the option has no ellipsis, the action you select takes place right away.

✦ When you see a key command listed on the right side of the menu — usually the Command (⌘) symbol and a character for Macintosh or Ctrl plus a character for Windows, but sometimes the ⌘ symbol [Ctrl] or another modifier key plus a character — you can type that key command instead of using the mouse to pull down this menu. Using key commands for menu items works just like clicking the menu bar and pulling down to that item.

✦ If you see a little triangle next to a menu item, it means the menu has a submenu associated with it. You can choose items in the submenu by pulling over to the menu and then pulling up or down to select the menu item needed. Submenus usually appear on the right side of the menu, but due to space limitations on your monitor, they may appear on the left side for certain menus.

Palette menus

In addition to the main interface menus, many palettes have their own menus. In the upper right corner of many palettes is a round button with an arrow on it. This button will open a fly-away menu of palette options. Figure 1-10 shows the Color palette with its palette menu visible.

Tips for Using Menus Effectively

If you can never remember what is on which menu and you are constantly holding down the mouse button while slowly running along the menu bar, reading every menu item and looking for a certain command, you have a disease. Every year millions of people become afflicted with Menu Bar Scanning Syndrome (MBSS), defined as "the pathological need of users to continually search and hunt for special menu items that they just can't remember the locations of."

MBSS is a disease that can be treated fairly easily, but it wastes valuable production time, costing companies billions of dollars a year. Don't be surprised if the next time you flip to *60 Minutes*, Steve Kroft is doing an inside investigation into the mysteries of MBSS.

MBSS is deadly not only because it wastes time, but because the user is forced to read every single menu and pop-up menu. Sure, in the File menu you *know* that Document Setup is where to go to change the size of the page, but as you work your way over, things begin to get a little fuzzy. By the time you get to the Filter menu, your mind is mush. You see the Distort category and figure that all the submenu items are legal functions. If you can manage to get to the Windows menu, thewordswouldjustruntogether, making no sense whatsoever.

You can help prevent MBSS by doing one of two things:

✦ **Memorize what is in each menu.** This is the hardest thing to do, but a few hours spent memorizing each menu item and where it goes will eventually prevent countless MBSS-related searches. Make sentences out of the first letters of each menu item, if it helps. The File menu is either, "New, Open, Open Recent Files, Revert, Close, Save, Save As, Save a Copy, Save for Web, Place, Export, Preview AlterCast in Browser, Manage Workgroup, Scripts, Document Setup, Document Color Mode, File Info, Separation Setup, Print Setup, Print, Exit" or "Nine Old Odd Red Cats See Seven Severely Silly People Eating Purple Mashed Sour Damp Danish Flowered Soggy Pieces of Pruned Eggplant." (Yeah, yeah—you're not supposed to eat pruned eggplant when it's damp. That's why these seven people are *silly*.) Of course, having to learn a new crazy sentence like this every time a new version is released becomes more and more difficult as new commands are added.

✦ **Use the menus as little as possible.** Instead, memorize key commands. Most of the menu items have them, so you only need to go up to the menu bar when a menu item doesn't have a key command. If you set your own keyboard commands using the Keyboard Shortcuts command (choose Edit ➪ Keyboard Shortcuts), you can set a keyboard command for *every* menu item in Illustrator.

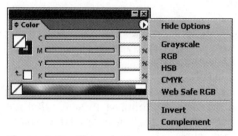

Figure 1-10: The palette menu offers additional options

Context-sensitive menus

Illustrator provides context-sensitive menus that appear right under your cursor as you're working. Control+click [right-click] with a cursor anywhere in the document window, and a context-sensitive menu appears. These menus contain commands that relate to the type of work you're doing and the specific tool you have. Figure 1-11 shows a context-sensitive menu that appears in a document when a rectangle shape is created and selected. This menu would look different if some other object were selected.

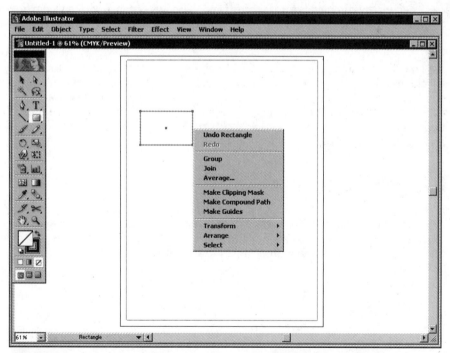

Figure 1-11: A context-sensitive menu appears by right-clicking in the document window.

Typing keyboard commands

Keyboard commands are shortcuts for common activities that you perform in Illustrator. These shortcuts typically use the ⌘ [Ctrl] key in combination with other keys.

Many of the Illustrator menu items have keyboard shortcuts listed next to their names. Pressing the key combination does the same thing as choosing that menu item from the menu. Some menu items do not have keyboard commands; usually, you have to choose those items from the menu.

On a Macintosh, common keys that are used with the ⌘ key are the Option key (located handily next to the ⌘ key) and the Shift key. The Control key is used only to simulate the right mouse button that Windows users have (OS X also supports a multi-button mouse). By default, no keyboard commands use the Control key, although you can assign them if you wish. You hold down these keys while you press another key or click the mouse to perform a specific function.

On a Windows system, the Ctrl key is used along with the Alt and Shift keys. If you press certain combinations of these keys while pressing another key or clicking the mouse, the related function activates.

In Appendix B, "Shortcuts in Illustrator 10," you can find a complete listing of the default key commands for Macintosh and Windows systems. You can learn how to make your own custom keyboard shortcuts in Chapter 15, "Customizing and Optimizing Illustrator."

Keyboard commands are as important to an Illustrator artist as the mouse is; with a little practice, you can learn them quickly. Besides, many of the default keyboard commands are the same from program to program, which will make you an instant expert in software that you haven't used yet! Good examples of this are the Cut/Copy/Paste set of commands (⌘+X, C, V [Ctrl+X, C, V]), Select All (⌘+A [Ctrl+A]), and Save (⌘+S [Ctrl+S]).

Using the status bar

In the lower-left corner is the status bar, which includes a Zoom drop-down list and a button that displays all sorts of neat information you just can't get anywhere else. The default is usually set to display the name of the current tool, but if you click on the status bar, you can select from the following options:

✦ **Current Tool:** Displays the name of the selected tool.

✦ **Date and Time:** Displays the current date and time.

✦ **Free Memory:** Displays a percentage and the amount of RAM that is free and available.

✦ **Number of Undos:** Displays the number of undos and redos that are queued.

✦ **Document Color Profile:** Displays the current Color Profile.

Mousing Around in Illustrator

Illustrator requires the use of a mouse for selecting items, pulling down menus, moving objects, and clicking buttons. Learning to use the mouse efficiently requires patience, practice, and persistence. In most programs, you can master using the mouse quickly, but using the mouse with Illustrator's Pen tool can be difficult at first. If you're unfamiliar with using a mouse, a fun way to get used to working with one is by playing a mouse-driven game. After several hours of play (providing you don't get fired by your employer or kicked out of the house by your irritated spouse), you'll become Master of Your Mousepad, King of Your Klicker, and so on.

The mouse is used to perform five basic functions in Illustrator:

✦ **Pointing**, which is moving the cursor around the screen by moving the mouse around your mousepad.

✦ **Clicking**, which is pressing and releasing the mouse button in one step. Clicking is used to select points, paths, and objects, and to make windows active. (Windows users: "Clicking" means clicking with the *left* mouse button, unless you've reconfigured your mouse.)

✦ **Dragging**, which is pressing the mouse button and keeping it pressed while you move the mouse. You drag the cursor to choose items from menus, select contiguous characters of text, move objects, and create marquees.

✦ **Double-clicking**, which is quickly pressing and releasing the mouse button twice in the same location. Double-clicking is used to select a word of text, select a text field with a value in it, access a dialog box for a tool, and run Illustrator (by double-clicking its icon).

✦ **Control+clicking [right-clicking]**, which displays a context-sensitive menu when you press Control and click on the Mac (Windows users only need to press the right mouse button).

The cursor is the little icon (usually an arrow) that moves in the same direction as the mouse. (If the cursor seems to be moving in the opposite direction from the mouse, check that the mouse isn't upside down, or, heaven forbid, that you aren't upside down yourself.) In Illustrator, the cursor often takes the form of a tool that you are using. When the computer is busy doing whatever a computer does when it is busy, an ugly little watch or a multicolored spinning circle (Macintosh) or hourglass (Windows) takes its place.

Navigating Around Your Document

Being able to move through a document easily is a key skill in Illustrator. Rarely can you fit an entire illustration in the document window at a sufficient magnification to see much of the image's detail. Usually you are zooming in, zooming out, or moving off to the side, above, or below to focus in on certain areas of the document.

Who's zoomin' who?

The most basic navigational concept in Illustrator is the ability to zoom to different magnification levels. Illustrator's magnification levels work like a magnifying glass. In the real world, you use a magnifying glass to see details that aren't readily visible without it. In the Illustrator world, you use the different magnification levels to see details that aren't readily visible at the 100-percent view.

Changing the magnification levels of Illustrator does not affect the illustration itself. If you zoom in to 200 percent and print, the illustration will still print at the same size as it would if the view were 100 percent. It will *not* print twice as large. Figure 1-12 shows the same Illustrator document at 100 and 200 percent magnification.

Figure 1-12: An Illustrator document at 100 percent (left) and 200 percent (right) magnifications

In Illustrator, 100 percent magnification means that the artwork you see on the screen has the same physical dimensions it will have when it prints. If you were to put a printout next to the onscreen image at 100 percent magnification, it would appear to be exactly the same size, depending on your monitor resolution (the higher the resolution, the smaller the document will look onscreen). If you're designing for the Web, 100 percent works correctly (the result will be at 100 percent as well), because the Save for Web feature automatically converts images to 72 ppi (the "standard" screen resolution for cross-platform viewing).

In Photoshop, 100-percent view is different from Illustrator. In Photoshop, each pixel onscreen is equal to one pixel in the image. Unless the pixels per inch (ppi) of the image match those of the screen (and they would if Web graphics were being designed), the 100-percent view tends to be larger than the printed dimensions of the image.

Using the Zoom tool

Perhaps the easiest way to control the magnification of your artwork is with the Zoom tool. This tool (which looks like a magnifying glass and is located in the right column of the Toolbox) can magnify a certain area of artwork and then return to the standard view.

To use the Zoom tool to magnify an area, select it in the toolbox by clicking it once. The Zoom cursor takes the place of the Arrow cursor (or whatever tool was previously selected). It looks like a magnifying glass with a plus sign in it. Clicking any spot in the illustration enlarges the illustration to the next magnification level, with the place you clicked centered on your screen. The highest magnification level is 6,400 percent — which, as all you math aficionados know, is 64 times (not 6,400 times!) bigger than the original.

Where you click with the Zoom tool is very important. Clicking the center of the window enlarges the illustration to the next magnification level, but the edges (top, bottom, left, and right) of the document (and possibly some or all of your artwork) will disappear as the magnification increases. Clicking the upper-right corner hides mostly the lower-left edges, and so forth. If you are interested in seeing a particular part of the document close up, click that part at each magnification level to ensure that it remains in the window.

If you zoom in too far, you can use the Zoom tool to zoom out again. To zoom out, press the Option [Alt] key when you have the Zoom tool active (releasing the Option [Alt] key restores the Zoom In tool). Clicking with the Zoom Out tool reduces the magnification level to the next lowest level. You can zoom out to 3.13 percent (1/32 actual size). When you hold down the Option [Alt] key the Zoom cursor displays a minus sign within the magnifying glass.

When you use the Zoom tool, you magnify everything in the document, not just the illustration. You magnify all paths, objects, the artboard, and the Page Setup boundaries equally. However, the way certain objects appear (the thickness of path selections, points, handles, gridlines, guides, and Illustrator user interface (UI) components such as palettes and windows) does not change when you zoom in.

If you need to zoom in to see a specific area in the document window, use the Zoom tool to draw a marquee (by clicking and dragging diagonally) around the objects that you want to magnify. The area thus will magnify as much as possible so that everything inside the box just fits in the window that you have open, as shown in Figure 1-13. Dragging a box while holding down the Option [Alt] key to zoom out does nothing special; it works the same as if you had just clicked to zoom out.

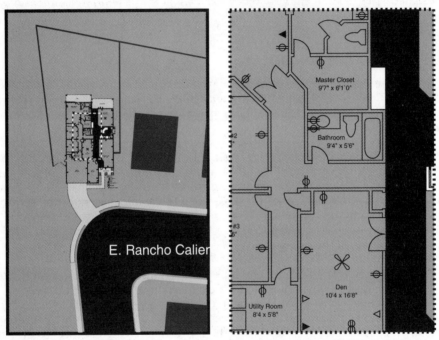

Figure 1-13: Zooming in to a certain area in the original image (left) results in the magnification and placement of the image as shown on the right.

Tip   To move a zoom marquee around while you're drawing it, press and hold the space-bar after you've begun drawing the marquee but before you release the mouse button. When you release the spacebar, you can continue to change the size of the marquee by dragging.

Other zooming techniques

You also can zoom in and out by using commands in the View menu. Choose View ➪ Zoom In (➪ cmd[Ctrl]++) to zoom in one level at a time until the magnification level is 6,400 percent. The Zoom In menu item zooms from the center out. Choose View ➪ Zoom Out (➪ cmd[Ctrl]+-) to zoom out one level at a time until the magnification level is 3.13 percent.

Even though Illustrator can zoom to any level, 17 default zoom levels are used when the Zoom tool is clicked, or when the Zoom In and Zoom Out menu items (or their respective keyboard commands) are accessed. Table 1-1 lists each of the default Zoom In and Zoom Out default levels.

Table 1-1			
Zoom In and Zoom Out Default Levels			
Zoom Out	**Ratio**	**Zoom In**	**Ratio**
100%	1:1	100%	1:1
66.67%	2:3	150%	3:2
50%	1:2	200%	2:1
33.33%	1:3	300%	3:1
25%	1:4	400%	4:1
16.67%	1:6	600%	6:1
12.5%	1:8	800%	8:1
8.33%	1:12	1,200%	12:1
6.25%	1:16	1,600%	16:1
4.17%	1:24	2,400%	24:1
3.13%	1:32	3,200%	32:1
		4,800%	48:1
		6,400%	64:1

Zooming to Actual Size

You can use several different methods to automatically zoom to 100-percent view. The first method is to double-click the Zoom tool slot in the toolbox. This action changes the view to 100 percent instantly. Selecting 100% from the Zoom drop-down list in the lower left corner of the interface will also size the document to 100 percent. But perhaps the best way to zoom to 100-percent magnification is to choose View ➪ Actual Size (⌘[Ctrl]+1), which not only changes the image size to 100 percent but also centers the page in the document window.

Zooming to Fit in Window size

You can choose from two different methods to change the document view to the Fit in Window size. Fit in Window instantly changes the magnification level of the document so that the entire artboard (not necessarily the artwork, if it isn't located on the page) fits in the window and is centered in it. One way to automatically change to the Fit in Window view is to choose View ⇨ Fit in Window (⇨ cmd[Ctrl]+0). Another way is to double-click the Hand tool slot.

Tip   You can quickly go to 3.13 percent by Command [Ctrl]+double-clicking the Zoom tool slot in the toolbox.

Zooming to a specific magnification

If you'd like to view a document at a specific zoom level, double-click the view area at the bottom-left corner of Illustrator's window (shown in Figure 1-14), type the magnification you wish to zoom to and press Enter or Return.

Figure 1-14: Enter the exact zoom level you wish to zoom to in the field at the lower-left corner of the document window.

You can never undo any type of magnification level change because zooming only changes the view of the document, it doesn't change the actual document in any way. Choosing Edit ⇨ Undo after zooming undoes the last change you made to the document before you changed the magnification level, *not* the magnification level change.

Zooming with the Navigator palette

Of course, being able to zoom in very closely to your artwork does have a pitfall: The more you zoom in on an illustration, the less of that illustration you see at one time. The Navigator palette (shown in Figure 1-15) helps you out by letting you see the entire illustration as well as the portion you're zoomed into (indicated by a red viewing rectangle). You can stay zoomed in and move easily to another section by dragging the red rectangle within the Navigator palette to another area. Access the Navigator palette by choosing Window ➪ Show Navigator.

Rectangle

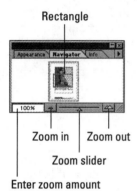

Zoom in   Zoom out

Zoom slider

Enter zoom amount

Figure 1-15: The Navigator palette

You can zoom in and out a preset amount (using the same amounts used by the Zoom In and Zoom Out tools and menu items) by pressing the Zoom In or Zoom Out button. Another way to zoom in and out is to drag the slider to the left or right. You can also type in an exact magnification level in the box in the lower-left corner of the Navigator palette.

The Navigator palette's fly-away menu includes a View Artboard Only option. This option sets the thumbnail in the Navigator palette to show only the extent of the artboard. If this option isn't set, then the thumbnail shows all objects included in the document.

Caution   The Navigator palette can slow down Illustrator if your artwork contains many patterns, gradients, and gradient mesh objects. To avoid this slowdown, you can close the Navigator palette using the Window ➪ Hide Navigator option.

Using the scroll bars to view your document

Sometimes, after you zoom in to a high magnification, part of the drawing that you want to see is outside the window area. Instead of zooming in and out repeatedly, you can use one of two different scrolling techniques to move around inside the document.

The scroll bar on the right side of the document window controls where you are *vertically* in the document. Clicking the up arrow displays what is above the window's boundaries by pushing everything in the window *down* in little increments. Clicking the down arrow displays what is below the window's boundaries by pushing the document *up* in little increments.

Dragging the thumb (sometimes called an *elevator box*) up displays what is above the window's boundaries proportionately by whatever distance you drag it. (Be careful not to drag too far or you will be previewing beyond the top of the artboard.) Dragging the thumb down displays what is below the window's boundaries proportionately by whatever distance you drag it. Clicking the gray bar above the thumb and between the arrows displays what is above the window's boundaries in big chunks. Clicking the gray bar below thumb, between the arrows, displays what is below the window's boundaries in big chunks.

Note For Mac OS X systems, you can set in the System Preferences, the amount of scrolling that happens when you click within the scrollbar.

The gray area of the right scroll bar is proportionate to the vertical size of the *pasteboard* (the space around the artboard). If the little elevator box is at the top of the scroll bar, then you are viewing the top edge of the pasteboard. If it is centered, you are viewing the vertical center of the pasteboard.

The scroll bar on the bottom of the document window controls where you are *horizontally* in the document. Clicking the left arrow displays what is to the left of the window's boundaries by pushing everything in the window to the *right* in little increments. Clicking the right arrow displays what is to the right of the window's boundaries by pushing the document to the *left* in little increments. Dragging the thumb to the left displays what is to the left of the window's boundaries proportionately by whatever distance you drag it. Dragging the thumb to the right displays what is to the right of the window boundaries proportionally by whatever distance you drag it. Clicking the gray bar, between the arrows, that is to the left of the thumb displays what is to the left of the window's boundaries in big chunks. Clicking the gray bar, between the arrows, that is to the right of the thumb displays what is to the right of the window's boundaries in big chunks.

Scrolling with the Hand tool

The Hand tool, which looks like a hand (surprise, surprise), improves on the scroll bars. Instead of being limited to horizontal and vertical movement only, you can use the Hand tool to scroll in any direction, including diagonally. It is especially useful for finding your way around a document when you're viewing it at a high magnification level. The higher the magnification level, the more you're likely to use the Hand tool.

To use the Hand tool, select it from the Hand tool slot in the toolbox.

To quickly access the Hand tool, press H, or press and hold the spacebar. Clicking and dragging the page moves the document around inside the document window while the spacebar is held down. If you release the spacebar, then you return to the previous tool. This works for all tools, but the Type tool works a little differently. If you're currently using the Type tool in a text area, press ⌘+spacebar [Ctrl+spacebar] to access the Zoom tool, and release ⌘ [Ctrl] while keeping the spacebar pressed to gain access to the Hand tool.

When you click in the document, be sure to click the side that you want to see. Clicking at the top of the document and dragging down enables you to scroll down through almost an entire document at a height of one window. Clicking in the center and dragging enables you to scroll through only half a window's size at a time. If the window of the document does not take up the entire screen space, you can continue to drag right off the window into the empty screen space. Just be sure to click first within the document that you want to scroll.

Be warned that Illustrator doesn't include support for a scrolling mouse except in Mac OS X. A scrolling mouse includes a wheel button in between the two buttons (if it's a two-button mouse typical with Windows) that you can use to quickly scroll around a page. The scrolling wheel has no effect on an Illustrator document. We can hope that Adobe will support this type of mouse in the future. Mac OS X includes support for the scrolling mouse as part of the operating system.

The best thing about the Hand tool is that it works live. As you drag, the document moves under "your Hand." If you don't like where it is going you can drag it back, still live. The second best thing is that accessing it requires only one keystroke, a press of the spacebar.

You cannot use Undo to reverse scrolling that you have done with the scroll bars and the Hand tool.

Scrolling with the Navigator palette

Use the red viewing rectangle in the Navigator palette to scroll quickly to another location within a document. Clicking and dragging within the red rectangle moves the viewing area around "live," whereas clicking outside the rectangle "snaps" the view to a new location.

The red rectangle can be changed to another color by choosing the Palette Options in the Navigator palette pop-up menu.

Opening a new window

So now you've learned how to zoom and pan around the document window, so you probably have many different sections of your artwork that you want to focus on. Illustrator will let you create a number of windows for the current artwork using the Window ➪ New Window option.

This option will create a new window that is the same size as the current window. You can then zoom and pan within this new window while maintaining the previous window. These windows can then be placed side by side to see the artwork from two unique perspectives. Each new window will be given a different reference number that appears in the title bar.

Working in Outline mode versus Preview mode

In the old days, everyone worked in Outline mode (previously called Artwork mode). In Outline mode you see only the "guts" of the artwork—the paths without the fills and strokes applied. To see what the illustration looked like with the fills and strokes applied, you had to switch to Preview mode. Usually the preview was not quite what you had in mind, but to make changes, you had to switch back to Outline, and then to Preview again to check, and so forth. Many users of Illustrator from that time refer to it as the golden age, with not a little trace of sarcasm.

Today, Illustrator 10 enables you to edit your work in both Outline and Preview modes, each shown in Figure 1-16. You can print a document from either mode. Saving the document while you are in Outline mode does not affect anything in the document, but the next time you open it, it will display in Outline mode. The same thing applies to Preview mode: Whatever mode you are in is saved with the artwork.

You cannot undo a Preview or Outline mode change (going from Preview to Outline, for example). If you make a Preview or Outline mode change and then close your document, Illustrator asks you if you want to save changes, which in this case would refer only to the view change.

The current view mode is always displayed in the title bar next to the document name.

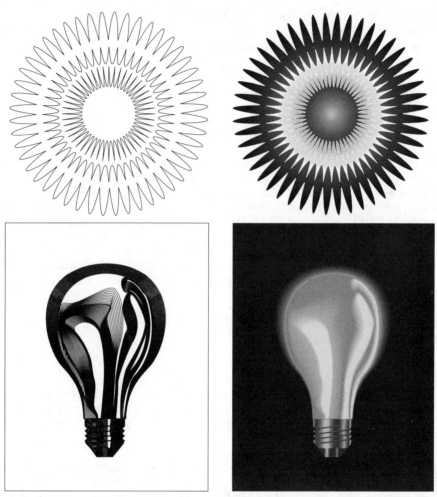

Figure 1-16: Artwork shown in both Outline mode (left) and Preview mode (right)

Outline mode

To change the current document to Outline mode, choose View ➪ Outline. If you are already in Outline mode, the view menu contains only an option to change to Preview mode. In Outline mode, the illustration disappears and is replaced onscreen by outlines of all the filled and stroked paths. Text that has yet to be converted into outlines looks fine, although it is always black. Depending on your choice in the Document Setup dialog box (choose File ➪ Document Setup), a placed image is displayed as a box (if Show Placed Images option is not checked) or as a black-and-white-only image surrounded by a box (if Show Placed Images option is checked).

Working with a drawing in Outline mode can be significantly faster than working with it in Preview mode. In more complex drawings, the difference between Outline mode and Preview mode is significant; on very slow computers, working in Preview mode is next to impossible.

Outline mode enables you to see every path that isn't directly overlapping another path; in Preview mode, many paths can be hidden. In addition, invisible masks are normally visible as paths in Outline mode. Outline mode is much closer to what the printer sees — paths that define the edges of the objects you are working with.

Placed artwork is displayed in black and white only, and templates are grayer than before. The main advantage to working in Outline mode is the speed increase over Preview mode when you're working with a complex image. The speed that you gain is even greater when the artwork contains gradients, patterns, placed artwork, and blends. In addition, you can select paths that were hidden by the fills of other objects.

Outline mode can take some getting used to. To select paths in Outline mode, you must click the paths directly or draw a marquee across them.

Outline mode can be better than Preview because it's faster, and also because your brain can learn to know what the drawing looks like from seeing just the outlines, which show *all* of the paths.

Preview mode

Choosing View ➪ Preview changes the view to Preview mode. If you are already in Preview mode, then the View menu contains only a menu option to change to Outline mode. In Preview mode, the document looks just the way it will look when you print it.

Note In Preview mode, the color you see on the screen only marginally represents what the actual output will be because of the differences between the way computer monitors work (red, green, and blue colors — the more of each color, the brighter each pixel appears) and the way printing works (cyan, magenta, yellow, and black colors — the more of each color, the darker each area appears). Monitor manufacturers make a number of calibration tools that decrease the difference between what you see on the monitor and the actual output. You can also use software solutions. One solution, CIE calibration, is built into Adobe Illustrator (choose Edit ➪ Color Settings). Mac users can use ColorSync, which is part of the OS.

In Preview mode, you can see which objects overlap, which objects are in front and in back, where gradations begin and end, and how patterns are set up.

Instead of selecting a path by clicking it, you can select entire paths by clicking the insides of those paths in a filled area. It becomes a little more difficult to select certain points on paths, because the strokes on those paths are also visible. Sometimes so much stuff appears on your screen in Preview mode that you don't know what to click. The option that enables you to select an entire path by clicking in a filled area is called Area Select, which is activated by a checkbox (turned on by default) in the General Preferences dialog box, which you can access by choosing Edit ⇨ Preferences ⇨ General.

You can stop screen redraw by pressing ⌘+Y [Ctrl+Y] at any time. This is useful if you would like to make a small change and would have to wait too long for the redraw. Of course, pressing ⌘+Y [Ctrl+Y] dumps you into Outline mode, but the redraw happens pretty much instantaneously.

Overprint Preview mode

When producing color separations, you can specify overprinting features using the Attributes palette. When colors are overlapped, the top color typically covers or knocks out the colors underneath. However, when you use the Overprint feature, the ink for the top color is printed on top of the lower colors. This process is easier and mostly cheaper for printers to produce, but it can affect the overall color of the objects. To view the results of specifying an overprint, you can use the Overprint Preview option by selecting the View ⇨ Overprint Preview option.

You can learn more about overprinting in Chapter 6, "Working with Color," and in Chapter 16, "Understanding Printing, Separations, and Trapping."

Pixel Preview mode

Illustrator 10 includes many features to help designers create graphics for Web pages. Web page graphics are typically pixel-based images. To help designers view their pixel-based images before saving them to a Web graphics format, Illustrator 10 includes a Pixel Preview mode.

You can find more information about creating Web graphics in Chapter 17, "Using Illustrator to Generate Web Graphics."

You can enable the Pixel Preview option using the View menu. This option is toggled on or off every time it is selected. If it is enabled, a checkmark appears next to the menu option. When the Pixel Preview option is enabled, the current document is displayed as a raster image (see Figure 1-17).

Figure 1-17: This document is displayed in normal Preview mode (left) and using Pixel Preview mode (right).

Combining Outline and Preview modes

Using the Layers palette, you can easily combine Outline mode with either Preview or Preview Selection mode. You can force individual layers to display in Preview mode while other layers remain in Outline mode. This feature can be useful when you have a layer with a placed image, gradients, or patterns (or all three) that would normally slow down screen redraw, and your workflow. You can place those images on their own layer and set that layer to Outline mode.

Cross-Reference   To learn more about using layers, check out Chapter 7, "Organizing Artwork."

Using custom views

Illustrator has a special feature called custom views that enables you to save special views of an illustration. Custom views contain view information, including magnification, location, and whether the illustration is in Outline or Preview mode. If you have various layers or layer sets in Preview mode and others in Outline mode, custom views can also save that information. Custom views, however, do not record whether templates, rulers, page tiling, edges, or guides are shown or hidden.

To create a new view, set up the document in the way that you would like to save the view. Then choose View ⇨ New View and name the view in the New View dialog box, shown in Figure 1-18. Each new view name appears at the bottom of the View menu. No default keyboard shortcuts exist for these views, but you can create your own shortcuts using the Keyboard Shortcuts dialog box, available under the Edit menu. You can create up to 25 custom views. Custom views are saved with a document as long as you save it using the Illustrator format.

Figure 1-18: This simple dialog box lets you name the new view.

If you find yourself continually going to a certain part of a document, zooming in or out, and changing back and forth between Preview and Outline mode, that document is a prime candidate for creating custom views. Custom views are helpful for showing clients artwork that you created in Illustrator. Instead of fumbling around in the client's presence, you can, for example, show the detail in a logo instantly if you have preset the zoom factor and position, and have saved the image in a custom view.

Once views are created, you can edit the view name or delete them using the View ⇨ Edit Views option. This will open the Edit Views dialog box, shown in Figure 1-19. To rename the view, select it and type the new name in the Name field. To delete a view, select it and press the Delete button.

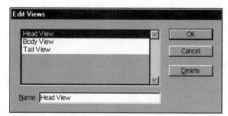

Figure 1-19: The Edit Views dialog box can be used to rename or delete custom views.

Using screen modes

So you've been working on an illustration for an important client (actually they all are important) and they scheduled an appointment to see your progress, but the best part of the work is hidden behind the palettes and the Toolbox. These can be easily turned off using the Window menu or you could use the F keyboard shortcut to switch between the different screen modes.

Illustrator uses three different screen modes represented by the three icon buttons at the bottom of the Toolbox. They are Standard Screen Mode, Full Screen Mode with Menu Bar and Full Screen Mode. You can toggle between these modes using the F keyboard shortcut. Figure 1-20 shows Nichiro Newt in Full Screen Mode with Menu Bar.

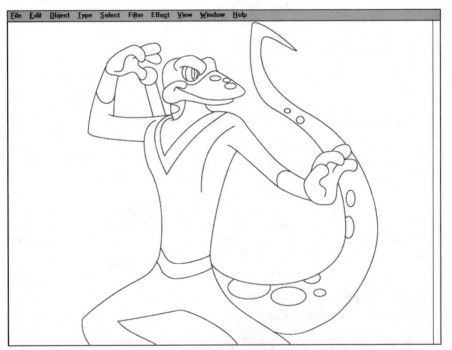

Figure 1-20: Full Screen Mode with Menu Bar maximizes the document window to fill the entire screen eliminating all interface elements except for the menu bar.

Using the Edit Commands

In most software, including Illustrator, many of the most basic functions of the Edit menu work the same way. If you've used the Edit menu in Photoshop or Microsoft

Word, for example, you should have no trouble using the same functions in Illustrator, because the menu options are located in the same place in each program.

Using the Clear command

The most simplistic Edit command is Clear, which in Illustrator works almost exactly like the Delete [Backspace] key on the keyboard. When something is selected, choosing Clear deletes, or gets rid of, what is selected.

You're probably asking yourself, "If the Delete [Backspace] key does the same thing, why do we need Clear?" or "Why didn't they just call the Clear command Delete [Backspace]?" Ah, the makers of Illustrator are a step ahead of you in this respect. Note that we said "almost" the same way; there actually is a subtle yet important difference in what the Clear command does and what the Delete [Backspace] key does, due to Illustrator's abundant use of palettes.

If you are working on a palette and have just typed a value in an editable text field, the Delete [Backspace] key deletes the last character typed. If you tabbed down or up to an editable text field, highlighting text, or dragged across text in an editable text field, highlighting text, then the Delete [Backspace] key deletes the highlighted characters. In all three situations, the Clear command deletes anything that is selected in the document.

Cutting, copying, and pasting

The Cut, Copy, and Paste commands in Illustrator are very handy. Copying and cutting selected objects places them on the clipboard, which is a temporary holding place for objects that have been cut or copied. After an object is on the clipboard, it may be pasted into the center of the same document, the same location as the cut or copied object, or another document in Illustrator, InDesign, Photoshop, Dimensions, or Streamline.

Choosing Cut from the Edit menu deletes the selected objects and copies them to the clipboard, where they are stored until another object is cut or copied or the computer is shut down or restarted. Quitting Illustrator does not remove objects from the clipboard. Cut is not available when no object is selected.

Choosing Copy from the Edit menu works like Cut, but it doesn't delete the selected objects. Instead, it just copies them to the clipboard, at which time you can choose Paste and slap another copy onto your document.

Choosing Paste from the Edit menu places any objects on the clipboard into the center of the document window. If type is selected with the Type tool, or copied from another application to the pasteboard, either a Rectangle type, Area type, Path type, or point type area must be selected with the Type tool. Paste is not available if nothing is in the clipboard.

Note   Illustrator also includes Paste in Front (⌘/Ctrl+F) and Paste in Back (⌘/Ctrl+B) options that can be used to control the position of the object being pasted relative to the other objects.

Now, the really cool part: Just because you've pasted the object somewhere doesn't mean it isn't in the clipboard anymore. It is! You can paste again and again, and keep on pasting until you get bored, or until your page is an indecipherable mess, whichever comes first. The most important rule to remember about Cut, Copy, and Paste is that whatever is currently in the clipboard will be replaced by anything that subsequently gets cut or copied to the clipboard.

Cut, Copy, and Paste also work with text that you type in a document. Using the Type tools, you can select type, cut or copy it, and then paste it. When you're pasting type, it will go wherever your blinking text cursor is located. If you have type selected (highlighted) and you choose Paste, the type that was selected is replaced by whatever you had on the clipboard.

You can cut or copy as much or as little of an illustration as you choose; you are only limited by your hard disk space (which is only used if you run out of RAM). A good rule of thumb is that, if you ever get a message saying you can't cut or copy because you are out of hard disk space, it's time to start throwing out stuff on your hard drive that you don't need. Or, simply get a bigger hard drive.

Thanks to the Adobe PostScript capability on the clipboard, Illustrator can copy paths to other Adobe software, including InDesign, Dimensions, Streamline, and Photoshop. Paths created in those packages (with the exception of InDesign) can be pasted into Illustrator. With Photoshop, you have the option of pasting your clipboard contents as rasterized pixels instead of as paths.

You have the ability to drag Illustrator artwork from an Illustrator document right into a Photoshop document. In addition, because Adobe lets you move things in both directions, you can drag a Photoshop selection from any Photoshop document right into an Illustrator document.

Undoing and redoing

You can keep undoing in Illustrator until you run out of either computer memory or patience. After you undo, you can redo by choosing Redo, which is found right below Undo in the Edit menu. And, guess what — you can redo everything you've undone.

Choosing Undo from the Edit menu undoes the last activity that was performed on the document. Successive undos undo more and more activities, until the document is at the point where it was opened or created or you have run out of memory.

The default minimum number of remembered undos is five. To change the minimum number of undos, go to the Units and Undo Preferences dialog box (Illustrator [Edit] ➪ Preferences ➪ Units and Undo) and type in the minimum number of undos that you want. You *can* set the minimum undo levels to zero, but we wouldn't recommend it; this might disallow any undo or redo operations in certain situations and is like tightrope walking without a safety net.

Choosing Redo from the Edit menu redoes the last undo. You can continue to redo undos until you are back to the point where you started undoing or you perform another activity, at which time you can no longer redo any previous undos.

If you undo a couple of times and then *do* something, you won't be able to redo. You have to undo the last thing you did and then actually do everything again. In other words, all the steps that you undid are gone. It's fine to use the Undo feature to go back and check out what you did, but after you have used multiple undos, don't do anything if you want to redo back to where you started undoing from. Got that?

Summary

In this chapter, you learned

- ✦ Illustrator may seem difficult to learn at first, but with this book and a bit of dedication, you can master it.

- ✦ Many of the user interface elements that are found in Illustrator are common among Adobe products.

- ✦ Common user interface elements include the document window, the toolbox, palettes, menus, and the status bar.

- ✦ You can view Illustrator documents at virtually any magnification level without actually changing them.

- ✦ The Hand tool is used to pan the document window.

- ✦ Illustrator's Outline mode lets you see paths without their strokes and fills.

- ✦ The Edit menu commands can be used to undo and redo commands, as well as cutting, copying, and pasting objects.

- ✦ Illustrator provides virtually unlimited undos and redos.

✦   ✦   ✦

Working with Illustrator Documents

Illustrator is used to create documents. These documents can be sent to a printer to produce a hard copy, converted into a Web graphics standard for publishing on the Web, or just saved on the local hard drive for more work at a later time. Whatever your intent, you'll need to work with Illustrator documents. This chapter covers managing, saving, exporting and obtaining information on Illustrator files.

Setting Up a New Document

The first thing you'll want to do after launching Illustrator is to create a new document to work on — unless you've launched the program by double-clicking an Illustrator document, which already brings up *that* specific document. Choosing File ➪ New (⌘+N [Ctrl+N]) when you're already in Illustrator creates a brand new document and makes that new document the *active* document (by *active document* we're referring to the document that is in front of all other documents, and that is affected by anything you do in Illustrator, such as choosing menu commands). This also opens the New Document dialog box, as shown in Figure 2-1, in which you can specify the document Name, Size, Units, artboard dimensions, orientation and which Color Mode to work in. The *artboard* defines the printable section of the document. Illustrator 10 enables you to work in two different color modes — CMYK for traditional print media and RGB for online images such as Web graphics.

Cross-Reference Chapter 6, "Working with Color," covers CMYK and RGB color modes in greater detail.

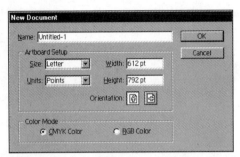

Figure 2-1: The New Document dialog box appears when you create a new document.

Many other graphics and desktop-publishing programs, including InDesign, Photoshop, and QuarkXPress, ask you to set up your document size before the document is created. When you create a new Illustrator document with the File ⇨ New command, the dialog box defaults to the size of the startup document that is located in the Plug-Ins folder. By default, this document is 8.5×11 inches, and appears in the *portrait* orientation (meaning that the width is less than the height).

 Cross-Reference See Chapter 15, "Customizing and Optimizing Illustrator," for more information on altering the startup document.

After clicking the OK button in the New Document dialog box, the document window shows up at Fit in Window size, as shown in Figure 2-2. In the title bar at the top of the window, you see Untitled-1 @61% (or whatever percentage the document is displayed at). As soon as you save the document, the title bar contains the name of the document. In addition to the document name, the title bar includes information such as the zoom percentage, and the Color and View Modes.

Although many aspects of the Illustrator environment can be altered, you cannot change the way some items appear when you first start Illustrator. For example, the Selection tool is always selected in the toolbox. Another unchangeable item is the initial Paint Style that you begin drawing with: a Fill of white and a Stroke of 1-point Black. The character attributes are always the same: 12-point Helvetica, Auto Leading, Flush Left alignment. In addition, the initial layer color is always light blue (a color that is just dark enough so that it doesn't conflict with cyan).

 Cross-Reference See Chapter 15, "Customizing and Optimizing Illustrator," for more information on customizing the environment.

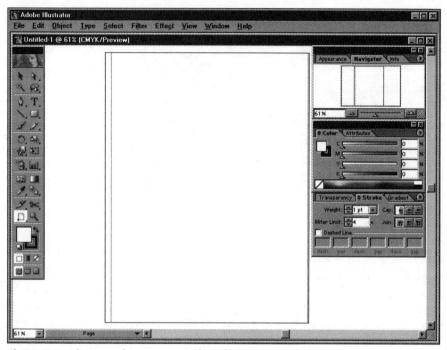

Figure 2-2: The new document window that appears after specifying the document dimensions

Changing the Document Setup

To change almost anything about the document structure and how you work with that document, you need to go to the Document Setup dialog box (see Figure 2-3) by choosing File ➪ Document Setup or pressing ⌘+Option+P [Ctrl+Alt+P]. In this dialog box, you can change the size of the artboard (the maximum drawing area that can be printed), define how and when paths are split, change the ruler units, and change the way that printable page edges, patterns, and placed images are viewed.

The following sections describe the various options that you'll find in the Document Setup dialog box. Any changes that you make to these options are saved with the document. The Document Setup dialog box consists of three separate option screens: Artboard, Printing & Export, and Transparency. You can select which screen to view using the popup menu/drop-down list at the top of the dialog box. You can also cycle through the various screens using the Previous and/or Next buttons to the right of the dialog box.

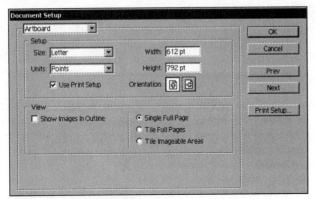

Figure 2-3: The Document Setup dialog box

Artboard options

In Illustrator, as mentioned previously, the *artboard* defines the maximum drawing area that can be printed. The artboard is useful as a guide to where objects on a page belong. In older versions of Illustrator, the maximum printable size was 11×17 inches; with version 6, it increased to 227.5×227.5 inches or about 360 square feet (provided that you can find a printer that prints paper that big) and it remains that size today.

Note   Illustrator's separation setup ignores the artboard and places crop marks around the entire imageable area. The *imageable area*, according to this dialog box, is only the area where artwork exists. It may be within the artboard, but it also may extend onto the pasteboard (the area outside the artboard, where you can store items that aren't part of the final design). When you export an illustration to another program, such as QuarkXPress, the artboard is ignored entirely.

You can view a document in points, picas, inches, centimeters, millimeters or pixels. The measurement units affect the numbers on the rulers and the locations of the hash marks on those same rulers. The measurement system also changes the way measurements are displayed in the Info palette and in all dialog boxes where you enter a measurement (other than a percentage).

The measurement system is changed in either the Units & Undo Preferences dialog box (choose Illustrator [Edit] ➪ Preferences ➪ Units & Undo) for all documents, or in the Document Setup dialog box (choose File ➪ Document Setup, or press ⌘+Option+P [Ctrl+Alt+P]) for the currently active document.

Choose the size of the artboard by selecting one of the following preset sizes in the Size pop-up menu:

✦ **Custom:** whatever size you type in the Dimensions text fields

✦ **640 X 480:** 640 pixels by 480 pixels

- ✦ **800 X 600:** 800 pixels by 600 pixels
- ✦ **468 X 60:** 468 pixels by 60 pixels
- ✦ **Letter:** 8.5×11 inches
- ✦ **Legal:** 8.5×14 inches
- ✦ **Tabloid:** 11×17 inches
- ✦ **A4:** 8.268×11.693 inches (21×29.7 centimeters)
- ✦ **A3:** 11.693×16.535 inches (29.7×42 centimeters)
- ✦ **B5:** 7.165×10 inches (18.2×25.4 centimeters)
- ✦ **B4:** 10.118×14.331 inches (55.7×36.4 centimeters)

 Note A4, A3, B5, and B4 are European paper sizes and A4 is also a Japanese standard.

You define the orientation of your artboard by choosing one of the two Orientation pages. On the left is Portrait orientation, where the shorter of the two dimensions goes across the page from left to right, and the longer of the two dimensions goes from top to bottom. On the right is Landscape orientation, where the longer of the two dimensions goes across the page from left to right, and the shorter of the two dimensions goes from top to bottom.

The Dark Ages

Creating a new document hasn't always been easy. Back in the days of Illustrator 88, and even Illustrator 3 to some extent, creating new illustrations was rather annoying. Choosing New Document brought up a dialog box that politely, yet sternly, asked you to choose a template to trace in Illustrator. Most of the time, though, you didn't want a template, so you had to click the little None button in the dialog box. If you pressed Return, Illustrator would attempt to open a template.

Illustrator 3 was a little more flexible. It let you create a new document without having to deal with the dialog box that asked you to choose a template. You could either press ⌘+Option+N [Ctrl+Alt+N] or hold down the Option [Alt] key when you chose File ➪ New. If you forgot about the Option [Alt] key, you had another chance. Pressing ⌘+N [Ctrl+N] when you were in the dialog box would send the box away and create a new document with no template — as long as you didn't have Directory Assistance, Super Boomerang, or any other utilities that created a new open folder when you pressed ⌘+N [Ctrl+N].

Adobe slowly realized that you neither wanted nor needed a template to do everything, and now, fortunately, template-forcing is a thing of the past.

In fact, opening templates has been removed entirely, leaving you the one option of placing an image on the background layer. A layer can act as a template. Select Template in the Layers Options dialog box.

If you check the Use Page Setup box (the Use Print Setup box in Windows), then the artboard defaults to the page size and orientation that is selected in the Page Setup dialog box.

You can control how certain items in Illustrator are viewed by checking the appropriate boxes:

✦ The **Show Images In Outline** option makes placed EPS (Encapsulated PostScript) images visible in Outline mode. Although the image is visible, it will be displayed in grayscale, as shown in Figure 2-4. When the Show Images in Outline option is disabled, only the border outline of -the image is visible.

Note   Although only a grayscale representation of the image is visible, a full color version of the image can be seen in the Navigation palette.

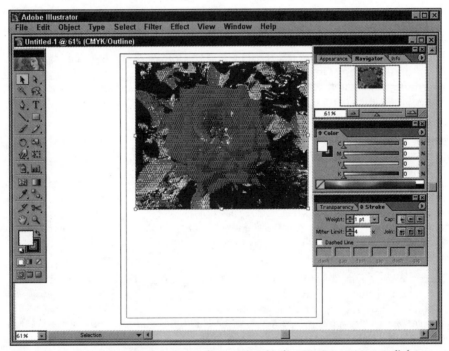

Figure 2-4: If the Show Images in Outline option in the Document Setup dialog box is enabled, images are displayed in grayscale.

✦ The **Single Full Page** option creates one Page Setup size outline on the page. This is the default option.

✦ The **Tile Full Pages** option creates as many page outlines (from Page Setup) as will completely print. For example, if the artboard is landscape, 11×17 inches, and the selected page size in Page Setup is portrait, 8.5×11 inches, then two page outlines appear side-by-side in the document, as shown in Figure 2-5.

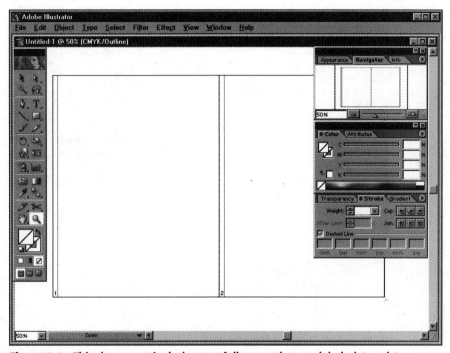

Figure 2-5: This document includes two full pages that are labeled 1 and 2.

✦ The **Tile Imageable Areas** option creates a grid on the document, with the size of each *block* equal to the page size that is chosen in the Page Setup dialog box. Little page numbers appear in the lower-left corner of each block, representing the pages you enter in the page *x* to page *x* fields in the Print dialog box. For example, if the artboard is 11 × 17 inches and a #10 Envelope is selected in the Page Setup dialog box, then the imageable areas will be displayed as shown in Figure 2-6. You could then print the bottom row of full envelopes using pages 10 through 15.

To move the page outlines, select the Page tool and click and drag in the artboard. You can drag with this tool by clicking and dragging the lower-left corner of the page.

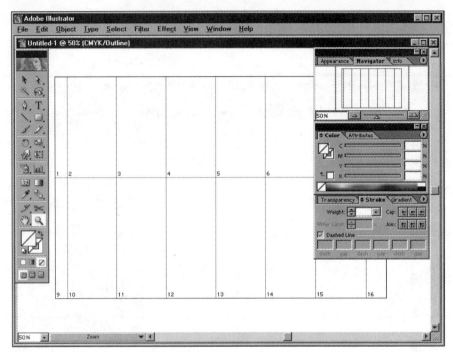

Figure 2-6: The Tile Imageable Areas split the artboard into a grid.

Printing & Export options

The second screen of options is labeled Printing & Export. This screen includes path options for setting the output resolution and splitting long paths. It also includes some print options, discussed later. Selecting Printing & Export in the popup menu/drop-down list at the top of the dialog box lets you access these options, as shown in Figure 2-7.

Path-splitting options

Robot would be screaming his bubble-head off if Will Robinson ever thought about clicking the Split Long Paths checkbox. The checkbox looks friendly enough, but the results of checking it can be deadly. If you are quick enough, you can always undo the split paths function, but the actual splitting of paths doesn't always happen when and where you expect it to happen.

Instead, it happens only when you save or print a document. This feature presents some very interesting problems. If you save the document and close it right after you save it, the paths are split permanently, and you cannot undo the damage the next time you open the document. Another problem arises when you are working in Preview mode: If you forget whether you checked the option, it's not always easy to determine whether paths have been split.

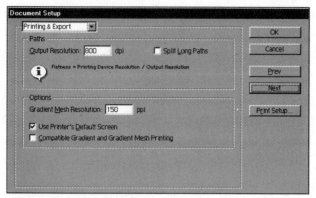

Figure 2-7: The Printing & Export options in the Document Setup dialog box

The Split Long Paths function tries to fix paths that are too long or too complex for your laser printer to handle. By entering the final output resolution for the Illustrator document, you can ensure that it will have a better chance of printing than if paths are not split. Every curve in Illustrator is made of tiny straight segments. The higher the resolution of the output device, the more straight segments that are needed to create the curve. The processing power of the laser printer limits how many little straight segments can be in one path. If you exceed that limit, Illustrator chops away at the paths, splitting them into several smaller sections. Because this problem occurs more frequently with low-resolution devices, the greater the number you enter in the Output resolution field, the more paths will be split. Figure 2-8 shows an original document and several examples of path splitting.

The only reason to use the Split Long Paths function is if a document fails to print because of a PostScript error (usually a limit check error). But instead of just checking the Split Long Paths checkbox, first make a copy of the entire document (doing a Save As or Save a Copy with another name will do this quickly) and then split paths in the new document. The original file will not contain split paths. Split paths are extremely difficult to reassemble, and the results from split paths can be horrifying. Please use caution when you split paths.

Using the Printer Default Screen

For gradients on low-resolution printers (600 dpi or less) when composite printing only, Illustrator uses a dither pattern called Adobe Screens (not to be confused with Adobe Accurate Screens) when Use Printer Default Screen is unchecked. This increases the apparent levels of gray by fracturing the halftone cells. When checking Use Printer Default Screens, you're just disabling Adobe Screens; you are *not* telling Illustrator to image the file at the printer's default line screen. Output software can still set the printer's line screen for the Illustrator file.

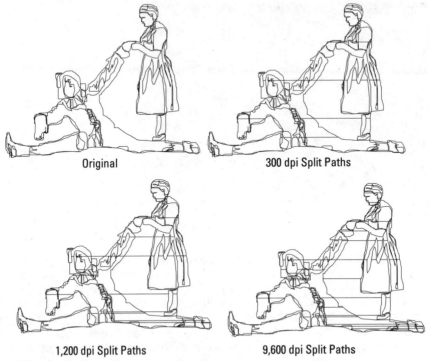

Original   300 dpi Split Paths

1,200 dpi Split Paths   9,600 dpi Split Paths

Figure 2-8: A document before and after path-splitting at different output resolutions

Compatible Gradient and Gradient Mesh printing

The Compatible Gradient and Gradient Mesh Printing option should be checked if you are printing to a non-PostScript Level 3 device. It automatically generates a JPEG file for any areas that contain Gradient Mesh Fills, as PostScript Level 1 and Level 2 devices cannot print Gradient Meshes properly.

Note   Some PostScript Level 3 printers are unable to print Gradient Mesh as well; Post-Script versions 3.010.105 and earlier are affected.

Transparency options

The Transparency options screen includes settings for controlling transparency. You can locate these options by selecting Transparency from the popup menu/drop-down list at the top of the Document Setup dialog box. The transparency options are shown in Figure 2-9.

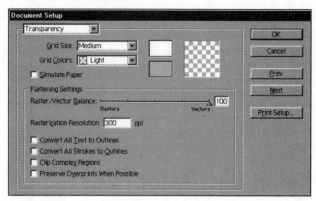

Figure 2-9: The Transparency options in the Document Setup dialog box

 Cross-Reference Transparency features are covered in depth in Chapter 12, "Understanding Transparency."

The Transparency options screen includes popup menus/drop-down lists for setting the Grid Size and Grid Color. You can set Grid Size to Small, Medium, or Large, and Grid Colors include an assortment of colors and a Custom option for selecting your own grid color. To the right of these options are two color swatches. Clicking these boxes opens the color selector dialog box. From this dialog box you can select custom transparency grid colors. A preview of the transparency grid is also shown. The default transparency grid colors are white and light gray.

The Simulate Colored Paper setting changes the entire artboard to the color of the lower transparency grid color swatch. This lets you see your artwork as it would look if it were printed on color paper. The colors of the artwork mix with the simulated paper color. For example, a red rectangle on top of a simulated yellow piece of colored paper will appear orange.

Because of the complexities that transparent sections add to a document, Illustrator will flatten transparent sections prior to printing, although you do have some control over how the flattening occurs. The Transparency option screen also includes a slider for setting the balance between rasters and vectors. This will determine the quality and speed of printing the transparent regions. Complex transparent regions can be rasterized when printed to speed the printing process. This process reduces the quality of the transparent region. To maintain the vector data while printing, you can set the Raster/Vector Balance slider to the right, which takes considerably more time to print, but results in quality printing. If the printing document includes any transparent sections that you want rasterized, you can set the resolution of the rasterized section by using the Rasterization Resolution setting.

At the bottom of this screen you'll see several options that affect the speed and quality of the printing. These options include

✦ Convert All Text to Outlines

✦ Convert All Strokes to Outlines

✦ Clip Complex Regions

✦ Preserve Overprints When Possible

Opening and Closing Illustrator Files

Opening files in Illustrator is fairly simple. Illustrator can open and manipulate a great variety of vector format files. It can also open an assortment of raster formats, but they will be pixel-based.

Files placed in Illustrator can be almost any of the most widely used raster file formats. PostScript files that are printed to disk usually can't be placed in Illustrator, although PostScript Level 1 files can be opened in Illustrator.

Other important file issues: Illustrator opens a pixel file as a new Illustrator document with the pixels inside. Arbitrary PostScript Level 1 files can be opened with the built-in PostScript Interpreter. Illustrator files can be saved directly into pixel formats.

You can open an assortment of vector and raster-based formats into Illustrator including Illustrator files saved in any previous Illustrator version. When you choose File➪Open or press ⌘+O [Ctrl+O], the Open dialog box, shown in Figure 2-10 and Figure 2-11, appears. This dialog box will let you locate and open into Illustrator any displayed file by double-clicking on it to have it open into a document window on the screen. Notice that this dialog box is slightly different between Windows and Mac systems.

You can see all the various formats that can be opened into Illustrator by looking in the Files of Type drop down list at the bottom of the dialog box for Windows. Selecting a single file type will filter all the files and only show the files of that type. The default is All Formats, which will show all files that can be opened into Illustrator.

Caution   If you try to open an unsupported file format, Illustrator will display an error.

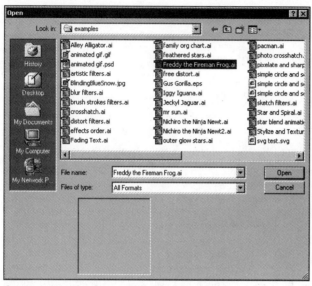

Figure 2-10: The Open dialog box for Windows

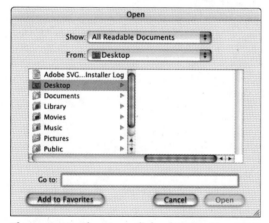

Figure 2-11: The Open dialog box for Mac OS X

Supported file formats

The file types that can be opened into Illustrator include the following. The extension is listed in parenthesis:

+ Adobe PDF (PDF)
+ AutoCAD Drawing (DWG)
+ AutoCAD Interchange File (DXF)
+ Windows Bitmap (BMP, RLE)
+ Computer Graphics Metafile (CGM)
+ CorelDRAW (CDR)

Note   Illustrator can open CorelDRAW documents from version 5 through version 10.

+ Encapsulated Postscript (EPS)
+ Enhance Metafile (EMF)
+ Filmstrip (FLM)
+ Freehand (FH4 – FH9)
+ Graphics Interchange Format, version 89a (GIF)
+ Illustrator (AI)
+ Illustrator EPS (EPS, EPSF, PS)
+ JPEG (JPG)
+ Kodak PhotoCD (PCD)
+ Macintosh PICT (PIC, PCT)
+ Microsoft RTF (RTF)
+ Microsoft World (DOC)
+ PCX (PCX)
+ Photoshop (PSD, PDD)
+ Pixar (PXR)
+ Portable Network Graphics (PNG)
+ Scalable Vector Graphics (SVG)
+ Compressed SVG (SVGZ)
+ Targa (TGA, VDA, ICB, VST)
+ Text (TXT)
+ Windows Metafile (WMF)

Always interested in saving you time, Illustrator is smart and courteous enough to keep track of your most recently opened files. Selecting the File ➪ Open Recent Files will present a list of the most recently opened files.

Closing files

To close the active Illustrator file, choose File ➪ Close (⌘+W [Ctrl+W]). The active document is the one that is in front of all other documents and has by default for the Mac OS, a title bar with lines on it and text in black. Nonactive documents don't display any lines in their title bar, and the text in the title bar is gray unless you've changed your system colors. Closing an Illustrator document does not close Illustrator; it continues running until you choose Quit [Exit].

If you saved the file prior to closing it, it just disappears. If you have modified the file since the last time you saved it, a dialog box appears, asking whether you want to save changes before closing. If you press Return or Enter to save the file, it is updated. If you have not saved the file at all, the Save As dialog box appears so that you can name the file, choose a location for it, and choose Preview and Compatibility options for the file. If you click the Don't Save button (D while the dialog box is showing), then any changes that you made to the document since you last saved it (or if you have never saved it, all the changes you made since you created it) are lost. Clicking Cancel (⌘+. (period) [Ctrl+. (period)] or Esc) takes you back to the drawing, where you can continue to work on it.

Saving Files

Saving Illustrator documents is the most important Illustrator activity you do. Saving often prevents damage to your computer — by keeping you from picking it up and sending it flying across the room. Saving often makes your life less stressful, and backing up your saved files helps you sleep better.

Caution

Unlike other software packages, Illustrator does not have an Auto Backup feature. Such a feature would automatically save a temporary copy of a document at regular intervals. These temporary copies can be salvaged if the power to the computer were cut; only the work since the last Auto Backup would be lost. Some of the better implementations of this feature enable the user to specify the backup interval and the temporary file locations. We can only hope that Adobe will include such a feature in future versions.

Controlling how files are saved in Illustrator can be a little daunting at first. Although you have many different options for saving file types, you need to follow one basic rule: Save as an EPS with a color preview if you are going to take the file into other applications. This type of file is not the smallest file type, but it is compatible with most software.

The amount of space that a saved Illustrator file takes up on a hard drive depends on two factors: the complexity of the drawing and the Preview option (if any) that you've selected. Tiny Illustrator files take up the smallest amount, about 10K or so.

The biggest illustrations are limited only by your storage space, but they can regularly exceed 2MB. As a practice, when you are working on a drawing, save it to the hard drive, not to a floppy disk or a removable cartridge. Hard drives are faster and much more reliable. If you need to place a file on a floppy disk, Zip, or Jaz disk, copy it there by dragging the icon of the file from the hard drive to the disk or cartridge. Because Illustrator uses *virtual memory* (the hard drive as RAM), you may want to keep additional hard drive space available, especially if you plan on working with lots of embedded images.

You should only save the file to another disk if you run out of room on the hard drive. To ensure that you never run out of room, always keep at least 10 percent of the hard drive space free. A hard drive that is too full can cause many problems that are more serious than being unable to save a file.

To save a file, choose File ➪ Save (⌘+S [Ctrl+S]). If you have previously saved the file, then updating the existing file with the changes that you have made takes just a fraction of a second. If you have not yet saved the file, the Save As dialog box, shown in Figure 2-12 or Figure 2-13 appears.

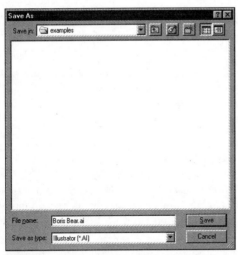

Figure 2-12: The Save As dialog box for Windows

If you click on the Format popup menu [Save as Type drop down list], you will see the formats that the document can be saved as. These formats include the following:

✦ Adobe Portable Document Format (PDF)

✦ Illustrator (AI)

✦ Encapsulated Postscript (EPS)

✦ Scalable Vector Graphics (SVG)

✦ Compressed SVG (SVGZ)

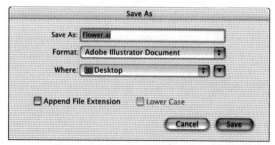

Figure 2-13: The Save As dialog box for Mac OS X

After clicking the Save button in the Save As dialog box, another dialog box of options will appear depending on the selected format type. The available format types and their options will be discussed in the "Format types and options" section to follow.

Consider these issues when saving a file:

✦ Decide how you are going to save the file. Choose the correct Preview and Compatibility options for the file. (See the descriptions in the "Format types and options" section, later in this chapter.)

✦ Decide where you are going to save the file and make sure that the name of the folder where you want to save it is at the top of the file list window. Saving your working files in a location other than the Illustrator folder is a good habit. Otherwise, you can have trouble figuring out which files are yours, which files are tutorial files, and so on.

✦ Name the file something distinctive so that if you look for it six months from now you will recognize it. Avoid using Untitled Art 1, Untitled Art 2, and so on. Such names are nondescriptive and, besides, you can too easily replace the file at a later date with a file of the same name. For the same reasons, do not use Document 1, Document 2, and so on. Also avoid using Test1 (if we had a nickel for every Test1 we've seen on people's hard drives, we'd have . . . well, we'd have a lot of nickels), stuff, #$*&!! (insert your favorite four-letter word here), picture, drawing, or your first name. A file name can have up to 31 characters, and you can use all the letters, numbers, and special characters (except a colon [:], the forward or backwards slashes [/ and \], or the pipe character [|]) that are found on your keyboard, so make the most of them and describe the file. It's not a good idea to use the @ symbol either because it could be confused with an e-mail address.

When Should I Save?

You really can't save too often. Whenever you put off saving for "just a few minutes," that's when the system locks up, crashes, or gives you a Type 1 error. Depending on your work habits, you may need to save more frequently than other people do. Here are some golden rules about when to save:

✦ Save as soon as you create a new file. Get it out of the way. The toughest part of saving is deciding how and where you are going to save the file and naming it. If you get those details out of the way in the beginning, pressing ⌘+S [Ctrl+S] later is fairly painless.

✦ Save before you print.

✦ Save before you switch to another application. Jostling stuff around in a computer's RAM is an open invitation for the whole system to poop out.

✦ Save right after you do something that you never want to have to do again — such as getting the kerning "just right" on a logo or matching all of the colors in your gradients so that they meet seamlessly.

✦ Save after you use a filter that takes more than a few seconds to complete.

✦ Save before you create a new document or go to another document.

✦ Save at least every 15 minutes.

✦ Save before you leave the computer. If you step away even to get a drink or to go to the restroom, you never know exactly how soon you can get back to your computer. It seems that every time I step away from my computer, I get roped into some meeting or emergency.

The Save As command

In addition to being used the first time a file is saved, the Save As command (⌘+ Shift+S [Ctrl+Shift+S]) also enables you to save multiple versions of the document at different stages of progress. If you choose Save As and do not rename the file or change the save location, you are prompted to replace the existing file. If you choose Replace, the file that you saved before is erased and replaced with the new file that you are saving. Most disk and trash recovery utilities cannot recover a file that you delete this way.

The Save As command is also useful for changing the Preview and Compatibility options (which are described in the "File types and options" and "Compatibility options" sections later in this chapter). If you have saved in Omit Header Preview and want to change to Color Preview, choose File ➪ Save As — don't change the file name or file location — and choose Color from the Preview pop-up menu.

The Save a Copy command

The Save a Copy command (⌘+Option+S [Ctrl+Alt+S]) saves a copy of your document in its current state without affecting your document or its name. Here's the scoop: Let's say you've designed a fairly nice logo—Whittles Logo—for Dr. Whittles, the plastic surgeon down the street. Dr. Whittles is pretty conservative, but his patients aren't. You need to show him both a basic logo and the same logo but spruced up. Once you've created the basic logo, you can Save a Copy as *Basic Logo* and continue working on *Whittles Logo*. The next time you press ⌘+S [Ctrl+S], your changes will be saved to Whittles Logo, and Basic Logo won't be affected at all.

Reverting to the last saved version

Choosing File ➪ Revert is an option that automatically closes the document and opens the last saved version of it. This option is grayed out if the file has not yet been saved. When it is selected, a dialog box appears, asking you to confirm that you *do* want to revert to the last saved version of the document.

Caution   A Revert action cannot be undone, and you won't be able to redo anything you've done up to that point with the document.

The Save for Web command

Choosing File ➪ Save for Web (⌘+Shift+Option+S [Ctrl+Shift+Alt+S]) opens the Save for Web dialog box, shown in Figure 2-14, where you can compare many different saving options to address the quality versus file size issue that is so important for Web graphics.

Cross-Reference   Saving graphics for the Web is a common job for designers nowadays. Illustrator 10 includes many new features that make this task much easier. Chapter 17, "Using Illustrator to Generate Web Graphics," covers this topic in much more depth, including the various features of the Save for Web dialog box.

 Along the top of the Save for Web dialog box are four tabs—Original, Optimized, 2-Up and 4-Up (sorry to report for you soft-drink fans that there isn't a 7-Up tab). Using these tabs, you can see your original work, an optimized version, and either two or four different versions side by side. For all optimized versions, the exact file sizes and download times for various modem speeds are displayed.

On the right side of the dialog box are settings for controlling the file format, dithering, palette, colors, and image size. You can also select and save setting profiles that can be reused by selecting them from a drop-down list.

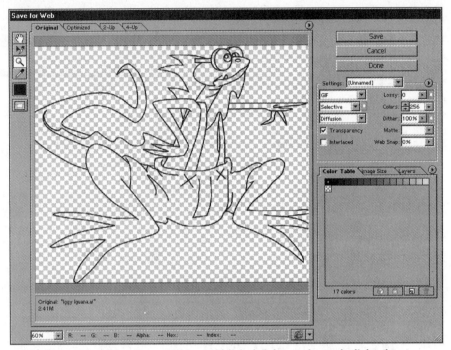

Figure 2-14: The rather large and incredibly helpful Save for Web dialog box

File types and options

You can save Illustrator 10 files in several ways. Actually, you can save them to almost 30 different formats. Each format will present a dialog box full of options.

Saving an Illustrator file with the wrong options can dramatically affect whether that file can be opened or placed in other software, as well as what features are included with the file when it is reopened in Illustrator. Saving a document as an older version of Illustrator may alter the document if the older version was missing features you used in your document.

Tip   If you plan on exporting your work for use in another vector-based software package, the best choice is EPS. This format can be read by more other packages than any other format.

As a rule, unless you're going to take your Illustrator document into another program, you can save it as an Illustrator file (AI) without any problems. This keeps the file size down and makes saving and opening the file much quicker.

Compatibility options for the AI format

Illustrator is one of the few software programs that is almost fully backward compatible. If you open a file in Illustrator 88 that you created in Illustrator 10, it looks almost exactly the same. Some software packages are forward compatible for one major version, but Illustrator is novel in that you can open an Illustrator 1.1 file in version 10 of the software, even though more than ten years have passed between those product versions.

When saving to the Illustrator (AI) format, the Illustrator Native Format Options dialog box, shown in Figure 2-15, will appear.

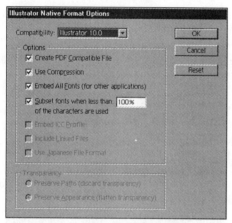

Figure 2-15: The Illustrator Native Format Options dialog box for the AI format enables you to save the document to any previous Illustrator version.

A number of reasons exist to save illustrations in older versions of Illustrator. The following list provides information about saving files in each version:

✦ **Illustrator 9** saves the file along with any transparency information. It also supports any saved color profile that is attached to the document.

✦ **Illustrator 8** saves the file in a cross-platform (Mac and Windows) format. Illustrator 8 includes support for EMF file format, and drag-and-drop to Microsoft Office products (Windows), Japanese-format FreeHand files, and DXF file formats. The drag-and-drop feature lets you drag objects from Illustrator and drop them into a Microsoft Office application such as Word without having to save them to the hard drive.

✦ **Illustrator 7** saves the file in a cross-platform (Mac and Windows) Illustrator 7 format. Illustrator 7 supports several bitmap file formats that Illustrator 6 does not. In addition, RGB color is not supported in previous versions of Illustrator.

✦ **Illustrator 6** saves the file in the Illustrator 6 format. The major file structure difference between Illustrator 6 and Illustrator 5.x is Illustrator 6's capability to import almost any type of raster image, while 5.x only supports EPS images. Other, not-so-obvious changes have to do with advanced object labels that plug-in developers use to achieve all sorts of effects.

✦ **Illustrator 5** saves the file in the Illustrator 5 format, which includes both Illustrator 5.0 and 5.5. The features that were added to version 5.5 do not affect file content. Thus, files created in version 5.5 have the same structure as files created in version 5.0.

✦ **Illustrator 4** saves the file in the Illustrator 4 format, which is a version that is available only for Windows users. Saving a file in the Illustrator 4 format ensures that Illustrator 4 for Windows will open that Illustrator file. Gradients, views, layers, and custom artboard sizes are not supported by the Illustrator 4 format. Technically, no real difference exists between the Illustrator 3 and 4 formats.

✦ **Illustrator 3** saves the file in the Illustrator 3 format. In fact, you can use the Illustrator 3 format for a lot of cheating — doing things that Illustrator normally doesn't enable you to do. For example, technically, you can't put gradients or masks into patterns. But if you save a gradient as an Illustrator 3 file and reopen it in Illustrator 7, the gradient becomes a blend, which you can use in a pattern (although Illustrator's Expand feature is quicker for this sort of task).

✦ **Illustrator 88** saves the file in the Illustrator 88 format, which, for about four years (1988 to 1991), was the Illustrator standard. Much clip art was created and saved in the Illustrator 88 format. The main problem with saving in the Illustrator 88 format is that type changes occurred between Illustrator 88 and Illustrator 3. Illustrator 88 cannot handle type on a curve (called path type, which it turns into individual segments), and it doesn't deal correctly with compound paths (type converted to outlines is made up of several compound paths, one for each character).

✦ **Illustrator 1.1** saves the file in the oldest of Adobe Illustrator formats, version 1.1. Saving in the Illustrator 1.1 format is useful when you want to take files into older versions of FreeHand and many other older drawing programs. Illustrator 1.1 format doesn't support custom colors or masks.

Saving as Illustrator EPS

If you do have to place your Illustrator document in another program, such as QuarkXPress, you need to save the file as Illustrator EPS. After you select the Illustrator EPS option in the Save As box and name the file, clicking the Save button brings up yet another dialog box, shown in Figure 2-16.

File Extensions

If you're using Illustrator on a Macintosh, be sure to append the two- or three-letter extension to your file name. While you may think that your files will never see a PC, they might, and since OS X supports extensions, it's a good idea to append the following extensions to file types:

+ .ai for Illustrator native format

+ .jpg for Illustrator EPS

+ .pdf for Portable Document Format (Acrobat) files

In addition, it's always a good idea to append the necessary extensions to raster formats as well (for example, .jpg for JPEG, .gif for GIF, .jpg for TIFF, and so on).

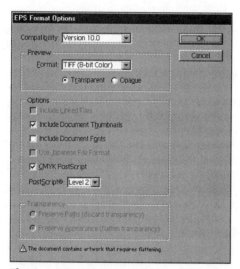

Figure 2-16: EPS Format Options dialog box

At the top of the EPS Format Options dialog box is a popup menu/drop-down list that enables you to select the Compatibility version. Available options include Illustrator versions all the way back to 3.0 and 3.2.

The following Preview options in Illustrator 10 affect the way that other software programs see Illustrator files when they are saved as Illustrator EPS files. Because files saved in the EPS format can include both vector and bitmap graphics, previews can be saved in bitmap formats in order to be displayed in other programs. These previews can be viewed as Transparent or Opaque images:

✦ **None** lets most software programs recognize the Illustrator document as an EPS file, but instead of viewing it in their software, you see a box with an X in it. Usually, this box is the same size as the illustration and includes any stray anchor points or control handles. The file will print fine from other software.

✦ **TIFF (Black & White)** saves the EPS file with a TIFF file preview as part of the EPS file. A TIFF image is embedded within the EPS file; you do not have two separate files. Page-layout and other software programs display this illustration in a black-and-white preview with no shades of gray in it. This file may take up substantially more space than the Include EPSF Header file requires because of the TIFF preview file. The larger the illustration measures, the more storage space it uses.

✦ **TIFF (8-bit Color)** saves the file with a color preview that is an embedded TIFF image. Page-layout and other software programs display this file in 8-bit color (256 colors) when you place it in a document. An Illustrator file that you save with a color preview takes up more file space than a file saved with any other option.

If your document includes transparency, you can select to preserve the appearance that is displayed by flattening the transparency, or you can preserve the integrity of the paths by discarding the transparency. These two options are disabled if the document doesn't contain any transparency.

Saving files in PDF format

The PDF format option saves files in Adobe Acrobat–compatible Portable Document Format (PDF). An Illustrator document saved as a PDF file becomes a page when opened in Acrobat. Acrobat Reader is free on most online services.

The Adobe PDF Format Options dialog box, shown in Figure 2-17, includes an option to save the file using the Acrobat 4.0 and 5.0 formats.

Selecting the General popup menu/drop-down list at the top of the dialog box will let you choose the Compression options, shown in Figure 2-18. This panel of options will let you select a compression format and quality as well as how bitmap images are handled.

Saving files with the SVG formats

The Scalable Vector Graphics (SVG) format is a new format that was created with broad industry support. It is an XML-based format that enables vector images to be saved and displayed online using a web browser.

Cross-Reference   The SVG format is covered in more detail in Chapter 17, "Using Illustrator to Generate Web Graphics."

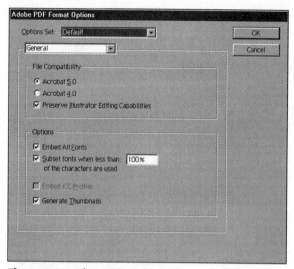

Figure 2-17: The options for saving a document using the PDF format.

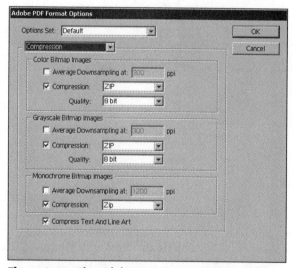

Figure 2-18: The Adobe PDF Format Options dialog box includes a second panel of compression options.

Figure 2-19 shows the options for saving an SVG file. These options include how to handle fonts and images. The Advanced button will display another dialog box of options, shown in Figure 2-20, which can be used to define how style sheets are used. These dialog boxes are used for both the SVG and the SVGZ formats.

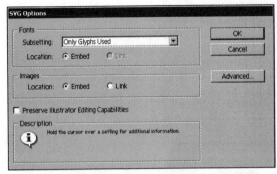

Figure 2-19: The SVG Options dialog box includes options for handling fonts and images.

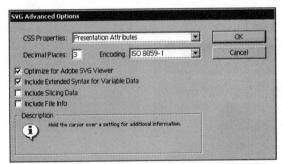

Figure 2-20: The SVG Advanced Options dialog box includes additional SVG settings

Exporting Files

Although the File ⇨ Save command only includes a limited number of formats, the File ⇨ Export option includes a large number of formats. Adobe Illustrator 10 enables you to export to several different file formats. Most of the export formats are bitmap formats such as TIFF, JPEG, and PICT, but some are vector formats.

Caution   Exporting an Illustrator document to any of these formats will change the document so that it can no longer be edited in Illustrator. Before exporting the document, be sure to save the document using the Save As command.

The complete list of export formats includes:

✦ AutoCAD Drawing (DWG)

✦ AutoCAD Interchange File (DXF)

✦ Windows Bitmap (BMP)

✦ Computer Graphics Metafile (CGM)

✦ Enhance Metafile (EMF)

✦ JPEG (JPG)

✦ Macintosh PICT (PIC)

✦ Macromedia Flash (SWF)

✦ PCX (PCX)

✦ Photoshop (PSD)

✦ Pixar (PXR)

✦ Targa (TGA)

✦ Text (TXT)

✦ TIFF (TIF)

✦ Windows Metafile (WMF)

Each export format will have its own dialog box of options that will control how the document is exported. For example, exporting an Illustrator document to a Photoshop (PSD) format will open a dialog box shown in Figure 2-21.

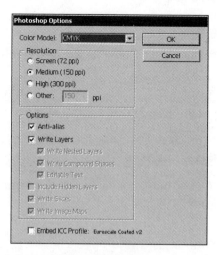

Figure 2-21: The Photoshop Options dialog box includes options for exporting an Illustrator file to the PSD format.

Placing Art

File formats that you can place or import into Illustrator are the same formats that can be opened using the File ⇨ Open menu. To place files, choose File ⇨ Place. A standard Open dialog box appears, as shown in Figure 2-22. Only files that can be placed appear in the file window and a preview of the image is displayed if available.

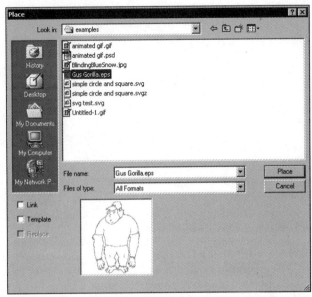

Figure 2-22: The Place dialog box will display a thumbnail of certain images.

After you place art into Illustrator, you can transform it (move, scale, rotate, reflect, and shear it) in any way.

The quality of placed art is as good as the original; if the original file was bitmapped (created or saved in a paint program such as Photoshop), then the quality lessens as the file is scaled up, and the quality increases as the file is scaled down. If the file was in PostScript outline format (created in Illustrator or FreeHand, EPS only), then the quality stays consistent as the file changes in size.

Note   You can use placed raster images for tracing, but the Auto Trace tool does not recognize EPS and does not automatically surround it.

Illustrator shows placed art differently in Outline mode and in Preview mode. In Outline mode, placed art is in black and white, or just shows up as a box.

When you save a document with placed art in it with a preview, you can link the placed art to Illustrator or include it in the Illustrator file. Normally, including the placed art within the Illustrator file is the better choice. This method prevents the two files from being separated; if you have one and not the other, you are out of luck. But you may want to link the file instead of including it for two reasons. First, placed art can be huge and may make your Illustrator file too large. Second, if you need to make changes to a placed art file that you have included in an Illustrator file that you have saved with a preview, you have to replace the placed art in the preview file with the new version. If you have linked the placed art instead of including it, the art is automatically updated when you make changes.

Tip Using linked placed files comes in handy if you are re-using an image in multiple documents. Then changing the placed image will automatically update the image in all documents without having to open and change each document individually.

You may want to replace placed art with new versions or completely different artwork. Illustrator has made this process painless. If placed artwork is selected, a dialog box appears asking if you would like to replace current artwork or place new artwork, not changing the selected artwork.

The really cool part about changing placed art this way is that if you have placed artwork that has been transformed, the artwork you exchange with it via the Place Art command will have the exact same transformation attributes! For example, if you scale down placed artwork to 50 percent and rotate it 45 degrees, artwork that is exchanged with that artwork is also scaled down 50 percent and rotated 45 degrees.

You can dim placed art by checking the Dim Images To checkbox in the Layer Options dialog box on the Layers palette and entering a Dim value. (By a Dim value we mean a percentage you want your image dimmed, not a half-witted value.) If you dim placed art, then a ghost of the image appears instead of the solid image. This feature makes manually tracing placed art easy. Dimming placed art does not affect its printed output.

Tip Another useful way to dim an image is to use the Transparency palette to reduce its Opacity value.

Placed art size issues

Be careful when importing artwork other than EPS images into Illustrator, as TIFF and most other bitmap formats increase the size of your document dramatically. The reason for this is that the image information for TIFFs and other formats is stored within the Illustrator document, and is not linked to the document in the way Placed EPS images are. Making the issue even stickier, duplicating TIFFs within Illustrator increases the document size by the size of that TIFF once again.

Using Document and File Information

Over time, your collection of Illustrator files will grow and quickly it will reach an unmanageable amount. This makes it difficult to find that one dog-show logo that you completed around two years ago or the image that used that really cool pattern. To help you with this problem, Illustrator includes several features that help you track important information about the document.

The Document Info palette includes a summary of the document including all the objects contained within the document as well as general information such as the size and color profile. The File Info dialog box can be used to record information about the document such as a detailed description and keywords.

Viewing Document Info

If you need to see a summary of a document, you can use the Document Info palette, shown in Figure 2-23, to see this information. From the palette menu (also shown in the figure), you can specify which type of information to access.

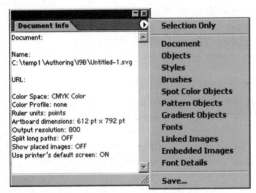

Figure 2-23: The Document Info palette displays information about the document.

The fly-away menu has eleven different information views for the active document:

- ✦ The first option, Document, shows the document setup of the active document. All the relevant options from the Document Setup dialog box are shown, including the Color Space and Profile, Ruler Units, Artboard Dimensions, and more, along with the name of the file.

- ✦ The second option is Objects, which lists how many paths, masks, transparent objects, styled objects, spot colors, patterns, gradients, fonts, and placed images are used in the document. This can be used as a rudimentary guide to how long a file may take to print.

✦ The remaining options show the names of any enclosed styles, brushes, spot colors, patterns, gradients, and fonts. The Linked and Embedded Images options list the name of the placed art and the disk path that tells Illustrator where to find it.

Note One option in the pop-up menu is Save. This Save option creates a simple text file with all categories of information about the document. To view the saved Document Info file, you must double-click the file name or open it within a text editor or a word processor.

Recording File Info

The File Info dialog box, shown in Figure 2-24, can be opened using the File ➪ File Info menu. Using the pane at the left, you can switch between the General, Keywords and Summary screens. Each screen includes text fields where you can enter information that will be stored with the file.

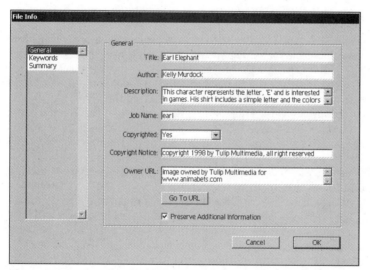

Figure 2-24: The File Info dialog box can hold information about the document.

Enabling Workgroup Collaboration

By establishing a workgroup, you can open and save documents to a location on the Internet that all members of the workgroup can access. This enables users from around the globe to work together on a project. For example, a designer in your California office could check out a document and add the logo design, then your editorial staff in New York could add text, then your layout specialist in London could position the elements on the page and finally, the publishing manager on vacation in Mexico could get online and sign off on the final layout before sending it to the publishing house.

To prevent one member of the workgroup from overwriting another members work, you need to check out the document from the Internet server before you can work on it. If another member of the workgroup has the file checked out, then you'll need to wait until there are finished with their updates and check the document back in before it becomes available for you.

Establishing a workgroup server

The first step in creating a workgroup is to setup a workgroup server on the Internet where the documents will reside. Illustrator uses a specialized type of Internet server that makes workgroup collaboration possible called the WebDAV server. WebDAV is an acronym for Web Based Distributed Authoring and Versioning. WebDAV servers are an industry standard server and you can find information about these servers at the WebDAV web site — www.webdav.org.

Note To setup a WebDAV server, you'll need to engage the help of your system administrator, who is responsible for setting up and configuring Web servers.

Once a WebDAV server is setup, you'll need to let your local version of Illustrator know where the server is located. This can be done using the File ➪ Manage Workgroup ➪ Workgroup Servers. This menu option will open the Workgroup Servers dialog box, shown in Figure 2-25. Click on the Choose button to select a folder on your local hard drive to which the workgroup files are checked out.

The Workgroup Servers dialog box displays a list of available servers. Illustrator can be set to point to several different workgroup servers. The New Server button will open a dialog box where you can give the server a nickname and define the server's URL, which is its address on the Web. The Edit Server button will let you change the server details and the Remove button will delete the selected server from the list. Within the New Server dialog box is a button labeled Advance Options. Clicking this button will open another dialog box where you can specify a custom workgroup file location and any alternate URLs for this server.

Once a workgroup server is setup, you can select it from the list to enable documents to be checked in and out from the server.

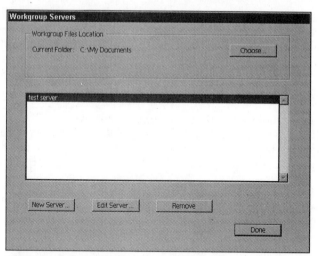

Figure 2-25: The Workgroup Servers dialog box is used to define the list of workgroup servers.

Setting workgroup preferences

The Preferences dialog box includes a panel for setting the workgroup options. Select Illustrator [Edit] ⇨ Preferences ⇨ Workgroup to open this dialog box, shown in Figure 2-26. At the top of the dialog box is a checkbox that is used to turn the workgroup features of Illustrator on and off.

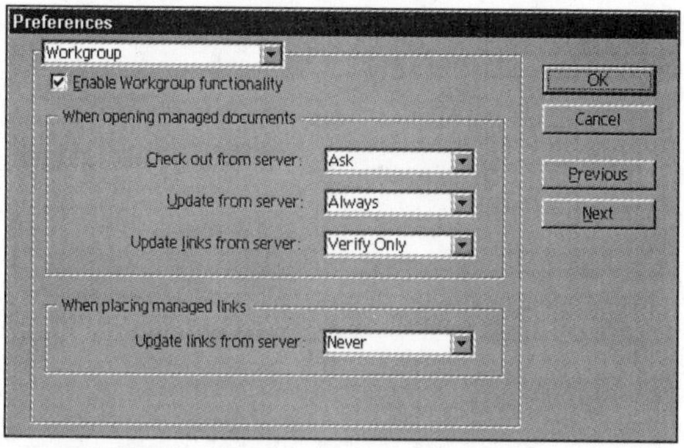

Figure 2-26: The Workgroup panel in the Preferences dialog box

Within the options are the settings for how Illustrator will handle checking out, updating and updating links from the server. The options include Ask, Never and Always. The Ask option will present a dialog box every time you check out, update or update linked files. The Never option will open the local copy of the documents without presenting a dialog box. The Always option will always automatically check out the requested document.

The Update Links options includes a fourth option, Verify Only, which will check with the server to see if any of the linked images are out of date. If any out of date images are found, then the images will be displayed as broken links in the Links palette.

Working with workgroup documents

With a server selected, you can get a workgroup managed document using the File ➪ Manage Workgroup ➪ Open menu option. This will present a dialog box showing the managed documents. Select the document that you wish to open and click Check Out to open and check out the document or Open if you wish to open a local copy without checking it out. Checked out files are locked so that no other users can make changes to it, but opened copies can be altered and the changes updated at a later time with the File ➪ Manage Workgroup ➪ Update menu option. If the document is already open, you can use the File ➪ Manage Workgroup ➪ Check Out menu option to check out the document.

Once you've made the needed changes, the File ➪ Manage Workgroup ➪ Check In menu option will check the document back in to the server and update the document with the changes you've made. If you do not wish to update the document, you can select the File ➪ Manage Workgroup ➪ Cancel Check Out option. This will release the document so others can work on it without updating your changes.

To add a document to the workgroup, use the File ➪ Manage Workgroup ➪ Save or Save As menu options. These options will open a file dialog box for the current server that will let you name and select a folder on the server where the file will be saved.

Managing links

The File ➪ Manage Workgroup ➪ Place menu option can be used to place a document as a link to a checked out document. All linked images will be listed in the Links palette, shown in Figure 2-27. You can save linked images to the workgroup server using the Save Workgroup Link menu option in the palette menu. The Verify Workgroup Link option will check with the server to see if any new documents have been updated on the server. These linked images will be marked by a small red triangle on the icon next to the image in the Links palette.

Caution Remember to upload any files that are linked to a checked out document or the person that checks out the document will not have access to the linked files.

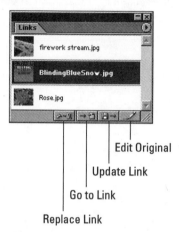

Edit Original

Update Link

Go to Link

Replace Link

Figure 2-27: The Links palette lists all the linked images for the current document.

To embed a linked image within the current document, use the Embed Image option in the palette menu. This will break the link and include the image file as part of the base document. The file size will also increase. The palette menu also includes options to update the links, edit the original and replace the linked image. The palette menu also includes an option labeled Information, which will open a dialog box like the one shown in Figure 2-28 that displays information about the linked image.

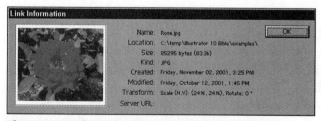

Figure 2-28: The Link Information dialog box displays information about the linked image.

If you select to replace an image that has different dimensions than the current linked image, you can select how the new image maps to the dimensions of the current image using the Placement Options dialog box, shown in Figure 2-29. The Preserve popup menu/drop-down list includes five options — Transforms, Proportions (Fit), Proportions (Fill), File Dimensions, and Bounds. Each of these options is explained in the dialog box. For each you can select the alignment corner (or edge) using the Alignment icon.

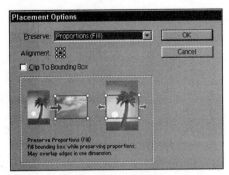

Figure 2-29: The Placement Options dialog box lets you decide how images are aligned when replaced.

The palette menu includes options for filtering the images that are displayed in the Links palette. These options include Show All, Show Missing, Show Modified, and Show Embedded. You can also sort the images by Name, Kind and Status. The Palette Options dialog box, which appears when the Palette Options menu option is selected in the palette menu, lets you select the size of the palette thumbnail size and the whether or not to Show Transparency Interactions.

Summary

If you refuse to work with documents, then you won't get very far with Illustrator. Every file needs to be opened and saved and that is what this chapter is all about. In this chapter, you learned:

✦ When a new document is created with the File ➪ New menu (⌘+N [Ctrl+N]), you can select the dimensions of the artboard and the color mode.

✦ The current document setup can be modified in the Document Setup dialog box, accessed by pressing ⌘+Option+P [Ctrl+Alt+P] or by choosing File ➪ Document Setup.

✦ You can automatically use the current Page Setup as your artwork size by selecting the Use Page Setup checkbox in the Document Setup dialog box, or you can access Page Setup by pressing ⌘+Shift+P [Ctrl+Shift+P].

✦ Path splitting is useful if you have several long paths and are getting PostScript limit check errors when printing.

✦ Unless you'll be importing the files into another application, you should save them as Illustrator 10 files.

✦ Illustrator files can be saved as AI, EPS, PDF and SVG files. They can also be exported into many different vector and raster-based formats.

✦ If you'll be importing files into another application, you probably want to save them as EPS, with an 8-bit preview.

✦ You can place any EPS image, bitmap, text, or vector file, by using the Place command, which is located in the File menu.

✦ Using the Document Info palette and the File Info dialog box, you can find and record information about a document that will help you locate it at a future date.

✦ Documents can be managed as part of a workgroup using a server that places files on the Web where a workgroup can check files in and out.

✦ All linked files within the current document are displayed within the Links palette.

✦   ✦   ✦

Drawing and Painting

The most effective (and challenging) way to create paths is to draw them with one of the drawing tools. The two main drawing tools include the Paintbrush and Pencil tools. Another useful drawing utility is the Brushes palette. Illustrator users looking for the Calligraphic, Scatter, Art, and Pattern brushes will find them in the Brushes palette menu. The Pencil tool, which includes the Smooth tool and the Erase tool in its pop-up menu, cuts editing time drastically.

Understanding Paths

Before you dive right in and start making a mess of your artboard, you need to learn all about the concept of paths. Once you understand this concept, all the squiggly lines will make some sense.

Drawing Paths

The most basic element in Illustrator is a *path*. A path in Illustrator must have at least two Anchor Points, and a line segment between those two Anchor Points (see Figure 3-1). At the same time, conceptually, no limit exists to the number of Anchor Points or segments that can be in any one path. Depending on the type of Anchor Points that are on either end of a line segment, the segment may be straight or curved.

Path types

Three major types of paths exist:

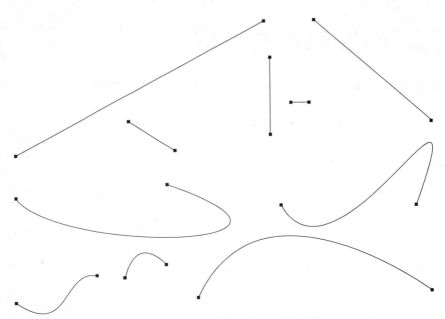

Figure 3-1: Paths consisting of two Anchor Points with a line segment between them

Path types

Three major types of paths exist:

✦ **Open paths** are paths that have two distinct End Points, with any number of Anchor Points in between.

✦ **Closed paths** are paths that are continuous. Such paths have no start or end and no End Points — they just continue around and around with a distinct inside and outside.

✦ **Compound paths** are paths that are made up of two or more open or closed paths.

Cross-Reference For a detailed look at compound paths, see Chapter 11, "Using Path Blends, Compound Paths, and Masks."

Viewing paths in Outline mode

When you work in Illustrator in Outline mode (View ➪ Outline), only paths are visible. In Preview mode (View ➪ Preview), fills and strokes applied to paths are visible. Unless a path is selected in Preview mode, that path (Anchor Points and line segments) isn't visible.

Paths in Illustrator can be filled with color, a pattern, a gradient, or a gradient mesh (which is gradient that is attached to a mesh that you can control). Closed paths always use the color to fill the *insides* of the shapes they form (see Figure 3-2). Paths can be stroked with a color, a pattern, or a brush.

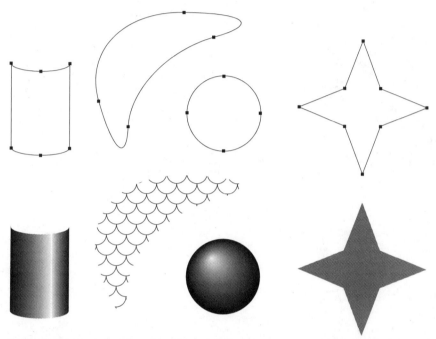

Figure 3-2: Closed paths with different fills: The top row shows how they appear in Outline mode, and the bottom row shows what they look like in Preview mode.

Filling and stroking paths

Open paths can also be filled; the fill goes straight across the two End Points of the path to enclose the object. Figure 3-3 displays different types of filled open paths. Filling an open path is usually not desirable, although in some circumstances it may be necessary.

Besides filling paths, you can also stroke paths with any tint of any color, or a pattern. These strokes can be any weight (thickness), and the width of the stroke is equally distributed over each side of the path. Open paths have ends on the strokes; these ends can be cropped, rounded, or extended past the end of each stroke by half the width of the stroke. Figure 3-4 shows several different paths with strokes.

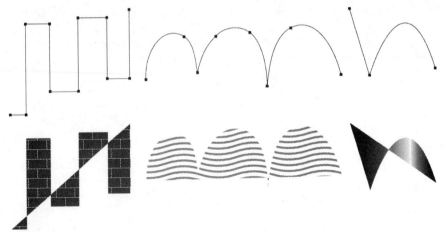

Figure 3-3: Open paths with different fills: The top row shows how they appear in Outline mode, and the bottom row shows how they appear in Preview mode.

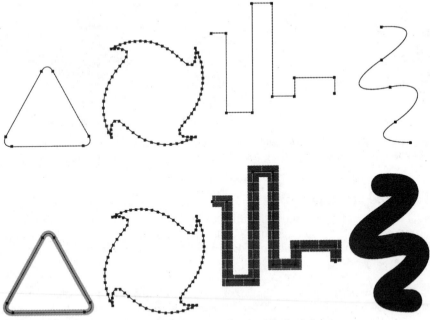

Figure 3-4: Various paths with different strokes applied to them

A single point, even though not a visible path, may contain the attributes of a path, but a single point in Illustrator can have no printable qualities (unless it has a brush applied to it). Having stray points floating around your document isn't readily noticeable because you *can* assign a fill or stroke color to a single point, although it still can't be seen in Preview mode or when printed. However, when the document is color separated, that single point of "fill," or color, will cause a separation of the color to print even if nothing else on that page is using the same color, and the separation will be blank. To be safe, if you think you might have individual Anchor Points floating around your illustration, you can select all of them at once by choosing Select ➪ Object ➪ Stray Points, and then delete them.

Fills and strokes in Illustrator can be any opaque color, which will knock out any color underneath. Fills and strokes may also be partially transparent, in which case the stroke or fill will not be opaque, which lets whatever is beneath "shine through." Partial transparency in Illustrator is achieved by the use of the Transparency palette.

Cross-Reference   Transparency is covered in more detail in Chapter 12, "Using Transparency."

Attaching anchor points

Paths are made up of a series of points and the line segments between those points. The points are commonly called *Anchor Points* because they anchor the path; paths *always* pass through or end at Anchor Points. Anchor Points come in two classes:

✦ **Smooth points** are Anchor Points that have a curved path flowing smoothly through them; most of the time you don't know where a smooth point is unless the path is selected. Smooth points keep the path from changing direction abruptly. Every smooth point has two linked *control handles*.

✦ **Corner points** are a class of Anchor Points in which the path changes direction noticeably at those specific points. Corner points come in three types:

  • *Straight corner points* are Anchor Points where two straight line segments meet at a distinct angle. This type of Anchor Point has no control handles.

  • *Curved corner points* are points where two curved line segments meet and abruptly change direction. Each curved corner point has two *independent control handles*.

  • *Combination corner points* are the meeting places for straight and curved line segments. A combination corner point has one independent control handle.

Figure 3-5 shows the different types of Anchor Points in Illustrator.

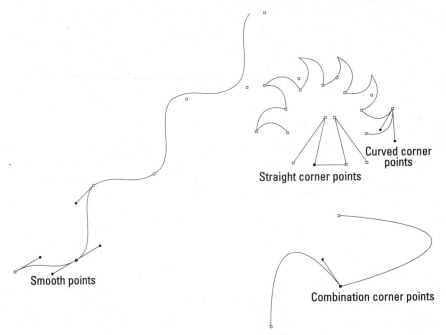

Figure 3-5: The different types of Anchor Points in Illustrator

Anchor Points, control handles, and control handle lines do not appear on the printed output of your artwork. In fact, they only appear in Illustrator, InDesign, QuarkXPress, and Photoshop — never on artwork imported into other applications. They also will only appear when a path or Anchor Point is selected.

Bending Bézier curves

PostScript curves are based on *Bézier curves* (pronounced *bez-ee-ay*), which were created by Pierre Bézier (see Figure 3-6) in the early 1970s as a way of controlling mechanical cutting devices, commonly known as Numerical Control. Bézier worked for Renault (the car manufacturer) in France, and his mission was to streamline the process by which machines were controlled.

A mathematician and engineer, Bézier developed a method for creating curves using four points for every curved segment. Two of these points lay at either end of the segment (we call them *Anchor Points* in Illustrator), and two points just floated around the curve segment, controlling the shape of the curve (*control handles*). Using these four points, one could conceivably create any curve; using multiple sets of these curves, one could create any possible shape. The two PostScriptateers, John Warnock and Chuck Geschke of Adobe, decided that using Bézier curves gave them the best method for creating curves in a page description language, and suddenly those curves became a fundamental part of high-end graphic design.

Figure 3-6: Pierre Bézier's groundwork indirectly resulted in Adobe Illustrator.

If an Anchor Point has a control handle coming out of it, the next segment will be curved. No control handle, no curve. Couldn't be simpler.

Control handles are connected to Anchor Points with *control handle lines*. Figure 3-7 shows what happens when an Anchor Point with no control handle, and an Anchor Point with a control handle, are connected to new Anchor Points.

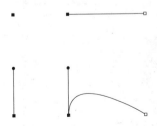

Figure 3-7: An Anchor Point without a control handle (top left) and an Anchor Point with a control handle (bottom left) are connected to new Anchor Points, resulting in a straight line segment (top right) and a curved line segment (bottom right).

The control handle lines themselves really have no function other than to show you which Anchor Points the control handles are attached to. You cannot select a control handle line. The only way to move a control handle line, or to change the length of a control handle line, is by moving its corresponding control handle. Figure 3-8 shows how control handles and lines work with curves and Anchor Points.

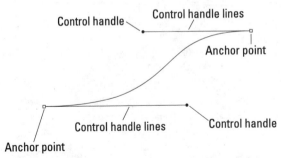

Figure 3-8: Anchor Points, control handles, and control handle lines along a path

The basic concept of control handles is that the control handles act as magnets, pulling the curve toward them (see Figure 3-9). This presents an interesting problem because each curved line segment usually has two control handles. As you might suspect, the control handle exerts the greatest amount of force on the half of the curved segment nearest to it. If only one control handle exists, then the segment is curved more on the side of the segment with the control handle than on the side with no control handle.

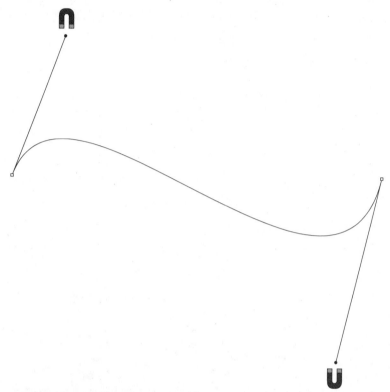

Figure 3-9: Control handles act as magnets, pulling the curve toward them.

The greater the distance between a control handle and its corresponding Anchor Point, the farther the curve (on that end of the curve segment) pulls away from an imaginary straight segment between the two points (see Figure 3-10). If the control handles on either end of the segment are on different sides of the curved segment, the curved segment will be somewhat S-shaped, as the bottom path in Figure 3-10 shows. If the control handles on the ends of the curved segment are on the same side, the curve will be somewhat U-shaped, as shown in the top path of Figure 3-10.

Control handle lines coming out of an Anchor Point are always *tangent* to the curved segment where they touch the Anchor Point, regardless of whether the Anchor Point is a Smooth point, a curved corner point, or a combination corner point. Tangent refers to the angle of both the control handle line and the angle of the curved segment as it crosses the Anchor Point (see Figure 3-11).

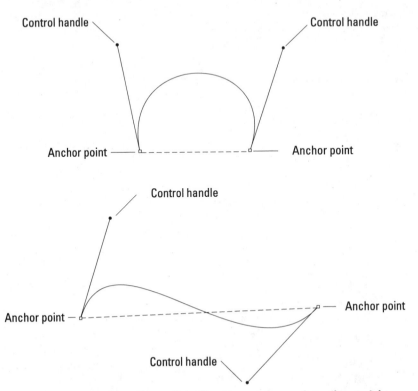

Control handle   Control handle

Anchor point   Anchor point

Control handle

Anchor point   Anchor point

Control handle

Figure 3-10: Control handles pull the line segment away from the straight line that would normally exist between them. The bottom path is an S shape because the control handles are being pulled in opposite directions.

Figure 3-11: Control handle lines run tangent to the path where the path meets the Anchor Point.

Using Illustrator Tools to Draw Paths

You can use many different drawing tools to draw paths. The Paintbrush tool offers the easiest way to create paths. It is even more amazing when you use it with a pressure-sensitive tablet. The Pencil tool is simple to use to create paths and, with its editing capabilities, it can be indispensable. The Pen tool is the most difficult to use, but its results can be better than the Paintbrush or the Pencil tool.

Each drawing tool does something better than any of the others, as well as having its own limitations. However tempting it may be, don't ignore any one of these tools because you think that another tool can perform the same function.

If we were gambling men, we'd bet that the one tool that you want to avoid is the Pen tool. Unfortunately, mastering Illustrator becomes impossible if you avoid learning how to use this tool. Hey, we won't kid you—mastering the Pen tool is like mastering calculus: It makes no sense at first and even less sense when people explain it to you. But, as with calculus, the more you use the Pen tool, the more you like it, and the more technically amazing things you can do with it. (Personally, we think the Pen tool is easier to learn than calculus, and, fortunately, this shaky analogy ends here.)

Note
Understanding how the Pen tool works helps you understand not only how Illustrator works, but also how PostScript and many other tools in other programs work. Adobe Photoshop also has a Pen tool that is virtually identical to Illustrator's Pen tool; so by understanding and using the Pen tool in Illustrator, you've already learned one of the most difficult tools to use in Photoshop.

Figure 3-12 was drawn using a combination of all three drawing tools. Throughout this chapter, we explain how the various parts of this illustration were drawn and how they were manipulated to produce the final drawing.

The Pencil tool

The Pencil tool initially seems to be a primitive version of the Paintbrush tool (which is covered later in the chapter). Like the Paintbrush tool, the Pencil tool draws a freeform stroked path wherever the cursor is dragged, but instead of creating a closed path that is a certain width, the result is a single path that approximately follows the route you've taken with the cursor. You can get the resulting path to follow your cursor-drawn line exactly by lowering the tolerance values found in the Pencil Tool Preferences dialog box, shown in Figure 3-13. You can open this dialog box by double-clicking the Pencil tool.

Figure 3-12: This illustration was drawn using the Paintbrush, Pencil, and Pen tools.

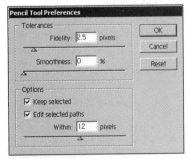

Figure 3-13: The Pencil Tool Preferences dialog box will let you set the Tolerances for the Pencil tool.

When you need to draw rough edges or realistic illustrations that don't look "computer-drawn," the Pencil tool is the tool to use. It draws a path wherever you drag the tool with the mouse, creating smooth curves or sharp corners relative to how you draw. Although the Pen tool is the tool to use to get precise, super-straight lines, it is difficult to use. The Pencil tool is much easier to use, but it draws lines that are far from perfect.

In addition to the Pencil tool, there are other drawing tools in the toolbox that can be used to draw lines. The Line Segment tool (\) can be used to draw perfectly straight lines and the Arc tool can draw nice sloping arc segments. Both these tools are covered in Chapter 4, "Working with Objects."

The Pencil tool has the unique capability to make the lines you draw with the cursor look . . . well . . . good. A swooping, uneven, jagged line that looks terrible as it is being drawn can be instantly transformed into a beautifully curved piece of artwork reminiscent of lines drawn traditionally with a French curve.

Still, the Pencil tool has some limitations. The main limitation is that, unlike the Pen tool, it is an *imprecise* path-drawing tool. It is difficult to draw a straight line with the Pencil tool. It is even more difficult to draw a shape with precise curves. The location of a path drawn with the Pencil tool is directly relevant to the direction and speed that the cursor is moving. To address these limitations, Adobe has added a couple of tools to the Pencil tool's pop-up options: the Smooth tool, which smoothes out lines of a selected path, and the Erase tool, which erases sections out of a selected path.

Drawing loosely with the Pencil tool

Before you use the Pencil tool for the first time, it's a good idea to change the Paint style attributes to a Fill of None and a Stroke of Black, 1 point. You can set a 1-point stroke using the Stroke palette. Having a Fill other than None while drawing with the Pencil tool often results in bizarre-looking shapes because area between the path edge and a line that connects the two end Anchor Points will be filled with the Fill color. You can quickly select these attributes by clicking on the Default Fill and Stroke icon (or by pressing D) to the lower left of the Fill and Stroke colors and then click on the None box (/).

To use the Pencil tool, select it from the toolbox, click in the document window, and begin dragging the mouse. As you drag, a series of dots follows the cursor. These dots show the approximate location of the path you have drawn. After you release the mouse button, the path of dots is transformed into a path with anchor points, all with control handle lines and control handles shooting off from them. The faster you draw with the Pencil tool, the fewer points are created. The slower you draw, the more points are used to define the path.

Follow these steps to draw paths with the Pencil tool:

1. Double-click the Pencil tool and set the Fidelity to 2.5 pixels and the Smoothness to 50 percent, which allows for detail in the paths without making all the segments straight lines. Using the Color and Stroke palettes, set the Fill to C100 Y70 and a Stroke of Black, 1 point.

2. You can create the short grass shown previously in Figure 3-12 by drawing three different clumps of grass (see the top of Figure 3-14) and then duplicating

the clumps to create the appearance of random blades. To do this, select the Pencil tool and drag up and down to create the blades; then drag across under the blades to connect the bottom to form a closed path. Repeat this procedure to create three or four clumps of different sizes. Be sure to change the Fill color to a slightly different greenish color each time.

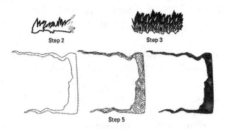

Figure 3-14: Clumps of grass and tree bark [GSL1]created with the Pencil tool

3. Using the Selection tool, click the clumps of grass and Option [Alt]+drag them side by side, overlapping them slightly. (Pressing the Option [Alt] key duplicates the dragged clumps.) Repeat this process until enough clumps exist to resemble a grassy area.

4. To create the tree, first change the Pencil Tool Preferences (by double-clicking the Pencil tool) fidelity to 2.5 pixels and the Smoothness to 100 percent. Drag with the Pencil tool to create the outline of the tree branch, trunk, and roots. Connect the ends of the path to close it and change the Fill to a dark brown (C75 M100 Y100 K25), keeping the Stroke set to Black.

5. To create the textured areas of the bark on the tree, change the Fill to None and the Stroke to a dark shade of Gray. Drag along the contours of the tree, which creates circles and wavy patterns.

Every anchor point created with the Pencil tool has two control handles shooting out of it; this means that you can't draw straight corner points with the Pencil tool. This lack of straight corner points makes constructing precise objects not only difficult, but also nearly impossible. Also, although they may appear to exist at first glance, smooth anchor points are not created with the Pencil tool, which can be especially deceiving when the Fidelity option is set to a high number and all the anchor points look like they are smooth points. This is *not* the case. In fact, most anchor points created with the Pencil tool — except for its end points — are *curved corner points*, which are anchor points with two independent control handles shooting out. If the Fidelity setting is high enough, you'll get smooth points as well. (See "Drawing Jagged versus Smooth Paths" later in this chapter for more information.) Normally, the Pencil tool resembles a little pencil when you are drawing, which is far better than having to draw with the little squiggle that appears in the toolbox. The line of dots that is drawn comes directly from the point (tip) of the pencil cursor.

Pressing the Caps Lock key (engaging it) changes the cursor from the pencil shape to cross-hairs, which looks suspiciously like the cross-hairs from the Paintbrush tool. The line of points comes from the dot in the center of the cross-hairs.

Tip   If you like using the cross-hairs cursor all the time, but get really mad every time you start typing because you forget to take off the Caps Lock key, you've got short-term memory problems. Fortunately, you can set your cursors to *always* be cross-hairs just by going to General Preferences (⌘+K [Ctrl+K]) and checking the Use Precise Cursors checkbox. When this option is checked, the Caps Lock key changes the cursor back to the regular tool.

Using the Pencil tool to draw open and closed paths

You can draw both open and closed paths with the Pencil tool. An *open path* has two separate, distinct end points. A *closed path* has no end points. To change an open path into a closed path, the end points must be joined together.

Cross-Reference   To learn more about joining end points, take a look at Chapter 5, "Selecting and Editing."

Paths in Illustrator may cross themselves. When these paths cross, the Fills may look a little unusual. Strokes look normal; they just overlap where paths cross.

To create an open path, draw a path with the Pencil tool, but make sure that the beginning and end of the path are two separate points at different locations. Open paths with Fills may look a little bizarre because Illustrator automatically fills in between the end points on the path, even if the imaginary line between the end points crosses the path itself. Figure 3-15 shows both open and closed paths drawn with the Pencil tool.

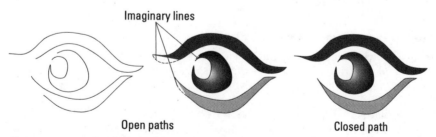

Imaginary lines

Open paths   Closed path

Figure 3-15: Paths drawn with the Pencil tool

To create a closed path, end your path at the same place where you started the path. When the pencil cursor is directly over the location where the line begins, a little circle appears to the lower-right of the pencil. This change means that the path is a closed path if you release the mouse button when that particular cursor is showing.

You can automatically create a closed path by holding down the Option [Alt] key while drawing with the Pencil tool. You will need to hold the Option [Alt] key down until you release the mouse button. Doing so creates a closed path regardless of where you stop drawing the path. A connecting segment is automatically drawn from the last point to the first.

Adding to an existing open path

To continue drawing on an existing path (which could have been drawn with the Pen tool or the Pencil tool), the existing path must first be an open path with two distinct end points. The path that you wish to extend needs to be selected. Select the Pencil tool and position the cursor on one of the path end points, and then draw the continued section while holding down the ⌘ [Ctrl] key. When the ⌘ [Ctrl] key is pressed, the cursor will look show a small rectangle with a line through it.

 Caution   You need to start drawing before pressing the ⌘ [Ctrl] key or you will simply drag the end anchor point.

Another way to continue a path is with the Caps Lock key. If this key is engaged, the cursor looks like cross-hairs and you can extend a path without using the ⌘ [Ctrl] key. Just position the cursor over an end point and drag to extend the path.

If you drag to the other open end of the existing path, you have the opportunity to make the path into a closed path. If you hold down the Option [Alt] key while extending the path, the path will be automatically closed.

You can add on only to end points on an existing path. Anchor points that are within paths cannot be connected to new (or existing, for that matter) segments. If you attempt to draw from an anchor point that is not an end point, you create an end point for the path you are drawing that is overlapping but not connected to the anchor point you clicked previously.

Drawing jagged versus smooth paths

Because drawing nice-looking paths with the Pencil tool and a mouse is just a tad difficult and frustrating ("Really?" you ask sarcastically), Illustrator provides a way to determine how rough or smooth your path will be *before* you draw it.

Normally, paths that appear from the dotted lines created with the Pencil tool are fairly similar to those dotted lines in direction and curves and such. When lines are being drawn, though, human error can cause all sorts of little bumps and skiddles (a *skiddle* is a little round misdrawn section resembling a small fruit-flavored candy) to appear, making the path look lumpy. In some cases, lumpy is good. More often than not, though, lumpy is an undesirable state for your illustrations.

The smoothness of the resulting paths drawn with the Pencil tool relies on the Fidelity and Smoothness options in the Pencil Tool Preferences dialog box, which determines how jagged or smooth each section will appear from the dotted line to the path.

The Fidelity setting controls the distance (measured in pixels) in which curves may stray from the original dotted line that you draw with the mouse. A low fidelity value results in sharper angles; a high fidelity value results in smoother curves. The smoothness setting controls the amount of smoothing (measured in percentage) to keep the path less bumpy or irregular. A low smoothness value results in a coarseangular path, while a high smoothness value results in a much smoother path with fewer anchor points (see Figure 3-16).

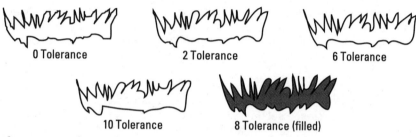

Figure 3-16: The results of different Fidelity Tolerance values

The Smooth tool

The Smooth tool is an extremely cool editing tool that makes changing any path a breeze. You can find the Smooth tool in the Pencil tool's pop-up tools. The Smooth tool works on any path regardless of what tool created it. To use the Smooth tool, you drag over a selected path to smooth out the line. The Smooth Tool Preferences dialog (which can be opened by double clicking on the Smooth tool) includes the same Fidelity and Smoothness values that were found in the Pencil Tool Preferences dialog box. A lower fidelity setting results in more mouse movement being recorded and more anchor points being added to the path. At a higher setting, fewer anchor points are used and the path is smoother. Figure 3-17 shows a path before and after using the Smooth tool. As you can see, the top path has more anchor points than the smoothed bottom path.

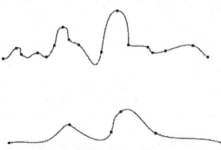

Figure 3-17: The path on the top is the original path. The path on the bottom is the same path after using the Smooth tool on it.

The Erase tool

The Erase tool is available in the Pencil tool's pop-up menu. Like the Smooth tool, the Erase tool works on any path, no matter how it was created. The Erase tool does what you'd think; it erases a path at the point where you have dragged the Erase tool over the path. You can use the Erase tool to cut a path by dragging across a section. The section you dragged over will be removed and new anchor points will be created on either end of the erased section.

You can use the Erase tool to cut a line the same way you would use the Scissors tool. If you just click one time on the path, the path would be cut exactly in that spot. Unlike Photoshop's clunky eraser-looking tool, Illustrator's Erase tool is much more refined.

The Eraser tool in some cases is much easier to use than the Scissors or Knife tools. The Scissors tool can only cut a path at an anchor point and the Knife tool can only separate enclosed sections. However, you can use the Eraser tool along any portion of a path regardless of anchor points.

Note   You cannot use the Eraser tool on text sections (unless they've been turned into outlines) or meshes.

The Pen tool

The Pen tool is the most powerful tool in Illustrator's arsenal because you are dealing more directly with Bézier curves than with any other tool. *Bézier curves* are a special type of curve that is mathematically defined and controlled using anchor points and control handles. It's one thing to adjust paths, anchor points, and control handles with the Direct Selection tool, but using the Pen tool to create paths out of nothing is dumbfounding.

During the first several months of our using Illustrator, we avoided the Pen tool like it was the plague. Then we slowly worked up to where we could draw straight lines with it comfortably and, finally, curved segments. Even after we had been drawing curved segments for a while, we really didn't understand how the tool worked, and we were missing out on a lot of its capabilities because of that lack of knowledge. The manuals for Illustrator really aren't very clear on how to use the Pen tool, and no one we knew could do any better. To learn how to use it, we forced ourselves to use the Pen tool to draw objects that we could have just traced with the Auto Trace tool.

While practicing with the Pen tool, we necessarily learned earlier in the chapter about the four types of anchor points — smooth points, straight corner points, curved corner points, and combination corner points. Because the key to using the Pen tool is understanding how anchor points work, these point types are worth covering again. A significant obstacle is to decide what type of anchor point you want to use. Remember, you have four different anchor points to choose from when drawing with the Pen tool:

✦ **Smooth points** are anchor points with two connected control handles sticking out, resulting in a path that moves smoothly through the anchor point. Changing the angle of one control handle changes the angle of the other control handle. Changing the length of the control handle line does not affect the other control handle. A smooth point guides the path along its journey but doesn't severely or suddenly alter that path's direction.

✦ **Straight corner points** are anchor points where two line segments meet in a corner. The line segments are not curved where they reach the anchor point, and no control handles exist. Straight corner points usually, but not always, distinctly change the direction of the path at the location where it passes through the anchor point.

✦ **Curved corner points** are anchor points where two different curved segments meet in a corner. Two control handles come out of a curved corner point, but the control handles are independent of each other. Moving one control handle does not affect the other.

✦ **Combination corner points** are anchor points where two segments meet, one curved and one straight. A combination corner point has one control handle. That control handle affects only the curved segment, not the straight segment.

If the path is smoothly curving, you use a smooth point. If a corner exists, use one of the corner points. Figure 3-18 shows each of the anchor point types.

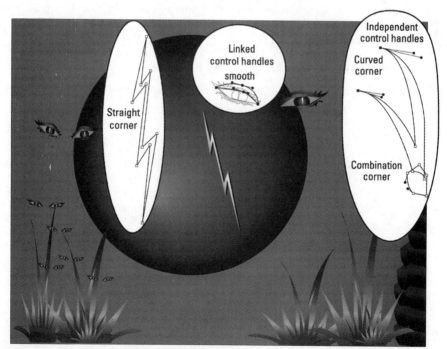

Figure 3-18: The four types of anchor points

Another obstacle arises when you decide that the anchor point should be anything but a straight corner point because all the other anchor points have control handles. The obstacle is figuring out how to drag the control handles, how far to drag them, and in which direction to drag them.

The Pen tool draws points one at a time. The first click of the Pen tool produces one anchor point. The second click (usually in a different location) creates a second anchor point that is joined to the first anchor point by a line segment. Clicking without dragging produces a straight corner point.

After you get the hang of it, the Pen tool isn't so bad — ask anyone who has been using Illustrator for, say, two years or longer. They like the Pen tool. We use the Pen tool more than the Paintbrush, Auto Trace, and Pencil tools combined.

We have approached this tool delicately because, although it is a little frustrating and confusing to use well, it is the most important tool to learn, and this is the one section of this book that you should really read carefully.

In the sample illustration (refer to Figure 3-1), the weeds in the upper-right corner were created with the Pen tool. The weeds are composed entirely of straight lines that were duplicated in clumps, just as the long and short grasses were. Figure 3-7 shows the process used for creating the mass of weeds in the illustration. Here are the steps:

1. Change the Paint style to a Fill of Black and a Stroke of None. Using the Pen tool, click (don't drag!) at the top of the first weed (1). Then click lower at the bottom-right corner of the first weed (2). Click to the left (3) and click back at the starting point (4) to complete the weed. When the last weed in the clump has been finished, click the first anchor point to close the path.

2. Repeat Step 1 to create additional weeds, making clumps of them similar to the one shown in Figure 3-19.

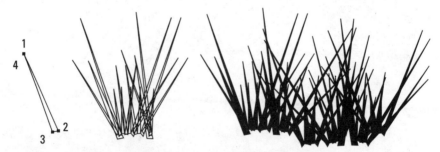

Figure 3-19: A clump of weeds drawn with the Pen tool

3. With the Selection tool, Option [Alt]+drag the clumps a few times to create a mass of weeds.

Note When drawing straight lines with the Pen tool, never drag with the mouse while pressing the button. Doing so results in at least one curved segment.

The Pen tool draws both curved and straight precise lines. With a little practice and by using the tips given on these pages, you can master the tool. In the process, you will understand Illustrator much better than is possible otherwise.

It would be really simple if the Pen tool did *all* the work, but you do have to do some of the labor involved in creating curves and straight lines yourself. Actually, using the Pen tool is easier than we have been letting on. All you have to do is place anchor points where you want the path to go, but it can be tricky to figure out where the anchor points need to go.

Two drawings with the same number of anchor points can look totally different depending on where they're placed. You have to think ahead to determine what the path will look like before you draw it.

Points should always be located where a change occurs in the path. That change can be a different curve or a corner. The three changes to look for are:

✦ A corner of any type.

✦ The point where a curve changes from clockwise to counterclockwise or vice versa.

✦ The point where a curve changes *intensity* — from tight to loose or loose to tight (by far, the hardest change to judge).

ASK TOULOUSE: Why Use the Pen Tool?

Vinnie: Why should I use the Pen tool instead of the other drawing tools?

Toulouse: The Pen draws paths *exactly* where you want them.

Vinnie: Yeah . . . that's it?

Toulouse: The Pen tool also draws curves.

Vinnie: I thought that's what the Pencil tool was for.

Toulouse: Yes, but the Pen draws *precise, perfect* curves.

Vinnie: Like the Ellipse tool.

Toulouse: Ah, there's a difference: The Pen draws curves one line segment at a time.

Vinnie: It sounds like a lot of work.

Toulouse: No, you just click and drag for each point. Once you get the hang of it, you'll be amazed that you ever used Illustrator without it.

Drawing straight lines with the Pen tool

The easiest way to start learning to use the Pen tool is by drawing straight lines. The lightning bolt in Figure 3-20 was created entirely with straight lines. The great thing about straight lines drawn with the Pen tool is that you have no control handles to worry about or fuss over.

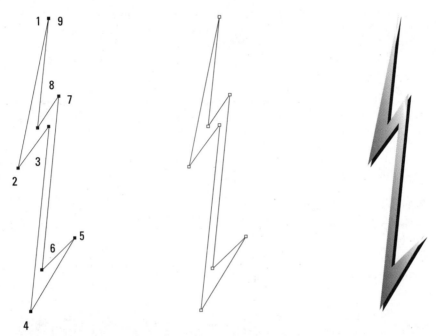

Figure 3-20: Straight lines drawn with the Pen tool

To draw the lightning bolt in Figure 3-20, click in order at each numbered point with the Pen tool. Before you click at number 9, the Pen tool changes to a pen cursor with a little circle in the lower-right corner. This change signifies that the path is going to close when you click this point.

The simplest straight line is a line drawn with only two anchor points. To draw a line like this, select the Pen tool and click and release where you want the first end point (the beginning of the line) to appear. Then click and release where you want the second end point (the end of the line) to appear. A line appears between the two points. Too easy, isn't it?

Tip   You can force the line to be angled to either 0, 45, or 90 degrees by holding down the Shift key.

To draw another separate line, first click the Pen tool in the toolbox or hold down the ⌘ [Ctrl] key and click. Either action tells Illustrator that you are done drawing the first line. Clicking and releasing again in one spot and then another draws a second line with two end points. Be careful not to drag when clicking the Pen tool to form straight lines.

Paths drawn with the Pen tool, as with the Pencil tool, may cross themselves. The only strange result you may see involves the Fills for objects whose paths cross. In open paths created with the Pen tool, Fills may look unusual because of the imaginary line between the two end points and any paths that the imaginary line crosses.

Closing paths with the Pen tool

If you want to create a closed path (one with no end points), return to the first anchor point in that segment and click. As the Pen tool crosses over the beginning anchor point, the cursor changes to a pen with a circle in the lower-right corner. After you have created a closed path, you have no need to click the Pen tool again. Instead, the next click of the Pen tool in the document automatically begins a new path.

You must have at least three anchor points to create a closed path with straight lines. You can change the identity of one of these points to a different type of anchor point by curving one of the segments and giving the closed path some substance.

Drawing curves with the Pen tool

Initially, the worst thing about drawing curves with the Pen tool is that the whole process is rather disorienting. You actually have to think differently to grasp what the Pen tool is doing. The difference that you notice right away between drawing straight lines and drawing curves is that, to draw a curve, you need to drag with the Pen tool; whereas, when drawing straight lines, you click and release.

The most basic of curves is the bump (a curved segment between just two points). A bump was used to create a path to fill the horses' rears (shown in Figure 3-12). Use the following steps to create the bump illustrated in Figure 3-21:

1. Click with the Pen tool and drag up about half an inch. You'll see an anchor point and a control handle line extending from it as you drag.

2. When you release the mouse button, you will see the anchor point and a line extending to where you dragged with a control handle at its end.

3. Position the cursor about an inch to the right of the place you first clicked.

4. Click with the mouse and drag down about half an inch. As you drag, you see a curve forming that resembles a bump. When you release the mouse, the curve is filled with the current Fill color. You also see the control handle you just dragged.

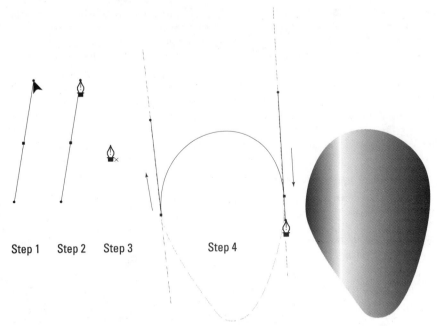

Figure 3-21: The four steps for creating a basic bump curve

Before you try to draw another curve, remember that the Pen tool is still in a mode that continues the current path; it does not start a new one. To start a new path, choose Deselect All (⌘+Shift+A [Ctrl+Shift+A]) or hold down ⌘ [Ctrl] and click an empty area onscreen. The next time you use the Pen tool, you will draw a separate path.

To create an S shape, one more set of steps is needed. The steps for creating the S shape are described here and illustrated in Figure 3-22:

1. Click and drag with the Pen tool about half an inch to the left.

2. Release the mouse button. You should see the anchor point and the control handle that you just drew with a control handle line between them.

3. Position the cursor about an inch below where you first clicked.

4. Click and drag to the right about half an inch.

5. Release the mouse button.

6. Position the cursor about half an inch below the last point you clicked.

7. Click and drag to the left, about half an inch. Now you have an S shape. To make the S look more like a real S, change the Fill to None and the Stroke to Black, 1 point.

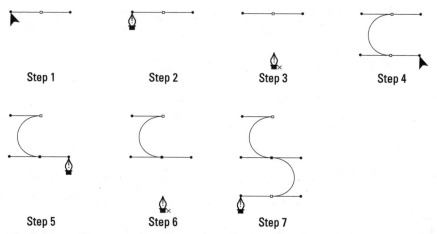

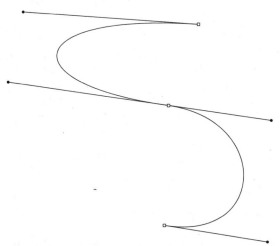

Figure 3-22: The seven steps to creating a basic S curve

All the anchor points we have created in these two examples are smooth points. The control handles were dragged in the direction of the next curve to be drawn, and the lengths of the control handle lines on either side of the anchor point were equal.

The lengths of the control handle lines on either side of the smooth point do not have to be the same. Instead, a smooth point may have both long and short control handle lines coming out of it. The length of the control handle line affects the curve, as shown on the S curve in Figure 3-23.

Figure 3-23: The length of the control handle lines controls the shape of the curve.

ASK TOULOUSE: Making Bad Waves with the Pen

Boom-Boom Washington: I'm having loads of trouble with my paths and the Pen tool.

Toulouse: What sort of trouble? Lines not connecting? Lumps everywhere? Pen running out of ink?

Boom-Boom Washington: Actually, I'm getting the "wave" thing happening, except my waves have . . .

Toulouse: Curved tips. I've been there. It isn't pretty.

Boom-Boom Washington: Wow, it's like you're in my head, looking out. . . .

Toulouse: The wave effect you're describing usually happens when you click and drag with the Pen tool. . . .

Boom-Boom Washington: Uh-huh . . .

Toulouse: And then let go, and the next click is right on top of the control handle you've dragged out. You drag out again, the next click is on the handle you've dragged out . . . and so on.

Boom-Boom Washington: So, how do I prevent it?

Toulouse: Just remember that each time you drag, you're setting the location of the control handle, not the path itself. Don't click the control handle; click far away from it.

Boom-Boom Washington: Like, if the first click is right in the middle of the page, the next click should be in, what, Jersey?

Toulouse: Not quite that far away. Now I know why you were 28 and still in 11th grade.

To create a smooth point with two control handle lines of different lengths, first create a smooth point along a path. Go back to this point and click and drag it again using the Direct Selection tool. You can adjust the angle for both control handle lines and the length for the new control handle line that you are dragging. Note that as you are dragging out this control handle line, the other control handle line wobbles to the angle that you are dragging. This happens because on any smooth point the control handle lines *must* be at the same angle, and as you drag out the new control handle line, you are changing the angle for both control handle lines simultaneously.

Knowing the Pen Commandments

The Pen Commandments are laws to live by — or, at least, to draw by — as shown dramatically in Figure 3-24 and described in detail in this section.

Figure 3-24: The Pen Commandments

The Pen Commandments are as follows:

✦ **Thou shalt drag approximately one-third of the length of the next curved segment.** What this means, as shown in Figure 3-25, is that the control handle you drag from the anchor point should be about one-third of the distance between this anchor point and the next one you click. (This technique takes some planning ahead.) In fact, you have to be aware of where the next anchor point is going to be located before you can determine the length of the control handle line you are dragging. Dragging by one-third is always an approximation — a little more or a little less doesn't hurt and, in fact, is sometimes quite necessary. You might run into trouble when the control handle line is more than half or less than one-quarter of the next segment. If your control handle line is too long or too short, chances are the line will curve erratically. Remember not to drag where the next point will be placed, just one-third of that distance.

Figure 3-25: Handles used for curving segments should be approximately one-third of the length of the curved segment.

✦ **Thou shalt remember that control handle lines are always tangent to the curved segment they are guiding.** Tangent? Well, a simpler way of putting this commandment may be that control handle lines go in the same direction as the curve and that they are always outside of the curve, as previously shown in Step 4 of Figure 3-22. Don't get the outside of the curve and the outside of the shape you are drawing confused — they may well be two different things. If your control handle lies inside the curve you are drawing, it will be too short and overpowered by the next anchor point. Control handles *pull* the curve toward themselves. If you fight this natural pull, your illustrations can look loopy and silly.

✦ **Thou shalt always drag the control handle in the direction that you want the curve to travel at that anchor point.** Once again, the control handle pulls the curve toward itself by its very nature; doing otherwise will certainly cause some trouble. If you drag backward toward the preceding segment, you will create a little curved spike that sticks out from the anchor point. This commandment applies *only* to smooth points, as previously shown in Step 4 of Figure 3-22. If the anchor point is to be a curved corner point, then the initial drag should be in the direction the curve was traveling, and the next drag (an Option [Alt]+drag) should go in the direction that the curve is going to travel. If the anchor point is a combination curve point and the next segment is straight, then the dragging motion should be in the direction that the curve was traveling; then the anchor point should be clicked and released. If the combination curve point's next segment is curved, the first click should be clicked and released, and the second click should be dragged in the direction of the next curve.

✦ **Thou shalt make segments as long as possible.** This is accomplished by using the fewest number of anchor points as possible. If your illustration calls for smooth, flowing curves, use very few anchor points. If, on the other hand, your illustration should be rough and gritty, use more anchor points. The fewer anchor points exist, the smoother the final result, as demonstrated in Figure 3-26. When only a few anchor points exist on a path, changing its shape is easier and faster. More anchor points mean a bigger file and longer printing times, as well. If you're not sure if you need more anchor points, don't add them. You can always add them later with the Add Anchor Point tool.

✦ **Thou shalt place anchor points at the beginning of each "different" curve.** Anchor points should be used as *transitional* points, where the curve either changes direction or increases or decreases in size dramatically. If it looks as though the curve will change from one type of curve to another, then the location to place an anchor point is in the middle of that transitional section. The top drawing in Figure 3-27 shows good locations to place anchor points on a curved path.

Figure 3-26: The path on the left was created with 12 anchor points; the path on the right was created with 60.

✦ **Thou shalt not overcompensate for a previously misdrawn curve.** If you really screw up on the last anchor point you've drawn, don't panic and try to undo the mistake by dragging in the wrong direction or by dragging the control handle out to some ridiculous length. Doing either of these two things may temporarily fix the preceding curve but usually wrecks the next curve, causing you to have to overcompensate yet again. The results of just minor overcompensation are shown in the bottom drawing in Figure 3-27.

Closing curved paths with the Pen tool

The majority of the paths you draw with the Pen tool will be closed paths, not the open ones we've drawn so far. Like open curved paths, any closed curved path must have at least two anchor points, just as paths with straight corner points need three distinct points to create a closed path.

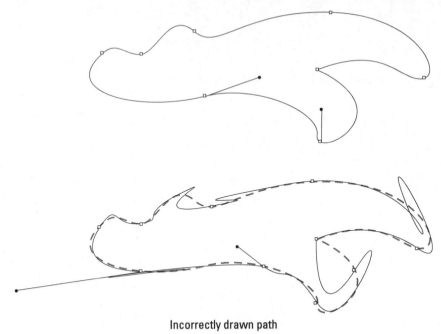

Incorrectly drawn path

Figure 3-27: The anchor points on the top path are placed where the curve changes. The path at the top was drawn correctly; the path on the bottom was drawn by overcompensating for previously misdrawn curves.

When the Pen tool is placed over the starting point of the path you've drawn, a little circle appears to the right of the pen shape. This is an indicator that the path will become a closed path if you click this anchor point.

Of course, to ensure that the initial anchor point remains a smooth point, you need to click and drag on the initial anchor point. Simply clicking produces a combination corner point, which has only one control handle associated with it.

Curved corner points

Curved corner points are points where two different, usually distinct, curved segments meet at an anchor point. Because the two curves meet this way, a smooth point does not provide the means for their joining correctly. Instead, a smooth point would make the two different curves blend into each other smoothly.

The main difference between a curved corner point and a smooth point is that a smooth point has two linked control handles on its ends; a curved corner point has two *independent* control handles. As the names indicate, control handles and their associated control handle lines move independently of each other, enabling two different, distinct types of curves to come from the same anchor point.

Points on a Path to Make a Figure 8

How few points does it take to create a basic curved shape? This is a good test of your abilities. The following infinity symbol was drawn with the least number of anchor points possible.

The number of points used to draw this shape was a number something less than infinity.

After you've tried to do this a few times, look ahead a couple of pages to see some of the different ways it can be done.

To create a curved corner point, create a smooth point in a path and then Option [Alt]+drag the control handle you just drew. As you Option [Alt]+drag the control handle, you are breaking the control handles independently. The next segment will curve as controlled by this control handle, not by the original one.

The clumps of grass shown previously in Figure 3-12 were created using curved corner points. The process is explained in the following steps:

1. As shown in Figure 3-28, click the first point (1) and drag up and to the left. Try to duplicate the locations of all the points for the best results.

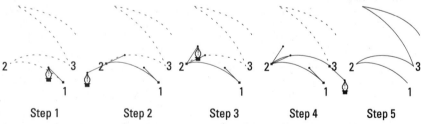

Figure 3-28: How to create paths with curved corner points

2. Click at (2) and drag left and down just a little bit, which creates the curved segment between (1) and (2). You won't see the control handle you are dragging on the figure on the right because Step 3 replaces it.

3. To create the first curved corner point, Option [Alt]+click at (2) and drag up and to the right.

4. Click at (3) and drag to the lower right.

5. Continue to Option [Alt]+drag control handles when drawing a new segment, effectively creating independent control handles until you have created a clump of grass. Option [Alt]+copy and transform the clumps to create several clumps of grass.

Tip

When creating curved corner points, you can press the Option [Alt] key (to create independent points) all the time, not just when starting a new segment.

Combination corner points

A combination corner point is a point where a curved segment and a straight segment meet each other. At this corner point, you'll find one control handle coming from the anchor point from the side where the curved segment is located and, on the other side, no control handle exists, indicating a straight segment.

To create a combination corner point with the Pen tool, draw a few curved segments and then go back to the last anchor point. Two linked control handles should be displayed at this point. Simply click the anchor point once and one of the two control handles will disappear. The next segment then starts out straight.

Tip

You can change existing smooth and curved corner points into combination corner points simply by dragging one of the control handles into the anchor points.

In the sample illustration shown in Figure 3-12, the Pen tool was used not only to draw the spiky weeds, but also to draw the horses on the hill and the Fill shapes for the hill. The horse outlines and the blade outlines were created with the Paintbrush tool.

To fill the hillside in the sample image in Figure 3-12, click where the left edge of the hill should begin and drag down and to the right about a half inch. Next, click at the top of the hill and drag just a tiny bit (less than a half inch) to the right. Click again at about halfway down the hill and drag at about the same angle as the hill. Click again at the base of the hill and drag to the right one inch. Click without dragging on the far side of the illustration. To finish off the hillside Fill, click the lower-right and lower-left corners and then click the starting point. Fill the path with a gradient that complements a hillside and change the Stroke to None.

To create the horse Fill shape, create a path with the Pen tool by using mostly smooth points that go right through the center of the horse outlines. Make separate shapes for the head area, manes, body area, and the tails. Fill the paths with gradients or solid colors and choose a Stroke of None.

Points on a Path to Make a Figure 8: The Answers

You have several ways to make a figure 8, as shown here.

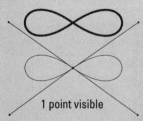

1 point visible

4 points

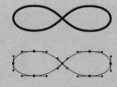

8 points

Compare these figures to the one you've drawn.

Your score is as follows:

✦ **One visible point (really two overlapping):** PenMaster

✦ **Two points, both visible:** Lots of Pentential

✦ **Three to four points:** ApPentice

✦ **Six or more points:** The sword is still mightier

To create the long grass blade Fills, use the Pen tool to draw paths that go right through the center of the blades of grass. Create separate paths for each blade, and Fill the blades with a green linear gradient.

Tip

The Pen tool includes two very handy controls. If you press the Option [Alt] key while dragging a control handle from an anchor point, you can freely change that control handle without affecting its mate (the control handle joined to it on the opposite side of the anchor point). The Pen tool also includes the capability to move the anchor point and control handle while dragging out a control handle by pressing the spacebar as you drag from the anchor point.

Painting in Illustrator

The Paintbrush tool is similar to paintbrush-type tools in painting programs; the Paintbrush is set to a certain width and you can paint with the paintbrush at this width anywhere in your document. The big difference between paint programs' paintbrushes and Illustrator's paintbrush is that when you finish drawing with Illustrator's Paintbrush tool, a stroked path has been created.

To use the Paintbrush tool, choose the tool, and then choose the brush from the Brush palette, and start drawing. A freeform path appears wherever you drag. That's all there is to it. Kinda. Figure 3-29 shows a drawing that was created with the Paintbrush tool set to a variable width with a pressure-sensitive stylus.

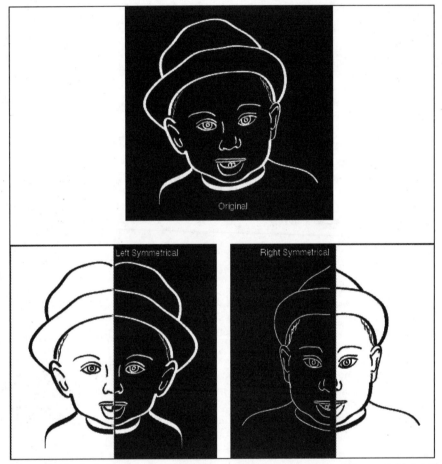

Figure 3-29: A drawing created with the Paintbrush tool using a Wacom tablet with a pressure-sensitive stylus

Drawing with the Paintbrush tool is a bit more complicated than we just explained. The most important consideration is the width of the paintbrush stroke. The paintbrush stroke can be as narrow as 0 points and as wide as 1,296 points (that's whopping 18 inches).

Although 0 is the smallest width, a paintbrush stroke drawn with a width of 0 points actually has a width bigger than 0 points. To change the paintbrush stroke width (the default is 9 points), double-click the brush in the Brush palette (*not* the tool-box) and enter a number in the Diameter text field. Remember that you are actually changing that default brush. If you want to create a totally new brush, choose New Brush from the Brushes palette pop-up menu and select the type of new brush you want to make.

Results achieved with the Paintbrush tool vary depending on two important characteristics: your artistic ability and your ability to control the mouse. If you can't draw with a pencil or other forms of traditional media, using a mouse is not likely to turn you into a Michelangelo (the artist, not the turtle). If Michelangelo had to use a mouse to draw, he probably would have become a philosopher or sunk so low as to be an editor for a Mac magazine, constantly complaining about the inefficient means by which cursors are controlled.

A mouse is *not* an intuitive drawing tool, and not being able to draw in the first place makes it even more difficult to draw with the Paintbrush tool. So, if artists have trouble with the mouse, what's the point of having the Paintbrush tool at all? Well, instead of a mouse, you can use several types of alternative drawing devices. The best of these is a pressure-sensitive tablet. Trackballs with locking buttons are also good for drawing with the Paintbrush tool (this device provides more control over the direction and speed of the paintbrush).

Note When you're drawing with any of the tools in Illustrator, dragging off the edge of the window causes the window to scroll, which creates a frightening effect for the uninitiated. If you don't want the window to remain where it scrolled to, don't let go of the mouse button; instead, drag in the opposite direction until the window returns to the original position. To scroll the other way while still using a tool, drag off the other side of the window.

To help you draw more precisely, you have the option of changing the cursor shape from the cute little brush into cross-hairs. Press the Caps Lock key (to engage it), and the cursor changes into cross-hairs with a dot in the center. Press the Caps Lock key again (to release it), and the cursor returns to the brush shape. The dot at the center of the cross-hairs is the center of any paintbrush stroke drawn with the Paintbrush tool. Normally, when the cursor is in the shape of a paintbrush, the tip is the center of the paintbrush stroke. Some people find it easier to draw when the paintbrush cursor is replaced with the precise cross-hairs.

Paintbrush types

In the Brushes palette, you see several different kinds of default brushes. Some of these are unique shapes are other are long stretched-out like someone has run their fingers down a chalkboard. All of these default brushes are broken down into four categories — Calligraphic, Scatter, Art and Pattern. Each of these categories have their own parameters and you can select with categories are displayed in the Brushes palette using the Brushes pop-up menu. Figure 3-30 shows the Brushes palette with each of the categories of brushes labeled.

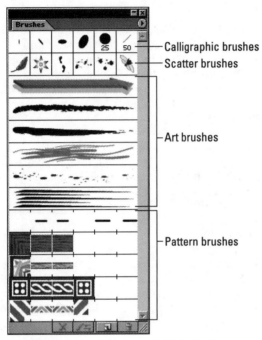

Figure 3-30: The Brushes palette includes four categories of brushes.

To set the parameters for the brush, double click on the brush to open a dialog box of options.

Writing with the Calligraphic Brush

A Calligraphic Brush was made to simulate the actual calligraphic pen tip. You set the angle and size and draw to your heart's content. You can also create a perfectly round brush in the Calligraphic Brush dialog box by not entering an angle and by keeping the Roundness at 100 percent.

The Calligraphic Brush Options (shown in Figure 3-31) are as follows:

✦ **Name.** This option lets you give your new brush a name or rename an existing brush (maximum of 30 characters).

✦ **Angle.** You can set the angle of the Calligraphic Brush. The angle you should choose depends on what is going to be drawn. To mimic hand-drawn lettering in a calligraphic style, the angle should be set to 45 degrees (or, if you're left-handed, it should be set to –45 degrees).

✦ **Roundness.** This does what you'd think it does. It sets the roundness of the brush. The higher the value, the rounder the brush.

✦ **Diameter.** The diameter option sets the maximum diameter of the brush.

✦ **Variation.** If you choose the Random option from the Angle or Roundness pop-up menu, you then enter a value for Variation. The Variation for the Angle value is in a degree that you want to vary from the original setting. The Variation for the Roundness is set in percentages. A slider sets the Variation for the Diameter or you can enter a number. The Diameter Variation goes from your original value up to the Variation value.

Tip   You can also change the parameters by dragging on the brush profile image that is displayed to the left of the dialog box between the Name and the Angle field.

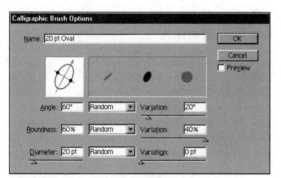

Figure 3-31: The Calligraphic Brush Options dialog box

Note   If you have a path selected when you open the brush options dialog box, a Preview checkbox will appear under the Cancel button. This checkbox will let you preview the path stroke as you change the brush parameters.

Defining a Calligraphic Brush

You have many ways to use the Calligraphic Brush. You can choose an existing brush and get started. If you load additional brush libraries, you'll find a variety of brushes to choose from. You can also create your own brush from an existing one or from scratch. To create a new brush, we use an existing style that we like, but that we want to alter. To create a brush like this, choose Duplicate Brush from the Brush palette pop-up menu. You first have to select the brush you want to duplicate. To edit that duplicated brush, double-click the duplicate brush, or select Brush Options from the pop-up menu. In the Brush Options dialog box, change the brush to your specifications.

Variable widths and pressure-sensitive tablets

If you have a pressure-sensitive tablet — some call them a Wacom (pronounced "walk 'em") tablet because a large majority tend to be made by Wacom — you can select the Pressure option beside the Diameter field in the Brush Options dialog box (accessed by double-clicking a brush in the Brushes palette). If you don't have a pressure-sensitive tablet, the Pressure option is grayed out (unselectable).

Tip

A *pressure-sensitive tablet* is a flat, rectangular device over which you pass a special stylus. The more pressure exerted by the stylus on the tablet, the wider a paintbrush stroke will be, providing the Pressure option in the Calligraphic dialog box is checked. When using the Pressure option, try to set the Variation different from the original specified diameter to see the difference when you press harder or lighter.

Scattering with the Scatter Brush

The Scatter Brush copies and scatters a predefined object along a path. You have some default Scatter Brushes to choose from such as Banana Leaf, Radial Star, Human Feet, Ink Splats and Flying Bug. Figure 3-32 shows an example of each default Scatter Brush.

The Scatter Brush Options (see Figure 3-33) are as follows:

✦ **Name.** You can name your brush with up to 30 characters.

✦ **Size.** In the size area, you have three pop-up options: Fixed, Random and Pressure. If you choose Fixed, then the size slider will only display the left options. The fixed size lets you enter a percentage so that all of the scattered images will be the exact same size. If you choose Random, the pop-up displays two sliders. With the Random option you can set up large and small scattered images by changing the sliders for each. If you want really big images and small images that vary in size, then drag the sliders in opposite directions. If you choose Pressure, then the size is determined by the pressure applied to a the graphics tablet.

✦ **Spacing.** This option adjusts the space between each object.

✦ **Scatter.** The Scatter option adjusts how the objects follow the original path on each side of the path. If you set a high amount, the objects are farther away from the original path.

✦ **Rotation.** This option adjusts how much the object will rotate from its original position.

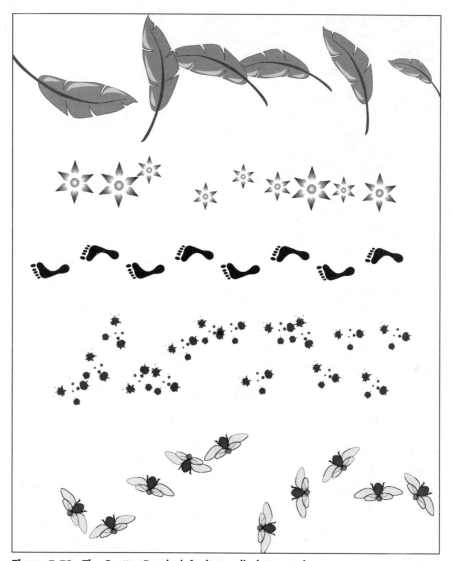

Figure 3-32: The Scatter Brush defaults applied to a path

✦ **Rotation relative to.** This option gives you two choices from a pop-up menu: Page and Path. The Page option rotates objects according to the page setup. The Path option rotates objects tangent to the path.

✦ **Colorization.** You have four Colorization choices: None, Tints, Tints and Shades, and Hue Shift. For more on colorization and colorization tips, see the "Using the Colorization Tips feature" section later in this chapter.

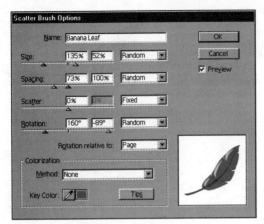

Figure 3-33: The Scatter Brush Options dialog box

Stretching with the Art Brush

The Art Brush, like the Scatter Brush, uses an object along a path. The difference is that the Art Brush stretches the object to the length of the path rather than repeat and scatter the object. The object is centered evenly over the path and then stretched. You can choose from the default Art Brushes or create an object of your own to use. Figure 3-34 shows the six default Art Brushes: Suspended Arrow, Charcoal, Fude, Dry Ink 2, Galaxy, and Scroll Pen 5.

The Art Brush Options (see Figure 3-35) are as follows:

✦ **Name.** You can name your new Art Brush or rename an existing Art Brush with up to 30 characters.

✦ **Direction.** This option lets you choose from four directions. The directions are relative to how you drag the paintbrush.

✦ **Size.** This option scales the art when it is stretched. You can choose Proportional to keep the object in proportion.

✦ **Flip.** The Flip option lets you flip your object along or across the path.

✦ **Colorization.** You have four Colorization choices: None, Tints, Tints and Shades, and Hue Shift. For more on colorization and colorization tips, see the "Using the Colorization Tips feature" section later in this chapter.

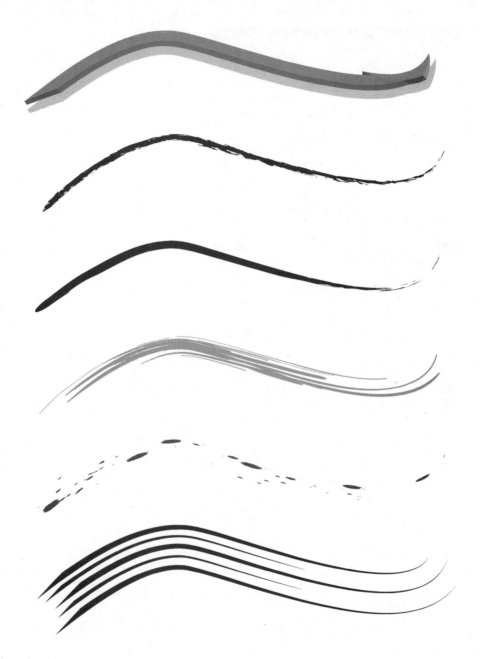

Figure 3-34: The Art Brush default brushes: Suspended Arrow, Charcoal, Fude, Dry Ink 2, Galaxy, and Scroll Pen 5.

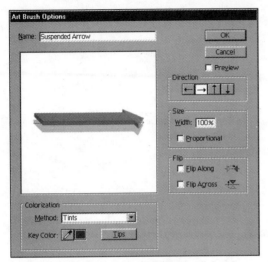

Figure 3-35: The Art Brush Options dialog box

Tiling with the Pattern Brush

The Pattern Brush repeats a tiled object along a path. The Pattern Brush can have tiles to display the sides, inner corner, outer corner, beginning, and end. If you think of a Pattern Brush as you would a regular Pattern tile, but keep in mind the corners, you'll have no problem creating your own interesting Pattern Brushes.

We like to take apart an existing pattern to see how it was created. To do this, select the Pattern Brush in the Brushes palette and drag it to an open area on your document. You'll see the individual tiles. Figure 3-36 shows the default Pattern Brushes including End to End Dash Stroke, Oak, Polynesian, Rectangles 1.9 and Samoan.

The Pattern Brush Options (see Figure 3-37) are as follows:

- ✦ **Name.** Enter a new name or change an existing name (up to 30 characters).
- ✦ **Tile button.** This is where you choose which of the five tiles you want to create.
- ✦ **Size.** This option lets you enter the size in proportion and the space between the tiles.
- ✦ **Flip.** This option lets you flip the pattern along or across the path.

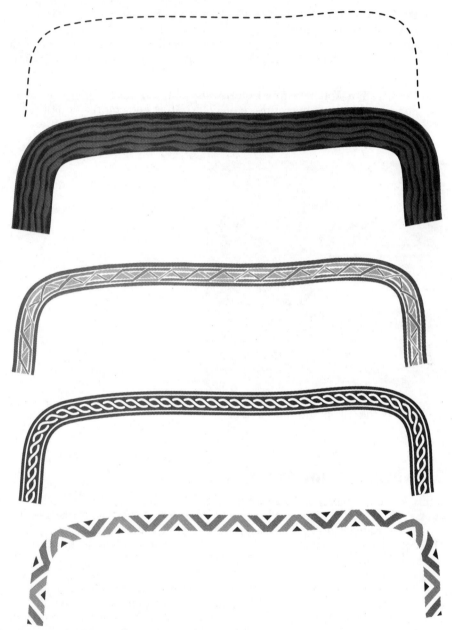

Figure 3-36: The default Pattern Brushes

✦ **Fit.** In this option, you can choose Stretch to Fit, Add Space to Fit, or Approximate Path. Stretch lengthens or shortens a tile to fit your object. Add Space adds a blank space between the tiles to fit the path proportionately. Approximate Path makes the tile fit as close to the original path without altering the tiles.

✦ **Colorization.** You have four Colorization choices: None, Tints, Tints and Shades, and Hue Shift. For more on colorization and colorization tips, see the "Using the Colorization Tips feature" section later in this chapter.

Figure 3-37: The Pattern Brush Options dialog box

Drawing with the Paintbrush tool

In this section, you create the grass and the horse outlines previously shown. Both can be drawn with or without a pressure-sensitive tablet (which is discussed in detail in "Variable widths and pressure-sensitive tablets," earlier in this chapter), although you can achieve better effects if you use a tablet. Follow these steps to create the grass and the horse outlines:

1. Choose the Paintbrush tool from the toolbar, and then choose a brush size from the Brushes palette. If the palette is not visible, choose Window ➪ Show Brushes. Choose New Brush from the Brushes palette pop-up menu and choose the New Calligraphic Brush. In the Calligraphic Brush Options dialog box, set the Roundness to 50 percent, the Angle to 45 degrees, the Diameter to 3 points, and the Variation to 0.5 point.

2. Using the Paintbrush tool, draw each piece of the basic shape of the horses, as shown in Figure 3-38. The more individual pieces you draw, the easier it is to use the Paintbrush tool. Long strokes are difficult to produce and aren't as appealing as shorter strokes. Don't worry about filling in the horses with color at this point. You are using the Paintbrush tool only to create the smoothly flowing outlines of the horses. If you make a mistake while drawing, choose Edit ➪ Undo (⌘+Z [Ctrl+Z]).

Step 2   Step 3

Figure 3-38: Horse and grass outlines created with the Paintbrush tool

3. To draw the tall blades of grass, just draw a few select blade outlines to create a clump of grass. For the best effects, drag the anchor points from the base of the clump up and outward with the Scale tool and the Option [Alt] key pressed.

Creating brushes

You have two ways to create a brush. If you like another brush, but not all aspects of it, duplicate that brush and edit its options to make it as you like. To edit a brush, double-click the brush, or choose Brush Options from the pop-up menu or icon at the bottom of the Brushes palette. The other way to create a brush is to choose New Brush from the pop-up menu or to click the New Brush icon at the bottom of the Brushes palette. This brings up a dialog box asking you to choose the type of brush you want to create (see Figure 3-39). You can create a Calligraphic Brush by filling in the text fields of the Calligraphic Brush dialog box. To create any of the other brushes, you have to have your art drawn first, and then choose New Brush.

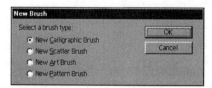

Figure 3-39: The New Brush dialog box

Creating a Scatter, Art, or Pattern Brush

With each brush you have brush options to choose from. The Calligraphic, Scatter, Art, and Pattern brushes are your brush choices and each brush has different options to choose from.

To create your own Scatter Brush design, first create the object that you want to use. Next, select all of the parts of the object that you want as a brush and choose New Brush from the Brushes palette pop-up menu. Then choose the type of brush you want to create. The Brush Options dialog box appears and you will see your new design there. Now all you have to do is set the rest of the options and you are ready to use this new brush. The following steps give an example of how to create a new Scatter Brush:

1. Select Window ➪ Symbols (Shift + F11) to open the Symbols palette. Drag one of the symbols to the document window. I've selected to use the puzzle piece.

2. With the symbol object selected, select New Brush from the Brushes palette menu. This will make the New Brush dialog box (shown in Figure 3-39) appear. Select the New Scatter Brush option and click the Ok button.

3. The Scatter Brush Options dialog box, shown in Figure 3-40 opens. Name the new brush Puzzle Piece Brush, set the Size, Spacing, Scatter and Rotation values all to 100 percent and make the Scatter and Rotation to Random with values of 50 percent. Then click the Ok button.

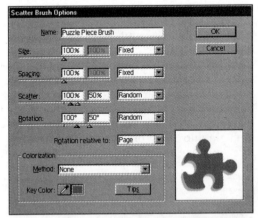

Figure 3-40: The new Scatter Brush Options dialog box lets you define how the puzzle pieces are scattered about the page.

4. In the toolbox, select the Paintbrush tool and drag a short path with the new brush selected in the Brushes palette. Figure 3-41 shows the results of the new brush.

Figure 3-41: This path was drawn using the newly created puzzle piece brush.

Using the Colorization Tips feature

The Tips button in the Colorization section of the Brush Options dialog box for the Scatter, Art and Pattern brushes displays the Colorization Tips dialog box, shown in Figure 3-42. This dialog box explains the different colorization options. Colorization has four example areas: None, Tints, Tints and Shades, and Hue Shift.

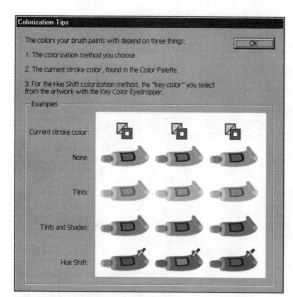

Figure 3-42: The Colorization Tips dialog box

To see how the Colorization options work, first create four copies of a brush using the Duplicate Brush menu option in the palette menu. For example, select a red arrow brush. Then draw four red arrows in the artboard. The first arrow uses the default Colorization Method of None. For the next three arrows change the Stroke color (you won't see anything happen yet). With the second arrow selected, double-click one of the arrow brush copies you made and select Tints as the Colorization Method. Then select the OK button. A dialog box will appear given you the choice to Apply to Stroke. The color should change at this point. Select the third arrow and double-click a different copy of the arrow brush and select Tints and Shades. Select the last arrow and double-click the last copy and select Hue Shift. All of the arrows should look different.

Browsing Brush Libraries

The Brush Library that appears when you choose the Brush palette is the default Library. You have seven additional Libraries to choose from. Adobe has really come up with some cool brushes for our creative pleasure. The Brush Libraries found under the Window menu include Animal Sample, Arrow Sample, Artistic Sample, Border Sample, Calligraphic, Default CMYK, Default RGB, Floral Sample, and Object Sample. Figure 3-43 shows all of the Brush Libraries you have to choose from.

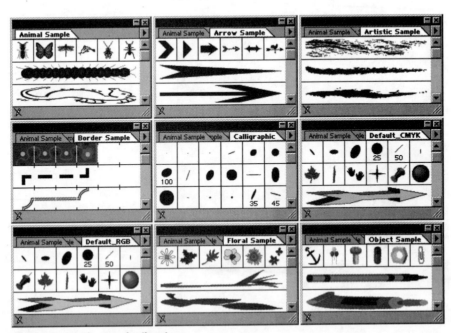

Figure 3-43: The Brush Libraries

Summary

Drawing and painting or painting and drawing (depending on the type of creation that you are most comfortable with), both offer the chance to create and communicate. Illustrator understands that you may need (or want) to use one or both of these techniques and has given you an array of powerful tools to accomplish this. Whether you start a drawing with the Pen, Pencil or Paintbrush tool, the other tools are there if you ever decide to select them. In this chapter, you learned many of the basics of using these critical tools:

✦ Illustrator uses four types of Anchor Points: straight corner points, smooth points, curved corner points, and combination corner points.

✦ Curved paths in Illustrator are modeled on Bézier curves, named after the French mathematician Pierre Bézier.

✦ Curved segments are controlled by manipulating control handles, which extend from Anchor Points at either end of the segment.

✦ The Pencil tool creates single paths that are open or closed.

✦ The Smooth tool smoothes any path by dragging a new path over a selected path.

✦ The Erase tool easily cuts or erases sections of an open or closed path.

✦ The Pen tool is the most powerful tool in Illustrator because it enables you to create perfectly formed curves and straight paths.

✦ Clicking with the Pen tool creates straight-line segments; dragging with the Pen tool creates curved segments.

✦ Keep the distance of control handle lines to about one-third the length of the affected curved line segment for the best results.

✦ The Paintbrush tool creates open paths that are Stroked.

✦ Use a pressure-sensitive tablet with the Paintbrush tool for the best results.

✦ The Scatter Brush can create repeating objects with various sizes and rotation along a path.

✦ The Art Brush stretches an object over a path.

✦ The Pattern Brush repeats a tile pattern on a path.

✦ You can create new brushes using the Brushes palette.

✦   ✦   ✦

Working with Objects

In This Chapter

Drawing rectangles, ellipses, polygons, stars, and flares

Drawing straight lines, arcs, spirals, rectangular and polar grids

Making, modifying, and enhancing basic graphs

Creating diagrams and flowcharts

Working with symbols

Technically, the name of this chapter should really be "Creating and Placing Preformatted Open and Closed Paths," but if it were, who would read it? This is an important chapter because it introduces many concepts that are built upon in later chapters. The following pages talk about how to use Illustrator's shape creation tools, graphs, symbols, and how to create diagrams using these and other tools.

Creating Different Shapes

Drawing the most basic shapes — rectangles, ovals, polygons, and stars — is precisely what a computer is for. Try drawing a perfect oval by hand. Troublesome, isn't it? How about a square that doesn't have ink bubbles or splotches at the corners? How about a nine-point star? Yuck. Drawing these objects and then coloring them in Illustrator is so easy and so basic that after a few weeks of using the program, you'll never be able to draw a shape by hand again without wincing. Figure 4-1 compares shapes drawn by hand with those drawn by a computer.

Getting rid of the shape you've drawn is even easier than creating it (delete it by selecting it and pressing the Delete [Backspace] key). And after the shape is created, it can be moved, rotated, scaled, and manipulated in any way you like.

Illustrator exemplifies the true power of *object-oriented drawing*. Object-oriented drawing is a procedure that increases productivity by reusing standard components (or objects) over and over without having to create new ones every time. No matter what you draw, you can adjust and move each piece of the drawing independently until it's just right. Don't like the sun so high in your background? Pull it down and tuck it in just a bit behind those mountains. Is the tree too small for the house in your illustration? Scale it up a bit. These features are great not only for artists, but also for your pesky client (or boss) who demands that everything be moved except that darned tree. Figure 4-2 shows an illustration drawn one way and then modified in a matter of seconds by moving and transforming existing elements.

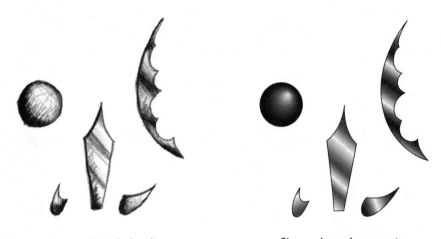

Shapes drawn by hand   Shapes drawn by computer

Figure 4-1: Hand-drawn shapes and their computer-drawn counterparts

Traditional bitmap paint applications do not have the capability to move pieces of a drawing (with the exception of those that use layers in software such as Photoshop). After an image is moved in a bitmap image, a hole appears in the place where the section used to be. And if anything exists under the section where the image was moved, that information is gone when the section is replaced with the new image.

Cross-Reference As if the various shapes presented in this chapter weren't enough, you can use the Pathfinder functions to create an unlimited number of shapes by combining and subtracting shapes from one another. The Pathfinder palette is covered in Chapter 5, "Selecting and Editing."

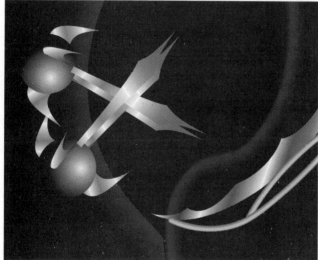

Figure 4-2: Illustrator objects moved from one drawing to the next

Drawing rectangles

The most basic shape you can draw is a rectangle. The following steps, and the illustration of these steps in Figure 4-3, explain how to draw a simple rectangle.

1. Select the Rectangle tool by clicking it in the toolbox or by pressing the M key.

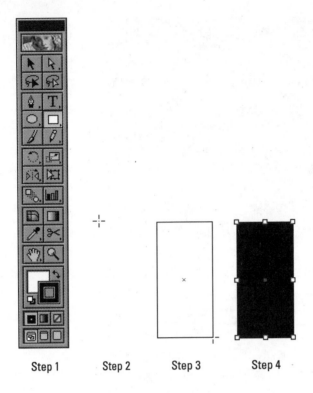

Step 1   Step 2   Step 3   Step 4

Figure 4-3: Steps for drawing a rectangle

2. Click to set the origin (starting point) and hold down the mouse button.

3. Drag diagonally (such as down and to the right) to the size you desire.

4. Release the mouse button. A rectangle is created. The farther the distance from the initial click until the point where you release the mouse button, the larger the rectangle.

After you release the mouse button, a white rectangle outlined in black (unless you have changed your default line and fill colors) appears with four blue points in the corners and one blue point in the center. The edge of the rectangle has thin blue lines surrounding it. The blue points in the corners are straight *Corner Anchor Points*. Anchor Points are the control points that enable you to edit the curve or shape. The blue point in the center is the center point. The blue lines are straight-line segments that connect the Anchor Points of the rectangle. The blue points and blue lines together are considered a *path*. In Outline mode, the rectangle has no fill or stroke, and the points and line appear black.

Note   If you aren't sure what View mode you're in, display the View menu by clicking View and keeping the mouse button down. If the top item of the menu reads Outline, you're in Preview mode. If it reads Preview, you're in Outline mode. If this seems a little backward, consider that choosing that menu item will change the viewing mode to the one you choose. So when you're in Preview mode, and you see and choose Outline, you're switched to Outline mode. An even easier way to determine this is to look on the title bar of the document window, which reveals the view mode and the color mode.

The initial click you make with the Rectangle tool is called the *origin point*. While you drag the mouse to create a rectangle, the origin point never moves; however, the rest of the rectangle is fluid, changing shape as you drag in different directions and to different distances with your mouse. Dragging horizontally with almost no vertical movement results in a long, flat rectangle. Dragging vertically with very little horizontal movement creates a rectangle that is tall and thin. Dragging at a 45-degree angle (diagonally) results in a squared rectangle.

You can draw rectangles from any corner by clicking and dragging in the direction opposite of where you want that corner to be. For instance, to draw a rectangle from the lower-right corner, click and drag up and to the left. As long as you have the Rectangle tool selected, dragging with it in the document window produces a new rectangle.

If you need to draw a rectangle that is an exact size, instead of dragging with the Rectangle tool, just click it once and release where you want the upper-left corner to be. The Rectangle dialog box shown in Figure 4-4 appears. Type in the width and height you want, click OK, and the rectangle draws itself, becoming precisely the size that you specified.

Figure 4-4: The Rectangle dialog box is used for specifying exact dimensions of a rectangle.

If you click with the Rounded Rectangle tool (which is explained in the sections to follow), you get a third text field. The third text field in the Rounded Rectangle dialog box is for the size of the corner radius. This option makes the corners of the rectangle curved, although leaving the setting at a value of 0 keeps the corners straight. Rectangles with sizes specified in the Rectangle dialog box are always drawn from the upper-left corner unless you press the Option [Alt] key while drawing (see the next section, "Drawing Rectangles from Their Centers"). The largest rectangle you can draw is about 19 feet by 19 feet. It's a wonder you can get anything done at all with these limitations!

When the Rectangle dialog box appears, values are usually already inside the text fields. Those numbers correspond to the size of the rectangle you last drew. To create another rectangle the same size, just click OK (or press Return or Enter). To make the rectangle a different size, replace the values with your own measurements. If a text field is highlighted, typing replaces the text in the text field and deletes what had been highlighted. To highlight the next field in a dialog box, press the Tab key. You can also highlight the preceding field in a dialog box by pressing Shift+Tab. If you'd like to highlight any text field instantly, double-click the value, or click the label next to that value. To accept the options in the dialog box, click OK or press Return or Enter.

When you first run Illustrator, all measurements are set to points. This means that the values inside the Rectangle dialog box appear in so many points (12 points in a pica). You can work in inches in three ways. The first way, before you bring up the Rectangle dialog box, is to choose Edit ➪ Preferences ➪ Units & Undo and choose inches as the measurement system. All dialog boxes in all new documents will then express their measurements in inches, not points. The second way is to choose File ➪ Document Setup and choose inches in the Units pop-up menu, which changes the units to inches in that document *only*. The third way is to type either the inch symbol (") or **in** (for inches) after the number, even though the text fields show points. Illustrator does conversions from points to inches and centimeters (and vice versa) on the fly, so after you enter a point value, the program converts the points into inches as soon as you press the Tab key. This little feature can be an excellent way for you to become more comfortable with points and picas.

To get out of the Rectangle dialog box without drawing a rectangle, click the Cancel button (or just press ⌘+. (period) if you are using a Mac, or press Esc if you are using Windows). Anything you have typed in that dialog box is then forgotten; the next time the dialog box is opened, it still has the size of the previously drawn rectangle inside it.

To create a basic drop-shadow box, follow these steps:

1. Using the Rectangle tool, draw a rectangle that is about one inch wide by one inch tall. Change the fill color of the rectangle to 100% Black by clicking the fill square in the toolbox, and then choosing Black in the Color palette. Change the stroke to black by clicking the stroke icon in the toolbox and then choosing Black in the Color palette.

2. Choose the Selection tool and drag up and to the right just a little while holding down the Option [Alt] key. (The farther you drag, the greater the depth of the drop shadow.)

3. After you release the mouse button, you should have two overlapping rectangles. Change the fill color of the rectangle on top to 50 percent gray by clicking the fill square in the toolbox, and then clicking 50% Black in the Color palette. Change the stroke to black by clicking the stroke icon in the toolbox and then choosing Black in the Color palette. Your illustration should now look like Figure 4-5.

Figure 4-5: A basic
drop-shadow box

Drawing rectangles from their centers

Instead of drawing a rectangle from a corner, you can also draw one from its center. Rectangles are often placed on top of or under certain other objects, and an even amount of space needs to separate the rectangle from the object it surrounds. Drawing from the corner forces you to "eyeball" the space around the object, while drawing from the center of the other object ensures that space surrounding the object is the same.

To draw a rectangle from its center, hold down the Option [Alt] key, click, and drag. The origin point is now the center of the rectangle. The farther you drag in one direction, the farther the edges of the rectangle go out in the opposite direction. Drawing from the center of a rectangle lets you draw a rectangle twice as big as the one you can draw if you drag from a corner. As long as the Option [Alt] key is pressed, the rectangle continues to be drawn from its center. If you release the Option [Alt] key before you release the mouse button, the origin of the rectangle changes back to a corner. You can press and release the Option [Alt] key at any time while drawing, toggling back and forth between drawing a corner rectangle and a centered rectangle.

Tip   If you click without dragging when the Option [Alt] key is pressed, the Rectangle dialog box appears. The center of the rectangle is now where you clicked (normally, the corner of the rectangle is where you click). Unlike manually drawing (dragging) centered rectangles, the values you enter for the width and height are the actual width and height of the rectangle. The value is *not* doubled, as it is when you are dragging a centered rectangle.

Drawing a perfect square

Few things in life really are perfect, but squares in Illustrator are pretty darn close. To create a perfect square, hold down the Shift key as you draw a rectangle. Holding down the Shift key forces Illustrator to draw a rectangle with four equal sides.

Tip   You can also use the Rectangle dialog box to draw a perfect square by entering equal values for the width and height.

To draw a square from its center, hold down the Option [Alt] and Shift keys while drawing. Make sure that *both* keys are still pressed when you release the mouse button.

Drawing rounded corners

Sometimes straight corners just aren't good enough. That's when it's time to create a rectangle with *rounded* corners. Why? Maybe you want your rectangles to look less like they were generated with a computer. A tiny bit of corner rounding (2 or 3 points) may be just what you need.

To draw a rectangle with rounded corners, choose the Rounded Rectangle tool (a pop-up tool that appears when you click the Rectangle tool in the toolbox), and drag to the right. Click and drag with this tool as if you were drawing a standard rectangle; the only difference is that this rectangle has rounded corners. The point at which you clicked is where the corner would be—if there were a corner. Of course, with rounded corners, no real corner exists, so the computer uses an imaginary point, called the *origin point*, as its onscreen corner reference.

The *corner radius* in Illustrator is the length from that imaginary corner (the origin point) to where the curve begins, as shown in Figure 4-6. The larger the value you enter in the Corner Radius field of the Rectangle dialog box, the farther the rectangle starts from the imaginary corner, and the bigger the curve is. For example, if you set the corner radius at one inch, the edge of the rectangle would start curving one inch from where a real corner would normally appear.

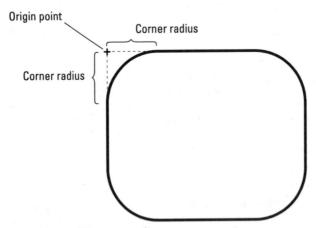

Figure 4-6: The corner radius

To draw a rounded rectangle from the center, press the Option [Alt] key and keep it pressed until you release the mouse button. To draw a rounded square, hold the Shift key while dragging and don't release it until after you release the mouse button. Drawing a rounded square from its center requires that you press and hold down both the Option [Alt] and Shift keys until you release the mouse button.

How the Corner Radius *Really* Works

For all you geometry buffs, this is the real way that this whole corner radius business works: The width of any circle is called the *diameter* of that circle. Half the diameter is the *radius* of the circle, as shown in the following figure.

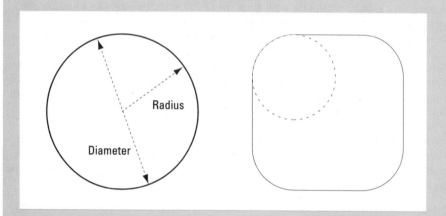

If you create a circle with a radius of one inch, the circle actually has a diameter of two inches. Put this two-inch circle into the corner of the rectangle, as in the preceding figure, and the curve of the circle matches the curve of the rounded rectangle that has a corner radius of one inch. Huh?

To realistically determine the way a round corner will look, use the method that measures the distance from the imaginary corner to the place where the curve starts.

The *roundness* of the corners is determined by either the corner radius used by the most recent rounded-corner rectangle drawn or the radius set in the General Preferences dialog box (Edit ➪ Preferences ➪ General). The corner radius in the General Preferences dialog box changes each time you change the radius with the Rounded Rectangle tool. To change the radius of the next rounded rectangle to be drawn, go to the General Preferences dialog box and enter the new corner radius value. All rounded rectangles are now drawn with this new corner radius until you change this value.

You can also change the corner radius by clicking once with the Rounded Rectangle tool anywhere in the document to display the Rectangle dialog box. Changing the value in the Corner Radius field not only changes the current rounded rectangle's corner radius, but also changes the radius in the General Preferences box. This corner radius is used for all subsequently drawn rounded rectangles until the radius value is changed again.

Tip If the corner radius is more than one-half the length of either the length or width of the rectangle, the rectangle will appear to have perfectly round ends on at least two sides. If the corner radius is more than one-half the length of either the length or width of the rectangle, then the rectangle will be a circle!

Using the Round Corners filter

If you have an existing rectangle with straight corners and you'd like to make the corners round, neither of the preceding methods will work. Instead, you must choose Filter ⇨ Stylize ⇨ Round Corners and enter the value of the corner radius you would like for the existing rectangle in the dialog box that appears. Using this filter enables you to change straight-corner rectangles to rounded-corner rectangles, but not rounded-corner rectangles to straight-corner rectangles. Using this filter on rectangles that already have rounded corners isn't recommended, as it will usually result in an unsightly (ugly) distortion.

Furthermore, this filter cannot change corners that have been rounded with either the Rounded Rectangle tool or by a previous use of the Round Corners dialog box. Using this dialog box affects corners that are *not* round. Figure 4-7 shows the Round Corners filter applied to various rectangles and the results.

Figure 4-7: Rounded corners on rectangles

Rounding corners backward

What if you want your corners to round inward instead of out? Well, it would seem that you are initially out of luck, for Illustrator doesn't provide any way for you to enter a negative value for a corner radius. Instead, you need to manipulate the corners manually. The following steps, and the illustration of these steps in Figure 4-8, explain how to create a reverse rounded-corner rectangle.

1. Choose Edit ⇨ Preferences ⇨ General and set the corner radius to **0.25"**. Draw a rounded rectangle that is about three inches wide by one inch tall.

2. Select the topmost point on the left side of the rounded rectangle with the Direct Selection tool (hollow arrow). One control handle appears, sticking out to the left.

3. Using the Rotate tool, click the Anchor Point once to set the origin. Click the control handle again and drag it down below the Anchor Point. Press the Shift key to ensure that the control handle line is perfectly vertical and then release the mouse button.

4. Select the second point from the top on the left side with the Direct Selection tool. A control handle appears, sticking straight up out of this Anchor Point.

5. Using the Rotate tool, click the Anchor Point once to set the origin. Click the control handle again and drag it to the right of the Anchor Point. Press the Shift key to ensure that the control handle line is perfectly horizontal and then release the mouse button.

6. Repeat these steps for each of the corners. After you get the hang of it, the points start flying into position almost by themselves.

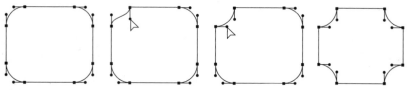

Figure 4-8: Steps for creating "backward" rounded corners on a rectangle

Drawing ellipses and circles

Drawing ellipses and circles is *almost* as easy as drawing rectangles and squares. You can create a variety of ellipses and circles in Illustrator.

Drawing an ellipse

To draw an ellipse, choose the Ellipse tool, click, and drag diagonally. The outline of an ellipse forms and when you release the mouse button, the ellipse itself appears onscreen. Ellipses, like rectangles, have four Anchor Points, but the Anchor Points on an ellipse are at the top, bottom, left, and right of the ellipse.

Drawing an ellipse is harder than drawing a rectangle because the point of origin on an ellipse is outside the ellipse. With a rectangle, the point of origin corresponds to either a corner of the rectangle, which also happens to be an Anchor Point, or the center of the rectangle. An ellipse has no corners. This means that clicking and dragging does not align the top or bottom, or left or right, but one of the 45-degree curves to the origin point (an *arc*). Figure 4-9 shows that the top of the curve extends above the origin point, the bottom of the curve extends below the origin point, the right edge extends to the right of the origin point, and the left edge extends to the left of the origin point. (More detailed — and largely unnecessary — math is available at the end of this section.)

Drawing an ellipse from its "corner" is a difficult task when the top, bottom, left, and right edges of the oval need to be at a specific location. On the other hand, tracing elliptical objects is easier because clicking and dragging on the edge of an existing elliptical object results in a close-to-perfect match, as shown in Figure 4-10.

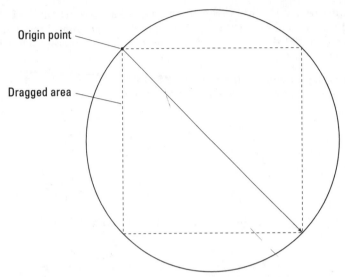

Figure 4-9: The curves of an ellipse extend beyond the boundaries of the dragged area.

Figure 4-10: Tracing a dimmed EPS image with the Rectangle and Ellipse tools

For easier tracing of circles, change the Constrain Angle value (Edit ➪ Preferences ➪ General) to 45 degrees. Now you can place the cursor on the top, bottom, or sides of the circle, and drag horizontally or vertically for a perfect fit. This technique doesn't work for ellipses because the ellipse will be angled at 45 degrees if drawn this way.

Here are the steps for using an image as a backdrop guide to help in the creation of an illustration such as the snowman shown in Figure 4-10:

1. Load the image that you want to trace (in this case we're using the snowman image). Choose Window ➪ Show Layers. In the Layers palette, double-click the layer that contains the image to trace and check the Dim Placed Images option and set the percentage to 50 percent.

2. Use the Rectangle tool to trace the frame of the image. Place the cursor in a corner of the object to be traced and drag toward the opposite corner.

3. Use the Rectangle, Ellipse, and Transform tools to duplicate the various elements of the image such as the snowman's hat, arms, and body.

To draw from the center of an ellipse, press the Option [Alt] key and drag. As long as you are holding down the Option [Alt] key when you release the mouse button, the ellipse uses the initial click as the origin point and is drawn from the center.

Note

Clicking without dragging with the Ellipse tool brings up the Ellipse dialog box, where you can enter any value for the width and height of your ellipse. The ellipse is drawn from the upper-left arc. Entering identical values results in a circle. Option [Alt]+clicking brings up the same dialog box, but the ellipse is then drawn from the center instead of the left arc.

Drawing a perfect circle

To draw a perfect circle, hold down the Shift key as you drag. The oval now has equal width and height, making it a circle. Make sure that you keep pressing the Shift key until you release the mouse button; otherwise, the ellipse loses its equal proportions. To draw a circle from the center with the Ellipse tool, hold down both the Option [Alt] and Shift keys and drag diagonally.

Ellipses are drawn from the upper-left corner and extend about 20 percent of the total height above the origin point and about 20 percent of the total width to the left of the origin point. It's not just a coincidence that the right edge and bottom also extend 20 percent past the release point. The way this works out in mathematics (numerophobics should skip ahead to the next paragraph now) is that the height and width of the ellipse will be the square root of 2 (about 1.414) times the height and width of the box that is dragged from corner to corner.

Only rectangles and ellipses were used to create the illustration in Figure 4-11. Through a creative use of fills, the illustration comes alive.

Moving rectangles and ellipses while drawing

While drawing a rectangle or ellipse, you may realize you want to move it. You can move any rectangle or ellipse by holding down the spacebar while your mouse button is depressed and dragging your shape to a new location. When you let up on the spacebar, you can continue to draw your object.

Follow these steps to create the juggler shown in Figure 4-11, using just ellipses and rectangles:

1. Change the paint style to a fill of None and a stroke of 1-point black.

2. Using the Ellipse tool, drag to create the juggler's body and then his head, as shown in Figure 4-12.

Figure 4-11: An illustration drawn with only rectangles and ellipses

3. To tilt the juggler's head backward, select the head oval and double-click the Rotate tool. Enter a value of **30** degrees, which angles the head backward.

4. Next, create one of the rings by pressing the Shift key and dragging to create a perfect circle.

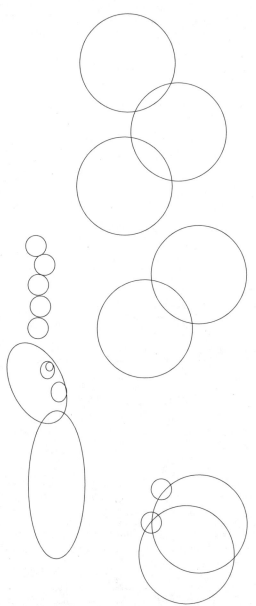

Figure 4-12: Ellipses and circles

5. Duplicate the circles by pressing the Option [Alt] key and dragging one of the circles to a new location. As long as the Option [Alt] key is pressed when you release the mouse button, the circle is duplicated rather than moved.

6. Draw a much smaller circle for one of the balls the juggler is balancing on his head. Using Option [Alt] and drag, duplicate the balls in the same way you duplicated the rings.

7. With Option [Alt], duplicate two more ball-sized circles to create hands, one for the white area of the eye, and one for the mouth.

8. Choose Edit ➪ Preferences ➪ General and change the Constrain Angle to 45 degrees.

9. Using the Rectangle tool, create first the top part of the hat and then the rim of the hat, as shown in Figure 4-13. The pieces will automatically be angled at 45 degrees.

10. Change the Constrain Angle back to 0 degrees and draw both arms. They may need to be rotated individually, depending on the location of the rings.

11. Draw the rectangular background and choose Object ➪ Arrange ➪ Send to Back.

12. Select individual paths and fill them with different colors and gradients.

Drawing Shapes at an Angle

Normally, when you draw a shape with a tool, it appears to be oriented with the document and the document window. For instance, the bottom of a rectangle is normally parallel to the bottom of the document window.

But what if you want to draw shapes that are all angled at 45 degrees on the page? Well, one possibility is to rotate them after they are drawn using the Transform Each command or the Rotate tool. Better than this alternative, however, is to set up your document so that every new shape is automatically angled.

The angle of the shapes is dependent on the *constrain angle*. Normally, the Constrain Angle is 0 degrees, where all shapes appear to align evenly with the borders of the document. To change the Constrain Angle, choose Edit ➪ Preferences ➪ General and enter a new value in the Constrain Angle text field inside the General Preferences dialog box.

When you are done drawing these angled shapes, make sure that you change the Constrain Angle setting back to 0 degrees, or all new shapes will be created at the altered Constrain Angle.

The Constrain Angle affects shapes and other objects created in Illustrator, such as type. In addition, dragging objects with the Shift key pressed constrains them to the current Constrain Angle or to a 45-degree or 90-degree variation of it. The Constrain Angle is much easier to see if you have Grids turned on (choose View ➪ Show Grids, or press ⌘+" [Ctrl+"]). The grid shown on the page is always aligned to the Constrain Angle.

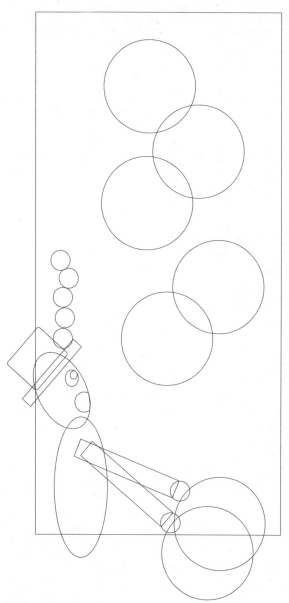

Figure 4-13: Adding rectangles to the illustration

Creating other cool shapes

Although it's loads of fun to create more and more ovals, rectangles, and rounded rectangles, sooner or later you're going to get bored. You can automatically create other, dare we say, *more interesting* shapes by using some of the additional shape tools that come with Illustrator. These additional shapes can be found as pop-up tools under the Rectangle tool, and include a Polygon tool and a Star tool.

Creating polygons

To create a polygon, select the Polygon tool (to the right of the Rectangle tool in the Rectangle tool slot) and click and drag in a document. As you drag, the polygon grows from its center and gets larger and larger.

To specify the number of sides for your polygon *before* you draw the polygon, click the left mouse button on the page without moving the mouse. This action brings up the Polygon dialog box (shown in Figure 4-14), where you can specify both the number of sides and the size of the polygon.

Figure 4-14: The Polygon dialog box

The radius is the distance from the center of the polygon to the corners of the polygon. For even-sided shapes (4, 6, 8, 10, and so on sides), the radius is half the width of the object, from one corner to the opposite corner. For odd-sided shapes, the radius is *not* half the width of the object, but instead, can *only* be measured by going from one corner point to the center.

All polygons created with the Polygon tool are equilateral polygons. We looked up *equilateral*, just to make sure we weren't spouting off multisyllabic words to sound impressive, and it means "sides of the same length." So every polygon you create has sides that are all the same. That's why every four-sided object you create is a square, and each six-sided object is a perfect hexagon. You may find the square capabilities of the Polygon tool useful (really); it can save you a step when you want to draw a perfect square that is tilted. That's something that can't be done with the Rectangle tool unless you change the Constrain Angle in General Preferences prior to drawing the square or use the Rotate tool on the square after it is drawn. We've found using the Polygon tool's square capabilities helpful on several occasions.

While drawing a polygon, you can change the number of sides on the fly. To increase the number of sides, press the up arrow. To decrease the number of sides, press the down arrow. Figure 4-15 shows different kinds of polygons you can draw with the Polygon tool.

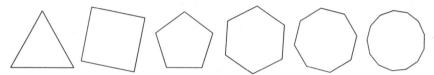

Figure 4-15: Polygons drawn with the Polygon tool

If you press the Shift key while dragging, the polygon you're creating is upright; it aligns to the current Constrain Angle (usually 0 degrees). This means that if you're creating a triangle and you press Shift, the triangle has one side that is perfectly horizontal (the bottom) unless you have a different Constrain Angle, in which case that edge of the triangle aligns to that angle.

Press the spacebar to move your polygon around when dragging with the Polygon tool. You can do this at any time during the creation of a polygon; when you release the spacebar, the tool functions as before.

Tip   Possibly the niftiest function of the Polygon (and the Star and Spiral tools) is the wonderful Spaz function that comes from using the back tick (`) key (on the same key as the tilde [~]). Press it when you're drawing and you'll see multiple instances of the shape appear on top of one another. As Figure 4-16 shows, Spazzing can create all sorts of questionable designs.

Seeing stars

To create stars, choose the Star tool from its hiding place next to the Polygon tool in the Rectangle tool slot and drag in the document. As you drag, a star is born. Figure 4-17 shows several kinds of stars.

Stars have several of the same controls as polygons when they're being drawn: Shift aligns the star to the constrain angle, the spacebar moves the star around, and the back tick key (`) makes millions of duplicates. The up and down arrows work a bit differently, however. Instead of adding and removing sides, the arrows add and remove entire points. So, in a way, they're actually adding or removing two sides. Stars have to have an even number of sides or they're not really stars, they're the pointy lumps you doodled during your Poly Sci classes as a sophomore.

The Star tool adds two additional keys for other functions. Pressing the Option [Alt] key makes every other side align with each other. It's hard to describe, but these stars look "perfect." Adobe refers to them as *fixed* stars, but we're not aware of any neutering or spaying taking place when the Option [Alt] key is pressed. ("It's the responsible thing to do; press the Option [Alt] key when you draw stars.") These fixed stars are shown in Figure 4-18. In case it's keeping you up at night, the Option [Alt] key has no effect on stars with four points, and it turns three-pointed stars into triangles.

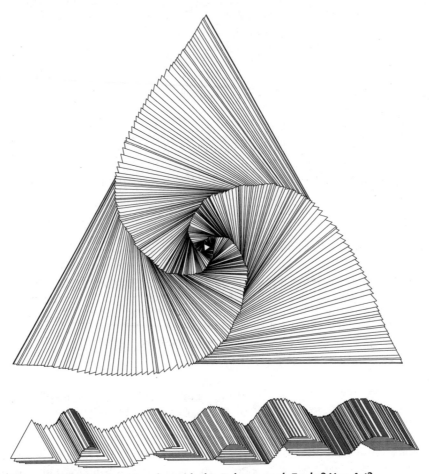

Figure 4-16: Spazzing triangles with the Polygon tool. Funky? Yes. Art? Hmmmmm.

Figure 4-17: A star is born.

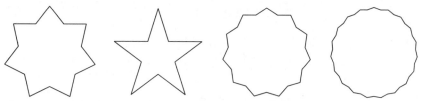

Figure 4-18: Fixed stars drawn while the Option [Alt] key is pressed

Stars can come in all shapes, not just the fixed and standard shapes. For example, the arms of a star could be very thin and long or they could be short and wide. You can create these various shapes by altering the relative distance between star points and the center of the star. In Illustrator, these different shapes are created by pressing the ⌘ [Ctrl] key when you drag. When you hold down the ⌘ [Ctrl] key, only the outer points of the star are extended while the interior points of the star remain fixed in place. Figure 4-19 shows the same star (points, rotation, size) with points extended differently.

Figure 4-19: These stars are the same except for the difference in the distance between the inner points and outer points.

You can also open the Star options dialog box by clicking with the Star tool on the page without moving the mouse. In this dialog box, you can enter the radius of the inner and outer points that make up the star, as well as the number of points.

Of course, all of these stars created with the Star tool consist of regular-looking stars. For a more dramatic-looking starburst, follow these steps:

1. Create a star with about 30 sides. Make it look something like the one shown in Figure 4-20.

2. Choose Filter ➪ Distort ➪ Roughen.

3. In the Roughen dialog box (see Figure 4-21), change the Size to 5 percent and select the Relative radio button. Then set the Detail to 0 (keeping the Detail at 0 prevents Roughen from adding Anchor Points). Check the Corner checkbox (so we don't have curves on our starburst) and click OK. You can also check the Preview checkbox; each time you check and uncheck it, a new random preview results; clicking OK uses the Roughen preview you see onscreen. The result appears in Figure 4-22.

Figure 4-20: A star about to become a starburst

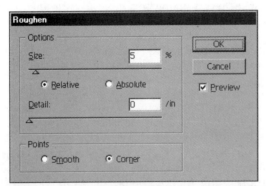

Figure 4-21: The Roughen dialog box set up
to change a star into a starburst

Figure 4-22: The resulting starburst

    4. Add any extras, such as a drop shadow, text, and so on. Figure 4-23 shows the end result.

Drawing Flares

If you get up early in the morning for a brisk jog before the sun comes up, the simulated spattering a rays as the sun breaks over the distance mountain is called a flare. Through the day, you can see flares as the sun reflects off shining surface, like the newly washed and waxed car.

 New Feature The Flare tool is new to this version and a powerful new addition to Illustrator.

Flares can be created in Illustrator using the Flare tool. Technically, flares in Illustrator aren't a shape, but rather a group of shapes made up of several circles with gradients in them, but the Flare tool is grouped with the other shapes as a pop-up tool under the Rectangle tool and many of the same controls for shapes work on the Flare tool.

Figure 4-23: The final, ready-for-stamping-on-the-front-of-the-book starburst

Flares, like the one that is shown is Figure 4-24, are made up of several parts including a Center, Rays, Halo and several Rings. Each of these parts has settings for controlling how they look.

Flares are created by clicking where the flare center is located and dragging to set the diameter of the rays and then clicking again to set the center of the final ring. A series of rings will be drawn between the flare center and the last ring's center. While dragging to set the rays diameter, you can hold down the ⌘ (Ctrl) key to change the halo width and the up and down arrows to add or subtract from the total number of rays. The ⌘ (Ctrl) can also be used to change the width of the rings when clicking to place the center of the rings.

Clicking in the document window without dragging or by double clicking on the Flare tool will make the Flare Tool Options dialog box appear, as shown in Figure 4-25. This dialog box will let you specify the Diameter, Opacity and Brightness of the flare center and the Growth and Fuzziness of the flare halo. Rays and Rings can be disabled using the checkboxes next to each.

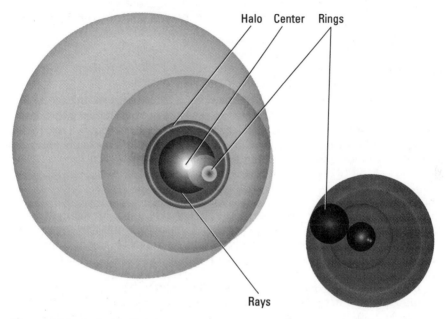

Figure 4-24: A simple flare

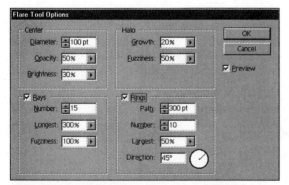

Figure 4-25: The Flare Tool Options dialog box includes settings for the various flare parts.

Once a flare is created, you can reposition the center of the flare or the center of the rings by moving the flare tool cursor over the top of the center location. When over each center, the cursor will change to include small arrows on its outside. When the cursor changes, you can click and drag to move the center's position.

To edit the flare settings, select the flare and double click on the Flare tool to open the Flare Tool Options dialog box where you can change the parameters of the flare. Using the Direct Selection tool, you can select the individual vertices of the halo or rings and edit them as desired. Using the Object ➪ Expand menu item, you can convert a flare object to individual objects. You'll need to ungroup the flare object to get access to the individual objects.

Creating unique lines

In addition to shapes, Illustrator includes several tools that can be used to draw specialized lines. These tools are meant to not replace, but enhance the Pencil, Pen and Paintbrush tools. These tools include the Line Segment tool (\), Arc tool, Spiral tool, Rectangular Grid tool and the Polar Grid tool. All these tools are located as pop-up tools under the Line Segment tool.

Drawing straight lines

I'm not sure how shaky your drawing hand is, but it is tough for me to draw a perfectly straight line by hand with the Pencil or Paintbrush tools. Yes, I can do it with the Pen tool, but there is an easier way. Directly to the left of the Rectangle tool in the toolbox is the Line Segment tool. This tool is selected directly using the (\) key.

Drawing straight-line segments with this tool is as simple as clicking to place the first end point and dragging to the location of the second end point and the line is drawn straight between these two points. Double clicking on the Line Segment tool or clicking once in the document window will open the Line Segment Tool Options dialog box, shown in Figure 4-26.

Figure 4-26: The Line Segment Tool Options dialog box lets you set the Length and Angle of the line segment.

Holding down the option (Alt) key while dragging will extend the line in both directions from the first end point. This is convenient if you know where the midline of the line needs to be. You can also use the Spacebar to move the line around as you drag it.

The Shift key, when held down, will constrain the line to 45-degree angles. This tool can also use the tick (`) key to produce a spaz effect of drawing multiple lines all at once. If you combine these two keys, you can quickly draw a simple star such as the one shown in Figure 4-27 by holding down the Shift and tilde (~) character while clicking and dragging around the origin point.

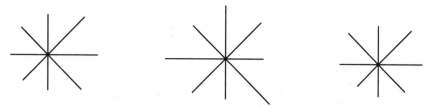

Figure 4-27: This star of lines was created by simply drawing multiple lines around an origin point constrained to 45 degrees.

Drawing Arcs

Another useful type of line is an arc. The Arc tool is the first pop-up tool under the Line Segment tool. Arcs are drawn within a rectangular box from one corner to the opposite corner. They can be either opened or closed. Closed arcs have two edges of the base rectangular displayed as shown in Figure 4-28. Holding down the C key while dragging to create an arc will switch an open arc to a closed arc and vice versa.

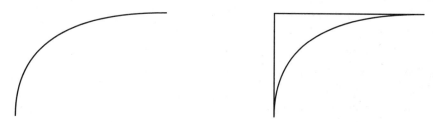

Figure 4-28: Arc segments can be either open (left) or closed (right).

The slope of the arc can be set to be any value between Concave and Convex. These two slopes are opposite of each other and higher values will push the arc towards the corner of the rectangle. Figure 4-29 shows two arcs with opposite slope values. A slope value of 0 will produce a straight line between the two corners of the rectangle. While dragging an arc, the up and down arrows can be used to increase or decrease the Slope value. Holding down the X key while dragging to create an arc will switch an concave arc to a convex arc and vice versa. The F key can be used while dragging to flip the arc.

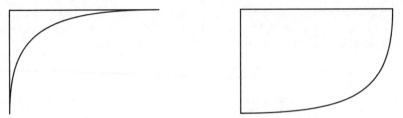

Figure 4-29: Arcs can be set to be either concave (left) or convex (right).

Just like other shapes, the Spacebar will let you move the arc while create it, the Shift key will draw an arc within a perfect square and the tick (`) key will create multiple copies of the arc. Finally, the Alt key will draw the arc from the center of the rectangle by extending both endpoints of the arc as you drag.

All settings for the arc segment can be set using the Arc Segment Tool Options dialog box, shown in Figure 4-30. The small square icon to the right of the Length X-Axis field designates the location of the origin point. The default is the lower left corner. You can click on the corners of the square icon to change the origin point.

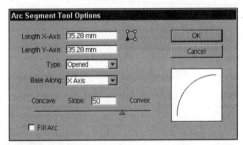

Figure 4-30: The Arc Segment Tool Options dialog box includes settings for the various flare parts.

Drawing spirals

If there's one really good thing to say about being able to draw spirals with the Spiral tool in Illustrator, it's that it was hellish to create spirals before a Spiral tool (or filter) existed. If there's another good thing to say, we haven't quite figured it out yet.

The Spiral tool (located as a pop-up to the Line Segment tool) makes spirals — all sorts of spirals. What would you use a spiral for? Well, we used the Spiral tool to create a simulated Lucy and the Rugrats' "Live Dinner LP," which included such classics as "Stop Making Excuses," "Watch Out, Tomcat," and the top-ten hit "Mercy, Mercy, Mercy." Of course, the path was exceedingly long and refused to

print on most imagesetters. Other than that, we've created lots of art for this and other Illustrator books using spirals. We're still waiting for a practical use to rear its twisted, spun head. Figure 4-31 shows several useless spirals we've manufactured with the Spiral tool.

Figure 4-31: Spiral madness

 Spirals beg to be stroked, not filled. Putting just a fill on a spiral makes it look like the circle you doodled in that Poly Sci class—lumpy and not quite round.

Here's a rundown of keys you can press while spiraling out of control with the Spiral tool:

✦ **Back tick (`)** duplicates here as well, but *don't* do it with spirals. The mess is usually disastrous on all but the most windless spirals.

✦ **Shift** keeps the spiral aligned to the Constrain Angle. Actually, it keeps the protruding line segment of the spiral aligned to a 45-degree variant of the Constrain Angle.

✦ **Option [Alt].** Pressing this key makes the spiral grow by adding or removing line segments (winds) to the spiral's outermost edge. Dragging away from the origin (where you initially clicked) adds segments; dragging toward the origin removes segments.

✦ **⌘ [Ctrl].** Pressing the ⌘ [Ctrl] key while dragging changes the tightness of the spiral (the "tightness" is also called the *decay* as the spiral gets less and less tight as the line spirals outward). Dragging away from the origin decreases the decay percentage, which makes the space between winds larger toward the outer edge of the spiral. Dragging toward the origin increases the decay percentage, which makes the space between winds similar from inside to outside. A decay of 100 percent results in a perfect circle. The decay can never be less than 5 percent.

✦ **Spacebar.** Pressing the spacebar lets you move the spiral around the screen.

If you click in your document with the Spiral tool, the Spiral dialog box (see Figure 4-32) appears, and you can enter specific values for a spiral. Handy for all those times your client or boss wants that 82.5 percent decay spiral.

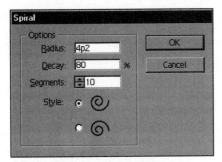

Figure 4-32: The Spiral dialog box

Drawing rectangular grids

Using the Grids feature, you can place a grid in the document window that covers everything like ants at a picnic, but there might be times when you want an actual grid object that has limits like localizing the ants to a certain area (ok, so the ants example doesn't work to well).

 The Rectangular and Polar Grid tools are both new with release 10.

The Rectangular Grid tool (located under the Line Segment tool) can create rectangular grids just like creating rectangles by dragging from one corner to the opposite corner. Holding down the Shift key will make a grid using a perfect square and the Option (Alt) key will create the grid from the center outward. The Spacebar allows you to move the grid while creating it. The up and down arrows will add or delete rows to the grid and the left and right arrow keys will add or delete columns.

Grids can be skewed (and they don't need to be weird to do it). A skewed grid will have the rows or columns near one edge closer together than the opposite edge. Grids can be skewed horizontally, vertically or both as shown in Figure 4-33. You can control the amount of horizontal skew is used while dragging with the F and V keys. The X and C keys control the amount of skew for the vertical direction.

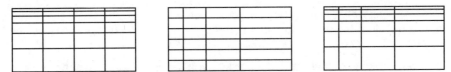

Figure 4-33: Rectangular grids can be skewed horizontally (left), vertically (center) or both (right).

Clicking without dragging on the document window will open the Rectangular Grid Tool Options dialog box, shown in Figure 4-34. This dialog box can be used to

change all the settings for the given grid. These changes will be used the next time the tool is used.

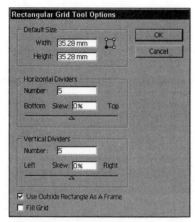

Figure 4-34: The Rectangular Grid Tool Options dialog box includes settings for the rectangular grid.

Drawing polar grids

Imagine you're in an airport control tower and that you spend all day looking at a radar screen (no, this isn't a nightmare). The radar screen is a circular screen with concentric circles and radial marks. Using these two sets of lines, you can determine the position of objects. This type of display isn't something new to Air Traffic Controllers, it is actually called a polar grid and Illustrator includes a tool that you can use to create polar grids.

The Polar Grid tool is located under the Line Segment tool and is very similar to the Rectangular Grid tool covered previously. The difference is that polar grids use circles instead of rectangles and concentric and radial lines instead of rows and columns. Figure 4-35 shows a sample polar grid. The concentric lines are the circles that grow larger from the center and the radial lines are those that extend from the grid center to the edge of the outermost circle.

The Polar Grid Tool Options are shown in Figure 4-36 and include many of the same parameters as the Rectangular Grid Tool Options dialog box. Like the rectangular grid, the polar grid can use the same keys to control how the polar grid is created.

The Shift key will constrain the polar grid to be positioned within a square yielding perfect circles and the option (Alt) key will create the grid from the center outward. The Spacebar will let you move the grid while you create it. The arrow keys can be used to add and subtract lines. The up and down arrows control the concentric lines and the left and right arrow keys control the number of radial lines.

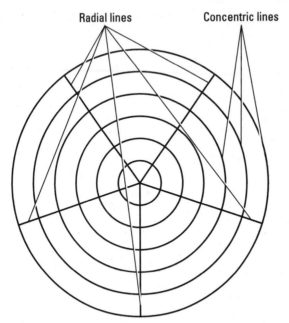

Radial lines   Concentric lines

Figure 4-35: A polar grid includes concentric and radial lines.

Polar grids, like rectangular grids, can also be skewed. While dragging, you can use the X and C keys to control the amount of skew for the concentric lines and the F and V keys for the radial lines.

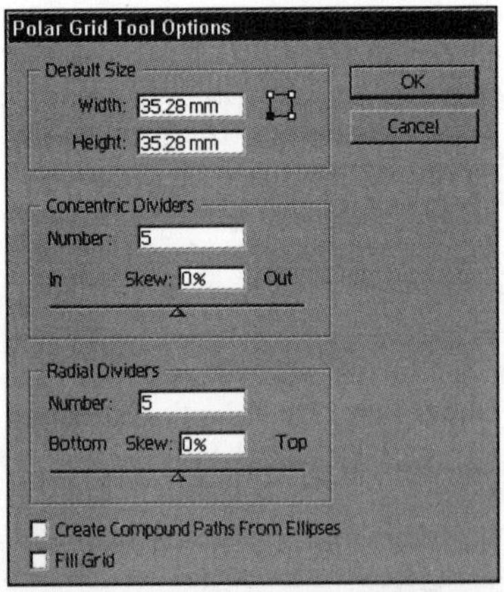

Figure 4-36: The Polar Grid Tool Options dialog box includes settings similar to its rectangular counterpart.

Constructing and Enhancing Graphs

The Graphs feature seems to be one of the most underused features in Illustrator, but they are objects and should be included along with a discussion of objects.

All the graph tools work in a manner similar to that of the shape creation tools: With the Graph tool selected, click and drag to set the size of the graph, or click to display the Graph Size dialog box and then enter the size information. If you press the Shift key while you drag, the graph is constrained to a perfect square (or to a circle, if it's a pie graph). If you press the Option [Alt] key while you drag, you drag from the center of the graph out. If you Option [Alt]+click, the graph you create is centered at the point you Option [Alt]+clicked. That's it. That's all you have to do to use the graph tools. Neat, huh?

Double-clicking the Graph tool brings up the Graph Type dialog box, shown in Figure 4-37. This dialog box has three different screens — Graph Options, where you can select the graph type; Value Axis, which includes options for the default vertical axis; and Category Axis, where you can set the options for the default horizontal axis. Using the drop-down list at the top of the dialog box, you can select from these different option screens.

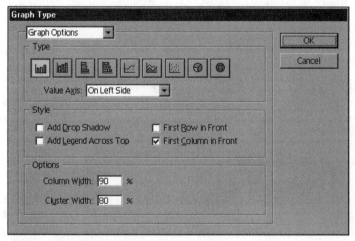

Figure 4-37: The Graph Type dialog box

Choosing a different graph type from the Graph Options screen and clicking OK changes the tool to represent the type of graph you selected. The various graph types are also available as pop-up tools. You can choose from nine graph types; the column graph is the default. You can also use the Graph Options dialog box to change an existing graph. To do this, just select the graph and double click on the graph tool and select the new graph type. The selected graph will be changed automatically.

One of the most exciting aspects of using graphs in Illustrator is their fluidity. Not only can you create graphs easily, but after you create them, you can change them easily. In addition, if the data that you used to create a graph changes, you can enter the new data and have it show up in the graph instantaneously.

Customizing graphs

When a graph is selected and the Graph Type dialog box is displayed, a number of options become available for most graphs:

✦ The **Value Axis** drop down list displays options for On Left Side, On Right Side and On Both Sides, which defines where the value axis is placed. The **On Both Sides** option puts the same axis on both sides.

✦ Checking the Add **Drop Shadow** option places a black shadow behind the graph objects. The shadow is offset up and to the right.

✦ The Add **Legend Across Top** option makes any existing legends appear across the top of the graph, instead of grouped together on the right side of the graph.

✦ The **First Row in Front** option places overlapping rows in order from left to right, wherever columns, clusters, or other objects overlap.

✦ The **First Column in Front** option places overlapping columns in order from left to right, wherever the rows overlap.

Each type of graph has its own customization options. The sections that follow will describe each type of graph explain those options.

Tip   To make visually striking graphs, use a combination of graph types. Simply use the Group Selection tool to select all the objects that are one legend type and then choose Object ➪ Graphs ➪ Graph Type and enter the new graph type for that legend.

Using the Graph Data dialog box

You can change the numbers and the text in the Graph Data dialog box (see Figure 4-38) at any time by selecting the graph and Object ➪ Graphs ➪ Data. Illustrator recreates the graph to reflect the changes you make. If you have moved some of the graph objects around, they may revert to their original locations when Illustrator recreates the graph. If a number does not have quotation marks around it, Illustrator assumes that you want the number to be entered as a value in the graph.

Tip   Make sure that the graph is never ungrouped, at least not until you have finished making all graph data and graph style changes. If you ungroup the graph, you will not be able to use any of the graph options to change the ex-graph because Illustrator will view it as just a set of paths and text.

Switch X/Y — ┌ Cell Style

Transpose row/column   Revert

Import Data   Apply

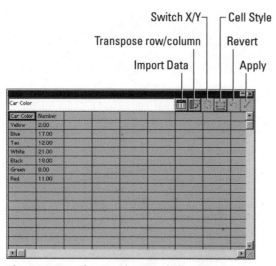

Figure 4-38: The Graph Data dialog box

Using one of the icon buttons at the top of the dialog box, you can import graph data in tab-delimited word processing files. Tab-delimited files are text and numbers that are separated by tabs and returns. To import data from another file, click the Import Data button in the Graph Data dialog box.

Illustrator is not really a graphing or spreadsheet program, so many of the usual controls for arranging data in such programs are not available, including inserting rows and columns and creating formulas.

The Cut, Copy, and Paste functions work within the Graph Data dialog box, so you can move and duplicate information on a very basic level.

One very useful feature in the Graph Data dialog box is the Transverse row/column button. This function switches the *x* and *y* axes of the data, reversing everything that you have entered. The Switch x/y button applies to Scatter graph types and can be used to switch x and y values.

The Cell Style button will open a simple dialog box where you can set the Number of decimals and the Column Width. The column width can be any number between 0 and 20. You can also place the cursor on the border between the cells and drag to increase the column width.

If you make a mistake, the Revert button will return the data and format to its original values. The Apply button will make the data values appear in the graph.

When to Use Graphs

Graphs are most useful when they show numerical information that would normally take several paragraphs to explain or that can't be expressed easily in words. Furthermore, you can express numerical information easily in graphs, and using graphs makes finding and understanding information easier than when the same information is presented in lines of text.

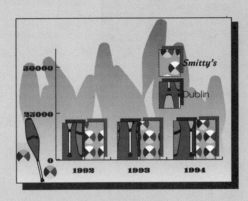

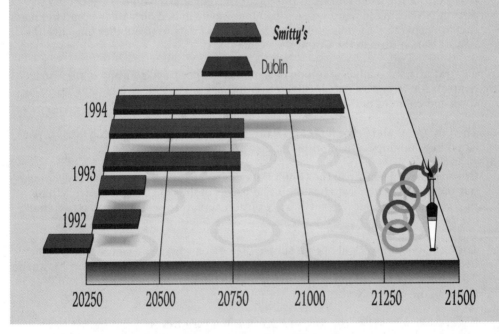

Numbers are fascinating concepts that most people have a good grasp of, but whose significance can be overlooked, especially when comparing different numbers. The numbers 2 and 9 are the same size when you type them; when used in a graph, however, they can represent a drastic difference.

Of course, although graphs are normally used to educate and inform, they are also well suited for misinforming. Stretching or crushing a graph can cause a great difference in the way the information appears. Even worse is the capability to stretch or compress information in just one part of the graph. The accompanying figure shows the same information in two radically different graphs.

The information for the top graph, created by the Smitty's people, shows them to be even with their competitors. The text for the numbers, the column drop shadows, and the distracting images cause the data to make less impact on the reader than the data does in the bottom graph. Dublin's graph indicates that Dublin is doing substantially better than Smitty's. The vast difference in the length of the bars is one way to show the difference, as is the numbering scheme, which starts at 20250, making the first Smitty's bar appear to be a negative number.

Creating and modifying graphs

The steps that follow describe the basics of creating and modifying a graph. The type of graph in this example is a grouped column graph, which is commonly used to compare quantities over time or between different categories.

1. Select the Graph tool and click and drag to form a rectangular area, in the same way that you use the Rectangle tool. The size of the rectangle that you create will be the size of the graph.

2. As soon as you release the mouse button, the Graph Data dialog box, shown in Figure 4-39, appears. Information that you enter in the Graph Data dialog box becomes formatted in graph form. The top row in the Graph Data dialog box worksheet area should contain the labels for comparison within the same set—in the example, we compare how many things a person can juggle to what the current world records are for juggling those particular objects. The items in the top row appear as *legends* outside the graph area. In the leftmost column, you can enter labels that appear at the bottom of the grouped column graph as *categories*—we entered the types of objects that are to be compared in the graph. In the remaining *cells*, enter the pertinent information.

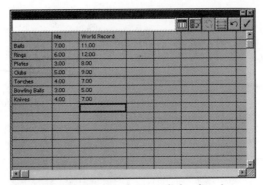

Figure 4-39: The Graph Data dialog box is where you enter the numerical data for the graph.

3. Close the window to have all the data that you entered used in the graph. The graph appears, and it should look something like the one in Figure 4-40.

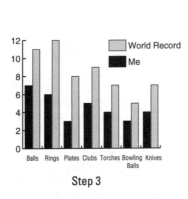

Step 3

Step 4

Figure 4-40: A simple column graph created in Illustrator

4. After we created the graph, we edited it by changing the paint style of the bars and legends, adding a background, changing the point sizes and font of the type in the graph, and adding the lightened circles at the top of each bar and legend to make the elements in the graph look more three-dimensional.

Making the most of various graph types

You can choose from nine different types of graphs in Illustrator. Each type gives a specific kind of information to the reader. Certain graphs are better for comparisons, others for growth, and so on. The following sections describe the graphs, explain how to create them, and tell how you can use them.

Grouped-column graphs

You primarily use grouped-column graphs to show how something changes over time. Often, they are referred to as *bar graphs* because the columns that make up the graphs resemble bars.

The previous example shows a grouped-column graph as created in Illustrator. This graph contains seven categories, and each of the seven categories is represented by two different totals. The height of the bars represents the number in each case, with higher bars representing higher values.

The real strength of a grouped-column graph is that it provides for the direct comparison of different types of statistics in the same graph. In the sample graph, the number of rings that the person can juggle is compared to the bowling ball juggling world record by the height of the bars.

Both column and cluster width are two customizable options for grouped-column graphs and stacked-column graphs. Column width refers to the width of individual columns, with 100 percent being wide enough to abut other columns in the cluster. Cluster width refers to how much of the available cluster space is taken up by the columns in the cluster. At 80 percent (the default), 20 percent of the available space is empty, leaving room between clusters.

You can widen columns and clusters to 1,000 percent of their size and condense them to 1 percent of the width of the original column or cluster.

Illustrator includes column graphs and bar graphs. The difference between the two is the orientation of the bars. Column graph bars run vertically and bar graph bars run horizontally.

Stacked-column graphs

Stacked-column graphs are good for presenting the total of a category and the contributing portions of each category. In Figure 4-41, we again used objects as categories and split each object into the number of those objects being juggled. The total of the time it takes (in weeks) to learn to juggle that number of objects is the height of the object's bar. The time for each number of objects juggled represents a certain portion of the entire time, reflected in each of the smaller sections of the bars.

 Tip To get the labels on the legends to read numbers only, we had to put quotation marks (" ") around each of the numbers. If we had not used quotation marks, the numbers would have been considered data, not labels.

This graph shows the same amount of information as the grouped-column graph, but the information is organized differently. The stacked-column graph is designed to display the total of all the legends, and the grouped-column graph is designed to aid comparison of all individual legends in each category.

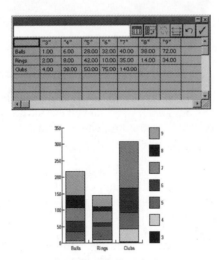

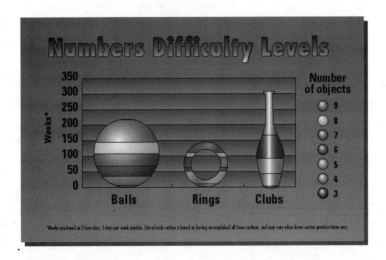

Figure 4-41: Data for a stacked-column graph, how the graph appears when it is first created in Illustrator, and the graph after it is altered

Illustrator also includes stacked column graphs and stacked bar graphs. The difference between these two is also the orientation of the bars. Stacked column graph bars run vertically and stacked bar graph bars run horizontally

Line graphs

Line graphs (also known as *line charts*) show trends over time. They are especially useful for determining progress and identifying radical changes. For example, the line graph in Figure 4-42 shows the average income of three street performers on successive weeks throughout the summer.

	Animated Suspension	The Flying Linguini	Disoriented Convolution
May	300	220	145
	240	190	120
	260	260	140
	320	300	200
June	380	360	150
	400	350	195
	395	320	230
	435	420	190
July	520	190	200
	600	290	195
	440	405	240
	380	340	150
August	300	210	200
	275	250	240
	360	280	230
	300	290	210
September	420	280	170
	220	140	110

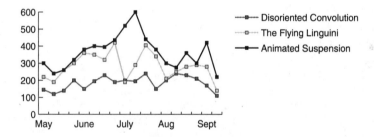

Figure 4-42: Line graph data (top), the graph as it first appears in Illustrator (center), and the graph after it is redesigned (bottom)

The Mark Data points option in the Options area of the Graph Type dialog box forces data points to appear as squares. If this box is not checked, the data points are visible only as direction changes in lines between the data points.

If the Connect Data points option is checked, lines are drawn between each pair of data points.

The Draw Filled Lines option and the corresponding text box for Line Width create a line that is filled with the data point legend color and that is outlined with black. The fill lines option changes the line from a single path with a stroke weight into a filled path with a black stroke.

The Edge to Edge Lines option stretches the lines out to the left and right edges of the graph. Although the result is technically incorrect, you can achieve better visual impact by using this feature.

Area graphs

On first glance, area graphs may appear to be just like filled line graphs. Like line graphs, area graphs show data points that are connected, but area graphs are stacked one on top of the other to show the total area of the legend subject in the graph. There are no additional options for Area graphs.

Scatter graphs

Scatter graphs, which are primarily used for scientific charting purposes, are quite different from all the other types of graphs. Each data point is given a location according to its *x-y* coordinates instead of by category and label. The points are connected, as are the points in line graphs, but the line created by the data point locations can cross itself and does not go in any specific direction. Scatter graphs have the same customization options as line graphs.

Pie graphs

Pie graphs are great for comparing percentages of the portions of a whole. In Figure 4-43, pie graphs show how much of a juggling performance was spent doing particular activities. The higher the percentage for a certain activity, the larger its wedge.

When you create pie graphs, you can remove the individual wedges from the central pie with the Group Selection tool to achieve an exploding pie effect.

The Legends in Wedges option is an option in the Graph Type dialog box that is specifically for pie graphs. If Legends in Wedges is selected, the name of each wedge will be centered within that wedge. However, Illustrator doesn't do a very good job of placing the legend names, many times overlapping neighboring names. In addition, the letters in the legend names are black, which can make reading some of the names difficult or impossible. Other customization options include Sort and Position.

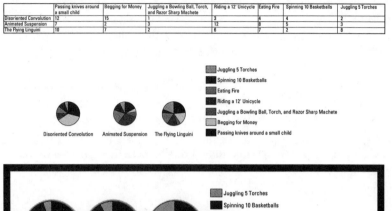

	Passing knives around a small child	Begging for Money	Juggling a Bowling Ball, Torch, and Razor Sharp Machete	Riding a 12' Unicycle	Eating Fire	Spinning 10 Basketballs	Juggling 5 Torches
Disoriented Convolution	12	15	1	3	4	4	2
Animated Suspension	7	2	3	12	8	5	3
The Flying Linguini	10	7	2	6	7	2	8

Figure 4-43: Pie graphs that show how much time each performer spent on certain activities were constructed from the data at the top.

Radar graphs

A radar graph compares values set at a certain point. This type of graph is viewed as a circle. Within the circle are spokes that mark the values. The graph includes a spoke for each number set that is graphed. The center of the circle marks the lowest value and the outer radius of the circle marks the maximum value. Radar graphs have the same options as the line graph.

Using marker and column designs

The most exciting part about the graphing functions in Illustrator is the capability to give column, line, and area graphs special icons to indicate values on the graphs.

On line and area graphs, marker designs are created, which you can use in place of the standard markers. For each value in the graph, the marker design is placed, adding visual impact to the graph.

Column designs are created for grouped-column graphs and stacked-column graphs. The strength of using column designs is most evident in grouped-column graphs, where images are placed side-by-side (see Figure 4-44). Here are the steps:

1. Create the graphic object in Illustrator. A good source of objects is the Symbols palette.

2. Draw a rectangle around the border of the object. Illustrator uses this border to determine the area of the object relative to the values entered for the graph.

3. Draw a horizontal line across the rectangle at a good place for the image to stretch. Make the horizontal line into a guide (View ➪ Make Guide). (This step is necessary only if you use the column design as a sliding design.)

4. Select the rectangle, object, and guide, and choose Object ➪ Graphs ➪ Design. This will open the Graph Design dialog box, shown in Figure 4-44. Click the New Design button to make the selected object appear in the window. Name the design and click the OK button.

Figure 4-44: The Graph Design dialog box can be used to specify graphic objects that can be used within graphs.

5. Select a single column or row using the Direct Selection tool and then select the Object ➪ Graphs ➪ Column menu option. This will open the Graph Column dialog box where you can select one the design elements added using the Graph Design dialog box. Repeat this step for each legend. Figure 4-45 shows several example graphs that use custom design elements.

You can combine column-design types by selecting a different type for each legend.

Creating charts manually

Illustrator has limited graphing tools, which means that sometimes the graph or chart you want can't be created using Illustrator's existing tools. For instance, if you wanted to create a chart with smooth lines instead of straight, angular lines, there's really no way to do this using just Illustrator's tools.

In most cases, the best thing to do is to create your graph "automatically" using Illustrator's built-in tools, and then either modify the results or trace over the graph created by Illustrator. Either way, you'll be stripping the graph of its "graph" qualities, meaning that you can't go back and edit it later.

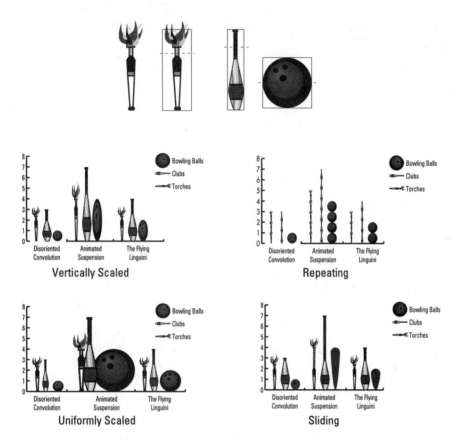

Figure 4-45: Creating a column design and using it in four different grouped-column graphs

Working with Symbols

As you begin to compile a portfolio of work, you'll create objects that are worth using again. If you save these individual objects as symbols, you'll be able to easily grab and reuse them as needed. Symbols are simply Illustrator objects that are placed in a virtual shoebox along with your favorite objects.

Symbols are stored naturally in the Symbols palette, shown in Figure 4-46. You can open this palette using the Window ➪ Symbols menu option or by pressing the Shift+F11 key combination.

 New Feature   Symbols and the Symbols palette are new to Illustrator 10.

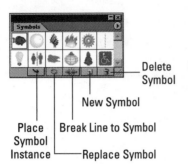

Figure 4-46: The Symbols palette

Delete Symbol

New Symbol

Break Line to Symbol

Place Symbol Instance

Replace Symbol

The palette menu includes three options for viewing the symbols — Thumbnail View, Small List View and Large List View. The list views display the thumbnail along with the symbol name.

Creating new symbols

New symbols can be created by dragging the created object into a slot in the Symbols palette. Wherever the object is dropped, the other symbols will move over to make room for the newcomer. If you drop the object with the Shift key held down, a dialog box will appear where you can name the symbol. Selecting New Symbol from the palette menu will open the same dialog box and the selected object will be added as a symbol. Finally, clicking the New Symbol icon at the bottom of the palette will make the selected object a symbol.

Symbols can be deleted from the Symbols palette by selecting the symbol and clicking on the Delete Symbol icon at the bottom of the palette.

Using symbols

To place an existing symbol in a document, simply drag it from the Symbols palette into the document window or you could click on the Place Symbol icon at the bottom of the palette to make the selected symbol appear in the document. This icon button is only available if a single symbol is selected.

If a symbol is selected in the document, you can replace it with a new selected symbol in the Symbols palette with the Replace button. Objects that are dragged from the Symbols palette retain a link as a symbol, but you can break this link with the Break Link button. This will make the symbol and editable object.

A single symbol can be used multiple times in a document and you can select all instances of a symbol by selecting the symbol and choosing Select All Instances in the palette menu.

The super selection of symbolism tools

Someone at Adobe really had the letter 'S' on their minds as they started to create a set of tools to use to modify a set of symbols. Call it creative or coincidence, but all the Symbolism tools begin with the letter 'S'. Before these tools can be used a symbol or a symbol set must be selected.

 New Feature The Symbolism tools are also all new in release 10.

The line-up includes the following:

✦ **Symbol Sprayer**: This tool creates a set of symbols by dragging the tool in the document window. All the symbols in the set are linked together.

✦ **Symbol Shifter**: This tool will move the symbols within the set in the direction of the tool. It can be used to reposition the symbols. Symbols closer to the center of the tool will move farther than a symbol that only touches the edge of the tool's diameter.

✦ **Symbol Scruncher**: This tool will pull all symbols in the set within the diameter of the tool towards the center of the tool. Holding down the Option [Alt] key will push the symbols away from the center of the tool.

✦ **Symbol Sizer**: This tool will resize the symbols that the tool is dragged over. The more the tool is dragged over the symbols, the larger (or smaller) the symbol becomes. Holding down the Option [Alt] key while dragging will make the symbols smaller.

✦ **Symbol Spinner**: This tool will rotate the symbols that it is dragged over. Dragging several times over a symbol will make it spin to a greater degree. The direction of the rotation depends on the direction that you drag the tool. All symbols will rotation about their own individual centers.

✦ **Symbol Stainer**: This tool will gradually alter the color of the symbol to match the Fill color. Holding down the Option [Alt] key will gradually alter the color back towards its original symbol color.

✦ **Symbol Screener**: This tool will gradually change the transparency value of the symbol. If the tool is used long enough, the symbol will eventually be completely transparent. The Option [Alt] key can reverse the application of transparency making the symbol opaque.

✦ **Symbol Styler**: This tool can only be used after a style is selected from the Style palette. The tool will then gradually apply the selected style to the symbols that are under the tool. The style can be gradually removed restoring the original look of the symbol with the Option [Alt] key.

Although these tools can be used on a single symbol instance, they really become powerful when you drag them over a set of symbols. Creating a set of symbols is accomplished with the Symbol Sprayer tool. To use this tool, you'll need to select a symbol from the Symbols palette. The selected symbol will be duplicated as the set is created.

Note You can add several different symbols to a symbol set, but the Symbolism tools will only affect the last symbols added to the set.

Once a symbol set has been created and selected, you can choose any of the Symbolism tools to alter the symbol's size, orientation, position, color, transparency, and style by dragging over the symbol set with the respective tool.

Once a symbol set has been altered using one or several of the Symbolism tools, you can use the Symbol Sprayer to add more symbols to the set. As you add more symbols to the set, the new symbols will assume the characteristics of the symbols that are around it. For example, if you've created a symbol set of fish that you've altered with the Symbol Sizer tool to range from large at the left to small at the right; then dragging with the Symbol Sprayer will over the set will add new fish that are the same relative size as their nearest neighboring symbol.

Figure 4-47 shows each of the Symbolism tools applied to a group of fish symbols.

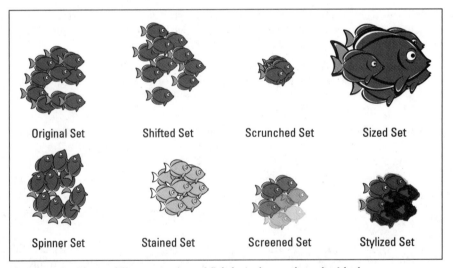

Figure 4-47: These different groups of fish have been altered with the Symbolism tools.

Creating Diagrams and Flowcharts

Diagrams are all about precision, just like Illustrator, making the two a perfect match for each other. Technical drawings need the accuracy that only Illustrator provides. Flowcharts are not as precise, but they still need an accurate, consistent look to them that you can easily accomplish with Illustrator.

You can find clip art that consists of "pieces" of all sorts of symbols for various types of diagramming, or build your own library. When we write books on Illustrator, we use a library of illustrations that contain tools, paths, points, and other Illustrator-specific objects.

Because we don't want a giant document for this purpose, we tend to use Illustrator's Eyedropper to "suck" attributes from items such as paths, control handle lines, and points. This means we can draw things and then use the settings that were applied to other artwork simply by clicking them with the Eyedropper tool. For example, if you've created a box that is used in a flowchart that has a unique Stroke, Fill, and text spacing, you can use the Eyedropper tool to obtain all the attributes of the flowchart box. Then you can drop those attributes on another box using the Paint Bucket tool to make it look the same.

Creating organizational charts

Creating organizational charts is easy in Illustrator, once you learn a few tricks. The chart shown in Figure 4-48 reflects a simple organizational chart in our home, and was done in Illustrator quite easily. The key to making it easy was to create a *template* box, and duplicate all the other boxes from there.

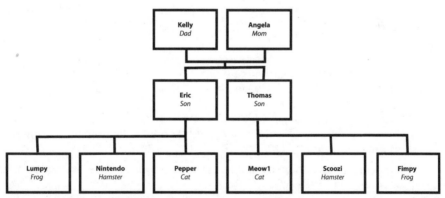

Figure 4-48: Our household organizational chart. Much to Angela's disappointment, she isn't placed at the very top, but instead Kelly splits the top honors with her. They both know who's really in charge anyway. . . .

The template box is simply a rectangle with text in it. We determined ahead of time that we'd like three lines of text in each box, bold text at the top and italic text underneath. We positioned the text by centering it. Then we selected just the box (with the Direct Selection tool) and gave the box a fill of white and a stroke of black with a width of 4. After entering the first name, we just Option [Alt]+copied the box for each additional name.

The Align palette helped get everything spaced properly, and we used the Pen tool to create "lines of authority" between people and animals.

What's nice about this approach is that if any changes occur (for instance, if Eric continues to forget to feed Nintendo, then the poor hamster might need to be removed altogether and despite the cats' plea, we don't plan on putting them in charge of the hamsters), we just have to move the lines around, and if necessary, the boxes. To make things even easier, dragging a Direct Selection tool marquee around a box with lines attached to it moves both the box and the End Point of the lines at that box.

Creating sitemaps

Sitemaps (for mapping out Web sites) can be created in a similar way to organizational charts, with the notable distinction that sitemaps tend to go from left to right, while organizational charts go from top to bottom.

Because sitemaps change so much, and take up so much space, a good practice is to set up your sitemap on the pasteboard using the Tile Pages option (in the Document Setup dialog box). This way you can print your site chart on several pages and then plaster them together with Scotch tape. Of course, if you're lucky enough to have a three or four foot wide plotter, you can set up an Illustrator document to be three or four feet high, and up to 19 feet wide, keeping everything on one page!

Summary

Objects in Illustrator come in many different shapes and sizes, but many of them work in the same manner. Learning to deal with objects will give you greater control over your artwork. In this chapter, you learned that

+ Illustrator provides basic drawing capabilities by enabling you to quickly draw basic objects with specialized tools, such as the Rectangle, Ellipse, Polygon, Star, and Flare tools.

+ Unique line tools can be used to create straight lines, arcs, spirals, rectangular grids and polar grids.

+ Graphs can be created in Illustrator just by entering the data.

+ Illustrator includes nine different graph types.

+ After a graph has been created, it can be adjusted and manipulated like any other path-based object.

+ Symbols can be used to capture an instance of an object that can be reused again and again.

+ Symbol sets can be altered using the Symbolism tools.

+ You can create diagrams and flowcharts by using shapes and paths to connect them.

✦   ✦   ✦

Selecting and Editing

Once you've created, traced, or even stolen someone else's artwork, there's always that period where you look at the artwork and you realize it's not quite right. For example, let's say you want to edit the paths of a company logo you made for a friend, which you plan to add to a Web page. However, you find the image is too big for the space. What do you do? That's where this chapter comes in. No, we won't do your finishing for you, but we'll show you how to take advantage of Illustrator's many tools to manipulate paths for the best end result. You'll learn how to make changes such as adding and deleting points to a path, simplifying a path, and working with multiple paths using the Pathfinder palette.

This chapter focuses on selecting and modifying individual paths and the points on those paths by cutting them, combining them, and adjusting them. Think of this chapter as the "portions of paths" chapter, while Chapter 3 ("Drawing and Painting") covers working with entire paths and multiple paths.

Selecting Your Path Before You Edit

Before you can edit a path, you first must be able to select the path. How you select a path determines how you can edit your artwork. In this section, you'll learn how to select paths in different ways using the many selection tools in Illustrator 10.

Choosing how to select your paths

You have several different ways to make selections in Illustrator, depending on what you wish to change:

✦ **InterPath selecting** means that at least one point or segment within a path is selected, usually with the Direct Selection tool. InterPath selecting is used to adjust individual points, segments, and series of points. Figure 5-1 shows InterPath selection.

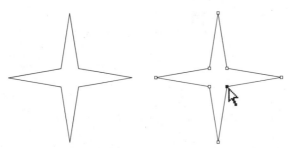

Figure 5-1: InterPath selection on paths

Even though just a portion of the path is selected, many changes will affect the entire path — not just the selected points. For example, most of the attributes available in the Object menu (including Pathfinder, Masking, and Compound Paths) affect the entire path even when only a point or segment is selected.

InterPath selecting also enables you to use most of the functions in the Arrange menu, such as hiding, locking, or grouping. But these options lock, hide, or group the entire path.

Selected Anchor Points on InterPath-selected paths are represented by solid squares; unselected points are hollow squares. Visible Control Handles and Control Handle Lines on either side of the segment indicate selected segments if the selected segment is curved. If the selected segment is a straight line, then it is not apparent that the segment is selected. One tricky way to determine which segment is selected is to delete the selection and then undo the deletion. If you delete a segment or point, the entire remaining path becomes selected.

✦ **Path selecting** means that all points and segments on a path are selected. When a path is clicked by using the Group Selection tool or the Selection tool, the entire path is automatically selected. (Dragging the mouse over the entire path with the Direct Selection tool also selects the entire path.)

All the capabilities from InterPath selecting are available, such as the entire Object menu and most of the functions in the Filter menu.

After you select a path, the entire path is affected by moving, transforming, cutting, copying and pasting, and deleting. Figure 5-2 shows an example of path selecting.

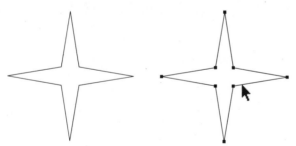

Figure 5-2: Path selection

✦ **Group selecting.** You can select and affect a series of grouped paths as if it were a single object by using Group selecting. All paths in the group are affected in the same way as paths that you select with Path selecting. The Selection tool selects entire grouped paths at once. If you use the Group Selection tool instead, you need a series of clicks to select a group of paths. Figure 5-3 shows what you can accomplish with Group selecting.

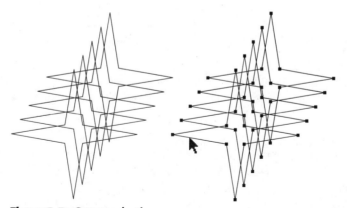

Figure 5-3: Group selection

✦ **InterGroup selecting.** You can select and affect groups of paths within other groups by using InterGroup selecting. All paths in the entire group of the object that is clicked on are affected in the same way as paths that you select with Path selection. Use the Group Selection tool to select a single path with a group, even if the path is within several groups. Each successive click on the same path selects all the paths in the group closest to the path that is clicked on. InterGroup selecting is demonstrated in Figure 5-4.

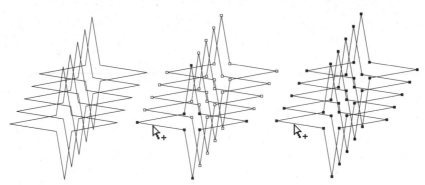

Figure 5-4: InterGroup selection

To select everything in your document that hasn't been hidden or locked, choose Select ➪ All (⌘+A [Ctrl+A]), which selects all the points and segments on every path in the document. You can also select everything in the document by drawing a marquee around all the paths with any selection tool.

Normally, after you select something new, everything that you have previously selected becomes *deselected*. To continue to select additional points, paths, or segments, you must hold down the Shift key while clicking.

The Shift key normally works as a toggle when used with a selection tool, selecting anything that is not selected and deselecting anything that is currently selected. Each selection tool works with the Shift key a little differently, as described in the following sections.

Tip   To deselect everything that is selected, click a part of the document that is empty (where you can see the pasteboard or artboard) without using the Shift key. You can also deselect everything by choosing Select ➪ Deselect (⌘+Shift+A [Ctrl+ Shift+A]).

You can use the selection tools for manually moving selected points, segments, and paths. Personally, the thought of manual labor terrifies us, but when we do something manually in Illustrator, we are usually referring to the process of dragging or clicking with the mouse. You use *automatic* or *computer-assisted manipulations* when you type in specific values in Transform palette, for example. The next few sections cover the selection tools and their functions.

Using Illustrator's selection tools

If you absolutely *must* have one group of tools in Illustrator, it's the set of three selection tools. As in most applications, to alter something (move, transform, and so on), you must first select it. When you draw a new path or when you paste in

Illustrator, the program automatically selects the object you're working on; however, as soon as you draw another path, the preceding object is deselected and Illustrator automatically selects the object with the new path. The selection tools enable you to select paths and perform additional manipulations on them. Illustrator has three selection tools: the Selection tool, the Direct Selection tool, and the Group Selection tool. All three of these tools are found in the top row of the toolbox. You can access the Group Selection tool by clicking the Direct Selection tool and dragging to the right in the pop-up menu.

Using the Selection tool

The Selection tool selects entire paths or complete groups at one time. You can't select just one point or a few points on a path with the Selection tool. Instead, the entire path on which that point lies is selected (all the Anchor Points turn black). Drawing a marquee (clicking and dragging as a box forms behind the cursor) around parts of paths or entire paths also selects entire paths.

The Bounding Box and Selection tool

A Bounding Box appears when using the Selection tool. This Bounding Box enables you to move or scale the selected objects by simply dragging. When an object is selected, a Bounding Box appears around the whole object. This Bounding Box has points on the four corners as well as points on the midline of each side of the box. These points enable you to scale the object any way you like. By holding down the Shift key and dragging one of the Corner Points, you can easily scale the selected object proportionately. You can show or hide the Bounding Box with the View ➪ Show/Hide Bounding Box (⌘+Shift+B [Ctrl+Shift+B]) command.

Using the Direct Selection tool

To select individual points, line segments, or a series of specific points within a path, you need to use the Direct Selection tool. It is one of the few tools that enable you to select something less than an entire path. You can also draw a marquee over a portion of a path to select only those points and segments within the area of the marquee. If the marquee surrounds an entire path, the entire path is selected. Individual points or a series of points on different paths can also be selected by drawing a marquee around just those points. You can permanently switch to the Direct Selection tool by pressing A on the keyboard. The Shift key is used with the Direct Selection tool to select additional points or segments or to deselect previously selected points. If only one segment or point on a path is selected and you Shift+click that segment or point with the Direct Selection tool, the entire path is deselected.

If you press the Shift key, the Selection tool works as a toggle between selecting and deselecting paths. While you hold down the Shift key and click paths that are not selected, they become selected. When paths that are selected are Shift+clicked, they become deselected. The Shift key can be used in this way to add to or subtract from a series of selected paths.

Selecting items with the Direct Selection tool can be a little intimidating because Anchor Points (the control points that make up the path) show up as *solid* when selected and *hollow* when deselected. Furthermore, a selected segment does not have any Anchor Points selected; instead, any Control Handles and Control Handle Lines associated with that segment become selected. If no Control Handles are associated with a segment, such as a segment that is in between two Straight Corner Points, then it is difficult to tell which segment is selected.

After you select a point or series of points, those selected points can be manipulated in a number of ways, including by being moved and transformed (via the transformation tools) and having certain filters applied to them. Individual segments and series of segments can be selected and modified in the same way points are transformed.

Using the Group Selection tool

Objects within Illustrator can be grouped with other objects and, in turn, the group of objects can be grouped with other objects to create a hierarchy of grouped objects. The Group Selection tool lets you select a single object within a group and then, with another click, you can select the entire initial group of objects. Each successive click selects the group of objects included in the above hierarchy. For example, if you create a circle object and group it with some text and then group the circle and the text with a filled rectangle, clicking once on the circle with the Group Selection tool selects the circle object. Clicking again selects the circle and the text, and a third click selects the circle, the text, and the filled rectangle.

For the Group Selection tool to work properly, choose the first path or paths by either clicking them or drawing a marquee around them. To select the group that a particular path is in, however, requires that you click one of the initially selected paths. To select the next group also requires a click; if you drag at any point, only the paths you drag over are selected.

This process may seem a little fuzzy at first, but it will get easier the more you use the Group Selection tool. Remember, the first time that you select something with the Group Selection tool, you are selecting only the paths that you click or drag over. The next time you click an already-selected path, all the paths in its group will be selected.

Note Still confused about how the Shift key selects and deselects paths? We can make it worse. The Shift key is an odd duck when used with the Group Selection tool. What happens when you click an unselected path with this tool while holding down the Shift key? The path is selected. But what happens when you click a selected path? The process deselects *just one path*. What would make more sense is if you would click again with the Shift key, and it then would deselect the entire group. Nope. Ain't gonna happen. The Shift key works as a toggle on the one path you are clicking — selecting it, deselecting it, and so on.

Dragging a marquee around paths with the Group Selection tool works only for the first series of clicks; dragging another marquee, even over the already-selected paths, just reselects those paths.

ASK TOULOUSE: Too Many Selection Tools?

Marcia: I'm getting mouse wrist because of all these different selection tools.

Toulouse: How so?

Marcia: It's such a pain to keep going up to the toolbox to select different selection tools. And then there are the other tools as well. . . .

Toulouse: You use the toolbox to access the selection tools?

Marcia: No, I have them flown in from Hackensack when I wanna use them. Of *course* I use the toolbox.

Toulouse: Actually, you can use the keyboard to jump around each of the selection tools.

Marcia: I have a keyboard. Tell me more.

Toulouse: No matter what tool is selected in the toolbox, holding down the ⌘ [Ctrl] key will toggle to the Selection tool.

Marcia: Wow! This is great!

Toulouse: You can toggle between the regular Selection tool and the Direct Selection tool by pressing Ctrl+Tab.

Marcia: No kidding.

Toulouse: When you have the Direct Selection tool, press Option [Alt] and you'll access the Group Selection tool!

Marcia: You should really write a book on this stuff.

Caution Pressing ⌘ + Tab on a Mac system will toggle between different applications. To switch between the Selection and Direct Selection tool, you need to use Ctrl+Tab.

If you have selected several paths at once, clicking a selected path selects only the group that the selected path is in. If other selected paths are in different groups, those groups are not selected until you click those paths with the Group Selection tool. However, clicking multiple times on any of the paths in the selected group continues to select "up" in the group that the selected path is part of.

The Group Selection tool is the most useful when dealing with graphs and blends, but you can use it in a number of other situations to greatly enhance your control of what is and is not selected. People who are always ungrouping and regrouping paths (who can be affectionately called *groupies*) can greatly benefit from using the Group Selection tool. In fact, proper use of this tool prevents you from ever having to ungroup and regroup objects for workflow reasons.

Using the Direct Select Lasso tool

The Direct Select Lasso tool provides a way to select an Anchor Point or a group of Anchor Points. This tool works just like the Direct Selection tool, except you can draw the selection path instead of using just a rectangular selection area, as shown in Figure 5-5. The default shortcut key for this tool is the Q key.

If you hold down the Shift key while drawing around additional objects, they will be added to the current selection. The Lasso tool cursor displays a small plus sign when the Shift key is held down. Holding down the Option [Alt] key while drawing around additional objects removes them from the current selection. The cursor for this option shows a small minus sign.

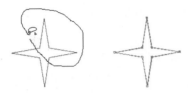

Figure 5-5: Selecting with the Direct Select Lasso tool.

Using the Lasso tool

The Lasso tool is located as a pop-up tool under the Direct Select Lasso tool. It provides a way to select irregularly shaped objects or groups of objects. To use the Lasso tool, draw a path around all the objects that you want to select. All objects that are within or intersected by the lasso path are selected.

The Shift and Option [Alt] keys work the same way as the Lasso tool for adding and subtracting objects from the current selection.

Selecting with the Magic Wand tool

The Magic Wand tool will select all objects that use the same fill color, stroke color, stroke weight, opacity or blending mode. The default shortcut key for this tool is the Y key. For example, if you have several shapes of all different fill colors, you could select all the shapes with a red fill color by clicking on one with the Magic Wand tool.

New Feature   The Magic Wand tool is new to Illustrator 10.

You can specify which characteristics are used to select similar objects using the Magic Wand palette. You can open this palette by double clicking on the Magic Wand tool or by selecting Window ⇨ Magic Wand. The Magic Wand palette is shown in Figure 5-6.

Figure 5-6: The Magic Wand palette lets you select which attributes must be similar and their corresponding Tolerance values.

The Magic Wand can select objects with similar attributes. These attributes include the following:

✦ Fill Color

✦ Stroke Color

✦ Stroke Weight

✦ Opacity

✦ Blending Mode

For all these attributes (except for the Blending Mode), you can select a Tolerance. Low Tolerance values make Illustrator pickier about how similar the attributes are and higher values make the selection more lenient. For example, a Tolerance value of 40 will select all the hues of a single color.

You can also use the Shift key with the Magic Wand tool to add to the current selection and the option (Alt) key to subtract selections from the current selection.

Selecting, moving, and deleting entire paths

Now that you've learned how to use the selection tools, you'll learn how to work with paths. Usually, the best way to select a path that is not currently selected is by clicking it with the regular Selection tool, which highlights all the points on the path and enables you to move, transform, or delete that entire path.

To select more than one path, you can use a number of different methods. The most basic method is to hold down the Shift key and click the successive paths with the Selection tool, selecting one more path with each Shift+click. Shift+clicking a selected path with the Selection tool deselects that particular path. Drawing a marquee around paths with the Selection tool selects all paths that at least partially fall into the area drawn by the marquee. When drawing a marquee, be sure to place the cursor in an area where nothing exists. Finding an empty spot may be difficult in Preview mode because Fills from various paths may cover any white space available. Drawing a marquee with the Selection tool when the Shift key is depressed selects nonselected paths and deselects currently selected paths.

If paths are part of either a compound path or a group, all other paths in that compound path or group are also selected.

To move a path, click the path and drag (in one motion) with the Selection tool. To move several paths, select the paths and then click an already-selected path with the regular Selection tool or the Direct Selection tool and drag.

Note If you have been selecting multiple paths by using the Shift key, be sure to release it before clicking and dragging the selection. If the Shift key is still pressed, the clicked path becomes deselected and no paths move. If this does happen, just Shift+click the paths that were deselected and drag.

To delete an entire path, select it with the Selection tool and press the Delete key. To delete multiple paths, select them and press the Delete key.

Often, many objects need to be moved and duplicated at the same time. To duplicate paths when moving them, hold down the Option [Alt] key while the mouse button is released.

Select and Deselect All

Choosing Select ➪ All (⌘+A [Ctrl+A] or ⌘+. (period) [Ctrl+. (period)] when the screen is not redrawing) selects all paths in the active document. If a type tool is selected and an insertion point exists in the text, all the type in that story will be selected.

Choosing Select ➪ Deselect (⌘+Shift+A [Ctrl+Shift+A]) deselects all selected objects. The Deselect menu does *not* work with type selected with a Type tool.

If you accidentally deselect the selection, you can return to the previous selection with the Select ➪ Reselect (⌘+6 [Ctrl+6]) menu option. This will reselect the previous selection.

Select Inverse

Choosing Select ➪ Inverse quickly selects all objects that are not currently selected. For example, if one object is selected and the document contains 15 other objects, the 15 objects will become selected, and the one object that was selected originally will become deselected.

Note Select ➪ Inverse does not cause locked or hidden objects to be selected and does not select guides unless guides are not locked. Objects on layers that are locked or hidden are not selected either.

Select ➪ Inverse is useful because selecting a few objects is usually quicker than selecting most objects. After you select the few objects, Select ➪ Inverse does all the nasty work of selecting everything else.

When no objects are selected, Select Inverse selects all the objects, just as Select ➪ All (⌘+A [Ctrl+A]) would. When all objects are selected, Select Inverse deselects all the objects, just as Select ➪ Deselect (⌘+Shift+A [Ctrl+Shift+A]) would.

Select Object Above and Below

As objects are placed in the document window, they have a relative stacking order. This order determines which object is visible if two objects are overlapped. Using the Object ➪ Arrange menu, you can change this stacking order. The Select menu includes two options for selecting the object that is immediately in above or below the current selection.

Select ➪ Next Object Above (⌘+Option+] [Ctrl+Alt+]]) will select the object that is above the current object in the stacking order. Select ➪ Next Object Below (⌘+Option+[[Ctrl+Alt+[]]) will select the object just below the current object in the stacking order.

If multiple objects are selected, then the object that is above the highest object (or below the lowest object) is selected when these menu options are used.

Selecting, moving, and deleting portions of paths

To select just a portion of a path, you *must* use the Direct Selection tool. To select an Anchor Point or a line segment, simply click it. To select several individual points or paths, click the points or paths to be selected while holding down the Shift key. Series of points and paths can be selected by dragging a marquee across the paths that are to be selected.

Individual points that are selected become solid squares. If these points are Smooth, Curved Corner, or Combination Corner Points, Control Handles appear from the selected Anchor Point.

Line segments that have at least one Anchor Point that is either a Smooth, Curved Corner, or Combination Corner Point may display a Control Handle Line and Control Handle coming out from that Anchor Point. Figure 5-7 shows samples of each of these selected types of Anchor Points.

To move selected points or paths, release the Shift key and click a selected path or point and drag.

Illustrator doesn't tell you when a straight-line segment is selected or which one is selected. The first time you click a straight-line segment, all the Anchor Points on the path appear as hollow squares, which is just telling you that something on that path is selected. Selected points turn black, and curved line segments have one or more Control Handles and Control Handle Lines sticking out from the ending Anchor Points, but straight-line segments don't do anything when selected. The inventive side of you may think that you can get around this problem by dragging the selected segments to a new location or by copying and pasting them and then undoing, but this solution doesn't work because of Illustrator's habit of selecting all points on paths when undoing operations on those paths. Another way to detect when a straight-line segment is selected is to delete the selection with the Delete key and then Undo the operation.

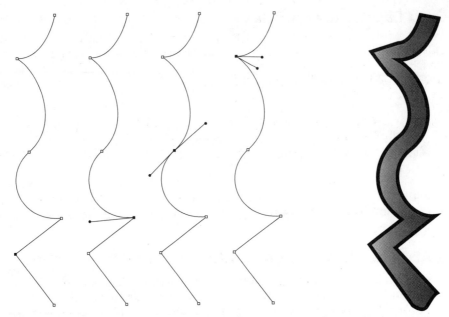

Figure 5-7: The four different types of Anchor Points when selected

Tip When you run into this problem of not knowing whether a straight-line segment is selected, do the following: Instead of moving, copying, or pasting, simply whack the good ol' Delete key and whatever disappears is what you had selected. Now when you undo, just the segments that were selected before the deletion are still selected, not the entire path.

To delete points and segments, select them as described previously and press Delete. Remember that line segments exist only when one point exists on either side of the segment. Even if the line segment is not selected, if one of its Anchor Points is deleted, the line segment is deleted as well. A path is made up of points, and those points are connected via segments. If the points are gone, the paths disappear along with them. But if you delete all the segments, all the points can still remain.

Portions of paths can be duplicated when pressing the Option [Alt] key while the mouse button is being released. Duplicating segments also duplicates the Anchor Points on either side of that segment.

Applying select functions

Illustrator has several special select functions (they were filters in Illustrator 5/6). The Select functions are used for selecting paths with common or specific attributes. The Select functions make mundane, repetitive tasks easy to accomplish by doing all the nasty work for you.

New Feature The Select menu has moved from being a submenu under the Edit menu to being its own menu.

To select objects that are similar (without using the Magic Wand tool), choose Select ⇨ Same and the appropriate selection function from that submenu.

 Tip You can redo the last selection type by choosing Select ⇨ Reselect (⌘+6 [Ctrl+6]).

The eight selection functions — Blending Mode, Fill & Stroke, Fill Color, Opacity, Stroke Color, Stroke Weight, Style, and Symbol Instance — use common attributes of currently selected objects to select additional objects. Using these functions makes object selection quick and intuitive. Many of these same attributes can be selected using the Magic Wand tool. The trick to using these functions is to identify specific attributes that are unique to the object or objects that you wish to select.

Below these same selection function options are several additional selection functions under the Object submenu. These include All on Same Layers, Direction Handles, Brush Strokes, Clipping Masks, Stray Points, and Text Objects. The Select Masks function makes the process of manipulating masks much easier by showing you where masks are in the document.

The Select Stray Points function selects all isolated Anchor Points. Individual Anchor Points don't print or preview, and you can see them in Preview mode only when they are selected. After you cut portions of line segments, stray points often appear. These individual points often interfere with connecting other segments. You can't use this selection function enough. If you regularly cut paths, it's a good habit to use this function to select and delete stray points.

The Brush Strokes function helps you to identify all the brush strokes in your document, regardless of their color, weight, and fill.

Select Same Blending Mode

The Same Blending Mode function (Select ⇨ Same ⇨ Blending Mode) selects objects that use the same Blending Mode. The selection is made regardless of style, Stroke color and weight, and Fill color.

The various Blending Modes include Smooth Color, Specified Steps, and Specified Distance. These are options that determine how the blend proceeds from one object to another.

 Cross-Reference Color blends are covered in Chapter 10, "Applying Unique and Interesting Fills," and the various path-blending modes are covered in more detail in Chapter 11, "Using Path Blends, Compound Paths, and Masks."

Select Same Fill & Stroke

Choosing Select ➪ Same ➪ Fill & Stroke selects objects that have both the same Fill and Stroke attributes as the currently selected object. This function combines two separate properties into a single selection criteria and enables you to make selections that would otherwise be difficult to make.

Select Same Fill Color

Choosing Select ➪ Same ➪ Fill Color selects objects that have the same Fill color as the currently selected object. This function selects objects regardless of their Stroke color, Stroke weight, or Stroke pattern. You cannot select objects with different Fills for Same Fill Color to work, but you may select two objects that have the same Fill.

Same Fill Color considers different tints of spot colors to be the same color. This function works in two ways. First, if you select one object with any tint value of a spot color, then Same Fill Color will select all other objects with the same spot color, regardless of the tint. Second, you can select more than one object, no matter what tint each object contains, provided that the selected objects have the same spot color. You can limit the Same File Color function to only select colors that have the same tint percentage values by using the Select Same Tint Percentage setting in the General panel of the Preferences dialog box. If this option is selected, then the colors must have equivalent tint percentage values to be selected.

Note   To be selected with Same Fill Color, process-color Fills have to have the same values as the original. Even single colors, such as yellow, have to be the same percentage. Same Fill Color considers 100% Yellow and 50% Yellow to be two separate colors.

If you use spot colors often, Select Same Fill Color is extremely useful. It enables you to instantly select all objects that are filled with the spot color, regardless of the tint of the selected object or the tints of the objects to be selected.

Note   Same Fill Color also selects objects that are filled with the same gradient, regardless of the angle or the starting or ending point of the gradient. This function does not, however, select objects that have the same pattern Fill.

Select Same Opacity

The Same Opacity function (Select ➪ Same ➪ Opacity) selects objects based on their opacity setting. An object's opacity can be set using the new Transparency tools. This transparency function is another unique way to select an object that isn't based on strokes, colors, or fills.

Cross-Reference   The Transparency tools are covered in detail in Chapter 12, "Understanding Transparency."

Select Same Stroke Color

Choosing Select ⇨ Same ⇨ Stroke Color selects objects that have the same Stroke color, regardless of the Stroke weight or style and regardless of the type of Fill.

The color limitations that are defined in the preceding "Select Same Fill Color" section also apply to Same Stroke Color.

Although you can choose a pattern for a Stroke that makes the Stroke look gray, Same Stroke Color does not select other objects that have the same Stroke pattern.

Select Same Stroke Weight

Illustrator's Same Stroke Weight function (Select ⇨ Same ⇨ Stroke Weight) selects objects that have the same Stroke weight, regardless of the Stroke color, the style, or the Fill color.

Even if the Stroke is a pattern, other paths that have the same Stroke weight as the patterned Stroke will be selected when you use Same Stroke Weight.

Don't select more than one Stroke weight if you select more than one object. If you select different Stroke weights, no paths will be selected. The best thing to do with Same Stroke Weight, as with Same Fill Color and Same Paint Style, is to select only one object.

Select Same Style

Choosing Select ⇨ Same ⇨ Style selects objects that have almost exactly the same style as the style of the selected object. The following information has to be the same:

✦ The Fill color (as defined in the "Select Same Fill Color" section)

✦ The Stroke color

✦ The Stroke weight

Some things in the object's Style that don't matter (that is, they don't prevent Same Style from selecting an object) are any of the Stroke style attributes and the overprinting options.

 Caution   If you select more than one object, don't select objects with different paint styles. If you have different paint styles selected, no object will be selected by the selection function. The best thing to do with Style, as with Fill Color, is to select only one object.

If the currently selected object doesn't have any style applied, then the Same Style function will not be available.

If you have a spot color selected, the Select functions will select all other occurrences of that spot color, regardless of the tint. This can be troublesome.

Select Same Symbols

The Same Symbol Instance function (Select ➪ Same ➪ Symbol Instance) selects symbols that are the same. Symbol objects are stored and applied from the Symbols palette.

Cross-Reference   Symbols and the Symbols palette are covered in detail in Chapter 7, "Organizing Artwork."

Custom Style Selections

Illustrator 10 lets you select multiple-type selections for objects with similar Fill and Stroke attributes. However, you cannot select at one time all of the objects that have the same Stroke color and Fill color but have different Stroke weights.

The Lock Unselected command (press ⌘+Option+Shift+2 [Ctrl+Alt+Shift+2]) is the key to specifying multiple selection criteria. The following instructions describe how to perform multiple-type selections in a few steps.

1. Select a representative object that has the Stroke and Fill color that you want.

2. Choose Select ➪ Same ➪ Fill Color. All objects that have the same Fill color as the original object will be selected, regardless of their Stroke color.

3. This step is the key step. Press ⌘+Option+Shift+2 [Ctrl+Alt+Shift+2] to lock any objects that are not selected. The only objects that you can modify or select now are the ones that have the same Fill color.

4. Select ➪ Deselect (⌘+Shift+A [Ctrl+Shift+A]) and select the original object, which has both the Fill color and the Stroke color that you want to select.

5. Choose Select ➪ Same ➪ Stroke Color. Only objects that have the same Stroke and Fill colors are selected.

Select All on Same Layer

The Select ➪ Object ➪ All on Same Layer menu option will select all the objects that share the same layer as the currently selected object. This makes it easy to select an entire layer if you have one or more object on a layer. If you have objects from several different layers selected, then several layers will be selected using this menu option.

Cross-Reference   Layers are covered in Chapter 7, "Organizing Artwork."

ASK TOULOUSE: Selecting More than One Color

Archie: How can I select all occurrences of two different Fill colors?

Toulouse: You'll need to use Same Fill Color.

Archie: I tried that, but it doesn't work.

Toulouse: Do it this way: Select a representative of the first color, and then run the function.

Archie: Okay, but now I'm stuck.

Toulouse: Not really. Lock those objects with ⌘+2 [Ctrl+2], then select a representative of the second Fill color, and then run Same Fill Color again.

Archie: I'm still stuck.

Toulouse: Ah . . . here's the tricky part. Lock those objects as well.

Archie: Excuse me for noticing, but now I *can't* select those objects. They're all locked.

Toulouse: Just Unlock All (⌘+Option+2 [Ctrl+Alt+2]) and they'll all be selected!

Archie: You know, I really don't think these different colors should be mixed.

Select Direction Handles

When an anchor point is selected with the Direct Selection tool, its direction handles are displayed. Using the Select ⇨ Object ⇨ Direction Handles will make all the direction handles for the current selected objects visible. This is handy if you need to look at many direction handles at the same time.

Select Brush Strokes

Choosing Select ⇨ Object ⇨ Brush Strokes selects all the current brush stroke path objects. This includes all objects created with the Paintbrush, Pencil, and Pen tools that haven't had a style applied to them. Any brush stroke paths that are locked or hidden will not be selected.

Select Clipping Masks

Choosing Select ⇨ Object ⇨ Clipping Masks selects all the objects that are currently being used as masks. The only masks in the document that are not selected are the masks that are locked or hidden and the masks that are on layers that are locked or hidden.

Select Stray Points

Choosing Select ⇨ Object ⇨ Stray Points selects Anchor Points in the document.

Individual Anchor Points are nasty beasts, because although they don't show in preview or printing, they contain Fills and Strokes that can cause separation software to print additional blank color separations that aren't needed.

Stray points can be created in various ways:

✦ Clicking once with the Pen tool creates a single Anchor Point.

✦ Deleting a line segment on a path that has two points by selecting the line segment with the Direct Selection tool and pressing Delete leaves behind the two Anchor Points.

✦ Using the Scissors tool to cut a path, and while deleting one side or another of the path, not selecting the points turns these points into stray points.

✦ Ungrouping an oval or rectangle in Illustrator 3.2 or older and then deleting just the frame of the shape leaves the center point in the document.

Bringing an Illustrator 4 or older document that has still-grouped rectangles or ovals into Illustrator 10 automatically deletes the center point and turns on the Show Center Point option in the Attributes palette (choose Window ➪ Show Attributes or press F11).

Be careful not to think that center points of objects are stray points — they aren't, and you cannot select them without selecting the object they belong to. Center points of objects are visible when the Show Center Point option is chosen in the Attributes palette. Selecting the center point of an object selects the entire object, and deleting the center point deletes the entire object.

Select Text Objects

The Select ➪ Object ➪ Text Objects menu option will select all text objects in the current document. This is useful if you want to make a major change to all the text at once such as spell checking all text in the document or changing the font.

Text and the text functions are covered in detail in Chapter 8, "Manipulating Type."

Saving and naming a selection

Let's say that you have a detailed illustration of a skyscraper and your client can't decide the color that the rivets should be, so you select painstakingly all the rivets in the entire illustration and you decide that you don't want to have to go through this selection process again and wished there was some way to save the selection. Well, you're in luck. The Select menu includes a way to save and retrieve selection sets.

The Select ➪ Save Selection and Select ➪ Edit Selection menu options are new in Illustrator 10.

If you select the Select ⇨ Save Selection menu option, a simple dialog box appears where you can give the selection a name. This named selection set will then appear at the bottom of the Select menu. Selecting a named selection set from the bottom of the Select menu will select all the objects in the selection set.

The Select ⇨ Edit Selection menu option will open the Edit Selection dialog box, shown in Figure 5-8. This dialog box will let you rename or delete the saved selection set.

Figure 5-8: The Edit Selection dialog box lets you rename or delete saved selection sets.

Using Illustrator to Edit Paths

Once you've selected your path, you are now ready to edit the path. Illustrator includes several tools that are used to complete the edits. These editing tools can be found as pop-up tools under the Pen and Pencil tools, as well as, the Scissors and Scale tools. Using these tools, you can do things such as dividing paths into two, adding and deleting points to a path, changing the Anchor Point type, and smoothing paths.

Using path editing tools

You can find the path-editing tools spread across several different tools including the Scissors tool and the Knife tool, which is a pop-up of the Scissors tool slot; the Reshape tool, which is a pop-up of the Scale tool slot; the Add Anchor Point, Delete Anchor Point, and Convert Anchor Point pop-up tools in the Pen tool slot; and the Smooth and the Erase pop-up tools in the Pencil tool slot. Clicking and holding down the Pen tool displays the Pen tool, Add Anchor Point, Delete Anchor Point, and Convert Anchor Point. Dragging out to a path-editing tool replaces the default Pen tool with the newly selected pop-up tool. If you press the Caps Lock key at the same time that you choose a path-editing tool, the tool cursor resembles a cross hair. The cross-hair cursors enable precision positioning of cursors.

The purpose of each path-editing tool is as follows:

✦ The **Scissors tool** is used for splitting paths. Clicking with the Scissors tool on a closed path makes that path an open path with the End Points directly overlapping each other where the click occurred. Using the Scissors tool on an open path splits that open path into two separate open paths, each with an End Point that overlaps the other open path's End Point.

✦ The **Knife tool** slices through *path areas*. The knife tool is the only path-editing tool that doesn't require that you have paths selected; it works on all unlocked paths that fall under the blade. You can slice very precisely with the Object ⇨ Slice function, which turns a selected path into a Knife path.

✦ The **Add Anchor Point** tool is used for adding Anchor Points to an existing path. If an Anchor Point is added to a straight segment (one that has no Control Handles on either end), then the Anchor Point will be a Straight Corner Point. If the segment is curved — meaning that you have at least one Control Handle for that segment — then the new Anchor Point will be a Smooth Point.

✦ The **Delete Anchor Point** tool gets rid of the Anchor Point you select. A new segment is created between the Anchor Points that were on either side of the Anchor Point you clicked. If the Anchor Point you clicked on is an End Point, no new segment is drawn; instead, the next Anchor Point on the path becomes the new End Point.

✦ The **Convert Anchor Point** tool has two functions. The first is to simply change an Anchor Point from its current type of Anchor Point to a Straight Corner Point by clicking and releasing it. You can also change the current type to Smooth by clicking and dragging the Anchor Point. The second function is to move Control Handles individually by changing Smooth Points to Curved Corner Points and by changing Combination Corner Points and Curved Corner Points to Smooth Points. (Straight Corner Points don't have any Control Handles, so using this method can't change them.)

✦ The **Smooth tool** does what it sounds like it should do. The Smooth tool enables you to smooth or redraw a selected path. When you drag the Smooth tool over a path to create a direction, a new path is created from where you started the path to where you ended the path. Figure 5-9 shows a path before and after smoothing.

✦ The **Erase tool** erases sections of a selected path. No matter how the path was drawn, you can erase sections of it with the Erase tool. In the case of an ellipse or rectangle, you have to ungroup the shape first. In many ways, we prefer to remove sections using this precise tool rather than the Knife tool.

✦ You can use the **Reshape tool** to select and move an Anchor Point or a line segment. If you select and drag a line segment, a new Anchor Point is added where you click the line and the line bends relative to the adjacent Anchor Points. This tool provides an easy way to modify line segments without moving the Anchor Points.

You can add and remove Anchor Points in two different ways. We mentioned one method in Chapter 3, "Drawing and Painting," where we demonstrated how to add Anchor Points with the drawing tools and remove them simply by selecting them and pressing the Delete key.

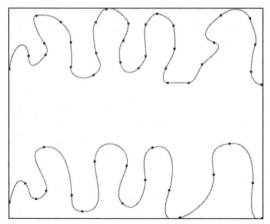

Figure 5-9: A path before and after using the Smooth tool

The techniques that we cover in this chapter are unlike the methods discussed previously. Instead of adding new points that create an extension to an existing path, you learn how to add points in the middle of existing paths. Instead of deleting points and the line segments connected to them, you learn how to remove points between two Anchor Points and watch as a new line segment connects those two Anchor Points.

In Figure 5-10, the top row shows a drawing with a point added, resulting in a new curved section. The second row shows a point being removed and then re-added. Adding points, even to the same areas where they were removed, will not change the path back to the shape that it was before the points were removed. That path will have to be altered to resemble the original path. We discuss these and other issues throughout this chapter.

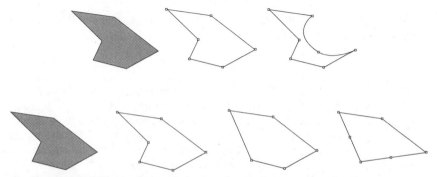

Figure 5-10: Adding Anchor Points after they've been removed will not return the shape to its original shape.

Figure 5-10 shows a very simple example. The Delete Anchor Point tool is most often used to remove unnecessary points from overly complicated drawings.

Using Anchor Points to edit a path

When you select a path, all the Anchor Points that make up the path are displayed as small filled squares. The path will always travel through these Anchor Points. By adding and deleting these Anchor Points, you can alter the path.

Adding Anchor Points

To add an Anchor Point to an existing path, select the Add Anchor Point tool and click a line segment of a path. You may not place an Anchor Point directly on top of another Anchor Point, but you can get pretty darn close. Figure 5-11 shows a path before and after several Anchor Points are added to it.

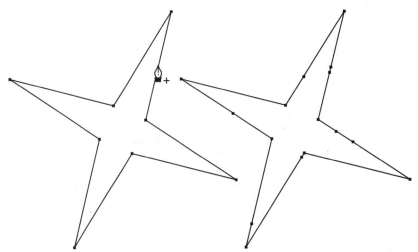

Figure 5-11: Adding Anchor Points to a path doesn't alter the shape of the path, but it *does* enable the path to be modified more easily than if the points had not been added.

Tip   We like to select the paths to which we are adding Anchor Points before we start actually adding the points. This technique ensures that we don't accidentally get the annoying message "Can't Add Anchor Point. Please use the Add Anchor Point tool on a segment of a path." It seems that if just one point exists in the middle of a path, that's where we end up clicking to add the point. After we add one point, the path becomes selected automatically.

Anchor Points added to paths via the Add Anchor Point tool are either Smooth Points or Straight Corner Points, depending on the segment where the new Anchor Point is added. If the segment has two Straight Corner Points on either side of it, then the new Anchor Point is a Straight Corner Point. If one of the Anchor Points is any type of Anchor Point other than a Straight Corner Point, the new Anchor Point is a Smooth Point.

The Add Anchor Points function

The Add Anchor Points function (choose Object ➪ Path ➪ Add Anchor Points) adds new Anchor Points between every pair of existing Anchor Points it can find. New Anchor Points are always added halfway between existing Anchor Points.

Note   Add Anchor Points is related to the Add Anchor Point tool. This function adds Anchor Points the same way as the tool does, only more efficiently. Points that are added to a smooth segment are automatically Smooth Points; points added to a straight segment are automatically Corner Points.

For example, if you have one line segment with an Anchor Point on each end, Add Anchor Points adds one Anchor Point to the segment, exactly in the middle of the two Anchor Points. If a rectangle is drawn and Add Anchor Points is applied, it will have four new Anchor Points: one at the top, one at the bottom, one on the left side, and one on the right side. Figure 5-12 shows an object that has had the Add Anchor Points function applied once, twice, and three times.

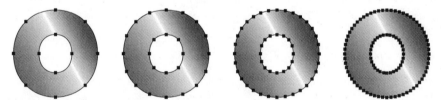

Figure 5-12: The Add Anchor Points function doubles the number of Anchor Points, adding new Anchor Points directly between existing points.

Note   Want to know how many points are being added to your path when Add Anchor Points is applied? Each time the function is reapplied, the number of Anchor Points doubles on a closed path and is one less than doubled on an open path.

Adding Anchor Points is useful before using the Punk & Bloat filter and the Scribble and Tweak filter, and before using any other filter that bases its results on the number and position of Anchor Points.

Tip   If you need to add a large number of Anchor Points quickly, use the Roughen filter with a size of 0 percent and the detail at how many Anchor Points you want per inch. The nice thing about Roughen is that the Anchor Points are equally distributed, regardless of where the original Anchor Points were in the selected path (as opposed to Add Anchor Points, which places new points between existing ones, resulting in "clumping" in detailed areas).

Removing Anchor Points

Removing Anchor Points is a little trickier than adding them. Depending on where you remove the Anchor Point, you may adversely change the flow of the line between the two Anchor Points on either side of it, as shown in Figure 5-13. If the point removed had any Control Handles, the removal usually results in a more drastic change than if the Anchor Point had been a Straight Corner Point. This situation occurs if Control Handles on the Anchor Point being removed controlled at least half the aspect of the curve. A Straight Corner Point affects only the location of the line, not the shape of its curve.

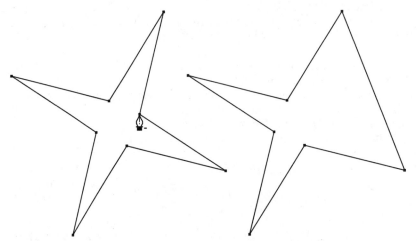

Figure 5-13: Removing an Anchor Point can dramatically alter the shape of a path.

To remove an Anchor Point, click an existing Anchor Point with the Delete Anchor Point tool. Like the Add Anchor Point tool, you can remove points without first selecting the path, but, of course, if the path is not selected, you can't see it or the points that you want to remove. If you miss and don't click an Anchor Point, you will get a message informing you that to remove an Anchor Point, you must click one.

After you remove Anchor Points, you cannot usually just add them back with the Add Anchor Point tool. Considering that the flow of the path will change when you remove a point, adding a point — even the correct type of point — will not give the same result as just undoing the point deletion.

If only two points exist on an *open* path, the Anchor Point you click is deleted and so is the segment connecting it to the sole remaining Anchor Point. If only two points exist on a *closed* path, both line segments from the Anchor Point you click are deleted along with that point, leaving only one Anchor Point remaining.

Simplifying paths by removing Anchor Points

Some artwork can be unnecessarily complicated, with many more Anchor Points than are actually needed. These additional Anchor Points most often occur with artwork that has been traced either by Illustrator's Auto Trace tool or by Streamline. Messy paths can be cleaned up using the Simplify function (choose Object ➪ Path ➪ Simplify). This function removes any unnecessary Anchor Points from the selected path. For example, if you use the Add Anchor Points function to add Anchor Points to a path and then immediately use the Simplify function, then the path will be returned to its former state.

When the Simplify function is selected, the Simplify dialog box is displayed. This dialog box, shown in Figure 5-14, lets you select Curve Precision and Angle Threshold values. The Curve Precision value determines how closely the simplified path should follow the original curve. Higher Curve Precision values result in more Anchor Points, while lower values remove a greater number of Anchor Points as it alters the curvature of the path. In some cases, depending on the complexity of the path, Anchor Points are added to the path if the Curve Precision value is set high. The Angle Threshold value is used to maintain sharp Corner Points. Any corner angles that are less than the Angle Threshold value will not be smoothed, but any Corner Points that have an angle that is greater than the Angle Threshold value may be smoothed as the path is simplified.

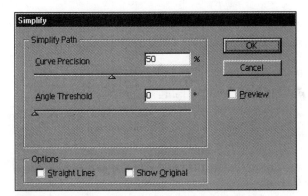

Figure 5-14: The Simplify dialog box enables you to reduce the total number of Anchor Points while maintaining the existing path curvature.

The Straight Lines option draws straight lines between each pair of Anchor Points. The Curve Precision setting is disabled when this option is selected. The Show Original option displays the original path behind the simplified path if the Preview checkbox is selected. This is useful to see how much the path will change prior to applying the changes. If the Preview checkbox is checked, then the number of points in the original path and the current path are displayed under the Angle Threshold setting, as shown in Figure 5-15.

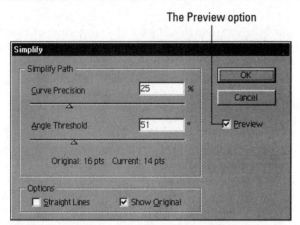

Figure 5-15: When you select the Preview option, the number of points in the original and current paths are displayed.

The Simplify command enables you to reduce the number of Anchor Points contained within a path. The following instructions describe how to simplify a messy path.

1. Select a path or group of paths that are needlessly complex.

2. Choose Object ⇨ Paths ⇨ Simplify. The Simplify dialog box appears.

3. Select the Preview option and set the Curve Precision value to 90 in order to match the original paths within 90 percent. Set the Angle Threshold value to 45. This setting maintains any Corner Points that have an angle less than 45 degrees.

4. Select the Show Original option to see the original path next to the simplified path. Figure 5-16 illustrates this.

5. If you are comfortable with the results that are displayed, click the OK button to apply the function.

Dividing and duplicating paths

Illustrator 10 provides several capabilities that allow for multiple types of dividing and duplicating of paths, even paths that aren't selected. This section discusses those different features, as well as the tools that make this possible: the Scissors and Knife tools.

Before simplify   After simplify

Figure 5-16: The original path, on the left, was reduced from 262 Anchor Points to 130 Anchor Points, on the right.

Splitting paths with the Scissors tool

To change a single path into two separate paths that together make up a path equal in length to the original, you must use the Scissors tool. You can also split paths by selecting and deleting Anchor Points or line segments, although this method shortens the overall length of the two paths.

To split a path with the Scissors tool, click anywhere on a path. Initially, it doesn't seem like much happens. If you clicked in the middle of a line segment, a new Anchor Point appears. (Actually, two will appear, but the second is directly on top of the first so you see only one.) If you click directly on top of an existing Anchor Point, nothing at all seems to happen, but Illustrator actually creates another Anchor Point on top of the one that you clicked.

After clicking with the Scissors tool, you have separated the path into two separate sections, but it still appears that only one path exists because the two sections are both selected. To see the individual paths, deselect them (⌘+Shift+A [Ctrl+Shift+A]) and select just one side with the Selection tool. After a path has been split, one half may be moved independently of the other half, as shown in Figure 5-17.

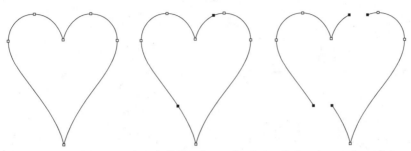

Figure 5-17: The original path (left), the path after splitting (center), and the path after the two pieces have been moved apart (right)

The Anchor Points created with the Scissors tool are either Smooth Points or Straight Corner Points, depending on the type of Anchor Point that is next along the path. If the line segment to the next Anchor Point has a Control Handle coming out of that Anchor Point that affects the line segment, then the new End Point will be a Smooth Point. If the line segment has no Control Handle, the End Point will be a Straight Corner Point.

Note You cannot use the Scissors tool on a line's End Point—only on segments and Anchor Points that are not End Points.

Tip Tired of those annoying warning boxes when you click where you shouldn't with the Scissors tool (or the Add Anchor Points tool, or the Delete Anchor Points tool, or the Convert Anchor Point tool)? You can turn those warnings off by clicking the Disable Warnings checkbox in the General Preferences dialog box. If the Disable Warning checkbox is enabled, then the warning dialog boxes are replaced with an audible warning that beeps whenever you click in the wrong place.

The Knife tool

You can find the Knife tool to the right of the Scissors tool. Access it by clicking and holding on the Scissors tool in the toolbox, and then dragging over to the Knife tool. The Knife tool divides paths into smaller sections as it slices through them. Those sections are initially selected, but they're not grouped. Figure 5-18 shows a path before and after it crosses paths with the Knife.

Pressing the Option [Alt] key when using the Knife tool constrains the tool to a straight line. This is handy if you need to make a straight edge cut.

Note Remember that the Knife tool works on *all* paths that are under the existing path, selected or not. It also works on groups of objects.

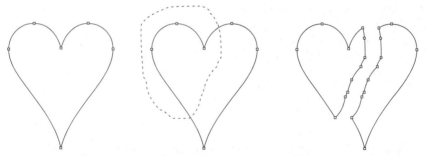

Figure 5-18: The original path (left), the path of the Knife tool (center), and the resulting paths (right) after being dragged apart, all shown in Outline mode

Slicing with other paths

The Knife tool can be useful, but sometimes you might want to divide or duplicate a portion of existing paths without having to draw them with the mouse and your unsteady shouldn't-have-drunk-and-illustrated right hand (maybe you need perfectly sized cuts or duplicates in the shape of text). That's where Slicing comes in. The Slice function takes any selected path and turns it into a knife path, slicing through all paths beneath it.

Using the Reshape tool

The Reshape tool can be found as a pop-up tool under the Scale tool next to the Shear tool, both of which are covered in Chapter 10, "Transforming and Distorting Artwork." To use the Reshape tool on any path, just click where you want to bend the path and drag. To use the Reshape tool on several paths at once, use the Reshape tool to select the points you wish to move. At least one point (that's not a Straight Corner Point) must be selected on each path. Then drag a Reshape-selected point; all the curved points will be moved as well. When you drag with the Reshape tool, the relative positions of the Anchor Points will be consistent. This maintains the general shape of the path as its being moved.

Using the Cleanup feature

Cleanup removes three unwanted elements from Illustrator documents: stray points, unpainted objects, and empty text paths. Cleanup works on the entire document, regardless of what is selected. Use Cleanup by choosing Object ⇨ Path ⇨ Cleanup. Figure 5-19 shows the Cleanup dialog box.

Cleanup doesn't work on locked or hidden paths, paths turned into guides, or paths on locked or hidden layers.

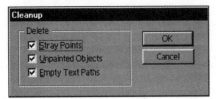

Figure 5-19: The Cleanup dialog box

The Delete options in the Cleanup dialog box are as follows:

✦ **Stray Points** selects and deletes any little points flying around. These points can cause all sorts of trouble, as a point can have paint attributes but can't print.

✦ **Unpainted Objects** gets rid of any paths that are filled and stroked with None, and that aren't masks (masks are always filled and stroked with None).

✦ **Empty Text Paths** finds any text paths with no characters and deletes them. This is *not* the same as the old Revert Text Paths from Illustrator 5/5.5, which changed empty text paths back into standard paths.

If you aren't sure if your document contains these three items, run Cleanup. If none of these items are found, a dialog box appears telling you so.

ASK TOULOUSE: Point Removal

Murray: Cleanup doesn't really work.

Toulouse: Maybe you just don't have the things it cleans up in your document.

Murray: Oh, sure, it gets rid of *those* things, but the paths still have too many points.

Toulouse: Unfortunately, Cleanup doesn't get rid of excess points on paths.

Murray: What? Why not?

Toulouse: Hey, I only write *about* the program.

Murray: Well, Streamline has had a Simplify command since version 3.0, which was released in 1993.

Toulouse: Well, we're in luck because you can use Illustrator's Simplify command. I guess good things come to those who wait.

Murray: Yeah, but why did we have to wait so long?

Drawing an offset path

Choosing Object ➪ Path ➪ Offset Path draws a new path around the outside or inside of an existing path. The distance from the existing path is the distance that you specify in the Offset Path dialog box, which is shown in Figure 5-20. In a sense, you are creating a Stroke, outlining it, and uniting it with the original all in one swoop. You can specify the distance the path is to be offset by entering a value in the Offset box.

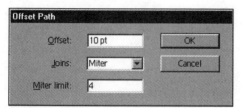

Figure 5-20: The Offset Path dialog box

A positive number in the Offset Path dialog box creates the new path *outside* the existing path, and a negative number creates the new path *inside* the existing path. When the path is closed, figuring out where the new path will be created is easy. For open paths, the outside is the left side of the path, as it runs from start to end, and the inside is the right side of the path, as it runs from start to end.

The Joins pop-up menu enables you to select from different types of joins at the corners of the new path. The choices are miter, round, and bevel, and the result is the same effect that you get if you choose those options as the stroke style for a Stroke.

The Miter Limit affects the miter size only when the Miter option is selected from the Joins pop-up menu, but the option is available when round and bevel joins are selected. Just ignore the Miter Limit when you are using round or bevel joins. (You cannot use a value that is less than 1.)

Often, when you are offsetting a path, the resulting new path will overlap itself, creating *skiddles* (small, undesirable bumps in a path). If the skiddles are within a closed-path area, select the new path and choose Unite from the Pathfinder palette. If the skiddles are outside the closed-path area, choose Divide from the Pathfinder palette and then select and delete each of the skiddles.

ASK TOULOUSE: Scaling Versus Offsetting

Ted: I don't know what the big deal is about Offset Path. I just use the Scale tool.

Toulouse: But the Scale tool does something totally different than Offset Path.

Ted: Not if you use Offset Path on a circle or a square.

Toulouse: Yes, in those few exceptions, it is exactly the same.

Ted: So why use it at all?

Toulouse: Well, let's say you wanted to make a rectangle bigger by one inch on each side.

Ted: I'd scale it up, pressing the Shift key.

Toulouse: That wouldn't work. The "shorter" dimension would be less than the larger one.

Ted: Then to hell with the Shift key. I'd eyeball it.

Toulouse: Oh, *that* would be exact. It would be easier to use Offset Path.

Ted: Okay, maybe in that isolated occurrence.

Toulouse: In almost every occurrence. Such as for text; try scaling versus offsetting and you'll see a huge difference.

Drawing an outline path

Outline Path creates a path around an existing path's Stroke. The width of the new path is directly related to the width of the Stroke.

We use Outline Path for two reasons. The first reason is the most obvious: to Fill a Stroke with a gradient or to be able to view a pattern that is inside a Stroke. The second reason is that when you transform an outlined Stroke, the effect is often different from the effect that results from transforming a Stroked path. Scaling an outlined Stroke changes the width of the Stroke in the direction of the scale. The same is true when using the Free Distort filter, which also changes the width of the Stroke in the direction of the scale, sometimes resulting in a nonuniform Stroke. Figure 5-21 shows the difference between transforming/distorting a Stroked path and an Outlined Stroke.

The End and Join attributes of the Stroke's style determine how the ends and joins of the resulting Stroke look.

Outline Path creates problems for tight corners. It causes overlaps that are similar to those generated by Offset Path.

Figure 5-21: The original Stroked path is to the left. The middle path has been transformed and distorted in various ways. The path on the right was outlined via Outline Path and then transformed and distorted exactly the same way as the middle path.

Use Unite to remove the skittles that result from overlapping paths. Not only does Unite make the drawing look better as artwork and prevent overlapping Strokes, but it also reduces the number of points in the file, making the illustration smaller so that it can print more quickly.

Note   Using a Dash pattern on the Stroke and using Outline Path changes the Stroke back to a solid line and then Outlines it.

Averaging points and joining

Averaging points is the process in which Illustrator determines the location of the points and figures out where the center of all the points will be on a mean basis. *Joining* is the process in which either a line segment is drawn between two End Points, or two End Points are merged into a single Anchor Point.

Averaging and joining are done together when two End Points need to change location to be one on top of the other and then merged into one point. You can perform these steps one at a time, or you can have Illustrator do both steps automatically by pressing ⌘+Option+Shift+J [Ctrl+Alt+Shift+J].

Averaging points

To line up a series of points either horizontally or vertically, use the Average command. The Average command also works to place selected points one on top of the other. Figure 5-22 shows the different types of averaging.

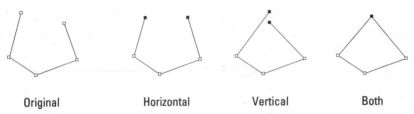

Original   Horizontal   Vertical   Both

Figure 5-22: Different types of averaging

To average points horizontally, select the points to be averaged with the Direct Selection tool and choose Object ➪ Path ➪ Average (⌘+Option+J [Ctrl+Alt+J]). The Average dialog box appears, asking which type of averaging you would like to do. In this case, choose Horizontal, which moves selected points only up and down.

Caution   Be sure to select the points to be averaged with the Direct Selection tool. If you select a path with either the Group Selection tool or the regular Selection tool, every point in the path will be averaged! This mistake can do quite a bit of damage when averaging both horizontally and vertically.

To average points vertically, choose the Vertical option in the Average dialog box. To average points both vertically and horizontally, choose Both. The Both option places all selected points on top of each other.

When averaging points, Illustrator uses the mean method to determine the center. No, Illustrator isn't nasty to the points that it averages; rather, Illustrator adds together the locations of the points and then divides by the number of points, which provides the mean location of the center of the points.

Cross-Reference   If you want to average entire paths, use the Align palette, which is covered in the "Aligning and Distributing Objects" section found in Chapter 7, "Organizing Artwork."

Joining points

Joining is a tricky area to define. Illustrator's Join feature does two entirely different things: It joins two End Points at different locations with a line segment, and it also combines two Anchor Points into one when they are placed one on top of the other.

To join two End Points with a line segment, select just two End Points in different locations (not on top of each other) with the Direct Selection tool and choose Object ➪ Path ➪ Join (⌘+J [Ctrl+J]). A line segment is formed between the two points, as shown in Figure 5-23.

To combine two End Points into a single Anchor Point, select the two points that are *directly* one over the other and choose Object ➪ Path ➪ Join (⌘+J [Ctrl+J]). The Join dialog box appears, asking what type of point should be created when the two

End Points become one Anchor Point. If you choose Smooth Point, then the point will become a Smooth Point with two linked Control Handles. If you choose Corner Point, the point will retain any Control Handle position that is part of it. And if no Control Handle is on the line, there will be no Control Handle on that side of the Anchor Point.

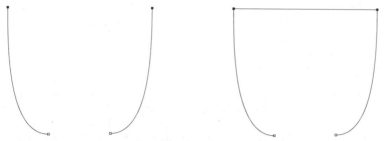

Figure 5-23: Joining two End Points with a line segment

Not only can you join two separate paths, but you can also join together the End Points on the same open path (overlapping End Points) to create a closed path in the same way that two End Points from different paths are joined.

To make sure that End Points are overlapping, turn on the Snap to Point feature in General Preferences and drag one End Point to the other with a selection tool. When the two points are close enough, the arrowhead cursor (normally black) becomes hollow. Release the mouse button when the arrowhead is hollow, and the two points will be directly one above the other.

Another way to ensure that the End Points are overlapping is to select them, choose Object ➪ Path ➪ Average (⌘+Option+J [Ctrl+Alt+J]), and select the Both option in the Average dialog box.

Note   When creating an Anchor Point out of two overlapping End Points, make sure that the two points are precisely overlapping. If they are even the smallest distance apart, a line segment will be drawn between the two points instead of transforming the two End Points into a single Anchor Point. You can tell immediately whether the points are overlapping correctly when you select Join. If a dialog box appears, the points are overlapping. If no dialog box appears, the points were not overlapping, and it is best to undo the join.

Tip   To make the points overlap and join at once, press ⌘+Option+Shift+J [Ctrl+Alt+Shift+J], which will both average and join the selected End Points. This method works only on End Points. The End Points are averaged both horizontally and vertically and are also joined into an Anchor Point that is a Corner Point, with Control Handle Lines and Control Handles unchanged.

Joining has these limitations:

✦ Joins may not take place when one path is part of a different group than the other path. If the two paths are in the same base group (that is, not in any other groups before being grouped to the other path, even grouped by themselves), the End Points can be joined.

✦ If one path is grouped to another object and the other object has not been previously grouped to the path, the End Points will not join.

✦ The End Points on text paths cannot be joined.

✦ The End Points of guides cannot be joined.

If all the points in an open path are selected (as if the path is selected with the regular Selection tool), then choosing Object ➪ Path ➪ Join (⌘+J [Ctrl+J]) automatically joins the End Points. If the two End Points are located directly one over the other, the Join dialog box appears, asking whether the new Anchor Point should be a Smooth Point or a Corner Point.

Joining is also useful for determining the location of End Points when the End Points are overlapping. Select the entire path, choose Object ➪ Path ➪ Join (⌘+J [Ctrl+J]), and choose Smooth Point. These steps usually alter one of the two segments on either side of the new Anchor Point. Undo the join and you will know the location of the overlapping End Points.

ASK TOULOUSE: Join Trouble

Mary: I can't join my two paths.

Toulouse: They're both open paths?

Mary: Yep.

Toulouse: You've selected just the End Points you want to join?

Mary: Yep.

Toulouse: You're choosing Join from the Object ➪ Path submenu?

Mary: Yep.

Toulouse: Are both paths ungrouped?

Mary: Yep. Uh . . . I mean . . . I'm not sure.

Toulouse: Select them both and Ungroup. Then try.

Mary: That was it!

Toulouse: Remember that you can't join paths when they're part of different groups.

Converting Anchor Points

This section deals with the Convert Anchor Point tool (Shift + C), which is a pop-up tool that is part of the Pen tool. This tool works differently with each type of Anchor Point. Figure 5-24 shows the different types of Anchor Points.

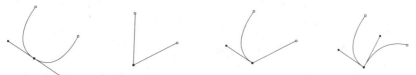

Smooth point   Straight corner point   Combination corner point   Curved corner point

Figure 5-24: The four types of Anchor Points

Cross-Reference For detailed definitions of the four different types of Anchor Points and how they're drawn with the Pen tool, take a look at Chapter 3, "Drawing and Painting."

You can use the Convert Anchor Point tool on either extended Control Handles or on Anchor Points. When two Control Handles exist on an Anchor Point, clicking either Control Handle with the Convert Anchor Point tool "breaks" the linked Control Handles (so that when the angle of one is changed, the other is changed as well), and makes them independent (the Control Handle's length from the Anchor Point and the angle can be altered individually).

Before learning how to convert between the various Anchor Points, it would be wise to recap the various types of Anchor Points. Anchor Points come in two classes:

✦ **Smooth Points** are Anchor Points that have a curved path flowing smoothly through them. Smooth Points keep the path from changing direction abruptly. Two linked *Control Handles* exist on every smooth point.

✦ **Corner Points** are a class of Anchor Points in which the path changes direction abruptly at those specific points. Corner Points come in three different types:

  • *Straight Corner Points* are Anchor Points where two straight line segments meet at a distinct angle. No Control Handles exist on this type of Anchor Point.

  • *Curved Corner Points* are points where two curved line segments meet and abruptly change direction. Two *independent Control Handles* exist on each Curved Corner Point.

  • *Combination Corner Points* are the meeting places for straight and curved line segments. One independent Control Handle exists on a Combination Corner Point.

Converting Smooth Points

Smooth Points can be changed into the other three types of Anchor Points by using both the Direct Selection tool and the Convert Anchor Point tool as follows:

✦ To convert Smooth Points into Combination Corner Points, use the Direct Selection tool or the Convert Anchor Point tool to drag one Control Handle into the Anchor Point.

✦ To convert Smooth Points into Curved Corner Points, use the Convert Anchor Point tool to drag one of the Control Handles. After being dragged with the Convert Anchor Point tool, the two Control Handles become independent of each other (the movement of one will not affect the other).

The following steps show you how you can use the Direct Selection tool and the Convert Anchor Point tool to change shapes — in this case, from a circle to a diamond.

1. Draw a circle with the Ellipse tool. Remember to keep the Shift key pressed so you end up with a perfect circle.

2. Select the Convert Anchor Point tool.

3. Click each of the Anchor Points and release. The diamond should look like the illustration in Figure 5-25.

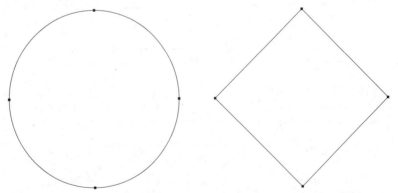

Figure 5-25: Convert the circle (left) to the diamond (right) by clicking each Anchor Point with the Convert Anchor Point tool.

Converting Straight Corner Points

You can change Straight Corner Points into one of the other three types of Anchor Points by using both the Convert Anchor Point tool and the Direct Selection tool as follows:

✦ To convert Straight Corner Points into Smooth Points, use the Convert Anchor Point tool to click and drag the Anchor Point. As you drag, linked Control Handles appear on both sides of the Anchor Point.

✦ To convert Straight Corner Points into Combination Corner Points, use the Convert Anchor Point tool to click and drag the Anchor Point. As you drag, linked Control Handles appear on both sides of the Anchor Point. Select one of the Control Handles with the Convert Anchor Point tool or the Direct Selection tool and drag it toward the Anchor Point until it disappears.

✦ To convert Straight Corner Points into Curved Corner Points, use the Convert Anchor Point tool to click and drag the Anchor Point. As you drag, linked Control Handles appear on both sides of the Anchor Point. Then use the Convert Anchor Point tool to drag one of the Control Handles. After being dragged with the Convert Anchor Point tool, the two Control Handles become independent of each other.

Converting Combination Corner Points

You can change Combination Corner Points into one of the other three types of Anchor Points by using both the Convert Anchor Point tool and the Direct Selection tool as follows:

✦ To convert Combination Corner Points into Smooth Points, use the Convert Anchor Point tool to click and drag the Anchor Point. As you drag, linked Control Handles appear on both sides of the Anchor Point.

✦ To convert Combination Corner Points into Straight Corner Points, use the Convert Anchor Point tool to click once on the Anchor Point. The Control Handle disappears.

✦ To convert Combination Corner Points into Curved Corner Points, use the Convert Anchor Point tool to click and drag the Anchor Point. As you drag, linked Control Handles appear on both sides of the Anchor Point. Then use the Convert Anchor Point tool to drag one of the Control Handles. After being dragged with the Convert Anchor Point tool, the two Control Handles become independent of each other.

The following steps are another example of how you can change shapes using the Direct Selection tool and the Convert Anchor Point tool — this time, a circle into a heart.

1. Draw a circle with the Ellipse tool. Remember to keep the Shift key pressed so that you end up with a perfect circle.

2. Click the lowest point on the circle with the Direct Selection tool.

3. Click the right Control Handle of that Anchor Point and drag it up, as shown in Figure 5-26.

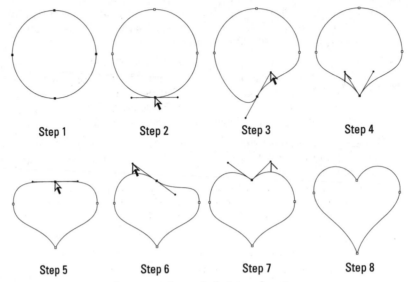

Figure 5-26: Steps for converting a circle into a heart

4. With the Convert Anchor Point tool, click the left Control Handle of that point and drag it up.

5. Click the Anchor Point at the top of the circle and drag it down a little.

6. With the Direct Selection tool, click the left Control Handle of the topmost point and drag it up.

7. Click the right Control Handle with the Convert Anchor Point tool and drag it down. If you turn the Grid on (⌘+' [Ctrl+']), you'll find making adjustments such as this much easier and more precise.

8. Adjust the Anchor Points and Control Handles until the heart looks really . . . well . . . nice.

Converting Curved Corner Points

You can change Curved Corner Points into one of the other three types of Anchor Points by using both the Convert Anchor Point tool and the Direct Selection tool as follows:

✦ To convert Curved Corner Points into Smooth Points, use the Convert Anchor Point tool to click and drag the Anchor Point. You can then use the Direct Selection tool to adjust the angle of both Control Handles at once.

✦ To convert Curved Corner Points into Straight Corner Points, use the Convert Anchor Point tool to click once on the Anchor Point. The Control Handles disappear.

✦ To convert Curved Corner Points into Combination Corner Points, use the Direct Selection tool to drag one Control Handle into the Anchor Point.

Using the Pencil tool

Two tools exist as pop-up tools under the Pencil tool. These are the Smooth tool and the Erase tool. The Smooth tool is unique and enables you to easily remove the sharp, pointed sections of a path. You can use the Erase tool to divide a path into several paths.

Smoothing a rough line

The Smooth tool is found in the Pencil tool's pop-up tools in the toolbar. This fabulous tool smoothes lines drawn with any tool. Whether you used the Pencil, Pen, or Brush tool, the Smooth tool can smooth any line just by dragging over it. The Smooth tool really helps if you have a smooth-hand or a pressure-sensitive tablet. Figure 5-27 shows a path before and after using the Smooth tool to even out the kinks. The Smooth tool will try to keep close to the shape you started with when you edit.

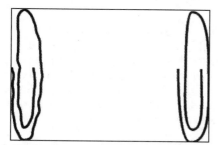

Figure 5-27: Before and after using the Smooth tool

Figure 5-28 shows the Smooth Tool Preferences dialog box, which you can access by double-clicking the Smooth tool. You can set Fidelity and Smoothness tolerances here. Tolerances are determined by pixels (yes, we know this is a vector-based program, but bear with us). The Tolerance setting follows the nuances of your hand moving the mouse or pressure-sensitive tablet pen. If you have a high setting of Fidelity and Smoothness, the lines will be smoother with fewer Anchor Points. If you choose a low setting for Fidelity and Smoothness, the lines will be bumpier with more Anchor Points. Figure 5-29 shows selected lines with a high Tolerance setting (left) and a low Tolerance setting (right), with the Bounding Box option turned off.

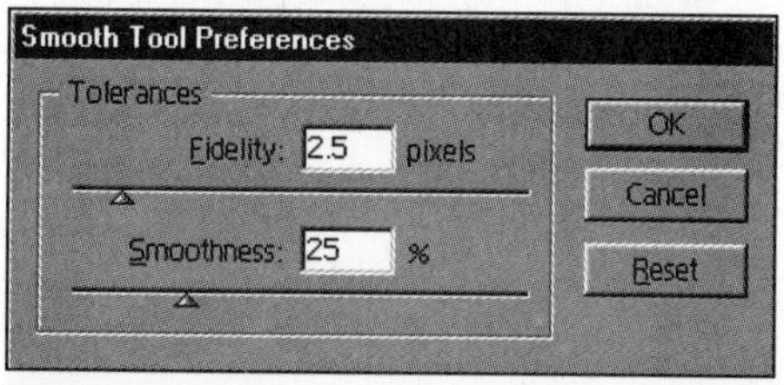

Smooth Tool Preferences

Tolerances

Fidelity: 2.5 pixels

Smoothness: 25 %

OK

Cancel

Reset

Figure 5-28: The Smooth Tool Preferences dialog box

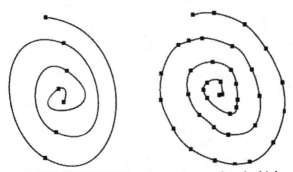

Figure 5-29: The left line shows the results of a high Tolerance setting and the right line shows the results of a low Tolerance setting in the Pencil/Smooth tools.

Erasing a section of a path

Another pop-up tool of the Pencil tool in the toolbox is the Erase tool. The Erase tool enables you to remove sections of a path just as if you were using a real eraser on paper. You drag over the area you want removed and it is deleted. This is a pretty cool tool. If you just click once over the path, it cuts the path, but does not remove a section. You can drag the two pieces apart. The longer you drag, the greater the number of parts of the path that will be erased. The Erase tool works on any path, but it doesn't work on text or a gradient mesh object.

Keep in mind that the Erase tool only works on the current selection. Dragging the Erase tool over the top of an unselected path does not have any effect.

Using Illustrator's Pathfinder Functions

The most powerful path functions in Illustrator are in the Pathfinder palette. They do things that would take hours to do using Illustrator's traditional tools and methods. The only drawback to the Pathfinder palette is that it has so many options that it's pretty darn hard to figure out which one to use for which job. Figure 5-30 shows the Pathfinder palette. Select Window ⇨ Show Pathfinder (Shift+F9) to open the Pathfinder palette.

The Pathfinder options take over most of the mundane tasks of path editing that could otherwise take hours. Everything that the Pathfinder options do can be done manually with Illustrator tools, but the Pathfinder options do them much more quickly. Common activities such as joining two paths together correctly and breaking a path into two pieces are done in a snap.

Add to shape area

Subtract from shape area

Intersect shape areas

Exclude overlapping shape areas

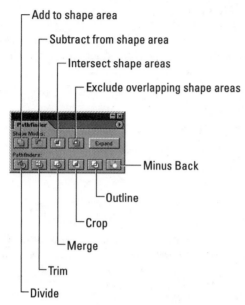

Minus Back

Outline

Crop

Merge

Trim

Divide

Figure 5-30: The Pathfinder palette

Caution The Pathfinder functions will not work with gradient mesh objects.

The Pathfinder options change the way that two or more paths interact. The cute little symbols on each of the Pathfinder options are supposed to clue you in to what each option can do, but the pictures are small and most don't accurately depict exactly how each option works. The tooltips for each button will help to describe the purpose of each button if you have the Hot Help [ToolTips] feature active, the name of each of the Pathfinder options pops up when you hold your cursor over its option symbol.

The Pathfinder palette is divided into two sets of buttons — Shape Modes and Pathfinders. The Shape Modes options can be used to combine overlapping shapes. They are what we call the "overlay" Pathfinders, because they generate results from two or more paths that overlap. The remaining Pathfinder options work with paths instead of closed shapes.

Note Now that the Pathfinder options are no longer on a pull-down menu (as in version 7), to reapply a Pathfinder function you can use the Repeat Pathfinder function found in the Pathfinder palette's pop-up menu.

The Pathfinder Options dialog box

To access the Pathfinder options, choose Pathfinder Options in the pop-up menu of the Pathfinder palette. This displays the Pathfinder Options dialog box, shown in Figure 5-31, which enables you to customize the way that the Pathfinders work.

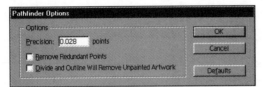

Figure 5-31: The Pathfinder Options dialog box

The value in the Precision text field tells Illustrator how precisely Pathfinders should operate. The more precisely they operate, the better and more accurate the results are, but the longer the processing time is. This speed differential is most apparent when you apply Pathfinders — especially Trap — to very complex objects. The default value is 0.028 points, which seems to be accurate enough for most work.

The Remove Redundant Points option gets rid of overlapping points that are side-by-side on the same path. We can't think of why you would want overlapping points, so keeping this option checked (the default) is a good idea.

If the "Divide & Outline will extract unpainted artwork" option is checked, it automatically deletes unpainted artwork. This relieves you from having to remove all those paths that Divide always seems to produce that are filled and stroked with None.

Note   Usually, the defaults in the Pathfinder Options dialog box are the best options for most situations. If you change the options, be aware that the Pathfinder Options dialog box will reset to the defaults when you quit Illustrator.

Add to Shape Area

Add to Shape Area unites the selected objects if they are overlapping. A new path outlines all the previously selected objects. No paths exist where the original paths intersected. The new object takes the Paint Style attributes of the topmost object. If any objects are within other objects, those objects will be assimilated. If "holes" exist in the object, the holes will become reversed out of a compound path.

You'll find that Add to Shape Area is one Pathfinder option that you'll use often. Play with combining various paths for a while so you know what to expect and you will develop a sense of when using Add to Shape Area is a better option than doing the same tasks manually.

ASK TOULOUSE: Creating Style Sheets with Unite

Phyllis: So, is that all Add to Shape Area is good for?

Toulouse: You mean joining abutting and overlapping paths?

Phyllis: Yeah. That's it?

Toulouse: Actually, no. You can use Add to Shape Area to create compound paths.

Phyllis: That's interesting.

Toulouse: You can also use Add to Shape Area to create pseudo style sheets.

Phyllis: How so?

Toulouse: If you want several paths to have the same paint style, and the paint style might change in the future, unite them. Make sure the topmost path is the color you want it to be.

Phyllis: And that works as a style sheet?

Toulouse: Sorta. By selecting any of those paths and changing the paint style, all the paths will change to that paint style. Of course, if you want real style sheets, you can use Alien Skin's full-featured Stylist plug-in, or VectorTools' Vector Object Style.

Add to Shape Area combines two or more paths into one path, as described in the following steps:

1. Create and select the artwork that you want to apply Unite to. In the example in Figure 5-32, the artwork is text converted into outlines. (Pathfinders work only with paths — you have to convert type into outlined paths, and you cannot use EPS (Encapsulated PostScript) images.)

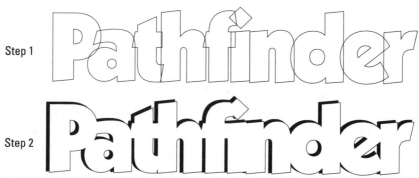

Figure 5-32: Using Add to Shape Area

2. Choose the Add to Shape Area option from the Pathfinder palette. Any overlapping artwork is united into one path. (The color of the united path is always the color of the path that was the topmost selected path before you used Unite.)

When you use Add to Shape Area, paths that don't overlap but are outside of other paths become part of a group. Illustrator draws paths between End Points of open paths before it unites those paths with other paths. Compound paths remain compound paths.

Subtract from Shape Area

The Subtract from Shape Area option will remove any overlapping top layer objects from the lowest level object. Figure 5-33 shows four rectangle shapes that are overlapped. The center rectangle is the furthest back object and the four corner rectangles are positioned on top of it. Using the Subtract from Shape Area option will remove the corners from the center rectangle.

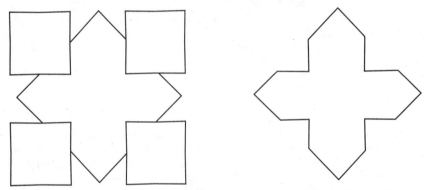

Figure 5-33: Using Subtract from Shape Area, before (left) and after (right)

The style of the combined shapes will be the same as the furthest back object that remains.

Intersect and Exclude Shape Areas

These two Shape Mode pathfinders are opposites. Using one results in the opposite of what you get from using the other. Kind of the "Punk & Bloat" of the Pathfinder variety.

Intersect creates only the intersection of the selected shapes. Any part of a selected path that does not intersect is deleted. If two paths are intersecting and selected, only the area that intersects between the two paths will remain. If three or more paths are selected, all must intersect at a common area for the function to produce results. If the paths selected do not intersect at all, nothing will happen. If one selected path is contained within all the other selected paths, the result will be that contained path. The resulting path will have the Paint Style attributes of the topmost path.

Exclude is pretty much the opposite of Intersect. Choosing Exclude deletes the intersecting areas, grouping together the outside pieces. If you are having trouble making a compound path, use Exclude; any path within another path will be reversed, creating a compound path automatically.

After you select two or more paths and click the Intersect button on the Pathfinder palette, only the overlapping portions of the paths remain. If you select three paths, the only area that remains will be the area where all three selected paths overlap each other.

If you use Exclude, only the areas that don't overlap will remain. Exclude follows the Winding Number rule, which is discussed in Chapter 11, "Using Path Blends, Compound Paths, and Masks."

The color of the intersected or excluded path is always the color of the path that was the topmost selected path before you used Intersect or Exclude. Figure 5-34 shows the results of both of these functions.

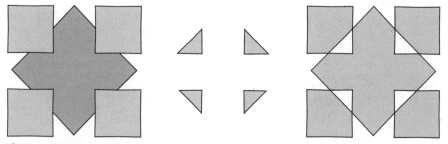

Figure 5-34: Using Intersect (middle) and Exclude (right) from Shape Area pathfinder functions. The shape on the left is the shapes before applying the functions.

The Expand Button

After a pathfinder option is used, all objects that are involved in the operation remain selected and grouped. You can use the Expand button to combine all the selected and grouped object into a single object. This button will perform the same function as the Object ➪ Expand menu option.

Divide

The Divide option in the Pathfinder palette checks to see where the selected paths overlap and then creates new paths at all intersections where the paths crossed, creating new paths if necessary. Fills are kept, but any Strokes are changed to None. In the process, Divide also groups the pieces of the Fill together. Divide also keeps sections their original colors; the illustration appears to look the same unless it previously had Strokes. To keep the Strokes, copy before using Divide, and then Paste in Back (⌘+B [Ctrl+B]).

Simply put, Divide divides overlaying paths into individual closed paths, as described in the following steps and illustrated in Figure 5-35.

1. Create the artwork that you want to divide into sections.

2. Create a path or paths where you want to divide the object. (If the division lines consist of more than one path, you do not need to make those paths into a compound path, although it doesn't hurt.)

3. Select all paths, both artwork and dividing paths, and choose the Divide option in the Pathfinder palette.

4. If you wish to move the pieces apart, you first have to ungroup them (Divide groups them automatically).

Figure 5-35: Using Divide

Trim

Trim removes sections of paths that are overlapped by other paths. Frontmost paths are the only ones that will remain. This Pathfinder is very useful for cleaning up complex overlapping illustrations, although it can take a bit of time to complete.

Tip   We'll often use Trim if we want to use a piece of artwork for one portion of the Soft Pathfinder (described later). This removes overlapping paths, which would otherwise change in color when Soft is applied.

Merge

Merge combines overlapping paths that have an identical Fill applied to them. Even if the Fill is different by as little as 1 percent, Merge creates two separate paths. This Pathfinder is much more efficient than Add to Shape Area for making areas of the same color into one object.

The following steps describe how to use Merge, and Figure 5-36 illustrates these steps.

1. Create the artwork that you want to use Merge for.

2. Select the artwork to be merged and choose the Merge option in the Pathfinder palette. All paths that were overlapped are removed, leaving only the paths that had nothing in front of them. All adjacent areas that contained identical colors are united.

Crop

Crop works in much the same way that masks work, except that anything outside the cropped area is deleted, not just masked. To use Crop, bring the object that you wish to use as a cropper to the front, select all the paths you wish to crop with it and the cropper itself, and choose the Crop option in the Pathfinder palette. Everything outside the cropper will be deleted. The objects that were cropped are grouped together in the shape of the crop.

Unlike masks, no outside shape remains after you crop. The cropper used to crop the image is deleted when Crop is chosen.

Figure 5-36: Using Merge

Outline

Outline creates small sections of paths wherever paths cross and color the Strokes, using the Fill of the path they were part of and giving the Strokes a weight of 1 point. Outline is useful for spot trapping as it automatically creates the sections needed that have to be chosen for overprinting, although many times the colors will be incorrect.

Outline creates smaller path pieces than Divide does; but instead of making each section a closed path, each path maintains its individuality, becoming separate from adjoining paths. The result of outlining is several small Stroke pieces. Instead of maintaining the Fill color of each piece, each piece is filled with None and stroked with the Fill color.

Minus Back

Each of these Pathfinders works on the principle that one path, typically the backmost of the paths selected, will have all the other overlapping paths subtracted from it.

Minus Back subtracts all the selected paths behind the frontmost selected path from the frontmost selected path. With two objects, it is also quite simple: The object in the back is deleted and the area where the object in back was placed is also deleted. This too gets a little more confusing when you have more objects, but it does the same thing, all at once to all the selected paths. If the area to be subtracted is totally within the path it will subtract *from*, then a compound path results.

ASK TOULOUSE: Strokes Are Gone

Ida: My Strokes are gone!

Toulouse: Yikes! What happened?

Ida: I was just Pathfindering around, and suddenly . . . no more Strokes.

Toulouse: Almost all Pathfinders zap your Strokes into oblivion.

Ida: I'd rather they didn't. What if I want to use Strokes from the paths *before* they're chopped up into little pieces?

Toulouse: The best thing to do is to copy the paths before you apply Pathfinders, and then Paste in Front.

Ida: But they'll cover up the new Pathfindered paths!

Toulouse: To see the paths underneath, change the Fill of the Paste in Front paths to None. Keep the Strokes as they are.

When you apply Minus Back, the color of the remaining path is the color of the frontmost path before you applied it.

Trap

The Trap pop-up menu option opens the Pathfinder Trap dialog box, shown in Figure 5-37. This feature takes some of the drudgery away from trapping. The only limitation for Trap is that it doesn't work well on extremely complex illustrations because of time and memory constraints. The other concern with Trap is that it leaves your illustrations "pseudo-uneditable" because it creates extra paths around your original trap and makes it really difficult to edit. It doesn't affect the existing paths, but if you do much editing, you'll have to delete the trap paths and retrap.

Tip Prior to trapping, we create a layer called *Traps*. Immediately after trapping, we move all the trap objects to the Traps layer. This keeps the traps together, in case we need to redo, adjust, or delete them.

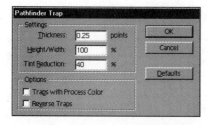

Figure 5-37: The Pathfinder Trap dialog box offers options for trapping objects.

Trap automatically creates a trap between abutting shapes of different colors. You set the amount (width) of trap in a dialog box that appears after choosing Trap. Here are the steps:

1. Create and select the artwork that you want to trap. (If the artwork is overly complex, you may want to select only a small portion of the artwork before you continue.)

2. Choose the Trap option in the Pathfinder palette's pop-up menu. In the Trap dialog box, enter the width of the trap in the Thickness text field (the default is 0.25 points). Enter the amount for how much you want the height of the trap to differ from the width, which allows for different paper-stretching errors. For example, entering the maximum, 400 percent, widens the horizontal thickness of the Stroke to four times the amount set in the Thickness text field and leaves the vertical thickness the same. Enter a Tint reduction value that specifies how much the lighter of the two colors should be tinted on that area. Check the Traps with Process Color checkbox to convert spot colors to process equivalents only in the resulting trap path that is generated from Trap. Check the Reverse Traps checkbox to convert any traps along the object that are Filled with 100% Black but no other colors to be less black and more of the lighter abutting color.

3. Click OK. Figure 5-38 shows the trap (the overlap of the colors).

All traps generated by Trap result in filled paths, not Strokes, and are automatically set to overprint in the Attributes palette.

ASK TOULOUSE: Trapping to Placed Images

Rhoda: Can I trap to placed images?

Toulouse: Oops. Uhhh . . . well, not really.

Rhoda: You're kidding me.

Toulouse: No, I wouldn't kid you about that.

Rhoda: Why can't I?

Toulouse: Think of it this way: When you bring in a placed image, it's this little self-contained image. It knocks out everything in its path (pun intended).

Rhoda: Anything I can do?

Toulouse: You might want to have your printer do it manually with the film separations.

Pathfinder

Figure 5-38: This figure shows the trap with a large point size and the trap darkened so you can see it.

Summary

As you work with paths, the chances that the first path you draw isn't going to be exactly what you want. But, by selecting and editing the path, you can get it closer to what the path should be. Illustrator includes many unique ways to edit paths from the various tools to the advanced pathfinder functions. In the chapter, you learned the following:

✦ Path editing is done in Illustrator by using the Direct Selection, Scissors, Smooth, Erase, and Convert Anchor Point tools.

✦ Adding Anchor Points alone never changes the shape of a path.

✦ Adding Anchor Points doubles the number of points on selected paths.

✦ You can use the Simplify function to reduce the number of points in the selected paths.

✦ Cleanup deletes unwanted path types from your entire document.

✦ Offset Path moves a path inward or outward by the number of points you specify.

✦ Outline Path creates a Filled path in the same location as a Stroke, at the size of the width of the Stroke.

✦ Removing Anchor Points can drastically change the shape of a path.

✦ Paths can be split one at a time with the Scissors tool.

✦ You can slice through paths with the Knife tool.

✦ You can erase through paths with the Erase tool.

✦ The Magic Wand tool selects objects with similar attributes.

✦ Quickly make duplicates of certain sections of paths by pressing Option [Alt] when using the Knife tool.

✦ Selected points can be aligned using the Average command.

✦ Use the Join command to join any two selected End Points.

✦ The Select menu includes many options for selecting objects.

✦ The Pathfinder palette options are path-specific.

✦ Add to Shape Area joins together abutting and overlapping paths.

✦ Subtract from Shape Area removes overlapping areas from the backmost shape.

✦ Intersect creates paths where all the selected paths overlap, deleting the rest of the paths.

✦ Exclude creates paths only where no overlap exists.

✦ Back Minus subtracts from the backmost or frontmost paths.

✦ Trap creates trapping in the amount you specify between abutting or overlapping paths.

✦   ✦   ✦

Working with Color and Gradients

This chapter is about color. Color in Illustrator comes in many different forms. Colors can be spot colors selected from the Color palette, preset colors from the Swatches palette or colors as part of a gradient. In Illustrator, colors are generally applied in two ways, as Fills and as Strokes.

No Illustrator book would be complete without a discussion of how to create gradients. Sure, you could create these three effects by the simple act of drawing them, but Illustrator has made their creation a breeze. Illustrator enables you to create custom gradients. Another useful type of gradient is the Gradient Mesh.

Even though this chapter is about color, we're not going to start with the Color palette, but rather with the Swatches palette because it contains some preset colors that can be selected and applied.

The Swatches Palette

View the Swatches palette (see Figure 6-1) by choosing Window ➪ Show Swatches. It includes an assortment of colors, patterns and gradients. You can think of it as the palette that a painter uses to mix and hold paints. Colors are selected by simply clicking on the color that you wish to use.

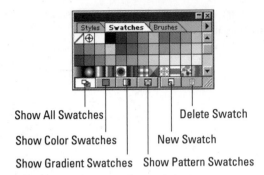

Figure 6-1: The Swatches palette

By default, the Swatches palette contains and displays several commonly used colors, patterns, and gradients. Change the display by clicking the icons along the bottom of the palette:

> ✦ **Show All Swatches** displays all color, gradient, and pattern swatches.
>
> ✦ **Show Color Swatches** displays only the color swatches.
>
> ✦ **Show Gradient Swatches** displays only the gradient swatches.
>
> ✦ **Show Pattern Swatches** displays only the pattern swatches.

You can also view the swatches in either small or large squares, or view all the swatches in a list, with names if they have them (see Figure 6-2). Change the view mode by choosing the appropriate option from the Swatches pop-up menu.

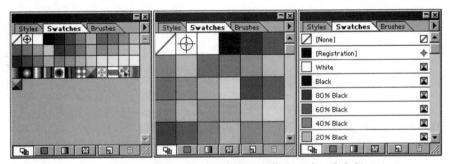

Figure 6-2: The Swatches palette displayed in Small Thumbnail (left), Large Thumbnail (middle), and List View (right)

Create a new swatch based on the current paint style (shown in the Paint Style section of the toolbox) by clicking the New Swatch icon along the bottom of the Swatches palette. If you press Option [Alt] when creating a new swatch, the New

Swatch dialog box appears, enabling you to initially name the swatch and set its color mode to either process (CMYK) or spot. You can also create a new swatch by choosing New Swatch from the Swatches palette pop-up menu.

Double-clicking a swatch displays the Swatch Options (shown in Figure 6-3) for that swatch. The Swatch Options dialog box lets you change the name of the swatch (primarily for use in Name view mode), set the color type of the swatch to either process or spot, and the color mode of CMYK, RGB, HSB, or Grayscale.

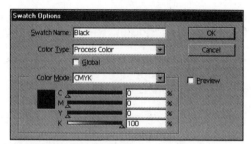

Figure 6-3: The Swatch Options dialog box

In addition, you can select one or more swatches to edit or duplicate, or you can remove them from the Swatches palette. Click a swatch to select it; a frame appears on the selected swatch. When a swatch is selected, choosing Swatch Options from the Swatch menu also displays the Swatch Options for the selected swatch.

Tip Regardless of the view mode you choose (Small Thumbnail, Large Thumbnail, or List), ⌘+Option+clicking [Ctrl+Alt+clicking] the Swatches palette makes the palette respond to keyboard entry for selecting swatches. For instance, if you wanted to use the swatch called PrenatalGoo you would ⌘+Option+click [Ctrl+Alt+click] in the Swatches palette and then type the first few letters of the swatch name; in this case the letters **PRE** should do it. When you stop typing, the swatch whose name is closest to the one you typed is highlighted, and pressing the Return [Enter] key makes that the active (selected) swatch in the Swatches palette. This is extremely useful for selecting Pantone colors in the huge Pantone Swatches palettes.

Choosing Duplicate Swatch from the pop-up menu duplicates the selected swatches. You can also drag a selected swatch to the New Swatch icon (the little piece of paper) to duplicate the swatch.

To delete a swatch, select the swatch and click the Trash icon or choose Delete Swatch from the Swatches palette pop-up menu. A warning dialog box (see Figure 6-4) appears, asking if you want to delete the swatch selection. Click Yes to delete the swatch.

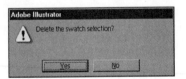

Figure 6-4: The Warning dialog box that appears when you attempt to delete a swatch

Note

If you accidentally throw away a needed swatch, you can always undo a swatch deletion. The unlimited undo capability applies to the Swatch palette deletions.

You can select more than one swatch by pressing the ⌘ [Ctrl] key and clicking additional swatches. If you press the Shift key and click additional swatches, a contiguous (connected) set of the swatches is selected, from where you initially clicked to where you Shift+clicked. Deselect individual swatches by ⌘ [Ctrl]+clicking selected swatches. Deselect all the swatches by clicking an empty area of the Swatches palette. By selecting multiple swatches, you can duplicate and delete several swatches at once.

The Swatches pop-up menu (shown in Figure 6-5) has other functions as well. Choosing Select All Unused selects the swatches in the Swatches palette that aren't being used in the current document. You can then delete those swatches if necessary. Sort By Name organizes the swatches (regardless of which viewing mode the swatch palette is in) alphabetically. Sort By Kind sorts the swatches to appear starting with color, then gradients, and then patterns.

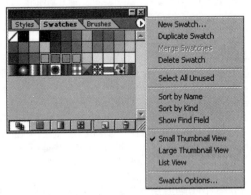

Figure 6-5: The Swatches palette pop-up menu

The Show Find Field option enables a searchable Find field at the top of the Swatch palette. By typing a color name in this field, you can search for and select swatches. The Find field automatically selects the swatch that matches the letters you type.

For example, if you type the letter **o**, an orange color swatch is selected, as shown in Figure 6-6.

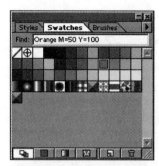

Figure 6-6: You can use the Find Field to search for and select swatches from the current Swatch palette.

If you want to sort the swatches manually, you can do so by selecting any number of swatches and dragging them to a new location within the Swatches palette.

The other Swatch Libraries

In addition to the standard Swatch Library palette, several other default Swatch Library palettes are accessible from the Swatch Libraries submenu of the Window menu (see Figure 6-7). You can also create a new Swatch Library palette from any Illustrator document.

To view one of the other default Swatches palettes, choose it from the Swatch Libraries submenu. You cannot edit these Swatch Libraries; you can only add swatches from these libraries to your main Swatches palette.

To add a swatch (or several selected swatches) to your main Swatches palette, select the swatches to be added and choose Add To Swatches from the library's pop-up menu, or drag the swatches to the main Swatches palette. Fortunately, the main Swatches palette is saved with your document; this way you can customize a palette for a specific document, or edit the Adobe Illustrator Startup document's Swatches palette to use a certain set of colors in each new document you create.

Cross-Reference Using and abusing the startup document is covered in Chapter 15, "Customizing and Optimizing Illustrator."

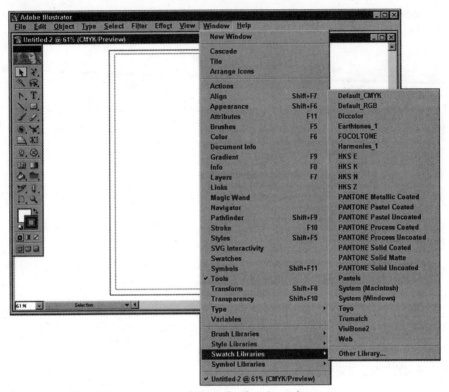

Figure 6-7: The Window menu and Swatch Libraries submenu

Otherwise, these Swatch Libraries work the same way as your main Swatches palette; you can choose colors for Fill and Stroke, sort the swatches by Kind or Name, and view the swatches by Name, Small Swatch, or Large Swatch. Figure 6-8 shows three Swatch Libraries in different views.

The Colors Palette

You can select various colors for Fills and Strokes from the Color palette. This palette, like the other palettes, can be opened by selecting Window ⇨ Show Color. You can also open this palette with the F6 key.

Choosing and mixing colors

You can create any color to be used in an illustration by defining it in the Color palette (shown in Figure 6-9). The Color palette provides basic color selection via the Color Ramp along the bottom of the palette, and more precise control via sliders and percentage entries in grayscale, RGB, CMYK, HSB, and spot color spaces.

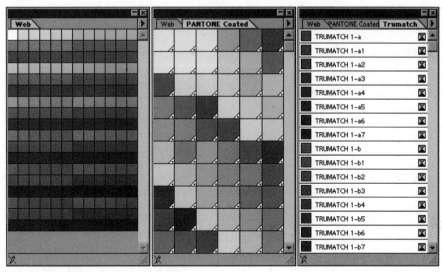

Figure 6-8: Three Swatch Libraries

You can create your own Swatch Library if you want. This technique works for all the different types of libraries. To create your own Swatch Library, edit the Swatch palette so it contains all the colors, gradients, and patterns that you wish to include in the new library. Save the document with the name that you wish to appear in the Swatch Library menu. Then move the file into the Swatch Libraries folder under the application folder. The file name will appear in the Swatch Library menu the next time Illustrator is restarted.

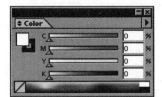

Figure 6-9: The Color palette

Note
In the Color palette, along the Color Ramp are the choices for None, Black, and White. When creating or mixing a color, you have the choice to have it applied to the Fill or Stroke swatch. When you apply None to either the Fill or Stroke, the Last Color option pops up in the Color palette (see Figure 6-10), which is a really cool function. This means you can apply the last color mixed by clicking the mouse to set the color.

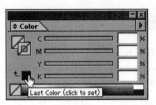

Figure 6-10: The Last Color option in the Color palette

The Color palette has a pop-up menu that enables you to display options and to choose from the available color spaces. The "options" are really the color mixing sliders; we've never found a reason to hide them. In fact, the sliders take up such a small amount of space that once they're in view, you'll probably never hide them either. If you choose to hide them, you can click the double arrows on the Color tab to toggle among three different palette sizes.

The color space options let you switch among the following:

✦ **Grayscale.** White to black with all shades of gray in between (see Figure 6-11).

Figure 6-11: The Color palette displaying grayscale color space

✦ **RGB.** Red, green, and blue. This is the color space used by computer moni-tors, and it's perfect for multimedia and Web-page graphics (see Figure 6-12). You can enter RGB values as percentages or as values from 0 to 255. Double-click to the right of the text fields to change the RGB measurement system from percentages to the numeric 0 to 255 system and back.

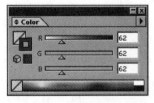

Figure 6-12: The Color palette displaying RGB color space

✦ **HSB.** Hue, Saturation, Brightness. This RGB-derived color space is best for adjusting RGB colors in brightness and saturation (see Figure 6-13).

Figure 6-13: The Color palette displaying HSB color space

✦ **CMYK.** Cyan, magenta, yellow, and black. These are considered typical printing process colors, although Illustrator calls any colors *process* that aren't *spot* (see Figure 6-14).

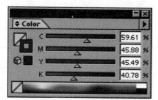

Figure 6-14: The Color palette displaying CMYK color space

✦ **Web Safe RGB.** This color mode automatically snaps to Web-safe colors. These colors will be viewed consistently in a browser regardless of the operating system (see Figure 6-15).

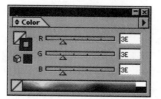

Figure 6-15: The Color palette displaying Web Safe RGB color space

When you change color spaces, the Color Ramp along the bottom of the palette changes as well to show the colors in that color space.

Tip

Shift+click the Color Ramp to cycle through the color spaces; this is much faster than choosing a color space from the pop-up menu.

As you drag a slider, the other sliders also change in color. This gives you a sort of preview for what would happen if you were to drag along the sliders. The icon to the left of the sliders shows the current color and whether you're adjusting the Fill (solid box) or Stroke (box with a hole). Instead of dragging, you can also just simply click a different location along the slider to change its value.

ASK TOULOUSE: The Color Purple

Cassiopeia: How can I make a purple color with the CMYK sliders?

Toulouse: Try 50 percent Cyan and 100 percent Magenta.

Cassiopeia: Wow, that was easy. How'd you know that?

Toulouse: Well, I sorta cheated. All the sliders in the Color palette are interactive.

Cassiopeia: They provide a real-to-life multimedia experience?

Toulouse: Not exactly. But the sliders change color relative to what the current color is. For instance, when I set Magenta to 100 percent, I looked at the other sliders, and saw there was purple in the middle of the Cyan slider bar. So I dragged the Cyan slider to 50 percent and voilà!

Cassiopeia: Voilà, indeed. You know, someone should stick that in a book somewhere. . . .

Toulouse: Good idea. . . .

You can also change the slider values by typing in values for each of the individual color channels (Cyan is a color channel in CMYK, for instance). Press the Tab key to highlight the next text field, or Shift+Tab to highlight the previous text field.

Tip Quickly highlight the text fields by clicking to the right of the text field, or by clicking the name of the text field on the other side of the slider.

Tip Most of Illustrator's Palettes' text fields are mathematically adept. You can add, subtract, multiply, and divide in them. This is useful when entering color percentages in the text fields of the Color palette. To add 5 percent to the current value, type **+5** after the current value. To subtract 5 percent, type **–5** after the current value. To divide the current value by 2, type **/2** after the current value. To multiple the current value by 2, type ***2** after the current value.

Tip Press Shift+Return/Enter after entering values to rehighlight the current text field. In this way you can type in different values without ever having to reselect the text field.

The Color Ramp

The Color Ramp enables you to quickly pick a color from the current color space. When you rest your cursor above the Color Ramp area, the cursor changes into an Eyedropper.

The Color palette also includes the None swatch. This is available in all Color Ramps. Click the None swatch to apply no color to the Fill or Stroke swatch. When you click the None swatch, you'll get the option to apply the last color that was previously in the swatch before you applied None.

Click any portion of the Color Ramp to select that color. In Illustrator 10, the RGB, HSB, and CMYK Color Ramps have fairly large rectangles of black and white to make choosing them easier. The grayscale ramp has large areas for both 0 percent and 100 percent to make selecting those percentages easier. You can also drag over the Color Ramp, watching the large square in the top of the Color palette (if Options are showing) to see the color you're dragging over. If Options aren't shown, look at the active Fill/Stroke icon in the toolbox to see the color you're currently positioned over (this *only* works when the mouse button is pressed as you pass across the Color Ramp). Fill and Stroke swatches are available in the Color Palette.

Tip

You can press the X key while dragging around the Color Ramp to switch between the Fill and Stroke focus. This way you can quickly select colors for both Fill and Stroke with *one* mouse click! If the Fill is in focus, click and drag through the Color Ramp to the appropriate color. Then, with the mouse button still pressed, press the X key; you'll now be picking a color for the Stroke. Want to change the Fill again? Just press X, keeping the mouse button down.

Tip

Here's a super-cool power tip: Option [Alt]+clicking anywhere on a Color Ramp affects the opposite attribute! For instance, if Stroke is in focus on the toolbox, Option [Alt]+clicking a Color Ramp changes the Fill color, not the Stroke. Be aware, however, that Option [Alt]+clicking a swatch in the Swatches palette does *not* affect the opposite attribute; this only works on a Color Ramp (and the color box in the Color palette).

ASK TOULOUSE: Tinting Process Colors

Starbuck: Why isn't there a tint control for process colors?

Toulouse: That would be too confusing: you'd have a 50 percent tint of 20 percent cyan, 50 percent magenta, and 10 percent black, which would really be 10 percent Cyan, 25 percent Magenta, and 5 percent Black.

Starbuck: Do I have to do all that math each time I want to change a process tint?

Toulouse: You can, but there's a shortcut. . . .

Starbuck: I thought all the letters on the keyboard were used up, but go ahead, tell me.

Toulouse: All you do is press Shift before you drag a slider, and all the sliders with values move along with the one you're dragging.

Starbuck: Wow! Great! Wait, it goes too fast, much too hard to control . . .

Toulouse: When adjusting the tint this way, be sure to move the slider with the largest percentage, as it gives you more control. The other sliders will move proportionately with that one.

Gamut trouble

If you choose certain colors in the RGB or HSB color spaces, a little icon appears near the lower-left corner of the Color palette (see Figure 6-16). This icon is indicating that the current color is out of gamut with CMYK color space. This issue is only important if you'll be printing the document using CMYK process colors. If you'll be using the image onscreen, such as in Web or multimedia publishing, it doesn't matter if the color is in gamut or not.

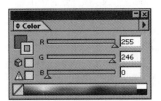

Figure 6-16: The Out of Gamut indicator (the exclamation mark inside a triangle) appears when the current color cannot be accurately converted into CMYK values.

The best way to reset the current color to CMYK color space is to click the Out of Gamut icon. The RGB or HSB values change so that the resulting color is well within CMYK color space. Another way to change the current color to CMYK color space is to choose CMYK from the Color palette pop-up menu.

Tip   If you want to change the color space of several objects — or perhaps your entire document — to CMYK, select the objects to be changed and choose Filter ➪ Colors ➪ Convert to CMYK. Filters are also available for changing the color space to grayscale and RGB.

Spot/process colors

Spot colors are colors in Illustrator that aren't separated into process colors (cyan, magenta, yellow, and black) when printed. Instead, they are printed on a different separation. A commercial printer uses special ink (commonly Pantone) for this spot color.

You can use as many spot colors in an illustration as you would like, though it isn't usually practical or desirable to have more than four in one document (because CMYK printing can duplicate most colors, process colors are often a better choice than four spot colors). Illustrator's default Swatch Libraries (choose Window ➪ Swatch Libraries ➪ Your Library) contain mostly spot colors that you can choose among, or you can create your own. To create your own Spot color, create a new swatch with the appearance (using the color sliders) you want. Then change the Swatch type from Process to Spot in the Swatch Options dialog box (access Swatch Options by double-clicking the swatch). When you use that swatch as a Fill or Stroke, it will be considered a spot color when it comes time to print.

Spot colors are indicated in the Swatches palette in Small Thumbnail and Large Thumbnail views by a white triangle containing a black dot in the lower right of the spot color swatch. List view shows a square with a circle inside of it (a "spot") on the right edge of the swatch listing. Figure 6-17 shows a palette of spot colors.

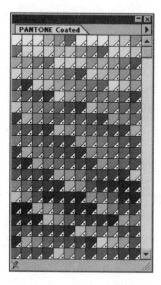

Figure 6-17: Spot colors are identified with a small white triangle with a black dot in the lower-right corner.

Tip

You can convert any spot color to a standard CMYK color (the color, not the swatch) by selecting the spot color and then changing the color space in the Color palette to CMYK. You can even change the color space to grayscale, RGB, or HSB in this way. This only works on the selected paths; the swatch itself is not affected.

Putting all the color palettes to use

Now you know how the palettes work, but how do you change the color of paths to what's in the palettes? The easiest thing to do is to select the path you want to change the Fill or Stroke (or both) of, change the focus (if necessary) of the Fill/Stroke icons, and select a color from either the Color or Swatches palette. Press X to change the color for the other (Fill or Stroke).

The key here is *selecting*. If you have the paths selected, any changes you make will affect those selected paths.

When you create a new path, it will be the Fill and Stroke that are currently displayed in the Paint Style section of the toolbox. To apply colors to text, you can either select an entire text area with a Selection tool, or select individual characters with a Type tool.

Caution

Selecting Type with a Selection tool can cause type paths and type areas to be filled and stroked as well as the type. You can use the Group Selection tool to deselect the associated paths or, better yet, just use the Type tool and drag across the characters you want to select.

Eyedropper/Paint Bucket tool

The Eyedropper and Paint Bucket tools are lifesavers for those of us who are constantly using up notes to jot down what the percentages of CMYK (cyan, magenta, yellow, and black) are in one path so that we can apply those same amounts to another path.

Illustrator has endowed these tools with additional features. You can use the Eyedropper tool to pick up the appearance and style of an object and use the Paint Bucket tool to apply the style to another object. Transferable attributes include Fill and Stroke settings, transparency, and effects.

You can specify which appearance attributes are transferred in the Eyedropper/ Paint Bucket Options dialog box. Double-clicking either tool brings up the Eyedropper/Paint Bucket Options dialog box (shown in Figure 6-18), where you can select or deselect multiple options regarding paint style information.

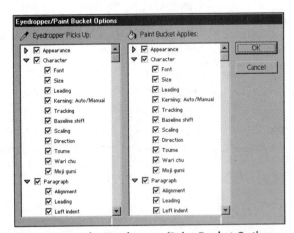

Figure 6-18: The Eyedropper/Paint Bucket Options dialog box

Note

You can also use the Eyedropper and Paint Bucket tools with Type. This makes it speedy to absorb and apply colors to type. For more on this feature see Chapter 8, "Manipulating Type."

The Eyedropper tool

The Eyedropper tool samples paint style information from a path or a placed image and stores it in the Paint Style Fill and Stroke boxes (on the toolbox), without selecting that path. The information stays there until you change the information in the color palette, select another path with different paint style information, or click any other path or placed image with a different paint style. Pressing the Shift key when the Eyedropper tool is active enables it to do *Direct Sucking*. Direct Sucking is used to pull colors from anywhere, including such areas within gradients.

Tip

If you have paths selected when you click with the Eyedropper tool, all selected objects in the document are changed to the paint style of the path that you clicked. If you hold down the Option [Alt] key, the Eyedropper tool toggles to the Paint Bucket tool.

The Paint Bucket tool

The Paint Bucket tool is used for applying the current paint style to both paths and 1-bit TIFF images.

Holding down the Shift key when clicking a path fills the Paint Bucket tool with the current paint style and also selects that path. If the path was already selected, a Shift+click deselects it. Pressing the Option [Alt] key toggles from the Paint Bucket tool to the Eyedropper tool.

ASK TOULOUSE: Why Use the Eyedropper and Paint Bucket Tools?

Baltazar: Why should I use the Paint Bucket and Eyedropper tools? It seems like a lot of work.

Toulouse: One reason is that you can be assured that your colors are consistent throughout the illustration. So, for example, if you used a custom color somewhere that you want to use again somewhere else, you don't try to duplicate it with a CMYK mix that may not be an exact match. And you don't have to select the objects you're clicking with the Paint Bucket tool.

Baltazar: What's all this nonsense about sampling colors from pixel-based images?

Toulouse: You can sample colors from any placed image by holding down the Shift key and clicking on the color you want.

Baltazar: Wow. Does the Eyedropper sample an average color, like that "other" illustration program?

Toulouse: No, it samples the exact pixel you click.

Baltazar: Thanks for the info. I won't tell the Cylons, honest.

Toulouse: Oh, sure, rat out your race but keep quiet about graphics applications. . . . I believe you.

Transparency Basics

One of the major advances included as part of Illustrator 9 was the inclusion of transparency features. These features let you set the Opacity for current object from 0 percent (fully transparent) to 100 percent (zero transparency). Transparency for the selected object can be set using the Transparency palette, shown in Figure 6-19. This palette can also set the blending mode for mixing the background colors and the transparent object colors.

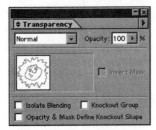

Figure 6-19: The Transparency palette

The Transparency palette includes a preview window where you can view the effects of the various settings on the current object.

Depending on the blending mode that is selected, the Opacity of an object affects the overall color of the object. For example, if a transparent blue object is placed over the top of a yellow object, the overlapped space would be colored green. Blending modes include Normal, Multiply, Screen, Overlay, Soft Light, Hard Light, Color Dodge, Color Burn, Lighten, Darken, Difference, Exclusion, Hue, Saturation, Color, and Luminosity.

Cross-Reference   You can find more information on Transparency and the various Blending modes in Chapter 12, "Understanding Transparency."

The Transparency palette also includes options to Isolate Blending, create a Knockout Group, and to enable the Opacity and Mask to define the knockout shape.

Figure 6-20 shows a transparent object — the nostalgic ghost from the Pacman arcade game. Because the ghost object is transparent, the dots behind it are visible.

Color Filters

The color filters in the Color submenu of the Filter menu really take Illustrator's color capabilities to the next level in many ways. Unfortunately, they fall far short of Photoshop's color capabilities, but they're making good headway.

Figure 6-20: Pacman had better get gobbling with this transparent ghost so close.

Adjust Colors

Adjust Colors increases and decreases process color Fills in each color component. The percentages entered in Adjust Colors are absolute changes, meaning that a 10 percent decrease of cyan when cyan is 100 percent results in 90 percent, and a 10 percent decrease of cyan when cyan is 50 percent results in 40 percent, not 45 percent. If the increase makes the tint of a color greater than 100 percent, it stays at 100 percent, but other colors may still increase if they are not yet at 100 percent. If the decrease makes the tint of a color less than 0 percent, that color remains at 0 percent, but other colors may still decrease, as long as they are not yet at 0 percent. For example, a 25 percent increase to both yellow and magenta to a path with 80 percent yellow and 50 percent magenta results in the colors being 100 percent yellow and 75 percent magenta. Reapplying this filter results in 100 percent yellow and 100 percent magenta. Reapplying this filter at this point results in no change at all.

Figure 6-21 shows the Adjust Colors filter.

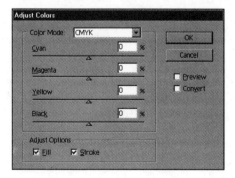

Figure 6-21: The Adjust Colors dialog box

At the bottom of the Adjust Colors dialog box are several options. The Preview checkbox lets you see the changes that have been applied so far. The checkbox automatically converts custom and Illustrator black-based colors to process equivalents.

Tip   You can adjust colors using any color model, even if your selected paths are a different model. Click the Convert checkbox and choose a different model.

The Color Blend filters

Blend Front to Back, Blend Horizontally, and Blend Vertically blend the colors of at least three objects whose ending objects are both process tints or both black tints. The Blend filters do not work with custom colors, patterns, or gradients. Using Blend filters is very similar to using the Blend tool, but instead of making different shape *and* color blends, the Blend filters create new colors between objects automatically. If the ending paths' colors are different color *types*, the Blend filters will produce undesirable results.

The main difference between each of these filters is how each determines what the end paths are, and in what direction the blend flows.

The Convert filters

The three Convert filters — Convert to CMYK, Convert to Grayscale, and Convert to RGB — enable you to change the color model of selected paths with a simple menu selection. In addition to switching between Grayscale, CMYK, and RGB, the Convert filters change custom colors to those color models as well.

The Invert Colors filter

Invert Colors works in strange and mysterious ways on selected paths. Whatever the color of the path, Invert Colors takes the first three colors in the Paint palette (cyan, magenta, and yellow) and subtracts them from 100. If the original color was a shade of Red (for example, where Cyan = 0 percent, Magenta = 100 percent, and Yellow = 100 percent), then Invert Colors makes the new color Cyan = 100 percent, Magenta = 0 percent, and Yellow = 0 percent.

Note   The percentage of black is not affected by Invert Colors. Therefore, this is *not* the same as getting a negative image. Although Invert works poorly with CMYK images, it works perfectly with both grayscale and RGB images.

To use the Invert Colors filter, select the art you wish to invert, and then choose Filter ⇨ Color ⇨ Convert to RGB, Invert Colors, or Convert to CMYK.

Caution   When using the Invert Colors filter, be aware that slight differences may result from changing the color mode of your artwork.

The Overprint Black plug-in

Choosing Filter ⇨ Color ⇨ Overprint Black displays the Overprint Black dialog box (shown in Figure 6-22), which enables you to apply overprinting of black to selected paths. You can select a number of options, including whether to add or remove overprinting from the selected objects. Another option lets you specify the amount of black percentage that is the minimum that will be used to overprint.

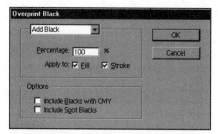

Figure 6-22: The Overprint options appear in the Overprint Black dialog box.

A mistake we have made in the past is thinking that if we select an 85 percent black to overprint then everything from 85 to 100 percent black in the illustration will overprint. But that is not the case — you have to select each object and enter the specific value for that object.

You can specify whether the overprint affects Fills or Strokes or both. The other options determine whether black will overprint when combined with CMY or when part of a spot color.

The Overprint Black filter adds overprinting only to selected objects that are not currently overprinted when the Add Black option is selected in the drop-down list at the top of the dialog box, and it removes overprinting from objects that currently have overprinting when the Remove Black option is selected. In no circumstance does it remove overprinting when the Add Black option is selected, even if the overprinting object does not fall within the parameters of the settings of the Overprint dialog box.

In the Attributes palette, the appropriate checkboxes are selected when you use the filter on selected objects.

The Saturate filter

Saturate adds or subtracts equal amounts of color to the selected objects. This filter does not correspond in any way to saturation changes made by Photoshop;

instead, the color added is proportional to each color in a path. Using Saturate works in much the same way as pressing the Shift key and dragging a triangle to the right in the Color palette. Saturate does not work with patterns or gradients.

The Saturate dialog box (shown in Figure 6-23) enables you to saturate or desaturate, depending on the direction you drag the slider. The Preview checkbox in this dialog box is quite helpful, letting you see what is happening to the paths in real time.

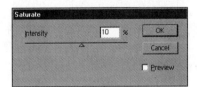

Figure 6-23: The Saturate
dialog box

Manipulating colors with the color filters

The color filters provide automated ways of changing colors for a variety of objects. Most of the filters work on paths that are filled with black or a process color, and some of them work on the Strokes of the paths as well. The following sections describe various uses for the color filters.

Techniques for creating shadows and highlights

You can use color filters to create shadows and highlights for black and process-color paths.

You create most shadows by simply creating a copy of the object and placing it under, and slightly offset from, the original. You can darken the copy in a number of ways, but the easiest way is to use the Adjust Colors filter. Figure 6-24 shows the four steps that you follow to create shadows and highlights. You create highlights the same way as you create shadows, but instead of darkening the copy, you lighten it.

1. Create an object that has several colors in it. Group the individual elements in the object.

2. Copy the object and choose Edit ➪ Paste in Back (⌘+B [Ctrl+B]). Offset the copy down and to the right.

3. Choose Filter ➪ Colors ➪ Adjust Colors. To darken the shadowed copy evenly, add 20 percent to Cyan, Magenta, and Yellow, and 40 percent to Black.

4. To create the highlight, choose Edit ➪ Paste in Back (⌘+B [Ctrl+B]) and offset the copy up and to the left. Decrease all four process colors by 40 percent if the

background is dark or 20 percent if the background is light. The background is dark, so we reduced the color in the highlight by 40 percent of each color.

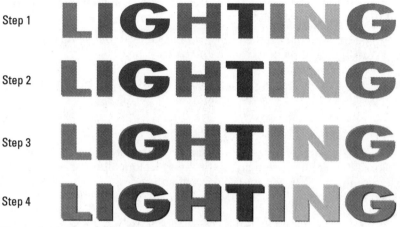

Figure 6-24: Steps for creating highlights and shadows on text

Creating extruded multiple path objects

Usually, you can make objects appear extruded by blending two objects together. If the objects contain multiple paths, however, you have to blend each of the paths separately. And if the objects contain compound paths, the blends that you create will not share the compound attributes of the original objects.

You can use the Blend Front to Back filter to make objects appear to be extruded, as described in the following steps.

1. Release any compound paths in the object and group all the paths in the object together.

2. In the Move dialog box (choose Object ➪ Transform ➪ Move), enter **0.25 pt** in the Horizontal text field and **0.1 pt** in the Vertical text field. Click the Copy button.

3. Choose Arrange ➪ Transform Again (⌘+D [Ctrl+D]) until the object has been duplicated far enough to appear 3D. Copy the final duplicate object. (It should still be selected.)

4. Change the color of the final duplicate object to be the color of the frontmost part of the blend. In this example, we made the final duplicate object black and left the rest of the objects red.

5. Select all the objects and choose Filter ➪ Colors ➪ Blend Front to Back.

6. Choose Edit ➪ Paste in Front (⌘+F [Ctrl+F]) and give a different color to the object just pasted. In the example, we used yellow. Choose Object ➪ Compound Path ➪ Make (⌘+8 [Ctrl+8]) and then Object ➪ Hide Selection (⌘+3 [Ctrl+3]).

7. Continue to select each grouped object, making each group a compound path and then hiding it, until all the paths are hidden.

8. After you have hidden all the paths, choose Object ➪ Show All (⌘+Option+3 [Ctrl+Alt+3]) and then group all the paths together.

Do not make all of the paths one compound path or the color information for each path will be lost.

Creating negatives with the color filters

You can produce negative images in Illustrator almost automatically by using the Invert Colors filter. For a process color, the Invert Colors filter subtracts the tints of cyan, magenta, and yellow from 100 percent and leaves Black as is. On an object that is filled or stroked with black only, the filter subtracts the tint of black from 100 percent.

To get around the way that this filter works when creating negatives, select all the objects that you want to reverse. Next, choose Filter ➪ Colors ➪ Invert Colors, select each path, and check whether the paths have a process color Fill that contains black. If you find any Fills that contain black, manually change black to the correct value.

After you check a path to see whether it is a process color that contains black, hide that path. Using this method can help you be sure that you have checked every path, and you do not have to worry about wasting time by rechecking paths.

Color Management

It can be disheartening to complete a complex project and have the colors displayed in the Illustrator environment not match the output device. A solution to this problem is to use a color-management system that can correctly convert among various color systems. For example, colors in an illustration drawn in the RGB color space that needs to be output to a CMYK printer will need to be accurately converted before the final piece is printed.

Illustrator offers a complete color-management system with several predefined system settings. You can access these settings from the Color Settings dialog box opened with the Edit ➪ Color Settings menu option. Figure 6-25 shows the Color Settings dialog box.

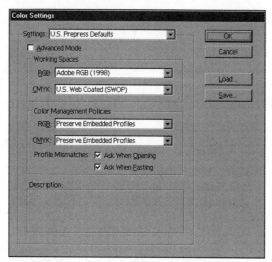

Figure 6-25: The Color Settings dialog box

From the Settings popup menu/drop-down list at the top of the Color Settings dialog box, you can select one of the predefined color-management systems. The options include the following:

✦ **Emulate Adobe Illustrator 6.0** maintains backward capability with previous Illustrator versions. If you have a color-management proofing system that has worked for you with previous projects, this option maintains the process.

✦ **Custom** lets you select your own options. If any of the predefined settings are altered, this option is automatically selected.

✦ **Color Management Off.** Projects that will not be ported to another device have no need for color management. This option turns off the color-management features.

✦ **Emulate Photoshop 4** duplicates the color-management system used by Photoshop 4 and earlier versions of Photoshop.

✦ **Europe Prepress Defaults.** Prepress shops in Europe typically use standard settings. This option matches these European standards.

✦ **Japan Prepress Defaults.** Prepress shops in Japan typically use standard settings. This option matches these Japanese standards.

✦ **Photoshop 5 Default Spaces** uses the color-management system used by Photoshop 5 and later.

✦ **U.S. Prepress Defaults.** Prepress shops in the United States typically use standard settings. This option matches these U.S. standards.

✦ **Web Graphics Defaults** manages the colors of content to be published online on the Web.

✦ **ColorSync Workflow** is available for the Macintosh OS only. It manages color using the ColorSync 3.0 system.

If none of these predefined systems works for you, then you can load your own color-management system (CMS) using the Load button. Or you could tweak the settings and save your own CMS.

The predefined CMS options will select the RGB and CMYK Working Spaces, which are the standard defined color spaces that are used in prepress shops around the world. You can also select a Color Management Policy for both RGB and CMYK color spaces. The policy choices include Off, Preserve Embedded Profiles, and Convert to Working Space. You can specify with checkboxes whether to Ask about Profile Mismatches when opening the file or when pasting objects into the current document.

Tip   When a warning dialog box appears informing you of profile mismatches, you can disable the warning dialog box by selecting the Don't Show Again option in the dialog box. This option disables any future profile mismatch warning dialog boxes. To view the warning boxes again, you will need to select the Reset All Warning Dialogs option in the Preferences dialog box.

At the top of the Color Settings dialog box is a checkbox labeled Advanced Mode. Enabling this checkbox opens the Conversion Options settings. These settings let you select the conversion Engine and the Intent, as shown in Figure 6-26. The Color Settings dialog box also includes a useful Description field. In this field, the various settings are described when the mouse cursor is placed over them.

Many output device manufacturers supply color profiles that can be loaded into Illustrator. Using these profiles helps insure consistent output from Illustrator to that particular device. To load these color profiles onto your system, copy the profile file into the ColorSync Profiles folder on Macintosh systems or into the Windows\System\Color directory on Windows-based machines.

At any time, you can change the Color Profile that is used by a project. To change the Color Profile, select Edit ➪ Assign Profile. The options, shown in Figure 6-27, include from Don't Color Manage This Document, to use the Working CMYK, or to select a new Profile from a drop-down list.

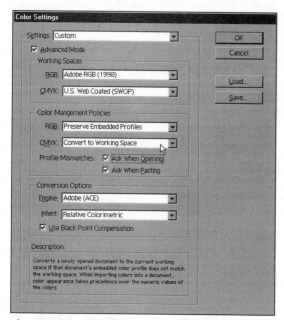

Figure 6-26: The Color Settings dialog box in Advanced Mode

Figure 6-27: The Assign Profile dialog box

Once a color profile is assigned, you can specify whether that profile is saved with the file. Figure 6-28 shows the Illustrator Native Format Options dialog box that appears when a document is saved using the File ⇨ Save command. One of the checkboxes in this dialog box is to Embed ICC Profile. The current profile is displayed next to the option.

When you print a document, the specified color profile is displayed along with the Intent setting. Prior to printing, you can specify a different color Profile and Intent. To open the Print dialog box, select File ⇨ Print.

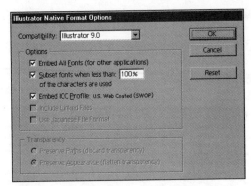

Figure 6-28: The Illustrator Native Format Options dialog box includes an option to Embed ICC Profile.

Gradients

The gradient feature has no rivals. It is by far the most powerful gradient-creating mechanism available for PostScript drawing programs. Gradients in Adobe Illustrator can have 32 different colors, from end to end in a linear gradient, and from center to edge in a radial gradient. Gradients can consist of custom colors, process colors, or just plain black and white. The midpoint of two adjacent colors can be adjusted smoothly and easily toward either color. The Gradient palette can be made available at all times because it is a floating palette, and you can access it or view it by pressing F9. And, for what they do, gradients are easier to use than blends.

You can apply gradients only to the Fills of paths, not to Strokes or text objects. Gradients cannot be used in patterns, either.

Checking the Compatible Gradients checkbox in the Document Setup box prevents most gradient problems from occurring. When you're printing to PostScript Level 1 printers, checking this box speeds gradient printing dramatically. Compatible gradients bypass a high-level imaging system within Illustrator that older printers and printers without genuine Adobe PostScript (commonly referred to as "PostScript clones") cannot understand. Checking this box may cause documents to print more slowly on printers that would ordinarily be able to print those documents without the checkbox.

The Gradient tool

You use the Gradient tool to change the angle and the starting and ending points for a linear gradient, as well as set the location of the center and edges of a radial gradient. The gradient applied with the Gradient tool will match the gradient displayed in the Gradient palette. The default gradient is black and white with white on the left and black on the right. The left side of the gradient is applied where the

Gradient tool is clicked. For the default gradient, this creates a white highlight if the Radial Gradient type is used.

Unlike blends, which you can create only with the Blend tool, gradients can survive quite nicely without the Gradient tool. Gradients are created with the Gradient palette if a setting is altered. They can also be applied by clicking the Gradient icon in the toolbox, which is the middle icon positioned under the Fill and Stroke boxes. The keyboard shortcut for this icon is the period (.) key. Double-clicking the Gradient tool displays the Gradient palette.

To use the Gradient tool, you must select at least one path that is filled with a gradient. Dragging with the Gradient Vector tool on linear gradients changes the angle and the length of the gradient, as well as the start and end points. Dragging with the Gradient tool on radial gradients determines the start position and end position of the gradient. Clicking with the Gradient tool resets the highlight to a new location.

Using preset gradients

To choose a preset gradient, select a path and make sure the Fill box is active in the toolbox. In the Swatches palette, click the gradient swatch icon at the bottom of the palette. The four default gradient presets appear alone in the swatches. None of the options are selected until you click one of them.

 Cross-Reference Preset gradients appear in Illustrator because they exist in the Illustrator startup file, which is discussed in Chapter 15, "Customizing and Optimizing Illustrator."

Using the Gradient palette

The Gradient palette, if nothing else, is really *neat* looking, with all sorts of nifty little controls at your disposal for creating and modifying gradients, as shown in Figure 6-29.

 Note By default, the Gradient palette is collapsed. You can expand the palette by clicking on the arrows to the left of the tab.

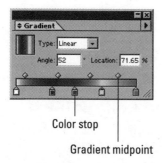

Color stop

Gradient midpoint

Figure 6-29: The Gradient palette

The bottom of the Gradient palette is where you control what colors appear in the gradient and where the colors are in relation to one another.

To add a new color to the bar, click below the bar where you want the new color to appear. The new color will be a step between the left color slider and the right color slider. The percentage depends on how close you click to either end. In other words, the closer you click to the left end, the closer that color will be to the left slider. Then change the settings in the Color palette to create the color you want for that *color stop.* You can enter up to 32 color stops between the two end colors. When a color stop is selected, entering a different percentage in the text field on the right changes the color stop's position.

Tip   You can copy a sample color to the Gradient palette by Shift+clicking with the Eyedropper anywhere on the screen.

The diamonds above the color bar show where the midpoint between two color stops is. By moving the midpoint left or right, you alter the halfway color between two color stops. When a diamond is selected, entering a different percentage in the text field on the right changes the diamond's position.

Here's an example of gradients in action:

1. Draw a series of vertical rectangles, some overlapping, with their bases horizontally even. In this example (see Figure 6-30), we angled the top of one of the rectangles.

2. Fill the rectangles with the Black & White gradient (by clicking it in the Swatches palette) and be sure that the gradient angle in the Gradient palette is 0 degrees.

3. In the Swatches palette, duplicate the Black & White gradient and name the copy "Buildings." In the Gradient palette, enter a new color stop at 31 percent across and make the color 70% Black. Change the color of the leftmost color stop to 85% Black. Apply the "Buildings" gradient to the rectangles.

4. Draw a rectangle and send it behind the buildings. Change the fill to the Black & White gradient and change the gradient angle to 90 degrees and the Position of the Midpoint to 80%.

For added dramatic impact in a cityscape, copy the buildings one by one and Paste in Front (⌘+F [Ctrl+F]). Fill the front copies with a custom pattern of lights with a transparent background.

Shadows, highlights, ghosting, and embossing

You can use gradients to simulate special effects by either duplicating and altering a gradient or by using the Gradient Vector tool on similar gradients.

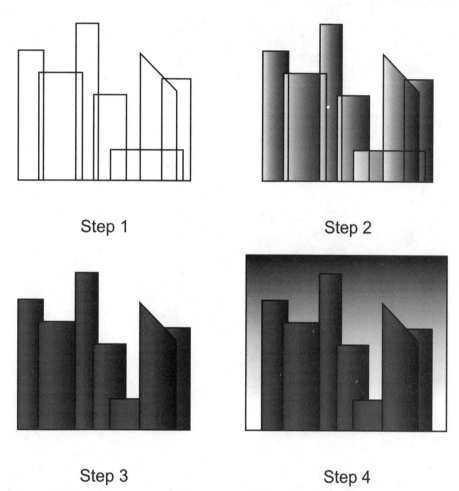

Step 1

Step 2

Step 3

Step 4

Figure 6-30: A cityscape created from rectangles and gradients

Making Ghosting

You can simulate ghosting by using the Gradient Vector tool to slightly alter the starting and ending locations of the gradient. Follow these steps to "ghost" some text:

1. Ghosting effects are easiest to see on text, so create a rectangle and then create large text on top of the rectangle.

2. Convert the type into outlines and position the type outline just to the right and below the center of the rectangle.

3. Select both the type and rectangle and apply a Gradient Fill to them. For Figure 6-31, we used the Red & Yellow gradient at 90 degrees (of course, the color isn't shown in Figure 6-31).

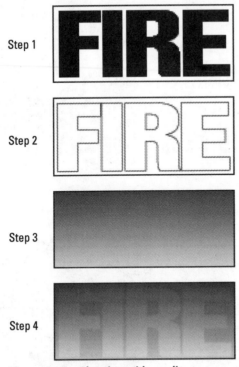

Step 1

Step 2

Step 3

Step 4

Figure 6-31: Ghosting with gradients

4. Move the type to the center of the rectangle. The type appears to be ghosted there, as shown in Figure 6-31.

Embossing

Offsetting two copies of the original graduated image creates embossed gradient images. In one offset image, the gradient is lightened; in the other, the gradient is darkened. Here's how to do it:

1. Create text and convert it to outlines.

2. Select the outlined type and choose Unite from the Pathfinder palette. Draw a rectangle around the type and send it to the back.

3. Select both the type outline and the rectangle and Fill them with a Gradient. Use a process gradient for this example. Drag the Gradient Vector tool across the rectangle (keeping both objects selected) to set the gradient length and angle.

4. In the Swatches palette, select the gradient used for both the rectangle and type outlines, and make two duplicates of it. Make one duplicate lighter by selecting each color stop and moving it to the left. Make one gradient darker than the original by moving each color stop to the right. Using the Move dialog

box, create a copy of the path that's offset a few points up and to the left. Create another copy offset a few points down and to the right.

5. Fill the upper-left path with the lighter gradient you created and the lower-right path with the darker one you made.

6. Select the middle type path and choose Object ➪ Arrange ➪ Bring to Front (⌘+Shift+] [Ctrl+Shift+]]). The type appears embossed, as shown in Figure 6-32.

Step 1

Step 2

Step 3

Step 4

Step 5

Step 6

Figure 6-32: Steps for making embossed type

Tip   To make embossed images seem sunken rather than raised, make the lighter image below and to the right and the darker image above and to the left. To make the image seem further raised or recessed, increase the distance between the original path and the offset images.

Simulating Shadows

You can simulate shadows by creating darker gradients based on an existing gradient. You create the new, darker gradient in a path that is the same shape as the object causing the shadow, as follows:

1. For this example, use the cityscape created in Figure 6-30. Create a rectangle at the bottom of the city and give it a gradient from light to dark. Send the rectangle behind the city. Duplicate the gradient and add some black to the color stops in the duplicate.

2. Select the city and choose the Reflect tool. Reflect a copy of the city across the base of the city.

3. Unite the reflected city buildings with Unite from the Pathfinder palette. Fill the united city with the darker gradient.

4. Using the Shear tool, adjust the shadow to more accurately resemble the light source. The result should resemble Figure 6-33.

Taking Gradients Where Gradients Fear to Go

Many software programs accept Illustrator files but don't care for gradients very much. Dimensions 3, for example, ignores gradients. And even Illustrator says "uh-uh" when you try to use a gradient in a pattern.

The solution to this problem is to use the Expand feature (Object ⇨ Expand), described in Chapter 9, "Applying Fills and Strokes." Expand converts gradients into blends automatically.

After expanding, select the blends and choose Merge from the Pathfinder palette, which gets rid of the overlapping areas always present with blends in Illustrator.

In addition, gradients cannot be used in Strokes of paths. To get around this limitation, select the path, make the Stroke the correct weight, and choose Object ⇨ Path ⇨ Outline Path. The Stroke is transformed into a closed path, which you can then fill with a gradient.

Before using Outline Path, be sure that the weight of the Stroke on the path to be outlined is the correct weight; otherwise, you have no way, short of undoing the whole thing, to convert outlined Strokes back into a single path.

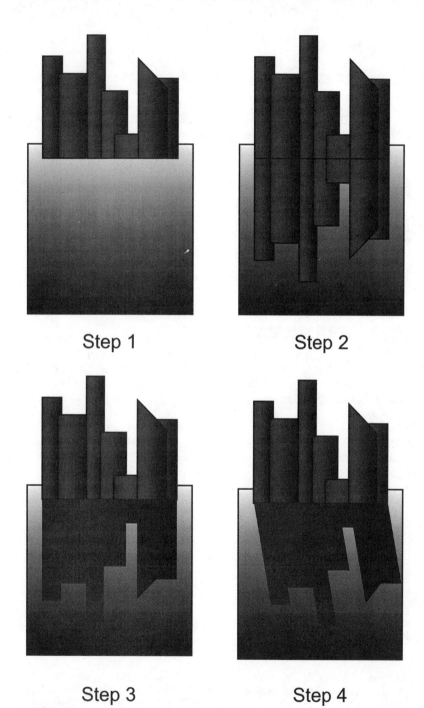

Figure 6-33: Creating a shadow on a gradient

Gradient Mesh

The Gradient Mesh tool changes a normal filled path into a multicolored object with the click of a button. You click and create a new color at the clicked point. The new color will blend smoothly into the object's original color. Use the Gradient Mesh tool to add highlights, shading, and three-dimensional effects. Figure 6-34 shows an object created with the Gradient Mesh tool.

Figure 6-34: An object created with the Gradient Mesh tool

Working with meshes

Mesh objects are created whenever the Gradient Mesh tool or the Object ⇨ Create Gradient Mesh menu option is used on a closed-path object. You can also change open paths into mesh objects. Open paths are automatically made into closed paths by connecting the starting and ending points.

When you use the Object ⇨ Create Gradient Mesh menu option, the Create Gradient Mesh dialog box, shown in Figure 6-35, appears. This dialog box lets you specify the number of rows and columns to include in the mesh. Between each row and column is a line that is known as a *mesh line*. These mesh lines are visible when you select the mesh object.

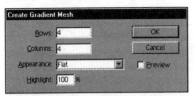

Figure 6-35: The Create Gradient Mesh dialog box

You can also specify its Appearance to be Flat, To Center, or To Edges. The Flat setting does not add a highlight to the mesh. The To Center option causes the center of the mesh to the have the brightest highlight, and the To Edges option makes the brightest highlights at the edges of the mesh. The Highlight value sets the maximum highlight value.

At the intersection of mesh lines are *mesh points*. These mesh points are similar to anchor points with a major difference. Mesh points can also be assigned a color. Mesh points are identified by a small diamond shape. You can add and delete mesh points using the Direct Selection tool the same way as adding and deleting anchor points on a path. You can also add anchor points on a mesh line. You can use these anchor points to change the curvature of the mesh lines. The Direct Selection tool can also be used to edit the position of the mesh points. The mesh lines will move along with the mesh points.

The areas in between mesh lines are called *mesh patches*. These mesh patches can also be given a color.

Adding highlights and color

Use the Gradient Mesh tool to add a highlight to an object or to add some shading. Always deselect the object you wish to add a point to, pick the color of the point in the Color palette, and then click to set the point. You can add color to a mesh patch by clicking in the middle of the mesh patch. Colors can be dragged and dropped from the Color or Swatches palettes onto a mesh point or patch. The Paint Bucket is also useful to place color.

You can also use the Gradient Mesh tool to add, delete, and edit mesh points. To add a mesh point to a mesh object without changing its color, hold down the Shift key while clicking the mesh object. Using the Option [Alt] key, you can delete a mesh point. To edit a mesh point, you simply need to drag it with the Gradient Mesh tool. Holding the Shift key down while dragging causes the point to move along the current mesh line without changing the mesh line's position.

Changing highlight color

With the Direct Selection tool, select a point on the mesh and change its color values in the Color palette. This action changes the color of the mesh point or mesh patch.

Adding multiple highlights

Clicking an object more than once with the Gradient Mesh tool adds more blends to the object. The strange thing about this is that each click creates a new horizontal and vertical axis. This is the reason the tool is called a "mesh"—the more clicks that are created, the more individual lines appear until the base object appears as a complex mesh of lines. Each intersection of lines is a point of color that can be changed. However, when you change a color, adjacent intersecting points aren't updated. The following steps give you an example of what happens when you add multiple highlights to an object.

1. Create a dark blue rectangle and deselect it.

2. Change the color in the Color palette to a bright yellow.

3. With the Gradient Mesh tool, click in the upper left quadrant of the rectangle. A yellow point of light appears, creating a sort of radial gradient.

4. Deselect, change the Fill color to bright green, and click another point in the lower right quadrant. When you do this, two additional points that are somewhere between the blue background and the yellow and green highlights appear, as shown in Figure 6-36.

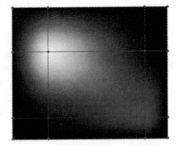

Figure 6-36: An object highlighted with a single highlight (left) and with two highlights (right) using the Gradient Mesh tool

You can create very complex Gradient Mesh objects with just a dozen or so clicks; these objects are editable, but you'll need to somehow keep track of which points were the originals, so that all the other ones will update automatically.

Tip   You can change the background color of the object you're editing after several highlights have been added by selecting *all* the points on the perimeter of the original object with the Direct Selection tool. Every click with the Gradient Mesh tool adds four points to the perimeter of the object.

Adding highlights to complex shapes

Adding a gradient mesh to a simple shape isn't that impressive, but when used on complex shapes with lots of curves, the Gradient Mesh really starts to shine. For a quick example, we've added some highlights to a group of balloons. The Gradient Mesh will make the highlight curve to follow the shape of the object.

1. Create a bunch of balloons with unique shapes using the Pencil tool. Make sure that the paths are closed. Holding down the Option [Alt] key will automatically close the path.

2. Change the Fill color in the toolbox for each balloon and select the strings to have no Fill color. The bunch of balloons before a Gradient Mesh is applied is shown on the left of Figure 6-37.

3. With the Selection tool, select one of the balloon objects and click on the Gradient Mesh tool. With the Gradient Mesh tool click near the right edge of the selected balloon object. Then click on the white color in the Color palette to make the highlight white.

4. Repeat step 3 for all the balloon shapes. The resulting balloons with highlights are shown on the right of Figure 6-37.

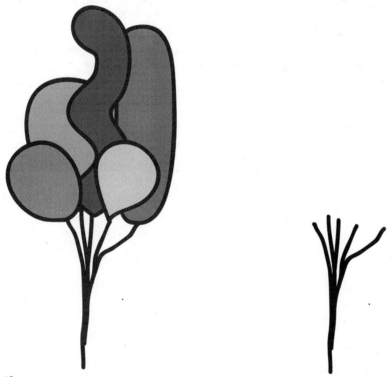

Figure 6-37: A set of balloons before (left) and after (right) applying Gradient Mesh

Summary

Despite all those design classes in college that taught how to use colors, you really can't apply correct colors unless you understand how Illustrator works with colors. This chapter presents these important details, including the following:

✦ Use the Swatches palette to store and apply commonly used colors.

✦ You can access Pantone colors by choosing Window ➪ Swatch Libraries ➪ Pantone.

✦ The Color palette enables you to choose colors from a Color Ramp and to mix colors using interactive sliders.

✦ Change the color space from grayscale to CMYK to RGB to HSB by selecting one option from the Color pop-up menu.

✦ The Stroke palette is used to change the Stroke weight, Cap and Join style, and Dash pattern.

✦ Paths and type can be colored quickly by using the Eyedropper tool (to sample colors from paths or placed images) and the Paint Bucket tool (to apply those sampled colors).

✦ Adjust Colors adds and subtracts various amounts of process colors from multiple colored objects.

✦ The color blend filters look at two opposite paths and blend between the two colors.

✦ Saturate increases or decreases the amount of color in selected paths.

✦ Color Management Profiles can be specified and saved with a document.

✦ The Gradient Mesh tool makes adding shadows, highlights, and shaping a breeze.

✦   ✦   ✦

Putting Illustrator to Work

Part II puts you to work learning about type and how to fine-tune those paths and objects you drew in Part I. It also gives you a chance to bend and distort paths. This part includes a healthy dose of the hard stuff, such as compound paths, masks, blends, patterns, and type.

Organizing Artwork

In addition to all the drawing tools that are available, Illustrator includes many features that don't actually create any objects in the document, but are useful for organizing objects. These features include grouping objects, working with layers, using grids and guides (including Smart Guides), and measuring. This chapter covers these features.

Locking and Hiding Objects

All objects in Illustrator can be locked or hidden — including guides. Locking and hiding are about the same, and the results are only marginally different. In a way, hiding is an "invisible lock."

Locking

Locked objects cannot be moved or changed, but they are always visible and will always print (locked objects cannot be hidden). To lock an object, select it and choose Object ➪ Lock ➪ Selection (⌘+2 [Ctrl+2]). The selected object is not only locked, but also deselected. In fact, an object is unselectable when locked. Because a locked object can't be selected, it can't be changed, and in Illustrator, objects are modifiable only when selected.

A locked object remains locked when the document is saved and closed. As a result, locked objects are still locked the next time you open the document. Locked objects print with no indication as to whether they are locked or not.

To unlock an object, choose Object ➪ Unlock All (⌘+Option+2 [Ctrl+Alt+2]). You have no way to unlock just a few objects locked with the Lock command.

The Object ➪ Lock menu also include options to lock All Artwork Above and to lock Other Layers. These options will let you lock all the objects that are above the current selection and all other layers so you can concentrate on the current one.

Tip A tricky way to invisibly "copyright" your illustration is to create a small text box in a far corner of the pasteboard with your copyright information in it, color the text white, and lock the text box. No one will know it is there, and it can't be easily selected. In fact, it'll even print if it is placed on top of a background in another program.

We like to lock objects under these circumstances:

✦ When the document is full of complex artwork, so we can do a Select All and not have to wait forever for the selection to finish.

✦ When we don't want to accidentally move or change certain artwork.

✦ When we can't easily select paths that are under other paths (in which case, we lock the ones on top).

✦ When we have to fit an illustration into a certain area (in which case, we create a box of that size and lock it so we have an instant boundary to work with).

Hiding

Sometimes you don't want to see certain objects on your document page—perhaps because they obstruct your view of other objects or they take a long time to redraw. In these cases, it's a good idea to hide the objects in question. To do so, select them and choose Object ➪ Hide ➪ Selection (⌘+3 [Ctrl+3]).

Hidden objects are invisible and unselectable; they still exist in the document, but they do not print. When a document is reopened, hidden objects reappear.

To show (and select) all hidden objects, choose Object ➪ Show All (⌘+Shift+3 [Ctrl+Shift+3]). Think of it as "unhide." You have no way to show just a few of the hidden objects when using the Show All command.

Like the Lock command, you can also select Object ➪ Hide ➪ All Artwork Above and Object ➪ Hide ➪ Other Layers.

Object information

Choosing Window ➪ Show Attributes (F11) brings up the Attributes palette, shown in Figure 7-1. In this palette, you can add notes to any selected object, set overprint options, reverse path direction (if the object is part of a compound path), display or hide the center point of the object, and change the mathematical formula which determines whether a filled section is a hole or not (this is know as the fill rule). At least one object must be selected in order to choose Attributes.

Don't Show Center

Show Center

Reverse Path Direction on/off

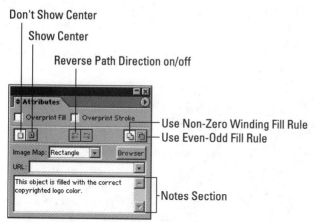

Use Non-Zero Winding Fill Rule
Use Even-Odd Fill Rule

Notes Section

Figure 7-1: The Attributes palette

Tip   A handy way to "copyright" your artwork is to select all the objects, and then go to the Attributes palette and enter your copyright information within the palette.

Cross-Reference   The Attributes palette includes some additional features that are useful for Web graphics such as specifying an image map, attaching a URL to the selected item and providing a button for opening a web browser. These features are covered in more detail in Chapter 17, "Using Illustrator to Generate Web Graphics."

Stacking Order

Stacking order is a crucial concept that you need to understand in the world of Adobe Illustrator. This concept is not the same as the layer concept that is discussed later in this chapter; rather it is the forward/backward relationship between objects within each layer.

After you create the first object in Illustrator, the next object is created *above* the first object, or on top of it. The third object is created above both the first and second objects. This cycle continues indefinitely, with objects being stacked one on top of another.

A great deal of planning goes into creating an illustration so that the first object you draw is on the bottom of the pile and the last object you draw ends up on the top. To make your life more pleasant, Illustrator has the capability to move objects up and down (forward or backward) through the stack of objects. In fact, Illustrator's method of moving objects up and down is so simple and basic that it is also quite limiting.

You can change the stacking order of objects in Illustrator relative to foreground and background, either all the way to the bottom or all the way to the top, or you can move objects up or down through the stacking order. Figure 7-2 shows the same illustration after various objects were moved in the stacking order.

Figure 7-2: The original art (left) and after the stacking order of various pieces has changed (right)

To move an object to the front, choose Object ⇨ Arrange ⇨ Bring to Front (⌘+Shift+] [Ctrl+Shift+]]). The selected object is brought forward so that it is in front of every other object (but only in that layer; layers are discussed later in this chapter). If more than one object is selected, the topmost object of the selected group is at the very top and the bottommost object of the selected group is beneath all the other selected objects — but all the selected objects will be on top of all the nonselected objects. Bring to Front is not available when no objects are selected. Multiple-selected paths and grouped paths still retain their front/back position relative to each other.

To move an object to the back, choose Object ⇨ Arrange ⇨ Send to Back (⌘+Shift+[[Ctrl+Shift+[]). The selected object is sent to the back so that it is behind every other object. Send to Back is not available when no objects are selected. Multiple selected paths and grouped paths still retain their front/back position relative to each other. Illustrator enables you to move selected objects through the stacking order one object at a time, forward or backward. To move selected objects forward one object at a time, choose Object ⇨ Arrange ⇨ Bring Forward (⌘+] [Ctrl+]]). To move selected objects backward one object at a time, choose Object ⇨ Arrange ⇨ Send Backward (⌘+[[Ctrl+[]).

Individual characters in a string of text work in a similar manner to their object cousins when it comes to front/back placement. The first character typed is placed at the bottom of the text block, and the last character typed is placed at the top, as shown in Figure 7-3. To move individual characters forward or backward, you must first choose Type ➪ Create Outlines (⌘+Shift+O [Ctrl+Shift+O]) and select the outline of the character you wish to arrange.

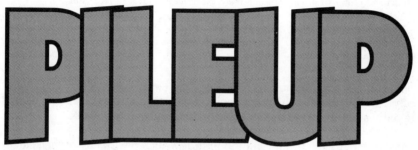

Figure 7-3: Text characters that overlap each other

Try as you may, you cannot change the forward/backward relationship of Strokes and Fills. Strokes are always in front of Fills for the same path. To get the Fill to cover or overlap the Stroke, you must copy the path, use the Paste in Front command (choose Edit ➪ Paste in Front or press ⌘+F [Ctrl+F]), and then remove the Stroke from the path you just pasted.

Pasting objects in front of and behind selected objects

Choosing Paste in Front (⌘+F [Ctrl+F]) from the Edit menu pastes any objects on the clipboard on top of any selected objects or on the top of the current layer if no objects are selected.

Choosing Paste in Back (⌘+B [Ctrl+B]) from the Edit menu pastes any objects on the clipboard behind any selected objects or on the bottom of the current layer if no objects are selected.

In addition, both Paste in Front and Paste in Back paste objects in the same location as the copied object, even from document to document. If the documents are different sizes, Illustrator pastes them in the same location relative to the center of each document. If the clipboard is empty, or if type selected with a Type tool is on the clipboard, these options are not available.

Note Copied items in Illustrator always retain their layer name and related layer information. For example, when you copy an item that is on a layer named "X-Flies" and paste that item in another document that contains an X-Flies layer, the item appears on the X-Flies layer. If the document doesn't contain that layer, a new layer is created with that name and the item appears on that layer. This only works if the Paste Remembers Layers option is checked in the Layers palette, which is discussed later in this chapter. Layers are covered later in this chapter.

Groups

Grouping is the process of putting together a series of objects that need to remain spatially constant in relationship to each other. Groups can be made up of as little as one path, and they may contain an unlimited number of objects.

To group objects together, they should first be selected with any of the selection tools. After you select the objects, choose Object ➪ Group (⌘+G [Ctrl+G]) to make the separate objects stay together when selected.

Selecting any object in a group with the regular Selection tool selects all the objects in that group and makes all the points in a path solid (selected). To see how the Group Selection tool works with selecting groups, see the "Using the Group Selection tool" section that follows.

Not only can several objects be grouped together, but groups can also be grouped together to form a group of groups in which a hierarchical series of grouped groups exists. In addition, groups can be grouped to individual objects or to several other objects.

After a set of objects or groups is grouped together, grouping it again produces no effect. The computer does not beep at you, display a dialog box, or otherwise indicate that the objects or groups you are attempting to group are already grouped. Of course, it never hurts to choose Object ➪ Group (⌘+G [Ctrl+G]) again if you are not sure if they are grouped. If they weren't grouped before, they now are, and if they were grouped before, nothing unusual or unexpected happens.

For an illustration that includes multiple paths as part of one item, the objects are much easier to manipulate if they are grouped. For example, in an illustration of horse grazing in a valley, you can group short grass together as one group, long grass as one group, the horse outlines and Fills as one group, and the hillside outline and Fills as one group. The tree outline and bark detail can be one group as well.

Tip If you are having trouble selecting all the objects for each type in a group, choose Select ➪ Same ➪ Style after one object is selected. This process usually (but not always) selects all the objects of one type.

Grouping similar areas is helpful for moving entire areas forward or backward as well as for doing any type of horizontal or vertical movement or transformation on a set of objects.

Caution

If you group several objects that are on different layers, all the objects move to the topmost layer and form a group there. This means that the perceived stacking order may change, and this can change the appearance of your Illustration.

Ungrouping

To ungroup groups (separate them into stand-alone paths and objects), choose Object ⇨ Ungroup (⌘+Shift+G [Ctrl+Shift+G]), and any selected groups become ungrouped. Ungrouping, like grouping, works on one set of groups at a time. For example, if you have two groups that are grouped together, ungrouping that group results in the two original groups. (Don't worry, we're just as confused as you are in this area.) If Ungroup is chosen again, those two groups also become ungrouped.

Tip

When you absolutely do not want anything in a group grouped with anything else — and you suspect that there may be several minigroups within the group you have selected — simply press ⌘+Shift+G [Ctrl+Shift+G] several times. You do not need to select the subgroups individually to ungroup them. To get rid of all the groups in your illustration, choose Select ⇨ All (⌘+A [Ctrl+A]) and then proceed to ungroup (⌘+Shift+G [Ctrl+Shift+G]) several times. To remove certain objects from a group or compound path, select just these objects, cut, and Paste in Front (or Paste in Back).

When you're ungrouping, groups must be selected with either the Group Selection tool or the regular Selection tool.

Using the Group Selection tool

The Group Selection tool is used primarily to select groups within other groups or individual paths within groups. To access the Group Selection tool, click the Direct Selection tool in the toolbox and drag to the right to the Group Selection tool. Clicking once with the Group Selection tool on any path selects that particular path. Clicking again with the Group Selection tool on the same path selects the group that path is in. Clicking yet again selects the group that the previously selected group is in.

To move a path that is part of a group, do not ungroup the path; instead, select the path with the Group Selection tool and move it.

Caution

If you select a path in a group with the Group Selection tool and then click the same path again to move it, the group that path is in is selected instead. To avoid this problem, either select and move the group at one time or use the Direct Selection tool to select and move the path.

If several different paths are selected with the Group Selection tool either by dragging a marquee or Shift+clicking, clicking again on a selected path or object selects the group that object is in. If that object's group is already selected, then the group that the selected group is in is selected.

The Group Selection tool also selects compound paths. The first click selects an individual path within the compound path, and the second click selects the entire compound path.

Using the Shift key with the Group Selection tool on selected paths or objects deselects just one path at a time. Shift+clicking a path that has just been deselected reselects that path; it does not deselect the group that path is in.

Tip   For quick access to the Group Selection tool, press the Option [Alt] key when the Direct Selection Tool is the active tool. But release the Option [Alt] key before the mouse button is released or you'll have a duplicated path or object. The Ctrl+Tab toggles between the Direct Selection and regular Selection tools. Pressing the ⌘ [Ctrl] and Option [Alt] keys together accesses the Group Selection tool, no matter which tool is selected in the toolbox!

Layers

The layering feature of Illustrator provides an easy and powerful way to separate artwork into individual sections. A *layer* is a separate section of the document that is on its own level, above, under, or in between other layers, but never on the same level as another layer. It is like have a separate document contained within the current document. Each layer has its own stacking order, which determines what appears on top of what. You can view these sections separately, locked, hidden, and rearranged around each other. Figure 7-4 shows objects that have been layered, along with a snazzy poem.

You create, control, and manipulate layers by using the Layers palette. Each layer can have its own color, and that color shows when all paths and points of objects are selected.

Note   You can create as many layers as you want, up to the limitations of application memory. To make sure that the Adobe people were on the up-and-up about this, we created 5,000 layers in one document. It worked without ever questioning the need for 5,000 layers. Why would you need 5,000 layers? We hope you wouldn't, but you shouldn't have any fears that you will not be able to create enough layers for an illustration. Of course, having all those layers to work with slowed the operation of Illustrator to a crawl. We had to click the mouse button and hold on the menu bar for about 3 seconds before the menu appeared. Suffice it to say, the more layers you create after a certain point (several hundred), the slower Illustrator runs.

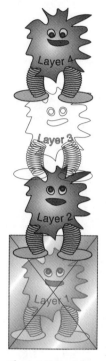

The Paths and Points and Handles
All of them wearing open-toed sandals
Had a dilemma, a confusing vector problem
That stumped even the most brightest of them
(Editors noted that this rhyming was sad
"It's unbalanced and ugly and just plain bad")

W'ever objects would meet, yet stay separated
They'd still be intermingled and some even dated
Groups were formed with a hierarchical slant
"We paths stick together" was their war cry and chant
Yet that wasn't enough, grouping groups was confusing
After keeping score for a while, the users were losing

Adobe Techs fielded support calls by the hundred zillions
So busy their Sega scores never made it to the millions
Suddenly the engineers assigned to make vectors better
Thought "We'll make layers, and make them to the letter"
Layers were magic and frosting and sugar and spice
The things of calories, tooth decay, and Disney mice

Vector objects rejoiced and cheered and screamed in glee,
"This is how life in a PostScript application should be"
Layers could be moved and previewed and printed
They could be colored and of course the fonts were still hinted
When the Paths and Points and Handles heard this great news
They ditched those open-toed sandals and bought leather dress shoes....

Figure 7-4: A layers' Seussian story

Getting started with layers

The Layers palette (shown in Figure 7-5) is the control center where all layer-related activities take place. Most activities occur on the main section of the Layers palette, which is always visible when the Layers palette is onscreen. Other activities take place in the pop-up menu that appears when you press the triangle in the upper-right corner of the palette.

The Layers palette includes some useful features. First is the capability to display only specific layers in the palette for those illustrations with tons of layers. Second is the capability to drag to a hidden layer. Third, a layer that is not set to print is displayed in italics so that you can see quickly what will print and what won't.

Using the layers palette

After you realize that you need to use layers, what do you do? The only way to create, manipulate, and delete layers is by using the Layers palette.

Visibility toggle

Lock toggle

Expand/Contract toggle

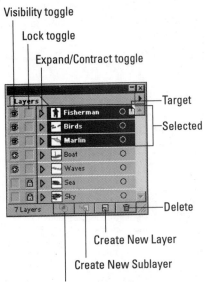

Target

Selected

Delete

Create New Layer

Create New Sublayer

Make/Release Clipping Mask

Figure 7-5: The Layers palette

These steps show how to create new layers, change layer names, set colors, and select and modify options:

1. If the Layers palette is not showing, choose Window ➪ Show Layers (F7). When you open the Layers palette for the first time in a new document, you see only Layer 1 listed.

2. To create a new layer, click the New Layer icon at the bottom of the palette (it looks like a piece of paper with the corner folded over). If you hold down the Option [Alt] key while clicking the New Layer icon, the Layer Options dialog box appears. You can also click the triangle in the upper-right corner of the palette to display a pop-up menu. Drag over to the first item, New Layer, to display the New Layer dialog box.

3. In the Layer Options dialog box, shown in Figure 7-6, the name of the new layer, Layer 2, is highlighted. To change this name, type a new name to replace the generic name. You can double-click the layer name to make this Layer Options dialog box appear.

Figure 7-6: The Layer Options palette

4. The options below the name affect how the layer works and is viewed. The first option is the color of the paths and points when objects on that layer are selected. Choose one of the preset colors from the pop-up menu/drop-down list or select the Other option to use a Custom Color. Each time you create a new layer, a different color (going in order from the list) is applied to that layer.

5. Select any of the options that you want for this layer. Show makes the objects in the layer visible. Lock prevents objects on this layer from being selected and prevents any objects from being put on this layer. Print enables you to print objects that are on this layer. The Preview option will display the layer objects in Preview mode. If the Preview option is disabled, then Outline mode is used. Dim Placed Images dims any placed images on the layer, making them about 50 percent lighter than normal.

6. Click OK after you choose all the options you want. The new layer appears above the existing layer in the Layers palette. If you want the objects on the new layer to appear below the objects on the existing layer, click the name of the new layer and drag it under Layer 1.

7. To modify the existing layer options, double-click on the layer row. You see the Layer Options dialog box again. Make the changes and choose the options that you want for this layer, and then click OK.

Tip

You can easily bypass the Layer Options dialog box when creating new layers. Clicking the New Layer icon (without pressing Option [Alt]), or pressing Option [Alt] while choosing New Layer from the Layer palette pop-up menu creates a new layer with the default naming scheme. You can always double-click that layer to access its Layer Options.

The main section of the Layers palette

Clicking the Close box in the upper-right corner closes the Layers palette. Another way to close the Layers palette is to choose Window ➪ Hide Layers (F7). To bring the Layers palette back to the screen, choose Window ➪ Show Layers (F7).

Clicking the Collapse box in the upper-right corner of the Layers palette resizes the palette to be collapsed, and then toggles to the previous height.

The left column controls how each layer is viewed. Solid eyes represent a layer that is in Preview mode. Hollow eyes mean that the layer is in Outline mode. No eye means that the layer is hidden. If the layer is a template, the icon of objects is displayed. Clicking a solid or hollow eye toggles it from showing to hidden. Clicking in the Show/Hide Column when no eye is present shows the layer. ⌘ [Ctrl]+clicking the eye changes it from solid (Preview mode) to hollow (Outline mode). Option [Alt]+clicking an eye shows or hides all other layers.

The second column on the left is the Lock/Unlock column. A small lock icon in this column signifies whether each layer is locked or unlocked. An empty column means that the layer is not locked. You can move items to hidden layers as long as those layers are not locked, but you cannot change anything that is already on a hidden layer.

The wide column on the right of the palette lists the names of all the layers in the document. When no documents are open, no layers are listed. The layer that is highlighted is the active layer. All new objects are created on the active layer. Select a range of layers by clicking one layer and holding down the Shift key while clicking another layer. Doing so selects all layers between the two selected layers. You can select layers individually by ⌘ [Ctrl]+clicking each layer to be selected. To deselect a layer, ⌘ [Ctrl]+click it while it is selected. One layer must always be selected.

Within the layer name column is an arrow icon (this arrow is called a disclosure triangle on Mac systems). Clicking this arrow icon displays all the sublayers that make up the layer. Each separate object within the layer is a separate sublayer, as shown in Figure 7-7. To roll the sublayers back up into the layer name, click again on the arrow icon for that layer. Sublayers can be named just like layers. To open the sublayer Options dialog box, double-click the sublayer. The Options dialog box for sublayers includes Show and Lock options.

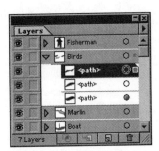

Figure 7-7: Clicking the
arrow icon reveals sublayers.

Between the arrow icon and the layer name is a small preview box. This box displays the contents of the layer.

The layer at the top of the column is the layer that is on top of all the other layers. The layer at the bottom of the column is the layer that is at the bottom of all the other layers. To move a layer (or layers) click it and drag it up or down. As you drag, a dark horizontal line indicates where the layer(s) will be placed when you release the mouse button.

You can undo all layer changes as they happen by choosing Edit ⇨ Undo (⌘+Z [Ctrl+Z]) right afterward.

To the right of the layer's name is a square that shows the layer color. This square appears in the row where at least one object on that layer is selected. You can drag selected objects from one layer to another by dragging on the square. You can select all objects in all layers if you click to the right of the small circle. The square contains the layer color. The layer color can be set using the Layer Options dialog box. These colors help identify all the elements of a layer. A new layer color is automatically selected each time you create a new layer.

Moving objects between layers

To the right of the layer color is a single radio button that appears filled in when the layer includes attributes set with the Appearance palette. You can also drag the appearance settings of an object on one layer to another layer by dragging the small circle to another layer. Here's how:

1. Select the objects that you want to move from one layer to another. If the objects are on one layer, group them together so that you can easily reselect them. (Do not group objects from different layers together or all objects will be placed on the topmost layer.)

2. Open the Layers palette by choosing Window ➪ Show Layers (F7). A square should appear next to one of the layers. The square represents the selected objects. (If you select objects on more than one layer, a square appears on each layer that has a selected object.)

3. Drag the square from its current layer to the target layer. The objects do not move left, right, up, or down, but now they may be in front of or behind other objects, depending on the layer that they are now on.

The Layers palette icons

Four icons appear along the bottom of the Layers palette that make layer manipulation much easier than ever before. The first icon (two overlapping shapes) is the Make/Release Clipping Mask icon. The second icon is the Create New Sublayer icon. The third icon (a little piece of paper) is the New Layer icon and the last icon is the Trash icon.

The Make/Release Clipping Mask icon is used to create a clipping mask for all the objects underneath the current layer. This icon works in the same way as the Object ➪ Clipping Mask menu options. The icon is a toggle button that makes the current layer a clipping mask or releases the clipping mask.

The Create New Sublayer icon adds a sublayer under the current layer. A single layer can contain many sublayers. Sublayers can also contain sublayers. If a parent layer is hidden or locked, all sublayers are also hidden or locked.

Clicking the New Layer icon creates a new layer instantly, without the New Layer dialog box appearing. Option [Alt]+clicking the New Layer icon creates a new layer by way of the New Layer dialog box. Dragging a layer or layers to the New Layer icon duplicates those layers and everything on them.

Clicking the Trash icon deletes the selected layers. If art exists on a layer that is about to be deleted, a dialog box appears to make sure that you really want to delete that layer. Option [Alt]+clicking the Trash icon deletes selected layers without a warning dialog box, whether or not art is on the selected layers. You can also drag a layer or layers to the Trash icon; the layers will be deleted without a warning dialog box.

The Layers palette pop-up menu

Clicking the triangle in the upper-right of the Layers palette displays a pop-up menu that shows the different options that are available relative to the selected layers (see Figure 7-8).

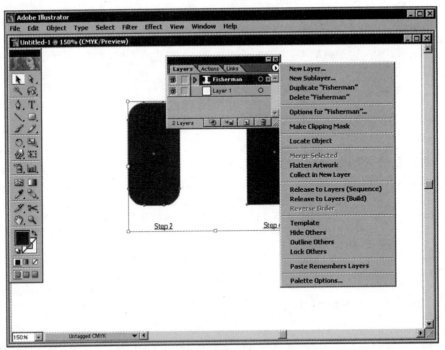

Figure 7-8: The Layers Palette pop-up menu

The first two options, New Layer and New Sublayer, create a new layer at the top of the list or a sublayer under the current selected layer. When either option is selected, the New Layer dialog box appears, which is the same as the Layer Options dialog box. When a new layer is created with Illustrator, it is automatically assigned the next color in the color list. New sublayers are automatically assigned a dark gray color.

If you press the Option [Alt] key before you click the pop-up menu triangle, the first menu item reads New Layer Above First Layer, or New Layer Above whatever the name of the active layer is.

The next menu option is Duplicate and the active layer's name, which duplicates selected layers, along with any objects that are on those layers. You can also duplicate select layers by dragging them to the New Layer icon at the bottom of the Layers palette.

The next option is Delete and the active layer's name, which deletes the layer and any artwork on the layer. If the layer to be deleted contains artwork, a dialog box warns you that you are about to delete it. If several layers are selected, the entry reads "Delete Layers" and all selected layers are deleted. You can undo layer deletions.

The fifth menu option is Options for Layer 1 (or Options for whatever the name of the active layer is) — the menu item reads "Options for Selection" if more than one layer is selected. Selecting Layer Options displays the Layer Options dialog box, in which you can choose a number of different options. If more than one layer is selected, the layer options affect all selected layers.

Tip   Double-clicking a layer name also brings up the Layer Options dialog box.

The next menu option is Make (or Release) Clipping Mask. This option converts the currently selected object into a clipping mask. The clipping mask must be above the object that it is clipping.

Below the Clipping Mask option is Locate Object. The option is convenient when the layer list becomes very large. It can locate the layer that a selected object is part of by scrolling the layer list until the layer containing the current object appears.

The next option in the Layers Palette pop-up menu is Merge Selected, which combines selected layers into one. Merge Layers does two important things: First, it places art that you want on the same layer together in one step. Second, it eliminates all those empty layers automatically. When you finish an illustration, if you know you won't need separate layers anymore, it's a great idea to select all your layers and Merge them into one. When layers are merged, the objects on the layer with the higher number are placed on top of the layer that is being merged.

The Flatten Artwork option works just like Photoshop's Flatten Layers. This takes all of your layers and combines them into one layer.

The Collect in New Layer creates a new layer and makes the current layer (and all its sublayers) a sublayer underneath the new layer.

The Release to Layers (Sequence) options makes all the sublayers under the current selected layer into new layers. For example, using the Release to Layers (Sequence) menu option on a layer with four separate objects would create four new layers with one object on each new layer. The Release to Layers (Build) will also create new layers, but the objects will be cumulatively placed on each layer. So, a layer with four objects will have all four objects on the first new layer, the second new layer will only have three objects and so on. The Reverse Order option becomes enabled if two or more layers are selected. This option switches the order of the selected layers. For example, if the top and second layers are selected and this option is used, the two layers switch places and the second layer is now the top layer.

The next four options are different ways of viewing templates and changing the locking:

✦ The first option, Template, is where you view the template.

✦ The next option reads either Show Others (if one or more is hidden) or Hide Others (if all are visible). Hide Others hides all the layers but the selected ones. This is like pressing the Option [Alt] key and clicking the column to the left of the selected layers.

✦ The next option is either Preview Others (if one or more is set to Outline view) or Outline Others, which changes all unselected layers to Outline view.

✦ The final option in this group is either Unlock Others, if any layers are locked, or Lock Others, which locks all layers but the selected ones. You can also lock or unlock layers from the Layers Palette by Option [Alt]+clicking the selected layers' Lock/Unlock column.

Checking the Paste Remembers Layers option causes all objects to be pasted on the layer they were copied from, regardless of which layer is currently active. Unchecking this menu item causes objects on the clipboard to be pasted on the current layer.

The final option is a pop-up menu that is the Palette Options option. This makes the Layers Palette Options dialog box appear, as shown in Figure 7-9. This dialog box lets you specify a Row Size including a Custom user-defined size. The advantage of having larger rows is that more of the layer preview is visible. You can also disable the preview Thumbnails to view only Layers, Groups, and/or Objects.

ASK TOULOUSE: Inverse on Specific Layers

Miguel: I want to select the inverse of the objects I selected that are just on specific layers.

Toulouse: You've already selected the inverse objects of the ones you want?

Miguel: Yep. How do I select just the inverse on certain layers only?

Toulouse: Easy. Run the Select ➪ Inverse function.

Miguel: But there are lots of paths selected that *aren't* on those layers.

Toulouse: Then just lock all the layers on which you don't want paths selected. Anything on a locked layer will deselect.

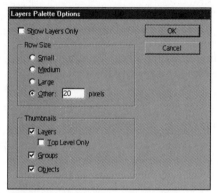

Figure 7-9: The Layers Palette Options dialog box

Tip

With many layers, it can take some time to update all the layer previews. If you don't need to view the thumbnails, disable them to speed up your system.

Layer advice and strategies

Layers take up RAM (Random Access Memory) and computer power, and the more layers you have, the slower your system will be.

Create layers when you believe that they help you better organize an illustration. Even setting up one additional layer can dramatically ease selection and moving problems. One of the best uses for layers is to trace placed images, which is covered in the next section.

Use vivid, distinct colors for each layer. You miss out on half the power of layers if you use the same colors for all layers. By choosing Select ➪ All (⌘+A [Ctrl+A]), you can quickly see which objects are on which layers, just by the color of the paths and points.

Using Templates in Illustrator

You can create a template in Illustrator by placing any image into a "template" layer. You can then use that image for tracing or as a guide for creating or adjusting artwork. Any layer in Illustrator can be used as a template layer; however, only raster images can be used as templates.

Creating a template layer

To create a template layer, double-click the layer you wish to modify. In the Layer Options dialog box, check the Template option. By default the "Dim Images" checkbox is checked, and all other options are grayed out. Enter a value in the Dim Images text field (the lower the percentage value, the lighter the image will appear in Illustrator).

Note   Paths that you place on template layers do not show when they're selected. An icon appears in the Layers palette "view" column to indicate that the current layer is a template layer. Template layers do not print.

Tip   You can make any vector artwork into a template by rasterizing it, and then setting that layer into a template layer.

Figure 7-10 shows an image before and after dimming.

Placed images work well as templates because their resolution is independent of the Illustrator document. You can scale placed images up or down, *changing their onscreen resolution* as you change their size. For instance, if you scale a 72-dpi (dots-per-inch) image down to one-fourth of its imported size (making the dpi of the placed image 4 times 72-dpi, or 288-dpi), you may zoom in on the image in Illustrator at 400 percent. At 400 percent, the placed image still has a 72-dpi resolution because one-fourth of 288-dpi is 72-dpi. The more the placed image's dpi is increased by scaling it down, the more you may zoom in to see the details of the image. If the placed image's dpi is already higher than 72, you'll be able to zoom in to a certain amount and retain quite a bit of detail automatically.

Another plus: A placed image "template" is a full-color template that keeps all the shading and colors and enables you to see all the fine details easily.

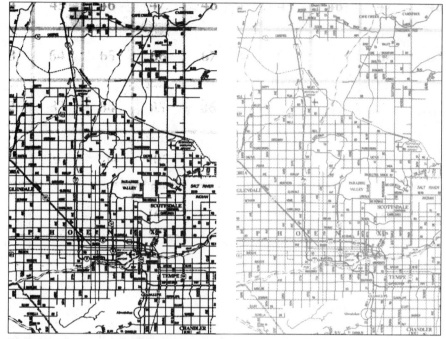

Figure 7-10: The original image (left) and after dimming (right)

Tracing a template layer

Now that you've got your template (placed image) all set up, you're ready to trace it — or so you would think. You have lots of different ways to go about tracing, and we've included the "best of the best" techniques in this section to help you push through the muddle.

You can trace templates in two ways: manually and automatically. Manually tracing consists of using the Pencil and Pen tools to tediously trace the edges of a template — often a very time-consuming task. Using the Auto Trace tool, though, speeds up the process. Unfortunately, the results may not be of the quality you desire.

Tracing placed images automatically

The Auto Trace tool (hidden in the same slot as the Blend tool) can be used for basic tracing of placed images, both black and white and full color. However, the results obtained by using this tool are usually less than satisfactory, requiring a great deal of time-consuming cleanup.

To use the Auto Trace tool, click the edge of a colored area of a placed image; the Auto Trace tool attempts to trace the edge of a solid area and applies the current Paint style to it.

Note Always use the Auto Trace tool from the outside in. This ensures that bigger paths around the outside don't overlap the inside paths.

The Auto Trace Tolerance setting in the Type & Auto Tracing screen of the Preferences dialog box (⌘+K [Ctrl+K]) directly affects the Auto Trace tool in much the same way that it affects the Pencil tool — the higher the number, the less precise the tracing. An Auto Trace Tolerance setting of 2 or 3 works pretty well for automatically tracing templates, but neither setting enables the Auto Trace tool to follow the ridges created from the template's diagonal and curved edges.

Note Adobe Streamline is the Auto Trace tool on a natural high (actually, it's more like a coke rush, we're told, but we hate to equate software to drugs . . . though both can be addicting and expensive). Anyway, Streamline can automatically trace full-color images, *retaining their color* automatically. Adobe Streamline is extremely cool. It takes tracing images to a whole 'nother plane.

Tracing placed images manually

Most designers prefer manually tracing templates. Using the Pen and Pencil tools provides illustrators with a level of precision not found with the Auto Trace tool. Furthermore, illustrators may add detail, remove oddities, and change curves, angles, and the like to their satisfaction (as opposed to an image that has been automatically traced, which gives it a more final appearance with less editability). For tracing artwork, a graphics tablet and stylus are very handy.

We've found that a combination of manual and automatic tracing works nicely for drawing fairly basic illustrations, especially those illustrations with type and straight lines. Automatically trace the basic shapes first and then use the path editing tools to add or remove anchor points and move paths so that the image has a consistent look. After fixing the traced section, use the Pen and Pencil tools to draw the intricate shapes.

Using layers for tracing

You can use layers for more than just dimming images for tracing. One of the unsung features of Illustrator's layers is the capability to show some layers in Preview mode and others in Outline mode. This is great for tracing because you can set the layer you're working on to Outline mode so objects you create aren't blocking out the template below. Just make sure your active "drawing" layer is above the template layer.

Aligning and Distributing Objects

The Align palette (see Figure 7-11) contains several buttons that are used for aligning and distributing objects. Align treats paths, type objects, and groups as single objects, allowing for quite a bit of flexibility when aligning and distributing.

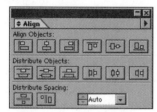

Figure 7-11: The Align palette

Objects can be aligned and distributed horizontally and vertically to the left, center, right, top, and bottom. To use the Align palette, select the objects you wish to align and/or distribute, and click the appropriate button in the palette. Each click in the palette counts as a change in Illustrator, which means that if you click 20 times, you'll need to undo 20 times to get back to where you started. The Distribute functions distribute objects along the edges or the center only. No reset button exists on the palette, so you'll have to undo if you click the wrong button.

The Align palette also includes two Distribute Spacing options — Distribute Vertical Spacing or Distribute Horizontal Spacing. These icons set the spacing between selected objects. Using the drop-down menu to the right of these icons, you can specify an exact spacing distance or select the Auto option. The Distribute Spacing section of the palette isn't visible by default. You'll need to click on the double arrows to the left of the palette title to make this section visible.

To align several square objects to make a checkerboard, follow these steps:

1. Create a square object with the Rectangle tool while holding down the Shift key to constrain the object to a square. Fill the square with White.

2. Duplicate the square object by dragging it with the Option [Alt] key pressed down. Fill the duplicated square with the color Red.

3. Open the Align palette and click the Vertical Align Center and Horizontally Align Center buttons while the two squares are selected. Then hold down the Shift key and move one of the squares to the right until the edges are aligned. Group the two squares with the Object ➪ Group command.

4. Duplicate the group of squares and rotate the group 180 degrees with the Shift key held down.

5. Select both groups and click the Horizontal Align Right button in the Align palette. With the Shift key held down, move the lower group of squares vertically until it is aligned with the lower edge of the other group.

You can then group the set of four squares and continue to duplicate and align groups of squares until you complete the checkerboard.

Measuring

You can measure distances in Illustrator in four ways:

✦ Using the Measure tool

✦ Using the rulers along the side of the document window

✦ Placing objects whose dimensions are known against the edges of the unknown object

✦ Eyeballing it (popular since the first artist painted his recollections of the preceding day's battle with the saber-toothed animals of his time)

The Measure tool

The fastest way to obtain a precise, exact measurement in Illustrator is to use the Measure tool, which looks like a ruler. The Measure tool pops up when you hold the cursor down on the Eyedropper tool and drag to the right. The results of the Measure tool are displayed in the Info palette (shown in Figure 7-12). These results include the distance between the location first clicked and the next location clicked or the distance between where the tool was first clicked and where the mouse was released after dragging. It also displays the angle of the measurement line. Double-clicking the Measure Tool pulls up the Guides and Grid Preferences dialog box (which is discussed and illustrated later in this chapter).

Figure 7-12: The Info palette

If the Snap To Point option in the View menu is checked, the Measure tool automatically snaps to nearby paths and points.

As soon as the Measure tool measures a distance, it routes that information to the Info palette. The Info palette displays the exact coordinate (X and Y) values, the Width (W) and Height (H) values, measured in the current units, and the distance (D) and angle measured with the Measure tool.

In addition to the measurement results, the Info palette also shows the current cursor location as X and Y values, the width and height of the dragged line and the values for the Fill and Stroke colors.

Note Know anything about PostScript? Well, one thing you absolutely have to know is that pages in PostScript are always measured from the lower-left corner of the page. This means that moving something along the *Y* axis with a positive number moves it up, not down. It's a math concept based on the Cartesian coordinate system. Your geometry teacher really knew what she was talking about.

If you hold down the Shift key, you can constrain the movement of the measuring line to the following:

✦ In Preview mode, the measuring line defines a 45- or 90-degree angle if no paths or Filled parts of paths are under the cursor.

✦ In Outline mode, your cursor snaps to the paths.

✦ In Preview mode, the cursor snaps to any Filled part of any path.

Sizing objects with the Transform palette

The Transform palette (choose Window ➪ Show Transform) shows the height, width, and location of any selected path or paths, as illustrated in Figure 7-13.

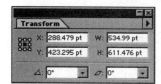

Figure 7-13: The Transform palette

X and *Y* show the location of the object on the page, measured (as always) from the lower-left corner.

W is the width of the selected object (or the total width of the selected objects when more than one is selected), while *H* is the height or total height of the selected object or objects.

The two angle values at the bottom of the palette are the amount of rotation (left) and the amount of skew (right).

All these measurements are in points — unless, of course, you know how to change the measurement units, which, coincidentally, is the topic of the next section.

Changing the measurement units

When you first use Illustrator, you are faced with points. That's great for type and numbering star tips, but when was the last time your art director said, "I'd like you to design a 360×288-point ad and make the logo at least 144 points high." (Or your grandmother said to you, "Gosh, you must be at least 5,600 points tall, maybe taller. You've grown at least 100 points since I last saw you. Does your mother let you wear *that* to school?!")

Points don't work for everything, so Adobe lets us change the measurement units to picas, inches, centimeters, or millimeters. The way to choose this is to temporarily indicate a different unit of measurement each time you enter a value, by appending a character or two to the end of your numerical value. For instance, to enter 2 inches you'd type **2 inch**, **2 in**, or **2"**. To enter 2 millimeters, you'd enter **2 mm**. To enter 2 points you'd enter **2 pt** or **p 2**. You can enter picas by putting a *p* after the number, such as **2p** for 2 picas. You can also combine picas and points by sticking a *p* between them, as in **2p6** for 2 picas, 6 points. For centimeters, type **2 cm**.

Centimeters and picas/points units of measure have been available since version 7 of Illustrator. The centimeter system has 100 centimeters in a meter and 10 millimeters in a centimeter (if you live in the United States and have not yet been metricized). The other system, which is much more significant to Illustrator users, is the pica/point system. When the pica measurement system is selected in the Units and Undo Preferences, measurements are displayed using the common (common to typesetters and designers, anyway) system of picas followed by points. So a distance of 3 picas and 6 points is displayed as 3p6. Such a measurement would be displayed as 42 points using the point system.

A quick refresher on measurement units and their relations:

1" =	6p =	72 pt =	25.4 mm =	2.54 cm
0.17" =	1p =	12 pt =	4.2 mm =	0.42 cm
0.01" =	p1 =	1 pt =	0.35 mm =	0.035 cm
0.04" =	p2.83 =	2.83 pt =	1 mm =	0.1 cm
0.39" =	2p4.35 =	28.35 pt =	10 mm =	1 cm

ASK TOULOUSE: Picas, Picas

Chrissy: I'm about to get fired.

Toulouse: I thought you had a stake in the ThighMaster thing. . . .

Chrissy: No, things I print don't measure correctly.

Toulouse: How so?

Chrissy: Well, picas don't equal picas.

Toulouse: Actually, that's a common occurrence. But you're not doing anything wrong.

Chrissy: Pardon me for asking, but why the hell does it happen?

Toulouse: Well, when you measure, you're probably using one of those pica sticks, right?

Chrissy: Sure. It's the weapon of the graphic artist.

Toulouse: Okay. The problem is that until just recently, most pica sticks were traditional picas, which aren't the same as new picas, which are sometimes called Adobe picas.

Chrissy: And traditional picas are different from Adobe picas?

Toulouse: Um, yeah . . . See, there are 72.27 points in an inch using traditional points and picas, and there are 72 points in an inch using Adobe points and picas. So picas, which are 12 points, are different sizes in each system.

Chrissy: So, which programs use Adobe picas and which ones use traditional picas?

Toulouse: Actually, by default, most software uses Adobe picas and points. Some programs, such as QuarkXPress, let you switch between them.

Chrissy: How confusing.

Toulouse: It is. You know, step by step . . .

To permanently alter your measurement units, choose Illustrator [Edit] ⇨ Preferences ⇨ Units and Undo and change the General pop-up menu in the Units section to the measurement system you want. Figure 7-14 shows the Units & Undo screen of the Preferences dialog box.

 Caution

If you've noticed that the Preferences option in the File menu is missing, don't despair. Adobe decided that it needed some new friends so it moved it to a new neighborhood. Its new locale is now under the Edit menu.

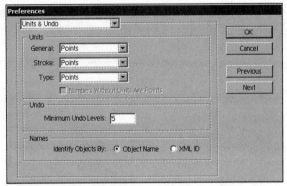

Figure 7-14: The Units & Undo screen of the Preferences dialog box

Using rulers

You can toggle rulers on and off by choosing View ➪ Show/Hide Rulers (⌘+R [Ctrl+R]). Normally, the rulers measure up and across from the document's lower-left corner; however, you can alter this orientation by dragging the ruler origin (where the zeros are) from its position in the upper-left corner, between where the two rulers meet. Because rulers take up valuable onscreen real estate, it's usually a good idea to leave them turned off unless you are constantly measuring or you want to display your illustration at a higher magnification. Rulers are easy to show and hide — just press ⌘+R [Ctrl+R] when you want to see them and press ⌘+R [Ctrl+R] again to lose them. To reset the rulers to their original location, double-click the origin box of the rulers.

Note   If you change the ruler origin to the middle of the document page, try to move it back to a corner when you are finished. When you zoom in, rulers may be the only indicators of your location within the document.

One of the rulers' nicest features is the display of dotted lines that correspond to the cursor's position. And yet, at times, measuring with rulers works no better than eyeballing; although measuring with rulers requires precision, you are limited by the rulers' hash marks in pinpointing the cursor's exact position. The rulers are best suited for measuring when the document is at a very high zoom level.

Measuring with objects

Using objects to compare distances can be more effective than using either the Measure tool or the rulers, especially when you need to place objects precisely — for example, when you want several objects to be the same distance from one another.

ASK TOULOUSE: Measuring Trouble

Jack: You know, my measurements never seem accurate.

Toulouse: Really? How far are they off?

Jack: It varies. Sometimes they'll be right on, and at other times they'll be half the size, twice as big. . . . Once they were ¹/₁₆ the actual size!

Toulouse: I hate to ask this, but what are you using to measure the onscreen objects?

Jack: The rulers on the monitor, of course.

Toulouse: Well, that's very weird. I've always found those rulers to be quite accurate.

Jack: You've used my computer?

Toulouse: No, but I have rulers on my system, too.

Jack: But how do you know they're the same as mine?

Toulouse: You know, I'm thinking there's a lack of communication somewhere here. . . .

Jack: The real problem was getting them to stay in place.

Toulouse: Huh?

Jack: Yeah, I ended up hot-gluing each ruler to the edges of the monitor. Duct tape would've been my next choice.

Toulouse: You know, there are rulers within Illustrator.

Jack: You're kidding me.

Toulouse: ⌘+R [Ctrl+R]. Check it out.

If you place a circle (that has the diameter equal to the distance that you want the objects away from each other) adjacent to an object (so that the objects' edges touch), you know that the second object is placed correctly when it's aligned to the circle's other side. (A circle is the object most commonly used because the diameter is constant.)

You can use other objects for measuring, including these:

✦ ___Squares — **when you need to measure horizontal and vertical distances**

✦ ___Rectangles — **when the horizontal and vertical distances are different**

✦ ___Lines — **when the distance applies to only one direction**

To enable better precision, turn the measuring object into a guide. (Guides are discussed in more detail later in this chapter.)

ASK TOULOUSE: More Measuring Woes

Furley: This isn't working. I'm no mathematician.

Toulouse: Trouble with rulers?

Furley: Yeah. I want to place objects at certain distances from the edges of different pieces of artwork.

Toulouse: Why's that a problem?

Furley: Well, my object is at about 2.3" across the page, and 6.7" from the bottom. I can't work this way.

Toulouse: You can reset the way the rulers measure, so you can measure from the top left of any artwork on the page.

Furley: Without doing the math?

Toulouse: No math. Just drag the origin (that's where the rulers meet at the top left of the page) to the point you want to measure from.

Furley: Wow! This is great! I haven't been this excited since Stanley took off for his own show! Which then bombed, of course, leaving me on a top-ten show.

Toulouse: If I recall, weren't the ratings at a high point before you came on the show?

Furley: I've never really done the math. . . .

Using Offset Path (for equidistant measuring)

There are times when you want to place several objects the same distance from a central object. Using any of the previously mentioned measuring techniques can be time-consuming and even inaccurate, especially when you deal with complex images. Illustrator's Offset Path feature (see Figure 7-15), however, enables you to automatically align objects equidistantly from a central object.

Figure 7-15: The Offset Path dialog box

First, select the central object. Then choose Object ➪ Path ➪ Offset Path and enter the desired distance (in points, millimeters, or inches) in the Offset text field. If the path curves close to itself, then creating an Offset Path causes any overlapping sections to appear as loops. After the new path is created, check the corner areas to see whether any overlapping areas appear as loops. If so, use Unite to eliminate these unsightly aberrations by choosing Unite from the Pathfinder palette. Change the new path into a guide and align your objects to this guide.

Grids

We've found nothing more useful on a day-to-day basis than the Grid feature. Grids act as a framework for your artwork, providing an easy method for aligning and positioning images. Figure 7-16 shows an Illustrator document that has grids turned on.

Figure 7-16: A document with Illustrator's Grid function turned on

Display grids by choosing View ➪ Show Grid (⌘+" [Ctrl+"]). Once grids are displayed, you can automatically snap to the grid points by turning on the Snap To feature: choose View ➪ Snap to Grid (⌘+Shift+" [Ctrl+Shift+"]). Turn off grids by choosing View ➪ Hide Grid (⌘+" [Ctrl+"]).

Grids start from the origin of your document (usually the lower-left corner). If you want to change the position of the grid, you can do so by dragging the origin point (at the Origin Marker where the rulers meet) to the new starting position for the grid. Reset the grid position (and the ruler origin) by double-clicking the Origin Marker.

Tip   If you would like grids to be displayed in each new document, open the Adobe Illustrator Startup file in your Illustrator Plug-Ins folder and turn on grids in that document. Then save the Startup file. All new documents will have grids displayed when you first create them.

Grid color, style, and spacing

You can customize the way grids look by changing the Grid preferences. Choose Illustrator [Edit] ➪ Preferences ➪ Guides & Grid, and the Guides & Grid Preferences dialog box (see Figure 7-17) appears. Here you can change the grid color and spacing. Pick a new color from the list of colors or choose Other to use the color picker to pick a new color for your grids. Because we're just too darn picky, we pick cyan, and then go to the color picker and lighten it substantially. The result is non-reproductive-blue-looking lines that make the grid resemble graph paper (which we've always thought should be called grid paper).

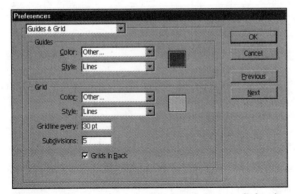

Figure 7-17: The Guides & Grid Preferences dialog box

You can also choose between lines and dots as the grid style. We prefer to use lines for our grids, as dots can turn an already busy-looking page into one with all sorts of, well, dots all over the place.

Illustrator 10 includes the Grids in Back checkbox in the Guides & Grid preference's panel. The box is checked by default so that the gridlines aren't running on top of your artwork.

To change the space between the major (darker) gridlines, enter a value in the Gridline Every text field. To create subdivisions (minor) between the dark values, enter a number for how many sections should be created between the main lines. If you enter 1 as the value, no subdivisions are created. Because you're defining the 0number of divisions, not the number of lines, entering 2 creates one line between the two main lines. The standard 1-inch gridline with eight subdivisions creates ⅛-inch squares.

The magically spinning grid

Your grid doesn't have to consist of just vertical and horizontal lines. You can rotate the grid to any angle you like by changing the Constrain Angle in General Preferences (⌘+K [Ctrl+K]). Figure 7-18 shows a grid set at an angle of 30 degrees. This is perfect for working with angled artwork; even if only a portion of the artwork is at an angle, the Constrain Angle can be set temporarily to the angle of the artwork.

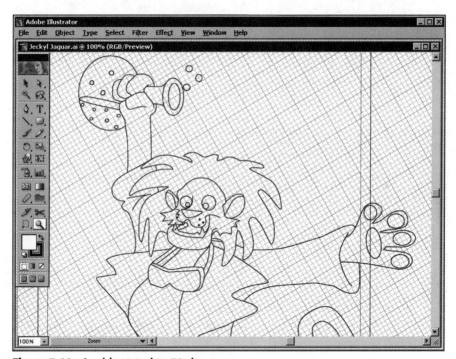

Figure 7-18: A grid rotated to 30 degrees

The secret power of grids

If what we listed previously were all that grids could do, we'd be way happy. After all, this feature makes Illustrator closer to CAD (computer-aided design) programs without losing any of its wonderful design capabilities. But the one secret feature of grids that Adobe doesn't want you to know about (actually, we're sure they don't really care either way) is this: Grids are the perfect transparency indicator layer.

What the heck are we talking about? Well, because Illustrator's paper color (the document and the artboard) is always white, it can be hard to tell whether paths are Filled with white, Filled with None, or are the hole part of a compound path. Displaying the grid ends the confusion instantly. Objects with a white Fill don't display the grid behind them; objects with a Fill of None or that are simply a hole in a compound path show the grid through their openings. Even if you aren't going to use the grid for alignment or snap-to, the transparency indicator feature is a great way to know *exactly* what's going on with questionably-filled paths. Figure 7-19 shows objects with Fills of white and None on a grid background.

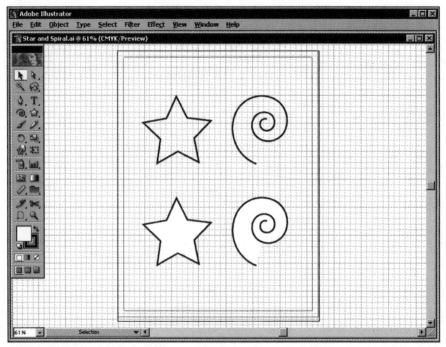

Figure 7-19: The top objects have a Fill of None and the bottom objects have a Fill of white.

Guides

Guides are teeny, tiny little people who show you around Illustrator. The more of them you make, the easier it is to use the program. (Uh huh . . . we know, let you know when the shuttle lands. . . . Sigh.)

Okay, actually, *guides* are dotted or solid lines that help you align artwork. Guides do not print, and they are saved with documents. In Illustrator and most desktop-publishing software, guides are straight lines extending from one edge of a document to the other. But in Illustrator, you can also turn *any* path into a guide (see the following section).

Creating guides

You can create guides in two ways: by pulling them out from the rulers and by creating them from paths.

To pull a guide from a ruler, first make the vertical and horizontal rulers visible by choosing View ➪ Show Rulers (⌘+R [Ctrl+R]). To create guides that span the entire pasteboard, click the vertical or horizontal ruler and drag out. The guide that is dragged out will be parallel to the ruler that it came from.

To transform an existing path into a guide, select the path and choose View ➪ Guides ➪ Make Guides (⌘+5 [Ctrl+5]).

Tip   And now a word about the Magic Rotating Guide (possibly the coolest tip you'll ever learn): When you drag a guide out from the vertical ruler, hold down Option [Alt] and the vertical guide becomes a horizontal guide. And vice versa.

Moving guides

Moving an unlocked guide is simple—click it and drag. If guides are locked, unlock them by choosing View ➪ Lock Guides (⌘+Option+5 [Ctrl+Alt+5]).

If you aren't sure whether the guides in your document are locked or unlocked, click and hold on the View menu. If you see a checkmark next to Lock Guides, the guides are locked (and all new guides will also be locked). To unlock all the document's guides, choose View ➪ Lock Guide; to lock guides again, choose View ➪ Lock Guide (yes, it's a toggle).

All guides in a document have a special status of "lockedness," where all guides are either locked or unlocked. Weirdly enough, however, guides can be locked and unlocked individually as well by selecting them and choosing Object ➪ Lock (⌘+2 [Ctrl+2]) and Object ➪ Unlock All (⌘+Option+2 [Ctrl+Alt+2]).

Releasing guides

To release a guide, or change it into a path, select the guide and choose View ➪ Guides ➪ Release Guides (⌘+Option+5 [Ctrl+Alt+5]).

To release multiple guides first, make sure that the guides are unlocked; in other words, make sure that there's no checkmark next to Lock Guides in the View menu. Then select the guides (in the same way you select multiple paths: either drag a marquee around the guides or Shift+click each guide) and choose View ➪ Guides ➪ Release Guides (⌘+Option+5 [Ctrl+Alt+5]).

Tip

Selecting *all* guides—even those that are currently paths—by dragging a marquee or Shift+clicking can be a chore. Here's another way: Make sure that the guides are not locked and choose Select ➪ All (⌘+A [Ctrl+A]). Then select View ➪ Guides ➪ Release Guides (⌘+Option+5) [Ctrl+Alt+5]). This releases all guides and, more importantly, selects all paths that were formerly guides (all other paths and objects are deselected). Then choose View ➪ Guides ➪ Make Guides (⌘+5 [Ctrl+5]) and all guides become guides again and are selected.

For the most part, guides behave exactly like their path counterparts. As long as guides are unlocked, you may select them, hide them, group them, and even paint them (although paint attributes are not visible onscreen or on a printout until the guides are converted back into paths).

Clearing guides

Let's say you have just finished a fantastic drawing that you created with the help of many guides. Now that the image is complete you want to delete those guides. Sure, you can unlock them and select them by holding down the Shift key. Or, if you were really thinking, you can put those guides on a layer, simply Select All and then Delete. By choosing View ➪ Guides ➪ Clear Guides, all guides are miraculously deleted.

Smart Guides

Illustrator 10 includes Smart Guides. These guides pop-up to help you create a shape with precision, align objects with accuracy, and move and transform objects with ease. These settings can be enabled from the Smart Guides & Slices screen of the Preferences dialog box, shown in Figure 7-20. You can open this screen in the Preferences dialog box by selecting Illustrator [Edit] ➪ Preferences ➪ Smart Guides.

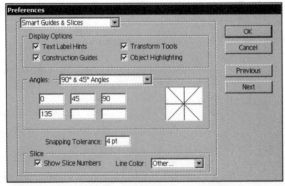

Figure 7-20: The Smart Guides screen of the Preferences dialog box

Some of the Smart Guide display options are:

✦ **Text Label Hints** pop up when you drag over your object. They tell you what each area is. For example, if you drag over a line, the hint pops-up with the word "path." If you drag over an anchor point, the hint says "anchor point."

✦ **Transform Tools.** When you are rotating, scaling, or shearing an object with this option checked, Smart Guides appear to help you out.

✦ **Construction Guides** let you view guidelines when using Smart Guides.

✦ **Object Highlighting** highlights the object you are pointing to.

Checkboxes enable you to turn these options on and off.

 Cross-Reference Slices and the slice options are covered along with web graphics in Chapter 17, "Using Illustrator to Generate Web Graphics."

Angles

The Smart Guides dialog box lets you pick what angles guides are displayed when you drag an object. You can choose from seven presets, which consist of a series of 90-, 45-, 30- and 60-degree angles, or create a Custom Angle of your own. For custom angles, you can select six different angles, which are shown in the Preview window to the right of the angles section in the dialog box.

Snapping Tolerance

Snapping Tolerance isn't how much patience you have with a spouse before you explode. Rather, it lets you choose how close you have to have an object to another object before the first object automatically "snaps" to the second object. You set the Snapping Tolerance in points — the lower the number, the closer you have to move the objects to each other. If the number is high, an object snaps to another object if it's merely passing by.

Guide preferences

In the Guide Preferences dialog box (choose Illustrator [Edit] ➪ Preferences ➪ Guides & Grid), you can change the style and the color of the guides. Choose a color from the pop-up menu or select Other to choose a color from the color picker. Unlike with grids, we like to use a darker, more vibrant color than a watered-down cyan. No matter which color you choose, keep it different from the Grid color and contrast it to colors you're using in your document.

Guide Style can be set to either dots or lines; which you choose is a matter of preference. However, you may want to pick the opposite of what you've chosen for grids, to further differentiate the two.

Measuring for Printing

Thinking ahead to the time your job will be printed is always good, and two of the most important areas of printing are the placement and the sizing of your artwork within the Illustrator document. This section deals with production-oriented issues you may face while using Illustrator to create printable pieces.

Stepping

Oftentimes, you'll create something that's quite small and you'll need to have several copies of the artwork on the page at once. Setting up your artwork for optimal spacing and printing is referred to as *stepping*.

Illustrator doesn't do stepping automatically, but it does provide the tools you need to step your artwork. The following procedure shows you how:

1. Make sure the Control palette is open. Select the finished artwork and open the Move dialog box (double-click the Selection tool).

2. Enter the width of the art in the Horizontal field. Enter 0 (zero) in the Vertical field. Click the Copy button (or press Option+Return [Alt+Enter]).

3. Choose Object ➪ Transform ➪ Transform Again (⌘+D [Ctrl+D]) to create another duplicate of the artwork. Press ⌘+D [Ctrl+D] until the right number of pieces exists across the page.

4. Select the entire row of artwork, and open the Move dialog box again.

5. Enter 0 (zero) in the Horizontal field, and enter the height of the art in the Vertical field. Click the Copy button (or press Option+Return [Alt+Enter]).

6. Choose Object ➪ Transform ➪ Transform Again (⌘+D [Ctrl+D]) to create another duplicate of the row of artwork. Press ⌘+D [Ctrl+D] until the right number of pieces exists down the page, as shown in Figure 7-21.

Creating crop marks

Crop marks are little lines that are designed to help you cut (or crop) along the edges of your illustration after the document has been printed (see Figure 7-22). Crops (that's the slang term; if you're even half cool you won't say "crop marks") don't intrude on the edges of the artwork, but instead are offset a bit from the corners where the edges meet.

Unfortunately, you can only create one set of crop marks per document. Making multiple crop marks by drawing them yourself or using the Trim Marks filter (Filter ➪ Create ➪ Trim Marks) isn't enough for color separations. Trim Marks can be used to mark where to cut for a single selected object. Black crop marks that you create by drawing may be 100 percent of process colors but do not contain any other spot color that you may have in your illustration. (This problem is the result of a serious limitation in Illustrator: The program does not let you choose "registration" as a color, which would print on every color plate.) Trim marks created with the Trim Marks filter are 100 percent black.

Figure 7-21: Artwork that has been stepped and repeated on a page

Figure 7-22: Crop marks indicate where to cut the paper along the edges of the illustration.

Here's a workaround: Choose the crop marks and/or trim marks you created and Stroke them with 100 percent of all four process colors when you are printing out four-color separations. If you are printing out spot-color separations, you must copy the crop marks, choose Edit ➪ Paste in Front (⌘+F [Ctrl+F]) or Edit ➪ Paste in Back (⌘+B [Ctrl+B]), and then color the Stroke of the crops with the spot color you are using, choosing the Overprint Strokes option in the Paint Style palette. Additional crop marks need to be pasted in front or pasted in back for every additional color separation in your document.

To transform a selected rectangle drawn with the rectangle tool into crop marks, choose Object ➪ Crop Marks ➪ Make.

Note   The rectangle can only be modified prior to becoming crop marks by moving it or resizing it via the Scale tool. If any transformation is done to the rectangle, a message appears saying that you can only make crop marks out of a single rectangle. If a rectangle is drawn with a Constrain Angle set to an angle other than 0, 90, 180, or 270 degrees (–90 degrees), you are not able to make crop marks out of that rectangle.

If you choose Object ➪ Crop Marks ➪ Make when nothing is selected, crop marks appear around the edge of the single full page. If Tile Imageable Areas is enabled in Document Setup, the crop marks appear only around the first page. If crops are set to the size of the page and the page is moved with the Page tool, or if the document has been resized with the Document Setup dialog box, the crop marks do not move.

To release selected crop marks, choose Object ➪ Crop Marks ➪ Release. If the crop marks were created from a rectangle, then that rectangle is an editable path that can be resized and changed back into crop marks, deleted, or modified. Any rectangle that has been changed back from being a set of crop marks has a Fill and Stroke of None.

Note   You cannot choose Object ➪ Crop Marks ➪ Release when no crop marks are in your document. In addition, Object ➪ Crop Marks ➪ Release does not release trim marks made with the Filter ➪ Create ➪ Trim Marks command.

Japanese crop marks and trim marks

Instead of using standard crop marks, you can choose to use Japanese crop marks, which are different looking, yet seemingly no more functional than regular crop marks. If you check the General Preference setting Japanese Crop Marks, both crop marks and trim marks take on the characteristics of Japanese crop marks (shown in Figure 7-23).

You can create a document that has both traditional and Japanese trim marks. To do so, select the object you would like traditional trim marks on and apply the Create Trim Marks filter (Filter ➪ Create ➪ Trim Marks). Then check the Japanese Crop Marks checkbox in General Preferences (Illustrator [Edit] ➪ Preferences ➪ General, ⌘+K [Ctrl+K]), select the next object, and reapply the filter (just press ⌘+Shift+E [Ctrl+E]). The second set of trim marks is Japanese.

We checked with several local printers and designers (in the United States) and most of them said that they would be able to use the Japanese crop marks, as well as traditional ones. Each, however, expressed concern that a greater chance exists of trimming or measuring incorrectly with Japanese crop marks because of their unfamiliarity with them.

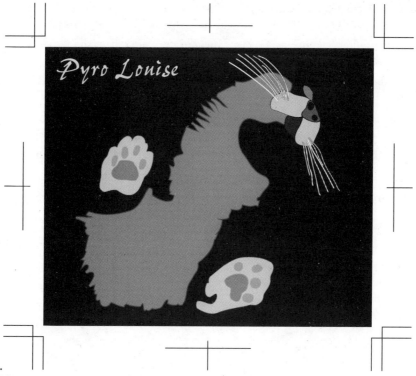

Figure 7-23: Japanese crop marks

Summary

As more paths and objects get added to a document, it can be tricky to isolate the exact objects that you want to select and edit. In this chapter, you learned about several features that make it easier to keep all your artwork organized including the following:

✦ Locking and hiding objects prevents paths from being selected or altered in any way.

✦ Group paths together by selecting more than one path and pressing ⌘+G [Ctrl+G]; ungroup selected groups by pressing ⌘+Shift+G [Ctrl+Shift+G].

✦ Use the Group Selection tool to select paths and groups within other groups.

✦ Layers can be used to effectively separate different sections of your artwork.

✦ The Align palette (Shift+F7) can line up objects relative to one another.

✦ The Measure tool provides a quick way to measure distances in your Illustrator documents.

✦ Measurements generated by the Measure tool appear in the Move dialog box the next time you open it.

✦ Guides can be created from any object by selecting the object and pressing ⌘+5 [Ctrl+5].

✦ You can quickly create document high/wide guides by dragging out from the rulers.

✦ Use the Copy button within the Move dialog box to step and repeat artwork.

✦ Use the Smart Guides feature to make editing much easier.

✦ Stepping and cropping are two features that help facilitate the printing process.

✦   ✦   ✦

Manipulating Type

T ype is a huge part of Illustrator. For the *Adobe Illustrator 10 Bible*, we've packed this chapter full of everything we could about type, to the point where this version of the *Adobe Illustrator Bible* is a little type-heavy, and severely off balance.

When we talk to Illustrator users, from veterans to those who are wet behind the ears, a lot of them tell us that the main reason why they use Illustrator is to manipulate type. So here's what can be the most important chapter in this book.

Typesetting Fonts

Before diving into type, it is helpful to learn about the various font types that Illustrator supports. For the seasoned graphic artist, the thousands of typefaces available provide a typesetting heaven on earth. For a newcomer to Illustrator and typesetting, the quantity and sheer variety of fonts can be overwhelming. Illustrator ships with about 300 Adobe PostScript Type 1 fonts, and others are available at costs that range from about $2 per face to hundreds of dollars for a family.

Fonts come in various formats, each format having advantages and disadvantages over other formats. Overall, fonts fall into the following categories:

+ Bitmap fonts, also known as screen fonts
+ PostScript fonts, also called Type 1 or Type 3
+ TrueType fonts
+ OpenType fonts
+ Multiple Master fonts

Bitmap fonts

A bitmap font is a font that is made up of a series of dots inside a grid pattern. Bitmap fonts were the original computer fonts. They worked well both onscreen and on the dot-matrix printers that were standard equipment when bitmap fonts were introduced. However, you won't find many bitmap fonts in use today.

Each character in a bitmap font has a certain number of square black dots that define its shape. Some bitmap fonts include different point sizes, with the smaller point sizes having fewer dots than the larger point sizes. The larger the point size of the bitmap fonts, the more detail is available and the better the letters look.

A problem arises when a point size is specified for which no corresponding bitmap font is available. Then dots from the point size that is closest to the specified size are scaled to the new size. The result is usually large, blocky-looking letters. The larger the size specified, the larger the "blocks."

Note

Sometimes Illustrator users, in their enthusiasm, start spouting off all manner of seemingly meaningless terms, such as RAM, Pantone colors, gigabytes, PostScript Level 3, dpi, and Option [Alt]+clicking. And power-users are into megahertz, terabytes, Bézier curves, line screens, and ⌘+Option+Shift+clicking [Ctrl+Alt+Shift+ clicking]. In this book, such terms are discussed as they come up.

PostScript fonts

PostScript fonts are the font format of choice for graphic designers, but they also are the most confusing and frustrating fonts to use because they have two parts: the *screen fonts* (which are really bitmap fonts) and the *printer fonts*.

Printer fonts are needed, as their name implies, for printing. Printer fonts consist of outlined shapes that get filled with as many dots as the printer can stuff into that particular space. Because these printer fonts are outlines based on mathematics, and not a certain number of dots, they make characters look good at any point size. In fact, PostScript printer fonts are *device-independent*, meaning that the quality of the type depends on the dpi of the printer (which is *device-dependent*). The higher the dpi, the smoother the curves and diagonal lines look. If printer fonts are missing, the printer either uses the corresponding bitmap font or substitutes another font whose printer font is available (usually Courier . . . yuck!).

PostScript fonts were developed by Adobe, which, just by coincidence, created the PostScript page description language, which is also, just by coincidence, based on outlines instead of dots. Adobe also created typefaces in PostScript format, called Type 1 format.

Since the rise of desktop publishing in the mid-eighties, the font standard had always been PostScript. However, in 1990, Apple developed a new font format, called TrueType, and licensed it to Microsoft. It is one of the most common font formats in use today.

TrueType Fonts

The greatest advantage of TrueType fonts over PostScript fonts is that they have only one component. Screen and printer fonts are not separate—just the TrueType font exists. (Actually, many TrueType fonts do include screen fonts, because hand-tuned screen fonts at small sizes tend to look better than filled outlines at screen resolution. The difference is that both the TrueType font and the bitmap are contained together.) The quality of TrueType fonts is comparable to, if not better than, that of PostScript typefaces. Apple and Microsoft include TrueType fonts as part of their operating systems.

OpenType fonts

OpenType fonts are an extension of the TrueType format that enables the font to include PostScript Type 1 data. The format was created jointly among several companies including Apple, Adobe, and Microsoft. The result is a robust font format that is compatible across several platforms. OpenType fonts include support for compression that makes them well suited for Web applications.

Multiple Master fonts

Multiple Master fonts, again from Adobe, provide an impressive, if not somewhat complex, way to vary typestyles. Normally, a typeface may come in several weights, such as bold, regular, light, and black. But what if you want a weight that is between bold and black? Usually, you're out of luck.

The theory behind Multiple Master fonts is that a font has two extremes—black and light, for example. Multiple Master technology creates any number of in-betweens that range from one extreme to the other. Multiple Masters don't stop with weights, though. They also work to step between regular and oblique, wide and condensed, and serif or sans serif.

Multiple Master font capabilities are built into many high-end graphics applications, such as Illustrator, Adobe PageMaker, and QuarkXPress. A special palette is included in Illustrator just for adjusting multiple master fonts.

Tip   You can control Multiple Master fonts with the MM Design palette, which is opened using the Window ⇨ Type ⇨ MM Design menu option. This palette is discussed in more detail later in the chapter.

The Type Palettes

Although there is a Type menu, many of the most frequently used type formatting options are found in the four type-specific palettes—Character, MM Design, Paragraph and Tab Ruler. Each of these palettes can be found as submenus to the Window ⇨ Type menu.

Character

Window ⇨ Type ⇨ Character (⌘+T [Ctrl+T]) brings up the Character palette with the Font field highlighted. In the Character palette, you can change fonts, styles, point size, leading, baseline shift, vertical scale, horizontal scale, and tracking/kerning values, all at once!

When you choose the Show Options item from the Character palette's pop-up menu, the Horizontal and Vertical scaling controls and the Baseline shift control are available (see Figure 8-1). Choosing Multilingual Options displays the Multilingual Options area in the bottom half of the palette. The Multilingual Options let you specify a Language, a writing Direction and several proportional spacing options such as Tsume, Moji Gumi and Wari-Chu.

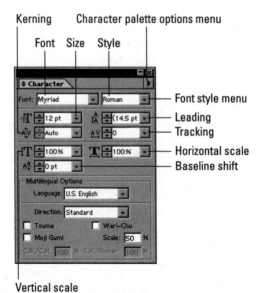

Figure 8-1: The Character palette, expanded to show both Options and Multilingual Options

If the Character palette is currently open, choosing the Character option or pressing ⌘+T [Ctrl+T] closes it.

Paragraph

Paragraph (⌘+M [Ctrl+M]) displays the Paragraph palette with the Left Indentation field highlighted by default (see Figure 8-2). You can use this palette to change the left, right, and first line indents, and to change the alignment by clicking the different alignment boxes. In addition, the Space before paragraph, Hang Punctuation, and Auto-Hyphenate options are available for all fonts, as well as Repeated Character Processing and Line Breaking options for the Japanese fonts. In the bottom part of the palette (choose Show Options from the pop-up menu of the palette to see the bottom part), you can set spacing limitations and guidelines.

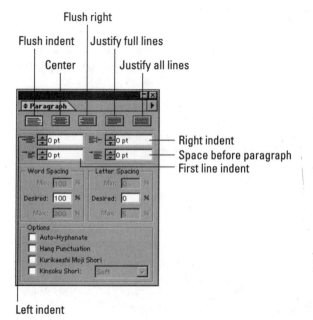

Figure 8-2: The Paragraph palette

If the Paragraph palette is currently open, choosing the Paragraph command or pressing ⌘+M [Ctrl+M] closes it. ⌘+~ (tilde) [Ctrl+~ (tilde)] takes you to the last entry field.

Choosing Hyphenation Options from the pop-up menu displays the Hyphenation Options dialog box (see Figure 8-3), where you can specify the number of letters before and after hyphens, and how many consecutive hyphens can appear in a paragraph. Kinsoku Shori (which is Japanese for line breaking) is also an option and is covered in the "Special Characters" section later in this chapter.

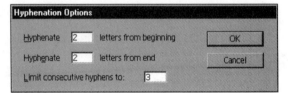

Figure 8-3: The Hyphenation Options dialog box

MM Design

Choosing Window ⇨ Type ⇨ MM Design displays the Multiple Master Design palette, where you can create variations of any installed Multiple Master fonts (see Figure 8-4). *Multiple Master fonts* are flexible fonts that can be modified in real time within Illustrator. These fonts have properties such as weight, serif, italics, and width that can be changed. The Multiple Master Design palette enables you to modify the axis available for each font.

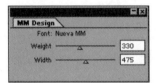

Figure 8-4: The Multiple Master Design palette when Nueva MM is selected — a Multiple Master font with two axes (Weight and Width)

The Tab Ruler palette

The Tab Ruler palette is used to set tabs the same way you would in your word-processing or page-layout software. To access the Tab Ruler palette, choose Window ⇨ Type ⇨ Tab Ruler or press ⌘+Shift+T [Ctrl+Shift+T]. The Tab Ruler palette is shown in Figure 8-5.

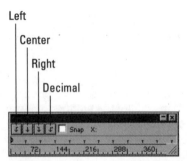

Figure 8-5: The Tab Ruler palette

To set tabs for type, select the type and choose Window ➪ Type ➪ Tab Ruler. The Tab Ruler palette appears above the type you have selected and automatically assumes the width of the type area.

To change the width of the Tab Ruler palette, click and drag on the Extend Tab Ruler button in the lower-right corner of the palette. The Tab Ruler palette can be made wider or thinner, but not taller. To reset the Tab Ruler palette to the exact size of the type area, click the Alignment box in the upper-right corner of the palette. The Alignment box is the one next to the Close icon marked with an "X". This box is only found on Windows-based computers.

Note　　　The Alignment box moves the Tab Ruler palette to make it flush left with the type and moves the palette up or down so that it is right above the selected text area.

Illustrator automatically sets tabs at every half inch. These are called *Auto tab stops*. Once you set a tab, all the Auto tab stops to the left of the tab you have set disappear. The Auto tab stops work like left-justified tabs.

If the Snap option box is checked, tab stops correspond to ruler tick marks. The measurement system shown on the ruler is the same system that is used by the rest of the document and can be changed in the Preferences dialog box.

Creating tabs

To set a tab, select a tab from the four Tab Style buttons on the upper-left corner of the Tab Ruler palette and click the ruler below to set exactly where you would like the new tab. Once the tab has been set, you can move it by dragging it along the ruler, or remove it by dragging it off any edge of the ruler.

You can set four types of tabs:

✦ **Left-justified** tabs align type to the right side of the tab, with the leftmost character aligning with the tab stop.

✦ **Center-aligned** tabs align type to the center of the tab, with the center character aligning with the tab stop.

✦ **Right-justified** tabs align type to the left side of the tab, with the rightmost character aligning with the tab stop.

✦ **Decimal-aligned** tabs align type to the left side of the tab, with a decimal or the rightmost character aligning with the tab stop.

To change a tab from one style to another, select a tab stop and click the Tab Style button that you wish to change to. To deselect all tabs, click in the area to the right of the Tab position box. (If you don't click far enough away from the Tab position box, you end up changing the units.) It is a good idea to get in the habit of deselecting tabs after they are set so that defining a new tab style for the next tab stop does not change the tab stop that was just set.

Note   You have no way to create dot leader tabs automatically by using the Tab Ruler palette.

Graphical tabs

Graphical tabs are tabs that flow around objects (paths) in Illustrator automatically. The following steps show you how to use graphical tabs:

1. Create a rectangle type area and type in five words separated by tabs. (Yes, each word is set at **1/2"** apart — we fix that shortly.) Press Return [Enter] after the last word entered.

2. Select All (⌘+A [Ctrl+A]) and Copy (⌘+C [Ctrl+C]). Then click the last line of type (it should be blank) and paste it a few times (press ⌘+V [Ctrl+V] a few times).

3. Using the Pencil tool, draw a series of four straight or curved vertical lines that extend above the top and below the bottom of the type area. Select the lines and the type area and choose Type ➪ Wrap ➪ Make. The type should be tabbed to the lines that you drew.

Tabs will tab to the other side of text wrap objects. Play with this a little and you'll discover that this method is much more flexible than standard word-processing tab stops.

Basic Type Technique

The Type menu, shown in Figure 8-6, contains most of Illustrator's type controls (with the exception of the Type tools). All the palettes that deal with type are located as a submenu under Window ➪ Type.

Most of the Type options can be changed in either the Character palette (choose Window ➪ Type ➪ Character or press ⌘+T [Ctrl+T]) or the Paragraph palette (choose Window ➪ Type ➪ Paragraph or press ⌘+M [Ctrl+M]), both of which are discussed later in this chapter.

Type is set in Illustrator in *stories*. A story is a set of continuous, linked text. When the term *paragraph* is mentioned, it is usually referring to the characters that are between Returns. If no Returns exist in a story, that story is said to have one paragraph. Returns end paragraphs and begin new ones. Exactly one more paragraph always exists in a story than there are Returns.

The following sections describe each of the Type menu options.

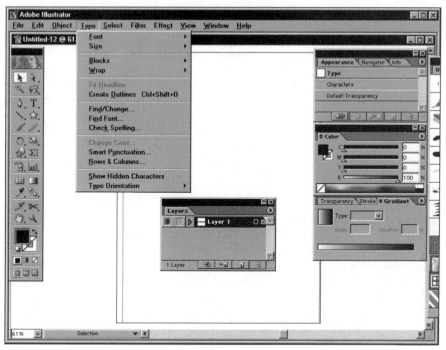

Figure 8-6: The Type menu

Font

Font displays a submenu with all the fonts that are currently installed on the computer you are using. Pressing ⌘+Option+Shift+F [Ctrl+Alt+Shift+F] or ⌘+Option+Shift+M [Ctrl+Alt+Shift+M] automatically highlights the Font field on the Character palette and shows the palette as well. A checkmark appears in the Type ➪ Font menu next to the font that is currently selected. If no checkmark appears next to any of the fonts, more than one font is currently selected.

Note If you are wondering why the folks at Adobe chose such an odd combination of keys and commands, you probably don't use QuarkXPress very much. Quark's key command for highlighting the font field in its measurement palette is ⌘+Option+Shift+M [Ctrl+Alt+Shift+M].

Size

Type Size displays a submenu with Other and various point sizes listed. When you choose Other, the Character palette appears with the Size field highlighted. You can type any point size from 0.1 to 1,296 in this field.

Note Type created in Illustrator may be scaled to any size, but to go beyond the size limits, you must convert the type into outline paths by selecting the type and using the Create Outlines command (⌘+Shift+O [Ctrl+Shift+O]). Once the text is converted to outlines, you can drag one of the corner control handles to increase its size.

A checkmark appears next to the point size that is currently selected. If the point size currently selected does not correspond to a point size in the Size submenu, a checkmark appears next to the Other menu item. Point size for type is measured from the top of the ascenders (like the top of a capital letter *T*) to the bottom of the descenders (like the bottom of a lowercase *p*). If no checkmark appears next to any of the sizes, more than one size is currently selected (even if the different sizes are all Other sizes).

You can increase the point size of type by using the keyboard shortcut ⌘+Shift+> [Ctrl+Shift+>], which increases the point size by the amount specified in the Keyboard Increments preferences. The Keyboard Increments value can be found in the General panel of the Preferences dialog box. Using ⌘+Shift+< [Ctrl+Shift+<] decreases the point size by the amount specified in the Keyboard Increments preferences.

Yet another way to change point size is to use the Scale tool. Using the Scale tool lets you change to any size; that size is displayed in the Character palette as soon as you are done scaling. Again, remember that the limit in scaling type is 1,296 points, and that you cannot exceed that limit even with the Scale tool unless the type has been converted to outlined paths.

Note Be sure to hold the Shift key down when scaling type to maintain the proportions. Distorting type makes a typographer cringe in sheer agony.

The Link Blocks option

The Link Blocks option (Type ➪ Blocks ➪ Link) links text from one area to another, continuing text from one area or rectangle to another (see Figure 8-7). Linked blocks act like groups, enabling you to use the regular Selection tool and click just one area to select all areas. (Individual blocks can still be selected with the Direct Selection tool.) Whenever more text is available than can fit into a text area, a tiny little plus sign in a box appears, alerting you that more text exists in the box than you see.

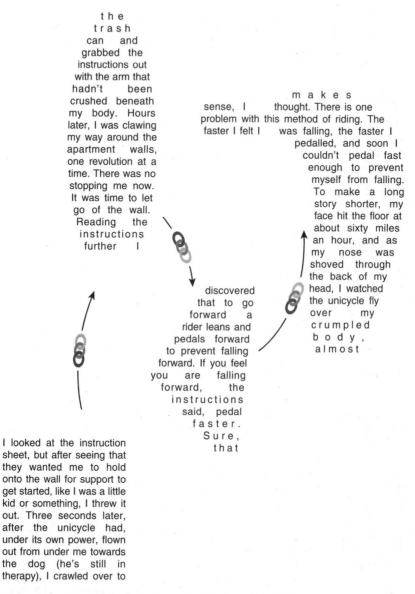

Figure 8-7: Text blocks linked together in the order of the arrows

To use Link Blocks, select a text area or rectangle and any other shapes, and choose Link Blocks. The text areas then act as if they are grouped. Text flows from the backmost shape to the frontmost in any group of linked blocks, so be careful to order your boxes correctly when setting up linked text. In fact, if you send a box to the back, the text starts from there, going to the next box forward, and then the next, and so on. You cannot select Link Blocks if at least one text area and one other path or text area are not selected.

The Unlink Blocks option

The Unlink Blocks option (Type ➪ Blocks ➪ Unlink) destroys the links made with the Link Blocks command. Blocks can only be unlinked when all boxes linked together are chosen. This is done easily with the regular Selection tool. When blocks are unlinked, the text inside them is split into several stories, one for each block. If the boxes are later relinked with the Link Blocks command, they are separated by paragraph returns.

The Make Wrap option

The Make Wrap option wraps text around any paths, as shown in Figure 8-8. To use Make Wrap, select both the type and the paths you want the type to wrap around. The paths that the type wraps around must be in front of the type in order for the text to wrap around the paths. Choose Type ➪ Wrap ➪ Make. The objects then act like a grouped object; you can use the regular Selection tool to select all objects in a Make Wrap area.

Make Wrap only works with Area type and Rectangle type (the option is dimmed for Path type and Point type).

Make Wrap works in levels: You can Make Wrap with one type area or rectangle to a path and then Make Wrap again with the same type area or rectangle to another path, and the type wraps around both paths.

Caution   Remember that Make Wrap only wraps around paths. Regardless of how thick the Stroke on your path is, the wrap does not change. This can cause the wrapping object to run into the text if the object has a heavy Stroke.

Additional objects can be used to wrap. Just place them in front of the type area, select both the type area and the new wrapping object, and choose Type ➪ Wrap ➪ Make.

Tip   Text wrapping objects need no Fill or Stroke, but they do need to be closed. If you want to use an existing path and that path is not closed, simply copy the path, choose Edit ➪ Paste In Front (⌘+F [Ctrl+F]), and change the Fill and Stroke to None.

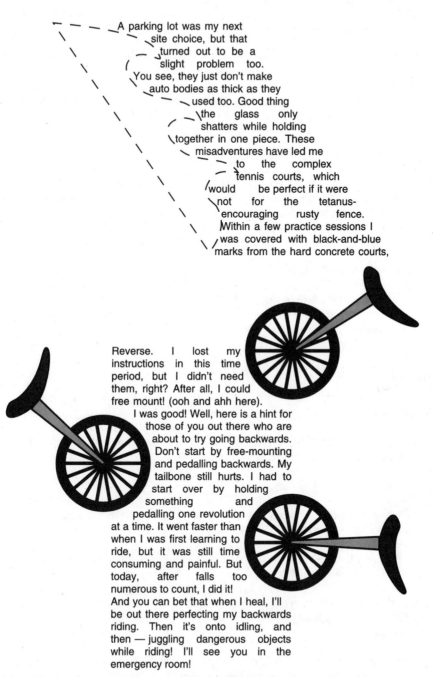

A parking lot was my next site choice, but that turned out to be a slight problem too. You see, they just don't make auto bodies as thick as they used too. Good thing the glass only shatters while holding together in one piece. These misadventures have led me to the complex tennis courts, which would be perfect if it were not for the tetanus-encouraging rusty fence. Within a few practice sessions I was covered with black-and-blue marks from the hard concrete courts,

Reverse. I lost my instructions in this time period, but I didn't need them, right? After all, I could free mount! (ooh and ahh here). I was good! Well, here is a hint for those of you out there who are about to try going backwards. Don't start by free-mounting and pedalling backwards. My tailbone still hurts. I had to start over by holding something and pedalling one revolution at a time. It went faster than when I was first learning to ride, but it was still time consuming and painful. But today, after falls too numerous to count, I did it! And you can bet that when I heal, I'll be out there perfecting my backwards riding. Then it's onto idling, and then — juggling dangerous objects while riding! I'll see you in the emergency room!

Figure 8-8: Text wrapped around different objects

The Release Wrap option

The Release Wrap (Choose Type ➪ Wrap ➪ Release) option releases any text wraps that are selected, all at one time. Release Wrap does *not* release wraps in the order that they were created. Because paths wrapped to type areas and rectangles do not lose or change attributes when they become wrapped paths, those paths retain their original Paint Style attributes when released.

The Fit Headline option

The Fit Headline option is designed to automatically increase the weight and width of type using Multiple Master fonts to fit type perfectly from the left side of a type area or rectangle to the right side of that same type area or rectangle. This feature can work for any fonts. You can do this by adjusting the tracking value of the applied font. The type must be placed within a type container before this option becomes available.

Note   If you don't have Multiple Master typefaces, you can still use Fit Headline. Although the command only increases the tracking of the type until it is justified, it actually does a lot better job than the Justify All Lines command (in the Paragraph palette), which only puts space between words. Select the type using the Type tool and choose Type ➪ Fit Headline.

The Create Outlines option

After your type is selected with a selection tool, not a type tool (and spelled correctly), choose Type ➪ Create Outlines (⌘+Shift+O [Ctrl+Shift+O]) and the type selected is converted into *editable paths* (see Figure 8-9). Each letter is its own compound path, and each path can be edited with the Direct Selection tool. This conversion turns the type into line art where it is no longer recognized as text, but as shapes and objects.

Note   Create Outlines only works with Type 1 PostScript and TrueType fonts, not bitmapped or Type 3 PostScript fonts. You must have both the screen and printer fonts for bitmapped and Type 3 fonts.

TrueType combines the screen and printer fonts into one file — if you can select a TrueType font in Illustrator, you can create outlines from it.

When type has been converted to outlines, you can apply gradients and patterns to its Fill by selecting the Gradient button in the toolbox or a pattern from the Swatches palette.

Caution   While you can undo Create Outlines, be forewarned that you have no way to convert back to type in case you made a spelling error or wish to change the font or any other type attribute.

All forms of type, including Point type, Path type, Area type, and Rectangle type, may be converted to outlines.

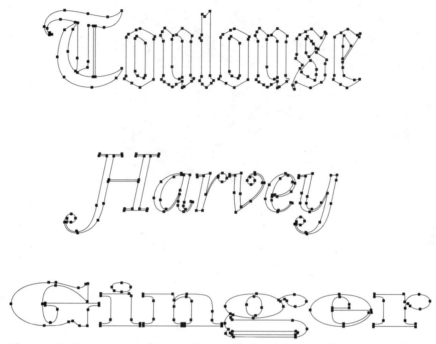

Figure 8-9: Type converted into outlines with the Create Outlines command

Tip

Creating outlines out of type is also very useful when you want to send the file to be outputted and the person doing the output does not have the font you are using. Simply use the Create Outlines option before you send the file, and the person outputting it should be able to print the type. (This is not advised for 4-point type or smaller, as described in the "Hinting" section later in this chapter). Another good tip is to group all the letters together. This helps keep the type organized.

Type outlines

Creating editable type outlines has many uses, including distorting mild-mannered characters into grotesque letters. More practical uses for editable type outlines include making type-based logos unique, *arcing* type (making one side flat and the other curved), creating special effects and masking, and avoiding font-compatibility problems.

To change type from being editable text into an Illustrator path (for that is what an editable type outline really is), select the type with a selection tool, not a type tool. Choose Type ➪ Create Outlines or press ⌘+Shift+O [Ctrl+Shift+O], and the type changes into paths that you can edit. Figure 8-10 shows the "CHO" logo before and after being converted into outlines.

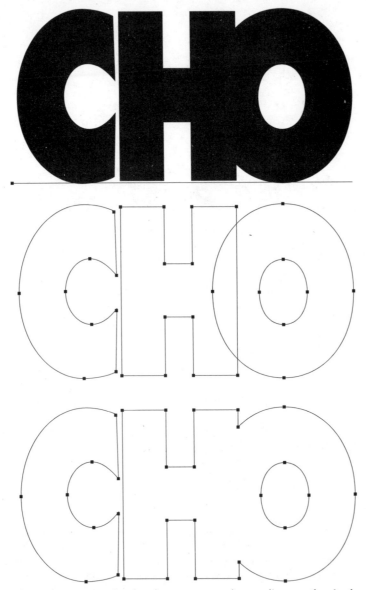

Figure 8-10: Type that has been converted to outlines and united
via the Unite function

Note   After type has been changed into Illustrator paths using Create Outlines, the only
way back is to use the Undo command (⌘+Z [Ctrl+Z]). No "Convert from Paths to
Type" function exists. Type cannot be edited in Outline mode. This means that if
you misspell something, it remains misspelled.

Initially, when type is converted into outlines, individual characters are turned into compound paths. This ensures that holes in letters, such as in a lowercase *a, b,* or *d,* are see-through, and not just white-filled paths placed on top of the original objects.

See Chapter 11, "Using Path Blends, Compound Paths, and Masks," for an in-depth discussion of compound paths.

Making letters that normally appear in your worst nightmares

After letters have been turned into outlines, nothing is stopping you from distorting them into shapes that only resemble letters in the most simplistic sense of the word.

The results of letter distortion usually aren't all that eye pleasing, but they can be *fun.* Few things in life are as pleasing as taking a boring letter Q and twisting it into "the letter that time forgot." Or fiddling around with your boss's name until the letters look as evil as your boss does. Or adding pointed ears and whiskers to a random array of letters and numbers and printing out several sheets of them with the words "Mutant kittens for sale." Some samples are shown in Figure 8-11.

When modifying existing letters, use the Direct Selection tool. Select the points or segments you wish to move, and drag them around to your heart's content. This can be great practice for adjusting paths, and you may accidentally stumble onto some cool designs.

Creating logos from type outlines

Type outlines provide you with the flexibility to turn an ordinary, boring, letters-only logo into a distinct symbol embodying a company's image.

Outlines are flexible enough that there really are no limits to what can be done with something as simple as a word of type.

The examples in Figure 8-12 show some logos that have been "touched up" by changing them into outlines and moving around the paths that comprise them.

Distorting words and phrases

Arced words are different from type on a circle. The letters in type on a circle are rotated individually, making each letter line up with one part of the circle. The letters in arced type are not rotated; instead, either the top or bottom of each letter is stretched to fit to a circular curve, as in the examples shown on the right side of Figure 8-12.

Arcing type is easier and creates better results when the type is created as all capital letters, especially when the tops of the letters are being curved to fit a circle.

Figure 8-11: Fun with type outlines

To arc type, first convert it into outlines, and then create an oval or circle above or below the outlines. As an example, the following steps arc type using the circle-below method.

1. Make sure that the tip of the top of the circle touches the center letters in the word so that these letters don't need to be changed. Always adjust the horizontal scaling to increase or decrease the font size prior to aligning the circle to the outlined type, as this prevents unnecessary adjustments.

2. Using the Scale tool, scale the first letter vertically only (hold down the Shift key) and drag until either the left or right side is even with the path of the circle. Do the same for the remaining letters.

3. After the letters are the correct approximate height, use the Direct Selection tool to adjust the bottoms of the letters to fit the curve well. This can take some time and a bit of practice to get the technique correct, but the results can be outstanding.

Tip   The best way to arc type is by using a third-party filter, such as the KPT (Kai Power Tools) Warp Frame filter in the KPT Vector Effects set of filters.

Figure 8-12: Type converted to outlines, edited, and ready to be used for logos

Arcing curved letters is much more difficult than arcing straight ones, and arcing letters with serifs is slightly more difficult than arcing sans serif letters.

Arcing letters just on one side of a curve can be started easily by selecting just those letters on that half and using the Free Transform tool. Select the letter you want to distort and using the Free Transform tool, click and hold a point of the bounding box and ⌘+Shift [Ctrl+Shift] to adjust the perspective. This does the scaling even more accurately than using the Scale tool because the letters are scaled proportionately and angled automatically.

Masking and other effects

Standard type or type that has been converted into outlines can then be used as a mask or filled with gradients or patterns, as shown in Figure 8-13.

Figure 8-13: Type that has been converted to outlines and is now filled with a pattern (left) and used as a masking path (right)

For words to work as a single mask, they must first be changed into a compound path. Usually, individual letters of converted type are changed into individual compound paths, whether the letter has a hole in it or not. For masks to work properly, you must select the entire word or words you want to use as a mask, and then choose Object ➪ Compound Paths ➪ Make (⌘+8 [Ctrl+8]). This changes all the selected letters into one compound path.

In some third-party (non-Adobe) and shareware typefaces, making a compound path out of a series of letters produces results where the holes are not transparent. This issue is usually one of path direction, which can be corrected by selecting the inner shape (the hole) and changing the direction with the path direction buttons on the Attributes palette.

After the words are a compound path, place them in front of the objects to be masked, select both the words and the masked objects, and then choose Object ➪ Masks ➪ Make (⌘+7 [Ctrl+7]).

Avoiding font conflicts by creating outlines

If you ever give your files to a service bureau or to clients, you've probably already run into some font-compatibility problems. A font-compatibility problem usually means that the place you gave your file to doesn't have a typeface that you used in your Illustrator document.

This is a problem for which no great solution exists, and the trouble seems to worsen as more font manufacturers spring up — TrueType fonts being the Windows standard, and PostScript Type 1 fonts being the Mac standard. And then consider shareware typefaces, some of which resemble Adobe originals to an uncanny degree of accuracy. All this leads to a great deal of confusion and frustration for the average Illustrator user.

But you do have a way around this problem, at least most of the time. Convert your typefaces into outlines *before* you send them to other people with other systems —

ASK TOULOUSE: Masking Type Mishaps

Kim: I can't get masking with text to work right.

Toulouse: What's happening?

Kim: Only the last letter in the word I'm using as a mask is working like a mask. The other letters disappear.

Toulouse: Did you make a compound path out of all the letters in your word before you masked?

Kim: Uh, no. That's bad, huh?

Toulouse: Actually, yes. What's happening now is that the last letter in the word, which is in front of all the other objects that are selected, is trying to mask everything else that's selected.

Kim: Ah, including the other letters.

Toulouse: Exactly. Illustrator has to see the word as one path, which is what making a compound path out of the entire word does.

Kim: So to fix it?

Toulouse: First, release the mask, select just the letters, and make them a compound. Then select everything and choose Object ➪ Mask ➪ Make.

they don't need your typefaces for the letters to print correctly. In fact, converted letters aren't really considered type anymore, just outlines or line art.

Tip   Save your file before converting the text to outlines and then save it as a different file name after converting the text to outlines. This enables you to do text editing later on the original file, if necessary.

Hinting

Most Type 1 fonts have *hinting* built into them. Hinting is a method for adjusting type at small point sizes, especially at low resolutions. Although hinting is built into the fonts, when those fonts are converted into paths via the Create Outlines command, the hinting functionality is gone. This is part of the reason that type converted to outlines looks heavier than it does otherwise.

Creating outlines shouldn't cause that much of a problem when the type is to be output to an imagesetter, because the high resolution of the imagesetter makes up for the loss of hinting. However, very small type — 4 points or less — can be adversely affected.

Note Converting typefaces to outlines removes the hinting system that Adobe has implemented. This hinting system makes small letters on low-resolution (less than 600 dpi) devices print more accurately, controlling the placement and visibility of serifs and other small, thin strokes in characters. Type at small point sizes looks quite different on laser printers, although it retains its shape and consistency when it is output to an imagesetter or an output scanner system.

Find

The Find/Change feature (Type ➪ Find/Change) uses the Find/Change dialog box that is shown in Figure 8-14 to search for and, if necessary, replace certain letters, words, or character combinations.

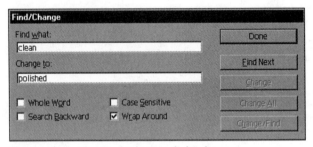

Figure 8-14: The Find/Change dialog box

The options available in the Find/Change dialog box are

✦ **Whole Word** tells Illustrator that the characters you type in the Find what box are an entire word, not part of a word.

✦ **Case Sensitive** selects the characters only if they have the same uppercase and lowercase attributes as the characters you type in the Find what text field.

✦ **Search Backward** tells Illustrator to look before the current word for the next instance of the characters, instead of using the default, which is to look after the current word.

✦ **Wrap Around** keeps Illustrator going through all the text blocks and makes Illustrator continue looking and finding the next occurrence throughout each text block. When it reaches the last text block, it starts where it originally began and continues finding the word or characters that you specified in the Find what box.

Finding and replacing text

The following steps describe how to use these options to find and replace text:

1. Choose Type ➪ Find/Change. The Find/Change dialog box appears.

2. Type the word, phrase, or characters that you want to find in the Find what text field. (You do not need to select areas of type with the Selection or Type tools — just make sure that the document that you want to search be the open and active document.)

3. Check the appropriate options (described in the bulleted list preceding these steps).

4. Click the Find Next button to find the first occurrence of the word or characters.

5. In the Change to box, type the word or characters that you want to use to replace the text that Illustrator found.

6. Click the Change button to replace the selected text. Click the Change/Find button, and then the Find button to replace the selected text and automatically highlight the next matching word or characters. Click the Change All button to replace all occurrences of the word or characters throughout the document.

Caution Illustrator cannot find words or characters that you have converted to outlines.

Find Font

Find Font looks for certain fonts in a document and replaces them with fonts you specify.

Select type with either a selection tool or with a type tool. Then choose Type ➪ Find Font. The Find Font dialog box appears, as shown in Figure 8-15.

To change all occurrences of a certain font to another font, select the font to be changed in the top window, titled Fonts in Document. Then select a font in the Replace Font From Document or System pop-up menu window and click the Change All button. To change one particular instance, click the Change button. To find the next occurrence of that font, select Find Next. The Skip button skips over the currently selected text and finds the next occurrence of that font.

Pressing the Save List button enables you to save your font list as a text file. After the fonts are found, you have to select type with the Type tool, no matter how it was selected before Find Font was used.

Figure 8-15: The Find Font dialog box

Check Spelling

Check Spelling checks all text in a document to see if it is spelled (and capitalized) correctly. To use this feature, choose Type ⇨ Check Spelling. The Check Spelling dialog box shown in Figure 8-16 appears.

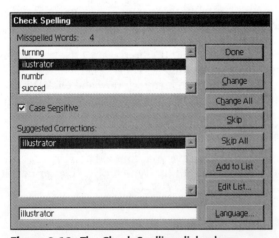

Figure 8-16: The Check Spelling dialog box

Note Check Spelling uses a standard user dictionary as well as all foreign language and hyphenation dictionaries.

If all words are spelled correctly, a message appears telling you "no spelling errors found."

If you have any misspelled words or words that are not in the spelling dictionaries, those words are listed at the top of the Check Spelling dialog box in the Misspelled Words window. Selecting a word in this list displays similar words below in the Suggested Corrections window.

If the Case Sensitive option is checked, the capitalization of words must match the words in the spell checker's dictionary, or they appear as misspelled words.

Adding words to the dictionary

Use the Add to List button when you would like to add the selected "misspelled" word to your custom dictionary. Clicking the Edit List button displays the Learned Words dialog box, showing you which words are currently in the user dictionary. The Learned Words dialog box enables you to add, remove, or change entries in the user dictionary.

1. To add a new entry to the user dictionary, select the Edit List button in the Check Spelling dialog box, which displays the Learned Words dialog box.

2. Type in the word that you would like to add to the user dictionary. Click the Add button, and the word is added to the list of words in the user dictionary. (Capitalization is very important when adding words, so be sure to place initial caps on proper nouns and to use correct capitalization on all words that require it.) If the word you are trying to add exists in the user dictionary or the main dictionary, a dialog box appears telling you that it is already a dictionary entry.

3. Repeat Step 2 until all the words have been added.

4. If at any time you make a mistake, you may change the spelling of an entered word by selecting it in the window above, typing in the correct spelling, and then clicking the Change button. If you wish to delete an entry that exists in the Learned Words window, select that word and click the Remove button.

5. When you are finished, click the Done button.

The user dictionary words are saved in a file called AI User Dictionary, which is stored in the Plug-Ins folder. The file is in text-compatible format, but the character that separates the words is indistinguishable (it appears as an open rectangle, which represents a symbol that is not available in that typeface), so you have no way to add words to the dictionary by using a word processor.

Caution

Be careful not to delete or remove the AI User Dictionary file when reinstalling the software or moving the files in the Plug-Ins folder. Doing so causes Illustrator to create a new user dictionary file with no words in it. You have no way to combine two different user dictionary files. You can drag the AI User Dictionary from the Plug-Ins folder of the old version of Illustrator to the Plug-Ins folder of the new version.

While you're checking your spelling in the Check Spelling dialog box, selecting the Change button replaces the misspelled word with the highlighted word in the Suggested Corrections list. Selecting the Change All button replaces all misspelled occurrences of that word throughout the entire document with the correctly spelled word.

Selecting the Skip button ignores that occurrence of the misspelled word. Selecting Skip All skips all occurrences of that word in the document.

Selecting the Language button uses a dictionary for the language you specify. Illustrator supplies dictionaries for the United States and the United Kingdom, both located in the Plug-In filters files.

Selecting the Done button closes the Check Spelling dialog box.

Change Case

Change Case converts selected text to one of a variety of case options. To use this filter, select type with a Type tool, and then choose Type ➪ Change Case. The Change Case dialog box appears, as shown in Figure 8-17.

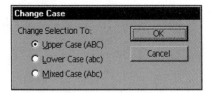

Figure 8-17: The Change Case dialog box

Type *must* be selected with a Type tool (characters must be highlighted) to use the Change Case feature. If type is selected with a Selection tool, the filter does not work and a dialog box stating this is displayed.

The three Change Case options affect only letters, not numbers, symbols, or punctuation. The options are as follows:

✦ **Upper Case (ABC)** converts all selected letters into uppercase, regardless of whether any letters were uppercase or lowercase.

✦ **Lower Case (abc)** converts all selected letters into lowercase, regardless of whether any letters were uppercase or lowercase. It also doesn't matter if the letters were originally uppercase because they were typed with the Caps Lock key engaged, or because of a style format.

✦ **Mixed Case (Abc)** converts all selected words into lowercase, with the first letter of each word becoming uppercase, regardless of whether any letters were originally uppercase or lowercase. It also doesn't matter if the letters were originally uppercase because they were typed with the Caps Lock key engaged, or because of a style format. The Mixed Case option separates words by making *any* character that is between letters end one word and begin another.

Smart Punctuation

The Smart Punctuation filter looks for certain fonts in a document and replaces them with fonts you specify. To use this filter, select type with either a Selection tool or with a Type tool. Then choose Type ➪ Smart Punctuation. The Smart Punctuation dialog box shown in Figure 8-18 appears.

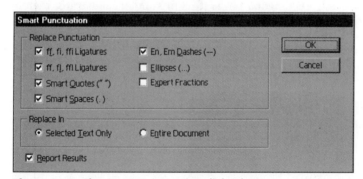

Figure 8-18: The Smart Punctuation dialog box

The Smart Punctuation filter works after the fact, making changes to text already in the Illustrator document. No settings exist, for instance, to convert quotes to curved quotes as you are typing them. The types of punctuation to be changed are determined by a set of checkboxes in the Smart Punctuation dialog box. A checked box means that Illustrator will look for these certain instances and, if it finds them, correct them with the proper punctuation.

The first two options are used for replacing ff, fi (or fl), and ffi (or ffl) with ligatures. Ligatures are certain letters joined together to form a single character, such as fi and ff. Most fonts have fi and fl ligatures, which look like fi and fl, respectively.

The remaining Smart Punctuation options work as follows:

✦ **Smart Quotes** replaces straight quotes (" " and ' ') with curly quotes, known as typesetter's quotes or printer's quotes (" " and ' ').

✦ **Smart Spaces** replaces multiple spaces after a period with one space. (In type-setting, there should only be one space following a period.)

✦ **En, Em Dashes** replaces hyphens (-) with en dashes (–) and double hyphens (--) with em dashes (—).

✦ **Ellipses** replaces three periods (...) with an ellipsis (. . .).

✦ **Expert Fractions** replaces fractions with expert fractions if you have the expert fractions for the font family you are using. Adobe sells "Expert Collection" fonts that contain these fractions. If you do not have expert fractions, your fractions remain unchanged.

Checking the Report Results box displays a dialog box when the filter is finished, telling you how many of the punctuation changes were made.

Rows & Columns

Rows & Columns divides rectangular paths (text or standard Illustrator rectangles) into even sections.

To use Rows & Columns, select a path and choose Type ➪ Rows & Columns. The Rows & Columns dialog box shown in Figure 8-19 appears.

Figure 8-19: The Rows & Columns dialog box

Any text path, open or closed, can be selected and divided into rows and columns, with one catch: the object becomes a rectangular shape, the size of the original path's *bounding box* (the smallest box that can completely contain the path). You have no way to divide a nonrectangular path automatically. See the steps later in this section for a way to do this without Illustrator knowing about it.

ASK TOULOUSE: But My Insertion Point Is Waaayyy Over There

Hawkeye: My insertion point is possessed.

Toulouse: Possessed, eh?

Hawkeye: When I enter text using the Text tool, my cursor floats two to six spaces to the right of its actual position in the line of text.

Toulouse: This usually happens when you have both TrueType and Type 1 versions of the same fonts installed.

Hawkeye: How can I fix it?

Toulouse: Just remove one or the other. I'd recommend keeping the PostScript Type 1 version.

The right side of the Rows & Columns dialog box determines the width of the columns. The left side determines the height of the rows. At the right of the dialog box is a Preview checkbox; checking this displays changes as you make them in the Rows & Columns dialog box.

Note All measurements in the Rows & Columns dialog box are displayed in the current measurement system being used by the program.

The first text field in the Rows section is the Number of Rows into which the original path is divided. The second text field, Height, is the height of each of the rows. The Height must be less than the Total (the fourth field) divided by the number of rows. The third text field is Gutter, which is the space between rows. The Total shows how high the entire rectangle is.

As the Row Height is increased, the Gutter decreases. When Row Height is decreased, the Gutter increases. Likewise, as the Gutter is increased, the Height decreases. When the Gutter is decreased, the Height increases.

In the Column section, Number determines how many columns the selected path is cut into. Below that, the Width text field determines the width of the columns. The Width must be less than the Total (fourth field) divided by the number of columns. The third text field is Gutter, which is the space between columns. The Total value is how wide the entire rectangle is.

As the Column Width is increased, the Gutter decreases. When Column Width is decreased, the Gutter increases. Likewise, as the Gutter is increased, the Column Width decreases. When the Gutter is decreased, the Column Width increases.

Remember that using the Rows & Columns feature actually divides the selected rectangle into several pieces.

The Text Flow options determine the direction of text as it flows from one section to the next. You may choose between text that starts along the top row and flows from left to right, and then goes to the next lowest row, flowing from left to right, and so on. The second option is to have text start in the left column, flowing from top to bottom, and then to the next column to the right, flowing from top to bottom. The third option causes text to flow from the upper-right to the upper-left, and to the lower-right to the lower-left. The fourth (rightmost) option flows the text from the upper-right to the lower-right to the upper-left to the lower-left.

The Add Guides checkbox creates guides that extend off each edge of the page. These guides align with the edges of each of the boxes created from the Rows & Columns feature.

Adding rows and columns to text

The following steps describe how to create rows and columns in a nonrectangular object, and Figure 8-20 illustrates these steps.

1. Create the object that you wish to divide into rows and columns. (In Figure 8-20, we used type converted to outlines and made the entire word one compound path.) Copy the object to the clipboard (choose Edit ➪ Copy or press ⌘+C [Ctrl+C]).

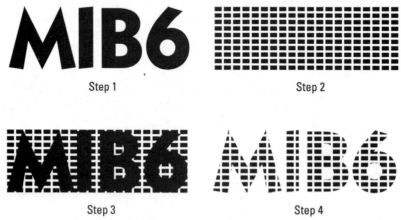

Step 1   Step 2

Step 3   Step 4

Figure 8-20: Steps for creating nonrectangular columns and rows

2. Choose Type ➪ Rows & Columns and divide the object into the number of rows and columns desired. Click OK. The object becomes rectangular.

3. Paste In Front. The original object appears in front of the rectangle that is divided into rows and columns.

4. Select all objects and choose Object ➪ Pathfinder ➪ Crop. The result is a non-rectangular shape that has been divided into rows and columns.

Creating angled rows and columns

The following steps describe how to create angled rows and columns, and Figure 8-21 illustrates these steps.

1. Create an oversized object that will become the rows and columns.

2. Choose Type ➪ Rows & Columns and divide the object into the rows and columns, but this time specify the size of the rows and columns, not how many you want. Click OK.

3. Rotate the columns and rows you have just created.

4. Create the object that will contain the angled rows and columns, and place it in front of the rows and columns. (In Figure 8-21, we used a plain rectangle.)

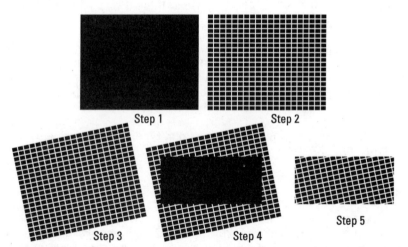

Figure 8-21: Steps for creating angled rows and columns (with outlined sections for easier viewing)

5. Select all objects and choose Object ➪ Pathfinder ➪ Crop. The result is an object with angled rows and columns within it.

Show Hidden Characters

Typically, you don't see characters such as spaces, returns, and tabs when you type. However, you can choose to view these hidden characters by choosing Show Hidden Characters from the Type menu. Enabling this option displays these non-visible characters.

Type Orientation

You can easily change the orientation of your type by choosing Type Orientation from the Type menu. That way, if you wanted to change horizontal type into vertical type, you can easily do so without retyping it. The Type Orientation option is only available if the type is selected using a Type tool.

Type Areas

For type to exist in Illustrator there must first be a *type area* defined. Type can never be outside these areas because type is treated very differently from any other object in Illustrator.

Four different kinds of type areas exist: Point type, Rectangle type, Area type, and Path type. Point type exists around a single point clicked with the standard Type tool. Rectangle type is type that is positioned within a rectangular area. Area type is type that flows within a specific open or closed path. Path type is type whose base-line is attached to a specific open or closed path.

Figure 8-22 shows the same sentence as Point type, Rectangle type, Area type, and Path type.

Using the Type tools

Initially, the six Type tools are used to create type. They can later be used to edit that very same type. The default tool is the standard Type tool, which creates both Point type and Area type. The tools on the tear-away Type palette (shown in Figure 8-23) are the Area Type tool, the Path Type tool, the Vertical Type tool, the Vertical Area Type tool, and the Vertical Path Type tool. (All of these tools are explained in detail in the following sections.) Each of the type tools displays a different cursor.

You can select type in Illustrator with the Selection tool, in which case *all* the type in the story is modified (a *story* is a contiguous set of type in Point type, Rectangle type, Area type, or Path type).

You select type with a Type tool by dragging across either characters or lines — every character from the initial click until the release of the mouse button is selected. Double-clicking with a Type tool selects the entire word you clicked, including the space after it. Triple-clicking (clicking three times in the same place) selects an entire paragraph.

These are the days you'll remember. Never before and never since, I promise, will the whole world be warm as this.

These   are
the   days
y o u ' l l
remember.
N e v e r
before and
never since,
I   promise,
will   the
whole world
be warm as
this.

T h e s e
are the days
you'll   remember.
Never   before   and
never since, I promise,
will the whole world
be   warm   as
this.

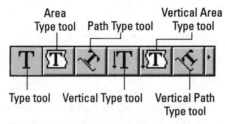

Figure 8-22: The same sentence as it appears (top to bottom) in Point type, Rectangle type, Area type, and Path type

Area
Type tool   Path Type tool   Vertical Area
Type tool

Type tool   Vertical Type tool   Vertical Path
Type tool

Figure 8-23: The Type tools

You can enter new type into an existing story by clicking with a Type tool where you want the new type to begin and then typing. If type is highlighted when you begin typing, the highlighted type is replaced with the new type.

The original reason for including a vertical type capability in Illustrator was for Japanese type (commonly referred to as Kanji) compatibility. Vertical type can have a number of specialized uses as well. The following sections that discuss the different types of type blocks (Point, Rectangle, Area, and Path) address both normal (horizontal) type and vertical type capabilities.

The Type tool

With the Type tool, you can do everything you need to do with type. Clicking in any empty part of your document creates *Point type*. Point type is aligned to an anchor point. Type created as Point type does not wrap automatically; instead, you must manually press the Return key and start typing the next line. Point type is usually used for creating smaller portions of type, like labels and headlines.

Clicking and dragging with the Type tool creates *Area type* — type that is bordered by a box, which you create when you click and drag the Type tool.

As the Type tool passes over a closed path, it changes automatically into the Area Type tool. Clicking a closed path results in type that fills the shape of the area you clicked. Holding down the Option [Alt] key as you pass over a closed path changes the tool into the Path Type tool. This intelligent switching of Type tools by Illustrator keeps you from having to choose different Type tools when you want a different kind of type.

If the Type tool crosses over an open path, it becomes the Path Type tool. Clicking an open path places type *on the path,* with the baseline of the type aligning along the curves and angles of the path. Holding down the Option [Alt] key when the Type tool is over an open path changes it into the Area Type tool.

The Type tool can be toggled to the Vertical Type tool by pressing the Shift key. In fact, pressing the Shift key with the Area Type and Path Type tools automatically toggles those tools to their Vertical Type counterparts. This holds true even if you press Shift along with the Option [Alt] key (when toggling between Area Type and Path Type tools).

The Area Type tool

The Area Type tool is used for Filling closed or open paths with type. Even compound paths can be Filled in Illustrator.

The Path Type tool

The Path Type tool is used for running type along any path in Illustrator. This is a great tool for putting type on the edges of a circle.

Tip

You can toggle between the Area Type tool and the Path Type tool by pressing the Option [Alt] key.

The Vertical Type tools

Vertical type? We were a little confused when we first saw this tool in version 7 (and its Area and Path counterparts). The easiest way to understand how the Vertical Type tools work is by example. Figure 8-24 shows the same line of type created with the regular Type tool and the Vertical Type tool. For the most part, the Vertical Type tool works like the regular Type tool, but instead of placing characters side by side, characters are placed from top to bottom. Because this area of Illustrator can be a little unusual, we've added a "Vertical Type" section later in this chapter that directly addresses vertical type and related issues.

Introducing the new
Static-O-Matic cat
fur brush. The only
brush actually made
out of cat fur. A great
practical joke for
your cat-allergic
friends.

```
f  y  g  m  T  i  I
r  o  r  a  h  c  n
i  u  e  d  e  -  t
e  r  a  e     O  r
n  t        o  -  o
d  c     o  n  M  d
s  a  p  u  l  a  u
.  t  r  t  y  t  c
   -  a        i  i
   a  c  o  b  c  n
   l  t  f  r     g
   l  i     u  c
   e  c  c  s  a  t
   r  a  a  h  t  h
   g  l  t        e
   i        a  f
   c  j  f  c  u  n
      o  u  t  r  e
      k  r  u     w
      e  .  a  b
            l  r  S
      f  A  l  u  t
      o     y  s  a
      r     h  t
               .  ı
```

Figure 8-24: Horizontal and vertical type

Point Type

To create type with a single point defining its location, use the Type tool and click a single location within the document window where no paths exist. A blinking *insertion point* appears, which signifies that type will appear where that point is located (see Figure 8-25). When you type on the keyboard, text appears in the document at that insertion point. Type cannot be entered when a Selection tool is being used. The second line of type in Figure 8-25 is selected with a Selection tool.

Insertion Point

CHO: The soft drink of the year 2000. And Beyond.

CHO: The soft drink of the year 2000. And Beyond.

Figure 8-25: Point type with an insertion point at the end of the line, and the same line of type selected with a Selection tool

Note   It used to be that every time Illustrator was launched, the text would default to 12-point Helvetica, Flush left, but with Illustrator10, the program remembers the type settings between sessions.

Point type that is flush left has its left side flush against the vertical location of the point initially clicked. Centered type is centered left to right on the vertical location of the point. Flush right type has its right edge flush with the vertical location of the point. Point type cannot be justified with either of the two methods available.

Caution   When creating Point type, remember that only a hard Return forces a new line of text to be created. If no Returns are used, text eventually runs right off the document. When importing text used as Point type, be sure that the text contains these hard Returns, or the text runs into oblivion. You can add hard Returns after importing, but it may be difficult to do so.

Area Type as a Rectangle

You have two ways to create Rectangle type (see Figure 8-26). The easiest way is by clicking and dragging the Type tool diagonally, which creates a rectangle as you drag. The blinking insertion point appears in the top row of text, with its horizontal location dependent on the text alignment choice. Choosing flush right forces the insertion point to appear in the upper-right corner; centered puts the insertion point in the center of the row; and flush left, or one of the justification methods, makes the insertion point appear in the upper-left corner.

Type the Right Way

Although at first it seems quite simple to outline characters of type using a 1-point Stroke in the Stroke palette, just slapping on a Stroke of a weight that seems to look good on the screen and changing the Fill to None or White is technically incorrect.

The right way to outline type is only a little bit more involved. First, select the type that you want outlined and give the type a Stroke that is twice the weight you want on the printed piece. Then Copy, Paste In Front, and give the new type a Stroke of None and a Fill of White. The White Fill knocks out the inside half of the Stroke, leaving the Stroke one-half the width you specified, which is what you really want.

The following figure shows both the right way and the wrong way to outline type. The top line is the original type. The middle line is outlined the wrong way with a 1-point Stroke and a Fill of white. The bottom part of the figure shows "100% Natural" outlined correctly, first with a White Fill and no Stroke, and then with a 2-point Stroke.

100% Natural
100% Natural
100% Natural

"Serif preservation," as it's known to a select few, requires a teeny bit of math, but it's worth the effort. The white area inside the Stroke is exactly the size of the character when done this way, as opposed to being smaller by half the width of the Stroke when done normally.

If you press the Shift key while drawing the rectangle, the rectangle is constrained to a perfect square. You don't have to drag from upper left to lower right — you can drag from any corner to its opposite, whichever way is most convenient.

To create type in a rectangle of specific proportions, draw a rectangle with the Rectangle tool by clicking once in the document window. The Rectangle Size dialog box appears, and you can enter the information needed. Then choose the Area Type tool and click the edge of the rectangle. The type fills the rectangle as you type.

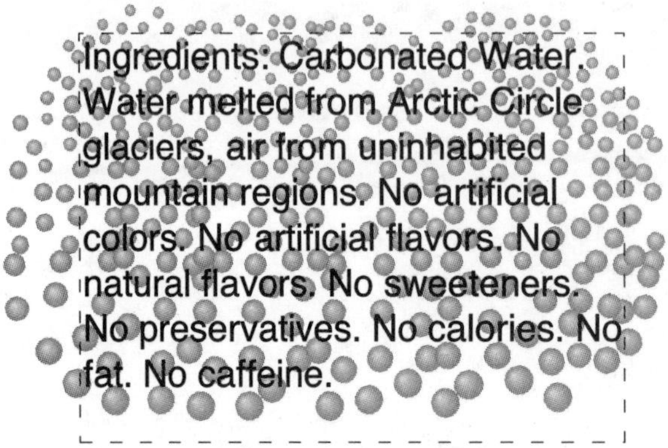

Ingredients: Carbonated Water, Water melted from Arctic Circle glaciers, air from uninhabited mountain regions. No artificial colors. No artificial flavors. No natural flavors. No sweeteners. No preservatives. No calories. No fat. No caffeine.

Figure 8-26: Area type (the dotted line is the border of the rectangle)

Here's how to create a Rectangle type area:

1. Using the Rectangle tool, click without dragging to get the Rectangle dialog box. Enter the exact dimensions of the type area.

2. Choose the Type tool and click the Type cursor on the edge of the rectangle. Any type entered into this box is constrained to that particular rectangle.

Note   Once a rectangle has been used as a type rectangle, it is always a type rectangle, even if the text is removed.

If you need to create a Rectangle type area that is a precise size but don't want to draw a rectangle first, open the Info palette by choosing Window ➪ Show Info (F8). As you drag the type cursor, watch the information in the Info palette, which displays the dimensions of the type area. When the W field is the width you want and the H field is the height you want, release the mouse button.

Area type

The capability of placing type within any area is one of the cooler features of Illustrator, right up there with the fact that the program comes in a trendy-looking box.

To create type within an area, first create the path that will be the area that confines the type. The path can be closed or open, and any size. Remember that the area of the path should be close to the size needed for the text (at the point size that it needs to fit). After the path has been created, choose the Area Type tool, position the type cursor over the edge of the path, and click.

The type in Figure 8-27 was flowed into the outline of the CHO logo. Using text wraps, the type exists only inside the letters yet reads across all of them.

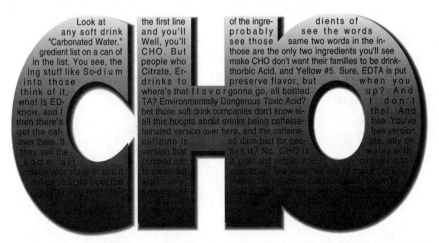

Figure 8-27: Area type created so that the text flows inside the outlines of "CHO"

Choosing good shapes for Area type

What exactly constitutes a "good" shape to be used for Area type? As a rule of thumb, gently curved shapes are better than harsh, jagged ones. Type tends to flow better into the larger lumps created by smoothly curving paths.

Try to avoid creating paths with wild or tight curves. Other designs that cause problems are "hourglass" shapes or any closed path that has an area where the sides are almost touching. Figure 8-28 shows how type flows into a smoothly curved area and how it has trouble flowing into a sharp, spiky shape.

Try to make the top and bottom boundaries of the path less "bumpy" than the sides. This reduces the number of times that type jumps from one area to another.

For best results with Area type, make the type small and Force Justify it (⌘+ Shift+J [Ctrl+Shift+J]). This ensures that the type flows up against the edges of the path.

Outlining areas of Area type

Placing a Stroke on the path surrounding Area type can be a great visual effect, but doing so and getting good results can be a bit tricky.

If the Stroke is thicker than 1 or 2 points, and you don't want the type to run into the edges of the Stroke, you can still do a few things.

Figure 8-28: Type flows much better into a smoothly curved area (left) than a sharp, spiky one.

The fastest way to do this (although it requires a bit of math) is to copy the Stroked path that contains the type and paste it in front. Fill the shape with the background color and a Stroke equal to twice the amount of white space you would like between the Stroke and the text. Hide the path and the type, and select the original path. Delete the text from this path and use the following formula to calculate the correct Stroke width:

$$\text{(Desired Width + White Space Size)} \times 2 = \text{Bottom Layer Stroke Weight}$$

For example, if you want a Stroke that is 6 points wide on a shape and has 3 points of white space between the Stroke and the text, the bottom shape will have a Stroke of $(6 + 3) \times 2 = 18$. The top layer will have a "white" Stroke of 6, with a Fill the same color as the Stroke.

Another way to do this is by using the Offset Path filter. This way is better for two reasons: First, it requires much less math, and second, you don't have to worry about background color (especially if the background is a bunch of other objects or a placed raster image). Of course, a catch exists: The path cannot be turned into a text area boundary before Offset Path is applied to it.

1. Create a path for your Area type with any drawing tool. Close the path for the best results when using Offset Path.

2. Do not make the path into a type area by clicking the path with a Type tool at this point. Select the path you wish to use for Area type with the Selection tool, and then choose Object ➪ Path ➪ Offset Path.

3. Determine the distance that you wish your text to be from the edge of the real path. If a Stroke exists on the edge of the real path, add half the width of the Stroke to your distance. In the Offset field, enter this distance in negative form. For example, if you want the distance from the edge of the path to be 6 points and the width of the Stroke is 10 points, you would enter **–11** points in the Offset field [6+(10/2)].

4. After you click OK, a new path is created inside the original. Click this path with the Area Type tool; the text appears "inside" the edge, with a buffer (see Figure 8-29).

Figure 8-29: Creating Area type with a buffer between the type and the edge

Doing bizarre things with Area type

Probably the most overlooked rule when it comes to manipulating Area type and the paths that create the type boundaries is the simple fact that the path and the type are treated equally, unless the path is chosen with the Direct Selection (or Group Selection) tool. Area type is selected when an underline exists under all the characters in the area.

When using the transformation tools, be sure to select just the path if you don't want to change any of the characteristics of the type. Use the Group Selection tool to click the deselected path once, and only the path is selected, not the type.

If the type is selected as well as the path, the transformations affect the type and the path. Figure 8-30 shows transformations occurring to both type and the surrounding path as opposed to transformations occurring to just the surrounding path.

Figure 8-30: The original (left); after both the type and the path have been transformed (top right); and after only the path has been transformed (bottom right)

Coloring type that is anchored to a path

When type is anchored to a path, either as Area type or Path type, you should think of some important considerations before Filling and Stroking the type.

First, if just the type or just the path is selected with the regular Selection tool, the other (path or type) is selected as well. Do you want to put a Stroke along that path that surrounds your type? If you select the path with the regular Selection tool, the type is also selected, and each character in the type area has the same Stroke you meant to apply to the path.

For changing just the Paint Style attributes of the path, be sure to use the Direct Selection tool to select the path. If an underline doesn't appear under the text, the text is *not* selected. To change all of the text, you must choose a Type tool, click within the text area, and then use the Select All command (⌘+A [Ctrl+A]). Only then will just the text be affected.

Changing the area, not the type

Many times, you may need to adjust the path that makes up the area of the Area type, like scaling that path up or down so that the text flows better. The trick here is to make sure that the entire path is selected without selecting any of the characters. To do this, deselect the type and select the path with the Group Selection tool (the hollow arrow with the + sign).

Now any changes you make only affect the path, so you can scale it, rotate it, or change its Paint Style attributes without directly affecting the text within it. Figure 8-31 shows a path that has been transformed, enabling the text inside to flow differently.

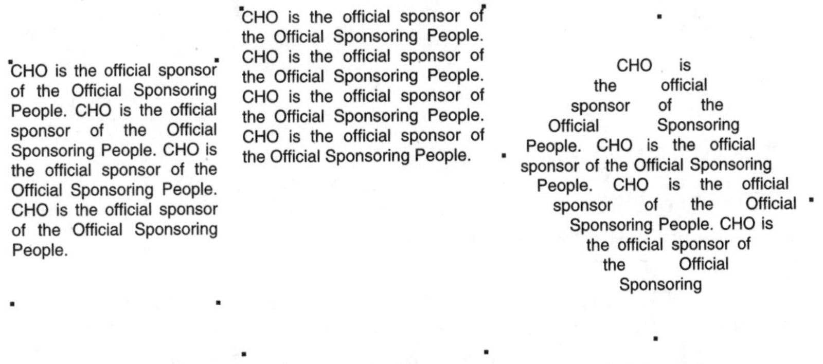

CHO is the official sponsor of the Official Sponsoring People. CHO is the official sponsor of the Official Sponsoring People. CHO is the official sponsor of the Official Sponsoring People. CHO is the official sponsor of the Official Sponsoring People.

CHO is the official sponsor of the Official Sponsoring People. CHO is the official sponsor of the Official Sponsoring People. CHO is the official sponsor of the Official Sponsoring People. CHO is the official sponsor of the Official Sponsoring People. CHO is the official sponsor of the Official Sponsoring People.

CHO is the official sponsor of the Official Sponsoring People. CHO is the official sponsor of the Official Sponsoring People. CHO is the official sponsor of the Official Sponsoring People. CHO is the official sponsor of the Official Sponsoring

Figure 8-31: Changing the size (middle) and rotation (right) of the original path (left) only affects the text flow, not the text itself.

Type Color and the Color of Type

The *color of type* is not the same as *type color*. Type can be painted in Illustrator to be any one of millions of different shades. The color of type, on the other hand, is the way the type appears in the document and is more indicative of the light or dark attributes of the text. The actual red-green-blue colors of the type do work into this appearance, but many times the weight of the type and the tracking and kerning have a much more profound effect on color.

To easily see the color of type, unfocus your eyes as you look at your document, or turn the page upside down. This works better on a printed piece than onscreen, but you can still get the gist of the way it will appear when viewing it on your monitor. Dark and light areas become much more apparent when you can't read the actual words on the path. This method of unfocusing your eyes to look at a page also works well when trying to see the "look" of a page and how it was designed. Many times, unfocusing or turning the page upside down emphasizes the fact that you don't have enough white space or that all the copy seems to blend together.

Heavy type weights, such as boldface, heavy, and black, make type appear darker on a page. Type kerned and tracked very tightly also seems to give the type a darker feel.

The x-height of type (the height to which the lowercase letters, such as an x, rise) is another factor that determines the color of type. Certain italic versions of typefaces can make the text seem lighter, although a few make text look darker because of the additional area that the thin strokes of the italic type covers.

Combined with red-green-blue colors, type can be made to stand out by appearing darker, or blend into the page when lighter. When you add smartly placed images near the type, your page comes alive with color.

Area type flowing into shapes

You can do all sorts of nifty things with type that has been flowed into areas — from unusual column designs to fascinating shapes.

Using nonrectangular columns easily livens up a publication. *Mondo 2000* magazine uses curved columns that are easy to read and lend a futuristic, hip look to the publication. Angled and curved columns are simple to create in Illustrator by creating the shape of the column and flowing Area type from one shape to the next.

Traditionally, forcing type into an irregular (nonrectangular) area was quite a task. The typesetter had to set several individual lines of type, each specified by the art director or client to be a certain length so that when all the text was put together, the text formed the shape (see Figure 8-32).

Figure 8-32: The subject matter fitted into a related shape

For example, you can give a report on toxic waste in New Jersey more impact by shaping the text into the form of a hypodermic needle. Or you can make a seasonal ad in the shape of a Christmas tree. Look at some of the Absolut Vodka ads to see what they've done to flow text into that all-too-familiar bottle.

Path Type

The unique thing about type on a path is that when the path is not visible, the type *becomes* the path, as shown in Figure 8-33. This produces some fascinating results, especially when combined with special characters and various fonts of different weights, styles, and colors.

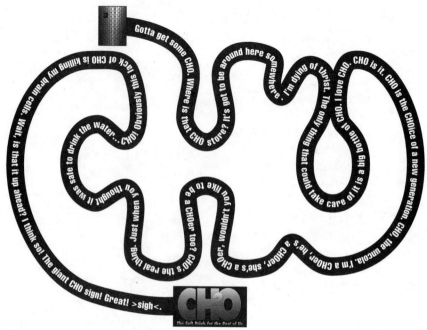

Figure 8-33: Type, when set on a path, actually *becomes* the path.

To create Path type, first create a path in your document. Then click the path with the Path Type tool to create an insertion point along the path. This works whether the path is a closed path or an open path.

The type aligns to the insertion point: If the type is set to flush left, the left edge of the type aligns to the location in which the Path Type tool was first clicked. Unlike Point type, where a hard Return sent the type to the next line, hard Returns work just like spaces in Path type.

You can flow Path type along the path to which it is aligned by clicking the Insertion bar (which resembles a little I-beam) with any Selection tool and dragging along the path. If you drag the Insertion bar to the other side of the path, the type flips over in the direction of the bar. For this reason, it is a good idea to click the topmost part of the I-bar before dragging.

Tip

As with other objects in Illustrator that can be moved by dragging, pressing the Option [Alt] key before releasing the mouse causes the object being dragged to duplicate instead of just move. This works with the Type I-bar, as well.

If you would like the type you are dragging to appear below the path but to not get flipped upside down and change direction, use baseline shift (found in the Character palette) to raise and lower the type to your liking. The key commands for baseline shift are Option+Shift+↑ [Alt+Shift+↑] and Option+Shift+↓ [Alt+Shift+↓] to move up and down by increments set in the Keyboard Increments Preferences dialog box. These commands are particularly useful when adjusting Path type.

Note

Although six different Type tools exist, you only need to choose one. If you have the standard Type tool, it changes into the Area Type tool when the cursor passes over a closed path and it changes into a Path Type tool when the cursor passes over an open path. You can access the Vertical types versions of these tools by pressing Shift.

Type on the top and bottom of a circle

Everyone's doing it. Peer pressure is going to make you succumb as well. If you can put type on the top and the bottom of a circle so that it runs along the same path, you are quite the designer. You can easily create the simple "Type on a Circle" shown in Figure 8-34.

Follow these steps (which are also illustrated in Figure 8-35) and with a little practice, you can create type on a circle in less than 15 seconds. Pretty impressive, even to those who understand how it's done. Here are the steps:

1. Draw a circle with the Ellipse tool (hold down the Shift key to make sure it is a perfect circle). Choose the Path Type tool and click the top center of the circle. The blinking insertion point appears at that point on the circle.

2. Type the text that is to appear at the top of the circle and press ⌘+Shift+C [Ctrl+Shift+C], which centers the type at the top of the circle.

3. Choose the Selection tool and click the top of the I-bar marker, dragging it down to the bottom center of the circle. Before letting go of the mouse button, center the type, making sure that it is readable from left to right, and press the Option [Alt] key. When you do release the mouse button, there will be type along the top and the bottom of the circle, but the type on the bottom will be inside the circle. (The Option [Alt] key duplicates the text and circle, moving them both to a new location in the process. If the Option [Alt] key were not pressed, the type would have just moved to the bottom of the circle.)

Figure 8-34: Type on the top and bottom of a circle

4. Select the bottom text with the Type tool and slowly scoot the type down below the baseline by pressing Option+Shift+↓ [Alt+Shift+↓]. This pushes the type down the baseline in the increments set in the General Preferences dialog box (the default is 2). Keep pressing the key combination until the type is vertically positioned to mimic the type on the top of the circle.

5. Select the text along the bottom of the circle with the Type tool. Type in the text that is to appear at the bottom of the circle. It replaces the selected text. You're finished. Amazing, isn't it? Just remember that you now have two circles with type on them, not one circle with two type paths (that can't happen).

Avoiding Path type trouble

The most common trouble with Path type usually occurs when the path has either corner anchor points or very sharp curves. Letters often *crash* (run into one another) when this occurs.

Besides the most obvious way to avoid this problem, which is to not use paths with corner anchor points and sharp curves, the areas where the letters crash can sometimes be kerned apart until they don't touch anymore.

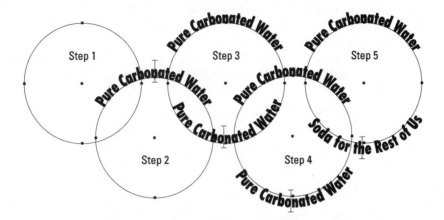

Figure 8-35: Steps for creating type on the top and bottom of a circle

When kerning Path type, be sure to kern from the flush side first. For instance, if the type is flush left, start your kerning from the left side and work to the right. If you start on the wrong end, the letters you kern apart move along the path until they aren't in an area that needs kerning, but other letters will appear there instead.

Another method of fixing crashed letters is to tweak the path with the Direct Selection tool. You can easily fix crashes and letters that have huge amounts of space between them by carefully adjusting both anchor points and control handles.

Tip

If the path that is the base of the letters doesn't need to be directly under the letters, use the baseline shift keyboard commands (Option+Shift+↓ [Alt+Shift+↓] and Option+Shift+↑_[Alt+Shift+↑]) to move the type until the path runs through the center of the text. This can automatically fix the spacing problems encountered by text that crashes over sharp turns and corners.

Path type

One of the most desirable effects with Path type (and, in our opinion, much cooler than type on a circle) is Path type that is reversed. The following steps, and Figure 8-36, describe how to create type reversed on a path:

1. Create the path you want to use for the Path type. In the example, we used a rounded rectangle. Your path can be open or closed.

2. Click the path with the Path Type tool and type in the text for the path. Type with no descenders works better than type with descenders.

3. Vertically center the type on the path by adjusting the baseline shift (Option+Shift+↑ or Option+Shift+↓ [Alt+Shift+↑ or Alt+Shift+↓]). If descenders exist, make sure the type is centered from ascender to descender.

4. Select the type with a Type tool and change the Fill to White. Select the path with the Direct Selection tool and change the Fill to None and the Stroke of the path to Black. Make the weight of the Stroke slightly greater than the point size of the type.

5. Add additional artwork to enhance the path type.

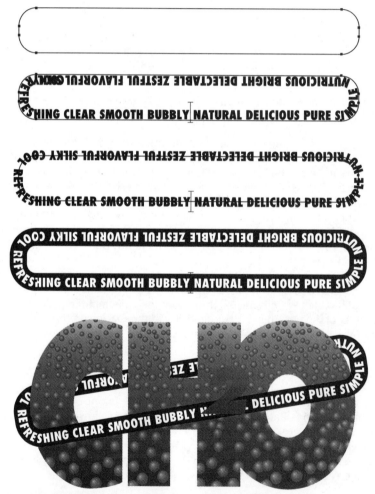

Figure 8-36: Steps for creating type reversed on a path

Selecting and Editing Type

Before you can make changes to text, you must first select it. You have two ways of selecting type: You can select type areas with a Selection tool, which selects every character in the type area, or you can select characters individually or in groups with any of the Type tools.

To select the entire type area or multiple type areas, click the baseline of a line of type within the type area you want to select. Any changes made in the Type menu, Font menu, Character palette, or Paragraph palette affect every character in the selected type areas.

Note If blank fields exist in any of the palettes or no menu items are checked (for instance, no font is checked) when type areas are selected, this means that different options exist for each of those fields or menu items within the type area (for instance, Helvetica for some characters, Times for others). Changing a blank field or unchecked menu item after a type area is selected affects all characters in that area.

To select characters within a type area, you must use a type tool. As you near text that has been typed in the document, the dotted lines surrounding the cursor disappear. The *hot point* of the type cursor is the place where the short horizontal bar crosses the vertical bar (see Figure 8-37). You should use this hot point when clicking with the type cursor.

To select an individual character, drag across the character. As a character is selected, its colors are inverted. To select more than one character, drag left or right across multiple characters; all characters from the location you originally clicked to the current location of the cursor are highlighted. If you drag up with the cursor over straight text, you select all the characters to the left and all the characters to the right of the cursor's current location. Dragging down does the reverse. The more lines you drag up or down, the more lines that are selected.

Hot point

Figure 8-37: The type cursor's hot point

To select one word at a time (and the space that follows it), double-click the word to be selected. The word and the space after it are reversed. The reason that the space following the word is selected is mainly due to the times you copy, cut, and paste words from within sentences. For example, to remove the word *Lazy* in the phrase "The Lazy Boy," you double-click the word *Lazy* and press Delete. The phrase is then "The Boy," which only has one space where the word *Lazy* used to be. To select several words, double-click and drag the type cursor across the words you want to select. Each word you touch with the cursor is selected, from the location initially double-clicked to the current location. Dragging to the previous or next line selects additional lines, with at least a word on the first line double-clicked and one word on the dragged-to line.

For the nimble-fingered clickers, you may also click three times to select a paragraph. Triple-click anywhere inside the paragraph and the entire paragraph is selected, including the hard Return at the end of the paragraph (if one exists). Triple-clicking and dragging selects successive paragraphs if the cursor is moved up or down while the mouse button is still pressed following the third click.

To select all the text within a type area with a Type tool, click once in the type area and choose Select ➪ All (⌘+A [Ctrl+A]). All the text in the type area is reversed. As in most programs, text can only be selected in contiguous blocks. You have no way to select two words in two different locations of the same type area without selecting all the text between them.

You can also select type by using the Shift key. Click one spot (let's call it the beginning), and then Shift+Click another spot. The characters between the beginning and

ASK TOULOUSE: Trouble with Path Type

Trisha: I'm having all sorts of trouble with Path type.

Toulouse: Aren't we all. Anything in particular?

Trisha: Well, for starters, I'm having a dickens of a time trying to move the little I-bar marker along the path.

Toulouse: The key to moving the I-bar marker is to click right at the top of it.

Trisha: Thanks. Also, it seems to flip over all the time.

Toulouse: Actually, grabbing the I-bar at the top fixes this as well.

Trisha: How come my type is sometimes below the path and sometimes above, but it reads the right way?

Toulouse: This usually happens after you've done something such as type on a circle, where you last changed the baseline shift to something less than 0. Change the baseline shift back to 0 and all will be well.

ASK TOULOUSE: I Can't Select My Type!

Winchester: This is really annoying. Every time I select my type, nothing happens.

Toulouse: Nothing's supposed to happen. Selecting doesn't "do" anything.

Winchester: I know that, but my type isn't being selected.

Toulouse: Have you talked to Frank?

Winchester: Yes, but I don't have any other text areas in the document. It can't be that.

Toulouse: Well, it might be . . .

Winchester: And the really spooky thing is that sometimes, when the type isn't selected, I can change the font and other type attributes.

Toulouse: Actually, the type is selected. . . . You just can't see it.

Winchester: I've been meaning to update my eyeglass prescription.

Toulouse: Actually, you probably have the Hide Edges option selected in the View menu.

Winchester: Whaddaya know, it *is* selected. But what does that have to do with my type?

Toulouse: Hide Edges doesn't just hide path edges and points, it hides the selection area when text is selected.

Winchester: That's silly.

Toulouse: Maybe, but it's a good way to change attributes of a few characters in a text story without having to see them in reverse.

the Shift+Click are selected. Successive Shift+Clicks select characters from the beginning to the current location of the most recent Shift+Click.

Illustrator has limited text-editing features. By clicking once within a type area, a blinking insertion point appears. If you begin typing, characters appear where the blinking insertion point is. If you press Delete, you delete the previous character (if one exists).

The arrow keys on your keyboard move the blinking insertion point around in the direction of the arrow. The right arrow moves the insertion point one character to the right, and the left arrow moves the insertion point one character to the left. The up arrow moves the insertion point to the previous line; the down arrow moves the insertion point to the next line.

Pressing the ⌘ [Ctrl] key speeds up the movement of the insertion point. ⌘+← [Ctrl+←] or ⌘+→ [Ctrl+→] moves the insertion point to the preceding or next word, and ⌘+↑ [Ctrl+↑] or ⌘+↓ [Ctrl+↓] moves the insertion point to the preceding or next paragraph.

Tip   Pressing the Shift key while moving the insertion point around with the arrows selects all the characters that the insertion point passes over. This works for the ⌘+arrow [Ctrl+arrow] movements as well.

When you select characters with a Type tool, typing anything deletes the selected characters and replaces them with what is currently being typed. Pressing the Delete key when characters are selected deletes all the selected characters. If you paste type (⌘+V [Ctrl+V]) when characters are selected, the selected characters are replaced with the pasted characters.

Anti-aliased type/artwork

Pixel-based software has always had the capability to display anti-aliased type onscreen, but Illustrator (as of version 9) now also has this capability. *Anti-aliasing* is a process of gradually changing the color of the pixels that lie close to the edge of an object in proportion to how close they are to the edge. The result is a smoother-looking line that isn't jagged. The main difference between anti-aliased type in Photoshop (or another pixel-based program) and Illustrator is that when you choose anti-alias in Photoshop, the text itself is anti-aliased. It appears onscreen and in print as anti-aliased type. In Illustrator, however, the anti-aliasing only takes place onscreen; printed text, based on PostScript, does not rely on anti-aliasing.

So the obvious question is "Why bother?" Well, think back to the late 1980s, before Adobe Type Manager. All type shown on screens had to be at the installed point sizes (usually 10, 12, 14, 18, and 24 points) or it looked terrible. Bigger and smaller type looked especially atrocious. Of course, this type printed wondrously, which was what was really important. Anyway, along came Adobe Type Manager, which made Type 1 PostScript fonts (at that time there was no TrueType) render perfectly onscreen. That was a huge jump forward in display capabilities. Now, however, the next huge jump is here.

Anti-aliased type (for onscreen display purposes only) looks amazingly better than standard type that has either black or white pixels. Part of the problem is that the resolution of a computer monitor is quite low; an average of 72 pixels per inch results in small type that is inherently ugly, regardless of the font. Anti-aliasing makes type edges look softer and enhances readability—at least it does at larger and very small point sizes. At onscreen sizes between 9 and 14 points, the effect is negligible.

You can turn on anti-aliasing within Illustrator by checking the Anti-Aliased Artwork option in File ➪ Preferences ➪ General.

Character Options

The easiest way to change the attributes of characters is by using the Character palette, shown in Figure 8-38. Many of the changes in the Character palette are available as options in the Type menu. As a rule, if you have more than one change to make, it is better to do it in the Character palette than the menu, just so that everything you need is in one place.

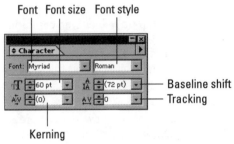

Figure 8-38: The Character palette shown with Options hidden

Character attribute changes affect only the letters that are selected, with the exception of leading (explained later), which should really be in the Paragraph palette.

Tip You can change several character attributes by increments. The increments are set in the Keyboard Increments Preferences dialog box (choose File ⇨ Preferences ⇨ Keyboard Increments). Increments can be changed for point size, leading, baseline shift, and tracking/kerning values. Where appropriate, the key commands for each attribute change are listed in the following sections.

The Character palette

The Character palette can be displayed in three different modes: Standard, With Options, or Multinational. Choose Show Options from the Character palette pop-up menu to display the Options section (which includes Horizontal Scaling, Vertical Scaling, and Baseline Shift). Choose Show Multinational to display the Multinational options: the language, character direction, and several different Kanji options. You can display both Options and the Multinational options at the same time (which some consider four total modes, but that's getting a bit picky, don't you think?). The Character palette remembers which mode the palette was in the last time it was displayed and shows that view the next time you display it.

You can use the Tab key to tab across the different text fields. When in partial display palette mode, the Tab key works only in the partial palette; when the last field (Tracking/Kerning) is selected, the Tab key goes back to the Font field. If a field in the lower part of the palette is highlighted when the palette is closed, the Font field is highlighted. When the palette is in full view, tabbing past the last field (Baseline Shift) highlights the Font field as well. In addition to the Tab key tabbing forward through the text fields, pressing Shift+Tab tabs backward through the text fields.

Choosing Edit ➪ Undo (⌘+Z [Ctrl+Z]) does not undo items typed in the Character palette while you are still in the text field. To undo something, you must first move along (tab) to the next field, undo, and then Shift+Tab back. Canceling (Esc) does not cancel what you have typed but instead highlights the text (if a Type tool is selected).

Note   All of the text fields in the Character palette have pop-up menus with common values in them for quick access and cute little up and down arrows to the left of each field. These arrows increase (up) and decrease (down) the values of each of the currently selected text fields. Pressing the Shift key while clicking the little arrow buttons makes the change with each press even greater.

You can use the keyboard to press these buttons. When the field is highlighted, press the up arrow on your keyboard to press the up arrow button; press the down arrow on your keyboard to press the down arrow button. Press Shift at the same time to increase the value to a greater amount.

Font and style changes

The first field on the Character palette (in the upper-left corner) is the Font family field. When you type the first couple of letters of the font you want to use, Illustrator fills in the rest of the name for you. What happens if you type in a font that you don't have? Illustrator just ignores you, for the most part. In a nice touch, you don't get silly dialog boxes telling you that no such typeface exists; instead, the blinking insertion point remains in the same location until a letter that works is typed.

Let's say you wanted to use the font TypoCity, but it isn't installed. You've highlighted the font field, and you start typing the name of the font. As you type the letter *T* the first font that starts with T is displayed, maybe Times. You type a *y* and discover to your horror that nothing happens. The blinking cursor remains between the *T* and the *i* in Times. You can verify that the font is indeed not installed by clicking the pop-up font menu on the Character palette. Automatically highlight the Font field (and display the Character palette, if it is not) by pressing either ⌘+Option+Shift+F [Ctrl+Alt+Shift+F], or ⌘+Option+Shift+M [Ctrl+Alt+Shift+M].

Note   For the Mac, there is only a single popup menu button to the right of the font and font style text boxes. This popup menu will display the fonts and their font style as submenus.

The field in the upper right, next to the Font field, is the Style field of the font family. The same rules for entering text in the Font field apply here. Type in the first couple of letters of the style, and Illustrator fills in the rest for you. Only if you have the font style installed on your system are you able to type it in. Illustrator is very strict when it comes to bold and italic versions of typefaces. If a specific type style does not exist for what you want, you will *not* be able to type it in, unlike most software programs, which have "bold" and "italic" checkboxes and that allow a font that isn't supposed to be bold to become bold. This can result in poor-quality output when printing.

Measuring Type

So, you've finally mastered this whole silly point/pica concept—you know that an inch has 72 points, and you think that you're ready to conquer the world. And you are, as long as no one asks you to spec type.

At 72 points, the letter I is about 50 points tall. In inches that would be just under ¾". To get better results for specially sized capital letters, a good rule of thumb is that every 100 points is about a 1-inch capital letter. This works for most typefaces, and only for the first several inches, but it is a good start to getting capital letters that are sized pretty accurately.

Curves in capital letters are yet another wrench thrown into the equation. In many typefaces, the bottom and top of the letter O go beneath the baseline and above the ascender height of most squared letters (see the following figure). Serifs on certain typefaces may also cross these lines.

Type is measured from the top of the ascenders (like the top of a capital T) to the bottom of the descender (like the bottom of a lowercase p) as shown in the figure. So when people tell you they want a capital I that is 1 inch high, you can't just say, "Oh, an inch has 72 points, so I will create a 72-point I for them."

Tip   For every text field, the information entered may be applied by either tabbing to the next or preceding text field, or by pressing Enter or Return.

To the right of the font and style text fields is a little pop-up menu triangle that, when pressed, displays a list of all the typefaces installed on your system. The families are displayed in the main list, and arrows show which families have different styles. To select a font, drag the cursor over it until it is highlighted. To select a specific style of a font family, drag the cursor to the font family name, and then drag to the right to select the style name. The fields to the pop-up menu's left are updated instantly.

Size changes

The field directly below the Font field is the Size field. Type in the desired point size (from 0.1 point to 1,296 points in increments of **1/10,000** of a point) and any selected characters increase or decrease to that particular point size. Next to the Size field is a pop-up menu triangle, which lists the standard point sizes available. Point size for type is always measured from the top of the ascenders to the bottom of the descenders. You can increase or decrease type point size from the keyboard by typing ⌘+Shift+> [Ctrl+Shift+>] to increase and ⌘+Shift+< [Ctrl+Shift+<] to decrease the point size by the increment specified in the General Preferences dialog box.

The keyboard commands for increasing and decreasing typographic attributes, such as point size, leading, baseline shift, and tracking, are more than just other ways to change those attributes. Instead, they are invaluable for making changes when the selected type has more than one different value of that attribute within it. For example, if some of the characters have a point size of 10 and some of them have a point size of 20, using the keyboard command (with an increment set to 2 points) changes the type to 12 and 22 points, respectively. This would be tedious to do separately, especially if multiple sizes exist or just a few sizes are scattered widely about.

Leading

Next to the Size field is the Leading text field. Enter the desired leading value (between 0.1 point and 1,296 points, in increments of **1/1000** of a point). To the right of the leading field is a pop-up menu triangle, from which common leading values can be chosen. In Illustrator, leading is measured from the baseline of the current line up to the baseline of the preceding line, as shown in Figure 8-39. The distance between these two baselines is the amount of leading.

Introducing CHO Light!

The world's best soft drink has just gotten better. — 23-Point Leading
Less Calories, Less Color, Less Carbonation, &
Less Filling means More that you can Drink! — 14.5-Point Leading

Figure 8-39: Leading is measured from baseline to baseline. The 23-point leading was set by selecting the second line and changing the leading. The 14.5-point leading was set by selecting the third and fourth lines and changing the leading.

If the Leading field is changed from the number that displays there by default, the Auto Leading entry in the Leading menu becomes unchecked. The Auto Leading box, when checked, makes the leading exactly 120 percent of the point size. This is just great when the type is 10 points because the leading is 12 points, a common point size-to-leading relationship. But as point size goes up, leading should become proportionately less, until, at around 72 points, it is less than the point size. Instead, when Auto Leading is checked, 72-point type has 86.5-point leading. That's a lot of unsightly white space.

Leading increments can be set in the General Preferences dialog box (⌘+K [Ctrl+K]). Press Option+↑ [Alt+↑] to increase the leading (which pushes lines farther apart) and Option+↓ [Alt+↓] to decrease the leading (which pushes lines closer together).

Kerning and tracking

Kerning is the amount of space between any specific pair of letters. Kerning values can only be changed when an insertion point is blinking between two characters.

Tracking is the amount of space between all the letters currently selected. If the type area is selected with a Selection tool, it refers to all the space between all the characters in the entire type area. If characters are selected with a Type tool, tracking only affects the space between the specific letters selected.

Although they are related and appear to do basically the same thing, tracking and kerning actually work independently of each other. They only *look* like they are affecting each other; they never actually change the amount of one if the other is altered. The Kerning field appears directly below the point size of the type, whereas the Tracking field appears below the leading (see Figure 8-40).

The Kerning field often reads Auto instead of a value when several letters are selected. If Auto appears in that field, the kerning built into the font is used automatically. Choosing a different value (if several letters are selected, only 0 can be chosen, but any number can be entered if a blinking insertion point appears between the letters) overrides the Auto setting and uses the value you type in. Auto Kerning works by reading the kerning values of the typeface that were embedded by the type designer when the typeface was originally created. The typeface designer normally defines the space between letters; different typefaces look like they have different amounts of space between letters. Usually a couple of hundred preset kerning pairs exist for common Adobe typefaces, although the expert sets have quite a few more. When Auto Kerning is in effect, you can see those preset kerning values by clicking between kerned letter pairs (capital *T* with most vowels is a good one to check) and reading the value in the Kerning field. If Auto Kerning is being used, the value is shown in parentheses.

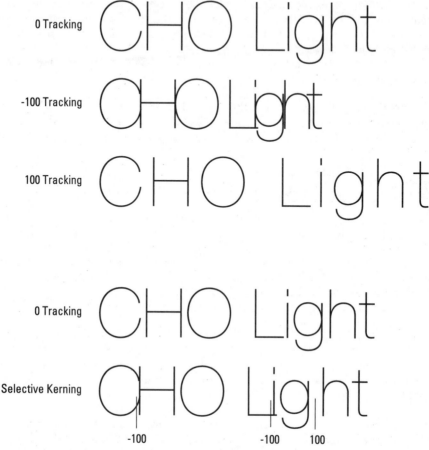

Figure 8-40: Examples of tracking and kerning

Different typefaces have different kerning pairs, and kerning pairs don't only change from typeface to typeface, but also from weight to weight and style to style. For example, a kerning pair of the letters *AV* in Adobe Garamond, when Auto Kerning is on, is set to –80. If you type in a value of –150, that value overrides the Auto Kerning, turning it off and using your new value of –150. Figure 8-41 shows the difference between a kerning of –80 and –150.

To increase or decrease the kerning or tracking by the increments specified in the Keyboard Increments Preferences dialog box, insert the Type tool between two letters and press Option+← [Alt+←] or Option+→ [Alt+→]. To increase or decrease the tracking or kerning by a factor of five times the amount in the General Preferences dialog box, press ⌘+Option+← [Alt+←] or ⌘+Option+→ [Alt+→].

Figure 8-41: The left letters are using Auto Kerning −80. The right letters are using −150 kerning.

Kerning and tracking values are based on **1/1000** *em space*. An em space is the width of two numbers (think of two zeros — they tend to be the widest-looking numbers) at that particular point size.

The values entered for tracking and kerning must be between −1,000 and 10,000. A value of −1,000 results in stacked letters. A value of 10,000 makes enough space between letters for 10 em spaces, or 20 numbers. That's a *lot* of space.

Note

Different software works with kerning and tracking differently. In programs that *do* offer numerical tracking, it is usually represented in some form of a fraction of an em space, but the denominator varies from software to software. In QuarkXPress, for example, tracking and kerning is measured in **1/200** of an em space. Check the documentation that comes with your software to determine the denominator used. This can get a little confusing when going from program to program, although the transformation from QuarkXPress to Illustrator is quite simple: To get the same tracking and kerning values in Quark that you used in Illustrator, divide the number you used in Illustrator by 5 (1,000/200 = 5).

The Options section of the Character palette contains the Baseline Shift field, which, unlike leading, moves individual characters up and down relative to their baseline (from leading). Positive numbers move the selected characters up, and negative numbers move the characters down by the amount specified. The maximum amount of baseline shift is 1,296 points in either direction. Baseline shift is especially useful for Path type. Baseline shift can be changed via the keyboard by selecting a letter with the Type tool and pressing Option+Shift+↑ [Alt+Shift+↑] to increase and Option+Shift+↓ [Alt+Shift+↓] to decrease the baseline shift in the increment specified in the General Preferences dialog box.

Vertical Scale and Horizontal Scale

Also in the Options section of the Character palette is the Horizontal Scale field. Horizontal scale controls the width of the type, causing it to become expanded or condensed horizontally. Values from 1 to 10,000 percent can be entered in this field. Like most other fields in the Character palette, the values entered are absolute values, so whatever the horizontal scale is, changing it back to 100 percent returns the type to its original proportions.

Tip You can quickly reset the Horizontal Scale field value to 100 percent by pressing ⌘+Shift+X [Ctrl+Shift+X].

The language barrier

If you're reading a translation of the *Adobe Illustrator 10 Bible* in a language other than English, we'd like to welcome you by saying hello in your native language: "Hello." Okay, we're probably not fooling you here; through the magic of translators who speak several languages much more fluently than we speak "westernized East-coast American English," our current language of choice, this book is translated into other languages without one iota of input from us.

If your language of choice is not English, you'll be interested in the Language option along the bottom of the Character palette. It enables you to change to the language you want, so that functions such as the spelling dictionary and hyphenation dictionary work for words that you type.

The other options along the bottom of the Character palette are specifically designed for Kanji character operations, with the exception of the Direction pop-up menu, which can be used with Roman characters to achieve various effects. The Direction pop-up menu is discussed later in this chapter in the "Vertical Type" section.

Paragraph Options

Some changes that are made to text affect entire paragraphs at the same time. Paragraph attributes include alignment, indentation, space before paragraphs, spacing, hyphenation, hanging punctuation, repeated character processing, and line breaking.

You can change paragraph attributes if you first select a type area using a Selection tool, in which case, the changes affect every paragraph within the entire type area. If you use the Type tool to select one or more characters, changes made to paragraph attributes affect the entire paragraphs of each of the selected characters.

To display the Paragraph palette (see Figure 8-42) using menu commands, choose Window ➪ Type ➪ Paragraph. To display the Paragraph palette with a key command, press ⌘+M [Ctrl+M].

Figure 8-42: The Paragraph palette shown with Options hidden

Pressing Tab tabs forward through the text fields and Shift+Tab tabs backward through the same text fields. Press Enter or Return to apply the changes that were made.

The bottom part of the Paragraph palette contains information that doesn't get changed too often, so for the most part, it doesn't need to be displayed. If you wish to display it, choose Show Options from the Paragraph palette pop-up menu.

Alignment

You can choose from five different types of paragraph alignment (see Figure 8-43). Each of them is represented by a graphical representation of what multiple lines of type look like when that particular alignment is applied.

The first alignment type is the most common: Flush Left, which experienced type-setters often refer to as ragged right due to the uneven right side of the text. You can also apply this type of alignment by pressing ⌘+Shift+L [Ctrl+Shift+L].

The next type of alignment is Centered, where all lines of type in the paragraph are centered relative to each other, to the point clicked, or to the location of the I-bar in Path type. You can also apply this type of alignment by pressing ⌘+Shift+C [Ctrl+Shift+C].

The middle alignment choice is Flush Right, in which type has a smooth, even right side and an uneven left side (no, ragged left isn't really a correct term). You can also apply this type of alignment by pressing ⌘+Shift+R [Ctrl+Shift+R].

The fourth type of alignment is Justified (Illustrator calls it Justify Full Lines), where both the left and right sides appear smooth and even. Extra space is added between letters and words, as defined in the "Spacing" section later in this chapter. The last line in a justified paragraph appears to be flush left. You can also apply this type of alignment by pressing ⌘+Shift+J [Ctrl+Shift+J].

The last alignment type is called Justify All Lines (commonly called Force Justify), which is the same as Justify Full Lines except that the last line of every paragraph is justified along with the other lines of the paragraph. This can create some really awful looking paragraphs if you're using one of the one of the Romantic languages, and is done mainly for artistic emphasis, not as a proper way to justify type. For many of the Asian languages like Japanese and Chinese, it is a common alignment type. Justify All Lines is particularly useful for stretching a single line of type across a certain width. You can also apply this type of alignment by pressing ⌘+Shift+B [Ctrl+Shift+B].

Note   Justification only works on Area type. Illustrator does not let you select Justify Full Lines or Justify All Lines for Path type or Point type.

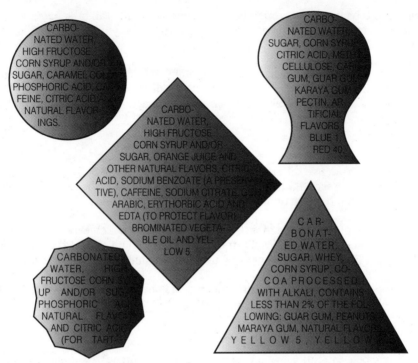

Figure 8-43: The five different types of alignment: Flush Left, Centered, Flush Right, Justify Full Lines, and Justify All Lines

Indentation

Paragraphs can be indented within the Paragraph palette by choosing different amounts of indentation for the left edge, right edge, and first line of each paragraph. The maximum indentation for all three fields is 1,296 points and the minimum is –1,296 points.

Using indents is a great way to offset type, such as quotes, that have smaller margins than the rest of the type surrounding the quote. Changing the indentation values is also useful for creating hanging indents, such as numbered or bulleted text.

To easily create hanging indents, make the Left Indent as large as the width of a bullet or a number and a space, and then make the First Line value the negative value of that. If the left indent is 2 picas, the first line would be –2 picas. This creates great hanging indents every time.

Space Before Paragraphs

Illustrator lets you place additional space between paragraphs by entering a number in the Space Before Paragraphs text field. This measurement is added to the leading to determine the distance from baseline to baseline before the selected paragraphs. You can also enter a negative number to decrease space between paragraphs, if necessary. Values for Space Before Paragraphs can be between –1,296 and 1,296 points.

Spacing

Illustrator enables you to control the spacing of letters and words in text by editing the Spacing fields in the middle of the Paragraph palette (see Figure 8-44).

Figure 8-44: The Spacing section of the Paragraph palette

Spacing affects the space between letters and words regardless of the alignment, although Justified text has even more spacing control than Flush Left, Flush Right, or Centered text.

When Flush Left, Flush Right, or Centered alignment is chosen, the only text fields that can be changed are the Desired fields for Letter Spacing and Word Spacing.

You can enter values ranging from 0 to 1,000 percent for Word Spacing. The Minimum must be less than the amount in the Desired box and the Maximum must be more than the amount in the Desired box. At 100 percent, the word space is normal; at less than 100 percent, the word space is reduced; and at a number greater than 100 percent, the word space is increased.

The values for Letter Spacing must be from –50 to 500 percent. The Minimum must be less than the amount in the Desired box and the Maximum must be more than the amount in the Desired box. At 0 percent, the letter space is normal; at less than 0 percent, the letter space is reduced; and at a number greater than 0 percent, the letter space is increased.

The Minimum and Maximum boxes in the Word Spacing and Letter Spacing areas are mainly used to control where the extra space goes and where it is removed from when stretching out and compressing lines of text.

Hyphenation

Hyphenation? In a drawing program? We couldn't believe it either, but there it was staring us in the face. A nice addition to Illustrator's text-handling capabilities, hyphenation works in the background, silently hyphenating when necessary.

To use Illustrator's hyphenation, you must check the Auto Hyphenate box in the lower-left of the Paragraph palette. After this is checked for selected text, that text hyphenates fairly well.

Hyphenation in Illustrator works from a set of hyphenation rules that you define in the Hyphenation Options dialog box (shown previously in Figure 8-3). View the Hyphenation dialog box by choosing Hyphenation from the Paragraph pop-up menu. Here you can specify how many letters must fall before the hyphen and how many letters must fall after the hyphen. You can also limit the number of consecutive hyphens to avoid the "ladder look" of multiple hyphens.

Tip   When you need to hyphenate a word at a place where Illustrator doesn't seem to want to hyphenate it, you can create a *discretionary hyphen*. Create a discretionary hyphen by placing the blinking insertion point where the word should break and typing ⌘+Shift+- (hyphen) [Ctrl+Shift+- (hyphen)]. This causes the word to hyphenate at a certain part of the word only if that word has to be hyphenated. If the word doesn't have to be hyphenated, no hyphen appears. This is much better than just typing a normal hyphen, as this works temporarily; but if the manually-hyphenated word is moved from the edge of the line, the hyphen remains within it.

Hang Punctuation

If Hang Punctuation is checked, punctuation at the left edge of a Flush Left, Justified, or Justified Last Line paragraph appears outside the type area, as shown in Figure 8-45. Punctuation on the right edge of a Flush Right, Justified, or Justified Last Line paragraph also appears outside the type area. Strangely enough, Illustrator is one of the few programs that supports this very hip feature.

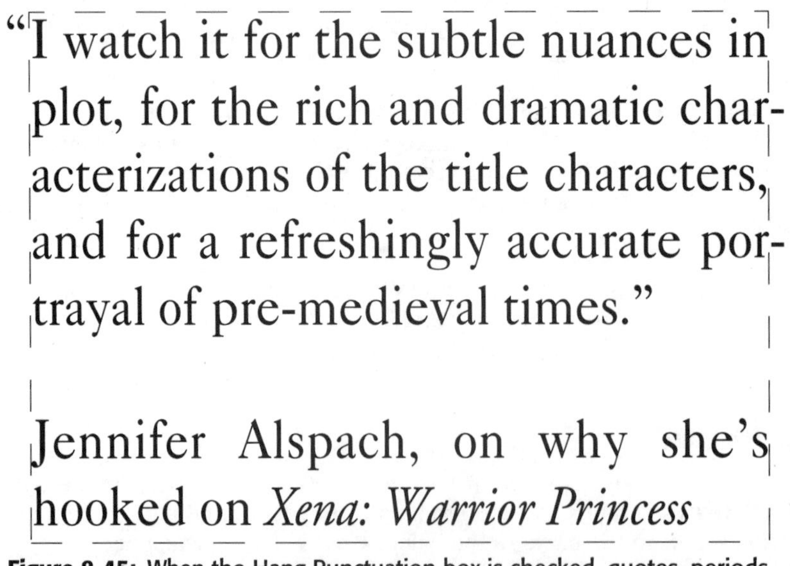

"I watch it for the subtle nuances in plot, for the rich and dramatic characterizations of the title characters, and for a refreshingly accurate portrayal of pre-medieval times."

Jennifer Alspach, on why she's hooked on *Xena: Warrior Princess*

Figure 8-45: When the Hang Punctuation box is checked, quotes, periods, commas, and hyphens fall outside the boundary of the type area.

Special Characters

Special characters are those characters that require special attention. They are the set of language-specific characters and symbols that aren't normally found on a standard keyboard. They can include diacritical marks, foreign language characters, Greek and Latin characters often used in mathematical equations, and common symbols such as the copyright and the cents symbols.

Those unusual options

Repeated Character Processing and Line Breaking % are two options that are only relevant to Kanji typefaces. They aren't available when a standard Roman typeface is being used. The Kurikaeshi Moji option lets you control the repeated Japanese text characters. By turning this option on, Illustrator inserts a repeat character rather than put in two identical characters after each other. The other option, Kinsoku Shori, lets you control the character's line breaking.

From the Paragraph palette menu, you can select a Kinsoku Shori option that opens the dialog box shown in Figure 8-46. This dialog box includes options for specifying whether punctuation marks can start a new line or if the text breaks to include a character on the next line.

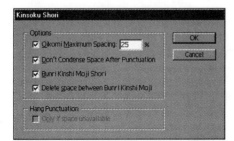

Figure 8-46: The Kinsoku Shori dialog box controls how line breaks are handled for Kanji text.

Special characters on a Mac

On a Macintosh OS, many special characters are available besides the standard letters, numbers, and symbols that appear on your keyboard. To show you these special characters, Apple's system software includes a desk accessory (Mac OS 9) or utility program (Mac OS X) called KeyCaps, which displays the keyboard you are using and shows what each character looks like in the typeface you choose.

Each font has essentially four sets of characters. The first set is obtained by normal typing of the keyboard keys, which include numbers, lowercase letters, and a few symbols. The second set is obtained by pressing the Shift key prior to pressing the keyboard key and includes capital letters and symbols that appear on the top half of the keyboard keys. The third set is obtained by pressing the Option key before pressing a keyboard key. This set consists primarily of the common special symbols, such as a bullet (•), the cents symbol (¢), an ellipsis (. . .), and the pi symbol (π). The fourth set of characters can only be obtained when both the Option and Shift keys are pressed before a keyboard key is pressed and includes less common symbols, like f ligatures (fi, fl), the double dagger (‡), and the Apple symbol (⌘).

While almost all typefaces have the first and second sets, many typefaces do not contain very many characters in the third and fourth sets. The list in Figure 8-47 shows the common symbols and their keyboard equivalents, but not all typefaces have all the symbols, and some of the symbols in some of the typefaces may have different keyboard commands.

Symbol typefaces on a Mac

Several symbol typefaces are available that contain symbols in place of letters and numbers. The most popular of these is the Symbol typeface, which has Greek letters and mathematical operands and symbols. The next most popular symbol font would have to be ZapfDingbats, which contains a variety of different symbols, as shown in Figure 8-48.

Some other typefaces that contain primarily symbols are Carta, the map symbol typeface; Bill's Dingbats, a shareware set of symbols that nicely complements ZapfDingbats; and Mathematical Pi, a math font containing math symbols.

One of the great things about Symbol typefaces is that individual characters can be turned into outline characters and edited to create different illustrations.

Special characters in Windows

To access special characters on a Windows system, you usually have to enter a code where you want the special character to be. You can enter codes in Illustrator by pressing and holding Alt, and then typing in the four-digit code for that character. Figure 8-49 shows all the hidden special characters (ones that aren't shown on the keyboard) and the code needed to type them.

To access a bullet, for instance, you would press Alt, type **0149**, and then release the Alt key. A bullet appears where your text cursor last was.

1st set	2nd set + Shift	3rd set + Option	4th set +Option+Shift
`	~	`	`
1	!	¡	⁄
2	@	™	¤
3	#	£	‹
4	$	¢	›
5	%	∞	ﬁ
6	^	§	ﬂ
7	&	¶	‡
8	*	•	°
9	(	ª	·
0	)	º	‚
-	_	–	—
=	+	≠	±
q	Q	œ	Œ
w	W	∑	„
e	E	®	‰
r	R	†	Â
t	T	¥	Ê
y	Y	¨	Á
u	U	^	¨
i	I	^	ˆ
o	O	ø	Ø
p	P	π	∏
[	{	"	”
]	}	'	’
\	|	«	»
a	A	å	Å
s	S	ß	Í
d	D	∂	Î
f	F	ƒ	Ï
g	G	©	˝
h	H	˙	Ó
j	J	∆	Ô
k	K	˚	
l	L	¬	Ò
;	:	…	Ú
'	"	æ	Æ
z	Z	Ω	¸
x	X	≈	˛
c	C	ç	Ç
v	V	√	◊
b	B	∫	ı
n	N	˜	˜
m	M	µ	Â
,	<	≤	¯
.	>	≥	˘
/	?	÷	¿

Figure 8-47: The standard Mac keyboard
set for most fonts

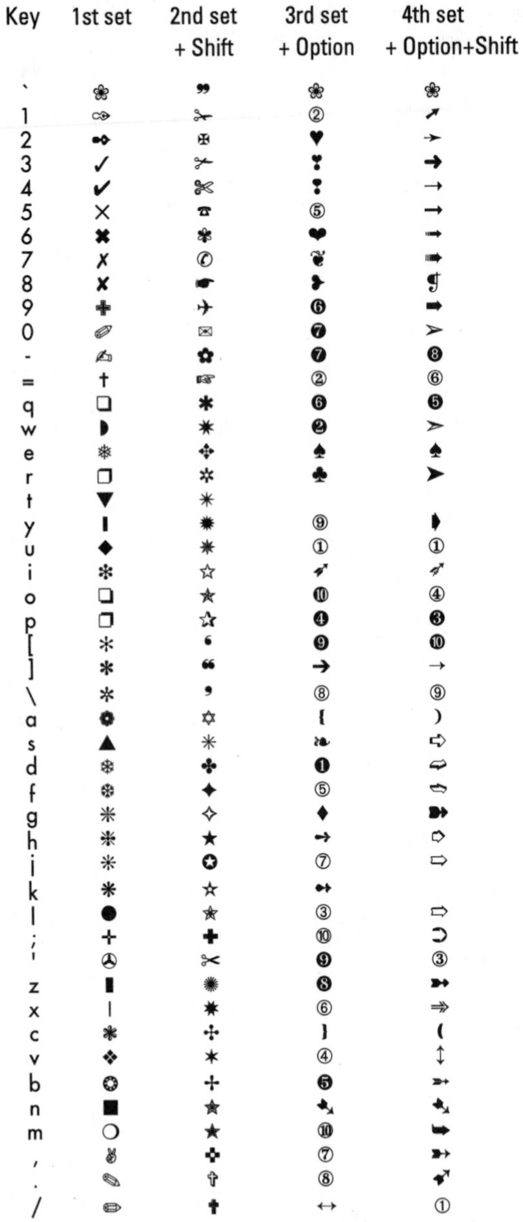
Key
1st set
2nd set + Shift
3rd set + Option
4th set + Option+Shift
` 1 2 3 4 5 6 7 8 9 0 - = q w e r t y u i o p [ ] \ a s d f g h j k l ; ' z x c v b n m , . /

Figure 8-48: The character set of ZapfDingbats

ƒ	0131	-	0173	×	0215
„	0132	®	0174	Ø	0216
…	0133	¯	0175	Ù	0217
†	0134	°	0176	Ú	0218
‡	0135	±	0177	Û	0219
ˆ	0136	²	0178	Ü	0220
‰	0137	³	0179	Ý	0221
Š	0138	´	0180	ß	0222
‹	0139			à	0223
Œ	0140	µ	0181	à	0224
	0141	¶	0182	á	0225
	0142	·	0183	â	0226
	0143		0184	ã	0227
	0144	¹	0185	ä	0228
'	0145	º	0186	å	0229
'	0146	»	0187	æ	0230
"	0147	¼	0188	ç	0231
"	0148	½	0189	è	0232
•	0149	¾	0190	é	0233
–	0150	¿	0191	ê	0234
—	0151	À	0192	ë	0235
~	0152	Á	0193	ì	0236
™	0153	Â	0194	í	0237
š	0154	Ã	0195	î	0238
›	0155	Ä	0196	ï	0239
œ	0156	Å	0197	ð	0240
	0157	Æ	0198	ñ	0241
	0158	Ç	0199	ò	0242
Ÿ	0159	È	0200	ó	0243
	0160	É	0201	ô	0244
¡	0161	Ê	0202	õ	0245
¢	0162	Ë	0203	ö	0246
£	0163	Ì	0204	÷	0247
¤	0164	Í	0205	ø	0248
¥	0165	Î	0206	ù	0249
¦	0166	Ï	0207	ú	0250
§	0167	Ð	0208	û	0251
¨	0168	Ñ	0209	ü	0252
©	0169	Ò	0210	ý	0253
ª	0170	Ó	0211	þ	0254
«	0171	Ô	0212	ÿ	0255
¬	0172	Õ	0213		
		Ö	0214		

Figure 8-49: The hidden special characters and their corresponding four-digit ANSI codes

Customizing Fonts

You can create and modify typefaces right on your computer, using tools very similar to the ones in Adobe Illustrator. Creating fonts is, in a way, the reverse process of outlining existing fonts because you are taking outlines and turning them into characters in typefaces. Figure 8-50 shows two of the most popular shareware fonts created through a combination of Illustrator and Fontographer: Lefty Casual and Ransom Note.

Figure 8-50: Lefty Casual and Ransom Note fonts

By using existing typefaces, you can customize the characters, creating a unique typeface. In a typeface you create, all the special characters can be ones you've designed especially for that face.

Caution   Check with the original typeface manufacturer before customizing, to ensure that you are not violating that particular font vendor's copyright.

Macromedia Fontographer is the most popular font-creation software currently available, boasting Multiple Master capabilities and very precise Bézier control tools.

Export/Place

To export text, select the text you want to export and choose File ➪ Export. A Save dialog box appears that asks in what format and to where you want to save the text.

You can save text in most of the common formats, and you can import it back into Illustrator with the Place command (choose File ➪ Place when a text area is active with a Type tool). Word-processing software, page-layout software, or any other software that can read text files can open and use text that you saved in Illustrator.

Vertical type

Vertical type is a fascinating capability in Illustrator. If you use Kanji characters, you'll find it invaluable. But even if you don't, you may find some interesting uses for setting type vertically, instead of horizontally.

You have two ways to make your type appear vertical instead of horizontal. You can create type using any of the three Vertical Type tools, or you can convert horizontal type into vertical type with Type ➪ Type Orientation ➪ Vertical. Figure 8-51 shows Rectangle type both horizontally and vertically. Note that Vertical type also flows from right to left and takes up more space than Horizontal type.

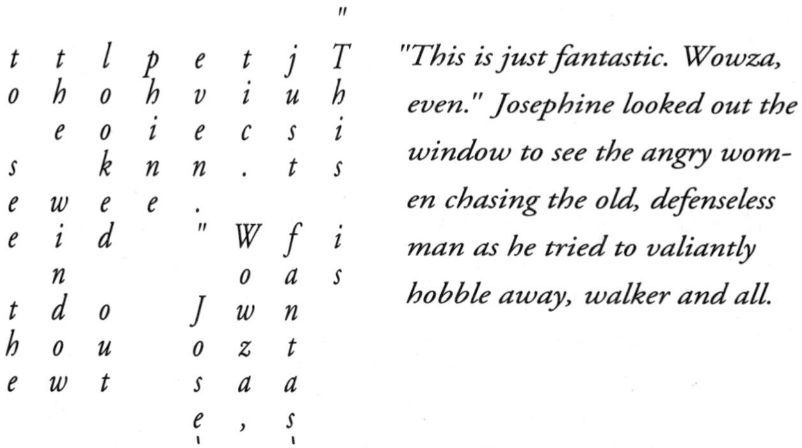

"*This is just fantastic. Wowza, even.*" *Josephine looked out the window to see the angry women chasing the old, defenseless man as he tried to valiantly hobble away, walker and all.*

Figure 8-51: Vertical type (left) and the same type reoriented to horizontal (right)

Most of Illustrator's standard character and paragraph palette changes work with vertical type, but not always in ways you would expect. For instance, type is set on a centerline, not a baseline. The centerline runs vertically through the center of each character. The following is a list of differences in the way each major function works:

✦ **Font.** Same

✦ **Size.** Same

✦ **Leading.** Changes the amount of space between the vertical "lines" of type, measured from centerline to centerline.

✦ **Kerning/Tracking.** Changes the amount of vertical space between each character. Because very few Roman characters have both ascenders and descenders, tracking and kerning substantially can help eliminate the excess white space between characters that makes vertical type so hard to read.

✦ **Vertical Scale.** Changes the width (horizontal scale) of the characters.

✦ **Horizontal Scale.** Changes the height (vertical scale) of the characters.

✦ **Baseline Shift.** Moves the type left (negative values) and right (positive values) along the centerline.

✦ **Flush Left.** Words are flush top.

✦ **Center.** Words are vertically centered.

✦ **Flush Right.** Words are flush bottom.

✦ **Justify Full Lines.** Words on full (vertical) lines are justified from top to bottom.

✦ **Justify All Lines.** All lines are vertically justified.

✦ **Left Indent.** Top indent. Positive numbers move the text down and negative numbers move the text up.

✦ **Right Indent.** Bottom indent, with numbers working like Left Indent.

✦ **First Line Indent.** The rightmost line indent. Once again, positive numbers move the text down and negative numbers move the text up.

✦ **Space Before Paragraph.** Paragraphs go from right to left, so this control increases the space to the right of the selected paragraph(s).

✦ **Auto Hyphenate.** Hyphenates words the same way as horizontal type, but the hyphens appear at the bottom of each line.

✦ **Hang Punctuation.** Punctuation is hung above and below the text area.

✦ **Tab Ruler.** Appears to the right of text areas in vertical form.

✦ **Create Outlines.** Same.

Changing the direction of type

Direction and Orientation completely differ from each other. The Orientation control is a text area control; changing it affects the entire text area. The Direction control is a character-based control, which can affect all characters or one character. This control really makes vertical type worth using.

You can choose from three options in the Direction pop-up menu (located in the Character palette):

✦ **Standard.** This keeps characters in the direction that is the default of the type area. This is usually displayed so that each character is "right side up."

✦ **Rotated.** This rotates characters –90 degrees.

✦ **Tate Chu Yoko.** This "direction" affects selected characters and groups the selected characters onto one horizontal line. In Figure 8-52, we've selected each word separately and applied the Tate Chu Yoko direction to them. In addition, we increased the leading so that the columns of text would be easier to read.

Type on a path takes on new life when you use vertical type. That, combined with Illustrator's capability to group characters (words and so forth) together along the chain of text provides additional text capabilities that can't be found anywhere else.

Other Type Considerations

When you're using type in Illustrator, remember the following points to get good results:

✦ Make sure that the person you are sending the Illustrator file to has the same fonts you have. It isn't enough just to have the same name of a font; you need the exact font that was created by the same manufacturer.

✦ Try not to mix TrueType fonts with PostScript fonts. This usually ends up confusing everyone involved.

✦ If the person you are sending Illustrator files to does *not* have your typeface, select the type in that font and choose Type ➪ Create Outlines (⌘+Shift+O [Ctrl+Shift+O]).

✦ When you're printing an Illustrator file that has been placed in other software, missing type styles may go unnoticed until after the job has printed. Be doubly sure that the person outputting the file has all the fonts in the embedded Illustrator file.

✦ If you are saving your illustration as an EPS file to be placed into another program and you are not going to open the file, you can select Include Document Fonts in the EPS Save dialog box. This forces any fonts used in the illustration to be saved with the illustration and enables the illustration to print as a placed image from within another program or to print from Illustrator as a placed EPS.

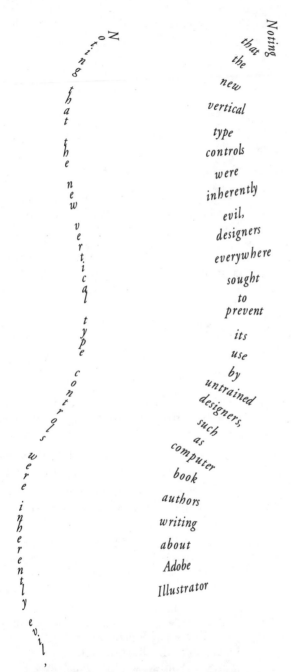

Figure 8-52: Vertical type on a curved path as it normally appears (left), and when each word has Tate Chu Yoko direction applied to it (right)

Summary

Type is a very important part of Illustrator and was used heavily to bring you this book. The assortment of type controls makes it possible to use individual characters as design objects. Whether you're using a menu option in the Type menu or one of the settings in Type palettes, you have complete control over how your text will look. In this chapter, you learned

✦ Illustrator supports several different types of fonts.

✦ Most of the options used to control type are found in the Type menu or the Window menu's Type submenu.

✦ You have four different ways to put type on a page: Point type, Rectangle type, Area type, and Path type.

✦ Point type has one point as its "anchor," and the type is aligned to that anchor point.

✦ Rectangle type exists within a rectangle drawn with the Type tool.

✦ Area type is type that exists within the confines of any path.

✦ Path type is type that runs along the edge of a path.

✦ Type can be selected all at once by clicking the path (or point) of the type with the Selection tool.

✦ Individual characters, words, and paragraphs can be selected by using any of the Type tools.

✦ The Character palette (accessed by pressing ⌘+T [Ctrl+T]) contains all the character-specific information about selected type and can be used to change that information.

✦ Illustrator doesn't have type "styles"; instead, you must select the exact font you wish to use.

✦ Tracking and kerning removes or adds space between groups or pairs of letters, respectively.

✦ The Paragraph palette (accessed by pressing ⌘+M [Ctrl+M]) contains all the paragraph-specific information about selected type and can be used to change that information.

✦ Type can be set to wrap around selected paths by using the Text Wrapping feature.

✦ Type can be set to jump from text block to text block by linking text blocks together.

✦ The Tab Ruler palette is used to set tabs for text areas.

✦ If you have both the screen font and the printer font of a Type 1 typeface, or if you have a TrueType font installed, you can convert the font into outlines via the Create Outlines command.

✦ Many special characters can be accessed in each font on a Mac or PC by pressing different keys or codes.

✦ Type can be orientated vertical as sentences or as characters.

✦　　✦　　✦

Applying Fills and Strokes

Every path that is drawn and every object that is created has two unique characteristics—a Fill and a Stroke. A Fill is a color that fills the path area or objects and the stroke is the color, thickness and style of the line that makes up the path. In addition to solid colors and gradients, objects and paths can be filled with patterns and textures. Patterns and textures could be created by the simple act of drawing them, but Illustrator has made their creation a breeze. Illustrator enables you to create a pattern and save that pattern for future use. And let's not leave out the capability to add textures to make your flat images pop up. The Pen and Ink option and the Photo Crosshatch option let you make those 2D images appear to have 3D qualities. There's a lot that you can do with strokes and the tail end of this chapter shows how to use them in many unique ways.

Fills

The *Fill* of an object is the color inside the shape. If a path is closed, the Fill exists only on the inside of the path. If the path is open (meaning that it has two End Points), the Fill exists between an imaginary line drawn from End Point to End Point and the path itself.

Fills in open paths can provide some very interesting results when the path crosses itself, or the imaginary line crosses the path. Figure 9-1 shows an example of Fills in open and closed paths and how the paths appear in Outline mode. For text, the Fill is the color of the text.

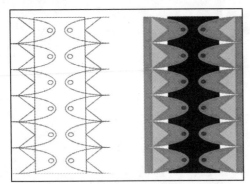

Figure 9-1: Open and closed paths in both
Outline mode (left) and Preview mode (right)

Note   Fills do not appear in Outline mode, only in Preview mode. Depending on the complexity of the path and the type of Fill, Illustrator may take a significant amount of time to preview the Fill. Working in Outline mode can overcome these time constraints.

The Fill color options include White, Black, Process Colors, Spot Colors, Patterns, Gradients, and Gradient Meshes. The Fill option for an object can also be set to None or to an Opacity setting from 0 to 100, where the Fill is transparent, semitransparent or completely opaque. This lets you see behind a path to what is underneath it when the Stroke of an object is the visible part.

To select a Fill color, you need to make sure that the Fill box in the toolbox is selected. You can select either the Fill box or the Stroke box. Pressing the X key toggles between these two boxes. When the Fill box is selected, it appears on top of the Stroke box. The Fill box displays the color or type of Fill.

Tip   You can tell if the Fill box is selected because it will be on top of the Stroke box in the toolbox.

The default Fill color is white. To select a different Fill color, you need to make sure the Fill box is selected, and then choose a new color in the Color palette. Another way to select a new Fill color is to double-click the Fill box. This opens the Color Picker dialog box where you can select a new Fill color. The various color modes and the Color Picker are covered in more detail in the "The Color Palette" section that comes later in the chapter.

Directly beneath the Fill and Stroke boxes in the toolbox are three icons. These icons specify the type of Fill that is to be used. The options include from left to right, Color (the default), Gradient, and None. The shortcut keystrokes for these options are < for Color, > for Gradient, and / for None. If the Color icon is selected, then the Fill box can hold either a color or a pattern, but if the Gradient icon is selected, then the Fill box will hold the gradient that is defined in the Gradient palette. If the None icon is selected, the fill will be removed from the selected object.

You can also change the Fill color and type using the Swatches palette. This palette can hold colors, gradients, and patterns. To select a swatch from the Swatch palette, just select the Fill box and click the swatch that you wish to use in the Swatch palette. The Color or Gradient icon will be selected automatically depending on the type of Swatch that was selected.

Another way to get Fill colors is with the Eyedropper tool. By selecting the Eyedropper tool and clicking a color in the current document, the color under the Eyedropper tool becomes the Fill color.

Selecting a style from the Styles palette will update both the Fill and Stroke boxes to the defined style. The style will be displayed in both the current selection and the Fill and Stroke boxes.

Strokes

The *Stroke* of an object is made up of three parts: color, weight, and style. Strokes appear where paths exist or around the edges of type. Like Fills, any one path or object may have only one type of Stroke on it; the color, weight, and style of the Stroke are consistent throughout the length of the path or the entire text object. (Individual characters in a text object can have different Strokes if they are selected with the Type tool when the Stroke attributes are applied.)

The Stroke color options are White, Black, Tints, Process Colors, Spot Colors, Patterns, Opacity, and None (the Stroke is off). When the Stroke color option is set to None, the object is said to have no Stroke and only the Fill color of the object is displayed.

Caution   Strokes cannot have gradients applied to them. If you click the Gradient icon when the Stroke box is selected, then the Fill box will be filled with a gradient.

The weight of a Stroke is how thick it is. On a path, the Stroke is centered on that path, with half the thickness of the Stroke on one side of the path and half the thickness on the other side of the path. Strokes can be anywhere from 0 to 1,000 points thick and can be specified as fractional amounts such as 4.25.

The style of a Stroke consists of several parts, including the cap style, join style, miter limit, and dash pattern. The *cap style* is the way that the ends of a Stroke look and can be either butt cap, rounded cap, or projected cap. The *join style* is the way that Corner Points on paths appear when stroked and can be either a mitered join, rounded join, or beveled join. Figure 9-2 shows examples of the cap styles.

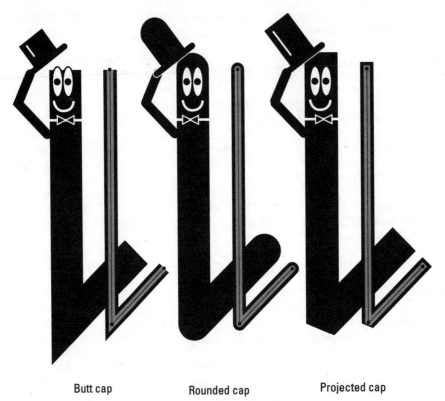

Butt cap   Rounded cap   Projected cap

Figure 9-2: The three different cap styles for Strokes

The *miter limit* is the length at which miter joins are cropped. If a path has a thick Stroke and a tight angle (like those that appear on some stars with a tiny inner radius and a large outer one), the point at which the outside edges of the Stroke would meet might be ridiculously far from where the points are set. Using a miter limit tells Illustrator that if the meeting point of the outside edges is more than so many times the thickness of the Stroke, to crop it off at the point. Figure 9-3 shows different miter limits on different corners.

Normally, the *dash pattern* for a Stroke is solid, but you can create various dash patterns for different effects. To enable a dash pattern, you must enable the Dashed Line option in the Stroke palette. You can then enter values for the dash and gap text fields. For example, entering 12pt in the first dash field and 6pt in the first gap will create a dashed line with dashes that are twice the width of the space between them.

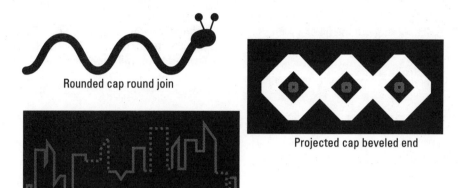

Figure 9-3: A sampling of all the different cap styles, join styles, miter limits, and dash patterns for Strokes

Combining Strokes with Fills

Many times, paths in Illustrator require both Fills and Strokes. When you give both a Fill and a Stroke to a single path, the Stroke knocks out the Fill at the edges of the path by one-half the weight of the Stroke. Figure 9-4 illustrates this.

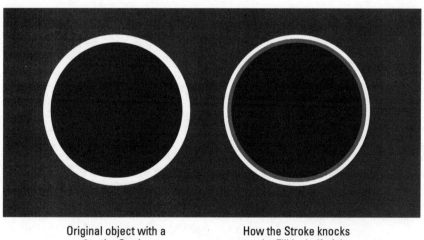

Original object with a
6-point Stroke
and a Black Fill

How the Stroke knocks
out the Fill by half of the
weight of the Stroke

Figure 9-4: A Stroke knocks out a Fill by one-half the weight of the Stroke.

Tip If knocking out the fill of a path presents a problem for your design, you can correct this problem by copying the path and pasting it in front, removing the frontmost path's Stroke. The Filled path, on top of the Stroked path, will knock out the "inner" half of the Stroke. This technique is discussed in detail in the next section.

Applying Fills and Strokes

The toolbox contains two icons, one for Fill and one for Stroke, located towards the bottom of the toolbox (see Figure 9-5).

Figure 9-5: The Paint Style section of the toolbox

Fill

Stroke

By default, the Fill is set to White and the Stroke is set to 1-point Black. In fact, at any time you can reset to the default Fill and Stroke by clicking the Default Fill and Stroke icon in the lower-left corner of the Paint Style section.

 Tip You can quickly reset the Fill and Stroke colors to their default by pressing the D key.

You can quickly swap between the colors in the Fill and Stroke icons by clicking the Swap Fill and Stroke icon located in the upper-right of the Paint Style section. Press Shift+X to swap the current Stroke with the current Fill.

When you first start Illustrator, the Fill icon is in front of the Stroke icon. This means that any changes made in the Color or Swatch palettes affect the Fill. When

A NEW KIND OF BUZZ

This illustration, created by Cole Gerst, is a good example of how raster images can work with Illustrator objects.

A SOUNDS ECLECTIC EVENING

SHELBY LYNNE ELLIOTT SMITH DJ SHADOW
OZOMATLI PETE YORN SPECIAL GUESTS

A BENEFIT CONCERT
AT THE WILTERN THEATER
NOVEMBER 9th, 2001

Created by Cole Gerst, this poster uses the Skew transform tool to change the orientation of the butterfly.

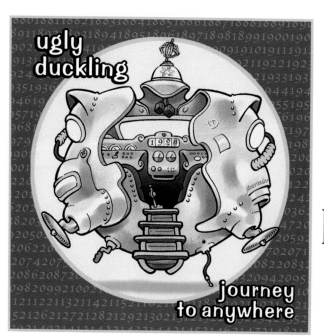

The upper-left and lower-right illustrations were created by Cole Gerst. Credit for the illustration that is used in the Ugly Duckling CD cover goes to Overton Lloyd. The upper-right logo was created by Lane Olsen and the lower-left logo was created by Joe Jones of Art Works Studio.

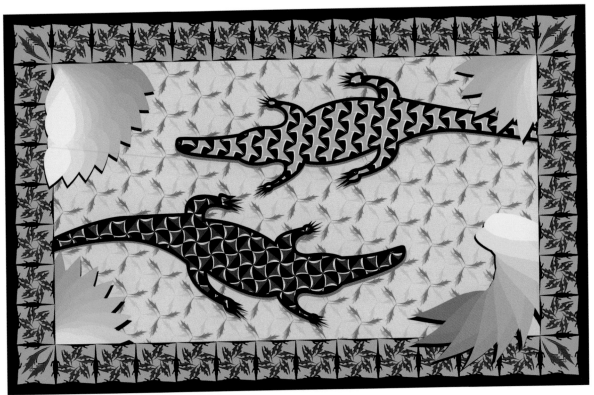

The file sizes of images such as these, created by Andreas Seidel, can be optimized by using symbols for repeating patterns and objects.

These two illustrations, also created by Andreas Seidel, use symbols around the outer border.

Republic P-47D Thunderbolt

BY MICHAEL HALBERT

4   X   4   D   O   D   G   E

T R U C K   1 / 2 - T O N   A M B U L A N C E

Michael Halbert created this authentic airplane and military ambulance using Illustrator's Transparency and Gradient Mesh features.

F4U-1A CORSAIR
BY MICHAEL HALBERT

Continuing with the military vehicles theme, these illustrations, also created by Michael Halbert, further showcase the capabilities of Illustrator.

Chris Spollen makes good use of the orbiting globe theme in these two illustrations. The lower illustration is Chris' studio logo.

These spreads, created by Joe Barsin, were used for featured articles for Web Hosting magazine. The open space on the right was used to place text.

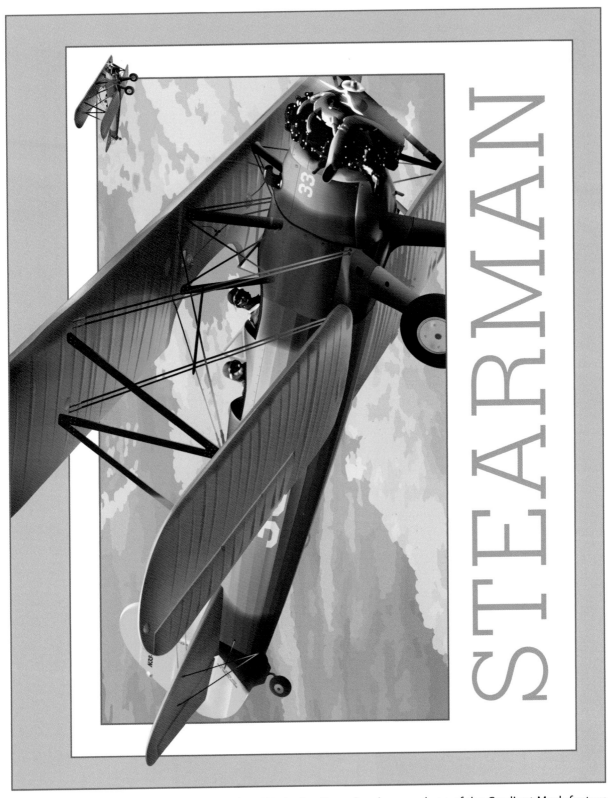

This illustration was created by Joe Jones of Art Works Studio and makes good use of the Gradient Mesh feature.

This image was also created by Joe Jones of Art Works Studio. You can find more of Joe's artwork on his Web site at www.artworksstudio.com.

These science fiction illustrations, created by Joe Jones, are entitled "Port Merillia" (top) and "Northern Outpost" (bottom). They were created using a 3D package, but the original designs began in Illustrator.

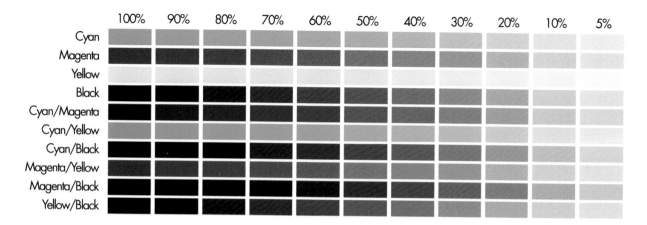

Coated Pantone Colors in Illustrator Chart

The chart on this and the next three pages shows the actual printing colors of the entire Pantone© process color library. Refer to this chart to see the actual printing color of any of the Pantone colors when they are being printed using process colors. These pages are included on the *Illustrator 10 Bible* CD-ROM in case you would like to directly compare them within Illustrator to the printed versions. Doing so may allow for more accurate calibration of your monitor. However, be advised that the colors represented here may vary from your end printing result due to variances in paper, ink quality, the press used for printing, and also the experience and skill of your commercial printer.

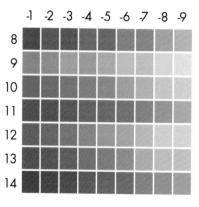

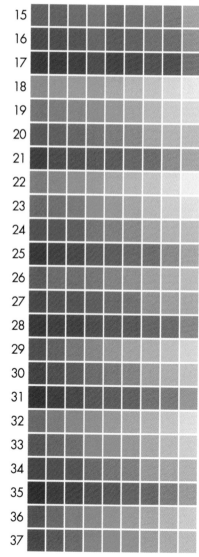

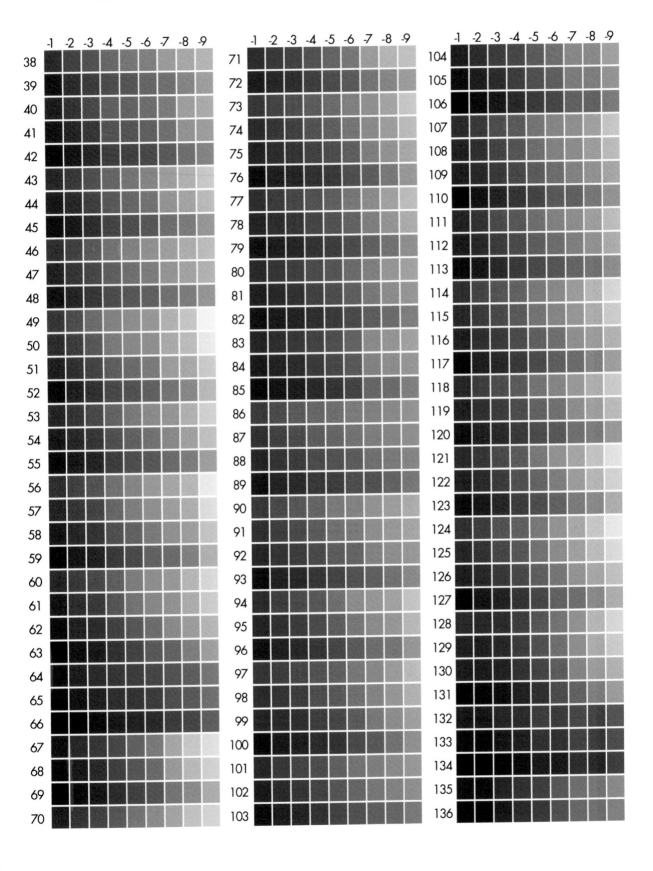

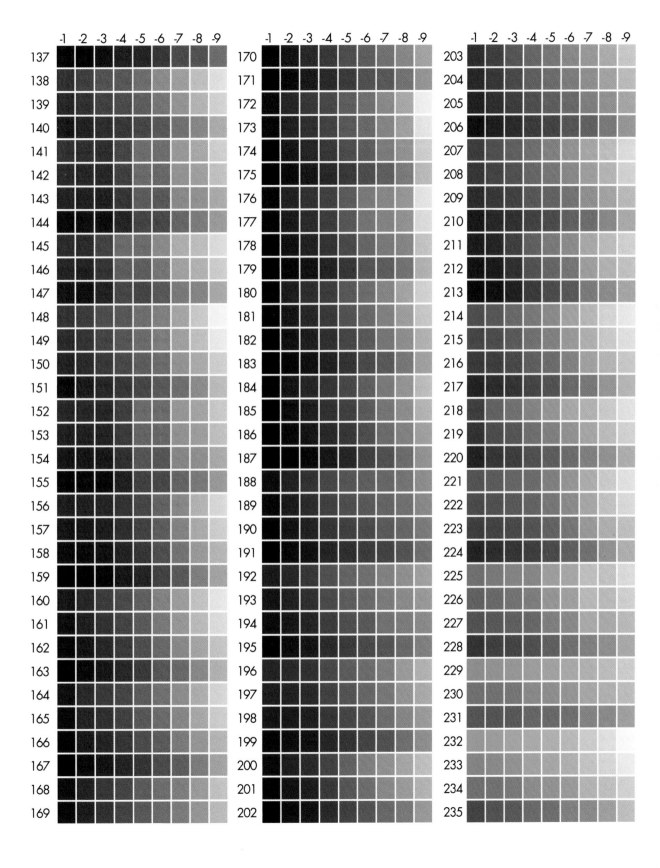

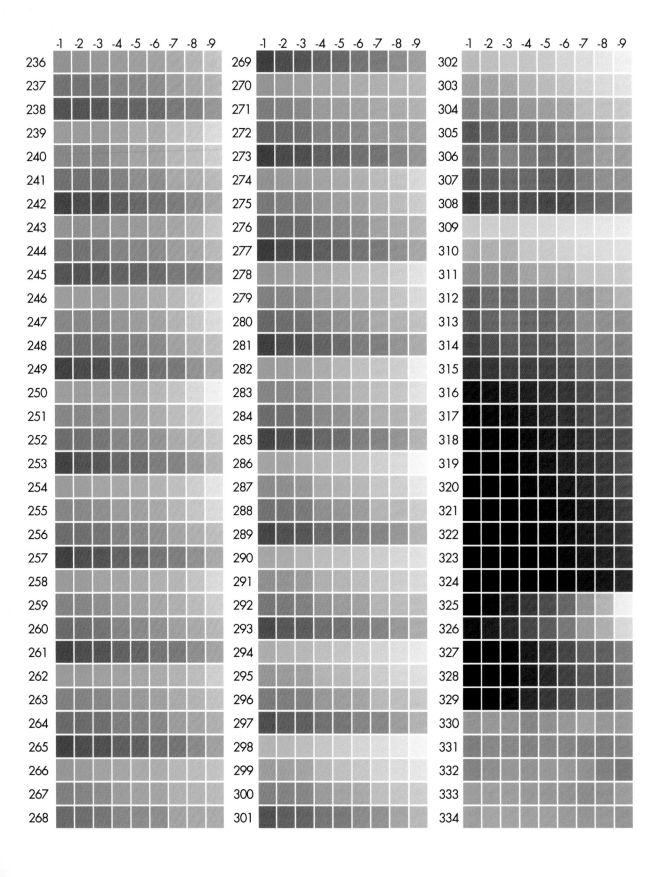

the Fill icon is in front of the Stroke icon, the Fill is said to be in *focus*. You can change the focus to the Stroke by either clicking the Stroke icon or by pressing the X key. Figure 9-6 shows the focus on the Stroke and the focus on the Fill. When the focus is on the Stroke, changes made in the Color or Swatch palettes affect the Stroke, not the Fill.

Figure 9-6: Focus on the Fill (left) and focus on the Stroke (right)

Tip   Use the X key to change the focus between Stroke and Fill. It's by the modifier keys (where your left hand should be anyway), and it's extremely handy, not to mention easier and faster than clicking the Stroke or Fill icons to change focus.

The Fill and Stroke icons change in appearance to match the current Fill and Stroke. For instance, if you have a green Fill and an orange Stroke, the Fill icon is green and the Stroke icon is orange, and you obviously slept through the color lectures in your design classes. The Fill icon displays a gradient or pattern if that is the current Fill.

The three icons at the bottom of the Paint Style section are used to determine the type of Fill or Stroke:

✦ Use the **Color** icon to change the Fill or Stroke to a solid color or a pattern. Press the comma key (,) on the keyboard to quickly select the color icon.

✦ Use the **Gradient** icon when the Fill contains a gradient. Strokes cannot be colored with gradients; clicking this icon when the Stroke icon is in focus changes the Fill to gradient and changes the focus to Fill as well. Press the period key (.) to quickly select the gradient icon.

✦ **None** creates an empty Fill or no Stroke. Fills of None are entirely transparent. Strokes of None are neither colored nor have any Stroke weight. Press the forward slash key (/) to quickly select the None icon.

Oddly enough, you don't need to determine the type of Fill when switching between color and gradient by using the color and gradient icons; you can simply click the appropriate swatch in the Swatches palette to change the Fill type. No swatch exists for None, however, so to change the Fill or Stroke to None you must either click the icon or press the forward slash key (/). Get used to the forward slash key; it will save you loads of time when changing colors for objects. We'll often do a quick combination of the X and / keys to change focus and apply None to the Stroke or Fill.

Incredibly intricate Strokes

Unfortunately, what you can do with Strokes is limited to the Stroke palette's options. Sometimes you'll wish you could do just a little bit more with Strokes. That's where Path Patterns come in. Path Patterns is a filter that enables you to place patterns on Strokes. These patterns increase in proportion as the Stroke changes shape.

Patterns

"The Perfect Pattern is one in which you cannot determine the borders of its tiles," so says the *Chinese Book of Patterns*. If this is true, you can use Adobe Illustrator to create perfect patterns.

The Pattern function in Illustrator is twofold. First, you can Fill or Stroke any path with a pattern. Second, you can edit existing patterns or create new ones from Illustrator objects. The real strength of Illustrator's pattern features is that you can create patterns as well as apply them onscreen in almost any way imaginable.

A pattern in Illustrator is a series of objects within a rectangle that is commonly referred to as a pattern tile. When you choose a pattern in the Swatches palette, the selected pattern is repeated on each horizontal and vertical side of the original pattern tile. Each successive tile is also surrounded with pattern tiles, as shown in Figure 9-7 (the original image is in the middle).

Illustrator places the pattern tiles together for you. After you apply a pattern to an object, you can use any of the transformation tools to transform it, and you can move within the object by using the Move command. You can move and transform patterns with or without the objects they are within.

Note   Tile patterns can either have a background color or they can be transparent. Transparent patterns can overlay other objects, including objects filled with patterns.

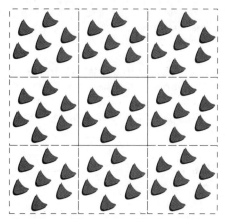

Figure 9-7: The area inside the solid rectangular outline in the center of the figure is the original pattern tile. The dotted-line rectangles represent additional pattern tiles that are aligned with the original to create the pattern and fill up the object.

Using the default patterns

The default Swatches palette includes six patterns that are available at all times. You can view these patterns by clicking on the Show Patterns Swatches icon at the bottom of the palette. The patterns are shown as large thumbnails in Figure 9-8.

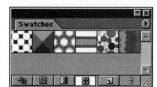

Figure 9-8: The default Fill patterns

You can open other libraries from the Swatch Libraries submenu of the Window menu. Under the Swatch Libraries submenu, you have many different libraries to choose from. The last option is the Other Library. Through Other Library, you can bring in saved libraries, as well as the sample libraries that ship with Illustrator.

To fill a path with a pattern, select that path, make sure the Fill icon is active, and click the corresponding pattern swatch in the Swatches palette. The path will be filled with the pattern indicated.

While only a limited number of different default Fill patterns exist, each one can take on a whole new perspective if you use the various transformation functions — move, rotate, scale, reflect, and skew — on them. Figure 9-9 shows what appear to be several patterns; it's really only the same four patterns with various transformations applied.

Figure 9-9: These patterns were created using the original four patterns by applying various transformations to them.

Patterns used as Strokes can send your printer to a crashing halt. A pattern-filled object has the object's path to figure out where to put the pattern when it is printed. The Stroke command in PostScript is a one-shot command that follows the path with thickness and a line join attribute. With a pattern in a Stroke, the PostScript interpreter must figure out where the Stroke should be and then fill it with a pattern. A better solution is to apply the Outline Path filter, Object ➪ Path ➪ Outline Path. This converts the Stroke into a compound path that can be filled with a pattern.

In addition to the default patterns, you can choose from the incredible variety of patterns included in the Adobe Illustrator Extras folder on the CD-ROM that ships with the Illustrator 10 software. This folder contains Action Sets, Brush Libraries, Patterns and Textures, and Templates. Open the pattern file to see large blocks that contain the patterns as well as the art that was used to create the patterns.

The default patterns are stored in the Adobe Illustrator Startup file. To learn how to modify the startup file to have a specific set of patterns available every time you use Illustrator, see Chapter 15, "Customizing and Optimizing Illustrator."

Creating custom patterns

In addition to using the patterns provided with Illustrator, you can create custom patterns by following the steps described below and shown in Figure 9-10. The pattern tile must have a bounding rectangle with a Fill and a Stroke set to None.

1. Create the artwork you would like to appear in the pattern tile. For this example, we created a bunch of different stars.

2. Select the artwork.

3. Drag the artwork into the Swatches palette.

Patterns in Illustrator 10

With the removal of the Pattern dialog box that was present in Illustrator versions earlier than 7, getting used to the Swatches palette is easy. Once you get the hang of it, you'll love this way of creating patterns. Until then, here are the changes to remember as you work with patterns in Illustrator 10:

✦ Patterns are now kept in the Swatches palette, which is used both to create and to apply patterns.

✦ Create patterns by dragging pattern elements to the Swatches palette. Select all the items to be in the pattern (including the boundary box if you have one), and drag them into the Swatches palette. A new swatch is created that contains that pattern.

✦ Apply patterns by clicking the pattern swatch when a path is selected. Make sure the appropriate Fill/Stroke icon is active.

✦ Access existing patterns by dragging the swatch to your document. Instead of using the old Paste button in the Patterns dialog box, you simply (and logically) drag the pattern swatch to your document.

✦ Duplicate patterns by dragging pattern swatches to the New Swatch icon.

✦ Delete patterns by dragging pattern swatches to the Delete icon.

✦ Name or rename patterns by double-clicking them.

Figure 9-10 also shows the artwork applied as the fill of another shape; the pattern was scaled down dramatically when placed in the larger star shape.

Note   The old Pattern dialog box is gone. Don't look for it, as you won't be able to find anything that even resembles the classic Illustrator pattern definition box. Instead, as of Illustrator 7, Adobe opted for the much more clever method of using the Swatches palette as the home for all patterns.

Creating patterns, although pretty easy initially, can actually be a little more time-consuming when it comes to specialty patterns. Patterns that need to appear symmetrical, random, or seamless require special steps. The following sections show different methods for creating these special pattern types.

Pattern backgrounds and boundaries

Any pattern tile you create can have the color background you specify, simply by making a rectangle the size of the tile and placing it behind the objects in the pattern. When the pattern is created, just select the background with the pattern objects to color the pattern background automatically.

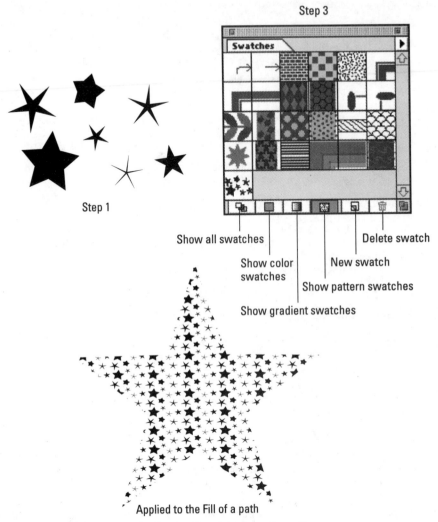

Figure 9-10: Steps 1 and 3 for creating a basic pattern tile

If you don't create a background rectangle, Illustrator uses the *bounding box* of the selected objects to determine the size of the pattern tile. The bounding box is a rectangle that is the exact size of all the selected paths in their current positions.

But what happens if you want the edge of the pattern tile to be somewhere inside the bounding box? Illustrator provides a way for you to define a boundary box to define pattern tiles that consist of objects that extend beyond the pattern edges. Create a boundary box by creating a Rectangle with the Rectangle tool, fill it with None, and make it the backmost object in the pattern tile.

ASK TOULOUSE: Changing Pattern Color

Julie: I can't change the color of the background of my pattern.

Toulouse: You have two ways to do that.

Julie: Tell me the easiest way first.

Toulouse: Okay, the first way is to duplicate the pattern and change the color.

Julie: Take me through it step by step.

Toulouse: First, drag the pattern swatch out of the Swatches palette and onto the document.

Julie: What does that do?

Toulouse: It puts a copy of the original pattern tile artwork in your document.

Julie: Cool.

Toulouse: Then select the background rectangle of the pattern and change its Fill color. Select the background and the rest of the pattern and drag them into the Swatches palette. You'll have another pattern with a different background color.

Julie: And the other way?

Toulouse: If you'll be changing colors all the time, or if you want to use a gradient or another pattern for your background. . . .

Julie: I thought you couldn't do that with patterns.

Toulouse: That's why you need to know this workaround.

Julie: Gotcha.

Toulouse: Go ahead and drag the Pattern swatch like before, but this time fill the background rectangle with None.

Julie: Ahhhhh. . . .

Toulouse: Yes. Now the new pattern won't have any background and you can paste a background behind the copy of the path that has the pattern.

To quickly make a boundary box for a pattern tile that is to have a background, make the background rectangle the size of the tile (with any objects in front sticking out if necessary), copy and Paste in Back, and whack the Slash (/) key to set the Fill to None. Make sure you select both the background rectangle and the boundary box along with your other pattern elements when creating a pattern.

Making seamless patterns

To make patterns seamless, you need to remember that objects that lie across the edge of the pattern border will be cut into two sections, the outside section of which will be invisible. You also need to make sure that lines that stretch from one edge of a pattern border to the other side connect to another line on the opposite edge of the boundary. The second problem is more difficult to deal with than the first one. To make a line match well from one side to the other, you usually have to move one or both of the ends up or down slightly.

Use the following steps to fix objects that get sliced apart at the edges of the pattern tile boundary.

1. Create the boundary (always the backmost rectangle) and the pattern tile objects. The objects may overlap any of the edges, including the corners. In the example that we created (see Figure 9-11), the stones overlap all four sides as well as one of the corners. We created a background rectangle so that you can see the boundary clearly.

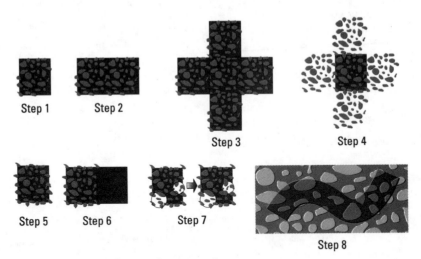

Step 1   Step 2

Step 3   Step 4

Step 5   Step 6   Step 7

Step 8

Figure 9-11: Steps for creating a seamless pattern

2. Select all of the objects, including the pattern boundary, and group them. Click the upper-left corner of the pattern and drag to the right until the arrow pointer is directly over the upper-right corner (it will turn hollow at this point indicating it is snapping into place). Press Option [Alt] and release the mouse button. A copy of the tile will be created to the right of the original.

3. Repeat the process in Step 2 until all four sides have copies of the pattern up against them.

4. Select all five sections and ungroup them. Select the boundary rectangles on the four copied sections and delete them.

5. Delete all the paths (stones, in the example) that don't cross the border of the rectangle.

6. Look at the corners of the rectangle. If an object overlaps any of the corners at all, it should overlap the other three corners. If it doesn't overlap the other three (as in the upper-right corner in the example), Option [Alt]+copy (drag the selected object, pressing the Option [Alt] key, and release the mouse button before releasing the Option [Alt] key) that piece and the boundary to cover the empty corners. Move the boundary with a corner as before so that the piece lines up perfectly. Delete the rectangle after you finish.

7. Look for any overlapping pieces of art in the artwork, including areas of objects that are too close for your liking. Move any pieces of art that are not overlapping a boundary.

8. Make the boundary and objects into a pattern by dragging them into the Swatch palette. Apply it to a shape and check the seams to make sure that it is correct. (If you are even the least bit doubtful that a pattern may be showing seams, zoom in to 1,600 percent to examine the questionable area.)

If you deleted the original pattern artwork, drag the pattern swatch to your document to place a copy of the original artwork on the screen.

To fix lines that cross the edges of the pattern tile boundary, you need to adjust both the lines and the boundary rectangle itself.

Follow these steps to create seamless patterns with continuous paths:

1. Create the artwork that you will use in the pattern.

2. Option [Alt]+copy all of the artwork to the right. At a few points inside the original tile boundary, use the Scissors tool to cut along each path in order to prevent any change to the location and angle of the lines as they meet the opposite edge. You must cut the paths inside the original boundary, not outside. Join the paths together, moving only the end point of the path in the original tile boundary.

3. Option [Alt]+copy both the original and the copied artwork down. Use the Scissors tool to cut along the inside bottom edge of the tile boundary and join the pieces, moving only the end point of the paths inside the original tile boundary.

4. Using the Scissors tool again, click about a quarter inch down the outside right and bottom edges of the tile boundary. Select all paths that do not go into the tile boundary and delete them.

5. Select the tile boundary rectangle and move it an eighth of an inch down and to the right. Make sure that no new paths are overlapped on the top and left edges; if they are, do not move the rectangle so far.

6. If you plan to use a blended line or a series of lines placed one on top of another, you may want to join the ends of the paths outside the rectangle to make the blends merge together and to keep layers of paths separate. We joined such ends in the example; if we hadn't, the pattern edges would not have lined up directly.

7. Add any other elements of the pattern and change the background color if necessary. In the example, we added meatballs and a sauce-color background. Select all the elements and make them into a pattern.

8. Fill a path with the pattern. Three variations on the pattern appear at the top of Figure 9-12.

Symmetrical patterns

You can easily create symmetrical patterns in Illustrator. The key to creating them is to draw the boundary box after you create the rest of the objects, drawing outward from the center point of one of the objects.

When you are creating symmetrical patterns, the main difficulty is judging the space between the objects in the pattern. Objects always seem too close together or too far apart, especially in patterns that have different amounts of space between the objects horizontally and vertically.

Tip   To have an equal amount of space from the center of one object to the center of the next object both vertically and horizontally, use a square as the pattern tile boundary.

Why Patterns Aren't Always Seamless

For patterns to appear seamless, the edges of the pattern cannot be apparent. Avoiding this problem sounds rather easy: You just avoid creating any objects that touch the edges of a background rectangle. Well, that technique will do it, but when you use such a pattern, the pattern tiles become evident because of the lack of any objects along the borders.

So, then, you do want objects to cross the edges of the pattern rectangle. The catch is that those objects cannot appear to be broken. Doing an illustration the wrong way can help you understand this principle.

Start by drawing a background rectangle with a Fill of None. Draw a 1-point black Stroked wavy path from left to right, overlapping both edges. Draw a circle that is filled with 50% Gray and that overlaps the bottom of the rectangle. Select all the objects and define the pattern.

When you fill an object with the new pattern, the edges of the pattern are very noticeable because the wavy path and the circle are both cut at the edges of the pattern boundary.

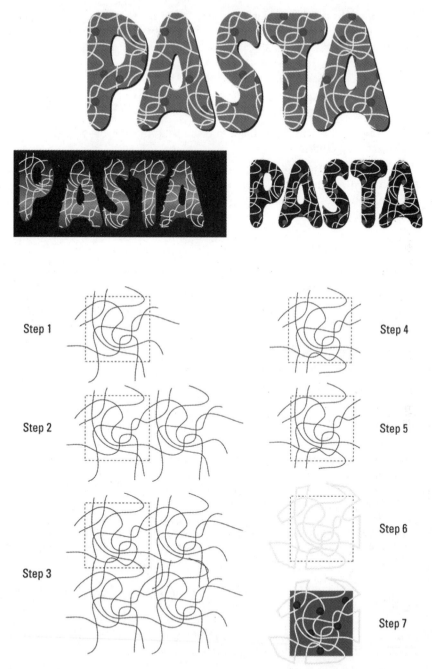

Figure 9-12: Steps for creating seamless patterns with continuous paths

Using the method described in the following steps (and illustrated in Figure 9-13), you can visually adjust the amount of space between objects before you make the objects a pattern. Here are the steps:

1. Create the artwork to use in the pattern.

2. Draw a rectangle from the center of the object so that the object is in the upper-left corner of the rectangle.

3. Option [Alt]+copy the object and the rectangle across and down. Delete the extra rectangles.

4. Using the Direct Selection tool, drag to select the objects on the right and Shift+drag (move the object with the Shift key pressed, releasing the mouse button before releasing the Shift key) them left or right to change the horizontal spacing.

5. Drag the Direct Selection tool to select the objects on the bottom and Shift+drag up or down to adjust the vertical spacing.

6. Move the rectangle so that it surrounds only the initial object and delete the other three objects.

7. Make the objects into a pattern and fill a path with it. The pattern is the background for Figure 9-13.

Line patterns and grids

Using lines and grids for patterns is ideal because they are so easy to create. The key in both types of patterns is the size of the bounding rectangle.

To create a line pattern with horizontal 1-point lines that are aligned on every half inch, do the following: Draw a rectangle that is exactly half an inch tall, at any width, with a Fill and Stroke of None. Draw a horizontal line with a Fill of None and a Stroke of 1 point from outside the left edge of the rectangle to outside the right edge of the rectangle.

Tip   Creating grids is even easier than creating evenly spaced lines. Create a rectangle that is the size of the grid holes (for a quarter-inch grid, the rectangle would be **1/4** inch by **1/4** inch) and apply a Stroke to the object. Make the Stroke the weight that you want the grid lines to be. Make that rectangle into a pattern. That's it. You now have a pattern grid that is as precise as possible.

Make a pattern out of the two objects. The new pattern consists of 1-point horizontal Strokes that are spaced half an inch apart.

You can use this technique with vertical lines, as well. Just make the bounding rectangle the width of the distance from line to line.

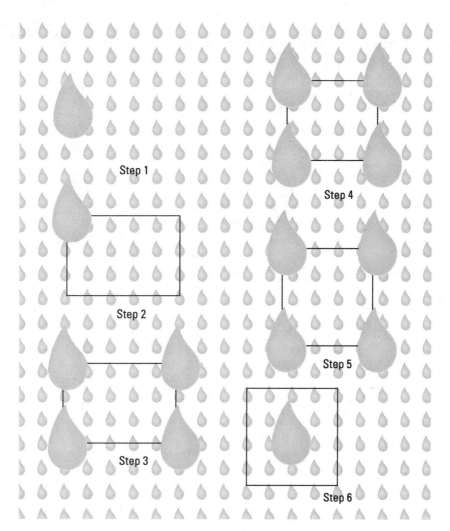

Figure 9-13: Creating perfectly symmetrical patterns

Tip If you want the space between grid lines to be an exact measurement, make the rectangle bigger by the Stroke weight. A quarter-inch grid (18 points) with 1-point grid lines requires a rectangle that is 19 points by 19 points. Remember that four of these grids combined don't equal an inch; instead, they equal 4 points more than an inch.

ASK TOULOUSE: Patterns to Paths

Isaac: Is there an easy way to convert patterns to paths that really works?

Toulouse: Well, you have several options: the Expand option in the Object menu, KPT Gradients/Patterns to Paths, and CSI Patterns to Paths.

Isaac: Which works the best?

Toulouse: Well, CSI gives you the option of keeping any transformations that were done to the patterns before they're converted.

Isaac: I sometimes get bad results converting patterns to paths.

Toulouse: Actually, because of the way Illustrator patterns work, the patterns are always offset a bit.

Isaac: Any way to fix this?

Toulouse: Just manually.

Diagonal-line and grid patterns

Creating diagonal-line and grid patterns can be difficult if you try to make a rectangle, draw a path at an angle, and then use the rectangle with the path in it as a pattern. Joining diagonal lines at the edges of the pattern is nearly impossible.

A better method is to create line and grid patterns in horizontal or vertical alignment, apply the pattern to a path, and then double-click the Rotate tool. In the Rotate dialog box, enter the angle to change the lines and uncheck the Object checkbox. The pattern rotates to the desired angle inside the path.

Tip

Using this technique is also a great way to avoid making several patterns when you need line patterns that are set at different angles. Just make one horizontal line pattern and rotate the patterns within the paths.

Transparency and patterns

To make the background of a pattern transparent, don't use a background rectangle. Only the objects in the pattern will be opaque.

To make the objects in a pattern transparent, make the background rectangle and the other objects into a compound path. Select the compound path and make the objects into a pattern. You can achieve some fascinating effects by using the transformation tools to make transformed copies of patterns.

Tip

When you make the bounding rectangle part of a compound path, it is no longer a rectangle and you cannot use it as the bounding rectangle. Always copy the rectangle before you make the objects and the rectangle into a compound path.

Another way to achieve interesting effects is by making a copy of the object behind the original. Select the object, choose Edit ➪ Copy (⌘+C [Ctrl+C]), and then choose Edit ➪ Paste in Back (⌘+B [Ctrl+B]). Change the Fill in the copy of the object to a solid or a gradient or change it to another pattern.

Modifying existing patterns

To change an existing pattern, drag the pattern swatch to your document. A copy of the original artwork will be placed in the document.

Select individual parts with any of the selection tools and change Fill and Stroke attributes or change the shape of any of the objects with selection or transformation tools.

After modifying the artwork, select all the pattern-related objects and drag them to the Swatches palette on top of the original version to replace the old swatch.

Putting patterns and gradients into patterns

Under normal circumstances, you cannot put gradients into patterns or patterns into other patterns. But if Illustrator doesn't think of the objects as patterns or gradients, you can put patterns and gradients into patterns.

To put a pattern into another pattern, drag the pattern that you want to put into the new pattern from the Swatches palette to your document. Group the pattern artwork and Option [Alt]+copy several squares. Draw a rectangle around the squares and add any additional artwork for the new pattern. Select the artwork and drag to the Swatches palette.

Including gradients in patterns is not quite so simple. First, create the object and fill it with the gradient. Expand the gradient with the Object ➪ Expand command. You can then use the blended object in any pattern.

When you transform gradients into blends via Expand for placement in a pattern, check for masked areas. You cannot use masks in patterns, so you need to release the mask before you incorporate the blend into the pattern. Also, try to keep the number of blend steps to a minimum.

Transforming patterns

After you create patterns and place them within paths, they may be too big or at the wrong angle, or they may start in an awkward location. You can use the transformation tools and the Move command to resolve these problems.

To transform a pattern inside a path, select the path and double-click the transformation tool that corresponds to the change that you want to make to the pattern. In the transformation tool's dialog box, uncheck the Object checkbox, which selects

---

ASK TOULOUSE: Pattern Printing Problems

Stubing: Why does it take so long to print patterns?

Toulouse: Well, if you think of what patterns actually are, you'll know.

Stubing: If I knew, would I be asking?

Toulouse: It's just that patterns are really bunches of masked sections of — get this — Type 3 fonts. The masks are rectangles.

Stubing: Which means . . . ?

Toulouse: Masks can always cause printing problems, as can Type 3 fonts, but if you do complex transformations to complex patterns, you're asking for trouble.

---

the Pattern checkbox. The Pattern and Objects checkboxes are grayed out if the selected object does not contain a pattern.

Any changes you make in the transformation tool's dialog box when only the Pattern checkbox is checked affect only the pattern, not the outside shape. The default (which cannot be changed) is for Objects to remain checked always.

If you are using any of the transformation tools manually, the pattern inside the selected object will transform with the object only if the Transform pattern tiles option in the General Preferences dialog box is checked.

To move a pattern within a path, choose Object ➪ Transform ➪ Move (or double-click the Selection tool). The Move dialog box also contains Pattern and Objects checkboxes.

Pen and Ink Filter Textures

One of the niftiest features in Illustrator is a filter called Pen and Ink. Pen and Ink takes basic Illustrator paths and turns them into random textures that you can control and manipulate through a variety of options.

To create a texture, select any path or paths and choose Filter ➪ Pen and Ink ➪ New Hatch. The New Hatch dialog box appears, as shown in Figure 9-14.

Click the New button and name your hatch. Click OK and you can use that hatch as a Pen and Ink Fill.

After you've created the hatch, you're ready to apply it as a Fill for any selected path. To do so, select the path you wish to fill and choose Filter ➪ Pen and Ink ➪ Hatch Effects. The Hatch Effects dialog box appears, as shown in Figure 9-15.

Figure 9-14: The New Hatch dialog box

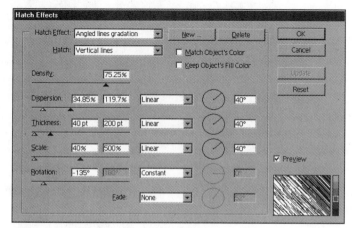

Figure 9-15: The Hatch Effects dialog box

Inside the Hatch Effects dialog box, you have a seemingly infinite number of combinations of various properties to apply to the hatch style. The effects are listed in the following sections, with figures showing the effects of various property settings chosen from the pop-up menu.

The texture that is created is actually a grouped mask of several paths. This enables you to change the paint attributes of the texture after it has been applied. In addition, you can then modify the individual paths just as you would modify any other path in Illustrator.

Note Remember that the paths that you use in a hatch style can have both Fills and Strokes, but the thickness property affects only Stroke width.

Tip The Hatch Effect pop-up menu is a collection of presaved settings made from a specific hatch. You can select a setting from the Hatch Effects dialog box and select a different hatch from the Hatch pop-up menu to make a new texture. If you like the texture, save the settings.

Density

Density is how closely packed together the elements of the hatch style are. The closer together the pieces, the darker or thicker the texture will appear. You can adjust the density by dragging the Density slider to the left and right; left is less dense, right is more dense. Figure 9-16 shows various amounts of density.

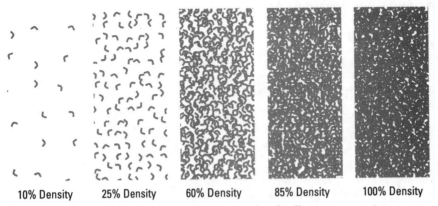

10% Density   25% Density   60% Density   85% Density   100% Density

Figure 9-16: Different amounts of density for a hatch effect

Dispersion

Dispersion controls how evenly the texture elements are spread within the Fill. Setting the dispersion to None results in a pattern-tile appearance that is very uniform, while increasing the dispersion randomizes the location and grouping of the pieces of the hatch style. Figure 9-17 shows various settings of the Dispersion slider.

Each of the six settings located on the right side of the Hatch Effects dialog box has different ways of creating each parameter. For instance, instead of a Constant dispersion, you can choose from None, Linear, Symmetrical, Reflected, or Random dispersion. Each of the other properties (with the exception of density) has these same controls.

The Hatch Effects dialog box options work as follows:

✦ **None** applies no effect to the setting.

✦ **Constant** keeps the setting the same throughout the entire Fill shape.

✦ **Linear** changes the amount of the effect across the Fill shape. The angle at which this is applied is changed in each effect section, either by moving the angle indicator or by entering a different angle in the Rotate field. You have two sliders to adjust, controlling the maximum and minimum amount of the effect.

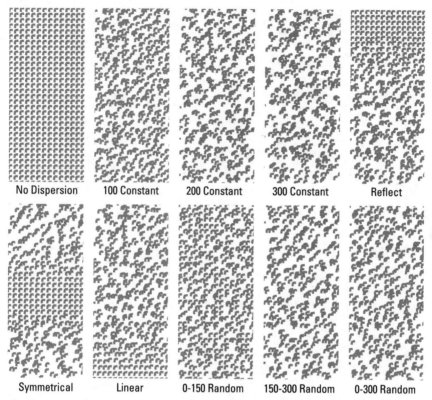

No Dispersion   100 Constant   200 Constant   300 Constant   Reflect

Symmetrical   Linear   0-150 Random   150-300 Random   0-300 Random

Figure 9-17: Different amounts of dispersion for a hatch effect

✦ **Reflect** increases or decreases the amount of the effect (somewhat like a double-linear effect). The angle and minimum and maximum amounts are controlled the same way as with the Linear option.

✦ **Symmetric** creates a symmetric pattern of the effect. The angle sets the angle of the hatch marks and the amount value determines how much of the effect is used. These settings are adjusted in the same way as they are with Linear and Reflect.

✦ **Random** generates random amounts of the effect, between the minimum and maximum amount that you specify.

Thickness

Thickness controls the Stroke thickness of the paths in the hatch style. Figure 9-18 shows some of the variations of Stroke thickness.

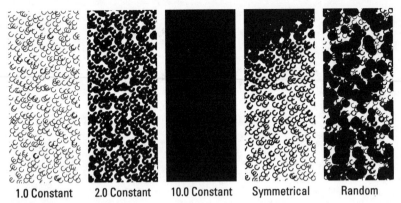

| 1.0 Constant | 2.0 Constant | 10.0 Constant | Symmetrical | Random |

Figure 9-18: Different thickness settings for a hatch effect

Rotation

Rotation controls the angle of the pieces in the hatch style. A constant amount of rotation rotates each of the pieces in the hatch style the same amount. Other rotation options vary the amount of rotation, as shown in Figure 9-19.

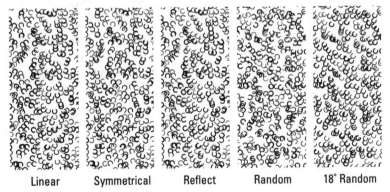

| Linear | Symmetrical | Reflect | Random | 18° Random |

Figure 9-19: Different settings for the Rotation property

To apply Rotation effects, follow these steps:

1. Start by creating the path you wish to fill with the symmetrical texture.

2. With the path selected, choose Filter ➪ Pen and Ink ➪ Hatch Effects, and select the hatch style to use.

3. Change the Rotation property setting to Linear, making the left and right sliders the same (for example 90, 90). Click the OK button to apply the texture to the path.

4. To finish, you may want to place a gradient behind the image, as we did in Figure 9-20.

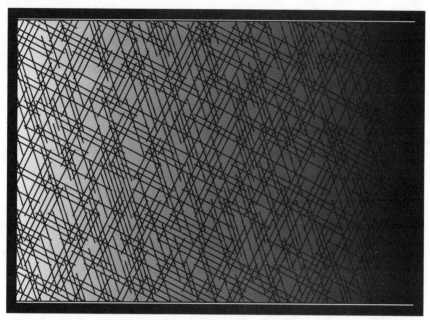

Figure 9-20: A crosshatch texture is created by applying rotation effects with the Hatch Effects dialog box

Scale

The Scale property changes the size of the hatch style pieces. It does *not* change the Stroke weight, however, just the size of the paths. Figure 9-21 shows sample scale settings.

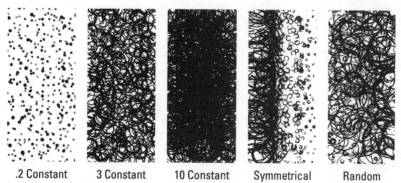

.2 Constant   3 Constant   10 Constant   Symmetrical   Random

Figure 9-21: Different settings for the Scale property

Tip If you are going to be using "lines" that you'd like to scale uniformly (that is, instead of just the length changing, you'd like the width to change as well), then create thin rectangles instead of single paths. That way, the width of the rectangle increases with its length. However, the Thickness property will then not have an effect on the hatch style.

Other ink pen Fill controls

Several other controls determine how your Fill interacts with the background. These controls are located next to the Hatch pop-up menu in the Hatch Effects dialog box.

Select the hatch style you'd like to use in the Hatch pop-up menu. The hatch color can Keep Object's Color (the color of the original paths when they were created as a hatch) or Keep Object's Fill Color of the selected path. The Background color of the original object is changed to None or White. The Fade pop-up menu controls the fade of the hatch style. The Fade Angle option controls the angle of the fade.

Figure 9-22 shows two examples of the Fade to White option with the background (a gradient) and no background.

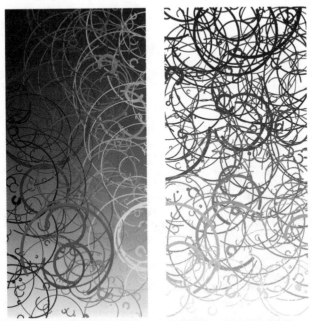

Figure 9-22: Fade to White with a gradient background (left) and with no background (right)

ASK TOULOUSE: Ink Pen Color Change

Gopher: I want to change the color of my hatch style.

Toulouse: After it's applied or before?

Gopher: Before, because I'm using the Fade to White option.

Toulouse: Okay. Open the Ink Pen Hatches dialog box.

Gopher: Done.

Toulouse: Then select the hatch style you wish to recolor.

Gopher: Done again.

Toulouse: Then click the Paste button.

Gopher: Paste does what?

Toulouse: Paste puts a copy of the hatch art in your document. Then change the color, go back to the Ink Pen Hatches, click New, and name your new hatch something else.

Photo hatch effects

The Pen and Ink filter also includes the capability to apply a Photo Crosshatch to any rasterized image. Adobe has made the Pen and Ink filter much easier to understand compared to its first introduction. This filter adds a texture of lines on top of your selected image or photo.

You can apply hatch effects to a photograph or any other rasterized image. The crosshatch effects are applied on top of the original image. The hatches are applied to the darkest areas of the image and feather out to the lightest areas.

Figure 9-23 shows the Photo Crosshatch dialog box.

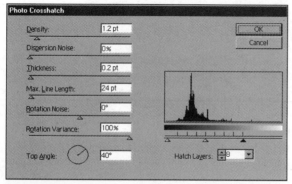

Figure 9-23: The Photo Crosshatch dialog box

You use this dialog box to set these options:

✦ **Density** controls how close the hatches are to each other.

✦ **Dispersion Noise** affects how evenly the hatch lines cover the fill area.

✦ **Thickness** controls the line thickness of the hatch lines.

✦ **Max. Line Length** sets the maximum length of a hatch line.

✦ **Rotation Noise** controls the random rotation of the hatch lines in the Hatch Layers.

✦ **Rotation Variance** controls the rotation amount of the layers from each other.

✦ **Top Angle** controls the angle of the top layer of the Hatch Layers.

✦ **Hatch Layers** controls the number of hatch color ranges. The higher the Hatch Layer, the more layers of hatches that are applied to the image. The hatch color ranges from 0 to 256 tones of black.

Figure 9-24 shows a rasterized image before applying a Hatch Effect to it. Figure 9-25 shows the image with the Photo Hatch filter applied to it using four different hatch level settings.

Figure 9-24: The original image

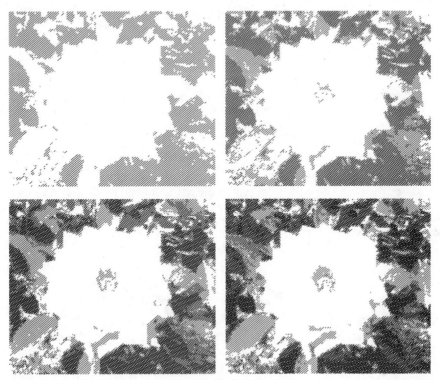

Figure 9-25: The Photo Crosshatch applied to Figure 9-24

Special Stroke Techniques

Now that we've covered the concepts of Fills and Strokes and they are fresh in your mind, we will look at a number of useful Stroke techniques.

You create most effects with Strokes by overlaying several Strokes on top of one another. By copying and choosing Edit ➪ Paste in Front (⌘+F [Ctrl+F]), you place an exact duplicate of the original path on top of itself.

Changing the weight and color of the top Stroke gives the appearance of a path that is a designer, or custom, Stroke. You can add Strokes on top of or under the original Stroke to make the pattern more complex or to add more colors or shapes.

The following steps describe how to create a specialty Stroke that looks like parallel Strokes, and Figure 9-26 illustrates these steps.

1. Use the Pencil tool to draw a short line. We usually set the Auto Trace Tolerance (choose Edit ➪ Preferences ➪ Type and Auto Tracing) to 10 points for a very smooth path. Change the Fill to None and Stroke the path with 18-point Black.

2. Copy the Stroke and paste the copy in front (⌘+F [Ctrl+F]). Change the copied (pasted in front) Stroke to 6-point White. Select both paths, copy them (⌘+C [Ctrl+C]), and lock them (⌘+L [Ctrl+L]). The 6-point Stroke looks as if it has been subtracted from the 18-point Stroke. The result appears to be two separate 6-point Black Strokes.

3. Choose Edit ➪ Paste in Back (⌘+B [Ctrl+B]). Deselect All (⌘+Shift+A [Ctrl+Shift+A]) and click the top path. Change the weight of the Stroke to 30 points. Lock the path and select the remaining path. Change the Stroke on this path to 42. The 30-point Stroke is 12 points more than the 18 points of the black Stroke, or 6 points on each side. The 42-point Stroke is 12 points more than the white 30-point Stroke.

Step 1   Step 2   Step 3

Figure 9-26: Creating parallel Strokes

This example is just the tip of the iceberg in creating custom Strokes. Not only can you have paths that overlap, but you can also give the Stroke on each path different dash patterns, joins, and caps. You can even add Fills to certain paths to make the Stroke different on both sides of the path. And if all of that isn't enough, you can use Outline Path to outline Strokes.

Note   When you are creating parallel Strokes, determine how thick each of the visible Strokes should be, multiply that number times the black *and* white visible Strokes that you want for the base Stroke, and work up from there. For example, if you want 10-point Strokes, and four white Strokes and five black Strokes exists, the first Stroke would be 90-points thick and black. The next Stroke would be 70-point White, and then 50-point Black, 30-point White, and 10-point Black.

Just knowing the secrets doesn't let you in on the really good stuff, though. Read on to learn how to apply these tricks to achieve truly amazing effects with Strokes.

Stroke Essentials

Strokes act and work differently than Fills. Remember these basic rules (no pun intended) when using Strokes:

✦ The most important thing to remember when using Strokes is that Stroke-weight width is evenly distributed on both sides of a path. In other words, on a Stroke with a 6-point weight, 3 points of the Stroke exist on both sides of the Stroke's path.

✦ Patterns can be put into Strokes, and starting with version 8 you can see the pattern on the Stroke unless you are using Outline mode.

✦ Gradients may not be used to color Strokes.

✦ Choosing Outline from the Pathfinder palette creates path outlines around the width of the Stroke. When a Stroke has been converted into an outline, it is really an outlined path object and can be Filled with patterns and gradients (both of which appear when previewing and printing).

✦ Stroke weight never varies on the same path.

✦ A Stroke with a color of None has no Stroke weight.

✦ Strokes are, for the most part, ignored when combining, splitting, or modifying paths with the Pathfinder functions. Strokes are never considered when the Pathfinder functions search for the locations of the paths.

Using the Stroke charts

The Stroke charts in Figures 9-27 through 9-30 show how some of the basic Stroke-dash patterns look with various options checked, at different weights, and in different combinations.

All the paths in the charts were taken from an original shape that included a straight segment, a corner, and a curve. The charts should help you determine when to use certain types of Stroke patterns because, as you can see, some patterns work better than others with curves and corners.

The first chart (Figure 9-27) consists of thirty-two 3-point Stroke paths that have a variety of dash patterns, end attributes, and join attributes. The second chart (Figure 9-28) shows eighteen 10-point Stroke paths with similar attributes. These two charts show Stroke effects with only one path. The area in the middle of each path in the chart describes the path.

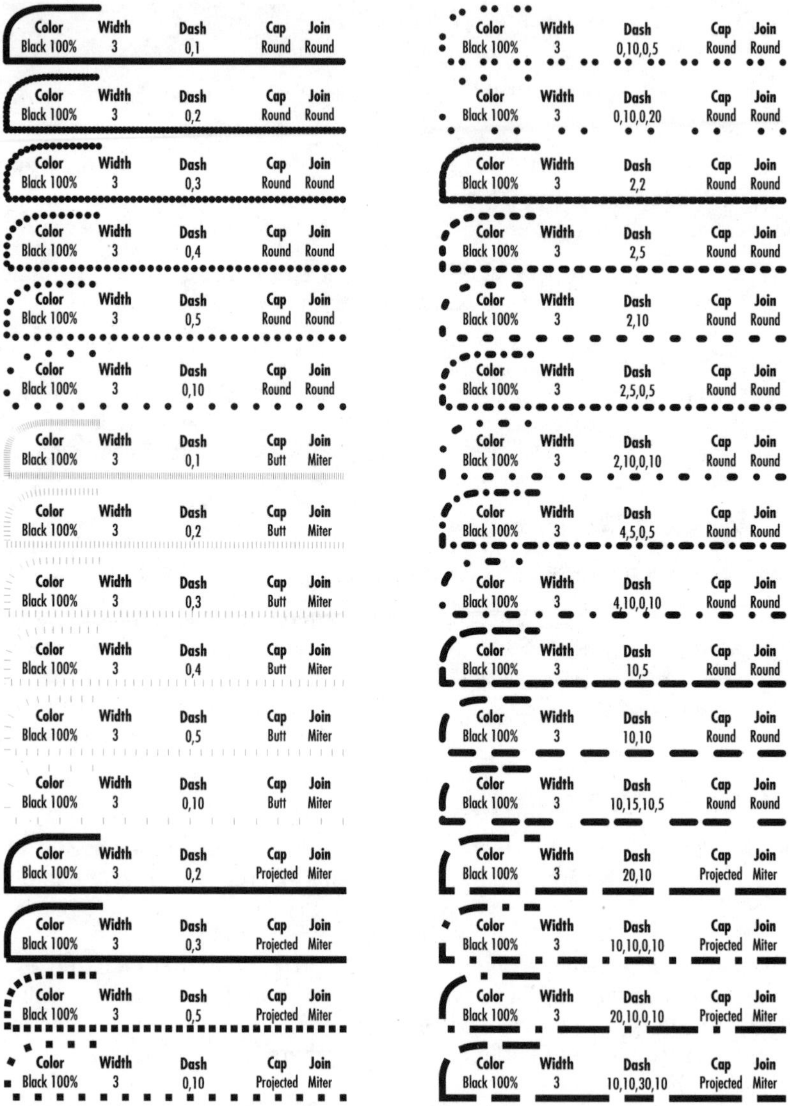

Figure 9-27: Thirty-two 3-point Stroke paths

The third (Figure 9-29) and fourth charts (Figure 9-30) contain paths that have been copied on top of the original by using the Paste in Front command. The paths are listed in the order that they were created. The first path is described at the top of the list. The first path is copied, pasted in front (⌘+F [Ctrl+F]), and given the Paint Style attributes of the second item in the list. The changes progress from the top left of each chart to the bottom left and then from the top right to the bottom right.

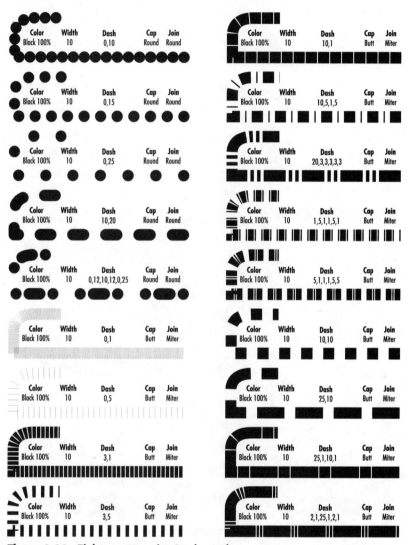

Figure 9-28: Eighteen 10-point Stroke paths

> **Note**
>
> In some cases, paths are blended from one to another. To be able to select an End Point on each Stroke (usually they will overlap), offset one of the paths by 0.1 point. When blending, use a number that is less than 100 for the number of blend steps, dividing the suggested number by 2 until it is small enough.

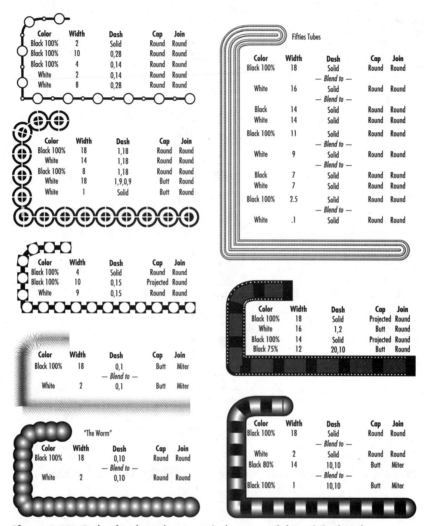

Figure 9-29: Paths that have been copied on top of the original paths

When you create a Stroke pattern, frequently the original path is selected, copied, and then pasted in front or back (⌘+F [Ctrl+F] or ⌘+B [Ctrl+B]) several times. You usually don't need to recopy the original path after it has been copied. You can continue to paste it again and again on top of or under the original path.

In the middle of the right-hand column in the third Stroke chart (Figure 9-29) is a Stroke that looks like a strip of film. The following steps describe how to create this film Stroke, which is a basic Stroke that produces a stunning effect.

1. Draw a wavy path with the Pencil tool.

2. Change the Stroke of the path to 18-point Black and the Fill to None.

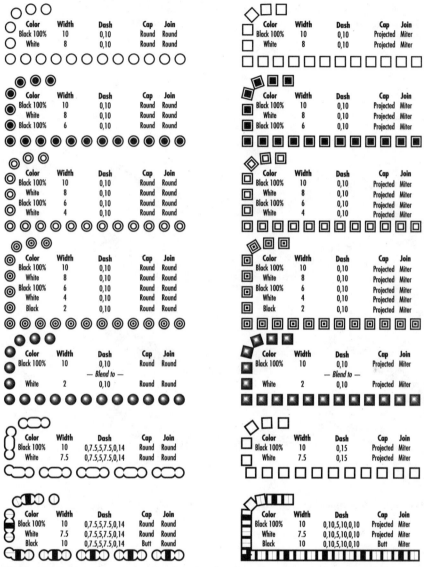

Figure 9-30: Another example of paths that have been copied on top of the original paths

3. Copy (⌘+C [Ctrl+C]) the path and choose Edit ➪ Paste in Front (⌘+F [Ctrl+F]). Change the Stroke to 16-point White, and use a Dash Pattern of Dash 1, Gap 2.

4. Choose Edit ➪ Paste in Front (⌘+F [Ctrl+F]) again and change the Stroke to 14-point Black, Solid.

5. Choose Edit ➪ Paste in Front (⌘+F [Ctrl+F]) once more and change the Stroke to 75% Black, 12 points, with a Dash Pattern of Dash 20, Gap 10.

Figure 9-31 shows these steps. You can use this procedure to create any of the Strokes in the third Stroke chart (Figure 9-29) by substituting the values that are listed in the chart for the Stroke that you want.

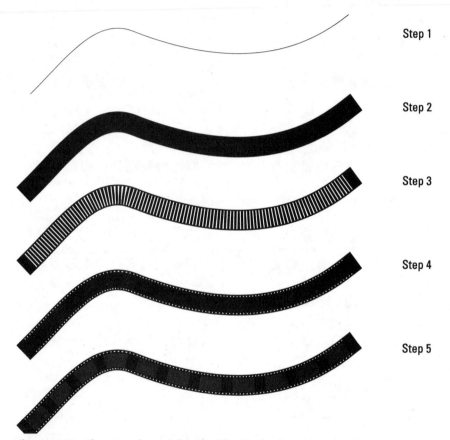

Step 1

Step 2

Step 3

Step 4

Step 5

Figure 9-31: The steps for creating the film Stroke from Figure 9-29

Type

You can use Strokes to enhance type in a number of ways. The first example, described in the following steps and shown in Figure 9-32, is based on Stroke blends.

1. Type a few words in a heavy-weighted font such as Helvetica Black, Futura Extra Bold, or Kabel Ultra.

2. Select the type with the Selection tool. Choose Type ➪ Create Outlines (⌘+Shift+O [Ctrl+Shift+O]) and change the Fill to None and the Stroke to Black or a light shade of gray. Change the weight of the Stroke to 0.1 point.

3. Copy (⌘+C [Ctrl+C]) the words and choose Edit ➪ Paste in Back (⌘+B [Ctrl+B]). Move the copy a few points up and to the right. Change the Stroke on the copy to 4-point White and blend each set of paths together with the Blend tool.

4. Choose Edit ➪ Paste in Front (⌘+F [Ctrl+F]) and change the Fill to White and the Stroke to None.

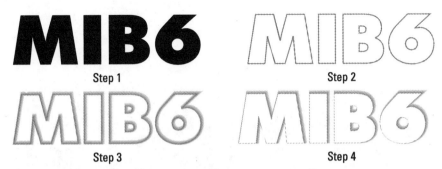

Step 1

Step 2

Step 3

Step 4

Figure 9-32: Steps for creating ghosted type

Cross-Reference

For more information on Stroke blends, see Chapter 11, "Using Path Blends, Compound Paths, and Masks"; for more information on type, see Chapter 8, " Manipulating Type."

Another popular effect for type (okay, it was popular in the 1970s) is produced by creating several Strokes for each stroke of a letter, as described in the following steps and shown in Figure 9-33.

1. Create a word or words in a lightweight typeface.

2. Use the Pen tool to re-create the letters in the typeface. In Figure 9-33, we colored the letters in the original word light red and then locked those letters in place so that we could trace the letters more easily.

3. Group all the paths that you have drawn and give them a heavy Stroke. (We used 18 points.) Change the join and cap style in the Stroke palette to rounded.

4. Copy (⌘+C [Ctrl+C]) and paste in front (⌘+F [Ctrl+F]) in gradually decreasing Stroke weights. Change between white and a darker color as the weight decreases.

Step 1

Step 2

Step 3

Step 4

Figure 9-33: Making type that has multiple Strokes

Creating rough edges

You can create some of the most interesting Stroke effects by using the Roughen filter in combination with a heavy-weighted Stroke. Even with a Roughen filter setting of 1 or 2 percent, a heavy-weighted Stroke can have many sharp, long points, as described in the following steps.

1. Create an object to which you want to add jagged or explosive edges. We used text that was converted to outlines (Type ➪ Create Outlines) in the example (shown at the top of Figure 9-34). Copy the text off to the side before continuing.

Figure 9-34: Creating roughened paths with Strokes

2. Use Object ➪ Path ➪ Offset Path to create a path that is offset by 20 points or more. This step is shown as the second row in Figure 9-34. Select all the paths

and click the Add Shapes button from the Pathfinder palette to combine all the shapes into a single object.

3. Before going in further, use the Edit ➪ Copy to create a copy of the unified object before its roughened. Then, apply the Roughen filter (Fitler ➪ Distort ➪ Roughen) to the unified object with a Size value of 20 percent. Select a different Fill color for the roughened object and give it a Stroke width of 40 pts. This resulting object is shown in the third row of Figure 9-34.

4. Paste in front the copied object with the Edit ➪ Paste in Front menu option and roughen as before, but give the Stroke a lesser weight and Fill the path with the same color as the Stroke. Place the original art (which you copied off to the side in Step 1) on top of the roughened paths. The final effect is shown at the bottom of Figure 9-34.

Half-stroked paths

One technique that we don't think is used enough is hiding one side of the Stroke as the path layers are built up. To hide half of the Stroke at any level, paste in front as you normally do and then select Lock Others from the Layers palette pop-up menu. This command locks everything that isn't selected; in other words, only the path that you just pasted (and which is currently selected) will not be locked.

Using the Pen tool, connect the ends of the just-pasted path and Fill it with the background color and give it a Stroke of None. This action obliterates one side of the Stroke because the file of the path covers the "inside" part of the Stroked path. Any Strokes that you place on top of this object will be visible on both sides of the path.

Workin' on the railroad

Several effects that you can create with paths have a traveling theme, mainly because a path starts somewhere and finishes somewhere else. Railroad tracks, roads, highways, trails, and rivers all have a tendency to conform very nicely to Stroke effects with paths.

One of the trickiest traveling paths to create is a railroad track. To get the real railroad-track look, some advanced cheating is necessary, as described in the following steps.

1. Draw a path to represent the railroad. Create a background shape and Fill the background with a color. In the example (see Figure 9-35), I used dark green.

2. Copy the path. Give the path a Stroke weight of 30 points. Choose Edit ➪ Paste in Front (⌘+F [Ctrl+F]) and give this path a Stroke weight of 20 points.

3. Select both paths. Choose Outline from the Pathfinder palette to change the paths into outlined paths because Strokes cannot contain gradients. Fill the paths with a metallic gradient.

Step 1

Step 2

Step 3

Step 4

Step 5

Step 6

Step 7

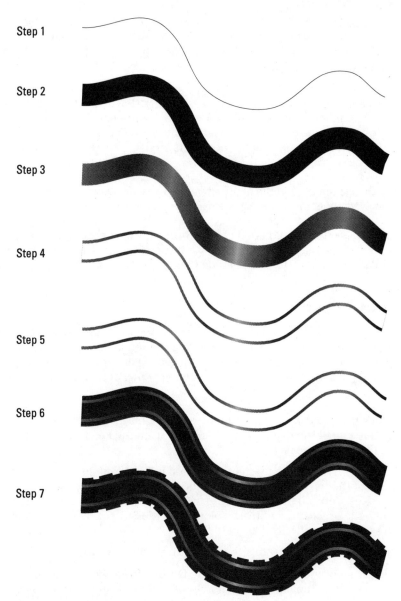

Figure 9-35: Steps for creating railroad tracks

4. Select both paths and choose Exclude from the Pathfinder palette. This command subtracts the inner section of the track from the two outer sections.

5. Check the ends of the path and delete any excess paths that are not part of the tracks. In the example, we also joined the ends on each individual track.

6. Paste in back (⌘+B [Ctrl+B]) and give the new path a Stroke weight of 40 points. Choose Outline from the Pathfinder palette. Stroke and Fill this path with a gradient consisting of several wood-like browns. This path is the wood that underlies the tracks.

7. The last thing to do is to split the pieces of wood into individual railroad ties. Select the wood path and choose Edit ⇨ Paste in Front (⌘+F [Ctrl+F]). This command pastes a path right on top of the wooden area. Give this Stroke the same color as the background and give it a Dash Pattern of Dash 20, Gap 10. The gaps will be the see-through areas, showing the wood-filled path below them.

Tip   To change the color of the new path in Step 7 easily, select the new path, choose the Eyedropper tool, and click the background.

Outline Path is often used on this type of Stroke design because Strokes can't have gradient Fills. The reason that the railroad ties were not given a dash pattern before Outline Path was applied is that Outline Path doesn't work with dash patterns.

The wild river

A wild river is another path that you can create easily using Strokes. One problem in getting rivers to look good is that creating the rough, in-out texture of a river's bank is difficult. Also, because different parts of rivers are different weights, connecting the parts smoothly is difficult. The following steps describe how to create a river.

1. Draw the paths for the river. In the example (see Figure 9-36), we created a Y at one end of the river and an island. We used the Pen tool to draw additional paths next to the river.

2. Give the river a Stroke weight and color. In the example, we gave the main part of the river a Stroke of 18 points and the two additional parts 14-point Strokes. Copy all the paths, paste in front, and color the copy a little darker than the original river Stroke color. Make the Strokes on the copy a few points less wide than the Strokes on the original.

3. Blend the two Strokes together, using three blend steps.

4. Select all of the Strokes and choose Outline from the Pathfinder palette. Select one of the new paths and choose Edit ⇨ Select ⇨ Same Fill Color. Choose Unite from the Pathfinder palette. Repeat this process for each of the five different colors.

5. Select all of the paths and choose Filter ⇨ Distort ⇨ Roughen. In the Roughen dialog box, enter 0.3 and 40 segments per inch and then click OK. The edges of the river are now a little ragged, and they appear to have ripples, or waves, in them.

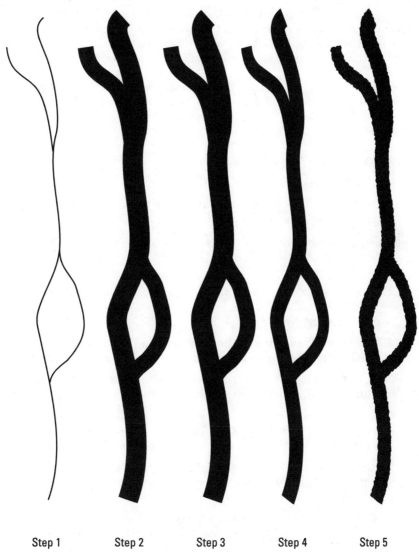

| Step 1 | Step 2 | Step 3 | Step 4 | Step 5 |

Figure 9-36: Steps for making a river

The highway

The following steps demonstrate a Stroke design that we discovered a few years back while playing with Illustrator. It has the makings of a cute parlor magic trick that you can use to impress your friends. Back when you had to work in Outline mode, that is, before Illustrator 5.0, creating designs with Strokes was much more difficult. Artists couldn't see what they were drawing onscreen, so they had to envision it in their minds. Editing dashes and weights is almost a pleasure now that you can use the Stroke palette and undo multiple changes.

After creating the railroad track Stroke design, which we thought was pretty clever, we yearned for a similar effect — turning one path into some form of artwork. We especially liked the effect of doing several paths and several Stroke attributes in Outline mode and then switching to Preview mode when we finished.

Figures 9-37 and 9-38 show the steps to create a four-lane highway by drawing just one path. These steps are described here.

1. Use the Pencil tool to draw a slightly wavy path from the left side of the artboard to the right side and then group the path.

2. Change the Path to a Fill of None and create a 400-point Stroke that is colored as follows: Cyan 100, Magenta 25, and Yellow 100. This path is the grass next to the highway.

3. Copy the path and paste in front. Change the paint style of the Stroke to Cyan 25, Yellow 25, and Black 85, with a weight of 240 points. This path is the shoulder of the highway.

4. Paste in front and change the paint style to Cyan 5 and Black 10, with a weight of 165 points. This path is the white line at the edge of the highway.

5. Paste in front and change the paint style to Cyan 15, Yellow 10, and Black 50, with a weight of 160 points. This path is the highway's road surface.

6. To create the dashed white lines for passing, paste in front, and change the paint style to Cyan 5 and Black 10, with a weight of 85 points, a dash of 20, and a gap of 20.

7. Paste in front and change the paint style to Cyan 15, Yellow 10, and Black 50, with a weight of 80 points. This path is the inner part of the highway's road surface.

8. To create the double yellow line, paste in front and change the paint style to Cyan 15, Magenta 20, and Yellow 100, with a weight of 8 points.

9. Paste in front and change the paint style to Cyan 15, Yellow 10, and Black 50, with a weight of 3 points. This path is the piece of highway that divides the double yellow line.

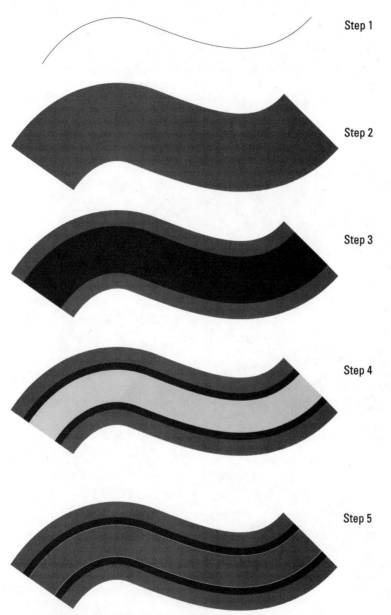

Figure 9-37: The first five steps in creating a highway

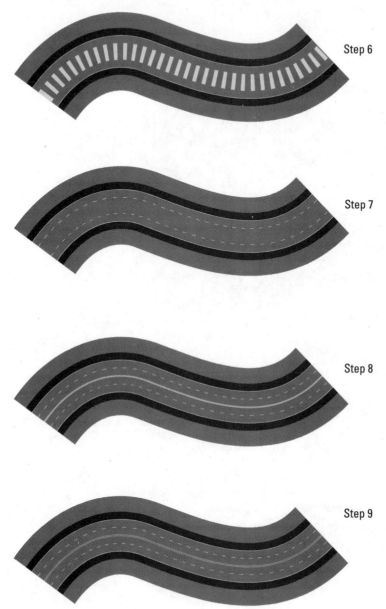

Figure 9-38: The last four steps in creating a highway

With Outline Path, we've taken the highway concept a step or two further by adding a passing zone to the highway. Use the following steps and the illustration in Figure 9-39 to create the passing zone.

1. Delete the top two paths of the original highway. Select all the paths and choose Object ⇨ Hide Selection (⌘+3 [Ctrl+3]) to hide the base of the road temporarily. You don't need to change anything about these parts of the highway to create the passing zone effect.

2. Paste in front and change the paint style to Cyan 15, Magenta 20, and Yellow 100, with a weight of 8 points. This path is the same double yellow line as the one in Step 8 of the preceding instructions, but it is not yet split.

3. Copy and paste in front. Keep the paint style at Cyan 15, Magenta 20, and Yellow 100, but change the weight to 3 points. This line is the same width as the road from Step 9 in the preceding instructions, but the color is the double-yellow-line color.

4. Choose Select ⇨ All (⌘+A [Ctrl+A]). This command selects the last two paths that you placed on the illustration. Choose Outline Stroke from the Pathfinder palette. This command creates outlines around the edges of the Stroke so that it results in two Filled objects instead of two overlapping Stroked paths.

5. Choose Exclude from the Pathfinder palette. This command subtracts the top object (the 3-point path) from the bottom one, resulting in two Filled objects that are grouped together. Ungroup the two objects by choosing Object ⇨ Ungroup (⌘+Shift+G [Ctrl+Shift+G]).

6. Deselect one of the two paths by Shift+clicking it once and deleting the selected object.

7. Paste in front to put the line with the double-yellow-line Stroke in front of the remaining Filled object. Change the paint style to Dash 20, Gap 20.

8. Paste in front and change the paint style to Cyan 15, Yellow 10, and Black 50, with a weight of 3 points. These settings create a gray line that divides the dashed section from the solid section of line. The dashed section is actually on both sides of the 3-point gray divider line, but you cannot see the part that overlays the solid line because it is the same color and size as the solid line.

9. Choose Object ⇨ Show All. The highway now has a dashed/solid yellow line.

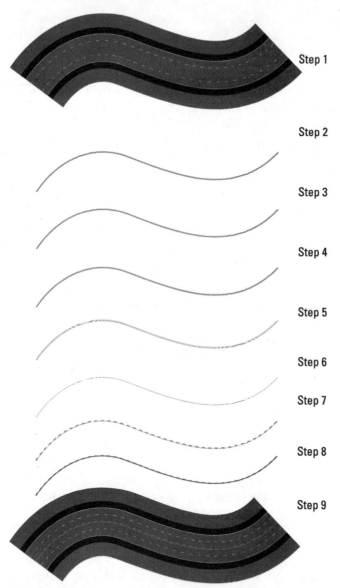

Step 1

Step 2

Step 3

Step 4

Step 5

Step 6

Step 7

Step 8

Step 9

Figure 9-39: Steps for creating a passing zone for the highway

Type into Strokes

You can put type into Strokes by creating Path type and giving the path a heavy enough Stroke weight to surround the type, as described in the following steps. Using symbols and special typefaces, you can create almost any pattern when you put type inside Strokes.

1. Draw the path on which you want the type to appear.

2. Click the path with the Path Type tool. Type the letters, numbers, or symbols that will make up the pattern.

3. Select the characters, copy, and paste. Paste until the path is full of characters.

4. Using the Type tool, change the Fill on the characters. Using the Group Selection tool, change the Stroke of the path.

Cross-Reference   For more information on creating Path type, see Chapter 8, "Manipulating Type."

If you are blessed to own font-creation software, such as Macromedia's Fontographer, you can achieve even better results. Simply incorporate any artwork that you create in Illustrator into a font and then use that artwork as Path type by using that font when you type.

Summary

Fills and Strokes are the two main ways that are used to add color, patterns and gradients to objects, but they open up many more doorways than just color. Hopefully, the techniques in this chapter have given you an idea of the way Fills and Strokes can be used. In this chapter, you learned

✦ Fill color can be added to an object.

✦ Strokes can be formatted with color, width and style.

✦ Patterns are a type of Fill that provides texture to any path.

✦ Several default patterns are supplied with Illustrator. These patterns can be transformed in the same ways that other Illustrator objects can be transformed.

✦ Almost anything in Illustrator can be used as a pattern, with the exception of masks, gradients, placed images, and other patterns.

✦ Diagonal-line patterns can be created by creating a horizontal-line pattern and rotating it with the Rotate tool while the pattern is filling a path.

✦ Textures can be created with the Pen and Ink Hatch Effects command.

✦ Cool effects can now be made to rasterized images with Photo Hatch Effects.

✦ The most attractive aspect of Strokes is that they can be used together, on top of one another.

✦ The Stroke charts provided in this chapter show some of what can be done with Strokes.

✦ Use Outline Path to create filled paths out of Strokes.

✦ Use Fills to create half-stroked paths.

✦   ✦   ✦

Transforming and Distorting Artwork

In Illustrator you have many ways to transform and distort an object. Using the Transformation tools found under the Object ➪ Transform menu and in the toolbox, you can rotate, scale, reflect, shear, and distort objects. Another common way to distort objects is with filters and effects. You have many different ways to transform and distort objects and many different tools to do it. This chapter covers these various ways and tools.

Transforming Objects

PostScript has the capability to transform any PostScript object by scaling it, rotating it, reflecting it, and shearing it. Illustrator takes this power and enhances it by providing you the flexibility of using certain tools, each of which does one of those transformations.

The toolbox includes five tools that can be used to transform objects. These tools are Rotate (which can be selected with the R key), Reflect (accessible with the O key), Scale (selected with the S key), Shear and Free Transform (which is accessed with the E key). Rotate, Scale and Free Transform are default tools, but the Reflect tool is found as a pop-up tool under the Rotate tool and the Shear tool can be found as a pop-up under the Scale tool. The Free Transform tool doesn't have any pop-up tools. Before you can select any of these tools, however, one or more objects (including paths, points, and segments) must be selected. The selected paths are the paths that are transformed. The toolbox icons for each of these tools can be seen in Figure 10-1.

Note There is actually a sixth transformation that doesn't have a tool associated with it. The Move function can be accomplished with the Selection tool, the Transform menu or the Transform palette.

Cross-Reference The Twist tool is another pop-up tool under the Rotate tool. This tool is covered later in the chapter in the "Distorting Objects," section. The Reshape tool is a pop-up tool under the Scale tool. It is covered along with the section on editing paths in Chapter 5, "Selecting and Editing."

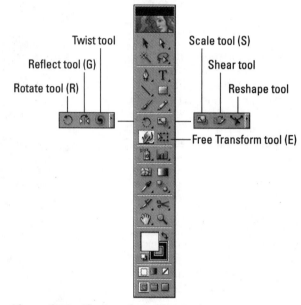

Twist tool
Reflect tool (G)
Rotate tool (R)
Scale tool (S)
Shear tool
Reshape tool
Free Transform tool (E)

Figure 10-1: The transformation tools

Note The Free Transform tool provides the capability to scale, rotate, skew, and reflect at one time.

You have five ways to transform selected objects:

✦ Click with the transformation tool to set an origin point and then drag from a different location. (This is called a *manual transformation*.) This will only work with the Rotate, Scale, and Reflect tools.

✦ Click and drag in one motion to transform the object from its center point (or last origin point).

✦ Option [Alt]+click to set the origin and then enter exact information in the tool's transformation dialog box. (This method is more precise than manual transformation.)

✦ Double-click a transformation tool to set the origin in the center of the selected object; then you can enter information in the tool's transformation dialog box.

✦ Use the Transform palette (where several transformation functions are located).

All the transformation tools work on a relative basis. For instance, if an object is scaled by 150 percent and then is scaled again by 150 percent, the object is now 225 percent of its original size (150% × 150% = 225%). If the object is initially scaled to 150 percent of its original size, and you want to return it to that original size, you must do the math and figure out what percentage is needed to resize it — in this case, 66.7 percent (100% ÷ 150% = 66.7%). Entering 100 percent in the Scale dialog box leaves the selected objects unchanged.

Illustrator automatically creates a visible origin point when you are using a transformation tool. Because the origin is in the center of the selection, if you just drag with the transformation tool, the origin point is visible as soon as you select the transformation tool. If you click without dragging to set the origin, it shows up at that location until the origin is reset. Having the origin point visible (as a blue cross-hair) makes the transformation tools much more usable and functional. Figure 10-2 shows a star object being rotated about an origin point that is below the shape.

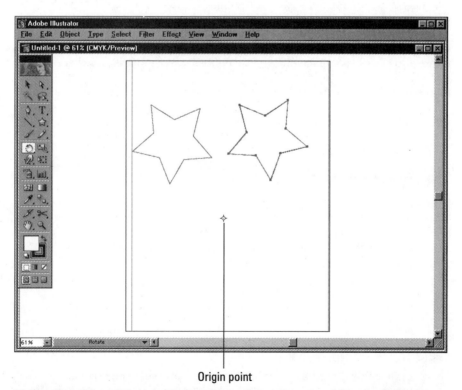

Origin point

Figure 10-2: The origin point that appears when using any of the transformation tools is the point about which the transformation happens.

Note The Free Transform and warp tools do not have an origin point.

When manually transforming objects, you can make a copy of the selected object (and thus leave the original untransformed) by holding down the Option [Alt] key before and after releasing the mouse button. In a transformation dialog box, you can make a copy by clicking the Copy button, pressing Option+Return [Alt+Enter], or Option [Alt]+clicking OK.

If the Patterns checkbox is available (you must have a pattern in one of the selected paths for this option not to be grayed out) inside any of the transformation dialog boxes, you can check its option box to transform your pattern along with the object. You can also transform the pattern only, leaving the object untransformed, by unchecking the Objects box.

Tip You can manually transform just patterns (and not the objects themselves) by pressing the tilde (~) key while using any of the transformation tools (including the Selection tool for moving).

Manually transforming objects is fairly simple if you remember that the first place you click (the point of origin) and the second place should be a fair distance apart. The farther your second click is from the point of origin, the more control you have when dragging to transform. The Shear tool is an exception—although it does matter where you click—because you can lose control of your shape anywhere.

All the transformation tools perform certain operations that rely on the Constrain Angle setting as a point of reference. Normally, this setting is set to 0 degrees, which makes your Illustrator world act normally. You can change the setting by choosing Edit ⇨ Preferences ⇨ General (⌘+K [Ctrl+K]) and entering a new value.

The Transform menu

In addition to the tools in the toolbox, you can transform objects using the Object ⇨ Transform submenu. Doubling clicking on a transformation tool will open a dialog box of options that can precisely transform the objects using values that you enter. You can access each of these transformation dialog boxes from the Object ⇨ Transform submenu (see Figure 10-3).

The Object ⇨ Transform submenu also includes other options that are quite useful such as the Transform Again and Transform Each. These features are covered later in the chapter.

Resetting the Bounding Box

The Bounding Box is the blue box that surrounds any selected objects. The Bounding Box is a visual reminder of the selected objects. After any transformation, the Bounding Box will be distorted. You can reset the Bounding Box from its distorted position to an enclosing square Bounding Box once again using the Object ➪ Transform ➪ Reset Bounding Box menu command.

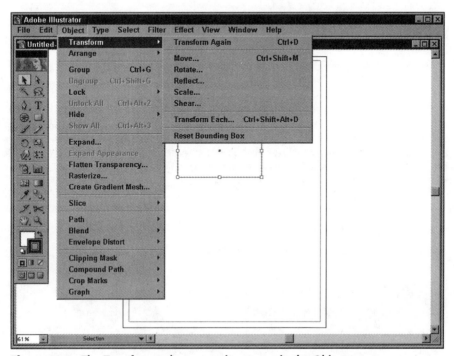

Figure 10-3: The Transform submenu as it appears in the Object menu

The Rotate tool

The Rotate tool rotates selected objects within a document. Double-clicking the Rotate tool displays the Rotate dialog box, where the precise angle of the selected item's rotation can be entered in the Angle box. The object rotates around its origin, which by default is located at the center of the object's Bounding Box. A positive number from 0 to 180 rotates the object counterclockwise by that many degrees. A negative number from 0 to –180 rotates the selected object clockwise. The Rotate tool works on a standard 360-degree circle of rotation, although it is usually easier to type in numbers from 0 to 180 or 0 to –180, than numbers such as 270, which is the same as –90 degrees.

Holding down the Option [Alt] key and clicking somewhere in the document also brings up the Rotate dialog box (see Figure 10-4); however, the object now rotates around the point where the Rotate tool was clicked. This point can be on or off the selected object. Be careful, because it is easy to rotate an object right out of your viewing area! Illustrator has many precautions, however, to prevent you from transforming or moving an object off the drawing area.

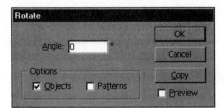

Figure 10-4: The Rotate dialog box

Click once to set the origin point from where the object's center of rotation should be and then click fairly far from the origin and drag in a circle. The selected object spins along with the cursor. To constrain the angle to 45-degree increments as you are dragging, hold down the Shift key. This angle depends on the Constrain Angle box (Edit ➪ Preferences ➪ General or ⌘+K [Ctrl+K]), and is in 45-degree increments plus the angle in this box. Figure 10-5 shows an illustration before and after rotation.

Figure 10-5: An illustration before (left) and after (right) rotation

The Reflect tool

The Reflect tool makes a mirror image of the selected objects, reflected across an axis of reflection. Double-clicking the Reflect tool reflects selected objects across an axis of reflection that runs through the center of the selected objects. In the Reflect dialog box, you can enter the axis of rotation. If you want to rotate the object along either the horizontal or vertical axis, click the appropriate button.

Tip   Option [Alt]+clicking in the document window also brings up the Reflect dialog box, but the axis of reflection is now not in the center of the selected object, but in the location in the document where you Option [Alt]+clicked.

Manual reflecting is done by clicking once to set the origin point (the center of the axis of reflection) and again somewhere along the axis of reflection. If you click and drag after setting your origin point, you can rotate the axis of reflection and see what your objects look like reflected across various axes. The Shift key constrains the axis of reflection to 90-degree angles relative to the constrain angle (Illustrator [Edit] ⇨ Preferences ⇨ General or ⌘+K [Ctrl+K]). Holding down the Option [Alt] key during the release of the click leaves a copy of the original object. Figure 10-6 shows an illustration before and after being reflected.

Figure 10-6: An illustration before (left) and after (right) being reflected across the vertical axis

The Scale tool

The Scale tool resizes objects both uniformly and nonuniformly. You can also use the Scale tool to flip objects, but without the precision of the Reflect tool. (It is impossible to keep both the size and proportions of an object constant while flipping and scaling.)

Double-clicking the Scale tool brings up the Scale dialog box, shown in Figure 10-7. All selected objects are scaled from their origins, which by default are located at the center of each object's Bounding Box. If the Uniform option is chosen, numbers typed into the text field result in proportionately scaled objects (where the width and height of the object remain proportional to each other). Numbers less than 100 percent shrink the object; numbers greater than 100 percent enlarge it. You may also check the box called Scale Strokes & Effects. This will cause any strokes and/or effects to scale proportionally to the object scaling. For instance, if two strokes of different weights are scaled, then the weights of the strokes are scaled along with their sizes, so that the relative difference between the strokes remains constant.

Nonuniform scaling resizes the horizontal and vertical dimensions of the selected objects separately, distorting the image. The way nonuniform scaling works is related to the Constrain Angle box (Illustrator [Edit] ⇨ Preferences ⇨ General or ⌘+K [Ctrl+K]), where the angle set there is the horizontal scaling, and the vertical scaling is 90 degrees from that angle.

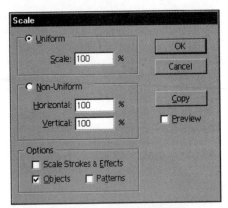

Figure 10-7: The Scale dialog box

Tip　Pressing the Option [Alt] key and clicking in the document window also brings up the Scale dialog box, but in this case the objects are scaled from the location in the document that was Option [Alt]+clicked.

Manual resizing is achieved by clicking your point of origin and then clicking away and dragging to scale. If you cross the horizontal or vertical axis of the point of origin, the selected object flips over in that direction. Holding down the Shift key constrains the objects to equal proportions (if the cursor is dragged at approximately 45 degrees from the point of origin) or constrains the scaling to either horizontal or vertical scaling only (providing the cursor is being dragged along at about a 90-degree angle from the point of origin relative to the constrain angle).

The Shear tool

This tool should actually be called the "Swear" tool because it causes more cursing (no, not cursoring; that's different) than any other tool (except perhaps for the mighty Pen tool). Another good name for the Shear tool (one that we have heard many people use) is the "Stupid" tool, because that's usually how you feel when trying to get good results from it. It's a terrifying feeling to see the artwork you spent an hour touching up until it's just right go zinging off the screen, seemingly all by itself.

Despite the criticism, the Shear tool works by moving one edge of an object while keeping the other one fixed. For example, if you have a square object and you shear the top edge, then the two side edges will be bent at an angle. The resulting shape will be a parallelogram.

The Shear tool is found in the pop-up menu with the Reflect tool. This tool is rightfully distrusted because using it manually is usually a quick lesson in futility. Double-clicking the Shear tool brings up the Shear dialog box, shown in Figure 10-8, which is much more controllable. Double-clicking causes the origin to be in the center of the selected object. The Shear Angle box is simple enough; in its text box, enter the angle amount the object should shear. Any amount over 75 degrees or less than

–75 degrees renders the object into an indecipherable mess, because at this angle or higher the art has been "flattened." The Shear tool reverses the positive-numbers-are-counterclockwise rule: To shear an object clockwise, enter a positive number; to shear counterclockwise, enter a negative number. The Axis Angle box is for shearing an object along a specified axis.

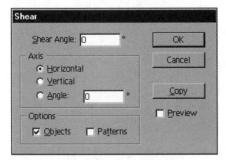

Figure 10-8: The Shear dialog box

 Tip Option [Alt]+clicking in the document window also brings up the Shear dialog box, with the origin of the shear being the location of the preceding Option [Alt]+click.

Manual shearing is something else again because you are doing two things at once: changing both the angle of shearing (the distance from the beginning of the second click until it is released) and the angle of the axis of shearing (the angle the mouse is dragged during the second click). Usually, it's best to start your second click fairly far away from the point of origin. Holding down the Shift key constrains the axis of shearing to a 45-degree angle relative to the constraining angle. Figure 10-9 shows an illustration before and after being sheared.

Figure 10-9: An illustration before (left) and after (right) being sheared

The Free Transform tool

The Free Transform tool enables you to rotate, scale, reflect, and shear all with one tool. This way you can create multiple transformations at one time.

What is unique about this tool is that you can select more than one object to change the size, shape, and placement in one step. The Free Transform tool replaces the Free Distort filter (if you check out the Filter menu, you'll find that the Free Distort filter is gone). Using this cool tool to create distorted effects is easier than using the Free Distort filter.

When you select the Free Transform tool, the object is surrounded with a Bounding Box. This box has control handles on every corner and in the middle of every edge. To scale with the Free Transform tool, you simply need to drag the corner control handles.

If you drag on the side control handles, you can distort the object. If you press ⌘+Option [Ctrl+Alt] while dragging one of the side control handles, then you can shear the object. Holding down only ⌘ [Ctrl] will move only the selected edge. If you drag a side control handle through the opposite side, the object will be reflected.

You can rotate objects with the Free Transform tool by positioning the cursor near one of the control handles until it changes from a straight double-headed arrow to a curved double-headed arrow cursor. If you drag when with the curved cursor is near a control handle, then the object will be rotated.

To distort a single corner of an object, hold down ⌘ [Ctrl] while dragging a corner control handle. You can distort the perspective of an object by holding down ⌘+Option+Shift [Ctrl+Alt+Shift]. Distortions using these keys will only work on the corner control handles.

Note   When using the Free Transform tool, you need to select and begin dragging a control handle before using a keyboard combination in order to get the desired effect. If you press the keyboard keys before beginning to drag the control handle, the effect will not work.

Moving

The most common way to move an object is to use a Selection tool and drag the selected points, segments, and paths from one location to another.

The precise way to move an object is to use the Move dialog box (see Figure 10-10) or the Transform palette (see the following section). Select the object you want to move and then choose Object ➪ Transform ➪ Move. The Move dialog box appears, and you can enter the appropriate values in either the horizontal or vertical text fields. If you want to move an object diagonally, enter a number in the Distance text field and then enter the angle of movement direction in the Angle text field.

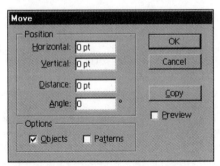

Figure 10-10: The Move dialog box

Any selected object (except for text selected with a Type tool) can be moved via the Move dialog box, including individual Anchor Points and line segments.

By default, the Move dialog box contains the distance and angle that you last moved an object, whether manually (with a Selection tool) or in the Move dialog box. If you used the Measure tool prior to using the Move dialog box, the numbers in the Move dialog box correspond to the numbers that appeared in the Info palette when you used the Measure tool.

> **Tip**   Double-clicking the Selection tool in the toolbox displays the Move dialog box.

In the Move dialog box, positive numbers in the Horizontal text field move an object from left to right, while negative numbers move an object from right to left. Positive numbers in the Vertical text field move an object from bottom to top, while negative numbers move an object from top to bottom. Negative numbers in the Distance text field move an object in the opposite direction of the Angle text field. The Angle text field works a bit differently. Negative numbers in the Angle text field move the angle in the opposite direction from 0 degrees (so entering –45 degrees is the same as entering 315 degrees and entering –180 degrees is the same as entering 180 degrees).

The measurement system in the Move dialog box matches the system set in the General Preferences dialog box. To enter a measurement different from the current measurement system, use these indicators:

    ✦ **For inches:** 1" or 1in (1 inch)

    ✦ **For picas:** 1p or 1pica (1 pica)

    ✦ **For points:** 1pt or 0p1 (1 point)

    ✦ **For picas/points:** 1p1 (1 pica, 1 point)

    ✦ **For millimeters:** 1mm (1 millimeter)

    ✦ **For centimeters:** 1cm (1 centimeter)

The Horizontal and Vertical text fields are linked to the Distance and Angle text fields; when one of the fields is changed, the others are altered accordingly.

Pressing the Copy button duplicates selected objects in the direction and distance indicated, just as holding down Option [Alt] when dragging duplicates the selected objects.

Tip

The Move dialog box is a great place to enter everything via the keyboard. Press Tab to move from text field to text field, press Return [Enter] to push the OK button, and press ⌘+. (period) [Esc] to push the Cancel button. Pressing Option+ Return [Alt+Enter] or pressing Option [Alt] while clicking OK pushes the Copy button. The same is true for all of the transformation dialog boxes.

The Transform Palette

Imagine, if you will, a palette that combines four of Illustrator's transformation capabilities into one place. Then take a look at Figure 10-11, which shows Illustrator's Transform palette in all its glory.

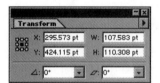

Figure 10-11: The Transform palette

The Transform palette provides a way to move, scale, rotate, and shear selected artwork. There's no Reflect option (you'll need to use the tool or the Transform submenu option to reflect artwork). Instead of manually setting an origin point or transforming from the center by default, the Transform palette gives you nine "fixed" origin points based on the Bounding Box of the selected objects. Choose an origin point before entering values in the palette, and the transformations will originate from the corner, center of a side, or the center of selected objects.

The text fields in the Transform palette are as follows:

✦ **X:** This is the horizontal location of the artwork, measured from the left edge of the document (or horizontal ruler origin if it has been moved from the left edge).

✦ **Y:** This is the vertical location of the artwork, measured from the bottom edge of the document (or vertical ruler origin if it has been moved from the bottom edge).

✦ **W:** This is the width of the artwork's Bounding Box.

✦ **H:** This is the height of the artwork's Bounding Box.

✦ **Rotation:** This field lets you apply a rotation to the selected artwork.

✦ **Shear:** This field lets you apply a shear to the selected artwork.

To use the palette, type the new value you'd like to use in any field and then press Return [Enter]. If you have another value to enter, press the Tab key to go to the next text field (or Shift+Tab to go back a field). Pressing Option [Alt] when you press Return [Enter] creates a duplicate of the selected artwork with the transformations you specified.

For Scaling, you can enter either absolute measurements (the size in inches, picas, and so on, that you want the artwork to be), or by percentage by adding the % symbol after your value. You can also force Illustrator to scale uniformly, regardless of whether you're using absolute measurements or percentages, by pressing ⌘ [Ctrl] when you press the Return [Enter] keys.

Transform Palette Wish-List

Okay, time for us to 'fess up. We're not big fans of the Transform palette (although it is getting better with each new release), and here's why:

✦ **No Reflect option.** Although the palette menu includes Flip Horizontal and Flip Vertical options, couldn't we have a button enabling us to enter a negative scale value to reflect across the horizontal/vertical axis?

✦ **Each option.** Transform Each is hard to get to, and this would've provided an easy way to do these transformations.

✦ **No Random option.** Transformations are perfect for random values, as evidenced by Transform Each's Random checkbox.

✦ **No Keyboard commands to highlight the text fields.** Even the transformation tools can be accessed by pressing the keyboard keys.

✦ **After rotating and shearing, the value reverts back to 0 degrees instantly.** We'd like the values here to show how far the art has been transformed since it was created. A few technical issues would need to be worked out here (groups? compound paths? portions of paths? objects pasted?), but we're sure Adobe could figure them out.

✦ **No automated repeat function.** A text field for number of duplicates would be handy (we hate pressing ⌘+D [Ctrl+D] 34 times when we want to duplicate/rotate an object around a circle at 10-degree increments).

✦ **No floating origin point.** We have to use one of the nine presets—and there's no way to change them automatically or revert to center using the keyboard.

Okay, sure, many of the things we don't like about the Transform palette are wish-list features and Adobe has addressed some of them in this new version, such as a keyboard command to show/hide the palette—Shift+F8. But if we're going to have this palette sucking up valuable screen real estate, we want something back for it. Most of Illustrator's other palettes are worthy of taking up chunks of pixels; the Transform palette isn't (at least not yet).

Note The "Transform Palette Wish-List" sidebar comments are here for two reasons. First, because we think you should know that, while we love Illustrator (our program of choice if we were to be stuck on a desert island with a computer), we still don't like a few things, or we feel they could be improved. The second reason is to show a sample of the types of communication that Adobe and other software companies use to determine what features take priority for future implementation. If instead of listing what we don't like and would like to see in the next version of Illustrator we just said, "We don't like the transformation palette," Adobe would just shrug and ignore us. But its concern is to make the best software it can, and that means addressing its customers' needs. If you have suggestions or ideas for Adobe (or for third-party plug-in developers such as Extensis), make sure you're both as concise and descriptive as possible.

Transform Each

Transform Each provides a way to do several transformations in one shot, but that's only the beginning. The unique thing about Transform Each is that each selected object is transformed independently, as opposed to having all the selected objects transformed together. Figure 10-12 shows the difference between "normal" rotating and scaling, and the Rotate and Scale functions in Transform Each.

Figure 10-12: An illustration (left) after being rotated and scaled (right top), and then after using the same values with the Rotate and Scale functions within Transform Each (right bottom)

To access the Transform Each dialog box (see Figure 10-13), choose Object ➪ Transform ➪ Transform Each. In the dialog box, use the sliders/dial or type in values for each of the transformations. The Random checkbox on the right side of the dialog box gives each object selected a random value that falls within the default (100 percent for Scale; 0 points for Move and Rotate) and the value set by the slider/dial.

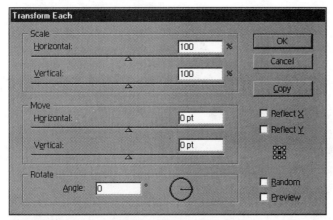

Figure 10-13: The Transform Each dialog box

Of all options in the Transform Each dialog box, the randomize function is the most powerful. Checking the Random checkbox can turn a grid into a distinct random texture, as shown in Figure 10-14.

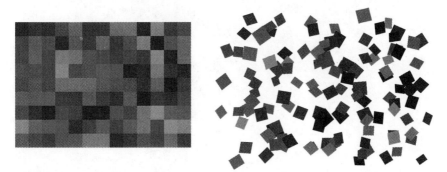

Figure 10-14: Transform Each's Random function applied to a checkerboard of colored squares

The following steps show you how to use the Transform Each function, and Figure 10-15 illustrates these steps.

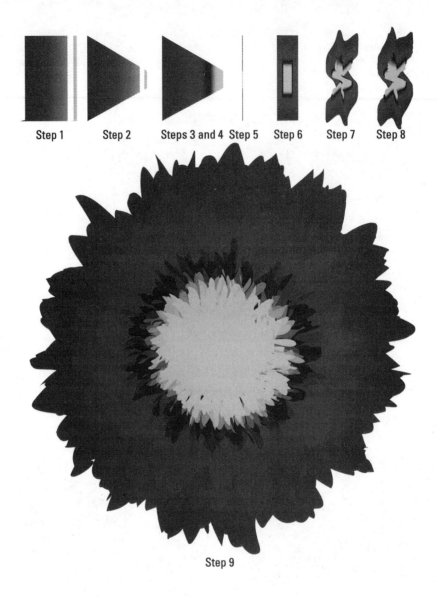

Step 1   Step 2   Steps 3 and 4 Step 5   Step 6   Step 7   Step 8

Step 9

Figure 10-15: Steps for creating a flower using Transform Each

1. Create a rectangle (like the one shown in Figure 10-15) and fill it with the Purple, Red, Yellow gradient.

2. Use the Direct Selection tool to move the upper-right point down and the lower-right point up.

3. Add a color stop to the gradient (in the Gradient palette) that's black.

4. Expand the Gradient (Choose Object ➪ Expand) using 100 blend steps. Choose Crop from the Pathfinder palette. This setting crops the blend along the angles you defined in Step 2.

5. In the Align palette, choose the Align Vertically button (second from the left, top row).

6. Horizontally scale the objects.

7. Choose Filter ➪ Distort ➪ Zig Zag, and enter 10 percent, 2 segments, and Smooth.

8. Choose Filter ➪ Distort ➪ Scribble and Tweak, and Scribble at 5 percent Horizontal, 5 percent Vertical, with all options checked.

9. Choose Object ➪ Transform ➪ Transform Each, enter a rotation of 180 degrees, and check the Random box. This setting rotates the objects anywhere from 0 to 180 degrees.

Transformation Techniques

The transformation tools open a world of possibilities within Illustrator. The following tips and ideas should give you a head start in exploring the amazing power of transformations.

Choosing Transform Again (⌘-D [Ctrl+D]) from the Transform submenu of the Object menu redoes the last transformation that was done to a selected object. Transformations include Move, Rotate, Scale, Reflect, Shear, and Transform Each. Transform Again also makes a transformed copy if a copy was made either manually or by clicking the Copy button in the prior transformation dialog box.

Tip   Transform Again remembers the last transformation no matter what else you do in the meantime, and it can apply that same transformation to other objects or reapply it to the existing transformed objects.

Creating shadows

You can create all sorts of shadows by using the Scale, Reflect, and Shear tools, as shown in the illustrations in Figure 10-16. Follow these steps to create shadows:

1. Select the path where you want to apply the shadow and click the bottom of the path once with the Reflect tool. This action sets the origin of reflection at the base of the image. Drag down while pressing the Shift key. The image flips over, creating a mirror image under the original. Press the Option [Alt] key (keeping the Shift key pressed) before and during the release of the mouse button.

2. Using the Shear tool, click the base of the reflected copy to set the origin. Click and drag left or right at the other side of the reflection to set the angle of the reflection.

3. Using the Scale tool, click once again on the base of the reflected copy to set the origin. Click and drag up or down at the other side of the reflection.

4. Color the shadow darker than its background and apply a gradient to the shadow.

Figure 10-16: Creating shadows with the transformation tools

To create a shadow for type, you must first vertically scale a copy of the type. Hold down the Option [Alt] key when you release the mouse button to make the copy, and hold down the Shift key to constrain the scaling to vertical as you drag the mouse up or down. Setting the origin of the scale to the baseline of the type helps, as does using all caps or type with no descenders.

Send the copy to the back (⌘+Shift+[[Ctrl+Shift+[]) and shear the shadow off to one side or the other, once again setting the origin at the baseline of the type. Holding down Shift as you shear prevents the baseline of the copy from angling up or down.

If you want the shadow in front of the type (making it appear as if the light source is coming from behind the type), use the Reflect tool to flip the copy of the type across the baseline of the type.

Transforming gradients

You can transform gradients in the same way that you transform objects that are colored by gradients. All of the transformation tools affect gradients, but the best effects are achieved by scaling and shearing gradients, especially radial gradients, as shown in Figure 10-17.

To create an effect similar to that of Figure 10-17, create a radial gradient inside a circle with no Stroke. (Use a circle so that no portions of it are cropped outside of the shape when it is distorted.) Scale and shear the circle with the radial gradient, and the radial gradient becomes scaled and sheared as well.

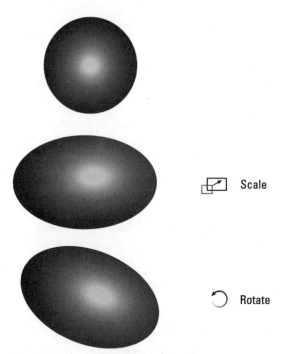

Scale

Rotate

Figure 10-17: Transforming a gradient

Rotating into a path

Clever use of the Rotate tool can create a realistic, winding path by duplicating the same object at different rotational intervals, rotated from different origins.

Start by creating an object of some sort. (The illustration in Figure 10-18 uses paw prints.) Select the objects (it's often best to group them together) and choose the Rotate tool. Click to set an origin a little distance from the side of the object. Click the other side of the object and drag. As you drag, you see the outline of the shape of the object that you are dragging. When the object is a good distance away, press the Option [Alt] key (to copy) and release the mouse button; then release the Option [Alt] key. A copy of the object appears. Press ⌘+D [Ctrl+D] (Transform Again) to create another object the same distance away.

After using the Transform Again command (⌘+D [Ctrl+D]) a few times, click with the Rotate tool on the other side of the object to set another origin. Click and drag the outline of the object about the same distance; then press the Option [Alt] key and release the mouse button. Use the Transform Again command a few more times.

Figure 10-18: Paw prints that have been rotated into a path the old-fashioned way

The farther you click from the objects to set the origin, the smaller the curve of the path of objects. Clicking right next to the objects causes them to turn sharply.

Making tiles using the Reflect tool

You can make symmetrical tiles with the Reflect tool. You can use a set of four differently positioned, yet identical, objects to create artwork with a floor-tile look, as shown in Figure 10-19. Here are the steps:

1. Create the path (or paths) that you will make into the symmetrical tile. Group the artwork together.

2. Using the Reflect tool, click off to the right of the object to set the origin. Click and drag on the left edge of the object and drag to the right while pressing the Shift and Option [Alt] keys. (Using the Shift key reflects the image at only 45-degree angles.) When the object has been reflected to the right side, let go of the mouse button, still pressing the Option [Alt] key. Release the Option [Alt] key. You now have two versions of the object.

3. Select the original and reflected object and reflect again, this time across the bottom of the objects. Four objects now exist, each mirrored a little differently, that make up a "tile." You can now use this tile to create symmetrical patterns.

Using Transformation tools on portions of paths

When using the transformation tools, you don't need to select an entire path. Instead, try experimenting with other effects by selecting single Anchor Points, line segments, and combinations of selected Anchor Points and segments. Another idea is to select portions of paths on different objects.

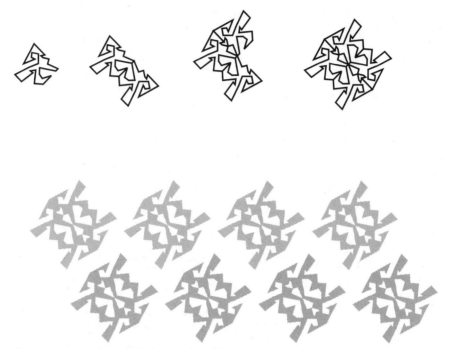

Figure 10-19: Creating tiles with the Reflect tool

Tip   When you're working with portions of paths, one of the most useful transformation tool procedures is to select a smooth point with the Direct Selection tool and then choose a transformation tool.

You can achieve precise control with the Rotate tool. Click the center of the Anchor Point and drag around the Anchor Point. Both control handles move, but the distance from the control handles to the Anchor Point remains the same. You can also use just the Direct Selection tool to accomplish the same task, but it is very difficult to perform.

You can accomplish the exact lengthening of control handle lines by using the Scale tool. Click the Anchor Point to set the origin and then drag out from one of the control handles. Both control handles will grow from the Anchor Point in equal proportions.

When working on a smooth point, you can use the Reflect tool to switch lengths and angles between the two control handles.

Here are some more portion-of-path transformation ideas:

✦ Select all the points in an open path except for the End Points and use all the different transformation tools on the selected areas.

✦ Select the bottommost or topmost Anchor Point in text converted to outlines, and scale, rotate, and shear for interesting effects.

✦ Select two Anchor Points on a rectangle and scale and skew copies into a cube.

If you have ever wondered how to create a splendid spirograph image, the following steps and Figure 10-20 will show you how.

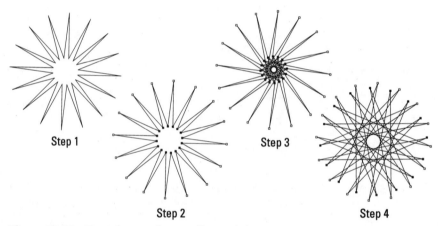

Figure 10-20: Steps for creating a spirograph image

1. Create a star with lots of points, and a fairly tight inner radius.

2. Select just the middle points with the Direct Selection tool.

3. Use the Rotate tool to "twist" the inner points around.

4. Use the Scale tool to invert the inner points outside of the outer ones.

Rotating into kaleidoscopes

By rotating and duplicating objects that have Strokes, you can make kaleidoscopic illustrations, such as the one in Figure 10-21. You may have trouble working with the last two or three objects, but this section shows you how to work through any difficulties.

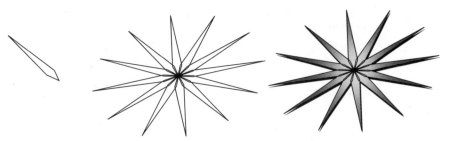

Figure 10-21: Objects that have been rotated into kaleidoscopes

First, select the object that you wish to rotate and duplicate. Choose the Rotate tool and Option [Alt]+click at one end or corner of the object. In the Rotate dialog box, enter an angle that goes into 360 degrees evenly, such as 18 degrees ($20 \times 18 = 360$), and press the Copy button (Option+Return [Alt+Enter]). Choose Transform Again (⌘+D [Ctrl+D]) until the object circles around the origin back to the beginning.

The trouble that you may run into here is that if the objects have a Fill and they overlap at all, the last object looks as if it's on the top and the original object looks as if it's on the bottom, which destroys the perspective of the kaleidoscope. So either the original or the last object has to be fixed. It is generally easier to fix the original (bottommost) object.

Start by selecting the bottommost (original) object. Copy it (⌘-C [Ctrl+C]) and paste it in front (⌘+F [Ctrl+F]). Then create two breaks in the path of the object with the Scissors tool, one on either side of the area where the two objects overlap. Remove that portion of the path by deselecting all (⌘+Shift+A [Ctrl+Shift+A]) and selecting it, and then delete just that portion. Many times this step alone fixes the path. If a Fill and a Stroke exists, however, your problems may not go away quite so easily. Copy the remaining piece of the copied object, choose Paste in Front again (⌘+F [Ctrl+F]), and change the Fill to None. This procedure corrects any Stroke deficiencies from the first copy.

Transforming patterns

The option in all transformation dialog boxes (and the Move dialog box) to apply transformations to patterns can produce some very interesting results, as shown in Figure 10-22.

One of the most interesting effects results from using patterns that have transparent Fills. Select an object that has a pattern Fill and double-click a transformation tool. Enter a value, check the Pattern tiles box, uncheck the Objects box, and then click Copy. A new object (which is unchanged) will overlap the original object, but the pattern in the new object will have changed. If desired, use the Transform Again command (⌘+D [Ctrl+D]) to create additional copies with patterns that have been transformed even more.

Figure 10-22: A pattern that has been scaled up inside the text and rotated

 Tip   You can transform patterns "live" by pressing the tilde key (~) while dragging with any transformation tool (including the Selection tool for moving).

Distorting Objects

There are many different ways to distort your face when looking in the mirror. You can scrunch up your nose, pull the corners of your mouth in to a frown or squint your eyes real good. In Illustrator, there are also several different ways to distort objects and artwork—you could use tools like the Twist or Warp, scrunch objects into the shape of an envelope, or apply any one of many interesting filters or effects. The best part is that mom's threat that your face will freeze like that won't come true.

In addition to the Twist tool, there are several distortion tools available under the Warp tool. Under the Warp tool (which is accessed with the Shift+R key) are the Twirl, Pucker, Bloat, Scallop, Crystallize and Wrinkle tools. These tools collectively are called the Liquify tools because they are used to distort locally the paths that make up an object in different ways.

 New Feature   The Liquify tools are all new to Illustrator 10.

The Twist tool

Have you ever wanted to twist your artwork around its middle continuously until you couldn't make out what the original artwork was? Neither have we. The Twist tool was incorporated into Illustrator, hiding to the right of the Rotate tool.

To use the Twist tool, click and drag either left or right. Any selected artwork will spin around the center of the combined objects. Figure 10-23 shows a simple array of diamonds that have been twisted to varying degrees.

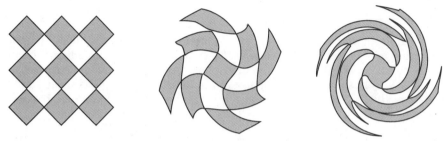

Figure 10-23: Artwork before (left) and after twisting with the Twist tool to different extents (middle and right)

You can twist around any origin simply by clicking to set an origin point and then dragging. The artwork will twist around the origin point you set. We took the original artwork from Figure 10-23 and twisted it around the lower-left diamond a couple of times to get the funhouse effect shown in Figure 10-24.

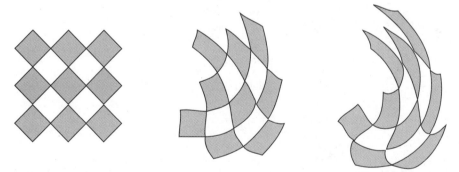

Figure 10-24: The funhouse effect achieved by twisting around the lower-left diamond of Figure 10-23

Tip

To twist a specific amount, Option [Alt]+click at the origin point you wish to twist around. This opens the Twist dialog box where you can enter the value of the Twist Angle.

Using the Liquify tools

When you were working with real ink, did you ever accidentally brush against a newly created drawing and actually find that the resulting drawing was actually improved? (Well, it never happened to me, but it might have happened to some-one.) One aspect of working with real ink is that the ink is actually a liquid and in certain ways, you could use this to your advantage. Just consider the many abstract artists that splash ink on a canvas and voila. Illustrator has developed a set of tools that enable you to warp, twirl, and distort your artwork as if it were still wet on the canvas.

These tools are collectively called the Liquify tools and they are all found under the Warp tool in the toolbox. These tools, shown in Figure 10-25, include the following: Warp, Twirl, Pucker, Bloat, Scallop, Crystallize and Wrinkle (even the names sound fun). You'll notice many of these names from the Filter and Effects menus and those respective filters and effects still exist, but the tools give you much more control over these effects.

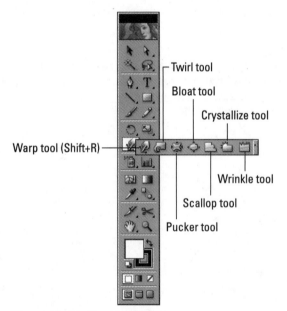

Figure 10-25: The Liquify tools

Each of the Liquify tools lets you define a circular brush with a given width, height, angle and intensity. These values can be set using the various tool option dialog boxes. This dialog box can be opened by double clicking on the tool icon in the toolbox. For example, with the Warp tool selected, you can open the Warp Tool Options dialog box, shown in Figure 10-26, with a double click on the tool's icon. The brush defining values are the same for all liquify tools.

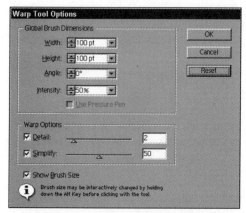

Figure 10-26: The Warp Tool Options dialog box displays options for defining how the brush looks and the resulting detail of the path.

The Width and Height values define the dimensions of a rectangle that contains the brush. The Angle value will rotate any elliptical shaped brush to the given angle. At the bottom of the dialog box is the Show Brush Size option. Enabling this box will make an outline of the brush visible while you work with the tool. The Intensity value determines how quickly the distortion takes place. Higher Intensity values will produce a more radical distortion for a small cursor movement. The Use Pressure Pen option will adjust the Intensity value based the pressure applied to the stylus of a graphics palette.

Another way to change the brush dimensions is to hold down the Option [Alt] key while dragging in the document window. This will interactively change the brush's shape. Holding down the Shift and Option [Alt] key will proportionally increase or decrease the size of the brush. Holding the Shift key by itself while dragging will constrain the brush's movement to be horizontal or vertical.

The Warp tool

Although the warp tool sounds like something that should be part of the Starship Enterprise, it has also found its way into Illustrator. So now, you can bold say, "Mr. Sulu, give me warp 6," but your co-workers may look at you funny. If you've watched Star Trek, you'll know that engaging a warp drive will distort the starship and the similar behavior can done with the Warp tool in Illustrator.

Clicking on the Warp tool will enable a brush with a visible area. As you click and drag this brush, the selected objects will bend outward around the center of the brush. One of the nice features of the warp tool is that as the object bends, its path stays intact like a rubberband that is stretched. Figure 10-27 shows a grid of diamonds that has been distorted with the Warp tool.

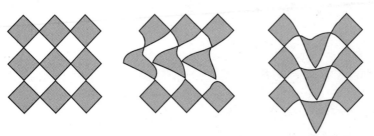

Figure 10-27: The Warp tool was dragged from right to left on the middle grid and from top to bottom on the right grid.

If you double click on the Warp tool, the Warp Tool Options dialog box, shown previously in Figure 10-26, appears. Using this dialog box, you can change the dimensions, orientation and Intensity of the warp tool brush. As the path is bent, additional anchor points are automatically added as needed. You can also set values for the Detail and Simplify sliders of the effected path. A High Detail value will place more anchor points closer together. A higher Simplify value will represent the path in the fewest number of points.

The Twirl tool

The Twirl tool (not to be confused with the Twist tool) will spiral the points near the cursor around the brush's center, but only for the area covered by the brush. This local distortion is different from the Twist tool, which spirals the entire object about an origin point. Figure 10-28 shows how the Twirl tool can be used.

Caution

Be cautious to not confuse the new Twirl tool with the Twist tool. The Twist tool was previously referred to as the Twirl tool.

Figure 10-28: The Twirl tool can be used to distort the circle shape on the left into shapes like the ones on the right.

In addition to the Detail and Simplify values, the Twirl Tool Options dialog box also includes a Twirl Rate value. This value can range between –180 and 180. Negative values will rotate the swirls in the clockwise direction while positive values will twirl in the counterclockwise direction. Higher values will twirl more aggressively as the cursor is dragged than values closer to 0.

The Pucker tool

The Pucker tool sounds lost without the Bloat tool and don't worry the Bloat tool is coming right behind it. The Pucker tool will pull paths and points toward the center of the tool's brush. The closer the path segment and/or anchor point gets towards the center of the brush, the greater its movement. But, once the point or path reaches the center of the brush it stops its movement.

Figure 10-29 shows two squares that have been puckered with the Pucker tool. The middle square was created by dragging the Pucker tool from the top and bottom to the square's center. The right square was created by dragging the Pucker from the left and right side of the square toward its center.

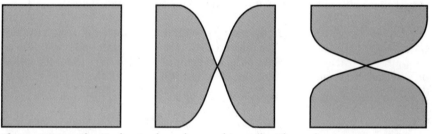

Figure 10-29: The Pucker tool can be used to pull paths and points toward the center of the brush.

The Pucker Tool Options dialog box includes the same values as the Warp Tool Options dialog box including Detail and Simplify values.

The Bloat tool

Following close on the heals of the Pucker tool, is its close cousin, the Bloat tool. The Bloat tool is actually the opposite of the Pucker tool. It will push paths outward from its center location. As the path is pushed outward, it will conform to the shape of the brush. Figure 10-30 shows two square shapes that have been affected by the Bloat tool. The middle square has had the Bloat tool moved from its center toward the top and bottom of the shape. This has pushed the upper and lower edges of the square outward. The right square was pushed to the left and right.

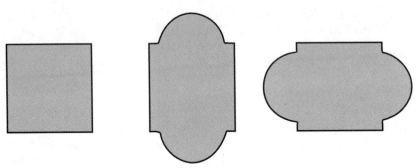

Figure 10-30: The Bloat tool can be used to push paths away from the center of the brush.

The Scallop tool

Although the Scallop tool sounds like something a seafood-lover would like, it actually doesn't have anything to do with food. But you can think of seashells and it would make sense. When the Scallop tool is dragged across a path, the path will raise scalloped bumps that move towards the center of the brush.

The paths in Figure 10-31 were traced over with the Scallop tool, which pulled scallops from the path outward. The middle path traced the path on its left side and the right path was traced on its right side. Dragging the brush over the path on one side will pull the scallops toward the side that the center of the brush is.

Figure 10-31: The Scallop tool will pull small bumps away from the path.

The Scallop Tool Options dialog box, shown in Figure 10-32, includes several options that control the shape of the scallops. The Complexity value sets the density of the bumps. Higher values will result in dense collections of bumps that are close together. By selecting to have the brush affect the tangent handles (either In or Out), the resulting scallops are smoother. Selecting the Brush Affects Anchors Points will make the scallops sharper at their ends and more spike-like.

Scallop Tool Options

Global Brush Dimensions

Width: 100 pt

Height: 100 pt

Angle: 0°

Intensity: 50%

☐ Use Pressure Pen

Scallop Options

Complexity: 1

☑ Detail: 2

☑ Brush Affects Anchor Points

☐ Brush Affects In Tangent Handles

☐ Brush Affects Out Tangent Handles

☑ Show Brush Size

ⓘ Brush size may be interactively changed by holding down the Alt Key before clicking with the tool.

OK

Cancel

Reset

Figure 10-32: The Scallop Tool Options dialog box includes additional options that control how the scallops look.

The Crystallize tool

The Crystallize tool is the opposite of the Scallop tool in that it will push bumps away from the brush center. These bumps can be either smooth or spiky based on whether the affect tangent handles options in the Crystallize Tool Options dialog box are enabled. The Crystallize Tool Options dialog box has the exact same options as the Scallop Tool Options dialog box.

Figure 10-33 shows a circle that has been traced on the inside with the Crystallize tool, which has pushed the bumps outward. For the middle circle, the Brush Affect Anchor Points option in the Crystallize Tool Options dialog box has been selected and for the right circle, the Brush Affects In and Out Tangent Handles options have been enabled.

Figure 10-33: The Crystallize Tool Options dialog box options can turn this shape into a sun or a flower.

The Wrinkle tool

The last of the Liquify tools will do something that is cursed by housewives the world over — add wrinkles to objects. The Wrinkle tool is like a cross between the Scallop and Crystallize tools. It will add small perturbations to each side of a path. This tool can be used to add some irregularity to a path to make it look like it was handwritten.

The Wrinkle Tool Options dialog box includes the same options as the Scallop and Crystallize tools, but the Wrinkle tools include two additional values for defining the percentage of wrinkle in the Horizontal and Vertical directions. Figure 10-34 shows a path that has been wrinkled. The middle path has been wrinkled with a Complexity value of 1 and the right path has a Complexity value of 4. Notice how the right path includes more details.

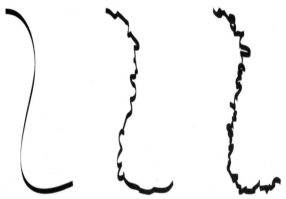

Figure 10-34: The Wrinkle tool can wrinkle paths by both pulling and pushing the path.

Creating a heart

One of the uses of the Liquify tools is to quickly and easily make common symbols. Just in time for Valentine's Day, these steps will show you how to use the Liquify tools to create a heart. Figure 10-35 shows how a simple heart can be created with the Liquify tools.

1. Create a circle with the Ellipse tool by holding down the Shift key while you drag in the document window.

2. Select the Pucker tool and drag the tool from the top of the circle towards the center and again from just below the center of the circle to below the circle.

3. Select the Bloat tool and drag from around the center of the heart up to the left and again up towards the right to round out the upper half of the heart.

4. For the final refining, select the Warp tool and drag from inside the heart towards the outside around the bottom vertex to gradually reshape the heart.

Figure 10-35: The steps to create a heart using the Liquify tools

Distortion Filters

In addition to the Liquify tools, you can distort objects using the various filters found in the Filter ⇨ Distort menu. The Distort submenu includes the following filters: Free Distort, Pucker & Bloat, Roughen, Scribble & Tweak, Twist, and Zig Zag. Each of these filters will open a dialog box where you can control the parameters of the filter.

Cross-Reference Chapter 13, "Using Styles, Effects and Filters," presents all the other filters listed in the Filter menu.

Free Distort filter

The Free Distort filter works like the Free Transform tool in that it enables you to move the corners of the Bounding Box to distort the perspective of the selected object. The main difference is that the Free Distort filter enables the corner control handles to be moved independently.

Selecting Filter ⇨ Distort ⇨ Free Distort opens the Free Distort dialog box, shown in Figure 10-36. This dialog box lets you interactively move the Bounding Box corner control handles and preview the changes as you make them.

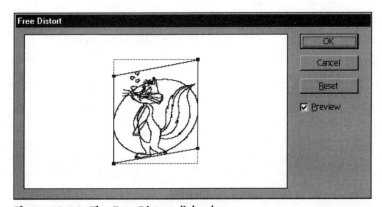

Figure 10-36: The Free Distort dialog box

Figure 10-37 shows some artwork that has been distorted using the Free Distort filter. Notice how this image has a different result from the Shear tool.

Figure 10-37: Artwork before (left) and after (right) the Free Distort filter has been applied

The Punk and Bloat filter

Although the Punk and Bloat filter undoubtedly has the coolest sounding name that Illustrator has to offer, this filter is also one of the least practical. But Illustrator is a fun program, right? And these filters make it lots of fun.

Punking makes objects appear to have pointy tips sticking out everywhere, and *bloating* creates lumps outside of objects. Punking and bloating are inverses of each other; a negative punk is a bloat, and a negative bloat is a punk. If you are bewildered by these functions, stop reading right here. The following information spoils everything.

Selecting Punk and Bloat opens the Punk and Bloat dialog box, where you may specify a percentage that you want the selected paths to be punked or bloated by either typing in the amount or dragging a slider.

Bloating causes the segments between Anchor Points to expand outwards. The higher the percentage, the more bloated the selection. You can bloat from –200 percent to +200 percent. While Bloat makes rounded, bubblelike extrusions appear on the surface of your object, Punk makes tall spikes appear on its path. When you drag toward Punk, you can enter how much you want to punk the drawing. Punk amounts can range from –200 percent to +200 percent. The number of spikes is based on the number of Anchor Points in your drawing. Figure 10-38 shows a few punked and bloated objects.

Original   Punk   Bloat

Figure 10-38: Punked and bloated objects

The Punk and Bloat filter moves Anchor Points in one direction and creates two independent direction points on either side of each Anchor Point. The direction points are moved in the opposite direction of the Anchor Points, and the direction of movement is always toward or away from the center of the object.

The distance moved is the only thing that you control when you use the Punk and Bloat filter. Entering a percentage moves the points by that percentage.

 Note Nothing about the Punk and Bloat filter is random. Everything about it is 100 percent controllable and, to some extent, predictable.

Follow these steps to punk an object:

1. Create and select the artwork that you want to punk, as shown in Figure 10-39.

2. Add Anchor Points or use the Roughen filter at 0 percent to create additional Anchor Points if necessary. We chose Object ⇨ Add Anchor Points twice, increasing the number of Anchor Points from 4 to 16. Although the extra Anchor Points may not be visible, they will give the circle object more points that can move during the Punk and Bloat operation.

3. Choose Filter ⇨ Stylize ⇨ Punk and Bloat. In the dialog box, enter the amount that you want to punk or bloat the object, or drag the slider in the appropriate direction.

Figure 10-39: Steps for punking and bloating

4. Check to see whether the result is what you intended.

5. Add other artwork to the punked or bloated object.

The Roughen filter

The Roughen filter does two tricks at once. First, it adds Anchor Points until the selection has the number of points per inch that you define. Second, it randomly moves all the points around, changing them into straight corner points or smooth points, whichever you specify.

Because the Roughen filters work randomly, you get different results when you apply the same settings of the same filter to two separate, identical objects. In fact, the results will probably never be duplicated (if you do get an exact duplicate, you probably win a lot of lotteries, too). This filter is a good reason for having the Undo command, so you can apply the filter, undo, and reapply until you achieve the desired effect.

ASK TOULOUSE: I Can't Get Punked Stuff Back to Normal

Squiggy: After I punk, I can never get the paths back to normal.

Toulouse: Undo doesn't work?

Squiggy: Sure, but I like changing things I've saved, closed, and reopened.

Toulouse: Undo won't work in that case.

Squiggy: So, I'm trying to bloat the paths I punked, because Bloat is the opposite of Punk.

Toulouse: It just doesn't work that way.

Squiggy: Why?

Toulouse: Punk and Bloat change each Anchor Point into a curved corner point. Each point has two independent handles, and those handles are moved with Punk and Bloat.

Squiggy: Wouldn't bloating punked paths move the handles back to where they started?

Toulouse: No, because originally, many of those points didn't have handles at all.

Squiggy: Anything else that can be done?

Toulouse: Redraw or, if you have the patience, edit each of the points, unless you added Anchor Points before punking.

Tip Using the keyboard, you can continually reapply any filter that works randomly and get different results. Select the object and apply the filter by choosing the menu item and entering the values. If you don't like the result, press ⌘+Z [Ctrl+Z] (Undo) and then ⌘+E [Ctrl+E] (reapply last filter).

One important limitation of the Roughen filters is that they work on entire paths, even if only part of the path is selected. The best way to get around this limitation is to use the Scissors tool to cut the path into different sections.

Selecting Roughen opens the Roughen dialog box (see Figure 10-40), where you can enter information to roughen up the illustration—literally.

The Roughen dialog box has three options:

✦ **Size.** How far points may move when roughened, relative to the width or height (whichever is greater) of the selected path. This value can be a percentage of the total width or height if the Relative option is selected or it may be a distance measured in points if the Absolute option is selected.

✦ **Detail.** How many points are moved. For example, if you have a 1-inch × 1-inch square, the number of points added is 36. (Four inches at the top, bottom, left, and right at 10 points per inch equals 40 points. A rectangle already has four points, so you only need 36 more points.)

✦ **Points.** If you select Smooth, all the Anchor Points added will be smooth points. If you select Corner, all the points added will be straight corner points.

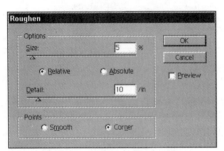

Figure 10-40: The Roughen dialog box

ASK TOULOUSE: Not the Same Effect

Carmine: You know, one thing that bugs me about Illustrator is its inconsistency.

Toulouse: What's inconsistent?

Carmine: The Roughen filter, for one thing.

Toulouse: It's supposed to be inconsistent. After all, it does random stuff.

Carmine: But let's say I want to duplicate a roughen effect.

Toulouse: I think you're out of luck.

Carmine: How does Illustrator come up with the random values? Surely there's a chart somewhere.

Toulouse: Actually, most "random" numbers are generated based on the time and date. Because this always changes, you'll get a different "result" each time.

Carmine: So if I went back in time to when I applied the Roughen filter the first time, it would be the same.

Toulouse: Well, you'd have to do it at the exact moment when you applied it before. Which would be almost as hard as traveling back in time in the first place.

Carmine: I could change my system clock, couldn't I?

Toulouse: Yes, but still, we're talking fractions of a second. The odds are you won't be able to do it right, unfortunately.

Roughen never takes away Points when roughening a path.

Tip
You can use the Roughen filter as a very hip version of the Add Anchor Points filter. If the Size box is set at 0 percent, all points added will be added along the existing path all at once. Instead of going to Add Anchor Points again and again, just try entering a value of 25 in the segments per inch field of the Roughen filter. You have instant multiple Add Anchor Points. This is a great technique for Scribble and Tweak or anything else where you need a bunch of Anchor Points quickly.

Using the Roughen filter on a path is fairly straightforward, but using it on a portion of artwork is not. Figure 10-41 and the following steps take you through setting up artwork so that the Roughen filter affects only a portion of the artwork.

1. Create the artwork that you intend to "tear."

2. Select the Pen tool and click from one edge of the artwork to another, crossing the path that you want to tear. If you don't want the tear to be straight, click additional points to change direction. If you want a curved tear, make the path curved. Connect the path by continuing around the outside of the artwork.

3. Select the artwork and the path. Choose Divide from the Pathfinder palette. Ungroup (⌘+Shift+G [Ctrl+Shift+G]) and choose Select ⇨ Deselect (⌘-Shift+A [Ctrl+Shift+A]). Select the paths on one side of the tear and drag them away from the remaining paths.

4. Using the Scissors tool, click the ends of the tear on one side of the split path. Drag the cut section away from the rest of the path. On the other half of the tear, cut that tear away and delete it as well.

5. Choose Filter ⇨ Distort ⇨ Roughen to see the Roughen dialog box. In the Size text field, enter the percentage that you want the Anchor Points to be moved. (In the example, we used 2 percent to move the points just slightly.) Next, determine how many points you want to add to the tear. (We chose 30 points per inch.) Then decide on the type of roughen: Rounded or Jagged. A Rounded roughen produces smooth points with control handles that stick out a very small amount from the Anchor Point, and a Jagged roughen has only straight corner points.

6. Click OK and check the newly roughened path to ensure that it is roughened correctly. If it isn't, or if you don't like the random movement of the anchor Points, choose Edit ⇨ Undo (⌘+Z [Ctrl+Z]) and select the Filter dialog box again (press Option [Alt] and choose Filter ⇨ Distort ⇨ Roughen). Continue undoing and roughening until the artwork is the way you want it or just adjust the Anchor Points with the Direct Selection tool.

7. Option [Alt]+copy the roughened path to the edge of the path that it was torn from. The best way to perform this task is to click an End Point with the Selection tool and drag to the End Point of the existing path with the Option [Alt] key pressed. Average and join the points (⌘+Option+Shift+J

[Ctrl+Alt+Shift+J]). Move the original roughened path to the other side of the path and average and join both points. (It's a good idea to zoom in, perhaps as much as 1,600 percent, to make sure that the two points are on top of each other and that only two points are selected.)

8. Add any other artwork to the torn paths. In the example, we rotated each of the halves a small amount.

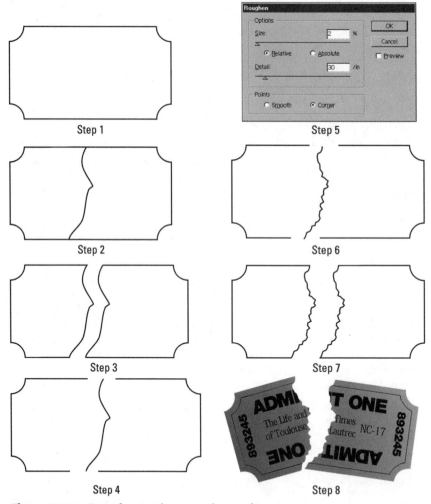

Figure 10-41: Steps for creating a tear in a path

The Roughen filter has a secret function that very few people know about: You can use it to add Anchor Points to paths. Simply enter **0** in the first text field and the points that are added will not be moved at all. This method is especially useful as a substitute for Add Anchor Points when some of the paths in a compound path don't need as many additional Anchor Points as others. The Roughen filter evens out the number of points for each of the paths in a compound path.

If you want roughened edges to be *really* rounded, don't choose the Rounded option in the Roughen dialog box. Instead, choose the Jagged option and then choose Filter ⇨ Stylize ⇨ Round Corners. The Round Corners option changes only straight corner points, so it changes all the points in the Jagged roughened object to smooth curves.

If you choose the Rounded option in the Roughen dialog box, the Round Corners filter has no effect on the roughened object.

The Scribble and Tweak filter

Although it sounds like characters from *Animaniacs*, the Scribble and Tweak filter, as is true for most filters, creates effects that would take a long and impractical amount of time to do manually.

One important detail needs to be made clear right away: The Scribble and Tweak filter does one thing. The only difference between scribbling and tweaking is in the way that you enter the amount of random movement. When Scribble is selected, you enter percentages that are based on the size of the object's Bounding Box; when Tweak is selected, points are moved based on absolute measurements that you enter.

The Scribble and Tweak filter, like the Roughen filter, will have a different result every time it is applied to a path, so keep the Undo option handy.

Selecting Scribble and Tweak displays the Scribble and Tweak dialog box. When the Scribble option is selected, you define the amount of scribble, including how much horizontal and vertical scribble and which points are moved—Anchor Points, In Control Points, or Out Control Points. (The *In Control Points* are the points on one side of the Anchor Point; *Out Control Points* refers to the points on the other side of the Anchor Point.)

Because of the measuring system that Tweak uses, selecting the Tweak option is usually much easier than using the Scribble option. Having to enter percentages when Scribble is selected can be very confusing, especially because you have to be concerned with both horizontal and vertical proportions.

Note   No Anchor Points are added with the Scribble dialog box.

For Scribble, horizontal and vertical percentages correspond to the movement of the selected points. If you enter 0 percent in either field, no movement will occur in that direction. The percentage is based on the width or height of the shape, whichever is greater. If Anchor Points is checked, then all Anchor Points on the selected path are moved in a random distance corresponding to the amounts set in the Horizontal and Vertical text fields. If either In Control Points or Out Control Points is checked, then those points are moved the specified distance as well.

Selecting Tweak displays the Tweak options. Instead of specifying a distance based on a percentage, the Tweak option lets you enter the distance in real measurements (such as picas or inches) in whatever unit your measurement system is currently using. All Tweak options have the same effects as the Scribble options.

Tip   We use the Scribble option when we're not sure of the size of the selected artwork, or when we can determine only that we want points moved a certain portion of the whole, but cannot determine an absolute measurement.

Follow these steps to Scribble and Tweak (as shown in Figure 10-42):

1. Create the artwork that you want to use with the filter. In this example, the text has been converted to outlines.

Note   The Scribble and Tweak filter does not work with type that has not been converted to outlines or with placed images; nor does it affect patterns or gradients that are being used as Fills.

2. Choose Filter ➪ Distort ➪ Scribble and Tweak. In the Scribble and Tweak dialog box, enter the amount that you want points to be moved, both horizontally and vertically. (Moving the points a large amount usually results in overlapping, crisscrossing paths that aren't very attractive.) Check the options that correspond to the points that you want to move randomly (for example, checking the Anchor Points checkbox moves Anchor Points randomly). Check the In Control Points or Out Control Points checkbox to move the control handles. The In Control Points are the control handles that affect the segment that precedes the Anchor Point relative to the path direction; the Out Control Points are the control handles that affect the segment that appears after each Anchor Point relative to the path direction.

Cross-Reference   Path direction is explained in Chapter 5, "Selecting and Editing."

3. Click OK. If the artwork isn't what you expected, choose Edit ➪ Undo (⌘+Z [Ctrl+Z]) and then either reapply the filter (⌘+E [Ctrl+E]) or press Option and enter new values in the dialog box (choose Filter ➪ Distort ➪ Scribble and Tweak).

4. Add any further artwork to the completed object.

Step 1

Step 3

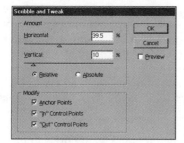

Step 2

Step 4

Figure 10-42: Steps for using the Scribble and Tweak filter, plus eight variations of the results

At the bottom of Figure 10-42 are eight different versions of the artwork. Each version has the same settings, but the points have been moved randomly eight different times.

The percentages you enter in the Scribble dialog box move points relative to the size of the Bounding Box. The Bounding Box is an invisible box that surrounds each object. If the Bounding Box is 5 inches wide and 2 inches tall and you enter a percentage of 10 percent for width and height in the Scribble dialog box, the filter moves the points randomly up to 0.5 inches horizontally and 0.2 inches vertically in either direction.

When the Scribble option is checked, the most important thing to remember when entering horizontal and vertical percentages is that the height and width of any object are usually different. As a result, entering the same percentage in each box usually causes different amounts of movement for each dimension.

Twist filter

Like the Punk and Bloat filter, the Twist filter reshapes objects in ways that would be time-consuming and tedious if you were using conventional Illustrator methods. The Twist filter moves the innermost points a certain number of degrees around a circle. The farther away the points are from the center of the circle, the less they move; points at the outermost edges of the object hardly rotate at all.

The Twist tool, covered earlier in this chapter, provides quick access to the Twist function, and the functionality is roughly the same as the Twist filter. It is quite different than the new Twirl tool though.

Selecting Twist displays the Twist dialog box, where you specify how much the selected objects will spin. You can set the twist angle from –4,000 degrees up to +4,000 degrees. The very center of the selected objects rotates the degree specified, while the objects on the edges rotate around the center very little. Positive values rotate the selected paths clockwise; negative values rotate the selected paths counterclockwise. Figure 10-43 shows an object before and after being twisted. One of this filter's drawbacks is that you cannot rotate around a point other than the center of the selection. To rotate about an off-center point, use the Twist tool that is found in the toolbox to the right of the Rotate tool.

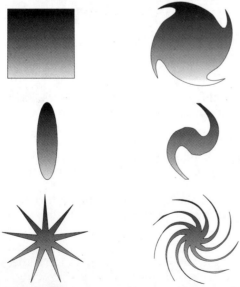

Figure 10-43: The original paths (left) are twisted (right).

Note Until Illustrator 7's version of Twirl (which is now called Twist), adding more Anchor Points to your path didn't necessarily result in a better effect. We used to apply Add Anchor Points several times or add Anchor Points via the Roughen filter before applying the Twirl filter. Now, however, the Twist filter is "smart" and curves paths automatically.

The Twist filter can twist single paths or multiple paths. When it twists multiple paths, the twisting takes place from the center of the entire group of objects, not from within each object.

Note The constraints on the Twist filter are similar to the constraints on the Free Distort filter. You cannot twist placed images, type that has not been converted to outlines, or patterns and gradients that are used as Fills.

Follow these steps to twist an object:

1. Create the artwork that you want to use with the Twist filter. In the example in Figure 10-44, we created a star with several points and a tiny first (inner) radius. Then we selected the center points with the Direct Selection tool and dragged them down and to the left.

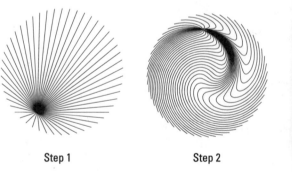

Step 1   Step 2

Figure 10-44: Steps for twisting artwork

2. Choose Filter ➪ Distort ➪ Twist to see the Twist dialog box. Enter the number of degrees that you want to twist objects. In the example, we used 300 degrees. Entering a positive number in the Angle text field twists the object clockwise; entering a negative number twists the object counterclockwise (which is opposite from how the degree setting for the Rotate tool works).

We wanted the twisted artwork in the example to resemble a fingerprint, so we used the Scale and Rotate tools, and then the Scribble and Tweak filter (see the "The Scribble and Tweak filter," section later in this chapter) to achieve the desired effect. After scribbling the artwork just 0.5 percent horizontally and vertically, we added the background and the accompanying text. You can twist paths up to 4,000 degrees in both directions (+4,000 and –4,000). The Twist filter by itself enables you to create many different effects. By moving different objects to different positions, the Twist filter can produce entirely different results. For example, you can use the following steps to create an arc in an illustration.

1. Create the type that you want to arc and convert it to outlines.

2. Make a copy of the type to the left of the original type and place an object between the two areas of type. Then place the same object at either end of the words. At this point, the illustration looks like Step 2 of Figure 10-45.

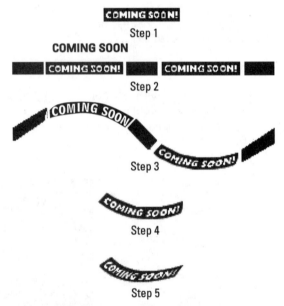

Figure 10-45: Steps for creating arced illustrations with the Twist filter

3. Select the objects and choose Filter ➪ Twist. In the Twist dialog box, enter **90** degrees and click OK.

4. Delete all the portions of the path except for the one shown.

5. Select the remaining portion and use the Free Transform tool. Use ⌘+Option+ Shift [Ctrl+Alt+Shift] after you click a corner of the Bounding Box.

The Zig Zag filter

The Zig Zag filter changes normally straight paths into zigzagged versions of those paths. When you first select Zig Zag, the Zig Zag dialog box, shown in Figure 10-46, appears.

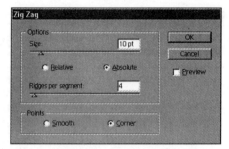

Figure 10-46: The Zig Zag dialog box

The Zig Zag dialog box enables you to specify various parameters of the zigzag effect, including the Amount, which is how large each zigzag is, and the number of Ridges, which is how many zigzags exist. In addition, you can specify whether you want the zigzags to be curved (choose Smooth) or pointed (choose Corner). Like most of the other Illustrator filters, Zig Zag has a handy Preview checkbox. Figure 10-47 shows an example of zigzagged artwork.

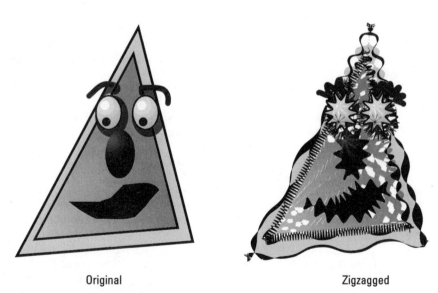

Original   Zigzagged

Figure 10-47: Zigzagged art

Tip

Don't keep the Preview checkbox checked while you're changing values in the Zig Zag dialog box. Instead, change your settings first, and *then* click the Preview checkbox. This prevents massive slowdowns that can occur when the Preview checkbox is checked.

Transformation and Distortion Effects

And now for the special effects, or *Live Effects* as Adobe is calling them. These Live Effects provide the same functionality as the filters, but a key difference is that the object isn't permanently altered and can still be modified without having to undo the effect. For example, if you draw a path with the Paintbrush tool and modify it with the Roughen filter, then you will no longer be able to modify the path using the control handles for the path. However, if you select the Roughen effect, then the path control handles are still accessible.

For example, if you have a textual heading that you want to distort, you could apply the Effect ⇨ Distort & Transform ⇨ Free Distort option to distort the text, but the text is still recognized as text. You can use the Text tool to change the text or the Type menu options to spell check the text regardless of the effect that it includes.

Tip   So should you use an effect or a filter? That depends on whether you plan on revisiting the effect. If you want to retain the option to delete the effect or to edit the underlying objects, then you should use an effect, but if you fairly confident that the effect is fine as it is and you want to conserve the memory required to hold the effect, use a filter.

Effects can be applied to objects, groups, and layers. The effects found in the Effect ⇨ Distort & Transform menu include Free Distort, Punk and Bloat, Roughen, Squiggle and Tweak, Transform, Twist and Zig Zag. These effects are exactly the same as those found in the Filter ⇨ Distort menu, except for the Transform option. The Transform effect found in the Effect ⇨ Distort & Transform menu will open a dialog that is identical to the Transform Each dialog box discussed earlier in this chapter, except the transform is applied as an effect.

Note   Illustrator offers a great feature with effects, but it can be confusing when you see the same functions over and over. New users can become quite confused when they see the same features as filters and as effects. In future versions, we can only hope that these features will be combined into a unified dialog box where the user can specify whether they want the modification applied as an effect or permanently as a filter.

Another nice feature is the idea of styles. Once you've added all the desired effects to an object, you can save the settings as a style, which can be placed in a library for easy recall.

Cross-Reference   For complete coverage of effects and styles, see Chapter 13, "Using Styles, Effects, and Filters."

Using Warp Effects

Now that I've mentioned effects, don't run off to Chapter 13 so quickly, there are several effects that specifically distort and warp the selected object and they are all conveniently located under the Effect ➪ Warp submenu.

Each of these effects will open the same dialog box, as shown in Figure 10-48. From the Style drop-down list at the top of this dialog box, you can select any one of the warp effects (regardless of the menu option you selected). You can also specify whether to Bend in the Horizontal or Vertical direction and the amount and to distort the object horizontally or vertically and the respective amounts. These options give you a lot of flexibility over distorting your objects.

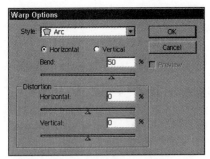

Figure 10-48: The Warp Options dialog box lets you distort objects vertically and horizontally.

Creating, editing, and deleting warp effects

Once the Warp Options dialog box is open, you can apply the effect by selecting the desired options and clicking Ok. The effect will be displayed as a line in the Appearance palette. You can edit the effect at any time by selecting the object and double clicking on the effect listed in the Appearance palette. This will open the Warp Options dialog box again where you can change the effect's options or even the effect type.

You can delete the warp effect by selecting is from the list of attributes in the Appearance palette and clicking on the Delete Selected Item icon at the bottom of the palette (the icon looks like a garbage can). You can delete all appearance items at once with the Reduce to Basic Appearance icon.

Warp effect types

The Warp effects include the following: Arc, Arc Lower, Arc Upper, Arch, Bulge, Shell Lower, Shell Upper, Flag, Wave, Fish, Rise, Fisheye, Inflate, Squeeze, and Twist. Figure 10-49 shows a simple logo before any warp effects are applied.

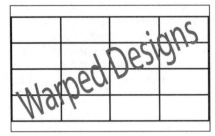

Figure 10-49: Original logo

Arc

The Arc warp effect will distort the object as if it were being wrapped around a circular object. For text, it will maintain the letter size and the spacing between each letter. Figure 10-50 shows the Arc warp effect applied using two different Bend values. A Bend value of 100 will wrap the object around a perfect half circle.

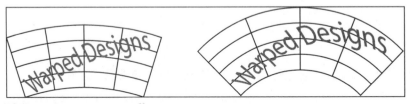

Figure 10-50: Arc warp effect

Arc Lower and Arc Upper

The Arc Lower and Arc Upper warp effects are the opposite of each other. Arc Upper will bulge the top edge of the object while Arc Lower will bulge the lower edge of the object. All other edges will remain unchanged. A Bend value of 100 in the Vertical direction will arc the top edge within an area equal in height to the height of the original object. Figure 10-51 shows the Arc Lower warp effect on the left and the Arc Upper warp effect on the right.

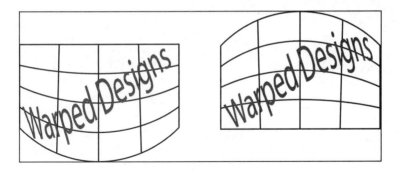

Figure 10-51: Arc Lower and Arc Upper warp effects

Arch

The Arch warp effect, like the Arc warp effect, will bend the object around a circular area, except the side edges of the object will not be distorted. This will cause the object to be scrunched at its sides and elongated at either end. Figure 10-52 shows the Arch warp effect with two different Bend values. A Bend value of 100 in the Vertical direction will arc the top edge within an area equal in height to the height of the original object.

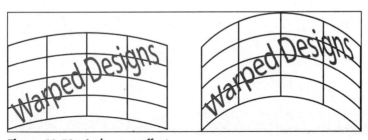

Figure 10-52: Arch warp effect

Bulge

The Bulge warp effect will bulge the object equally at opposite sides like using the Arc Lower and Arc Upper warp effects together. The midline of the object will not change at all, but either end will distort away from the center. Figure 10-53 shows the Bulge warp effect applied with different Bend values.

Figure 10-53: Bulge warp effect

Shell Lower and Shell Upper

The Shell Lower and Shell Upper warp effects will fan out the object in the shape of a shell. The sides of the object will be distorted and will end up curved. The top (or bottom edge) will be distorted into a circular section. Figure 10-54 shows the Shell Lower and Shell Upper warp effects applied to the logo. The Shell Lower warp effect is shown on the left and the Shell Upper is shown on the right.

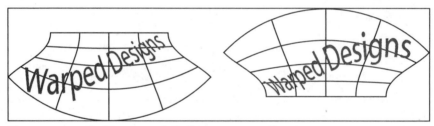

Figure 10-54: Shell Lower and Shell Upper warp effects

Flag

The Flag warp effect will make the selected object look like, well, a flag. This is accomplished by distorting the left half (or top half depending on the selected direction) downward and distorting the right half of the object upward. The vertical centered vertical line (or horizontal line) will be undisturbed. Figure 10-55 shows the Flag warp effect applied to the logo with two different Bend values.

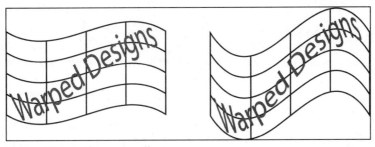

Figure 10-55: Flag warp effect

Wave

The Wave warp effect is more subtle than the Flag warp effect because it doesn't distort the exterior shape of an object. But, the internal lines within the object will be distorted the same as the Flag warp effect with one side rising up and the other side drooping down. Figure 10-56 shows the Wave warp effect. Notice how the rectangle of the logo is intact, but that the interior lines and text is warped.

Figure 10-56: Wave warp effect

Fish

The Fish warp effect bulges one side of the object and pulls the opposite side into the center of the object. The end result looks kind of like a fish. Figure 10-57 shows the Fish warp effect applied to the logo with different Bend values.

Figure 10-57: Fish warp effect

Rise

The Rise warp effect bends either side of the object like the Flag warp effect, but the entire object is also slanted to rise at an angle. High Bend values will result in a steep rising angle. Figure 10-58 shows the Rise warp effect at two different Bend values.

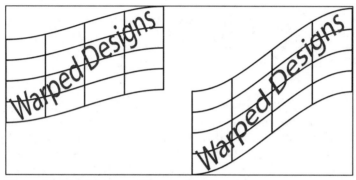

Figure 10-58: Rise warp effect

Fisheye

The Fisheye warp effect, like the Wave warp effect, only affects the internal portions of the object. Although the external outline of the object remains undistorted, the internal lines and text will bow out towards the edges as if the object were being stretched over a ball. Figure 10-59 shows two logos with the Fisheye warp effect applied. Notice how the very center of the object is unchanged.

Figure 10-59: Fisheye warp effect

Inflate

The Inflate warp effect will bow the internal portions of the object outward like the Fisheye warp effect, but the external outlines will also be affected. The outer edges of the object will curve away from the center of the object. The net result is to make the shape look like it was being stretched by its edges over a ball. Figure 10-60 shows the results of this warp effect at two different Bend values.

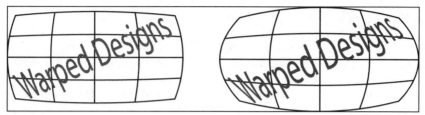

Figure 10-60: Inflate warp effect

Squeeze

The Squeeze warp effect will pull two opposite edge in towards the center of the object and push the adjacent opposite edges away from the center of the object. The interior lines and text will bend to follow edges and the center point of the object will be unchanged. Figure 10-61 shows the logo being squeezed with the Squeeze warp effect.

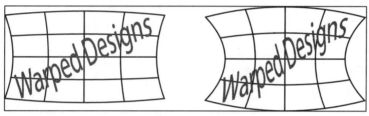

Figure 10-61: Squeeze warp effect

Twist

The Twist warp effect, like the Wave and Fisheye warp effects, will twist the internal portions of the object without affecting the external lines that make up the shape. The internal lines will twist about the center point. Figure 10-62 shows two logos being twisted.

Figure 10-62: Twist warp effect

Working with Envelopes

When sending a letter to a distant address, you first need to cram the letter into an envelope. The letter will then conform to the shape of the envelope. Illustrator has added envelopes as a new feature. Illustrator envelopes define a shape that other objects can fit inside. For example, if you create an outline of a train engine, you could make this outline path into an envelope. A paragraph of text could then be placed inside the envelope that would conform to the outlined shape.

New Feature Creating Envelopes and making an existing path act like an envelope are new features to Illustrator 10.

Figure 10-63 shows how an envelope can be used. A Mesh Envelope was applied to this heart and some of the interior envelope points have been moved. The heart object (which is the content of the envelope) will distort along with the mesh. For this object, the distorted heart as well as the overlying envelope are visible.

Figure 10-63: Envelopes provide a powerful way to distort objects.

Envelope Types

In Illustrator, there are actually three different envelope types — a Warp Envelope, a Mesh Envelope and a Top Object Envelope. Each of these types is unique and offers different ways to distort objects.

Warp Envelopes

Warp Envelopes need to start with a selected object. You can then select the Object ➪ Envelope Distort ➪ Make with Warp (⌘[Ctrl]+Option[Alt]+W) menu option. This menu option will open the Warp Options dialog box. This dialog box is the same dialog box that was shown earlier in the Warp Effects section. The same Warp options are available for this dialog box as with the Warp effects, except the warp is applied as an envelope. Figure 10-64 shows an Arc Warp Envelope applied to the heart object. Each point on the arc envelope can be moved to further distort the heart object.

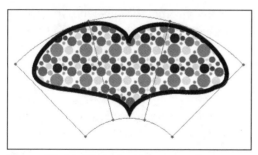

Figure 10-64: Warp Envelopes use the same shapes as the warp effects.

Mesh Envelopes

A second type of envelope, the Mesh Envelope, can also only be applied to a selected object. It is applied using the Object ⇨ Envelope Distort ⇨ Make with Mesh (⌘[Ctrl]+Option[Alt]+M) menu option. This opens a dialog box where you can specify the number of Rows and Columns to include in the mesh. After clicking Ok in the dialog box, a mesh appears over the top of the selected object.

Top-Object Envelopes

The final type of envelope is limited to a given set of warp effects or to a rectangular mesh, but rather allows you to use any object as an envelope. Using this envelope type requires that at least two objects are selected. With objects selected, the Object ⇨ Envelope Distort ⇨ Make with Top Object (⌘[Ctrl]+Option[Alt]+C) menu option will create the envelope. The topmost object will be used as the envelope and all selected objects underneath it will be placed within the envelope. Figure 10-65 shows a Top-Object Envelope that was created by applying the Roughen filter to the heart object.

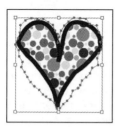

Figure 10-65: Top Object Envelopes can be made from any shaped object.

Editing Envelopes

Envelopes are fully editable using the Direct Selection tools and as the envelope's points are moved, the attached object is distorted to match the envelopes profile.

If you want to edit the actual objects contained within the envelope, you can select the Object ➪ Envelope Distort ➪ Edit Contents (⌘[Ctrl]+Option[Alt]+V) menu option. This will hide the envelope and allow you to edit the envelope's contents. You can return to editing the envelope with the same menu option.

Selecting Object ➪ Envelope Distort ➪ Envelope Options will open a dialog box of options, shown in Figure 10-66. Using this dialog box, you can enable Anti-Aliasing for raster images that are distorted. The Fidelity sets how many anchor points get reduced as the object is distorted. You also have the option to distort the object's Appearance, Linear Gradient and/or its Pattern Fills.

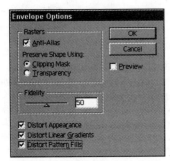

Figure 10-66: The Envelope Options dialog box

You can release an envelop at any time with the Object ➪ Envelope Distort ➪ Release command. This will return the object to their previous undistorted state although any content editing that you've done will remain.

The Object ➪ Envelope Distort ➪ Expand menu option will eliminate the envelope and maintain the distortion caused by the envelope.

Placing a Genie in a Lamp

The lamp craftsmen in ancient Arabia put a lot of work into the creation of everyday oil lamps and the net result is that no two lamps look alike. So, when the time comes to place a genie inside a lamp, it can difficult. This is where the envelope feature comes in handy. Naturally, you'll want to give the poor genie as much room as possible in their cramped quarters and make the lamp an envelope will maximize the living space for the trapped genie. The steps are as follows.

1. With the Paintbrush tool, draw a rough outline of a lamp as three parts — the lamp, its handle, and its stand.

2. With the Text tool, type the word Genie and resize it to be at least as tall as the main lamp part. Figure 10-67 shows the lamp pieces and the text side by side.

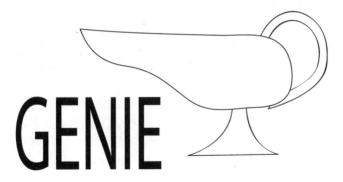

Figure 10-67: The object parts before the envelope is created

3. To use the Top-Object envelope, you'll need to make sure that the lamp is the top object. Select the lamp and use the Object ➪ Arrange ➪ Bring to Front (⌘ [Ctrl]+Shift+]) menu option. Then select the text and use the opposite Object ➪ Arrange ➪ Send to Back (⌘ [Ctrl]+Shift+[) menu option.

4. With the Selection tool, drag an outline over both the lamp's main piece and the text to select both objects. Don't select the handle or the lamp stand.

5. Select the Object ➪ Envelope Distort ➪ Make with Top Object (⌘ [Ctrl]+Option [Alt]+C) menu option to place the text within the envelope. Figure 10-68 shows the results.

Figure 10-68: The object parts after the envelope is created

Summary

Once you've finally drawn your artwork perfectly, this chapter comes along and teaches you how to move and distort your perfection. Using transformations and distortions, you can make your perfect art perfect in other ways. In this chapter, you learned

✦ The five major types of PostScript transformations are represented by four tools — Rotate, Scale, Reflect, and Shear — and the Move dialog box.

✦ You can do many transformations at one time with the Free Transform tool.

✦ Transform Each incorporates the Move, Scale, and Rotate functions that work on selected objects independently.

✦ Creating shadows, transforming gradients, and making tiles are some common transformation techniques.

✦ The Liquify tools provide an interactive method to distort objects by dragging over them.

✦ The Free Distort filter works by moving points anchor points that surround the object.

✦ The Punk and Bloat filter creates spiked and bubbled effects.

✦ You can use the Roughen filter to intelligently add Anchor Points.

✦ Use the Scribble and Tweak filter to move existing points and control handles randomly.

✦ You have two ways to twist artwork: with the Twist filter or with the Twist tool.

✦ Twisting adds Anchor Points as needed when twisting.

✦ Zig Zag creates even wavy or spiky paths.

✦ Another way to distort and transform objects is with effects.

✦ Using Warp Effects, objects can be distorted in several different ways including arcs, shells, flags, and so on.

✦ Illustrator includes three different types of envelopes — Warp Envelopes, Mesh Envelopes and Top Object Envelopes.

✦　　✦　　✦

Using Path Blends, Compound Paths, and Masks

Two of the most difficult areas of Illustrator to master are masks and compound paths. Of course, these are also two of the program's most powerful functions. A "mask" is used to hide portions of an image (mask them out), and compound paths are paths that consist of two or more separate paths that Illustrator treats as a single path. This chapter also deals with blends, which allow you to morph from one path to another.

Understanding Path Blends

At first glance, gradients and blends appear to be the same, except gradients are easy to use and blends seem to be much more difficult. This begs the question: Is it necessary to have a Blend tool or a Blend function? Our students, clients, and the occasional passerby have asked this question often, and they seem to have a good point at first. Upon further study, however, it becomes apparent that blends are quite different from gradients, both in form and function.

Gradients are used only as Fills. Gradients can be either linear or radial, meaning that color can change from side to side, top to bottom, or from the center to the outside. Every gradient can have as many distinct colors in it as you can create, limited only by RAM.

Blends, on the other hand, are series of transformed paths between two *end paths*. The paths between the end paths mutate from one end path into the other. All the attributes of the end paths change throughout the transformed paths, including shape, size, and all Paint Style attributes. The major benefit of blends is that you can blend multiple colors at one time.

Note   Two blending choices exist: You can blend either by using the Blend tool or by choosing Object ➪ Blend ➪ Make (⌘+Option+B [Ctrl+Alt+B]). You can create a blend with multiple shapes by pressing the right combination of keyboard commands.

To summarize, creating gradients is an easier way to create blends that change only in color, not in shape or size. Figure 11-1 shows how you can use blends and gradients to create a similar result. In this figure, the images at the left show the objects in Outline mode and the images on the right show the results in Preview mode. The first and third rows were created using blends and the second and fourth rows were created using gradients. Notice that the results are roughly the same, but that the objects with gradients are much simpler.

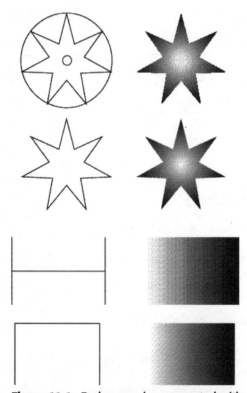

Figure 11-1: Each example was created with a blend (first and third rows) or a gradient (second and fourth rows).

If you remember that gradients work only with color, not with shapes, you should already have an idea of when to use which function. Linear and radial gradients usually look better than their blended counterparts because the quality is better and more colors can be added and manipulated. You can change color more easily with gradients than with blends. In addition, you can more easily change angles and placements of the gradients than move and reposition blend objects.

One drawback to using gradients is their "computer" look. Gradients are exact blends that are even from start to finish. Of course, with a little practice, you can add additional colors or tints, and you can offset the midpoint balance between two adjacent colors, giving the blend a more natural look. In general, though, realistic effects aren't all that easy to achieve with gradients.

Cross-Reference   Gradients are covered along with color in Chapter 6, "Working with Color."

Blends, on the other hand, can be incredibly flexible when it comes to creating photorealistic changes in color, if you plan ahead. Changes to blends aren't really changes at all; instead, they are deletions of the transformed objects and changes in the attributes of the end paths. If you know what you want, blends can take on an incredibly realistic look when you change the shapes of the blend's end paths just slightly.

But even more useful than creating realistic changes in color is blending's capability to transform shapes from one shape to another, as shown in the examples in Figure 11-2. With a bit of practice (and the information in this chapter), you can transform any illustration into another illustration. A limit exists to the complexity of the illustrations that can be transformed, but the limit is due more to the time it takes to create the blends than to limitations inherent in Illustrator.

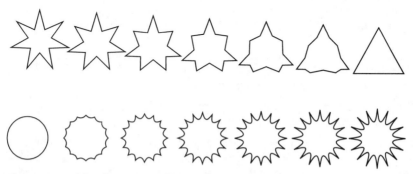

Figure 11-2: Blending to transform a shape

Because blends work on both Stroke and Fill attributes of objects, you can create some exciting effects that aren't possible using any other technique, electronic or traditional. In many ways, blend can be compared to morphing.

In past versions of Illustrator, blends were used predominantly for what gradients are used for now: to blend between, normally two, different colors, But some artists took it on themselves to stretch the capabilities of the Blend tool to create fantastic effects that amazed even the creators of the tool.

Originally, Adobe marketed the Blend tool (which was new to version 88) as a tool whose primary purpose was to transform shapes, not blend colors. Yeah, that's cool, designers said, but instead they used the tool for blending colors to create what were known as *vignettes*, or what traditional artists called *gradients*.

The Blend tool creates in-between steps in the area between two paths, where the paint style and shape of one path transform themselves into the paint style and shape of the second path.

Tip   One key blending feature is that blends are live, or editable. This characteristic enables users to change the color, shape, and location of the blend shapes and the results are immediately visible. Another great feature is that blends can follow a path.

Although any blend takes into account color and shape, we treat color and shape separately because people using the Blend tool are often trying to obtain *either* a color effect *or* a shape effect, rather than both at once.

Creating a blend

The Blend tool is used to create *blends*, which are a group of paths (commonly referred to as *blend steps*) that change shape and color as each path is created closer to the opposite *end path*. Follow these steps to create a blend:

1. Using the Rectangle tool, create a small (1-inch) vertical rectangle. With the Selection tool, Option [Alt]+copy the path a few inches to the side. Press Shift as you drag horizontally to constrain the movement of the path.

2. On the left rectangle, change the Fill to Black and the Stroke to None. Change the right rectangle to a Fill of White and a Stroke of None.

3. Choose the Blend tool (press the W key). Click the top-left point of the left path and then the top-left point of the right path. This step tells Illustrator to blend between these two paths and it uses the center points as reference. The Blend tool cursor changes from x to + in the lower-right corner.

4. A spine is created between the two end paths (which are now transparent). Press ⌘+Shift+A [Ctrl+Shift+A] to deselect all selected paths. The blend is

made up of 256 paths, including the two end paths. Each path is a slightly different tint of black. The default Blend Option creates smooth color between the two shapes. This may take some time depending on the complexity of the shapes involved, the number of steps and the speed of your computer.

5. You can edit the individual paths that make up the blend if you expand the blend object using the Object ➪ Expand option.

Note Adobe has changed the way you select blends. Gone is the annoying cross-hair with the next-to-invisible ellipses. Replacing the cross-hair is a small image of the Blend tool with an x in the lower-right corner. The cursor is white until you pass over an anchor point. When the cursor is black, you are over an anchor point that you can use to blend. A plus sign shows in the lower-right corner of the Blend tool after you click the first shape and it is in front of the second shape.

You must use the Blend tool to click from one path to another path on each of two different paths. Paths can be open or closed.

Creating Linear Blends

Color blends are made by creating two end paths, usually identical in shape and size, giving each path different Paint Style attributes, and creating a series of steps between them with the Blend tool. The more end paths that are created, the more colors you can create.

The following steps describe how to create a basic linear blend and Figure 11-3 illustrates these steps.

1. Draw a vertical path with the Pen tool. Give it a Fill of None and a Stroke of 2 points black.

2. Option [Alt]+copy the path to the right. Give the new path a Stroke of 2 points white.

3. With the Blend tool, click the path on the left and then the path on the right.

4. Deselect all (⌘+Shift+A [Ctrl+Shift+A]) to see the result.

Tip The examples in this chapter are easier to understand when you are working in Preview mode.

The blend depends on the Blend Options. To change the Blend Options, select the objects with the selection tool, and double-click the Blend tool in the toolbox to open the Blend Options dialog box.

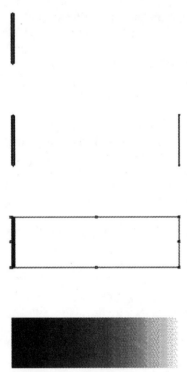

Figure 11-3: The steps needed to create a linear blend

Blend Options

Adobe has enhanced the Blending functions of Illustrator by improving the Blend tool and by adding a Blend submenu under the Object menu. The Blend submenu options are Make, Release, Blend Options, Expand, Replace Spine, Reverse Spine, and Reverse Front to Back. The Blend tool enables you to blend between specific points, and with Illustrator's Live Blend capability, you do not need to release a blend to change it. Live Blending enables you to change the shape or color of a blend and update it automatically. You can use the Direct Selection tool to select the path and edit or change the color and the blend updates.

Another update (found in the Transparency palette) is that you can select from various Blending Modes. These Blending Modes define how overlapping colors are combined when transparency is applied. You also have the option to Isolate Blending, which constrains the Blending Mode to only objects contained within the group.

Cross-Reference   You can find more details about the Transparency palette and the various Blending Modes in Chapter 12, "Understanding Transparency."

Illustrator 10 can blend multiple objects and paths simultaneously.

Using the Blend option

After choosing Object ➪ Blend ➪ Blend Options, or by double clicking on the Blend tool, you can access the Blend Options dialog box, shown in Figure 11-4. This dialog box includes three Spacing options, which are Smooth Color, Specified Steps, and Specified Distance. The Orientation options are Align to Page and Align to Path.

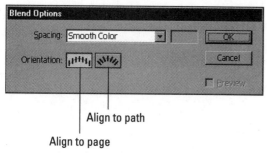

Align to path

Align to page

Figure 11-4: The Blend Options dialog box

The Blend options work as follows:

✦ **Smooth Color** automatically determines the number of steps needed to make this blend look as smooth as possible.

✦ **Specified Steps** lets you choose how far apart each blend step is from another blend step.

✦ **Specified Distance** enables you to type in the distance between the steps.

✦ **Align to Page** runs the blend vertically or horizontally depending on your page orientation.

✦ **Align to Path** runs the blend perpendicular to the path.

Blending multiple objects

To blend multiple objects in one step, select all the objects you want to blend and choose Object ➪ Blend ➪ Make. You can also use the Blend tool and click all the objects you want to blend.

Editing blends

The Blend tool enables you to edit blends without having to redo the entire blend. You have many different ways to edit a blend, such as moving the blend objects, replacing the blend spline with another path, or releasing or reversing the blend.

Changing blend colors on the fly

The Live Blend option lets you change the colors of a blend without having to redo the whole blend. With the Direct Selection tool, select the path that you want to change the color of in the blended shape. Select a new Fill or Stroke color. The blend is updated instantly with the new color.

Moving a blended object

Another great aspect of Live Blends is its capability to edit the blend at any time and have it automatically update on the fly. A spine is created when a blend is made. With the Direct Selection tool you can select an anchor point on the spline and move it. This changes the location of that point and the blend updates accordingly.

Editing a blended object

Now you can edit lines by adding, deleting, or moving any part of your blend and it updates automatically. You can delete and add points or change the shape of a path with the Direct Selection tool. Figure 11-5 shows a figure before and after editing the blend.

Figure 11-5: Before and after editing a blend

Adjusting the blend options

The Blend Options dialog box lets you change the Spacing and Orientation aspects. Select the blend you want to adjust and either double-click the Blend tool or choose Object ⇨ Blend ⇨ Blend Options to open the dialog box to change the settings.

Expanding a blend

If you want to edit the individual elements of a blend, you have to release it first. By choosing Object ⇨ Blend ⇨ Expand, the blend expands into a mess of shapes. The shapes will all still be grouped, but you can edit them individually after Ungrouping them. You can tell when a group of objects is no longer a blend because the spline will no longer be visible.

Replacing the spine

The Replace Spine option enables you to apply a blend to a selected path. To apply this effect, select the Stroked path and your blend and choose Replace Spine from the Blends submenu. Figure 11-6 shows the before and after of applying a blend to a path. Draw a path in the shape you want the spine of the blend to follow. Select the blend with the spine you want to change, and the new path that is to become the new spine. Choose Object ⇨ Blend ⇨ Replace Spine. The blend updates automatically.

Reversing the spine

This option reverses the sequence of the objects you are blending. If you have a rectangle on the right blended to a circle on the left, choosing Reverse Spine puts the circle on the right and the rectangle on the left. Reversing the spine flips the position of the shapes on the spine.

Reversing front to back

The Reverse Front to Back option reverses the order in which your paths were drawn when you created your blend. If you drew a circle first and a star second, choosing Reverse Front to Back displays the star on top and the circle underneath (see Figure 11-7).

Changing into filled shapes

Choosing the Expand option enables you to change any blend or gradient into filled shapes.

Nonlinear blends

End paths created with two end points that make up blends don't have to be just horizontal or vertical. In addition, when you create multiple color blends, the intermediate end paths don't have to be aligned the same way as the end paths are aligned.

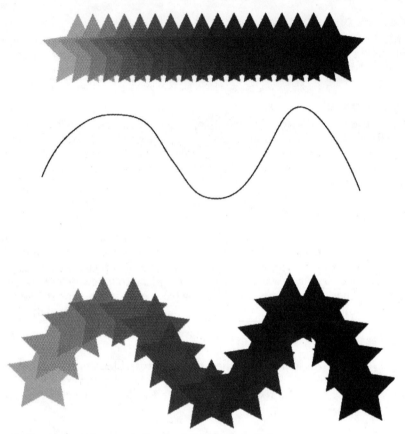

Figure 11-6: Before and after applying Replace Spine

Careful setup of intermediate blends can create many interesting effects, such as circular and wavy appearances, all created with straight paths.

Note End paths that cross usually produce undesirable effects; if carefully constructed, however, the resulting blends can be quite intriguing. Blending crossed end paths creates the appearance of a three-dimensional blend, where one of the end paths blends "up" into the other.

To create nonlinear blends, set up the end paths and either rotate them or change their orientation by using the Direct Selection tool on one of the end points. Then blend from one end path to the intermediate end paths and then to the other end path. Figure 11-8 shows two examples of nonlinear blends.

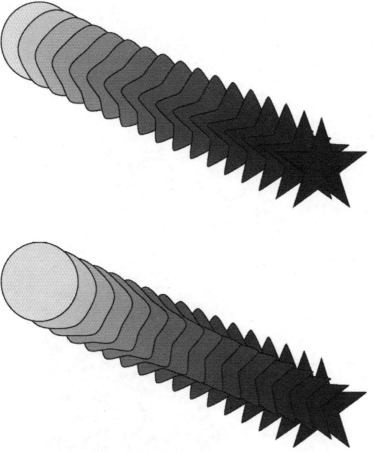

Figure 11-7: Before and after applying Reverse Front to Back

Masking blends

Blends by themselves are great, but when masked by other paths, they can take on a life of their own. Use the following steps to create a color wheel that illustrates this concept (see Figure 11-9).

1. Using the Pen tool, draw a straight segment and give it a 2-point green (100% Cyan, 100% Yellow) Stroke and a Fill of None in the Color palette.

2. Choose the Rotate tool, press Option [Alt], and click one end point of the path to set the origin. Type **60** for the angle in the Rotate dialog box and press the Copy button (Option+Return [Alt+Enter]). This procedure creates a copy of the Stroke at a 60-degree angle, with one end point directly on top of one of the existing ones.

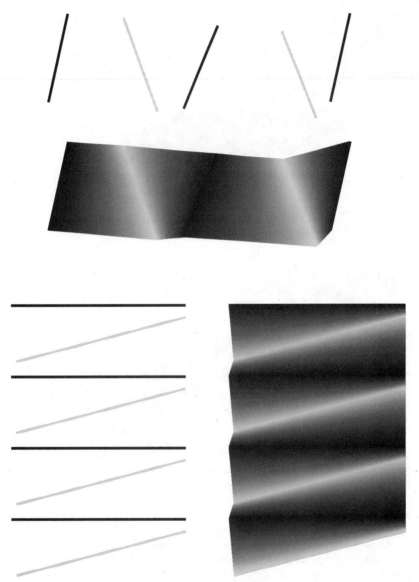

Figure 11-8: Blending to make a nonlinear blend

3. Choose Object ➪ Transform ➪ Transform Again (⌘+D [Ctrl+D]). Another Stroke is created at a 60-degree angle from the second. Continue to choose Transform Again until six Strokes exist. Each of these Strokes is used as an end path.

4. Color each Stroke as follows, moving clockwise: 1. Green (100% Cyan, 100% Yellow); 2. Yellow (100% Yellow); 3. Red (100% Magenta, 100% Yellow);

4. Magenta (100% Magenta); 5. Blue (100% Cyan, 100% Magenta); 6. Cyan (100% Cyan).

5. Blend each pair of end paths together either using the Blend tool on each end path, or by choosing (⌘+Option+B [Ctrl+Alt+B]). The only catch in using the Blend function from the Object menu is that you still have to manually blend the last end points. When all the end paths are blended together, the result is a beautifully-colored hexagon. Because of the shape, the end paths really stand out as points on the hexagon.

6. To complete the illusion of a perfect color wheel, the blend needs to be a circle. Using the Ellipse tool, draw a circle so that the edges are just inside the flat sides of the hexagon, with its center corresponding to the center of the hexagon. This process is easiest to do by Option [Alt]+clicking with the Ellipse tool at the center of the hexagon and pressing the Shift key as the oval is being drawn. Select the circle, the blend steps, and the end paths, and choose Object ⇨ Clipping Masks ⇨ Make (⌘+7 [Ctrl+7]).

7. For a more realistic color wheel effect (one that resembles Apple's color wheel), create a Black Stroke on the mask and a small circle at the center that has a Fill of White and a Stroke of Black.

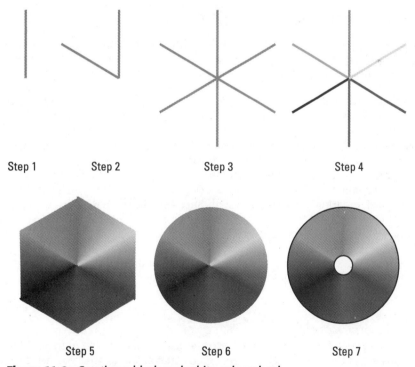

Figure 11-9: Creating a black-and-white color wheel

Tip Blends can be masked with any object. For some great effects, mask your blends with text (converted to outlines).

Pseudolinear blends

The end product of straight-line linear blends and linear gradients differs very little. Both are very "computery" looking, but gradients are a little easier to manipulate. The important thing about blends is that the end paths of linear blends *don't have to be straight lines.*

If you use a smoothly curving line, the blend takes on a fluidity and life of its own, gently caressing the objects it is behind, next to, or masked by. The curves (especially if the end paths are masked off) are not always visible to the eye, and this creates an effect that is both realistic and surreal, giving depth to your illustration in a way that flat linear blends can't.

Instead of smoothly curving lines, try broken, jagged paths, which add fierce highlights to a blend. Again, this type of blend is even more effective when the end paths are masked off. Figure 11-10 shows two examples of masked pseudolinear blends.

End paths for linear blends

In the previous linear blend example, we used lines with Stroke weights to create the blend. You can also use rectangles with Fills and no Strokes to achieve the same printed result. Figure 11-11 shows both lines and rectangles used for end paths.

No good reason exists to use a rectangle as an end path instead of a single line with two end points (at least, none that we can dig up). In fact, lines are better than rectangles for three reasons. First, lines use half as much information as rectangles because two anchor points exist on a line while four exist on a rectangle. Second, the width of a line (Stroke weight) is much easier to change after the blend has been created (just select the lines and enter a new weight in the Stroke palette) than it is to change the width of rectangles (you would have to use the Scale Each option). Third, creating a linear blend with lines (Strokes) creates a thick mess of paths, but creating a linear blend with rectangles creates a thicker mess, so much so that it is difficult to select specific rectangles.

Tip An open path can be blended with a closed path and vice versa. Choose Object ➪ Blend ➪ Make or use the Blend tool to blend open or closed paths to any path.

Calculating the number of steps

Whenever you create a blend, Illustrator provides a default value in the Specified Steps text field of the Blend Options dialog box that assumes that you are printing your illustration to an imagesetter or other high-resolution device capable of printing all 256 levels of gray that PostScript allows.

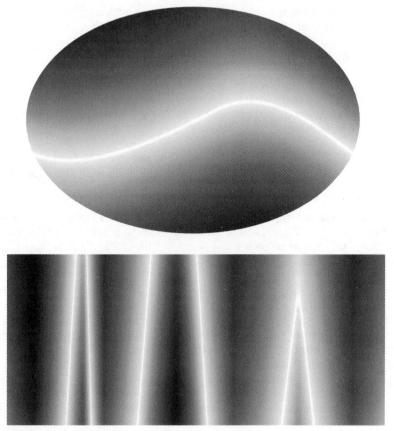

Figure 11-10: Masked pseudolinear blends

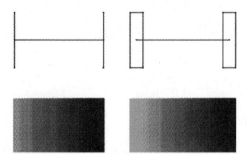

Figure 11-11: Lines (left) and rectangles (right) used for end paths in both artwork and final output

The formula Illustrator uses is quite simple. It takes the largest change that any one color goes through from end path to end path and multiplies that percentage by 256. The formula looks like this: 256 × largest color change percentage = the number of steps to be created.

For instance, using our linear blend example, the difference in tint values is 100 percent (100% – 0% = 100%). Multiply 100 percent by 256, and you get 256. Because the total number of grays must be 256 or fewer, only 254 were created. When added to the two ends, 256 tints exist.

In the second example, where the first line was changed to a 10% Stroke, the difference in tint values is 10 percent (10% – 0% = 10%). 10% × 256 is 26, the number of steps Illustrator calculates.

In a process color example, if the first end path is 20% Cyan, 100% Magenta, and 40% Yellow, and the second end path is 60% Cyan, 50% Magenta, and 0% Yellow, the largest difference in any one color is Cyan (100% – 50% = 50%). The number of steps created is 128 or 50% × 256.

But, of course, not everything you create is output on an Imagesetter. Your laser printer, for example, cannot print 256 grays unless the line screen is set extremely low. To determine how many grays your laser printer can produce, you need to know both the dpi (dots per inch) and the line screen. In some software packages, you can specify the line screen, but unless the printer is a high-end model, it is usually difficult to specify or change the dpi. Use the following formula to find out how many grays your printer can produce:

$$(\text{dpi/line screen}) \times (\text{dpi/line screen}) = \text{number of grays}$$

For a 300-dpi printer with a typical (for 300-dpi) line screen of 53, the formula looks like this:

$$(300/53) \times (300/53) = 5.66 \times 5.66 = 32$$

A 400-dpi printer with a line screen of 65 has the following formula:

$$(400/65) \times (400/65) = 6.15 \times 6.15 = 38$$

A 600-dpi printer with 75 lines per inch uses this formula:

$$(600/75) \times (600/75) = 8 \times 8 = 64$$

Sometimes you may want to reduce the number of blend steps in a blend from the default because either your printer can't display that many grays or the distance from one end path to another is extremely small (see "Airbrushing and the Magic of Stroke Blends," later in this chapter).

When reducing the number of blends, start by dividing the default by two and then continue dividing by two until you have a number of steps that you are comfortable with. If you aren't sure how many steps you need, do a quick test of that blend with different numbers of steps specified and print it out. If you are printing to an Imagesetter, don't divide by two more than twice or banding (oh no!) can occur (see the following sidebar, "Avoiding Banding," for more information.)

Creating radial blends

To create a radial blend, make a 2-inch circle, filled with 100% Black. Make a smaller circle inside the larger circle and fill it with White. Select both shapes and choose Object ➪ Blend ➪ Make. To change the number of steps, choose Object ➪ Blend ➪ Blend Options. The Blend Options dialog box defaults to a value that ensures a smooth transition.

Radial blends can be created with objects other than circles. In Figure 11-12, the radial blend was created with a star.

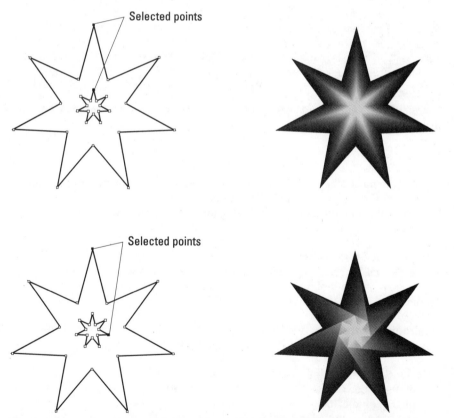

Figure 11-12: The top example was blended choosing the same position points in the images and the bottom example was blended choosing different position points in the images. The left side shows the images in Outline mode; the right side shows them in Preview mode.

Avoiding Banding

The graphic artist's worst nightmare: Smooth blends and gradations turn into large chunks of tints, as shown in the accompanying figure, and suddenly get darker or lighter instead of staying nice and smooth. *Banding*, as this nightmare is called, is an area of a blend where the difference from one tint to the next tint changes abruptly and displays a defining line showing the difference between the two tints. Individual tints appear as solid areas called *bands*.

These causes pretty much make sense. Take the linear blend example earlier in this chapter. If only three intermediate steps exist between end paths, there are only five colors in the blend, thus resulting in five bands. If the end paths are each on one side of a 17-inch span, each blend step created would take up the 5 points of width of the Stroke, making each shade of gray 5 points wide — a noticeable size. If the color on the left were 10% Black instead of 100% Black, there would be only 26 color steps between the two end paths.

So, to avoid banding, use the recommended number of steps over a short area with a great variation of color.

If you find it hard to fix the banding problem and the blend is made of process colors, try adding a small amount of an unused color (Black, for instance) to cover up the banding breaks. A 5 to 30 percent change over distances may provide just enough dots to hide those bands. Keeping this in mind, more chance for banding exists if you use the same tints for different process colors. Alter the tint values for one of the colors at one of the end paths just a little, and this alteration staggers the bands enough to remove them from sight.

See "Calculating the Number of Steps", earlier in this chapter, for more information on banding.

Caution   As with most other blends, when blending from two identically-shaped end paths, always click the anchor point in the same position on each object. Figure 11-12 shows the difference between clicking the anchor points in the same position and clicking those that are not in the same position.

One of the nice things about creating radial blends manually (not using the gradient feature) is that by changing the location and the size of the inner object, the gradient can be made to look vastly different. The larger the inner object, the smaller the blended area.

The Gradient feature enables you to change the highlight point on a radial Gradient without changing the source or angle of the highlight.

Cross-Reference   The Gradient Mesh tool enables you to create easy highlights with the click of a mouse. See "Gradient Mesh" in Chapter 6, "Working with Color," for more information on this tool.

Creating Color Blends

Although there are many different ways to use blends, one aspect of blending directly relates to the Fill colors — Color Blends. These have some functionality that is uniquely different from gradients such as defining a different path along which the colors can change.

Multiple colors with linear blends

To create linear blends that have multiple colors, you must create intermediate end paths, one for each additional color within the blend, as follows:

1. Create two end paths at the edges of where you want the entire blend to begin and end. Don't worry about colors at this time.

2. Select the two paths and choose Object ➪ Blends ➪ Make (⌘+Option+B [Ctrl+ Alt+B]). Then choose Object ➪ Blends ➪ Blend Options. Change the Smooth Options to Specified Steps. Choose your orientation and enter a number for the steps. (We entered 3 to create three evenly spaced paths between the two end paths.)

3. Expand the newly created Strokes by choosing Object ➪ Blends ➪ Expand, color each of the Strokes of the paths differently, and give them a weight of 2 points. Select all of the paths and choose Object ➪ Blends ➪ Make (⌘+Option+ B [Ctrl+Alt+B]).

4. The result should look like the blend of colors shown at the bottom of Figure 11-13.

Note In Illustrator 10, the blend automatically attaches itself to the original paths. The only way to select the original paths is to expand them first using the Expand feature of the Blends submenu.

Guidelines for creating color linear blends

Although the preceding procedure should have gone smoothly with no problems, follow these guidelines when creating blends to get good results each time you print:

✦ For linear blends, use either rectangles with only four anchor points or a basic 2-point path. If you use a shape with any more anchor points or if you use a curved shape with any paths that aren't perfectly straight, you get extra information that isn't needed to create the blend, and printing takes much longer than usual.

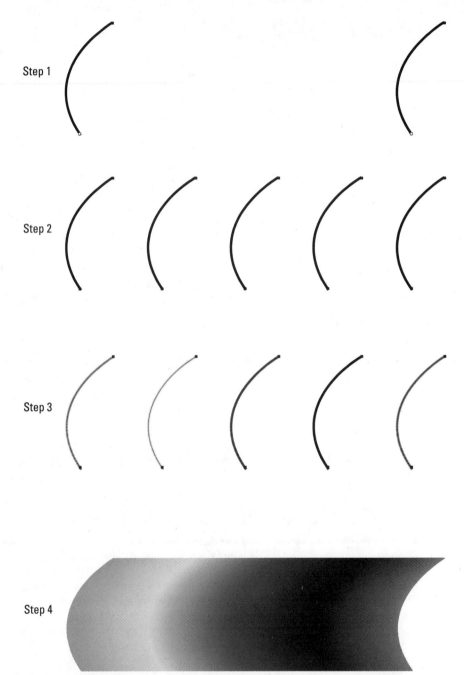

Figure 11-13: The steps to create a multiple-color linear blend

✦ When creating linear blends, use one rectangle per end path and color the Fills of the paths, not the Strokes. Coloring the Strokes may appear to work, but it usually results in a moiré pattern when printed. Make sure that the Stroke is set to None, regardless of what the Fill is.

✦ Don't change the number that appears in the Specified Steps text field in the Blend dialog box if you want smooth color. Making the number higher creates additional paths that can't be printed; making the number lower causes banding when printed (see the "Avoiding Banding" sidebar, earlier in this chapter).

Creating Shape Blends

The difference between color blends and shape blends is their emphasis. Color blends emphasize a color change; shape blends emphasize blending between different shapes.

You should remember a number of things when creating the end paths that form a shape blend. Both paths must be either open or closed. If open, only end points can be clicked to blend between the two paths. If the shapes also change color, be sure to follow the guidelines in the earlier section, "Guidelines to creating color linear blends."

For the best results, both paths should have the same number of anchor points selected before blending, and the selected points should be in a relatively similar location. Illustrator pairs up points on end paths and the segments between them so that when it creates the blend steps, the lines are in about the same position.

Shape blend 1: Computer vents

Look on the side of your monitor or on the side of a computer or hard drive case. You undoubtedly see vents or simulated vents running back along these items for design purposes. This type of blend (changing the angle of straight lines) is the most basic of shape blends and is easy to create, so we've added an extra tip at the end of this section to make these blends more realistic. The following steps describe the process for creating computer vents and Figure 11-14 illustrates this process.

1. Draw a rectangular shape that has been distorted to appear like the side of your monitor (use the Pen tool). Choose a Fill of 25% Black and a Stroke of 0.5-point, 50% Black.

2. Select the shape and double-click the Scale tool. Enter **90** percent in the Uniform field of the Scale dialog box and click Copy (Option [Alt]+Return).

3. With the Direct Selection tool, select and delete the two vertical segments of the shape. Select both of the horizontal segments and change the Fill to None.

4. Blend the two paths together. Then choose Object ⇨ Blend ⇨ Blend Options and change the Spacing to Specified Steps and the number to 15. One side of a monitor is now complete.

5. Select all the paths and copy them up 0.5-point by using the Copy button in the Move dialog box. Change the Stroke to 75% Gray.

6. Draw a circle over the center of the group and select the group and the circle. Choose Object ⇨ Masks ⇨ Make and you have a "real" vent in the simulated one.

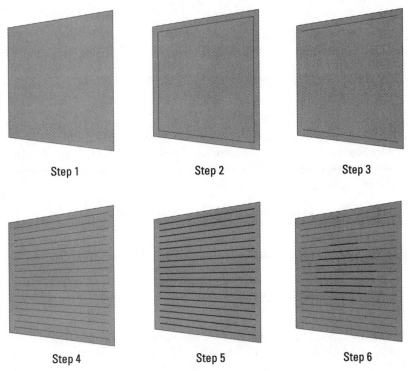

Step 1   Step 2   Step 3

Step 4   Step 5   Step 6

Figure 11-14: A computer vent blend

Shape blend 2: Circle to star

The preceding blend slowly transformed one path to another, but the paths were basically the same. The real power of the Blend tool is evident when it is used to generate intermediate paths between two totally different, distinct paths, as in the following example.

1. Create a 1-inch circle with the Ellipse tool. Create a 5-point star by clicking with the Star tool and entering **5** in the Points text field. Enter **0.19"** in the First Radius text field and **0.5"** in the Second Radius text field.

2. Fill both shapes with a color (we used light gray) and give each of them a 2-point Stroke of another color. Change the view to Fit In Window (⌘+0 [Ctrl+0]) and place the two objects as far apart onscreen as possible.

3. Choose the Direct Selection tool and select the entire circle. Press the Shift key and click the four points on the star that closely match the four points on the circle. If you accidentally click a point that you decide should not be selected, just click it again with the Direct Selection tool. As long as the Shift key is pressed, the tool deselects only that point while all the other points remain selected.

4. After four points are selected on both the circle and the star, blend them together with the Blend tool. Click the corresponding points on each, such as the topmost points, and then choose Object ➪ Blend ➪ Blend Options. Change the Spacing to Specified Steps and the number to 7.

To see what happens if a different number of points are selected on each path, select both paths with the Selection tool. Click the topmost point of the circle with the Blend tool and then click the topmost point of the star. In the Blend dialog box, enter **7** in the Specified Steps text field and then click OK. The star appears to work its way out of a growth on the circle. Figure 11-15 shows the difference between blending with a corresponding number of anchor points selected and without a corresponding number of anchor points selected on each path.

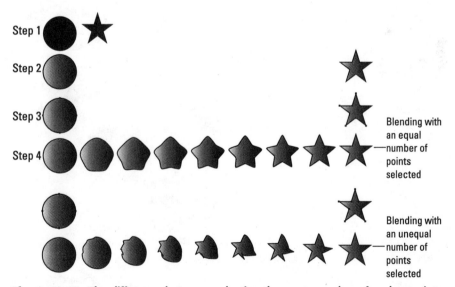

Figure 11-15: The difference between selecting the same number of anchor points on each path in a shape blend (top) and selecting a different number of anchor points on each path (bottom)

Tip Another way to get a smooth transformation between two paths with different numbers of anchor points is to add anchor points strategically to the path with fewer points. By selecting both of the paths with the Selection tool, you can get results that are similar to selecting similarly positioned points. The results can actually be better when anchor points are added because they can be added in positions that correspond to the anchor points on the other path.

Complex-shape blending

Whenever a shape is complex (that is, it isn't a perfectly symmetrical shape, such as a circle or a star), you may have to do several things to create realistic and eye-pleasing effects. Figure 11-16 shows a complex-shape blend.

Figure 11-16: Complex-shape blending

One thing you can do to make the blend better is to add or remove anchor points from the end paths. Even if the same number of points are selected and those points are in similar areas on each path, the results can be anything but acceptable.

The Add Anchor Point and Delete Anchor Point tools are useful here. By adding points in strategic locations, you can often fool Illustrator into creating an accurate blend; otherwise, the blend steps can resemble a total disaster.

Tip In general, adding anchor points does not disturb the composition of the graphic as much as removing them. On most paths, removing any anchor points changes the shape of the path dramatically.

Another method of getting the paths to blend more accurately is to shorten them by splitting a long, complex path into one or two smaller sections that aren't nearly as complex. Each path has to be blended, which can be done in one step by choosing Object ⇨ Blend ⇨ Make.

And then you have the third method of blending paths, cheating, which the next section describes.

Shape blend 3: Cheating

At times, blending together two different shapes produces results that are grotesque no matter what you do with the anchor points. In these cases, a little fixing (which we call "cheating") is in order: The more blend steps you need, the more you benefit from this method.

To get more aesthetically pleasing results from shape blending, it is sometimes easier to create one or more intermediate (middle) end paths. Instead of blending from end to end, you blend from end to middle and then middle to end. Keep in mind that the middle should contain aspects of both end paths. Figure 11-17 shows how a blend naturally appears (Steps 1 and 2) and how it appears after cheating (Steps 3 through 7).

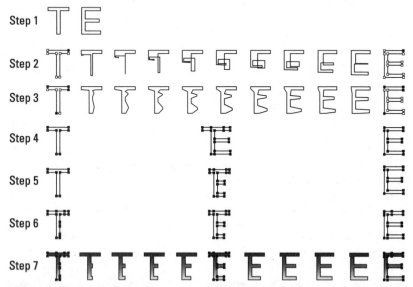

Figure 11-17: Blending a *T* to an *E* without cheating (Steps 1 and 2) and with cheating (Steps 3 through 7)

The following steps show you how to blend a *T* to an *E* with and without cheating:

1. In this example, create a text area with a 100-point T and E in any font (a sans serif font, such as Helvetica, is easier than a serif one, such as Times). Select the type with a Selection tool and choose Type ➪ Create Outlines (⌘+Shift+O [Ctrl+Shift+O]). You are blending between these two letters. Change the Fill to None and the Stroke to 1-point Black.

2. Choose View ➪ Fit in Window (⌘+0 [Ctrl+0]) and put each letter on either side of the document. Select both of them with the regular Selection tool and then blend them together with ten steps by choosing the upper-right point in each object and changing the Specified Steps in the Blend Options dialog box. The results are quite ugly. A common shape-blending problem called *blend arcing* occurs when you choose very few or no anchor points on either the top or bottom of end paths. In this case, you select an anchor point along the top and no anchor points along the bottom, so the blend arc forms along the bottom of the letters.

3. Undo the blend. You achieve a better blending effect by selecting the two upper-right points, the upper-left point, and the lower-left point of the T and the E (previously shown in Figure 11-17), but then the blend takes on an ugly, lumpy look.

4. Undo the blend again. The best thing to do in this case is to create an intermediate end path. Copy the T and E and place them so that one is over the top of the other and between the two original letters.

5. Select the overlapping letters and choose Unite from the Pathfinder palette. The two paths merge into one. Bring in the horizontal bars about halfway by using the Direct Selection tool.

6. Select both the T and the merged letters. Make sure that corresponding points exist for each path by adding anchor points to the T with the Add Anchor Point tool. Both paths should have the same number of anchor points. Add corresponding anchor points to the E, as well.

7. Blend the T to the merged path with the Blend tool by clicking the lower-right point of each and entering **4** in the Specified Steps field of the Blend Options dialog box. Blend the E to the merged path by clicking the lower-right point of each and entering **4** in the Specified Steps field of the Blend Options dialog box. The transformation should be almost perfect. If necessary, you can touch up individual points with the Direct Selection tool.

Remember that cheating is apparent only to you. The client or your boss will never know from seeing the final output that the results were forced. Surprisingly, many illustrators actually feel guilty about creating another end path using this method. If you can't live with yourself, by all means continue trying to select just the right points. However, we'll let you in on a secret: Adobe cheats too. In one of the earlier ads for Illustrator and in the accompanying videotape (watch it and check for the poor splicing!), you see an *S* transformed into a swan. Of course, in Adobe's case, it was misrepresenting the capabilities of the Blend tool by making it look as if the tool automatically made eye-pleasing middle paths when, in reality, the "blended" paths were only loosely based on the real blends.

Note You can achieve some really interesting effects by using the Rotate tool or the Rotate section of the Transform Each dialog box, which makes the paths appear to spin as they are transforming from one shape into another. Using these tools also masks any anomalies in the blend steps.

Creating realism with shape blends

To create a realistic effect with shape blends, the paths used to create the blends need to resemble objects you see in life. Look around you and try to find a solid-colored object — doesn't the color appear to change from one part of the object to another? Shadows and reflections are everywhere. Colors change gradually from light to dark, not in straight lines but in smooth, rounded curves.

Blends can be used to simulate reflections and shadows. Reflections are usually created with shape blends; shadows are usually created with Stroke blends.

In the following example, we show you how to simulate reflections with shape blends. This procedure is a little tricky for any artist because the environment determines the reflection. The artwork you create will be viewed in any number of environments, so the reflections have to compensate for these differences. Fortunately, unless you are creating a mirror angled directly at the viewer (impossible, even if you know who the viewer is in advance), you can get the person seeing the artwork to perceive reflection without really being aware of it.

The chrome-like type in the word *DON'T* in Figure 11-18 was created by masking shape blends designed to look like a reflective surface. The following procedure shows you how to achieve this:

1. Type the word or words you want to use for masking the reflective surface. The typeface and the word itself have an impact on how the finished artwork is perceived. We chose the word *DON'T* and the typeface Madrone. We also did a great deal of tracking and kerning so that all the letters touched, which makes the word look like one piece of material. In addition, we used baseline shift to move the apostrophe up several points.

2. Choose Type ➪ Create Outlines (⌘+Shift+O [Ctrl+Shift+O]). Choose a Fill of White for the text and a Stroke of Black. At this point, most of the serifs on the letters overlap.

3. Select all the letters and choose Unite from the Pathfinder palette. This command gets rid of any unsightly seams between the letters. Create a rectangle and place it behind the letters.

4. Set the Auto Trace Tolerance option to 2 in the General Preferences dialog box (Edit ➪ Preferences ➪ General or ⌘+K [Ctrl+K]). Using the Pencil tool, draw a horizontal line from left to right across the rectangle. With a low Auto Trace Tolerance setting, this step should result in a path with many points.

5. Option [Alt]+copy several paths from the original down to the bottom of the rectangle. An easy way to copy the paths is to Option [Alt]+drag down just a bit and then choose Object ➪ Transform ➪ Transform Again (⌘+D [Ctrl+D]) several times. In this example, we created five more paths. With the Direct Selection tool, randomly move around individual anchor points and direction points on each path, but try to avoid overlapping paths. We left the third and fourth paths virtually identical and kept them close together so that there would be a swift change in color that brings out a "shine." Color the Stroke of each path differently, going from dark to light to dark. In this example, we went from dark to light to dark to light and back to dark again.

6. Blend the Stroked paths together and mask them with the type outlines. In this example, we did this step twice. The first time, we created the front piece; the second time, we used lighter-color Strokes for a highlight, which we offset slightly up and to the left and placed behind the original type.

In the preceding steps, we Option [Alt]+copied the path not only because it was easy, but also to ensure that the end paths in the blends have the same points in the same locations. This technique is much more effective than adding or deleting points from a path.

Tip   With slight transformations, you can use the same reflection blend for other objects in the same illustration and no one will be the wiser. A method that we often use is to reflect the original, scale it to 200 percent, and then use only a portion of the blend in the next mask.

In the next example, we use shape blends to create the glowing surface of a light bulb (see Figure 11-19). The key to achieving this effect successfully is to draw the light bulb first, and then use a copy of exactly the same path for the highlights. The relative locations of anchor points stay the same and the number of anchor points never changes.

Follow these steps to create the glowing surface of a light bulb:

1. Draw a light bulb. Take your time and get it exactly the way you want it, because this path is the basis for everything else in this example. Fill the light bulb with 30% Magenta, 80% Yellow, and a Stroke of None. The first four steps in Figure 11-19 show the light bulb in Outline mode.

2. Option [Alt]+scale the light bulb down just a little bit, setting the origin on the base of the bulb. Option [Alt]+scale two more copies of the light bulb. Use the Direct Selection tool to change the shape of the paths until they resemble the paths in Step 2 of Figure 11-19. These paths are the basis for blends within the light bulb. Don't change the color of these paths.

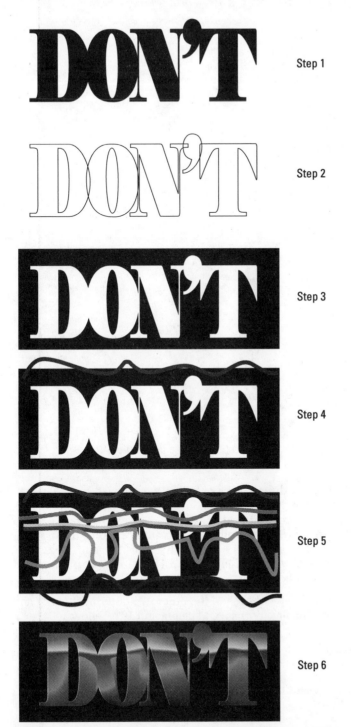

Step 1

Step 2

Step 3

Step 4

Step 5

Step 6

Figure 11-18: Steps for creating type with a reflective surface

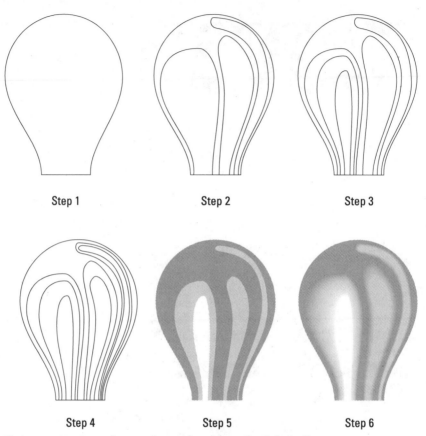

Figure 11-19: Steps for creating real surfaces of a light bulb

3. Option [Alt]+scale down three copies of the path on the left and shape as displayed in Figure 11-19. While your paths do not have to be exactly like the ones in the picture, be sure that each smaller path does not overlap the larger path. Color the paths as follows, from inside to outside: Color the first (inside) path as 5% Magenta, 10% Yellow; the next path as 10% Magenta, 30% Yellow; and the last path as 15% Magenta, 40% Yellow. The outermost path should still be 30% Magenta, 80% Yellow.

4. Option [Alt]+scale one copy of each of the other two outermost paths and reshape them. Color the new paths 5% Magenta and 10% Yellow.

5. The paths should be in the correct top-to-bottom order, but if they are not, fix them. To see if they are in the correct order, go to Preview mode. If the smaller paths are not visible, then send the outer paths to the back.

6. Blend the paths together by selecting similar anchor point locations on each step.

Airbrushing and the Magic of Stroke Blends

After wading through all the technical mumbo-jumbo about blending information, you are ready to enjoy your newfound blending powers. Blending can create effects that are usually reserved for bitmap graphics software, such as Adobe Photoshop, but without the limitation of pixels.

Blending identical overlapping paths together and varying their Stroke weights and colors creates most of the effects described in this section. This technique provides some of the best effects that Illustrator has to offer.

Usually, the bottommost Stroke has a heavier weight than the topmost Stroke, and as the color changes from bottom Stroke to top Stroke the colors appear to blend in from the outside.

Tubular blends

Creating tubular blends with the Blend tool is quite often easier than creating any other type of Stroke blend for one simple reason: The two paths, while identical, are not placed *directly* one over the other, but instead are offset just slightly, giving the tube a three-dimensional appearance. If you prefer the exactly-over-the-top method, you can simply omit the moving part in Step 2 of the following procedure and blend the objects using Object ➪ Blend ➪ Make command (⌘+Option+B [Ctrl+Alt+B]). Follow these steps to create Tubular blends:

1. Draw a path with the Pencil tool. Smooth curves work better than corners, so make the Auto Trace Tolerance high (7 to 10) in the Type and Auto Tracing dialog box before drawing the curves. Change the Fill to None and the Stroke to 50% Yellow, with a weight of 0.25 point in the Paint Style palette. The path may cross itself.

ASK TOULOUSE: Complex Realistic Blends

Freddy: My blends aren't . . . well, they look fake.

Toulouse: So, they don't look like real blends?

Freddy: No, they don't look *real*.

Toulouse: An important key to getting shape blends to look really good is to blend from the background color of the shape to the first blend, or to make that first blend the background color.

Freddy: What'll that do?

Toulouse: That'll smooth the blend into the background, so you can't tell exactly where the blend starts and stops.

2. Copy the path and Paste in Back (⌘+B [Ctrl+B]). Offset the copy about half a point up and to the right by selecting Object ⇨ Transform ⇨ Move and entering the appropriate values in the text fields. Change the stroke on the copy to 50% Yellow and 100% Black with a weight of 4 points.

3. Blend the two paths together. Create a Black rectangle and send it to the back. The result should look similar to the tube in Figure 11-20.

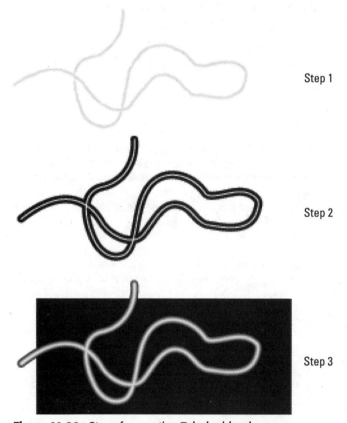

Step 1

Step 2

Step 3

Figure 11-20: Steps for creating Tubular blends

Note   When you're creating Stroke blends, the number of steps usually doesn't need to exceed 100. If the default is more than 100, divide it by 2 (as explained in the earlier section, "Calculating the number of steps") until the number is less than 100.

To see the end points better on Stroke-blend end paths, draw a tiny marquee around one of the ends with the Zoom tool. If you still can't see the end points, switch to Outline mode while creating the blend. You can also choose Object ⇨ Blend ⇨ Make command (⌘+Option+B [Ctrl+Alt+B]).

To create a Stroke blend that has more shine to it, make the Stroke lighter and thinner and do not offset it as far as in the preceding example.

To create a color Stroke blend that has more depth, make two end paths and color the bottom darker and wider and the top lighter and thinner. Then blend the paths together with one step between the end paths. Add a bit of Black (20 to 40 percent) to the bottommost Stroke and then blend from the bottom to the middle and from the middle to the top. The extra Black usually creates a much more realistic appearance of depth than using just two colors, and it keeps Black from being in the upper half of the tube.

 Caution   Try not to use White as your topmost path when creating tubes, because White can cause problems when you print. The more subtle your color change, the more realistic your results. If necessary, you can always add highlights of much lighter colors after the Stroke has been blended.

Many shapes exist besides free-flowing tubes that benefit from this type of Stroke effect, including stars, spirals, and line drawings. Objects that appear in everyday life that can be created with tube-like Stroke blends include wires, rods, paper clips, hangers, antennas, pins, and needles. The next section explains how to make one of the most confusing types of objects with blends — the spring tube.

Spring-tube blends

To create the curly section of a telephone cord (a spring tube), use the Spiral Tool to create a spiral with two winds and get rid of the inner spiral. Select the outer spiral and go through the steps to create a tube. Make this particular tube look like a section of a telephone cord, as shown in Figure 11-21.

After you've created the spring tube, group the entire tube together and Option [Alt]+copy it until one side of the spiral lines up with the other side of the spiral. Choose Object ➪ Transform ➪ Transform Again (⌘+D [Ctrl+D]) until the telephone cord is the desired length. To curve the phone cord, draw a marquee around one of the ends with the Direct Selection tool and move it, if necessary. Then use the Rotate tool to change the direction of the curve. Option [Alt]+copy the next section and rotate that section into place.

For quicker but less effective changes in direction, select a small section of the telephone cord and just rotate that section.

Airbrushed shadows

To create a realistic shadow effect, the edges of an object must be a little fuzzy. The amount of fuzziness on the edges of the path is relative to the distance of the object from its shadow and the strength of the light source. These two areas also affect how dark the shadow is.

Figure 11-21: A telephone cord created with tubular blends

To make really cool shadows, you can use either Soft Mix from the Pathfinder palette, which can be used to darken areas, or the Color Adjust filter, which can be used to change the types of color in a selected area. The Drop Shadow filter creates hard-edged shadows, which are usually good only for quickly creating text shadows.

If you work a lot with shadows, check out the new Drop Shadow effect that is covered in Chapter 13, "Using Styles, Effects, and Filters."

A second way to create cool shadows is to use Stroke blends. Stroke blends can make the shadows fade smoothly into the background with a Gaussian Blur-like effect. You can combine Stroke blends with the Soft Mix option from the Pathfinder palette for even better effects.

For information on using the Soft Mix option from the Pathfinder palette to create shadows, see Chapter 5, "Selecting and Editing."

The following procedure shows how to create shadows with linear blends:

1. Create a path (or copy it from an original object) for which you want to create a shadow. At this point, you may want to hide the object from which the shadow is being made so that it doesn't get in your way, especially if this object is right above where the shadow is. Fill the shadowed path with the color you want the shadow to be and then make the Stroke the same color, with a 0.5-point Stroke weight.

2. Copy the shadow, choose Edit ➪ Paste in Back (⌘+B [Ctrl+B]), and then change the Stroke color to whatever the background color is (usually White, unless something else is under the shadow). Make the Stroke weight twice the distance you want the shadow to fade out to. In this example, we made the Stroke 12 points.

3. Now blend these two paths. This has been made easy with the Blend tool. Watch for the cursor to change from an x to a +. The shadow slowly fades in from the background color to the shadow color. Show the hidden objects (you may have to bring them to the front), and you've created your shadow effect (see Figure 11-22).

Figure 11-22: Airbrushed shadows with linear blends

Creating glows

Glows are very similar to soft-edged shadows, but instead of a dark area fading into the background, a lighter area fades into the background. You can create a glow for the light bulb that appeared previously in Figure 11-19 by using Stroke blending. Follow these steps to create a glow for the light bulb:

1. Select the edge of the object on which you want to create the glow. In this example, we use the light bulb that was shown in Figure 11-19 previously. Copy the edge, Paste in Back (⌘+B [Ctrl+B]), and press ⌘+Option+Shift+2 [Ctrl+Alt+Shift+2]. These steps lock everything that is not selected. Give the copied edge a Stroke of 6% Magenta and 62% Yellow, and a Weight of 1 point.

2. Draw a Black rectangle around the outside edge of the object and send it to the back. Copy the edge of the light bulb and Paste in Back (⌘+B [Ctrl+B]) again. Change the Stroke to 6% Magenta, 60% Yellow, and 100% Black and

make the Stroke about 40 points wide. Move this path about ½ point to the right and up.

3. Blend the two edge paths together to create the glow of the light bulb (see Figure 11-23). The larger the Weight of the second copied path from Step 2, the bigger the glow.

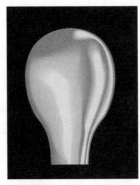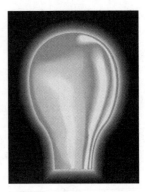

Figure 11-23: Creating a glow around the light bulb

An even easier way to create glows is with the new Glow effect features. These effects are covered in Chapter 13, "Using Styles, Effects, and Filters."

When creating glows, make the initial glow area (around the edge of the object) *lighter* than the object edges if bright highlights exist in the object. Make the initial glow *darker* than the edges if the edges of the object are the brightest part of the object.

Softening edges

Softening object edges of is similar to creating shadows. Edges are softened to remove the hard, computer-like borders from objects in your illustration. Softening edges can be done to an extreme measure so that the object appears out of focus, or just a tiny bit for an almost imperceptible change.

When determining how much distance should be softened, look at the whole illustration, not just that one image. Usually, the softening area is no more than one or two points (unless the object is being blurred).

To soften edges on an object, select the object, copy it, and then hide the original object. Choose Edit ➪ Paste in Back (⌘+B [Ctrl+B]) and then make the Stroke on the object 0.1 point, the same color as the Fill. Copy again, Paste in Back, make the Stroke the color of the background, and make the Weight 2 points (which makes the softening edge 1-point thick).

When softening objects, rather than moving the entire path in the background, try moving one anchor point out just far enough to be able to click it. Blend the two paths together, and then show the original object (it may have to be brought to the front).

To blur an object, make the bottom layer Stroke extremely wide (12 to 20 points or more, depending on the size of the illustration) and blend as described in the preceding paragraphs.

Neon effects

To create neon effects with Stroke blends, you need to create two distinct parts. The first part is the neon tubing, which by itself is nice, but it doesn't really have a neon effect. The second part is the tubing's reflection off the background, which usually appears as a glowing area. These two separate blends give the illusion of lit neon.

Note   Neon effects work much better when the background is very dark, although some interesting effects can be achieved with light backgrounds.

Follow these steps to create a neon effect using the candle and flame paths:

1. To make the tubing, create a path that will be the neon. In Figure 11-24, we use two paths: a candle and a flame. Give the Stroke of the paths a Weight of 4 and color them 100% Yellow. Make sure that the Fill is set to None. Change the cap of the Stroke to round and the join of the Stroke to curved.

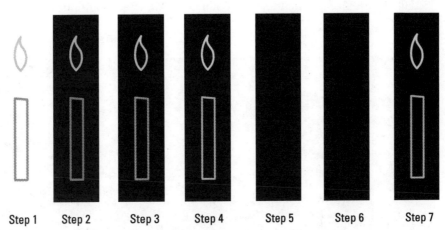

Figure 11-24: Steps for creating neon candles

2. Create a rectangle that is larger than the area of the path. Send it to the back and set the Fill to Black.

3. Select the neon path, copy it, and choose Edit ➪ Paste in Front (⌘+F [Ctrl+F]). Offset the copy by 0.25 point and change the Weight of the copy to 0.25 point. Hold down the Shift key and change the color of the Stroke by dragging the sliders to the left to make the color lighter. Do not make the copy White, but make it noticeably lighter than the neon color.

4. Blend the two paths together. This is the neon tube part of the illustration. Hide this tube.

5. To create the reflected area of the background, choose Edit ➪ Paste in Back (⌘+B [Ctrl+B]). This step pastes a copy of the original path behind the bottom part of the existing neon tube. Give the path a Stroke of 4 and change the color to 100% Yellow and 75% Black.

6. Copy the Stroke and Paste in Back (⌘+B [Ctrl+B]) again, changing the color of the Stroke to the same as the background and then making the weight of the Stroke 24 points. Offset this copy by 0.25 point and blend the two together.

7. Choose View Object ➪ Show All (⌘+Option+3 [Ctrl+Alt+3]). Your result should look similar to Figure 11-24.

Tip   Try crossing paths with neon or, for an even more realistic look, create "unlit" portions of neon by using darker shading with no reflective glow.

Backlighting

You can achieve backlighting effects by simply creating a glow for an object and then placing that same object on top of the glow. By making the topmost object Filled with Black or another dark color, a backlit effect is produced, as shown in Figure 11-25.

Figure 11-25: Backlighting the word *DARK*

Compound Paths

Compound paths are one of the least understood areas of Illustrator, but after you grasp a few simple guidelines and rules, manipulating and using compound paths correctly is simple.

Compound paths are paths made up of two or more open or closed paths. Where the paths cross or every other Fill area exists, a transparent hole occurs. You specify which paths create the holes by changing the direction of the paths via the Reverse option in the Attributes palette. The general rule is that paths traveling in the opposite direction of any adjoining paths form holes. Compound paths can be fun or frustrating, depending on the location of Pluto relative to Saturn, Jupiter, and Mickey.

Creating compound paths

You can create all types of compound paths by following the steps described here (which are also illustrated in Figure 11-26). It's a good idea to make sure that none of the paths are currently compound paths or grouped paths before creating a new compound path.

1. Create all the paths that you need for the compound path, including the outside path and the holes.

2. Select all the paths and choose Object ➪ Compound Paths ➪ Make (⌘+8 [Ctrl+8]). Illustrator now treats the paths as one path. When you click one of the paths with the Selection tool, the other paths in the compound path are selected as well. Fill the object with any Fill. (We used a custom radial gradient for the illustration in Figure 11-27.)

3. Place the compound path over any other object. (We used a placed EPS image for this example.) The inner paths act like holes that enable you to see the object underneath.

You can select individual paths by clicking them once with the Group Selection tool. As always, you can select points and segments within each path by using the Direct Selection tool.

Clicking only once with the Group Selection tool on paths that you wish to select is important. Clicking those paths more than once with the Group Selection tool selects all the other paths in the compound path. To click (for moving or copying purposes) the selected individual paths after the Group Selection tool has clicked them once, use the Direct Selection tool.

Figure 11-26: The frame of this window is a compound path with several holes in it.

Step 1   Step 2   Step 3

Figure 11-27: The steps for creating a compound path

Paths belonging to different groups cannot be made into a compound path unless all paths in all the groups are selected.

When you create a compound path, it takes on the Paint Style attributes of the bottommost path of all the paths that were selected and have become part of that compound path.

You can create a compound path that is only one path, though few reasons exist to do so. If the singular compound path is selected as part of a larger compound path (with either the Direct Selection tool or Group Selection tool), the path directions may be altered. If you aren't sure whether an individual path is a compound path, select the path and choose Object ⇨ Compound Path. If the Release option is available, the path is a compound path; if it is not available, the path is not a compound path.

Compound paths do not work in a hierarchical process as groups do. If a path is part of a compound path, it is part of that compound path only. If a compound path becomes part of another compound path, the paths in the original compound path are compounded only with the new compound path.

Tip You can blend between multiple-path compound paths. Select the Blend tool and click from one compound shape to the other shape. While the initial blend between the two objects is still selected, double-click the Blend tool in the toolbox to open the Blend Options dialog box. Select the Spacing pop-up menu and choose Specified Step and enter a number. Select Preview to see the results before you close the dialog box. The larger the number, the smoother the blend. For cool results make sure the two objects are different colors. For the smoothest blends make sure you don't have a stroke color applied to your shapes.

Releasing compound paths

When you want to release a compound path, select the path and choose Object ➪ Compound Path ➪ Release (⌘+Option+8 [Ctrl+Alt+8]). The path changes into regular paths.

If any of the paths appear as holes, they are, instead, filled with the Fill of the rest of the compound path. The results may be a little confusing because these holes then seem to blend right into the outer shape of the compound paths, as shown in Figure 11-28.

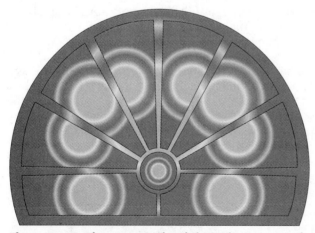

Figure 11-28: The compound path from Figure 11-27, after you release the path. The circles are the radial gradients that the compound path uses.

If the compound path that you are releasing contains other compound paths, they are released as well because Illustrator doesn't recognize compound paths that are within other compound paths.

Understanding holes

Holes for donuts, Life Savers, and rings are quite simple to create. Just select two circles, one smaller than, and totally within, a larger circle, and choose Object ⇨ Compound Path ⇨ Make (⌘+8 [Ctrl+8]). The inside circle is then a hole.

A compound path considers every path within it to lie along the borders of the compound path. Path edges within an object appear to you to be on the inside of an object, but they appear to Illustrator to be just another edge of the path.

With this concept in mind, you can create a compound path that has several holes, such as a slice of Swiss cheese or a snowflake. Just create the outermost paths and the paths that will be holes, select all the paths, and then select Object ⇨ Compound Path ⇨ Make.

Tip   You aren't limited to one set of holes. You can create a compound path with a hole that has an object inside it with a hole. In that hole can be an object with a hole, and so on.

Overlapping holes

Holes, if they really are paths that are supposed to be empty areas of an object, should not overlap. If several paths that are suppose to be holes do overlap, you can combine them using the Unite feature in the Pathfinder palette.

If holes within a compound path do overlap, the result is a solid area with the same Fill color as the rest of the object. If multiple holes overlap, the results can be quite unusual, as shown in Figure 11-29. (See "Reversing path directions," later in this chapter, to learn more about multiple overlapping holes.)

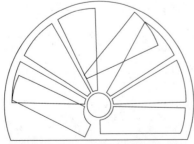

Figure 11-29: Overlapping holes in compound paths, in Outline mode (left) and Preview mode (right)

Note In most cases, you get the desired results with holes only if the outermost path contains all the holes. As a rule, Illustrator uses the topmost objects to "poke" holes out of the bottommost objects. If you want holes to overlap, make sure that the holes are above the outside border.

Creating compound paths from separate sets of paths

Compound paths are very flexible. You can choose two sets of paths, each with an outline and a hole, and make them into one compound path. This technique is especially useful for making masks, but you also can use it to alleviate the repetition of creating several compound paths and selecting one of them at a time.

For example, if you have two shapes, a square and a circle, and want a round hole in each of them, you draw two smaller circles and put them into place. After you position the two shapes in the correct locations, you select them and the round paths inside each of them, and then you choose Object ⇨ Compound Path ⇨ Make (⌘+8 [Ctrl+8]). Each of the objects now has a hole and they act as if they are grouped.

To move separate objects that are part of the same compound path, select each object with the Group Selection tool, which selects an entire path at a time, and then move them. Remember that once they're selected, you should use the Direct Selection tool to move the selected portions of a compound path.

Type and compound paths

You have been using compound paths as long as you have been using computer PostScript typefaces. All PostScript typefaces are made of characters that are compound paths. Letters that have holes, such as uppercase *B, D,* and *P* and lowercase *a, b,* and *d,* benefit from being compound paths. When you place them in front of other objects, you can see through the empty areas to objects behind them that are visible in those holes.

Each character in a PostScript typeface is a compound path. When you convert characters to editable outlines in Illustrator, each character is still a compound path. If you release the compound paths, the characters with empty areas appear to fill with the same color as the rest of the character, as shown in Figure 11-30, because the holes are no longer knocked out of the letters.

Tropical

Tropical

Figure 11-30: Type as it normally appears after you convert it to outlines (top) and after you release compound paths (bottom)

Note

Many times, type is used as a mask, but all the letters used in the mask need to be one compound path. Simply select all the letters and choose Object ⇨ Compound Path ⇨ Make (⌘+8 [Ctrl+8]). This action creates a compound path in which all of the letters form the compound path. Usually, all the holes stay the same as they were as separate compound paths.

Any letters that overlap in a word that you make into a compound path can change path directions and thus affect the "emptiness" of some paths. If letters have to overlap, use Unite on them first, and then select all the letters and choose Object ⇨ Compound Path ⇨ Make (⌘+8 [Ctrl+8]).

Cross-Reference

Compound paths can be combined using the Pathfinder tools. These tools are covered in Chapter 5, "Selecting and Editing."

Path Directions

Each path in Illustrator has a direction. For paths that you draw with the Pen or Pencil tool, the direction of the path is the direction in which you draw the path. When Illustrator creates an oval or a rectangle, the direction of the path is counter-clockwise.

Note

If you're curious about which way a path travels, click any spot of the path with the Scissors tool and then choose Filter ⇨ Stylize ⇨ Add Arrowheads. In the Add Arrowheads dialog box, make sure that the End button is selected and click OK. An arrowhead appears, going in the direction of the path. (Figure 11-31 shows several paths and arrowheads appearing for each path.) If the path is Filled and not Stroked, you see only half the arrowhead in Preview mode. Choose the Undo command twice (once for the arrowhead and once for the path splitting) to go back to where you started. You can also check the path direction in the Attributes palette. Select Window ⇨ Attributes and select one path with the Group Selection tool and notice the Reverse Path Direction. Select the hole and notice it shows the path in the opposite direction.

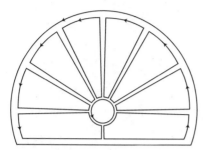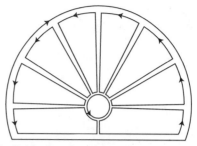

Figure 11-31: The paths on the left are individual paths. The paths on the right make up a compound path. The arrows represent the direction of the paths. Notice that the only difference in direction is on the outermost path.

Paths have directions for one purpose (one purpose that you need to know about, anyway), and that is to determine the solid and empty areas of a compound path. The individual paths in a compound path that create holes from solid paths go in opposite directions.

To see how this works, create a large circle and put a smaller circle within it. Both circles are traveling in the same direction — counterclockwise. Select both of them and choose Object ➪ Compound Path ➪ Make (⌘+8 [Ctrl+8]). The outside circle changes its direction to clockwise so that the two circles can work together to form a doughnut-like shape.

If two smaller circles are inside the larger circle, they still punch holes in the larger circle because both of them are traveling in the same direction. But what happens when the two inside circles overlap? The area where they overlap is inside the empty area, but both holes go in the same direction. The intersection of the two holes is solid because of the winding path rule.

The Winding Numbers Rule, or what happened to my Fills?

Understanding the Winding Numbers Rule is helpful when you are dealing with compound paths. The Winding Numbers Rule counts surrounded areas, starting with zero (outside the outermost edge) and working its way in. Any area with an odd number is Filled, and any area with an even number (such as zero, the outside of the path) is empty, or a hole.

You can apply this rule to most compound paths — although taking the time to diagram the paths you've drawn and placing little numbers in them to figure out what is going to be Filled and what isn't is usually more time-consuming than doing it wrong, undoing it, and doing it right. We've done the work for you in Figure 11-32.

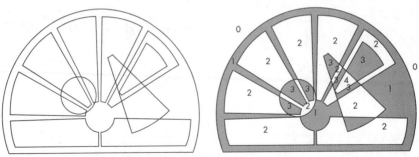

Figure 11-32: As the paths wind in from the outside, odd-numbered areas are Filled and even-numbered areas are empty.

Reversing path directions

To change the direction of a path, use the Group Selection tool to select just the path and choose Window ➪ Attributes (F11). In the Attributes palette box (see Figure 11-33), click the direction button that is not darkened.

Figure 11-33: The Attributes palette box

Reverse Path Direction Off

Reverse Path Direction On

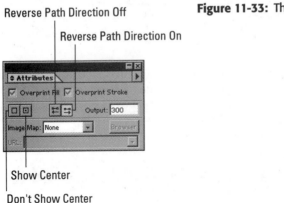

Show Center

Don't Show Center

When paths are changed into compound paths, their direction may change. The strange thing about this is that the Reverse Path Direction button is usually on for objects that are traveling counterclockwise. The outermost path does not change direction from counterclockwise to clockwise until more than one overlapping path is made into a compound path. The paths that make up the holes don't change direction. They're still counterclockwise, but when you look at their Attributes, Reverse Path Direction is on.

One thing that is consistent when dealing with path directions is that holes must travel in the opposite direction from the outside path. As a result, if the Reverse Path Direction button is on for the holes, it is not on for the outside path. That scenario is the normal one when you create compound paths with holes. You can, if you so desire, check the Reverse Path Direction button for the outside path and uncheck it for the inside paths. The resulting image has the same holes that are produced by the reverse process. Figure 11-34 shows a compound path and its path directions before and after four of the paths are reversed.

Figure 11-34: Reversing the direction of the four paths in the illustration on the left fills those holes, as shown in the illustration on the right.

Caution

Never, never, never attempt to change path direction when all paths of a compound path are selected. Clicking once on either button makes all the paths in the compound path go in the same direction, which means that no holes appear.

Using Add to Shape Area to create compound paths

Another way to make compound paths is by using the Pathfinder's Add to Shape Area function. Add to Shape Area works a little differently from the Make Compound Path command. All the selected paths become a single compound path, but none of the path directions are reversed. This means that no holes are created when Add to Shape Area is applied.

Add to Shape Area is useful for creating compound paths when you don't want to accidentally create holes between overlapping pieces of paths, such as text converted to outlines.

In addition, Add to Shape Area removes any overlapping path areas that have Filled areas or holes. Thus, Stroking the object gives you a much better result than leaving the object as a plain compound path.

Faking a compound path

At times, using a compound path just doesn't work. You may need to cheat a little. Except in the most extreme circumstances, you can fake compound paths, but you need to make an effort.

If the background is part of a gradient, select the hole and the object that is painted with the gradient, apply the gradient, and use the Gradient tool to make the gradient spread across both objects in exactly the same way. This trick can fool even the experts.

ASK TOULOUSE: Can't Make a Compound

Mork: I can't make a compound out of my selected paths!

Toulouse: That often happens when one or more of the paths is already a compound path.

Mork: Huh? How would know if that's the case?

Toulouse: Well, you can check and fix it at the same time. First, select the paths you'd like to make into a compound path.

Mork: Got it.

Toulouse: Then, go under Object to Compound Path and hold.

Mork: Okay.

Toulouse: Is Release gray or black?

Mork: Black.

Toulouse: That means that at least one of the selected paths is already a compound. Drag over to Release.

Mork: Done.

Toulouse: Then choose Object ⇨ Compound Paths ⇨ Make.

Mork: It worked!

Toulouse: And what did you learn this week?

Tip   One way to fake a compound path is by selecting the background, making a copy of it, making the hole a mask of the background area, and grouping the mask to the copy of the background.

Masks

In Illustrator, you use masks to mask out parts of underlying objects that you don't want to see. The path that you draw in Illustrator defines the shape of the mask. Anything outside the mask is hidden from view in Preview mode and does not print.

Masks are objects that *mask* out everything but the paths made up by the mask (see Figure 11-35). Masks can be open, closed, or compound paths. The masking object is the object whose paths make up the mask, and this object must be in front of all the objects that are being masked.

You can make masks from any path, including compound paths and text. You can use masks to view portions of multiple objects, individual objects, and placed EPS (Encapsulated PostScript) images.

Figure 11-35: An object, its mask, and the resulting masked object

Creating masks

To create a mask, the masking object (the path that is in the shape of the mask) has to be in front of the objects that you want it to mask. You select the masking object and the objects that you want to mask. Then you choose Object ➪ Clipping Mask ➪ Make (⌘+7 [Ctrl+7]). In Preview mode, any areas of the objects that were outside the mask vanish, but the parts of the objects that are inside the mask remain the same. Figure 11-36 shows an illustration with masks and without them.

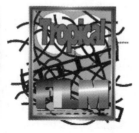

Figure 11-36: The image on the left uses masks to hide portions of objects. The image on the right is the result of releasing those masks.

Masks are much easier to use and understand in Preview mode than in Outline mode.

If you want to mask an object that is not currently being masked, you need to select the new object and all the objects in the mask, including the masking object. You then choose Object ➪ Clipping Mask ➪ Make (⌘+7 [Ctrl+7]). The mask then applies to the new object as well as to the objects that were previously masked. The new object, like all others being masked, must be behind the masking object.

Like compound paths, masking does not work in hierarchical levels. Each time you add an object to a mask, the old mask that didn't have that object is released, and a new mask is made that contains all of the original mask objects as well as the new object. Releasing a mask affects every object in the mask, as described in "Releasing Masks," later in this chapter.

Tip   Usually, grouping all the objects in a mask is a good idea, but group them only after you have created the mask. Grouping the objects makes moving the mask and its objects and selecting the objects easier when you want to add other objects to the mask.

Masking raster images

You have two different ways to mask raster images. The first method is to create a *clipping path* and save it as an EPS image in Photoshop. The second method is to use a mask in Illustrator.

Each of the two methods has its strengths and weaknesses, with the best solution being a combination of both methods. The main advantage to creating a clipping path in Photoshop is that the path can be adjusted while viewing the image clearly at a 16:1 ratio. (Viewing an image at 1,600 percent in Illustrator displays chunky, unrecognizable blocks of color.) In this manner, the path can be precisely positioned over the correct pixels so that the right pixels are selected for masking. One disadvantage to using Photoshop's clipping path is that the Path tool and path-editing controls in Photoshop are limited versions of Illustrator's Pen tool and path-editing controls, which makes it more difficult to create and edit a path. The second disadvantage to using a clipping path is that compound paths in Photoshop adhere to one of two different Fill rules, which control the way holes appear for differing path directions. Illustrator is much more flexible in this respect because you are able to change the path direction of each individual path with the Reverse Path Direction checkbox in the Attributes palette.

The best solution is to create the clipping path in Photoshop, and then, when the clipping path is selected, choose File ⇨ Export ⇨ Paths to Illustrator, which saves an Illustrator-compatible file with the clipping path intact. Save the Photoshop image as an EPS file and place it in Illustrator (File ⇨ Place). Then open the Illustrator file (that was created by Paths to Illustrator) and copy the path to the document with the raster image. The path is sized to fit directly onto the raster image.

Note   Copying the selected path in Photoshop enables you to paste it directly into Illustrator, even if you can run only one of those programs at a time. Just copy, quit Photoshop, run Illustrator, and paste it into the Illustrator document. This works when going from Illustrator to Photoshop (paths only) as well.

Masking other masks

You can mask objects that are masking other objects. Just make sure that you select all the objects in each mask and that, as with other objects, they are behind the path that you want to use for a masking object.

Stroking and Filling masking objects

Creating a basic mask requires four steps:

1. Select the path that you want to use as a mask and bring it to the front.

2. Select the mask and any objects that you want to mask and then choose Object ➪ Masks ➪ Make (⌘+7 [Ctrl+7]).

3. Group the masked objects with the mask for easier selecting in the future.

4. Using the Group Selection tool, select the mask. Then change the Stroke to 1-point Black. The mask now has a 1-point Black Stroke. The result should resemble Step 4 in Figure 11-37.

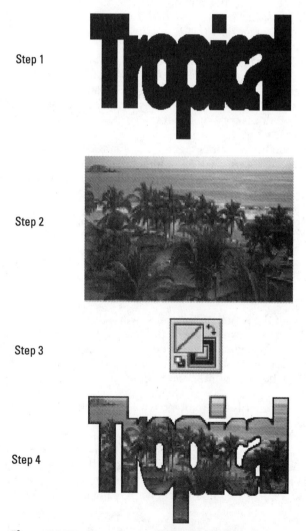

Step 1

Step 2

Step 3

Step 4

Figure 11-37: Steps for creating a Stroked mask

Note You can apply a Stroke or Fill to a masking object. A Fill and Stroke of None replace any Paint Style attributes that you applied to the object prior to transforming it into a mask. But if you select the object after it is a mask, you can apply a Stroke or Fill to that mask. If you release the mask, the path that was the masking object continues to have a Fill and Stroke of None.

Releasing masks

To release a mask, first select the masking object (you may select other objects as well). Then choose Object ⇨ Mask ⇨ Release (⌘+Option+7 [Ctrl+Alt+7]), and the masking object no longer is a mask.

If you aren't sure which object is the masking object or if you are having trouble selecting the masking object, choose Select ⇨ All (⌘+A [Ctrl+A]) and choose Object ⇨ Mask ⇨ Release (⌘+Option+7 [Ctrl+Alt+7]). Of course, this action releases any other masks that are in the document — unless they were separate masks that were being masked by other masks — got that?

To release all the masks in the document, even those masks that are being masked by other masks, Select ⇨ All (⌘+A [Ctrl+A]) and choose Release Mask repeatedly. Usually three Release Masks get everything, unless you went mask-happy in that particular document.

Masks and printing

As a rule, PostScript printers don't care too much for masks. They care even less for masks that mask other masks. And they really don't like masks that are compound paths.

Unfortunately, because of the way that Illustrator works, every part of every object in a mask is sent to the printer, even if only a tiny piece of an object is used. In addition, controlling where the masking object slices objects requires a great deal of computing power and memory. You may have a problem, for example, when you have more stuff to mask than the printer can handle.

More important than any other issue involved with masks and printing is the length and complexity of the masking path.

The more objects in a mask, the more complex it is. The more anchor points, the more complex it is. The more direction points coming off those anchor points, the more complex the mask is. In other words, your printer would enjoy a mask if the masking object was a rectangle and no objects were being masked.

Masks are usually incredibly complex. This complexity causes many problems for printers (especially ones equipped with PostScript Level 1 and PostScript clones) and often results in PostScript printing errors. In addition, be careful not to go mask-crazy (using hundreds of masks), or your document may never see toner.

Masks and compound paths

Creating masks from compound paths is especially useful when you are working with text and want several separate letters to mask a placed EPS image or a series of pictures that you created in Illustrator.

The reason that you need to transform separate objects into compound paths is that a masking object can only be one path. The topmost object of the selected objects becomes the masking object, and the others become objects within the mask. Creating a compound path from several paths makes the masking feature treat all the objects as one path and makes a masking object out of the entire compound path.

You can use compound paths for masking when you are working with objects that need to have holes, as well as when you are working with text and other separate objects. Figure 11-38 was created by making one compound path from all of the parts of the window frame and using that compound path as a mask for the space scene.

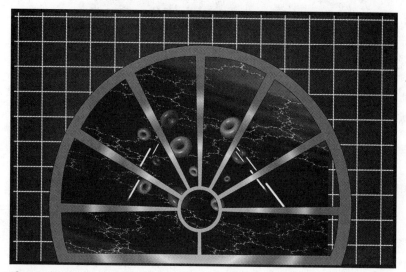

Figure 11-38: Creating a compound path out of all of the parts of the window frame made the window frame a mask for the space scene.

Using compound paths and masks in an illustration

We used several compound paths and masks to achieve the effects in Figure 11-39. The compound paths are the word *Tropical* and the large strips of film across the lower half of the illustration. The masks are the word *Tropical,* the binocular shape, and the outside frame of the poster.

Figure 11-39: Using several different compound paths and masks, we created this poster.

ASK TOULOUSE: Masking versus Cropping

Mearth: Should I mask or should I crop?

Toulouse: You mean with the Pathfinder Crop filter?

Mearth: No, I'm considering a career change in the direction of shucking corn.

Toulouse: I take it you're being sarcastic.

Mearth: Harrumph.

Toulouse: It really depends. Cropping has two serious advantages over masking.

Mearth: And those are . . . ?

Toulouse: First, unnecessary paths are deleted, and second, potential printing problems that may occur when a mask is being used are eliminated.

Mearth: So I should crop.

Toulouse: Actually, there's more in favor of masking.

Mearth: Aha!

Toulouse: Yep. Masking lets you edit the artwork in the future.

Mearth: That's a big one.

Toulouse: Real big. You can change the shape, size, whatever, of the mask and the masked objects.

Mearth: Good points.

Toulouse: And you can mask raster images and nonoutlined text.

Mearth: I'm sold.

Creating a film strip

In the first set of steps (described here and illustrated in Figure 11-40), you create the strip of film and place the island pictures into the film. You do not use masks in this process. We make this point so that you don't think that you always have to use masks, especially when another method is easier.

These steps show you how to create a compound path for a masking effect:

1. To create the film shape, draw a long, horizontal rectangle with the Rectangle tool and place five rounded-corner rectangles inside the long rectangle.

2. To create the sprocket holes in the film, place a right-side-up triangle next to an upside-down triangle and continue placing triangles until you have a row of triangles across the top of the film.

3. After you group all the triangles together, Option [Alt]+copy them (drag the triangles with the Option [Alt] key pressed, releasing the mouse button before releasing the Option [Alt] key) to create a second row of triangles along the bottom of the film.

4. Select all the pieces of the film and choose Object ➪ Compound Paths ➪ Make (⌘+8 [Ctrl+8]). Fill the compound path with a dark purple color that is not quite black.

5. This part looks as if you use a mask, but you don't need to do any masking here. Instead, place one image, size it so that it just covers the hole, and Option [Alt] +copy it across the remaining holes. Select each image in turn, choose File ➪ Place Art, and select a different image for each square. To complete the effect, simply bring the strip of film to the front.

6. Before you place the film into the poster, group the images and the film and rotate them slightly. Grouping them prevents the hassle of selecting each one later if you need to move or transform them.

Instead of making the film a compound path, you can mask each of the photos and place each masked photo on top of the film. The method described in the preceding steps makes changing photos easier and is less taxing on the output device.

The next set of steps describes how to use the word *Tropical* to show the tropical island.

1. Place an image in the document and create a masking path for the top of it. Before you make the objects into a mask, select the image and choose Edit ➪ Copy (⌘+C [Ctrl+C]). (You use this copy in Step 3.)

2. Select both the masking path and the image and choose Object ➪ Mask ➪ Make (⌘+7 [Ctrl+7]).

Tip   You can use the outline of the masking path as a shadow by Option [Alt]+copying it before you perform Steps 1 and 2. Change the Fill in the copy to Black and place the copy below and to the right of the original.

3. Choose Edit ➪ Paste in Back (⌘+B [Ctrl+B]) to position the image directly underneath the original image. Choose File ➪ Place Art and substitute a slightly varied version of the original image. The letters stand out decisively, as Figure 11-41 shows. The image behind the word Tropical was changed in Photoshop using a Mosaic filter.

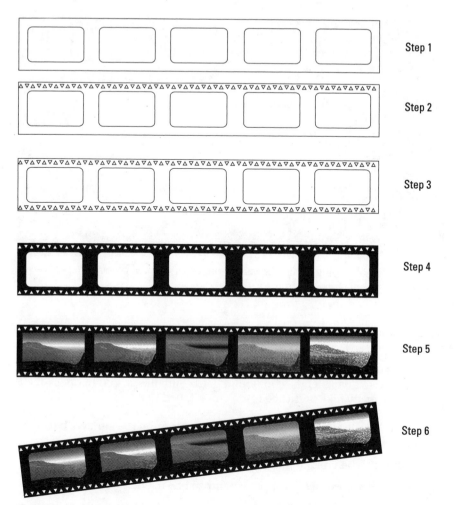

Step 1

Step 2

Step 3

Step 4

Step 5

Step 6

Figure 11-40: Steps for creating a complex compound path to achieve a masking effect

Figure 11-41: Using dissimilar raster images as masked objects makes the word *Tropical* stand out in the image.

Summary

The techniques covered in this chapter represent some of the more advanced topics in the book. Using blends, compound paths and masks, you're range of effects will increase many fold. In this chapter, you learned that

✦ Blends and gradients may resemble each other on the surface, but their capabilities and functionality are different.

✦ Blends can be created between any open and/or closed paths.

✦ Blends can be masked so that a blend can be used as a Fill.

✦ Shape blends can be created to transform an object from one shape to another.

✦ Blends can be used to create smooth airbrushing effects.

✦ Compound paths are one or more paths that Illustrator treats as a single path.

✦ Compound paths let you put holes in your paths.

✦ Changing the direction of a path via the Attributes palette can change the holes in the compound path.

✦ Each character of type converted to outlines consists of a compound path.

✦ Masks are paths that overlay other Illustrator objects, showing the objects only through the masking path.

✦ When using text outlines as a mask, make sure that all the paths that make up the text outlines are a single compound path.

✦   ✦   ✦

Mastering Illustrator

Part III contains the nitty-gritty—and we don't mean the dirt band. Hot topics such as using Illustrator styles, effects, filters, and techniques for creating fantastic graphics are presented. This part includes several newer features such as transparency and working with raster images. We even show you how to customize Illustrator to work better and faster.

Understanding Transparency

Now that Illustrator includes transparency, you will wonder how you ever survived without it. The concept of stacking things on top of one another is one that you learned as a child playing with blocks. It was also one of the early skills that you learned — or struggled to learn — as an Illustrator user. If you've ever lost an object and couldn't find it anywhere because it was hiding underneath some other larger object, then you know what we mean about struggling.

Arranging objects on top of one another always meant being careful to position objects so they would be visible. This also made it possible to hide the rough edges of an object. However, with the transparency feature, all the skeletons in the closet will be exposed. This opens up a world of possibilities, and means that we don't need to mess with Hot Door's plug-in anymore.

How Transparency Works

To understand transparency, it helps to think of a sheet of glass. If you look through the sheet of glass, then you can easily see objects on the other side, but if the glass sheet is painted, then you won't be able to see through it. An object that you can see through is transparent and an object that you can't see through is opaque. An object can't be both transparent and opaque, but it can have varying degrees of opacity.

So, how does transparency work in Illustrator? Transparency in Illustrator is essentially a single Opacity slider control that you can set from 0 to 100 percent. At 100 percent Opacity, no objects behind the current object can be seen; at 0 percent, the object is completely transparent.

When objects in Illustrator are stacked on top of each other, you can adjust the Opacity setting of the top object to make a lower object show through. The lower object will not be as clear as it would be if nothing were on top of it, but it will be visible. Figure 12-1 shows an image with a blue rectangle positioned on top of it. The Opacity of the rectangle is set to 50 percent, which lets the image underneath be visible.

Figure 12-1: Transparency lets objects that lie beneath be visible.

Transparency also affects the object color depending on the Blending Mode. Illustrator offers several different Blending Modes that can be used with transparent objects. This is further discussed in the "Blending Modes" section later in this chapter.

The Transparency palette

The Transparency palette (see Figure 12-2) doesn't come with a lot of flashy features, settings, or controls. You can open the Transparency palette with the Window ⇨ Show Transparency menu. You can also use the Shift+F10 keyboard shortcut.

Figure 12-2: The Transparency palette

The main setting is the Opacity value, which you can use to set the amount of opacity to apply to the object. Objects with an Opacity setting of 100 hide all objects behind them and objects with an Opacity setting of 0 are completely invisible.

The Transparency palette also includes a drop-down list of Blending Modes. These Blending Modes define how the colors of background objects are mixed with transparent objects. All the Blending Modes will be covered later in the chapter.

The Transparency palette also includes a preview pane where you can see a thumbnail result of the current setting. This preview pane includes space to show the selected shaped and any Opacity Masks that are applied.

The palette includes settings for making an object an Opacity Mask. Opacity Masks aren't visible, but they apply their Opacity setting to all objects that they cover. You can use the pop-up menu, which is accessible via the right-pointing arrow icon in the upper-right corner of the palette, to make and release Opacity Masks. You can also easily invert the Opacity Mask by selecting the Invert Mask option. The Clip option will make the Opacity Mask double for a clipping mask also.

At the bottom of the Transparency palette are checkboxes for three options. The Isolate Blending checkbox causes the Opacity setting to affect only the other objects within the current group or layer. The Knockout Group option causes the transparency settings to not affect the other objects in the current group or layer. The background objects are still affected by the transparency though.

For the Opacity & Mask Define Knockout Shape, you can use the Opacity Mask to define how much the object's transparency has an effect. If the Opacity Mask is 100 percent, then the area will be completely knocked out or the transparency will not have any effect on the other objects in the group. However, if the Opacity Mask is 0 percent, then the transparency setting will have full effect over the other objects in the group or layer. These options will be covered in more detail later in the chapter.

ASK TOULOUSE: Why Did It Take So Long to Include Transparency in Illustrator?

Twiggy: These transparency features are great.

Toulouse: Yes, it adds a whole new dimension to the product.

Twiggy: Why didn't transparency show up a couple of versions ago?

Toulouse: Well, the Adobe team has worked hard to include powerful features in each new Illustrator release. Transparency wasn't included until it was ready.

Twiggy: What was so tricky about including transparency?

Toulouse: The trickiest part about transparency is determining how to mix the colors of the current object with the objects that show through underneath.

Twiggy: Isn't that what the Blending Modes are for?

Toulouse: Yes, the Blending Modes offer several different ways to mix the color.

Twiggy: I understand it was tricky, but why the delay?

Toulouse: You don't sound very grateful.

Twiggy: Oh, I'm grateful. I finally have a way to make spaceships disappear.

Toulouse: Printing transparent objects was another major hurdle to overcome.

Twiggy: Did I say that I'm grateful?

Object versus group and layer transparency

Transparency can be set for an individual object, a group, or a layer. The selection that the transparency is being applied to is displayed in the thumbnail within the Transparency palette. The transparency settings for individual objects are additive. For example, if you set an object's Opacity to 50 and the object also belongs to a layer whose Opacity setting is 50, then the object's overall transparency will be twice the other objects in the layer.

You can control the transparency of the entire layer by targeting the layer and adjusting the Opacity slider. To target a layer, you simply need to click in the small circle located to the right of the layer name in the Layer palette. This affects the global setting for the layer including all the objects contained on that layer and any future objects that are added to the layer.

Blending Modes

The Transparency palette also includes many different Blending Modes. These are applied using the drop-down list found near the top-left corner of the Transparency palette. The Blending Mode affects how the colors of the overlapping objects will mix. The colors that are mixed are the *base color*, which is the color under the current transparent object, and the *blend color*, which is the color of the transparent object.

The various Blending Modes include the following:

- ✦ **Normal.** The blend color isn't affected by the base color.

- ✦ **Multiply.** The blend color is multiplied by the base color. This always results in a darker color.

- ✦ **Screen.** The inverse of the blend color is multiplied by the inverse of the base color. This always results in a lighter color.

- ✦ **Overlay.** The base color is mixed with the blend color to produce a lighter or darker color depending on the base color.

- ✦ **Soft Light.** The colors are lightened if the blend color is light, or darkened if the blend color is dark. This Blending Mode is like shining a soft light on the object.

- ✦ **Hard Light.** The colors are screened if the blend color is light, or multiplied if the blend color is dark. This Blending Mode is like shining a hard contrasting light on the object.

- ✦ **Color Dodge.** The colors are brightened toward the blend color.

- ✦ **Color Burn.** The colors are darkened toward the blend color.

- ✦ **Darken.** All colors lighter than the blend color are replaced with the blend color. Darker colors are left alone.

- ✦ **Lighten.** All colors darker than the blend color are replaced with the blend color. Lighter colors are left alone.

- ✦ **Difference.** Subtracts the brighter of the two colors from the other one.

- ✦ **Exclusion.** Also subtracts the brighter of the two colors from the other one, but results in greater contrast.

- ✦ **Hue.** Maintains the hue of the blend color while adopting the luminance and saturation of the base color.

- ✦ **Saturation.** Maintains the saturation of the blend color while adopting the luminance and the hue of the base color.

- ✦ **Color.** Maintains the hue and saturation of the blend color while adopting the luminance of the base color.

- ✦ **Luminosity.** Maintains the luminance of the blend color while adopting the hue and saturation of the base color.

You might notice how many of the Blending Mode options are opposites. For most of the transparency characteristics such as brightness, contrast, luminance, and saturation, you can increase or decrease the amount, but these characteristics are often more confusing than seeing the actual results of each Blending Mode. Over time as you gain experience, you will learn which Blending Mode to use at which time. Until then, experimentation is your best friend.

Figure 12-3 shows the various Blending Modes. The six-pointed star is placed underneath the circle shape. The circle Opacity setting is set to 50 percent and the various Blending Modes are selected. All of the available Blending Modes are shown in the following figure, except for the Color Blending Mode, which wouldn't show much when printed as a black-and-white image.

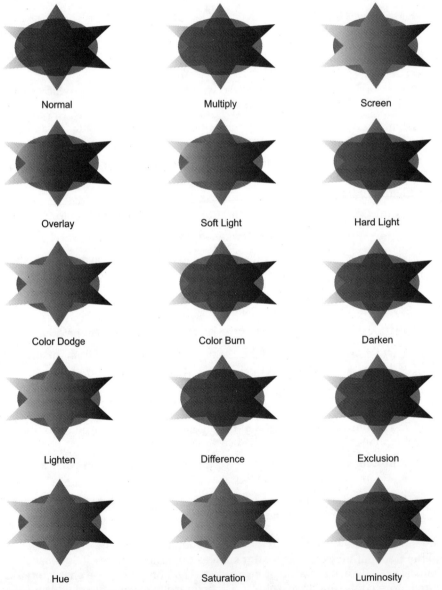

Figure 12-3: The different Blending Modes

Opacity Masks

Opacity Masks are similar to Clipping Masks that are created with the Object menu except that the transparency of the objects under the Opacity Mask are masked according to the luminance of the mask that appears above. Opacity Masks are created from the top object of the selected objects. If only a single object is selected, then the Opacity Mask has no effect.

 You can find more details on Clipping Masks in Chapter 7, "Organizing Artwork."

To create an Opacity Mask, select several objects with the mask object positioned on top of the other objects and choose Make Opacity Mask from the pop-up menu in the Transparency palette. You can access the pop-up menu by clicking the arrow icon in the upper-right corner of the palette. The Make Opacity Mask option makes the masked objects and the Opacity Mask visible as thumbnails in the Transparency palette, as shown in Figure 12-4.

Figure 12-4: The Transparency palette

You can edit the Opacity Mask by clicking its thumbnail in the Transparency palette. This selects the object that was used to create the Opacity Mask. You can also edit the transparency of the mask object by changing the Opacity setting and Blending Mode. When you finish editing the Opacity Mask, you can click the left thumbnail to exit from Opacity Mask editing mode.

Once an Opacity Mask is created, the object and the mask will be linked and will move together. If the link is broken, then the Opacity Mask can be moved independently of objects that it masks. Breaking a link can be done using the pop-up menu by selecting Unlink Opacity Mask or by clicking the link icon that appears between the two thumbnails.

To view the objects in their unmasked form, you can disable the Opacity Mask with the Disable Opacity Mask option in the pop-up menu. The Release Opacity Mask option in the pop-up menu removes any created Opacity Mask.

Caution   If you create an Opacity Mask using three or more objects, then for some reason, the option to Release the Opacity Mask does not appear. This could potentially leave you in a tricky spot. If you Ungroup the objects, then you can get back to the original objects, or using the Undo feature can also get you back. Hopefully, Adobe will fix this problem in a future release.

You can use the Invert Mask checkbox to make all object parts outside of the current Opacity Mask visible. Figure 12-5 shows two objects that use an Opacity Mask in which one is the inverse of the other. The object on the left uses both the Clip and Invert Mask options and the object on the right has both the Clip and Invert Mask options disabled and the Opacity for the mask set to 80 percent. The pop-up menu also has an option to make all new Opacity Masks inverted by default with the new Opacity Masks are Inverted option.

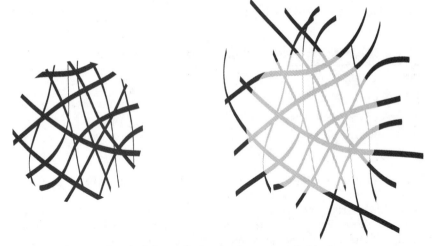

Figure 12-5: The Opacity Mask is applied to both groups of objects.

To apply an Opacity Mask to an object or group of objects, follow these steps:

1. Create an object on top of the objects to which you wish to apply the Opacity Mask.

2. Select the mask object along with all the objects that it will mask.

3. Select Make Opacity Mask from the pop-up menu in the Transparency palette.

Figure 12-6 shows a circular Opacity Mask applied to an object. The mask was filled with a grayscale gradient. Notice how the Opacity Mask has made the right side of the image more transparent than the left side.

Figure 12-6: A gradient Opacity Mask is applied to an object group. The left side is less transparent than the right side.

Printing and Exporting Transparency

The one sure way to export a document that contains transparency is to use the Photoshop (PSD) format. This format maintains transparency and layers.

The GIF and PNG formats that are used frequently on the Web include support for background transparency, but this type of transparency support is very different from Illustrator's new transparency features. These raster-based formats can only specify a single palette color that will be transparent. All pixels that use this specified color will appear transparent when the image is viewed within a browser.

Cross-Reference You can specify the background transparent color using the Save for Web window, which you can open using the File ➪ Save For Web menu option. Chapter 17, "Using Illustrator to Generate Web Graphics," explains this window and its features in detail.

All other formats flatten the transparent sections prior to exporting the document. The transparent sections will be dealt with depending on the settings in the Transparency screen of the Document Setup dialog box shown in Figure 12-7.

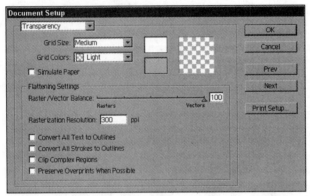

Figure 12-7: The Transparency screen of the Document Setup dialog box

You can open this dialog box by selecting File ➪ Document Setup. View the Transparency screen by selecting it from the popup menu/drop-down box at the top of the dialog box.

The Printing & Export slider has five different Quality/Speed settings ranging from Lower/Faster to Higher/Slower. These settings define how the transparent sections within a document are treated. Below the slider is a brief explanation of the current setting, as follows:

✦ For the leftmost setting, the entire document and all transparent sections are rasterized. This setting spools the image to the printer very quickly, but has the lowest resolution of all the settings.

✦ The second setting only maintains vector information for some of the simpler objects such as circles and rectangles. All transparent sections are rasterized. This improves the resolution for some objects and is still fairly fast when printing.

✦ The middle setting only rasterizes the most complex transparent sections. Most of the other objects are maintained as vector objects. This setting provides a good balance between speed and quality.

✦ The fourth setting keeps vector information on all but extremely complex transparent sections. This setting slows down print times dramatically, but results in good-quality output.

✦ The final setting exports all objects as vectors. If the document contains complex transparent sections, then the print times will be very long, but the quality will be maximized.

For all transparent sections that need to be rasterized, the setting in the Printing & Export panel of the Document Setup dialog box will determine the dpi. The default rasterization resolution is 300 dpi.

At any time you can flatten a transparent object using the Object ⇨ Flatten Transparency command. This command opens a simplified version of the Document Setup dialog box with a slider that you can use to change the Quality/Speed setting and the rasterization resolution value.

ASK TOULOUSE: Eliminating Color Stitching Artifacts

Buck Rogers: Why does it look like the raster and vector sections of my artwork don't line up?

Toulouse: It sounds like you've got a Color Stitching problem.

Buck Rogers: I'm a space explorer, not a seamstress. How could I have a stitching problem?

Toulouse: Some printers will have trouble where vector artwork appears adjacent to a raster section.

Buck Rogers: What causes this problem?

Toulouse: If you set the Quality/Speed slider in the Printing & Export panel of the Document Setup dialog box to the second setting, then quite likely portions of your artwork were rasterized when printed.

Buck Rogers: Hey, you're right. I did have it set to the second setting. Which setting should I use?

Toulouse: It should get better with higher settings. Try using the third setting and if that doesn't work, then try the fourth setting. You should also enable the Clip Complex Regions option.

Buck Rogers: What about the settings on either end of the slider?

Toulouse: Well, the first slider setting will cause the entire document to be rasterized, which could affect your quality. The final setting will maintain the entire document as vectors, which could take a long time to print.

Buck Rogers: In the 25th century, we shouldn't have these kinds of problems.

Toulouse: Sorry, you can only expect so much from Illustrator, version 2,307.

Buck Rogers: It's worth the money though.

The Document Setup dialog box also includes some convenient options that give the document a higher chance that it will print without any errors. These options include

✦ Convert All Text to Outlines

✦ Convert All Strokes to Outlines

✦ Clip Complex Regions

✦ Preserve Overprints When Possible

For more information about printing issues, see Chapter 16, "Understanding Printing, Separations, and Trapping."

Working with Transparency

You have many ways to use transparency with your artwork. The following is a sampling of what is possible. By experimenting, you will be able to find more possibilities.

Fading transparency with the Feather effect

The Feather effect, which is applied using the Effects ➪ Stylize ➪ Feather menu option, can be used to gradually fade an object from opaque to transparent. This is generally used to fade Fills, but you can use it on strokes as well. The Feather effect can also be applied to a group of objects or to a targeted layer.

You can find more information on using effects such as Feather in Chapter 13, "Using Styles, Effects, and Filters."

Creating a Knockout Group

When objects within a group are placed on top of one another, you can specify whether the top color covers the underlying objects within the group or whether the objects underneath are visible. This is accomplished using the Knockout Group.

Within the Transparency palette, you can select the Knockout Group checkbox to enable the knockout feature. To create a Knockout Group, follow these steps:

1. Select a group several objects into a group with the Object ➪ Group command.

2. Expand the layer in the Layers palette.

3. Target the group in the Layers palette by clicking the target radio button to the right of the group name.

4. Enable the Knockout Group option in the Transparency palette.

Figure 12-8 shows a group of objects with the Knockout Group option selected and the same group with the option not selected. Notice how objects within the Knockout group cover the other objects within the same group.

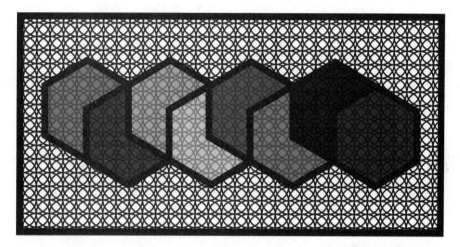

Knockout Group

No Knockout Group

Figure 12-8: Using a Knockout Group (top) and with no Knockout Group (bottom)

Stair-step gradient effect

Using transparency enables you to create some cool effects. Think of the invisible man. Now *that's* a cool effect. The transparency features won't let you make anyone invisible to wander the neighborhood, but it will let you make your objects invisible or slightly invisible. By the way, invisible objects don't add much to the visual aspect of your images.

You can simulate a stair-step gradient effect by gradually decreasing the transparency of an object. This trick makes the object seem to disappear into nothing. This is a quick effect that is easier to use than a complex gradient. It also has the advantage of having precise boundaries.

To create a stair-step gradient effect, follow these steps:

1. Create a shape to apply the effect to and duplicate several times.

2. Select the shape and scale each successive copy a given percentage.

3. Adjust the Opacity setting in the Transparency panel for each successive copy.

4. Select all the objects and align them vertically and horizontally using the Align palette.

Figure 12-9 shows a logo that uses this effect. The transparency feature in this effect only changes the color of the successive objects.

Figure 12-9: The stair-step gradient effect

Cutout shapes

Using an Opacity Mask, you can cut out a section of your image to highlight a certain area. Another cool trick is to use the Feather effect or gradients to gradually fade the visibility of an object to the edges of the cutout. The nice thing about this effect is that the cutout (or Opacity Mask) can be any shape.

To create a cutout shape, follow these steps:

1. Load an image that you intend to use the cutout on.

2. Add a shape or object that you want to use for the cutout and position it to cover the area that you wish to highlight.

3. Fill the shape with the color black. This maximizes the visibility of the center of the spotlight.

4. Apply the Feather effect to the shape (choose Effect ➪ Stylize ➪ Feather).

5. Select both the image and the shape. Make sure the shape appears on top of the image.

6. Select the Make Opacity Mask option from the Transparency palette pop-up menu.

Figure 12-10 shows the cutout effect applied to a raster image. For reference, the original image is shown above the cutout effect.

Figure 12-10: A feathered cutout is used to highlight a section of the original image.

Spotlight effect

Placing transparent objects with different Blending Modes on top of an image enables you to create some neat effects. For example, if you create a circle and assign it an Opacity that is less than 100 percent and set the Blending Mode to Overlay, then the circle will appear like a spotlight. We've always wanted to be placed in the middle of a bright hot spotlight and now we have the chance.

To create a spotlight effect, follow these steps:

1. Load an image that you intend to use the spotlight effect on.

2. Add a shape or object that you want to use for the spotlight and position it to cover the area that you wish to highlight.

3. Fill the shape with the color black.

4. In the Transparency palette, set the Opacity to 50 percent and select the Overlay Blending Mode.

Figure 12-11 shows the spotlight effect applied to a simple image. Depending on the image, you could also try to use the Soft Light, Hard Light, Lighten, or Luminosity Blending Modes to create a similar effect.

Figure 12-11: The spotlight effect

Fading text

Another good effect that you can accomplish with transparency is to cause text to fade away. You have a couple of different ways to do this. One way to fade text is to change the text to individual objects using the Type ⇨ Create Outlines command. You can then individually select each letter and apply a successively lesser Opacity value to each. The text on the top of Figure 12-12 shows this method.

Disappear
Disappear

Figure 12-12: Fading text

A more gradual method is to use an object with a gradient applied to it as an Opacity Mask, as follows:

1. Type some text using the Type tool and fill it with a color.

2. Using the Rectangle tool to create a rectangle that completely covers the text.

3. Fill the rectangle with a black-and-white gradient.

4. Select both the text and the gradient filled rectangle.

5. From the Transparency palette pop-up menu, select Make Opacity Mask.

The text on the bottom of Figure 12-12 shows the results of these steps. You can adjust how quickly the text fades by altering the midpoint for the gradient. This technique can be applied to bitmap images, text, or any other type of object.

Summary

Transparency deals with those things that you can see and things you can't see. Controlling the visibility of objects enables some interesting effects. In this chapter, you learned that

✦ The Opacity setting in the Transparency palette sets how transparent an object is.

✦ The Transparency palette includes many different controls for defining how transparency is applied to an object.

✦ Transparency can be applied to objects and groups of objects.

✦ If you target a layer, the entire layer can be made transparent.

✦ Illustrator includes a variety of Blending Modes that define how the colors mix.

✦ You can use Opacity Masks to set the transparency of the underlying objects based on their luminance.

✦ Opacity Masks can be unlinked, disabled, edited, and inverted using the controls in the Transparency palette.

✦ The Transparency screen of the Document Setup dialog box includes settings for how transparent sections are rasterized.

✦ You can use the Feather effect to fade Fills and Strokes from opaque to transparent.

✦ The Knockout Group option can hide the color of objects underneath objects within the same group.

✦ Effects such as stair-step gradients, highlighting with cutout shapes, spotlights, and fading text are possible with transparency.

✦   ✦   ✦

Using Styles, Effects, and Filters

The concept of styles is a powerful addition to Illustrator that enables defined appearance attributes to be saved and reapplied to other objects. This is an easy way to maintain consistency across a range of graphics.

Another useful set of features is classified as Effects. You can apply effects to objects to change their appearance, much like filters, but they don't change the underlying structure of the object, so text can still be edited as text and path can still be moved as desired while maintaining the effect. You can also modify and edit paths, which have an effect applied, like normal paths, in addition to removing and editing effects using the Appearance palette.

Filters are another way to change the appearance of objects, but they permanently change the structure of an object.

How Styles Work

Like they say in Hollywood — if you have style, you have it all. Actually, we don't know if anyone in Hollywood says that, but it certainly sounds like something they would say. Either way, Illustrator users are fortunate because the program brims with styles and you can even create your own styles if you like.

Before you run wild with style, you first need to learn about appearance. The appearance of an object is how it looks, but it is more than that. Appearance properties are object properties that you can edit and remove to return the object to its former state. This can include its Fill color, Stroke properties,

Transparency, or any effect that changes how it looks. Filters are not appearance properties because they cannot be changed back. All appearance attributes are controlled from the Appearance palette.

The Appearance palette

The Appearance palette is like the immunization record for an object. It contains a list of all the current attributes that have been applied to an object. These attributes include the Fill color, the Stroke color, the Stroke Width or Brush name, the Transparency setting and Blending Mode, and any effects that have been applied to the object.

The Appearance palette is divided into several sections. The top section shows the current selection. This can be an object, a layer, or a group or objects. Below the top section comes a list of Effects, Strokes, Fills, and Transparency that are applied to the current selection. The Fills and Strokes are listed according to their stacking order from front to back. The Appearance attributes (shown in Figure 13-1) applied to an object include a 4-pt black Stroke, a light-blue Fill color, and an Opacity setting of 70 percent.

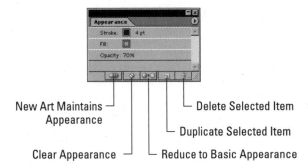

New Art Maintains Appearance

Clear Appearance

Delete Selected Item

Duplicate Selected Item

Reduce to Basic Appearance

Figure 13-1: The Appearance palette

Tip

Although it is hidden in the previous figure, you can make a small thumbnail image of the current selection visible to the left of the selection name at the top of the Appearance palette. You can hide or unhide this thumbnail image by selecting the Hide Thumbnail option in the pop-up menu.

You can rearrange the order of the attributes by dragging within the list that is in the Appearance palette. The order of the attributes affects the appearance of the object. Appearance attributes can only be moved within their respective sections. For example, effects can only be reordered with other effects and Fills and Strokes can only be reordered with other Fills and Strokes.

Figure 13-2 shows a star shape that has two effects applied to it — Roughen and Twirl. The star on the left has the Twirl effect applied first, followed by the Roughen effect. The star on the right is copied from the first one and the order of the Twirl and Roughen effects are switched in the Appearance palette.

Figure 13-2: The order of the effects affects the final appearance.

The Appearance palette also makes editing attributes easy. If you double-click an attribute, the palette or dialog box that was used to create the appearance opens, enabling you to edit the appearance. For example, the settings for many effects are set using a dialog box. The Effects dialog box appears whenever its attribute is double-clicked.

Using the Appearance palette's pop-up menu, which is accessed by clicking the arrow icon in the upper-right corner of the palette, or the icons at the bottom of the palette, you can add appearance attributes. To add a Stroke or a Fill, select Add New Fill or Add New Stroke from the pop-up menu. This creates a new Stroke or Fill above the other Strokes and Fills, using the current Stroke and Fill settings.

If the Fills or Strokes include multiple attributes such as color and transparency, an arrow appears to the left of the attribute that can be expanded to show all the attributes separately.

You can also delete and duplicate attributes using the pop-up menu or the icons at the bottom of the Appearance palette. To do so, select an attribute, and then use the Remove Item or Duplicate Item menu options. To clear the current object of all its current appearance attributes, choose Clear Appearance in the pop-up menu or click the Clear Appearance icon at the bottom of the palette.

The Reduce to Basic Appearance menu option and icon remove any effects and extra Fills and Strokes from the current selection. When this command is used, only the top Stroke and Fill colors remain and the Transparency is set to the default value (see Figure 13-3).

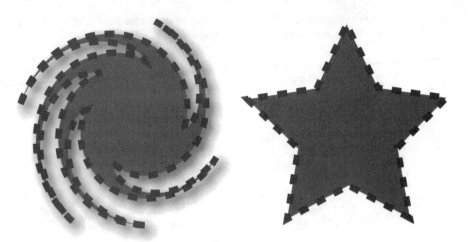

Figure 13-3: The appearance of the shape (left) is reduced to its basic appearance (right).

ASK TOULOUSE: Applying Styles

Shirley: Wow, I just used the Paint Bucket and the entire look of my object changed.

Toulouse: Yes, you just applied a style.

Shirley: Laverne always said that I have style.

Toulouse: You can pick up a style from another object using the Eyedropper.

Shirley: What?! Years in beauty school and you're telling me that all I need for style is an eyedropper?

Toulouse: I can't help your personal style, but in Illustrator, you can pick up styles using the Eyedropper tool and apply them with the Paint Bucket tool.

Shirley: What kind of styles can I pick up?

Toulouse: Styles include anything that is listed in the Appearance palette, including Fill and Stroke color, Transparency settings and any effects.

Shirley: Can I specify which styles to get?

Toulouse: Sure, just double-click the Eyedropper tool and the Eyedropper/Paint Bucket Options dialog box appears. From this dialog box, you can select which style attributes to pick and apply.

Shirley: Great! I'll never be short on style again.

Toulouse: Illustrator to the rescue once again.

Whenever new objects are created, the attributes that are currently set in the Appearance palette are used to create the new object. If you only want the basic appearance attributes to be used, you can select the New Art Has Basic Appearance menu option or icon in the Appearance palette. This causes any new object to be created using the basic appearance attributes.

Because colors can be added to groups and layers, you may run into trouble when individual objects within the group have different colors. The pop-up menu has a setting called Layer/Group Overrides Color. If this setting is enabled, any color that is applied to a group or layer overrides the current object color. If you don't want the object color to change, you can simply disable this setting.

The Styles palette

Once you have the perfect appearance attributes established for an object, you can save the style so it can be applied to another object at another time. Styles are simply a way of saving the settings of the Appearance palette. The Styles palette holds these styles and offers several preset styles. Figure 13-4 shows the default Styles palette.

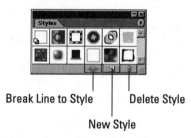

Break Line to Style   Delete Style

New Style

Figure 13-4: The Styles palette

You can apply styles in the Styles palette to an object by dragging the style from the Styles palette to the object that you want to apply it to. A style can be applied to an entire layer by targeting the layer, and selecting a style in the Styles palette. To target a layer, click the small radio button to the right of the layer name in the Layers palette.

You can also apply styles using the Eyedropper and Paint Bucket tools. Before you can use these tools to transfer styles, you need to specify that these tools pick up the style attributes. You can set this feature using the Eyedropper/Paint Bucket Options dialog box, as shown in Figure 13-5. Open this dialog box by double-clicking either the Eyedropper or Paint Bucket tools.

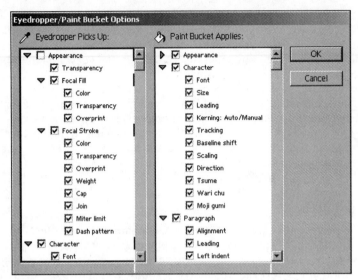

Figure 13-5: The Eyedropper/Paint Bucket Options dialog box

You can add styles to the Styles palette at any time by dragging the thumbnail image from the top of the Appearance palette to the Styles palette. Another way to create new styles is to click the New Style icon at the bottom of the Styles palette or select the New Style options from the pop-up menu accessible from the arrow icon in the upper-right corner of the palette. This actually duplicates the currently selected style. This duplicated style can then be edited to create a new style. To delete a style, click the Delete Style icon or select Delete Style from the pop-up menu.

Each style in the Styles palette can be named. Positioning the mouse over the top of the style displays the style name. If you double-click a style, the Style Options dialog box appears and you can change the name of a style. You can also display the Style Options dialog box by selecting Style Options from the pop-up menu.

The Styles palette can be set to three different views. Using the pop-up menu, you can select Swatch View, which is the default, Small List View, or Large List View. All views show a thumbnail of the style, but the last two also list the style name.

Several styles can be selected and merged into a single style. To select several styles, hold down the ⌘ [Ctrl] key while clicking several styles. A small black line frame appears around the thumbnail of the selected styles in Swatch View or the name is highlighted in the other views. When two or more styles are selected, Merge Styles appears in the pop-up menu. By selecting this command, you can merge style attributes into one style. This creates a new merged style at the end of the palette.

You can change the order of the styles in the Styles palette by dragging and dropping styles to their new location. The pop-up menu also includes some commands for rearranging the styles. The Sort by Name option sorts the styles alphabetically by name. The Select All Unused command inverts the current selection. This provides a way to quickly select all the styles.

When a style in the Styles palette is applied to an object, the attributes of that style appear in the Appearance palette. This creates a link between the selected object and the named style. If the style is changed in the Styles palette, all objects that have a link to the style are updated as the style is changed. You can break this link by clicking the Break Link to Style icon at the bottom of the palette or selecting the Break Link to Style option from the pop-up menu.

The Style Libraries

You can save styles into a library that is similar to the libraries for the Brush and Swatch Libraries. To view the available libraries, select Window ⇨ Style Libraries.

With a style library palette open, you can apply styles or move styles to the default Styles palette by dragging styles from the library. Dragging a style from a library to the Styles palette does not remove the style from the Library palette.

The files that make up the Style Libraries are located in the Style Libraries directory or folder where Illustrator is installed. If you select Window ⇨ Style Libraries ⇨ Other Library, a file dialog box opens where you can load a new library that is accessible by the Style Libraries menu. The library files need to be in Illustrator (AI) format.

Using Effects

Effects are like magic tricks in that they make something appear that isn't there. Effects can change the appearance of an object without permanently changing the object.

If you find an effect that works well and you want to use it again, the Effect ⇨ Apply Last Effect (⌘+Shift+E [Ctrl+Shift+E]) menu will apply the most recently applied effect to the current selection. You can also use this command to apply an effect multiple times. If you want to change the effect slightly, you can use the Effect ⇨ Last Effect (⌘+Shift+Option+E [Ctrl+Shift+Alt+E]) menu to open the dialog box of the last used effect. From the dialog box, you can change the settings and apply the effect.

Effects in the Effect menu can be applied to both raster bitmaps images and to vector objects. If a raster bitmaps image is affected by an effect, the settings in the Document Raster Effects Settings dialog box, shown in Figure 13-6, are used for the effect. This dialog box can be opened using the Effect ⇨ Document Raster Effects Settings menu option.

Using this dialog box, you can set the Color Model to be RGB or CMYK and also the resolution in Pixels per Inch (ppi). For web images, the Screen setting at 72 ppi is sufficient, but artwork that will find its way to a printer should be saved at a higher resolution setting. The Background of the resulting raster image can be set to White or Transparent. You can also set the image to be clipped (which is the same as setting the Background to Transparent). You can clear the image from any other objects by adding some space around the image. The Anti-Alias option will remove any stair-stepping artifacts.

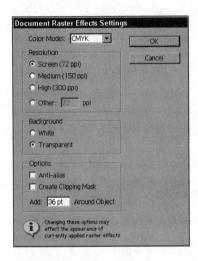

Figure 13-6: The Document Raster Effects Settings dialog box

Many different effects exist, categorized into several different groups. You can find all these effects in the Effect menu.

Convert to Shape effects

The Convert to Shape effects include Rectangle, Rounded Rectangle and Ellipse. The Shape Options dialog box, shown in Figure 13-7, that appears when you apply one of these effects lets you set the dimensions of the shape either Absolute or Relative. You can also select the Preview checkbox to see the effect applied within the document.

Framing an object

This effect can be used to frame the current object with one of the available shapes from the drop-down menu. Follow these steps to frame an object:

1. Select an object and duplicate it with the Copy and Paste commands.

2. Move the duplicated copy directly on top of the original object.

3. Select the Effect ⇨ Convert To Shape ⇨ Ellipse effect.

4. In the Shape Options dialog box, select the Relative radio button and enter Extra Width and Height values for the white space to appear between the object and the frame edge.

5. With the frame shape selected, select Object ⇨ Arrange ⇨ Send Backward to position the frame behind the object. Figure 13-8 shows the framed object.

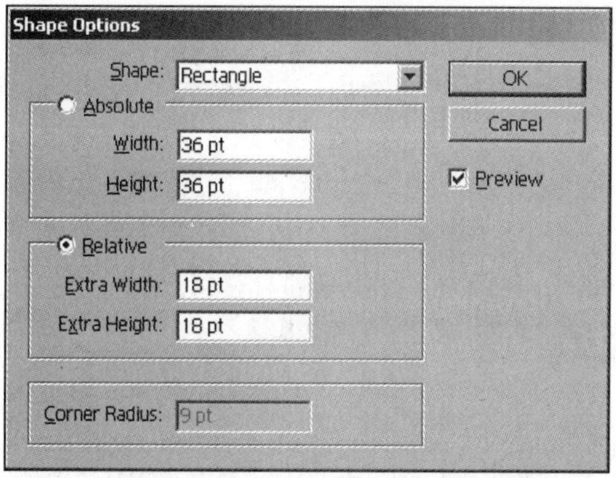

Figure 13-7: The Shape Options dialog box

Figure 13-8: An object framed using the Convert to Shape effect

Distort & Transform effects

The Distort & Transform effects are used to change the shape, orientation, and position of an object. You find these effects under the Effect ➪ Distort & Transform menu. This menu includes the following:

✦ **Free Distort** enables you to distort an object by moving one of its four corner points. This effect displays the current selection in a dialog box surrounded by a Bounding Box. On each corner of the Bounding Box is a control handle that can be moved within the dialog box. By moving the corner control handles, you can distort the object.

✦ **Pucker & Bloat** causes the path to move towards or away from the path's anchor points. The Pucker & Bloat dialog box includes a slider with Pucker and Bloat on opposite ends that lets you specify a percentage value.

✦ **Roughen** randomly moves points along the path, creating a rough, jagged look. The Roughen dialog box includes options for altering the Size, Detail, and Point type. The Size value determines the maximum possible movement of the path from its midline. The Detail value specifies the number of times per length of measurement the path is altered. The Point options can be either Smooth or Corner. The Corner Points option causes abrupt changes in the path to appear as sharp corners.

✦ **Scribble and Tweak** moves the path away from the anchor points in either a horizontal or vertical direction. The Scribble and Tweak dialog box includes sliders for the Horizontal and Vertical directions. These values can be either Relative or Absolute. You can also specify if the modifications allow Anchor, In, or Out Points to move.

✦ **Transform** lets you Scale, Move, or Rotate an object using a dialog box that is similar to the Transform Each dialog box available from the Object ➪ Transform menu. The Scale and Move transformations include sliders for the Horizontal and Vertical directions. You can also specify number of Copies, reflect the object along the X or Y axis, or set the transformations to be Random.

✦ **Twist** produces the same results as the Twist tool. The Twist dialog box includes an Angle value that determines how much the object is twisted.

✦ **Zig Zag** distorts the path using a regular pattern of back-and-forth distortions. The Zig Zag dialog box includes options for Size, Ridges per Segment, and Point type. The Size value determines the maximum distance that the path can be distorted from its midline. This value can be either a Relative or Absolute value. The Ridges per Segment setting determines the frequency of the distortions. The Point type can be Smooth or Corner. Using the Corner Point type causes the path distortions to be sharp corners.

Cross-Reference   Most of these effects, with the exception of the Transform effect, are the same as the Distort filters that are covered in Chapter 10, "Transforming and Distorting Artwork." You can find additional details on these effects in that chapter.

Path effects

The Path effects are used to offset and outline paths and strokes. They include the following:

✦ **Offset Path** duplicates a selected path and offsets both the duplicate and the original a specified distance. The two copies are then joined using the specified Join type. Applying the Offset Path effect to a closed path does not create a duplicate, but only offsets the original object. When selecting Effect ⇨ Path ⇨ Offset Path, the Offset Path dialog box appears. In this dialog box, you can specify the Offset value, the Join type, and Miter Limit. You can specify negative Offset values.

✦ **Outline Object** replaces an object with a filled object that matches the original object. This lets you work with a simplified outline rather than with a complex object. If applied as an effect, you can later remove the effect using the Appearance palette.

✦ **Outline Stroke** is the same as the Outline Object effect except it is applied to stroked objects.

Cross-Reference

These Path effects are identical to functions found in the Object ⇨ Path menu. You can get more information on these Path effects in Chapter 5, "Selecting and Editing," which discusses the Path menu options.

Pathfinder effects

The Pathfinder effects include a full range of features for combining, splitting, and isolating objects. These effects create an appearance that is similar to the features offered in the Object ⇨ Path menu and in the Pathfinder palette.

These effects can only be applied to groups, layers, or type objects. The Pathfinder effects include:

✦ **Add** traces the outline of the selected objects and combines them into a single object. Any interior objects are deleted.

✦ **Intersect** combines the overlapping areas of two objects. Objects that don't overlap are deleted.

✦ **Exclude** makes any overlapping areas transparent.

✦ **Subtract** subtracts the front object from the back object.

✦ **Minus Back** is the opposite of the Minus Front effect. It subtracts the back object from the front object.

✦ **Divide** splits an object into its various components. You can select to delete or save any unfilled objects.

✦ **Trim** deletes any portion of a filled object that is obscured.

✦ **Merge** also deletes any portion of a filled object that is obscured. It also combines any filled overlapping sections that are the same color.

✦ **Crop** divides the objects into their components and delete any object that are outside of the topmost object.

✦ **Outline** divides the object into separate line segments. You can select to delete or save any unfilled objects.

✦ **Hard Mix** combines objects by taking the highest color component value of each filled object.

✦ **Soft Mix** lets underlying colors define separate sections. The objects are then divided into their component color sections.

✦ **Trap** identifies the lighter areas and prints them on top of the darker areas.

These Pathfinder effects are covered in Chapter 5, "Selecting and Editing."

Rasterize effects

The Effect ➪ Rasterize menu option is very useful because the available effects create the appearance of rasterizing an object without the commitment of doing so. For Web graphics, this lets you see the results of rasterizing and working with the pixelated image without losing the object's editing capabilities. The Effect ➪ Rasterize menu opens the Rasterize dialog box where you can specify the Resolution, Background, and Options such as Anti-Alias and Create Clipping Mask.

These effects work in the same way as the Object ➪ Rasterize option that is covered in more detail in Chapter 14, "Working with Pixels."

Stylize effects

The Stylize effects are used to enhance paths and objects. The Stylize effects include Add Arrowheads, Drop Shadow, Feather, Inner Glow, Outer Glow, and Round Corners. Three of these — Add Arrowheads, Drop Shadow, and Round Corners are available as filters and are covered later in this chapter.

The Feather effect

The Feather effect fades the edges of an object from solid to transparent. The effect opens a simple dialog box where you can specify the number of pixels to include in the feather process. The higher the number of pixels, the smoother the transition. The feature effect applies to Strokes as well as Fills.

To feather an object, follow these steps:

1. Select an object to feather.

2. Select the Effect ⇨ Stylize ⇨ Feather command. This opens the Feather dialog box.

3. Set the number of pixels to feather. Figure 13-9 shows the feather effect applied to several objects.

Figure 13-9: Several shapes with the Feather effect applied

Inner and Outer Glows

The Inner and Outer Glow effects create the appearance of a color that glows on the inner or outer edge of an object. Selecting either Effect ⇨ Stylize ⇨ Inner Glow or Effect ⇨ Stylize ⇨ Outer Glow opens a dialog box where you can specify the Blending Mode, the Glow color, the Opacity, and the Blur distance. The Inner Glow dialog box also adds Center and Edge radio buttons. The Center option creates a glow from the center of the object and the Edge option cause the glow to emanate from the object edges. Figure 13-10 shows the Inner Glow dialog box.

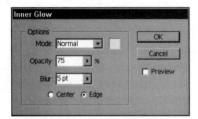

Figure 13-10: The Inner Glow dialog box

To apply an outer glow to an object, follow these steps:

1. Select an object to which you want to apply an outer glow.

2. Select Effect ⇨ Stylize ⇨ Outer Glow. This opens the Outer Glow dialog box.

3. Set the Blending Mode, the Glow color, the Opacity, and the Blur distance. Figure 13-11 shows the Outer Glow effect applied to several objects.

SVG Filters effects

Using the Effects ⇨ SVG Filters menu option, you can apply XML-defined filters to artwork.

The Effect ⇨ SVG Filters ⇨ Apply SVG Filter menu option will open a single dialog box that includes a list of all the available filters. From this dialog box, you can select any default or imported SVG filters. You can also maintain the available SVG filters by creating a new filter or deleting existing filters using the icons at the bottom of the dialog box. The list will only let you select a single filter at a time.

The Effect ⇨ Import SVG Filter will open a file dialog where you can select an SVG file to import. The imported SVG file will affect the selected objects and associate the needed XML code with the object.

Caution   Don't get confused with the menu option, SVG Filters, which is found in the Effect menu. The SVG format can define filters that affect how the object appears, but Illustrator applies these SVG filters as effects. The Filter menu doesn't contain any SVG Filters.

Figure 13-11: Several shapes with the Outer Glow effect applied

These effects will only be saved with the document if the file is saved using the SVG format. The default SVG Filter effects include

- ✦ **Alpha** adds some transparent turbulence to the object.
- ✦ **Bevel Shadow** adds a soft beveled shadow to the lower right of the object.
- ✦ **Cool Breeze** distorts the top edge of the object.
- ✦ **Dilate** increases the fill size of the object consistently around the outline of the object.
- ✦ **Erode** decreases the fill size of the object consistently around the outline of the object.

✦ **Gaussian Blur** blurs the object along its edges using the Gaussian algorithm.

✦ **Pixel Play** applies a lighting effect to the object.

✦ **Shadow** adds a hard shadow to the lower right of the object.

✦ **Static** replaces the fill color with transparent static interference.

✦ **Turbulence** adds transparent turbulent effects to the object.

✦ **Woodgrain** changes the fill color to be a woodgrain colored effect.

Chapter 17, "Using Illustrator to Generate Web Graphics," covers the details of the SVG format including how to use and edit SVG filters.

Warp effects

The Warp effects can be used to change the shape and outline of objects. Selecting any of the Warp effects from the Effect ➪ Warp submenu will open the Warp Options dialog box where you can select any of the Warp effects. You can also specify to distort the object Vertically or Horizontally and set the Bend amount.

In addition to the Warp tools, Illustrator 10 also includes a broad set of Warp effects.

The Warp effects, which can be selected from the Warp Options dialog box or directly from the Effect ➪ Warp submenu include the following:

✦ **Arc** distorts the object as if it were being wrapped around a circular shape.

✦ **Arc Lower and Arc Upper** bends the lower (or top) edge of the object outward and distorts the interior section of the object to follow these distorted edges.

✦ **Arch** bends the top and bottom edges of an object and distorts the object's interior.

✦ **Bulge** bows the top and bottom edges of the object outward.

✦ **Shell Lower and Shell Upper** change the shape of the object to resemble a shell with a larger (or smaller) base.

✦ **Flag** distorts the object to look like a flag.

✦ **Wave** distorts the interior portions of an object like the Flag effect without distorting its outer edges.

✦ **Fish** bows one side of the object outward and the opposite sides inward to resemble a fish.

✦ **Rise** makes the opposite edge of the object rise vertically and the connecting edges warp to connect the risen edge.

✦ **Fisheye** bows the interior of the object outward while keeping the edges from moving.

✦ **Inflate** bows all outer edges of the object outward as if the object were being filled with air.

✦ **Squeeze** bows all outer edges of the object inward as if the object were being deflated.

✦ **Twist** rotates the interior portions of the object while keeping the outer edges from moving.

Chapter 10, "Transforming and Distorting Artwork," covers the details and includes examples of the Warp effects.

Photoshop filter effects

All of the Photoshop effects that are available at the bottom of the Effect menu are also available as filters. The advantage of applying an effect over applying the same filter is that the effect can be removed by deleting the effect from the Appearance palette. Applying effects is much more demanding on your system memory. The benefit of using filters is similar to that of flattening layers — it can save valuable system resources such as internal memory.

All the Photoshop filters presented in the Effect menu are covered in Chapter 14, "Working with Pixels."

Filters in Illustrator

In addition to changing the appearance of images, most of the filters in Illustrator perform other tasks that took hours to do manually in previous versions of Illustrator. In a way, most of these filters work as intelligent macros, and they enable you to produce a variety of effects.

Some filters, such as the Zig Zag filter, seem to perform simple tasks. In reality, however, these filters are complex, math-based programs that accomplish certain tasks faster than the fastest illustrator can dream of performing without them.

So why are all these functions in the Filter menu, and not just functions within the software? Because none of them are really integrated into Illustrator; instead, each filter is an individual file called a *plug-in*, which resides in the Plug-Ins folder. For a filter to be available, the plug-in must be in the Plug-Ins folder or be in a folder that is recognized by the Preferences dialog box as a Plug-in folder.

Adobe, in its marketing wisdom, initially pushed two filters with grunge-like names: Punk and Bloat. To be honest, we rarely use either of these filters, though we were intrigued the first time we saw them demonstrated. Cool names, little functionality. The same thing applies to the Twist filter, which produces some amazing (but not very useful) effects.

The original Punk & Bloat and Twirl filters have actually been renamed Pucker & Bloat and Twist and can now be found in the Filter ⇨ Distort menu. Their function-ality has been added to two of the Warp tools also. They appear to be like a virus that is spreading through the software.

The Plug-Ins folder

All of the filters in Illustrator are in the Filter menu because a file with the same name as the filter is in the Plug-Ins folder (or in the folder designated to hold plug-ins). If the filter's file is not in the Plug-Ins folder, the filter does not appear in the Filter menu. You can add and remove plug-ins from the Filter menu by adding or moving the plug-in file from the Plug-In folder. The Plug-In folder can contain addi-tional folders also.

The way Illustrator is built, many standard features are implemented as plug-ins, so plug-ins may do more than just add a filter to the software. If you want to see a list of all the plug-ins, open the Illustrator [Help] ⇨ About Plug-Ins menu option. From the dialog box that opens, you should be able to recognize many of your favorite Illustrator features.

ASK TOULOUSE: What Are Filters?

Johnny: Now, how are filters in Illustrator different from the things I use to make sure all those little black things don't get in my coffee?

Toulouse: Filters in Illustrator do all sorts of amazing things that would be really difficult or time-consuming to normally do in the program.

Johnny: That's nice, but then why have all the hard ways to do things in Illustrator if you've got these filters hanging around?

Toulouse: A good example is the Roughen filter. It adds points to paths and then randomly moves them around.

Johnny: Wouldn't the easy thing be to just draw the paths using the Pencil tool with a low Curve Fitting Tolerance? Seems like you can avoid the Roughen filter altogether that way.

Toulouse: Ah, but what if you want to roughen existing artwork? The Roughen filter does this in just a few seconds.

The Plug-Ins folder is inside the first level of the Adobe Illustrator folder when Illustrator is installed. If you move the folder, you need to tell Illustrator where it is located. Here are the steps:

1. In the Finder, with Illustrator not running, move or copy the Plug-Ins folder to the desired location.

2. Double-click the Illustrator icon.

3. Choose Illustrator [Edit] ⇨ Preferences ⇨ Plug-Ins & Scratch Disk.

4. In the Plug-Ins dialog box, click the Choose button, find the Plug-Ins folder, and click the Select button at the bottom of the dialog box.

5. Quit Illustrator and double-click the Illustrator icon to restart Illustrator. The new Plug-Ins folder location is now used.

Why you can apply the last filter but never Apply Last Filter

Whenever you start Illustrator, the top menu item in the Filter menu reads "Apply Last Filter," but it is grayed out. This causes some confusion initially. After you use a filter, its name appears where the menu once listed "Apply Last Filter." Thereafter, the name of the last filter that you used appears at the top of the menu. The key command for reapplying the last filter is ⌘+E [Ctrl+E].

Tip   To return to the last filter's dialog box, select Filter ⇨ *[Name of Last Filter]*, located right below the Apply Last Filter option or press ⌘+Option+E [Ctrl+Alt+E].

Color filters

The Colors filters include a variety of filters that control object colors. Many of these filters let you blend and convert colors. These filters include Adjust Colors, Blend Front to Back, Blend Horizontally, Blend Vertically, Convert to CMYK, Convert to Grayscale, Convert to RGB, Invert Colors, Overprint Black, and Saturate.

Cross-Reference   The Color filters are covered in detail in Chapter 6, "Working with Color."

Create filters

There were a lot of Create filters in version 5.5 of Illustrator, but in Illustrator 10, the category is all but extinct, with only Object Mosaic and Trim Marks being the stragglers.

As with most filters, you can manually perform the functions that the two Create filters do, but using the filters is much easier.

Creating object mosaics

The Object Mosaic filter creates a series of tiles out of a placed bitmap image, as shown in Figure 13-12. Any size or color image may be used. When an image is converted through the Object Mosaic filter, it becomes a series of rectangles, each filled with a color corresponding to the image. If the selected object is a vector-based object, this Object Mosaic menu option will be grayed out. It can only be applied to raster bitmaps.

Figure 13-12: An original TIFF image (left) and the image after Object Mosaic has been applied (right)

In the Object Mosaic dialog box (see Figure 13-13), you can specify the number of tiles that the image is made up of and the space between the tiles. You also can specify a different size for the entire object mosaic.

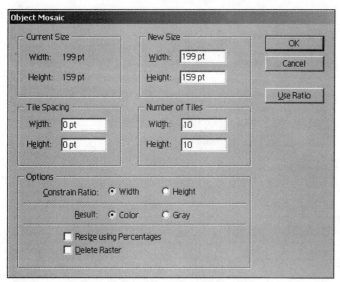

Figure 13-13: The Object Mosaic dialog box

Caution Be careful with Object Mosaic. This filter, unlike almost any other, runs out of memory if the source image or number of tiles is too large. This is the one filter in Illustrator that does almost exactly what its counterpart in Photoshop does.

The more rectangles there are, the more detail exists in the mosaic. Bitmapped images are mosaics of a sort, with each pixel equal to one square.

Tip If you need to apply Object Mosaic to an illustration you've created in Illustrator, you can rasterize it using the Object ⇨ Rasterize command. Do this at a low resolution (72 dpi works great for us), and then apply Object Mosaic to the rasterized image.

Use the following steps to create a fairly simple and basic mosaic in Illustrator.

1. Create a TIFF file and place it in Illustrator. You do not need to use a high-resolution TIFF file. The Illustrator object mosaic looks just as good when you convert a 72-dpi TIFF file as when you convert a 300-dpi TIFF file.

2. Choose Filter ⇨ Create ⇨ Object Mosaic. In the Object Mosaic dialog box, enter the size that you want the mosaic to be and also the number of tiles across and down. Click the Use Ratio button to keep the same proportions as in the original image.

3. Click OK when you are satisfied with the information that you have entered in the Object Mosaic dialog box. Step 3 in Figure 13-14 shows the results that are produced by entering three different tile widths and heights into the Number of Tiles boxes.

Step 1

333 × 419 Pixels
(139,527)

Step 2

Object Mosaic		

Current Size
Width: 126 pt
Height: 47 pt

New Size
Width: 126 pt
Height: 47 pt

OK
Cancel
Use Ratio

Tile Spacing
Width: 0 pt
Height: 0 pt

Number of Tiles
Width: 50
Height: 63

Options
Constrain Ratio: ● Width ○ Height

Result: ● Color ○ Gray

☐ Resize using Percentages
☐ Delete Raster

Step 3

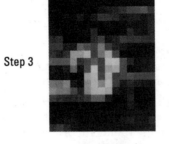  

15 × 19 Tiles	30 × 38 Tiles	80 × 101 Tiles
(285)	(1,140)	(8,080)

Figure 13-14: Steps for creating object mosaics

Caution The number of tiles that Illustrator can produce is strictly limited and is directly related to the amount of RAM allocated to Illustrator. Exceeding the limit causes Illustrator to create only a portion of the tiles.

You can create some very exciting effects with the Object Mosaic filter when you use it in conjunction with other filters. The best ones to use it with are Round Corners, all of the Distort filters, and most of the color filters, as well as the Transform Each function. The following example combines the Object Mosaic filter with the Round Corners filter and the Transform Each function:

1. Create an object mosaic with an average number of tiles (between 1,600 and 10,000 tiles, which would be from 40_× 40 to 100_×_100). In the example shown in Figure 13-15, we used an object mosaic with 50_×_63 tiles, or 3,150 tiles.

2. Select all the mosaic tiles and choose Filter ⇨ Stylize ⇨ Round Corners. In the Round Corners dialog box, enter a large number. We usually enter at least 10 points. As long as the tiles are not larger than 20 points wide, the Round Corners filter turns all the tiles into circles.

3. Copy all the tiles and choose Edit ⇨ Paste in Front (⌘+F [Ctrl+F]). Select all the tiles (the image now has 6,300 tiles) and choose Object ⇨ Transform ⇨ Transform Each. In the Move section of the dialog box, enter **5** in both text fields and check the Random checkbox. Click OK. If you want less white space between all the circles, choose Edit ⇨ Paste in Front (⌘+F [Ctrl+F]) again, and then choose Arrange ⇨ Transform Again (⌘+D [Ctrl+D]). The results should look similar to Step 3 in Figure 13-15.

The tiles created with the Object Mosaic filter are placed on the page from top-left to bottom-right. The top-left tile is underneath all the other tiles (in the back), and the bottom-right tile is on top of all the other tiles (in the front).

Because of the way that these tiles overlap, you can create a tiled or shingled roof quite easily. The following steps describe this process in detail:

1. Create a TIFF file to be used as the roof. In the example shown in Figure 13-16, we created the name of a restaurant. Then we rasterized it in Illustrator.

2. In Illustrator, rotate the image 135 degrees clockwise. Choose Filter ⇨ Create ⇨ Object Mosaic. Make the number of tiles across about 50 or more, and click the Use Ratio button.

3. Rotate the entire mosaic by 135 degrees. Using the Selection tool, draw a marquee around any white squares above, below, to the left, and to the right of the roof area to select them. Delete all white squares. Because the squares are white, you may need to switch to Outline mode to see them all.

Step 1

Step 2

Step 3

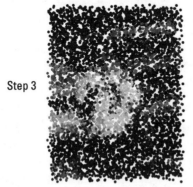

Figure 13-15: Creating a Seurat-like effect with the Object Mosaic filter

Figure 13-16: Creating a tiled roof with the Object Mosaic filter

4. Select the remaining tiles and group them. Choose Object ➪ Path ➪ Add Anchor Points to add one anchor point to every side of every square in the mosaic. Choose Filter ➪ Distort ➪ Pucker and Bloat and set the Bloat value to 3 to make all the points on each square jut out a little.

5. To round off the points and make the squares smoother, choose Filter ➪ Stylize ➪ Round Corners, and enter **10 pt** in the text field. Choose Object ➪ Transform ➪ Transform Each and enter **150** in both the Horizontal and Vertical fields of the Scale section of the Transform Each dialog box. Because the squares were scaled up, they now overlap.

6. Choose Object ➪ Transform ➪ Transform Each and enter **45°** in the Rotate section. In the Color and Stroke palettes, give each tile a Black Stroke of 0.25 point. Depending on the size of the tiles, the Stroke weight may vary.

7. Use the Free Transform tool to change the shape of the roof to be more . . . well . . . roof-like.

It may seem strange that the mosaic gets rotated twice in the previous procedure, but a method exists to this seemingly mad busywork. By placing the upper-left tiles on the bottom and the lower-right tiles on the top, the image is rotated first so that the lower parts of the image are turned into squares. By the way, if one of your authors hadn't helped put shingles on a roof recently (you have to work from the bottom up), he would never have been able to figure this out. So we guess that this is one of those "real-life" examples!

Overlapping tiles in a mosaic with no white space between them easily creates a background image or a funky illustration. These steps show how to overlap tiles with no whitespace:

1. Create an Object Mosaic from a raster image.

2. Choose Object ⇨ Transform ⇨ Transform Each, and enter the amount of movement for the tiles in the Move section. Check the Random checkbox. Measure one tile with the Measure tool. The tiles that we created for the example shown in Figure 13-17 are 3.3 points across, and the move distance that we used is 3.3 points. The most whitespace between any two tiles is 6.6 points.

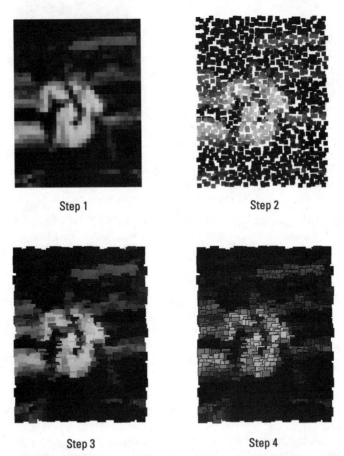

Step 1   Step 2

Step 3   Step 4

Figure 13-17: Steps for creating random overlapping tiles with no whitespace

3. Select Object ⇨ Transform ⇨ Transform Each. Enter the percentage that the tile must be scaled up to eliminate the white space in the Scale area. In this example, we entered 200 percent.

4. To see the edges of the tiles more easily, place a 0.25-point 100% Black Stroke on them.

By using the Object Mosaic filter in combination with the color blend filters, color sets that show all the colors of a palette as individual swatches can be created very easily. These color sets can be sampled for inclusion in the Swatch palette. Follow these steps to create color sets:

1. Create an Object Mosaic from any image, making the total number of tiles equal to the number of different tiles that you want in the color set.

2. Change the colors of the tiles that mark the beginning and end of each color set. In Figure 13-18, we used the primary colors and white as the beginning and end of each color set (although in this book you will see the color sets in black and white only).

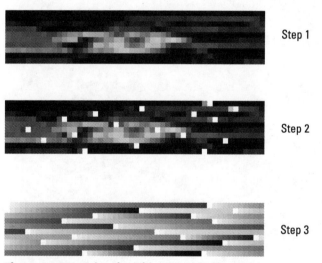

Step 1

Step 2

Step 3

Figure 13-18: Using the Object Mosaic filter to create color sets

3. Select one range of color and choose Filter ⇨ Color ⇨ Blend Front to Back to blend the colors from the upper-left tiles toward the lower-right tiles. Repeat this step for each range of colors.

Creating trim marks

The other filter in the Filter ⇨ Create menu is Trim Marks. This filter places trim marks around a set of objects. These marks specify a rectangular region that is to be cut after the document is printed. Trim marks are different than crop marks. Crop marks are created with the Object ⇨ Crop Marks ⇨ Make command. Crop marks mark the edges of the document that is represented by the artboard. Trim marks, on the other hand, can be placed multiple times with a single document. These marks identify sections or objects within the document that need to be trimmed once the document is printed.

Figure 13-19 shows a placed image with the Trim Marks filter applied.

Figure 13-19: The Trim Marks filter designates where the placed image should be cut.

Distort filters

The Distort filters are used to cause slight or major fluctuations in the paths of an object. These filters include Free Distort, Pucker & Bloat, Roughen, Scribble & Tweak, Twist, and Zig Zag. Each of these filters is described in the earlier section on Effects.

Detailed coverage of these filters can be found in Chapter 10, "Transforming and Distorting Artwork."

Pen and Ink filters

The Pen and Ink filters are unique in that they let you apply Hatch effects and Photo Crosshatch effects to images.

These filters are discussed in Chapter 9, "Applying Fills and Strokes."

Stylize filters

The Stylize filters are used for a variety of functions — kind of a catchall for filters that really can't go anywhere else. The three Stylize filters fall into two different categories. The first category contains the Add Arrowheads and Drop Shadow filters. These two filters create additional objects that are based on existing objects. Add Arrowheads puts all sorts of arrowheads onto the ends of open paths. Drop Shadow adds a darkened shadow to a selected path.

The Stylize filters in the second category work in much the same way as the Distort filters. The Round Corners filter removes corner points and replaces them with smooth points. This filter seems better suited to the Distort submenu, but Adobe has chosen to put it here.

Add arrowheads

The Add Arrowheads filter is a boon to technical artists, sign makers, and anyone else in need of a quick arrow. The number one complaint about the Add Arrowheads filter is that Illustrator offers too many arrowheads to choose from. Some complaint!

Choosing Filter ➪ Stylize ➪ Add Arrowheads adds an arrowhead (or two) to any selected open path. If more than one path is selected, arrowheads are added to each open path. To use Add Arrowheads, select an open path and choose Add Arrowheads. The Add Arrowheads dialog box appears, as shown in Figure 13-20. In this box, you can pick which of the 27 different arrowheads you want to stick on either end of your path. Scale refers to the size of the arrowhead relative to the Stroke weight of the path; you may enter any number from 1 to 1,000 percent in this box. Choosing Start places the arrowhead at the beginning of the path (where you first clicked to draw it). Choosing End places the arrowhead on the end of the path (where you last clicked to draw it); and choosing Start and End places the same arrowhead on both the beginning and end of the path. Reapplying this filter to the same paths continues to put arrowheads on top of arrowheads.

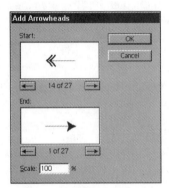

Figure 13-20: The Add Arrowheads dialog box

Note   Add Arrowheads does *not* work on closed paths.

Arrowheads are grouped to the paths that were selected when they were created; it is sometimes necessary to rotate the arrowhead by either ungrouping it or choosing it with the Direct Selection tool.

The size of the arrowheads is based on the width of the Stroke, but you can alter each arrowhead's dimensions in the Scale text field in the Add Arrowheads dialog box. Figure 13-21 shows you how to create and customize arrowheads.

Here are the steps for creating and customizing arrowheads:

1. Use the Pen or Pencil tool to create an open path. Set the width of the path to the width that you want it to be with an arrowhead attached to it. (You have to use an open path — nothing happens if you select a closed path and apply the Add Arrowheads filter. Even if you want just the arrowhead, and not the path, you still have to create a path first — you can delete the path after the arrowhead appears.)

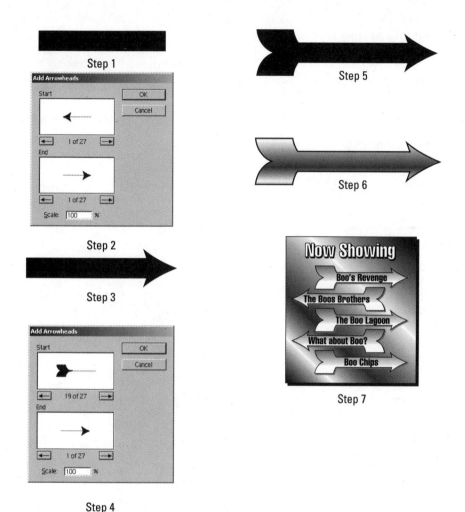

Figure 13-21: Steps for creating and customizing an arrowhead by using the Add Arrowheads filter

2. Choose Filter ➪ Stylize ➪ Add Arrowheads. The Add Arrowheads dialog box appears. Enter the size of the arrowhead (100 percent = normal size). Pick the end of the path where you want the arrowhead to appear. If you want the arrowhead on both ends of the path, click the Start and End option. (If you drew the path yourself with either the Pen or Freehand tool, the path direction is the direction that you drew the path — closed paths that were created

with the Rectangle or Oval tools or the Create filters and were then cut usually go in a counterclockwise direction.) Pick an arrowhead from the 27 options. (Press down and hold on the directional arrows to flip through the arrowheads quickly—after arrowhead #27, you see arrowhead #1. Figure 13-22 shows all the arrowheads.)

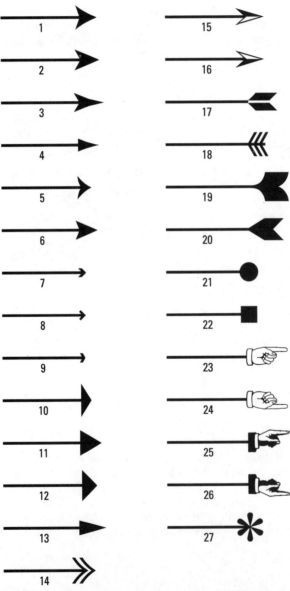

Figure 13-22: The arrowheads that are available in the Add Arrowheads dialog box

3. Click OK. The path now has an arrowhead. Whenever arrowheads are created, they are grouped to the path. You have to use the Group Selection tool to select individual pieces of the arrow, or choose Arrange ➪ Ungroup (⌘+Shift+ G [Ctrl+Shift+G]).

4. To add a different arrowhead to the other end of the path, select the path with the Direct Selection tool, and then choose Filter ➪ Stylize ➪ Add Arrowheads. Change the buttons to indicate that the new arrowhead should go at the other end of the path, and select the type of arrowhead.

5. Click OK. Make sure that the arrowhead is correct. If it isn't, choose Edit ➪ Undo (⌘+Z [Ctrl+Z]) and choose Filter ➪ Stylize ➪ Add Arrowheads. Then add a different arrowhead.

6. To make the arrowheads and path into one path, select the path and choose Object ➪ Path ➪ Outline Path. Then select both the new outlined path and the arrowheads and choose Unite from the Pathfinder palette.

7. Now you can Fill the new arrow object with anything, including gradients, and Stroke the entire object at once.

Drop Shadow filter

The Drop Shadow filter makes creating drop shadows for most paths a simple task.

Unlike most other filters, selecting Drop Shadow affects both Stroke *and* Fill. In the Drop Shadow dialog box (see Figure 13-23), you may specify the offset of the drop shadow by entering values for how far across the drop shadow should move (X Offset) and how far up or down it should move (Y Offset). Positive numbers move the shadow to the right and down; negative numbers move the shadow to the left and up.

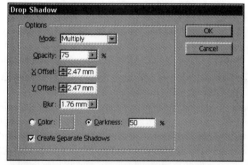

Figure 13-23: The Drop Shadow dialog box

The general rule in drop shadowing is that the more offset the drop shadow is, the higher the original object looks. To make an object look as if it is floating far above the page, enter high offset values.

You can also specify a Blending Mode, the Opacity, Color, and Blur distance of the drop shadow. The percentage entered in Darkness is how much Black is added to the Fill and Stroke colors. Darkness does not affect any of the other custom or process colors. If you check Create Separate Shadows, the drop shadow becomes a separate object from the selected object. This enables you to move the shadow independent of the object, which is a good idea, because you shouldn't just leave your shadow lying around.

Follow these steps to create a drop shadow:

1. Create and select the artwork to which you want to give a drop shadow.

2. Choose Filter ➪ Stylize ➪ Drop Shadow. The Drop Shadow dialog box appears, as shown in Figure 13-23.

3. Select a Blending Mode and an Opacity value. Enter the amount that you want the drop shadow to be offset. A positive value in the *X* text field puts the shadow to the right of the object; a negative value in the *X* text field puts the shadow to the left of the object. A positive value in the *Y* text field puts the shadow below the object; a negative value in the *Y* text field puts the shadow above the object. (The larger the offset amounts, the higher up the object appears to float above the original object.)

4. Enter a Blur distance and select the Darkness radio button. The value that you enter in the Darkness field determines how much black is added to the shadow to make it appear darker. If you don't check the Create Separate Shadows box, the shadow is grouped to the original object.

5. Click OK. If the shadow isn't what you want, use the Undo command (⌘+Z [Ctrl+Z]), choose Filter ➪ Stylize ➪ Drop Shadow, and create a new drop shadow.

The Round Corners filter

You can use the Round Corners filter to create round corners just like (snap your fingers) that. This filter works on any path that has corner points, but the best results seem to be on polygons and stars.

Selecting Round Corners changes all types of corner points to smooth points. In the Round Corners dialog box, you specify what the radius of the Round Corners should be. The larger the number you enter for the radius, the bigger the curve.

Note   Don't apply the Round Corners filter to a rounded rectangle to make the corners more rounded. Instead of the corners becoming rounder, the flat sides of the rectangle curve slightly.

Here are the steps to creating rounded corners:

1. Select the artwork that will have its corners rounded. We used type converted to outlines in the example in Figure 13-24.

ASK TOULOUSE: Extra Points?

Laverne: I keep getting extra points after I apply Round Corners.

Toulouse: That's what Round Corners does. It replaces most corner points with two smooth points.

Laverne: But I only want one point there.

Toulouse: Well, you can individually change each point to a smooth point.

Laverne: How long would that take?

Toulouse: Let's see. If you had 20 paths, each with 15 anchor points. . . .

Laverne: I have a Cray Supercomputer handy to help you figure this out.

Toulouse: That would be 300 anchor points. If you take 3 seconds on each, and 3 seconds to find the next point . . .

Laverne: The Cray is smoking. Too tough.

Toulouse: . . . it would take you half an hour of constant clicking.

Laverne: Isn't that a k. d. lang tune?

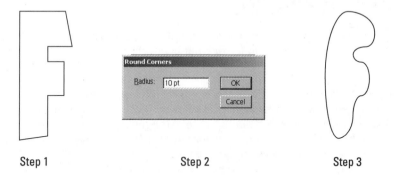

Step 1   Step 2   Step 3

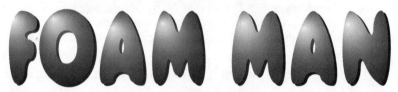

Step 4

Figure 13-24: Steps for creating rounded corners

2. Choose Filter ⇨ Stylize ⇨ Round Corners. The Round Corners dialog box appears. Enter the amount that you want the corners to be rounded. Entering a large number usually ensures that all points become as curved as possible. (We wanted the corners rounded as much as possible, so we entered 10 pt in the dialog box.)

3. Click OK.

4. Add other artwork to the final rounded artwork.

You can use the Round Corners filter to smooth out overly bumpy edges. Using the Round Corners filter with Roughen produces very smooth, flowing areas.

Photoshop filters

At the bottom of the Filter menu, below the horizontal spacer, are ten categories of filters ranging from Artistic to Video. These filters are unique because they all can be applied to raster-based images. These filters match the filters that are available in Photoshop.

Cross-Reference   Chapter 14, "Working with Pixels," covers these filters individually.

Third-Party Plug-ins

The following summary of the third-party plug-in sets available at the time of this writing gives you some examples of what is out there. You can find a more complete list in Appendix C, "Resources."

✦ **KPT Vector Effects.** This comprehensive filter set from Corel (formerly from MetaCreations), the maker of Kai's Power Tools (KPT), consists of several special-effects-oriented filters. Some of the highlights include KPT 3D Transform, which rotates and extrudes artwork in 3D; KPT ShatterBox, which fragments selected artwork into user-defined pieces; and KPT Warp Frame, an envelope-distortion filter. You can find more information on these filters at www. corel.com.

✦ **Letraset Envelopes.** This one-shot filter is an envelope-distortion filter with several presets.

✦ **CADtools.** This is an amazing set of actual *tools* that turns Illustrator into high-powered drafting and CAD software. Many of the tools can be used for other things besides CAD drawing, making this one of the most exciting plug-in sets to appear for Illustrator. For more information, visit www.hotdoor.com.

✦ **Vertigo 3D Words.** This is a one-shot plug-in that makes 3D words. The amazing thing about this plug-in is that the words are set onto paths that curve in 3D space — something no other plug-in (or even Adobe's own Dimensions) can do.

✦ **Vertigo Pop-Art.** This plug-in lets you create 3D images out of 2D objects. You can add light and depth to your art with ease — all from within Illustrator.

✦ **MAPublisher.** This is a set of tools for mapmaking created by Avenza. Cartographers will have a field day with the filters in this package. You can find more information on this product at www.avenza.com.

✦ **Toolbox.** These plug-ins created by Illom include a range of management tools for time tracking, as well as, transformation tools such as magnet.

✦ **3D Invigorator.** This set of plug-ins created by Zaxwerks let you add lighting, reflected surfaces, and views from different cameras.

✦ **FilterIt.** This plug-in includes several new live effects such as Emboss, Tiling, Explosion, and more.

✦ **Kimbo.** This plug-in includes several new drawing tools such as Rose, Wave, Rhombus, and others.

✦ **Vector Studio.** This plug-in lets you work with glass-like objects, morph brushes, and envelop meshes. You can also create gradient textures.

 Note   Other plug-ins are available and new plug-in sets are being developed all the time. Check with your favorite software store or search for new products online.

Illustrator Filters versus Photoshop Filters

The filters in Illustrator have to be different from the filters in Photoshop because Illustrator deals with vector-based images and Photoshop works with bitmapped graphics. Many electronic artists use Photoshop as a staple of their graphics work. For them, the word *filter* conjures up thoughts of blurring and sharpening, as well as some of the fantastic effects they can achieve by using filters from third parties, such as Kai's Power Tools or Alien Skin Eye Candy.

The term *filters* is based in photography terminology; filters are special lenses that are attached to cameras to achieve special effects. Photoshop's filters are based on this concept, and they take it quite a bit further, creating controls for variety and exactness that a camera lens can never match.

For this reason, filter isn't really the best term for the manipulations that Illustrator performs when you choose a filter. The following list compares some of the Illustrator filters with their Photoshop counterparts:

✦ **Illustrator:** Filter ⇨ Create ⇨ Object Mosaic; **Photoshop:** Filter ⇨ Stylize ⇨ Mosaic

The Mosaic filters take bitmap images and reduce the number of colored areas to large, single-colored squares. The filter does not work on vector-based objects unless they have first been rasterized.

Where Did All the Filters Go?

The Filter menu has been dramatically parsed down to only a few Illustrator-specific categories as well. Functions were not taken away, but many of them were either combined or moved from the Filter menu to other menus in Illustrator.

To help make this clear, we need to give you a little background story. In 1993, when Illustrator 5.0 (the first version to support plug-ins) was introduced, Adobe thought that any add-on functionality created from plug-ins should be placed in the Filter menu (as was the practice in Photoshop 2.5). While most of the new plug-in-based enhancements really weren't filters in a Photoshop sense of the word, they thought that because Illustrator was such a different product from Photoshop, these new features really can be considered "vector filters."

By the time Illustrator 6.0 was released, that thinking had changed substantially. The Illustrator engineers changed the API (Application Programming Interface) to let plug-ins be not just in the Filter menu, but also in any menu, or as a palette, or as a tool. Adobe started moving some things that were filters to tools (Spiral, Twirl, Polygon, Star), and others to palettes (align). With Illustrator 7, the only functions left in the Filter menu fell into the categories of Colors, Create (still not really filters), Distort, Ink Pen, and Stylize. The only change in Illustrator 8 was the addition of the Photo Crosshatch to the Pen and Ink filter (previously called Ink Pen), and the removal of some unnecessary filters. In Illustrator 9, the big addition was the Effects menu, which duplicates many of the filters found in the Filters menu. You can find more information on the Effects menu in Chapter 13, "Using Styles and Effects." And now with Illustrator 10, the shift has been continued with the Effect menu growing larger than the Filter menu with the additions of SVG Filters and Warp menus.

These two filters produce results that are the most alike of any of the Illustrator and Photoshop filters. The dialog boxes are a little different, but the results are functionally the same. One big difference is that stylizing a mosaic in Photoshop is a fast procedure, but creating an object mosaic in Illustrator is a complex task that eats up tons of RAM and can take up to ten minutes to complete.

✦ **Illustrator:** Filter ➪ Distort ➪ Twist; **Photoshop:** Filter ➪ Distort ➪ Twirl

Twirling/twisting spins an object or picture more in the center than around the edges.

Some features that you would expect to do the same thing in each program are not the same:

✦ **Illustrator:** Filter ➪ Colors ➪ Invert Colors; and **Photoshop:** Image ➪ Map ➪ Invert

Illustrator's Invert Colors filter is annoying because you expect a negative image but don't get it. Instead, you get Cyan, Magenta, and Yellow values that have been subtracted from 100, and a Black value that is untouched. Photoshop's Invert command creates a true negative, and it is a feature, not a filter.

✦ **Illustrator:** Filter ➪ Colors ➪ Saturate; and **Photoshop:** Image ➪ Adjust ➪ Hue/Saturation

The saturation filter in Illustrator increases or decreases the CMYK values for selected objects. In Photoshop, the color intensity is increased. Saturation in Illustrator is a misnomer, at least when compared to the functionality of Saturation in most other software packages.

 Coverage of the various Photoshop filters found in Illustrator is found in Chapter 14, "Working with Pixels."

Creating Illustrator Plug-ins

While this section is aimed at potential plug-in developers, casual readers may find it interesting to discover what exactly can be done in Illustrator via an add-on plug-in. These little pieces of software are quite amazing.

The Illustrator API and SDK

Illustrator API is one of the most advanced APIs (Application Program Interface) for any software, enabling plug-in developers to add features by creating modal-based functions, floating palettes, and tools anywhere in Illustrator.

Maybe you're asking yourself, why bother with a plug-in when I can just create an application that does what I want? Why bother spending the time to learn the API? For starters, creating a plug-in within Illustrator enables you to take advantage of Illustrator's file importing/exporting options. Illustrator supports all of Photoshop's pixel formats, as well as Illustrator-native EPS (Encapsulated PostScript), and PDF (Portable Document Format) files, in addition to printing issues. You don't need to worry about coding all of that boring stuff; instead, you get to dig into the meaty stuff that's fun to create—and use. The Illustrator API makes it easy to perform almost all of Illustrator's functions and features through simple programming functions.

Even better, the SDK (Software Developer's Kit), available from Adobe, includes plenty of sample plug-ins and source code. A more recent (postshipping) version of the SDK is available from Adobe's Web site.

To create a plug-in for Illustrator you must have a basic knowledge of C programming, and you must own a compiler of some sort. In general, most programmers and engineers use the Metrowerks CodeWarrior software.

Plug-in types

You can use three major plug-in types in Illustrator: menu-selectable modal dialog boxes, floating palettes, and tools. The following is a description of the three types:

✦ **Modal dialog boxes** are the standard filter type of plug-ins common to Photoshop. The user selects a menu item, and a dialog box appears. Corel's KPT Vector Effects, CSI's Socket Sets, and BeInfinite's InfiniteFX use modal dialog boxes for their plug-ins. Versions 5.0 and 5.5 of Illustrator only supported modal dialog box-based plug-ins, and they were only accessible via a submenu of the Filter menu. Versions 6 and later support putting menu items in *any* menu, not just the Filter menu.

✦ **Floating palettes** are fully supported by Illustrator 10. If you use the API to create a palette in Illustrator, the palette is treated as a standard Illustrator palette and follows the behavior of other palettes in Illustrator, including snapping to the edges of other palettes, snapping to the document window, and snapping to the edges of the screen. Palettes you create via the API are also hidden and shown automatically when you press the Tab key.

✦ **Tools** are plug-ins that add tools to the toolbox. Tools can interact with Illustrator objects in various ways. The Spiral, Polygon, Star, and Twirl tools were originally modal-based plug-ins (in Illustrator versions 5.0 and 5.5). Now, they are tools with added functionality (double-clicking the tools displays a dialog box that is eerily similar to the original filters).

Suites

One of the most useful API functions is that of suites. A *suite* is like a template that enables you to quickly create new plug-in functions. Illustrator has several integrated suites that provide a lot of additional functionality. The two suites that you may find especially helpful are the Path Construction Suite and the Shape Construction Suite. These two suites assist in creating and adjusting paths, and are especially helpful with distortion filters.

The most striking difference between the 5.0/5.5 distortion filter Twirl and its 6.0–10.0 counterpart (besides it also being a tool) is the way it works. Twirling a star in versions 5.0/5.5 resulted in a twirling of points only; the path shape was only affected in that the line segments followed the path. The Illustrator 6.0–10.0 Twirl/Twist filter (and tool) uses the Shape Construction Suite to adjust the entire path, not just the selected points, resulting in a smooth twirling effect.

The capabilities of each suite are documented in the SDK that is included on the application CD-ROM.

Plug-ins we'd like to see

Now that Illustrator has such a powerful API, all sorts of plug-ins can be created for it. Here are a few ideas of undeveloped plug-ins that Illustrator users have been clamoring for:

✦ **3D Transformation Tool, Find/Replace, Arc Tool.** FreeHand (that *other* illustrator program) has these features and many others that can be included in Illustrator using the Illustrator API. Of course, FreeHand is a little feature-heavy, but the best place to start is the competition.

✦ **Levels Color Controls.** We use Levels in Photoshop as much as (or more than) curves. Levels is perfect for quick "watermarking" of images.

✦ **Animation Plug-in.** Adobe Dimensions does basic key sequencing for animation, but Illustrator provides the tools that would enable a developer to create animation that can be viewed within Illustrator.

✦ **Simulated Animation.** A plug-in that takes a selection and applies virtual animation to it by creating a series of more transparent copies along a path.

✦ **Spotlight/Lighting Effects Tool.** A tool that can shine a spotlight on the artwork, creating a reflected light surface and a drop shadow.

✦ **Illustrator Document Viewer.** A plug-in that cycles through custom views, multiple documents, and more, using a simple VCR-style palette. Like a slide show, clicking on a mouse can advance images.

✦ **3D Path Splines.** Corel's KPT Vector Effects extrudes and Adobe Dimensions both extrudes and revolves. However, no tool enables paths to be constructed in three dimensions or to be displayed that way.

✦ **Stippling Tool.** A tool to create stippling effects in Illustrator, with varying intensity and color amounts.

✦ **Path Generator.** A plug-in that automatically generates random paths based on specific criteria. Perfect for backgrounds, random objects, and more.

✦ **Mosaic Creation.** A plug-in to create mosaic tiles from vector artwork; the current Object Mosaic is limited in the shape and control of the tiles.

✦ **Area Tool.** Illustrator's Measure tool is fine for measuring distance. An Area tool would measure the area within several clicked points or selected paths.

Many of these plug-ins can be created using little more than the tools provided with the Illustrator API. Other plug-ins require a higher level of complexity, but most, if not all of them, are do-able.

If you have plug-in ideas that you'd like to see developed, or if you've created a plug-in that you need marketed, contact the Adobe Developer's Association, which works with up-and-coming programmers to help them realize their plug-in goals. In addition, you may want to check with any of the existing plug-in developers, such as Adobe. They may be interested in licensing your technology for inclusion in a future product.

Summary

With styles, you can capture and add unique characteristics to many objects. Effects and filters can be used to add programmed functionality to objects. In this chapter, you learned:

- ✦ Change the appearance of objects using the Appearance palette.
- ✦ Save appearance settings as styles in the Styles palette.
- ✦ Load saved sets of styles using the Style Libraries.
- ✦ Use the Convert to Shapes effect to change objects into rectangles, rounded rectangles, and ellipses.
- ✦ Feather the interior Fill of an object with the Feather effect.
- ✦ Add Inner and Outer Glows to objects with the glow effects.
- ✦ Filters are loaded from the plug-in directory.
- ✦ The Object Mosaics filter can be used to create mosaic images.
- ✦ Trim marks are different from crop marks and can be placed multiple times throughout the document.
- ✦ Add Arrowheads creates arrowheads at the ends of open paths.
- ✦ Drop Shadow creates instant drop shadows.
- ✦ Round Corners changes Straight corner points into smooth points.
- ✦ Using the Illustrator API and SDK, you can create your own custom plug-ins.

✦　　✦　　✦

Working with Pixels

When we first learned that Illustrator would support Photoshop filters, all the wrong thoughts entered our brains. "Great, now we'll be able to Gaussian Blur our shadows without having to turn them into pixels first!" and "Wow, we wonder what'll happen with blends and some of the distort filters!"

Of course, we were misled (those silly press releases again, we're sure). Photoshop filters work only on *pixel-based* images, not vector-based images (paths and such). Fortunately, however, a command exists for making paths into pixel-based images — Rasterize. So, it's an extra step . . . but it works.

The plug-ins and filters included with Illustrator are nice, but the third-party plug-ins and filters really make it exciting. Plug-ins give Illustrator capabilities that users have wanted and dreamed about for years.

Vectors versus Pixel-based Images

In its original version, Illustrator was pure vector software. There was nary a pixel to be found round these parts. But with version 9, the border was crossed, and Illustrator is just this side of the pixel border (which is nowhere near as smooth as the vector border).

When you think vectors, think Illustrator's paths. Illustrator's paths consist of outlines. Sure, they're outlines that can be filled with various colors and gradients, but they're still outlines. And it is the manipulation of these outlines that is the essence of Illustrator. Outlines can be resized and transformed in almost any way imaginable. Also, when you create a curve in Illustrator, it's really a curve — not a jagged mass of pixels. Vector-based images can be stretched bigger and look better for it (except blends and gradients if they're scaled up too large).

When you think pixels, think Photoshop's little teeny-tiny squares of color — squares that never change position and that you don't add or delete. The only thing you change about pixels is their color. Pixels can only be square, and they take up space regardless of whether they're "empty" (filled with white or another background color) or "filled" (filled with a foreground color). Pixels exist on an immobile grid. Enlarging a pixel-based image results in giant, ugly squares of color.

Okay, we're not pixel people. If we were to be reincarnated as an electronic drawing tool, it wouldn't be as a Painter piece of chalk, but instead as Illustrator's Pen tool or Direct Selection tool. We're believers in vectors. Some say it's an obsession, but we're too busy staring at control handles to pay attention to that nonsense.

Fortunately, our minds are not so closed that we ignore the importance of pixels or their place in our electronic graphics society. So we're glad pixels exist in Illustrator. After all, you can do things to pixels in Illustrator that you *can't* do in Photoshop. Ah . . . now we've got your attention.

Even with its pixel capabilities, Illustrator is no Photoshop. Tools and features exist in Photoshop that are invaluable for adjusting pixel-based artwork. Adobe recognizes this, so it has provided several methods for moving pixels to Photoshop from Illustrator, and from Photoshop to Illustrator.

Placing Raster Images

The most rudimentary way of moving images, which has existed for several versions of both software packages, is to save art in a format the other program can read, and then to open or place the art in the other program. To place Illustrator art into Photoshop, save the art in Illustrator format, and then open the art in Photoshop. To place Photoshop art into Illustrator, save in Photoshop as a format that Illustrator can read, such as TIFF (Tagged Image File Format), and then in Illustrator choose File ➪ Place and select the file. Figure 14-1 shows the Place dialog box.

The Place dialog box includes a checkbox for including the image as a link. Linked images are not included within the Illustrator file, which results in a smaller file size. If the Link checkbox isn't checked, the placed image is embedded within the Illustrator file.

If the linked file cannot be found, Illustrator displays a warning dialog like the one shown in Figure 14-2. Clicking the Yes button enables you to select a replacement image and clicking the No button ignores the linked image. The placeholder for the linked image is still visible, but no image is displayed. You can load a new image into the placeholder by once again selecting the File ➪ Place option. In the Place dialog box, select the Replace checkbox to replace the current placeholder with a new linked image.

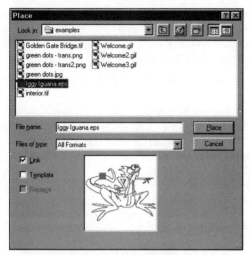

Figure 14-1: The Place dialog box

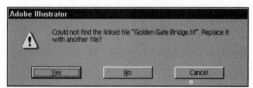

Figure 14-2: A warning dialog box appears if
the linked image cannot be found.

Note The key difference between opening an image file and placing an image file is that
the Open command opens the image as part of a new document, while the Place
command opens the image in the current layer of the existing document.

Using the clipboard

Another way to place images is through Adobe's wonderful PostScript process on
the clipboard, which allows for transferring artwork between Adobe software by
simply copying in one program and pasting in another. To place Illustrator art in
Photoshop, copy the art in Illustrator, switch to Photoshop, and paste the art in any
open document. To place Photoshop art in Illustrator, copy the art in Photoshop,
switch to Illustrator, and paste the art in any open document.

In the Files & Clipboard screen of the Preferences dialog box, accessed by the
Illustrator [Edit] ➪ Preferences ➪ Files & Clipboard menu option, you can specify

whether Illustrator transfers paths to the clipboard using the PDF (Portable Document Format) or AICB (Adobe Illustrator Clipboard) formats. Photoshop can handle both of these formats, but the difference is that the PDF format preserves the transparency of the objects while the AICB format does not.

Drag-and-drop

The easiest way to move art between these programs is to drag it from one program to the other. To drag art from Illustrator to Photoshop, select the art in Illustrator and drag it out of the Illustrator window onto a Photoshop window. To drag art from Photoshop to Illustrator, select the art in Photoshop and drag it out of the Photoshop window onto an Illustrator window.

Note   For drag-and-drop to work between programs, you must have a window from the "to" application showing when you start dragging.

You can also move just paths between the two programs. When opening or pasting Illustrator art in Photoshop, a Paste dialog box appears. Click the Paste As Paths option in this dialog box, as shown in Figure 14-3. Instead of Filled and Stroked paths appearing in Photoshop, paths appear that can be manipulated by the Path tools on the Paths palette.

Figure 14-3: The Paste dialog box

To place paths from Photoshop into Illustrator, select the paths in Photoshop with the Path Selection tool, copy the paths, and then paste them in Illustrator. If you hold down the ⌘ [Ctrl] key while dragging an object between the two programs, the object is copied as a path.

Another convenient place to use drag-and-drop is from the Windows Explorer window or the Macintosh desktop. If you select an image file, drag and drop it on an open Illustrator file, the image is placed within the open document just as if you had used the File ➪ Place command. For Windows systems, if you drop the image file on Illustrator's title bar, the image is opened as part of a new file. For the Mac OS, you can drop an image file on the Illustrator icon to open the file in Illustrator.

Rasterizing Illustrator Artwork

You have several ways to turn Illustrator art into pixels, the permanent way is to use the Object ➪ Rasterize command, which transforms any selected artwork into pixel-based artwork, at the resolution you specify.

Note
Another way to convert objects into pixels is with the Effect ⇨ Rasterize menu option. This method will change the appearance of the objects, but the rasterization can be deleted to return to the original objects.

The following steps tell you how to do this:

1. Create your artwork in Illustrator.

2. Select the artwork and choose Object ⇨ Rasterize. The Rasterize dialog box, shown in Figure 14-4 appears. Enter the ppi (pixels per inch) and click OK.

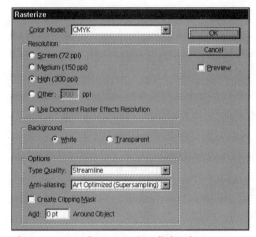

Figure 14-4: The Rasterize dialog box

3. Your artwork is rasterized. Figure 14-5 shows the artwork before and after being rasterized.

Figure 14-5: Artwork before
(left) and after rasterization (right)

The Rasterize dialog box can switch between CMYK, Grayscale and Bitmap Color Models. It also includes several preset ppi settings — Screen (72 ppi), Medium (150 ppi), and High (300 ppi). The Other setting allows you to set a custom ppi value. You also have the option to use the settings as defined in the Document Raster Effects Resolution dialog box. This dialog box can be opened using Effect ⇨ Document Raster Effects Settings and looks surprisingly close to the Rasterize dialog box.

The details of the Document Raster Effects Settings dialog box are presented in Chapter 13, "Using Styles, Effects and Filters."

The background of the rasterized object can be set to either White or Transparent. The dialog box also includes the options for setting the Type Quality to Streamline or Outline and the Anti-Aliasing to None, Art Optimized (Supersampling) or Type Optimized (Hinted). The Outline Type Quality option will make the type appear slightly heavier. The Anti-Aliasing options will soften the edges of the image you are rasterizing by adding a pixel color between the image and the background so the edges aren't jagged. The options can use different methods that are better for artwork or text.

A funky little checkbox in the Rasterize dialog box asks if you'd like to make a mask of your artwork. This can be a good thing to do for items where sharp edges are important, such as text. Checking the Create Clipping Mask option creates an automatic clipping mask around the edges of the artwork, and masks the image. In addition to keeping the edges nice and straight — because they're paths, not pixels — this masks off the areas of "white" or "empty" pixels, making those areas appear transparent. You can also specify the number of pixels to add around the object.

As an Illustrator user, you may not be familiar with having to decide resolution as you do in Photoshop. The quick rule of thumb is that the resolution of pixel-based images should be one- and-a-half to two times the line screen at which the piece will be printed. So if you are using a 133-line screen, your ppi should be between 199 and 266. It doesn't hurt to go higher than two times the line screen, but it is unnecessary. Because the math is easier, double the line screen for the resolution.

When you send Illustrator documents to a non-PostScript printer or you export to a raster format, all the objects within the document will be rasterized. You don't need to rasterize objects individually to print or export a document. The default rasterization resolution is specified in the Printing & Export screen of the Document Setup dialog box. Gradient Mesh objects, because of their complexity, have their own ppi setting in the Document Setup dialog box.

The Gradient Mesh object is described in more detail in Chapter 6, "Working with Color."

Applying raster effects

One of the drawbacks of rasterizing Illustrator objects is that you lose the ability to manipulate them. For example, if you rasterize a path, you can no longer select a point on the path and move it relative to the path. You can use the Auto Trace tool to convert the rasterized object into a controllable path again, but it will not be exactly like the original path. This problem probably makes you reluctant to

ASK TOULOUSE: Filters versus Effects?

Fred: Wilma?!?

Toulouse: Why the bellow?

Fred: I can't figure out these filters.

Toulouse: Maybe I can help?

Fred: I finally begin to figure out all the filters in Illustrator, and then these effects come along. I wish I were back in Bedrock mining rocks.

Toulouse: All your filters are still there, but many of them are also available as effects.

Fred: Isn't it inefficient to have the same feature repeated twice?

Toulouse: I suppose, but effects have a unique advantage — they don't change the structure of the object, only its appearance.

Fred: But, when I apply a filter, I know it's there.

Toulouse: Yes, but have you ever applied a filter, and then wanted to remove it a few steps later or edit it without undoing all your work and retracing your steps?

Fred: Yeah, that's happened a couple of times.

Toulouse: Using the Appearance palette, you can edit effects or remove them at any time and you'll still be able to edit the paths like normal.

Fred: So, why didn't effects just replace filters altogether?

Toulouse: Probably because Adobe didn't want you to feel lost when the filters were gone. You can still use many third-party filters, and effects can take up a lot of memory.

Fred: Hey, these filters are neat! I'm going to show these to Barney.

use the Rasterize feature without the Undo safety net. Illustrator presents a unique solution to this problem — the Rasterize Effect.

The Rasterize Effect can be used to rasterize an object, but only the appearance of the object is changed. The object still maintains all its object properties that enable it to be modified and controlled. Select Effect ⇨ Rasterize to apply this effect. This menu option opens the Rasterize dialog box that includes the same options as the Object ⇨ Rasterize menu.

Cross-Reference You can find more information about working with effects in Chapter 13, "Using Styles, Effects, and Filters."

Exporting raster images

Illustrator can export artwork to a number of different raster formats using the File ➪ Export command. For these raster formats, you can specify the Color Model, Resolution, and whether the artwork should be Anti-Aliased or not. These options are set in the Rasterize Options dialog box that appears when you export to a raster format. Figure 14-6 shows this dialog box.

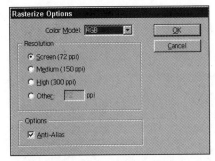

Figure 14-6: The Rasterize Options dialog box

This dialog box can include additional options depending on the specified format. For example, the TIFF format includes options for enabling LZW (Lempel Ziv Welch) compression, specifying Byte Order for IBM PC or Macintosh, and embedding an ICC (International Color Consortium) Profile.

Some raster formats supported by Illustrator include

✦ Amiga IFF (IFF)

✦ Bitmap (BMP)

✦ Filmstrip (FLM)

✦ Macintosh PICT (PIC)

✦ PCX (PCX)

✦ Photoshop (PSD)

✦ Pixar (PXR)

✦ Targa (TGA)

✦ TIFF (TIF)

Cross-Reference

You can find information on Web graphic formats, including GIF, JPEG, PNG, Flash, and SVG, in Chapter 17, "Using Illustrator to Generate Web Graphics." You can also find more information on the various supported formats in Chapter 5, "Selecting and Editing."

Working with Raster Images

Although raster images aren't native to Illustrator, they can be used alongside Illustrator artwork in several different ways. Understanding how to work with raster images can add many new dimensions to your artwork. Illustrator includes features that make working with raster images easier.

Viewing raster images

Illustrator includes a new preview mode for viewing raster images. You can select this preview mode with the View ⇨ Pixel Preview menu option. This mode displays all objects as raster images even if they are still Illustrator objects. The benefit of this preview mode is to see what the current artwork would look like if it were saved using a raster format.

Figure 14-7 shows the same image displayed in two windows. The window on the left is the standard preview mode and the window on the right is the Pixel Preview mode. Notice how the artwork on the right is pixelated.

Figure 14-7: Artwork in Preview mode (left) and Pixel Preview mode (right)

ASK TOULOUSE: Viewing Raster Images

Wilma: Betty, look at this invitation that I created for the Bedrock Barbecue next week. I just wish there was a way to view the image before printing it.

Toulouse: I'm not Betty, but I have your answer.

Wilma: Great! I can show this to Betty later.

Toulouse: Illustrator includes a Pixel Preview mode that can be used to view your document as a raster image.

Wilma: What's the catch?

Toulouse: No catch. You can use this mode by selecting View ⇨ Pixel Preview.

Wilma: Will this convert my artwork to a raster image?

Toulouse: No, it will only change the view of the artwork.

Wilma: Oh, that is handy.

Toulouse: The option is a toggle option that can be turned on or off.

In Pixel Preview mode, you can set objects to snap to the pixel grid when transformed. To enable pixel-snapping, select the View ⇨ Snap to Pixel option.

Colorizing 1-bit TIFF images

One-bit TIFF images (black and white only) can be colored in Illustrator. This effectively turns the black pixels into the color you specify. To color a 1-bit TIFF image, select the imported image, and change the Fill color to the desired color.

Tip You can create an unlimited number of colors in a 1-bit image by creating additional copies and applying different masks to each one.

The following steps describe how to color portions of a 1-bit image and Figure 14-8 illustrates these steps:

1. Select the imported image you wish to color and apply a color to it by changing the Fill on the Color palette.

2. Copy the image and paint the copy with a different color.

3. Create a mask over the portion of the copied object that should be the different color. Group the mask with the copied image.

4. Realign the copied image or mask with the original image.

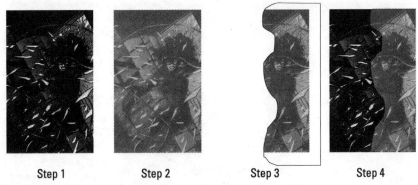

| Step 1 | Step 2 | Step 3 | Step 4 |

Figure 14-8: Steps for coloring a 1-bit image with multiple colors

Using scanned sketches

Another useful way to use raster images is to scan in a sketch of an image that is hand-drawn (yes, paper and pencil are still valid mediums). You can then use the scanned image as a backdrop for the paths that you will trace on top of the scanned image. You can set the transparency of the trace lines to 50 percent in order to see the backdrop beneath.

Tip

> To automatically trace a scanned image, use the Auto Trace tool, but at times you will only want to trace a limited selection of lines. In such a case, manually tracing the lines can be easier and more accurate than the Auto Trace tool.

Use the following steps to trace a scanned sketch:

1. Scan the sketched image and place it in a new document using the File ➪ Place command.

2. Select a tool to trace the scanned sketch, such as the Paintbrush or Pencil tool.

3. Set the Opacity slider in the Transparency palette to 50 percent and trace the lines in the scanned sketch. Figure 14-9 shows traced lines drawn on top of the scanned sketch image.

4. When finished tracing the relevant portions of the sketch, discard the sketch image and reset the Opacity to 100 percent.

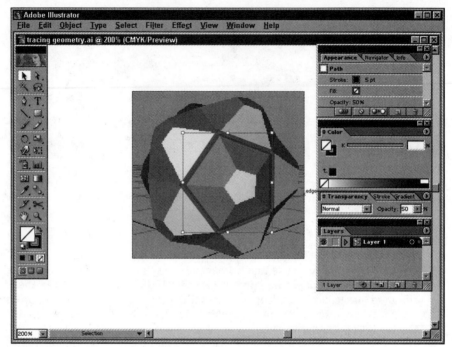

Figure 14-9: Traced lines on top of a scanned sketch image

Using Photoshop Filters in Illustrator

By themselves, these Photoshop filters are really neat. However, because many Illustrator users also have Photoshop, are they necessary?

For starters, these filters make things a bit easier than before Illustrator could use Photoshop filters, especially for creating things such as drop shadows and other special effects. Instead of having to allocate memory to Photoshop, you can do filter operations right in Illustrator.

But here's the very cool thing, the one advantage that Illustrator has over Photoshop when it comes to applying filters. It's so special that we've decided to offset it with one of those wonderful little icons. . . .

Note   Because Illustrator has multiple undos, you can apply several different filters to an imported image, and undo all of them in turn.

Photoshop filters work only on pixel-based images. If you'd like to apply a Photoshop filter to your Illustrator artwork, you have to first select it and choose Object ➪ Rasterize to turn it into a pixel-based image.

Tip

Photoshop filters can only be applied to a document that is in RGB Color Mode. If the document is in CMYK Color Mode, all the Photoshop filters will be disabled. You can change the Color Mode to RGB for the current document using File ➪ Document Color Mode ➪ RGB.

The following steps describe how to apply a Photoshop filter to an image and Figure 14-10 illustrates these steps.

1. Select the pixel-based image in Illustrator to which you'd like to apply the Photoshop filter.

2. Choose Filter ➪ *Name of Photoshop filter submenu* ➪ *Name of filter*. This can be, for instance, Filter ➪ Texture ➪ Mosaic Tiles. This will open the Mosaic Tiles dialog box, shown in Figure 14-10.

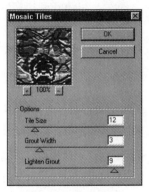

Figure 14-10: The Mosaic Tiles dialog box let you define the tile size.

3. In the Filter dialog box (if one exists), adjust the settings and values.

4. Click OK in the Filter dialog box to produce the effect shown in Figure 14-11.

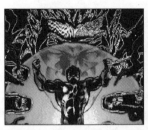

Figure 14-11: The images before (left) and after (right) applying the Mosaic Tiles filter.

One big limitation of using Photoshop filters in Illustrator is that you can't make any selections *within* the pixel-based image. A way around this is to create a copy of the image, apply the filter, and then mask the area you'd like that effect applied to.

Illustrator's Photoshop plug-ins

Illustrator includes all the Photoshop plug-ins that were originally Aldus Gallery Effects (back in the days before Adobe bought Aldus). They're separated from the vector filters and appear below the vector filters (the logic being that you won't be using them as much as Illustrator filters, so why let them get in the way).

Note Illustrator includes many of the Photoshop filters that ship with Photoshop. All the Photoshop (pixel-based) filters are set up to appear at the bottom of the Filter menu, while the vector-based filters appear at the top of the menu.

The plug-ins are primarily special-effect plug-ins, so we've included the following images to show the filter, the settings, and the result on the originally vector-based artwork, which is shown in Figure 14-12.

Figure 14-12: The original vector artwork

Note All these Photoshop filters can also be applied as an Effect. Applying an Effect only changes the appearance of the object; the object still retains its object properties. Effects are covered in detail in Chapter 13, "Using Styles, Effects, and Filters."

Artistic filters

The first category of Photoshop filters is the Artistic filters. These filters simulate many different artistic painting methods. The complete list of Artistic filters include

Colored Pencil, Cutout, Dry Brush, Film Grain, Fresco, Neon Glow, Paint Daubs, Palette Knife, Plastic Wrap, Poster Edges, Rough Pastels, Smudge Stick, Sponge, Underpainting, and Watercolor. Each of these filters opens with a dialog box that includes a preview window and several different option settings. Figure 14-13 shows a sampling of the Artistic filters.

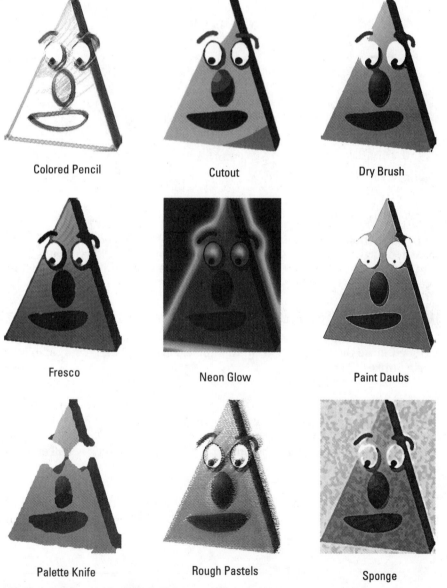

Figure 14-13: Sample Artistic filters

Blur filters

The Brush Strokes filters include a couple of filters that can be used to blur an object. These two filters are Gaussian and Radial Blur. Figure 14-14 shows these two filters.

Gaussian Blur   Radial Blur

Figure 14-14: Blur filters

Brush Strokes filters

The Brush Strokes filters include an assortment of brush and ink effects including Accented Edges, Angled Strokes, Crosshatch, Dark Strokes, Ink Outlines, Spatter, Sprayed Strokes, and Sumi-e. Figure 14-15 shows a sampling of the Brush Strokes filters.

Distort filters

The Distort filters can be used to add effects like looking through glass. They include Diffuse Glow, Glass, and Ocean Ripple. Figure 14-16 shows a sampling of the Brush Strokes filters.

Pixelate filters

The Pixelate filters change the characteristics of the individual pixels in an image. The filters include Color Halftone, Crystallize, Mezzotint, and Pointillize. Figure 14-17 shows these filters along with the Unsharpen Mask filter (which felt all alone in its own category).

Sharpen filters

Only a single Sharpen filter exists — Unsharpen Mask. This filter is also shown in Figure 14-17.

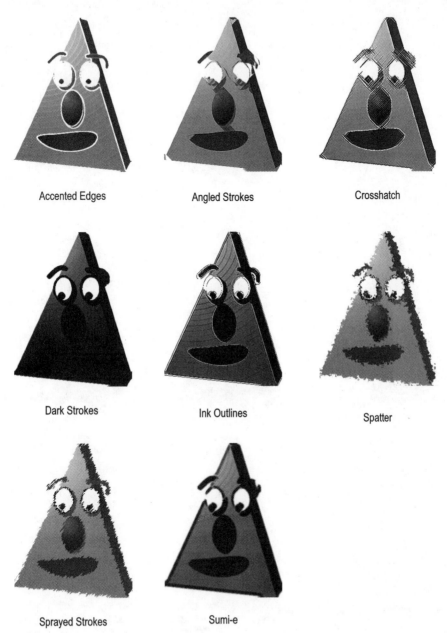

Accented Edges

Angled Strokes

Crosshatch

Dark Strokes

Ink Outlines

Spatter

Sprayed Strokes

Sumi-e

Figure 14-15: Brush Strokes filters

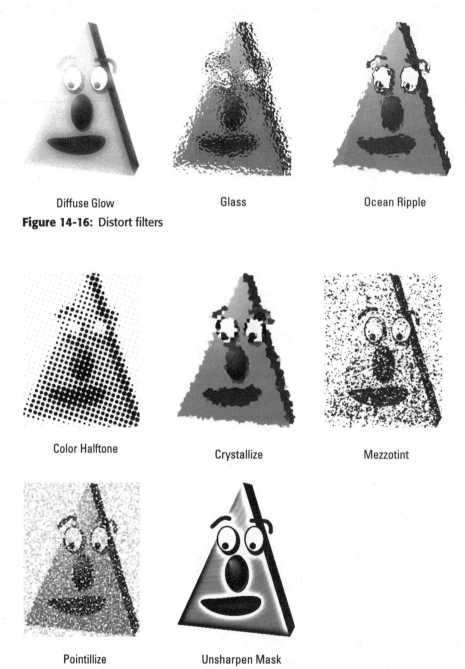

Diffuse Glow   Glass   Ocean Ripple

Figure 14-16: Distort filters

Color Halftone   Crystallize   Mezzotint

Pointillize   Unsharpen Mask

Figure 14-17: Pixelate and Sharpen filters

Sketch filters

The Sketch filters include another varied assortment of effects that simulate different artistic mediums, including Bas Relief, Chalk & Charcoal, Charcoal, Chrome,
Conté Crayon, Graphic Pen, Halftone Pattern, Note Paper, Photocopy, Plaster,
Reticulation, Stamp, Torn Edges, and Water Paper. Figure 14-18 shows a sampling
of the different Sketch filters.

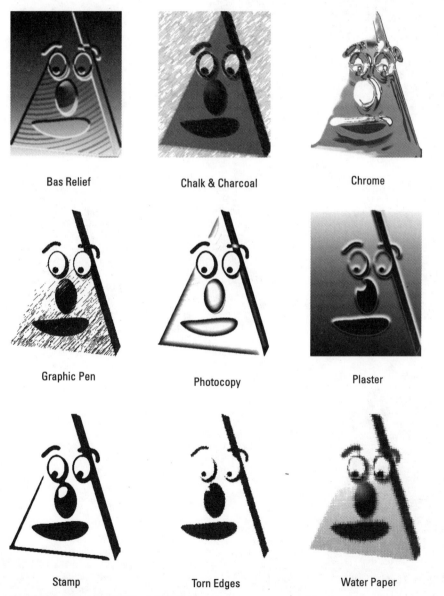

| Bas Relief | Chalk & Charcoal | Chrome |

| Graphic Pen | Photocopy | Plaster |

| Stamp | Torn Edges | Water Paper |

Figure 14-18: Sample Sketch filters

Stylize filters

The Stylize filters menu option only includes a single filter — Glowing Edges. This filter is shown in Figure 14-19 along with several Texture filters.

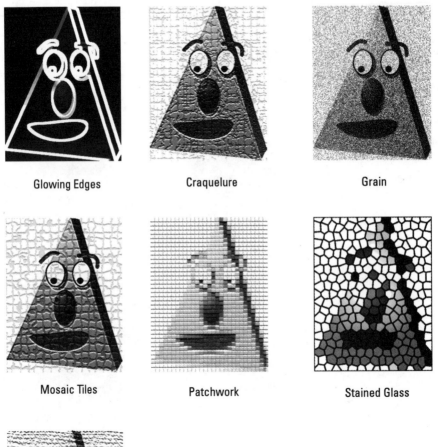

Glowing Edges   Craquelure   Grain

Mosaic Tiles   Patchwork   Stained Glass

Texturizer

Figure 14-19: Stylize and Texture filters

Texture filters

The Texture filters change an image by simulating drawing the image on different textured mediums. The filters include Craquelure, Grain, Mosaic Tiles, Patchwork, Stained Glass, and Texturizer. Figure 14-19 also shows these filters when they are applied to an image.

Note The Texturizer filter is unique because it enables you to load a separate grayscale image to use as a relief texture.

Video filters

The Video filters include De-Interlace and NTSC Colors. These two filters are used to prepare images for video output. The results of these filters aren't as noticeable as many of the other filters.

Other third-party Photoshop filters

Several Photoshop filter sets have been created by third parties, including Kai's Power Tools (KPT), KPT Convolver, and Alien Skin Eye Candy. You can find a comprehensive list of Photoshop compatible plug-ins on Adobe's Web site (www.adobe.com).

Using Illustrator to Create 3D Texture Maps

As you gain experience working with Illustrator, you will find ways to accomplish unique tasks. Another good way to learn new techniques is to ask other users. When we asked Joe Jones, one of the contributors to the color insert pages, how he created some of the images for the color insert, he offered to share the technique. We'd love to take credit for this technique, but all credit for this one belongs to Joe. You can see the final image printed in the color insert pages. For an explanation of this technique, we defer to Joe's own words (from here to the end of the chapter).

Though I would never claim to be one of the best texture mappers, 3D modelers, or science-fiction illustrators around, which I certainly aspire to be, the techniques I show here seem to work pretty well for me so far.

Very early on when I was experimenting in a 3D environment, I quickly realized the key to creating 3D images was to texture map with as much detail as possible. Creating a wireframe for every little intricate component that I wanted to show in my architecture would create incredibly huge files and probably take a couple weeks to render. Not the thing to do! For me, it was logistically impossible to model everything, so I had to quickly come up with a system to create the necessary level of detail in my illustrations. I am currently still refining my process of creating 3D illustrations, which has already taken several years of development. Incredibly difficult, but very fun stuff though!

Being able to have full control of each step and to see it all come together in 3D is nothing less than incredible to me. I've worked on every type of graphics and illustration projects you can imagine for over 18 years now, but nothing comes close to the intimacy that I feel when working on 3D texture images. Though I'm sure a psychiatrist would claim this is a form of escapism, I say hey, an artist has to dream!

Well, without further ado, here's a brief description of each of the steps involved:

Conceptualization

I first created a slew of small conceptual thumbnails, sketches, and studies. Figure 14-20 shows the original conceptual sketch that I worked from for this piece entitled "Port Merillia."

Figure 14-20: A sketch of the original concept

In the business of illustration, we have a saying: "Practice safe design and use the concept!" In the end, concept is everything. Although in 3D illustration true craftsmanship is in the model-making and texture mapping, the concept still has to pull it all together for the illustration to work. I first developed a large series of conceptual sketches (one of which is shown in Figure 14-21), and defined the look of my architecture. Then I designed and built all the outline parts for the shape of each building as paths in Illustrator, which were later used in the modeling process in Ray Dream Studio. The actual texture mapping for each building is a process that starts in Illustrator, which I discuss in a coming section.

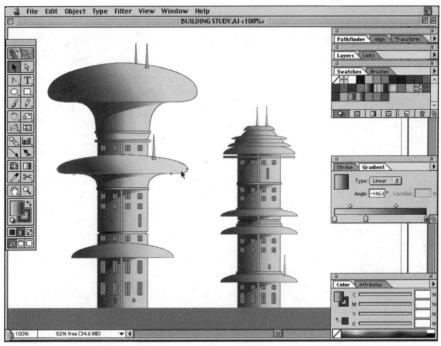

Figure 14-21: Structure study

Modeling

Yes, yes, I know, this is surely the poor boy's approach to 3D illustration. What can I say, it works and I'm still not quite ready to drop several thousand dollars on applications such as Maya or 3D Studio Max. Soon, maybe. Figure 14-22 is a conceptual vector study created in Illustrator. Here, I refine my composition and get a better feel for the pieces needed for each building. Here, I work on refining the scale, depth, color, and balance I want from this piece.

Figure 14-23 shows the actual wireframe model of the "Dome" element of just one structure after construction. It is now ready to be assembled with other modeled elements and texture mapped. To turn a basic shape into a 3D model you must generate at least two separate paths — one is the shape of how it would look from the side and the other is from the top. These paths are called *Cross Sections* and *Envelope Lines*, and are essential in extruding or lathing a shape into a 3D model.

Figure 14-22: Conceptual vector study

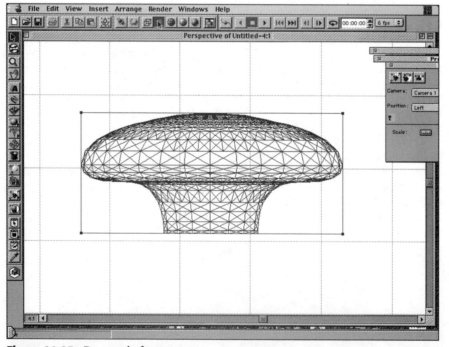

Figure 14-23: Dome wireframe

As you look at these illustrations, remember that for every single shape in each building I had to produce at least two precise paths in Illustrator. I created all line work for the models, as well as the artwork for the texture mapping, at the same time to ensure everything would fit and map correctly in the final steps. Very important!

Texture mapping

Figure 14-24 shows the wireframe model of the "Dome" element, quickly texture mapped for a better idea of its look, smoothness, and form.

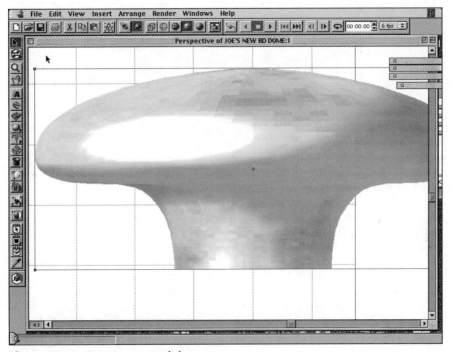

Figure 14-24: Texture-mapped dome

All of the custom mapping I created was based on my original sketches and more refined drawings, which had to be first carefully laid out in Illustrator, as shown in Figure 14-25. Starting with the circular base shape for the "Dome" on the first layer, I created the various panels, lights, and windows on separate layers for full control of these elements in Photoshop.

I carefully constructed each map to proportionately match the building models that were built. To maintain their layers, I then exported these Illustrator files into Photoshop, where I added additional weathering and edge effect treatments.

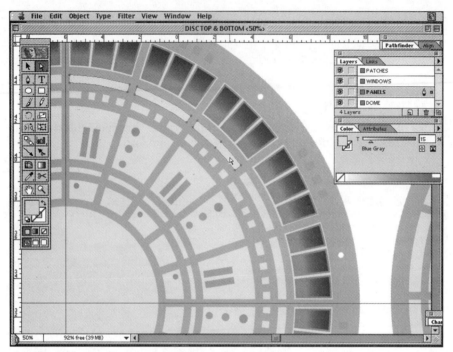

Figure 14-25: The dome texture map in Illustrator

Just like the "Dome" map, the Building map, shown in Figure 14-26, was created in a similar manner. Each element of the panels, patches, windows, and lights were set up on separate layers to be exported into Photoshop with the layers intact, to complete the final rendered map.

Figure 14-27 is the "Dome" map file being brought into Photoshop. I start with some color correction and create the custom brushes that are needed for painting the weathered appearance.

As any experienced texture map artist will tell you, the appearance of weathering and signs of aging is critical to creating an illusion of reality. Figure 14-28 shows the final "Dome" texture map with all of its edge effects and hand-painted weathering. I worked both in layers and Adjustments Layers in Photoshop to create this effect. When this map is applied to its model, it looks very convincing. Though the shapes in these maps are basic, this gives you some idea of the level of detail that can be created with a good texture map.

Figure 14-29 shows one of the many final building texture maps I had to create. Again, I created its edge effects and hand-painted weathering in layers and Adjustments Layers working in Photoshop.

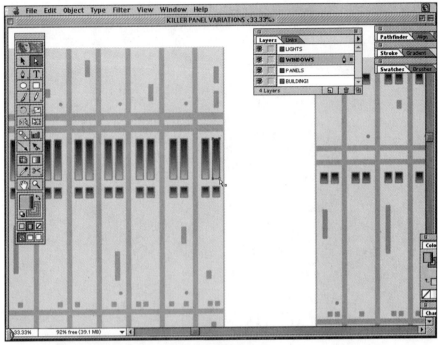

Figure 14-26: Building the texture map in Illustrator

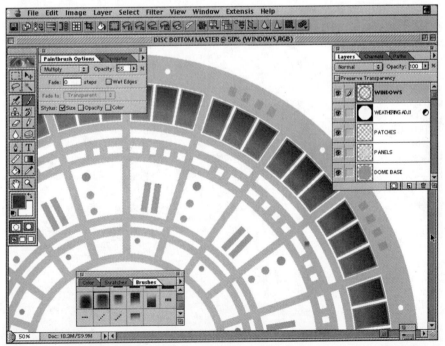

Figure 14-27: The dome texture map in Photoshop

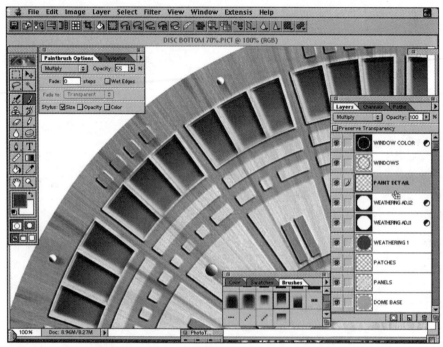

Figure 14-28: The weathered dome texture map in Photoshop

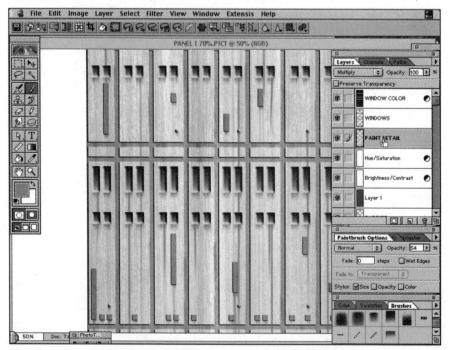

Figure 14-29: The weathered building texture map in Photoshop

To create certain effects, and especially the illusion of transparency and ambiance for the window and the lights, I first had to create this window mask for the "Dome" in Illustrator, as shown in Figure 14-30. I then rasterized it as a grayscale file to be mapped in later. If done right, this creates a convincing effect without the pains of extensive modeling.

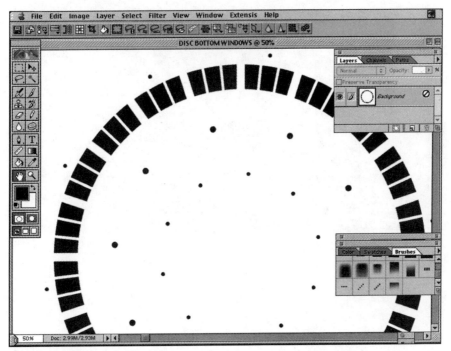

Figure 14-30: The dome window mask

Figure 14-31 shows four different texture maps applied to just one structure model. Add some light and atmosphere and we're well on our way. What'd I tell you, pretty convincing huh!

The final completed wireframe model partially rendered is shown in Figure 14-32. Of course, after all of the texture mapping is applied to all of the various models, this scene based on the original sketch needs to be built, lit, and then rendered. From there the file is brought into Photoshop where color correction and a ton of touch-up work is done. For example, the clothing for the figures is hand painted using a digital tablet. We're not in Kansas anymore!

You can view the finished image after all the final touch-ups in all its glory in the color insert pages.

Figure 14-31: The final dome texture maps

Figure 14-32: A sample of the final model

Summary

Although the world of pixel-based images really belong to Photoshop, Illustrator has added the functionality to work with pixel-based objects. In this chapter, you learned that

✦ You can incorporate pixel-based artwork into Illustrator by importing it, by copying and pasting it, or by dragging it out of Photoshop and dropping it into Illustrator.

✦ The quickest way to move images between Illustrator and Photoshop is to drag-and-drop them between windows in each program.

✦ You can also move paths back and forth between the two programs.

✦ You can colorize 1-bit images by selecting the image and changing the Fill color in the Color palette.

✦ Photoshop filters appear in the Filter menu underneath the Illustrator filters.

✦ You can use Illustrator to create realistic 3D texture maps.

✦   ✦   ✦

Customizing and Optimizing Illustrator

Having your system configured and personalized to meet your needs increases your efficiency as you work with Illustrator. Illustrator automatically remembers such settings as the location of your toolbox and palettes when you close down the application, but you have other ways to customize the environment. This chapter uncovers the tricks for customizing Illustrator so you can achieve valuable efficiency gains.

Preferences

No two illustrators work the same. To accommodate the vast differences in styles, techniques, and habits, Illustrator provides many settings that each user can change to personalize his or her software.

Illustrator provides the following four major ways to change preferences:

1. The most dramatic and difficult changes are to a small file called Adobe Illustrator Startup. The startup file changes how new documents appear and which custom colors, patterns, and gradients are available.

2. You can also control how Illustrator works by accessing the Preferences submenu (choose Illustrator [Edit] ➪ Preferences). You make most of these changes in the General Preferences dialog box, which you access by choosing Illustrator [Edit] ➪ Preferences ➪ General (⌘+K [Ctrl+K]). Within the Preferences dialog box, you can select different preference panels from the drop-down

menu at the top of the dialog box. You can go through each of the preference panels individually by clicking the Next and Previous buttons, or simply by choosing a preference panel from the Preferences submenu. The preference panels are General, Type & Auto Tracing, Units & Undo, Guides & Grid, Smart Guides & Slices, Hyphenation, Plug-Ins & Scratch Disk, Files & Clipboard, and Workgroup.

3. A third way to make changes is by changing preferences relative to each document. You usually make these changes in the Document Setup dialog box, but a few other options are available. More information on document-specific preferences appears later in this chapter.

4. The fourth way to customize preferences occurs automatically. When you quit Illustrator, it remembers many of the current settings for the next time you run it. These settings include palette placements and values in toolbox settings.

Illustrator has a few settings that you cannot customize. These features can really get under your skin because most of them seem like things that you should be able to customize. See the "Things You Can't Customize" section later in this chapter for a list of these settings.

Modifying the Startup Document

When you first run Illustrator, the program looks to the Illustrator startup file to check a number of preferences. Those preferences include window size and placement, as well as custom colors, gradients, patterns, zoom levels, tiling options, and graph designs.

As of Illustrator 10, there is not one startup file, but two. Which startup file you use depends on the Color Mode that you are using. When you create a new document, the New Document dialog box appears, where you can give the document a name, specify the artboard size and select the Color Mode. If you select the CMYK Color Mode, then the Adobe Illustrator Startup_CMYK.ai file is used. If you select the RGB Color Mode, then the Adobe Illustrator Startup_RGB.ai file is used.

New documents, as well as documents that are opened have all the gradients, custom colors, patterns, and graph designs of the startup file. Here's how you modify the startup file:

1. Open the startup file. It is either called Adobe Illustrator Startup_CMYK.ai or Adobe Illustrator Startup_RGB.ai, depending on the Color Mode, and is located in the Plug-Ins folder in the Adobe Illustrator folder. The file is an Adobe Illustrator 10 document, so double-clicking the file opens Illustrator as well.

2. Figure 15-1 shows the Adobe Illustrator Startup_CMYK.ai file. The document contains all the default swatches, styles and symbols. If you remove any of these elements, and then go to the Swatches, Styles or Symbols palette and delete the same element, then the element will not appear the next time you start Illustrator.

Caution If you delete a pattern, custom color, gradient, style or symbol from the startup file, it is gone. Kaput! The only way to get it back is to replace the startup file from the original disks or CD-ROM.

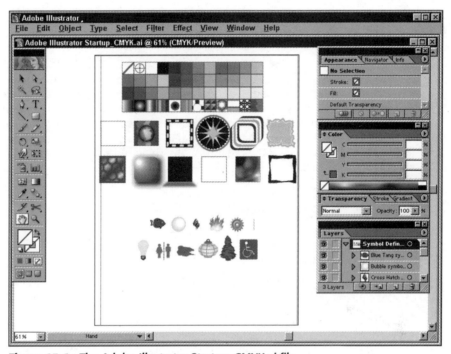

Figure 15-1: The Adobe Illustrator Startup_CMYK.ai file

3. To add a color, pattern, gradient, style or symbol to the startup file, simply add them to the Swatches palette. (To add a graph design, create the graph design and apply it to a graph. Then place the graph in the startup file.)

4. To change the window size, just save the startup file with the window size that you want new documents to have.

5. To change the color swatches on the Swatches palette, add, replace, or delete color swatches while the startup file is open, and then save the startup file.

If you delete the Adobe Illustrator Startup file, most patterns, gradients, and custom colors will not be available until you create a new startup file or place the original startup file from the disks or CD-ROM in the Plug-Ins folder.

To check whether changes that you made in the startup file work, quit Illustrator and run the program again. You cannot tell whether the changes are in place until you quit and reopen Illustrator.

You can change the window size of new documents and the viewing percentage. Most people like documents to fit in the window when it is created. For example, depending on your resolution, a 16- or 17-inch screen can comfortably use 66 percent, but 19- or 21-inch screens will likely use 100 percent.

Changing General Preferences

The General portion of the Preferences dialog box (choose Illustrator [Edit] ⇨ Preferences ⇨ General or press ⌘+K [Ctrl+K]) contains most of the *personalized* customizing options for Illustrator. The options in this box affect keyboard increments, measuring units, and the way that objects are drawn. These options are considered personalized options because they are specific to the way that each person uses the program. Few people have the same preference settings as others have (unless they never change the defaults). The General Preferences dialog box is shown in Figure 15-2.

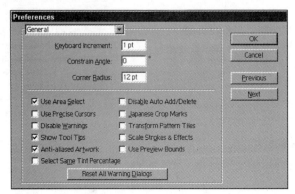

Figure 15-2: The General Preferences screen of the Preferences dialog box

Note   Although the Preferences dialog box was previously (in versions earlier than Illustrator 9) found in the File menu, it rests comfortably now under the Edit menu, unless you're running Illustrator in Apple's Mac OS X, in which case you'll find it under the Illustrator menu. If you have a habit of looking for the Preferences dialog box under the File menu, just remember the ⌘[Ctrl]+K keyboard shortcut.

The Keyboard Increment option

The cursor key increment that you specify in this option controls how far an object moves when you select it and press the keyboard arrows.

In our configuration, we have this increment set to 0.5 points because this is the smallest amount that we usually need to move things. The default for this setting is

1 point, which many people feel is small enough. We make the increment smaller when working in 800 or 1,600 percent views.

Tip While the arrow keys move selected objects the distance that is set in the Keyboard Increment option, pressing Option [Alt] plus the arrow key makes a copy of the object in that direction.

The Constrain Angle option

The Constrain Angle option controls the angle at which all objects are aligned. Rectangles are always drawn "flat," aligning themselves to the bottom, top, and sides of the document window. When you press the Shift key, lines that you draw with the Pen tool and objects that you move align to the constrain angle, or 45, 90, 135, or 180 degrees, plus or minus the constraining angle.

The constrain angle also affects how the four transformation tools transform objects. The Scale tool can be very hard to use when the Constrain Angle is not 0 degrees, and the Shear tool becomes even more difficult to use than normal at different constrain angles. Pressing Shift when you are using the Rotate tool constrains the rotational angle to 45-degree increments added to the constrain angle.

Cross-Reference Chapter 10, "Transforming and Distorting Artwork," discusses the Rotate tool and other transformational tools.

In Illustrator, 0 degrees is a horizontal line and 90 degrees is a vertical line. Figure 15-3 shows Illustrator angles.

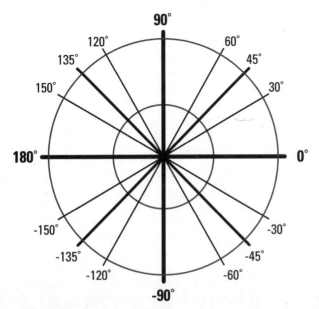

Figure 15-3: Angles in Illustrator

If you set the constrain angle at 20 degrees, objects are constrained to movements of 20, 65, 110, 155, and 200 degrees. Constrain angles of 90, 180, and –90 degrees (270 degrees) affect only type, patterns, gradients, and graphs; everything else works normally.

When Option [Alt]+copying objects, you can use the Shift key in conjunction with a constrain angle to duplicate objects at a specific angle. Option [Alt]+copy means to press the Option [Alt] key while dragging an object, and then to release the mouse button before releasing the Option [Alt] key to produce a duplicate of the object at the new location.

The Corner Radius option

The Corner Radius option affects the size of the curved corners on a rounded rectangle.

For a complete explanation of the corner radius and rounded rectangles, see Chapter 4, "Working with Objects."

Although the Constrain Angle and Corner Radius preference options affect many Illustrator's tools, keep in mind that some tools (such as the Rounded Rectangle tool) have their own Corner Radius (or Constrain Angle) option that takes precedence over the Preferences dialog box setting. You can access the tool options by double-clicking on the tool's icon in the toolbox.

The corner radius value changes each time you enter a new value in the Rectangle dialog box. This dialog box appears when you click the Rectangle or Rounded Rectangle tools without dragging in a document. If, for example, you create one rounded rectangle with a rounded-corner radius of 24 points, all rounded rectangles that you create from that point forward will have a radius of 24 points. The only ways to change the corner radius are to click a Rectangle tool without dragging in a document, and then enter a new value in the Rectangle dialog box, or to enter a new value in the Corner Radius text field in the General Preferences dialog box.

The real advantage to changing the corner radius in the General Preferences dialog box is that the corner radius immediately affects manually-created (dragged with the Rounded Rectangle tool) rounded rectangles. Changing the corner radius in the Rectangle dialog box requires that you know the exact dimensions of the rectangle or that you draw a rectangle by entering information in the Rectangle dialog box (clicking with the Rectangle tool without dragging) and specifying the corner radius. You must then delete the original rectangle in order to manually draw a rounded rectangle with the correct corner radius.

Because you can change the corner radius setting easily, be sure to check it before you draw a series of rounded rectangles manually. No easy or automatic way exists to change the corner radius on existing rounded rectangles.

If you use 0 point as the corner radius setting, the corners are not rounded at all. If you click with the Rounded Rectangle tool and enter 0 point as the corner radius, the corner radius setting in the General Preferences dialog box changes to 0 point.

General options

The 11 checkboxes in the General Options section of General Preferences are Illustrator's version of the *Battlestar Galactica* ragtag fleet of unwieldy spacefaring craft. Some are quite powerful; others seem like they aren't capable of transferring millions of people across the galaxy, much less defend themselves against the evil menace of the Cylon empire. Okay, that wasn't the best analogy. The fact is, no other place exists in Illustrator where so many totally unrelated options share the same dialog box, and we had to come up with a snazzy introduction to bring them all together.

The Use Area Select option

When the Use Area Select option is on, you can select an object in Preview mode by clicking the object's Fill. If the Use Area Select option is off, you select an object the same way that you select it in Outline and Preview Selection mode — by clicking paths or anchor points. The Use Area Select option has no effect on selecting objects in Preview Selection mode, but after you select them, you can move them by clicking and dragging a Filled area.

We have yet to have a good reason to turn this option off. The only reason that we can imagine for turning off this feature is if, for a particular illustration, we need to select specific paths from several overlapping, Filled objects. To be honest, selecting individual paths in Preview would still be difficult because you can't see most of them.

The Use Area Select option does not let you select paths by clicking Strokes, unless you click the center of the Stroke where the path is (in which case you would be clicking the path anyway). In addition, you can't select "through" a compound path; instead, clicking in the empty areas of a compound path selects the compound path itself.

The Use Precise Cursors option

Precise cursors are cursors that appear as variations of a cross-hair instead of in the shape of a tool. Figure 15-4 shows cursors that are different when the Use Precise Cursors option is on.

Name	Cursor	Precise Cursor or Cursor with Caps Lock
Pen tool		
Convert Direction Point with Pen tool		
Close path with Pen tool		
Add to existing path with Pen tool		
Connect to path with Pen tool		
Add Anchor Point tool		
Delete Anchor Point tool		
Eyedropper tool		
Select a Paint Style with Eyedropper tool		
Brush tool		
Freehand tool		
Paint Bucket tool		
Close open path with Freehand tool		
Connect an open path with Freehand tool		
Erase with Freehand tool		

Figure 15-4: The regular cursors are on the left; the precise cursors are on the right.

Note   The Caps Lock key toggles between standard cursors and precise cursors. When the Use Precise Cursors option is checked, the Caps Lock key makes the cursors standard. When the Use Precise Cursors option is not checked, the Caps Lock key activates the precise cursors.

We usually keep this option on and rarely engage the Caps Lock key to change the cursors back to normal. In particular, we've found the precise cursor for the Brush tool to be quite useful, seeing as how the standard Brush cursor is one giant amorphous blob.

The Disable Warnings option

This tiny little checkbox has the graphics community sending letters of thanks to Adobe. Version 6.0.1 of Illustrator enabled you to turn off some of the warnings, but it had to be done by editing the preference file, a task that most users found daunting at best. The warnings we're referring to are those handy little messages that appear when you've clicked in the wrong spot with the wrong tool. For instance, clicking with the Scissors tool off a path resulted in an ugly, overly long essay on the evils of clicking in empty space. Clicking with the Convert Direction Point tool brought up a dialog box condemning you for trying to convert something that wasn't a suitable anchor point. The first few times, the messages were helpful reminders. Years later, they became an annoying thorn in the side of experienced Illustrator users. Checking this box turns off the messages; instead of seeing a nagging dialog box, you hear a simple system beep noise. This noise is still a bit annoying, but it does let you know you've clicked in an unacceptable portion of the document. And if even the beep is too much, then you could disable the sound for your system.

The Show Tool Tips option

This option displays little pop-up names for each of the tools if you rest your cursor above them for one second. It's a great idea to keep this option on, as not only do you see the name of the tool, but you also see the key to press to access that tool.

Tip   Illustrator lets you see the name of swatches as you pass your cursor over them if you have Tool Tips active. These Tool tips will also display any keyboard shortcuts associated with the tool.

The Anti-Aliased Artwork option

The Anti-Aliased Artwork option turns on anti-aliasing for onscreen representation of vector objects. Aliased artifacts appear at the edge of a rasterized object when pixels near the edge are displayed using a single color. These jagged edges make the edge appear unsmooth. By enabling the Anti-Alias feature, the pixels around the edge are colored differently in order to produce a smoother edge. Curved and diagonal edges appear smooth instead of jagged (or "stair-stepped"). The resulting effect is for *onscreen* viewing only, and won't affect output or rasterization of your artwork.

The Select Same Tint Percentage option

When this option is enabled, selecting objects with stroked or filled colors using the Select menu bases the selection criteria on the tint percentage. This enables a wider selection of objects that match the stroke or fill color tint percentage that is used to designate process colors.

Disable Auto Add/Delete

This option refers to the Pen tool's automatic add/delete feature. The default is unchecked. When the box is not checked, you can add or delete points while drawing with the Pen tool. As you are drawing a path with the Pen tool, you can click the path to add more anchor points. You can also click an anchor point to delete it and continue to draw your path without having to switch tools. When you check this option, this feature is turned off.

The Japanese Crop Marks option

When checked, the Japanese Crop Marks option changes the standard crop marks. Create Japanese crop marks by going to Object ➪ Crop Marks ➪ Make (see Figure 15-5).

The Transform Pattern Tiles option

Check the Transform Pattern Tiles option if you want patterns in paths to be moved, scaled, rotated, sheared, and reflected when you use the transformation tools. When this option is checked, pulling up a transformation dialog box (Move, Rotate, Scale, Reflect, or Shear) automatically checks the Pattern checkbox. When the option is not checked, the Pattern checkbox is not checked in the transformation dialog box. This option controls whether selected patterns are transformed when the Transform palette is used.

The Transform palette is covered in detail in Chapter 10, "Transforming and Distorting Artwork."

We usually check the Transform Pattern Tiles box, which sets all patterns to automatically transform and move with the objects that are being transformed and moved. This feature is especially useful when you want to create perspective in objects because the transformations of patterns can enhance the intended perspective.

The Scale Strokes & Effects option

When the Scale Strokes & Effects feature is on, it automatically increases and reduces line weights relative to an object when you uniformly scale that object manually. For example, if a path has a Stroke weight of 1 point and you reduce the path uniformly by 50 percent, the Stroke weight changes to 0.5 point. This feature applies to Effects as well as strokes.

You can also select this option in the Transform palette pop-up menu.

Scaling objects nonuniformly (without the Shift key pressed) does not change the Stroke weight on an object, regardless of whether the Scale Line Weight feature is on or off.

Figure 15-5: Standard crop marks (top) and Japanese crop marks (bottom)

The Use Preview Bounds option

When a stroke is added to an object, the width of the stroke can change the dimensions of the object. This results in an inaccurate transformation if you're entering a transformation value in the Transform or Info palettes. If you enable the Use Preview Bounds option in the General Preferences dialog box, then the stroke width and effects are taken into account.

The Use Preview Bounds option also affects how an object will snap to a local grid intersection.

Type and Auto Tracing Preferences

The second screen in the Preferences dialog includes options for controlling type and the Auto Trace tool. As stated earlier, you can access this dialog box by going to Illustrator [Edit] ⇨ Preferences ⇨ Type & Auto Tracing preferences. Figure 15-6 illustrates the Type & Auto Tracing dialog box.

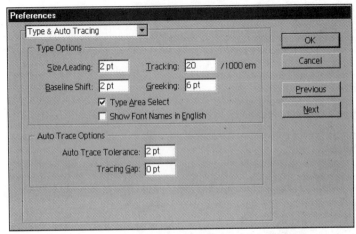

Figure 15-6: The Type & Auto Tracing screen of the Preferences dialog box

The Type options

You have six Type options to choose from. They include Size/Leading, Baseline Shift, Tracking, Greeking, Type Area Select, and Show Font Names in English.

The Size/Leading option

You can use the keyboard to increase and decrease type size by pressing ⌘+Shift+> [Ctrl+Shift+>] and ⌘+Shift+< [Ctrl+Shift+<], respectively. You can increase and decrease leading by pressing Option+↑ [Alt+↑] and Option+↓ [Alt+↓], respectively. In the Size/Leading text box, you specify the increment by which the size and leading change.

You can increase or decrease the type size and leading only until you reach the upper and lower limits of each. The upper limit for type size and leading is 1,296 points, and the lower limit for each is 0.1 point.

Tip We like to keep the settings fairly high, at 10 points, because we have found that when we change the font size, we typically need to change the point size drastically, usually quite a bit more than 10 points. Keeping the value high enables us to quickly make large point-size changes. If we need to do fine-tuning, we either type in the exact size that we want or use the Scale tool.

The Baseline Shift option

The Baseline Shift feature moves selected type up and down on the baseline, independent of the leading. The increment specified in this box determines how much the type is moved when you press the arrow keyboard commands. To move type up one increment, press Option+Shift+↑ [Alt+Shift+↑]. To move type down one increment, press Option+Shift+↓ [Alt+Shift+↓].

We keep the Baseline shift increment at 1 point so that we can adjust Path type better; specifically, we like to be able to adjust the baseline shift of type on a circle.

The Tracking option

Tracking changes the amount of space between selected characters, and the setting in this text field represents the amount of space (measured in thousandths of an em space) that the keyboard command adds or removes. To increase tracking, you press ⌘+→ [Ctrl+→]; to decrease it, you press ⌘+← [Ctrl+←].

Tip To increase the tracking by five times the increment in the General Preferences dialog box, press ⌘+Option+→ [Ctrl+Alt+→]. To decrease the tracking by five times the increment, press ⌘+Option+← [Ctrl+Alt+←].

The value in the Tracking text field also affects incremental changes in kerning. *Kerning* is the addition or removal of space between one pair of letters only. Kerning is done instead of tracking when a blinking insertion point is between two letters, as opposed to at least one selected character for tracking.

We set the Tracking increment to 10 because it produces a result that corresponds to twice the tracking generated by the QuarkXPress key command. In QuarkXPress, pressing ⌘+Option+Shift+[on the Mac and Ctrl+Alt+Shift+[in Windows or ⌘+Option+Shift+] on the Mac and Ctrl+Alt+Shift+] in Windows increases or decreases, respectively, tracking by @@bf1/200 em space.

The Greeking option

The number that you enter in this field defines the point at which Illustrator begins to greek text (see Figure 15-7). Illustrator *greeks* text — turns the letters into gray bars — when the text is so small that reading it on the screen would be hard or impossible. This change reduces screen redraw time dramatically, especially when the document contains a lot of text.

Figure 15-7: Text onscreen is so small that it is greeked.

The size in this text field is relative to the viewing magnification of the document. At a limit of 6 points, 6-point type at 100, 66, 50, 25 percent, or smaller is greeked; but 6-point type at 150 percent, 200 percent, or larger is readable. With the same limitations, 12-point type is greeked at 50 percent and smaller, but it is readable at 66 percent and larger.

The Type Area Select option

Turning this option on makes it possible to select text by clicking the text itself, instead of just the Baseline of the text (as in Illustrator versions 1.0 to 6.0). Some people (especially long-time Illustrator users) find this option annoying, and are outraged at Adobe's audacity to have it turned on by default. We like it, and we know it makes selecting text much easier for Illustrator newcomers. Besides, that's why it's a preference—if you don't like Type Area Select, just turn it off.

The Show Font Names in English option

If you have a font from another language installed on your system (such as Kanji, the Japanese character set), this option enables you to see these typefaces in the font/type menus as English words, rather than the indecipherable characters that double-bit fonts turn into when they're displayed in Roman characters.

The Auto Trace options

The Auto Trace section of the Type & Auto Tracing screen includes some options that affect how the Auto Trace and Pencil tools work.

The Auto Trace Tolerance option

The Auto Trace Tolerance setting controls the accuracy of paths that are created when tracing placed templates.

Cross-Reference Chapter 5, "Selecting and Editing," discusses Auto Trace settings and resulting paths.

The lower the Auto Trace setting, the more exact the resulting path. A higher setting results in smoother, less accurate paths. You can enter a value from 0 to 10, in increments of $\frac{1}{100}$ point (two decimal places).

The Auto Trace number is relative to the number of pixels on the screen that the resulting path may vary. A tolerance of 10 means that the resulting path may vary up to 10 pixels from the location of the actual dragged or traced area.

The Tracing Gap option

When you use the Auto Trace tool to trace a placed image, the tool may encounter *gaps*, or white space, between solid areas. The Tracing Gap option enables you to specify that if the Auto Trace tool runs into a white-space gap of 1 or 2 pixels, it can jump over the gap and continue tracing on the other side of it.

A value of 0 prevents the Auto Trace tool from tracing over gaps. If you use a value of 1, the Auto Trace tool traces over gaps that are up to 1 pixel wide. If you use a value of 2 (the highest allowed), it traces over gaps that are 2 pixels wide. The Tracing Gap setting not only goes over gaps, it also adheres less closely to the original template.

We usually use a setting of 0 because when tracing any image in Illustrator, we examine it closely in Photoshop to make sure that it does not have any gaps. We can then be sure that the resulting paths will not be misshapen because of image-tracing inaccuracies.

Units & Undo Preferences

The Units & Undo preferences enable you to select the measurement system you want to use and set the number of times you can use the Undo key in a row. You can also specify the objects by their object name or by their XML ID. Figure 15-8 illustrates the Units & Undo screen of the Preferences dialog box.

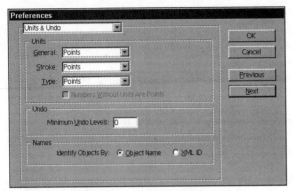

Figure 15-8: The Units & Undo screen of the Preferences dialog box

Units settings

The General pop-up menu in the Units section changes the measurement system for the current document and all future new documents. The three areas the measurement can be specified for are: General (which includes the Rulers), Stroke, and Type. Illustrator contains six different measurement units: inches, picas, pixels, points, millimeters, and centimeters. The ⌘+Control+U command (Macintosh only) toggles between all five units for the Rulers.

Caution   Changing the General units in the Units & Undo Preferences dialog box changes the Ruler units in the Document Setup dialog box (choose File ➪ Document Setup or press ⌘+Option+P [Ctrl+Alt+P]).

Being aware of which measurement system you are working in is important. When you enter a measurement in a dialog box, any numbers that are not measurement-system-specific are applied to the current unit of measurement. For example, if you want to move something 1 inch and you open the Move dialog box (choose Object ➪ Transform ➪ Move or double-click the Selection tool), you need to add either the inch symbol (") or the abbreviation *in* after you type a 1 in the dialog box if the measurement system is not inches. If the measurement system is points and picas, entering just a 1 moves the object 1 point, not 1 inch. If the measurement system is already in inches, entering just the number 1 is fine.

Usually, a corresponding letter or letters indicates the measurement system: *in* for inch, *pt* for points, and *cm* for centimeters.

We use the points/picas system for several reasons. First, using points and picas is easier because you can specify smaller increments exactly (ever try to figure out what $\frac{1}{12}$ of an inch is in decimals?). Second, type is measured in points, not inches. Third, points and picas are the standard in measuring systems for designers and printers.

Caution The default measurement is points and picas, so if you ever toss your preferences file or reinstall Illustrator, be aware that you may have to change the measurement system.

Undo settings

Illustrator can set the minimum number of undos — the number that makes sure you always have a certain number of undos available. The higher you set the number, the more steps you'll always be able to undo. Of course, the higher the number, the more memory that Illustrator needs to be able to undo that far. If you can provide Illustrator with gobs of RAM, then set your undos to at least 10, maybe even 20. But if you're working with a complex document on your favorite aunt's antiquated computer, you may want to keep the number to a more reasonable one or two.

Note Under Mac OS X, this isn't an issue. Every application has a 2GB virtual address space.

Identifying objects

The Names section of the Units & Undo screen will let you specify that objects are identified by their object name or by their XML ID. The XML ID is important if you are saving the file using the SVG format.

Cross-Reference Chapter 17, "Using Illustrator to Generate Web Graphics," covers the SVG format and XML IDs in more detail.

Guides & Grid Preferences

The Guides & Grid section of Preferences lets you control the color and style of your guide and grid lines. You can select from an array of colors and the Style options include lines or dots. The Color drop down list includes several preset color names or you can select the Other option, which will open the color selector where you can choose any color that you like. The selected color will appear in the color swatches to the right of the drop down lists. Double clicking on the color swatch will open the color selector.

The Grid section also includes values for specifying the spacing of your grid and the number of subdivisions. The Grids in Back option will place the grid lines behind all objects in the document if enabled. If disabled, the grids will penetrate all objects. Figure 15-9 illustrates the Guides & Grid screen of the Preferences dialog box.

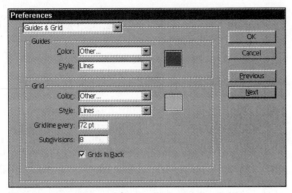

Figure 15-9: The Guides & Grid screen of the Preferences dialog box

Chapter 7, "Organizing Artwork," has the lowdown on getting the most out of grids and guides.

Even though Guides and Grids are specified in the Preferences dialog box, the grid and guide lines will only show up if they are enabled in the View menu.

Smart Guides & Slices Preferences

Smart Guides preferences enable you to check or uncheck four different Display Options as well as affect the angles and snapping tolerance. The Slice options let you set whether Slice Numbers are visible and the line colors. Figure 15-10 illustrates the Smart Guides & Slices screen of the Preferences dialog box.

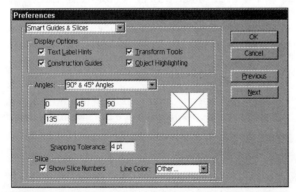

Figure 15-10: The Smart Guides & Slices screen of the Preferences dialog box

You can find more information on Smart Guides and how to use them in Chapter 7, "Organizing Artwork." Slices are covered in Chapter 17, "Using Illustrator to Generate Web Graphics."

The Display Options

The four Display Options are:

✦ ___Text Label Hints **pop up when you drag your mouse cursor over your object. They tell you what each area is. For example, if you drag your mouse cursor over a line, the hint pops up with the word "path." If you drag your mouse cursor over an anchor point, the hint says "anchor point."**

✦ ___Construction Guides **let you view guidelines when using Smart Guides.**

✦ ___Transform Tools. **Transform Tools enable you to rotate, scale, or shear an object. With this option checked, Smart Guides appears to help you out.**

✦ ___Object Highlighting **highlights the object to which you are pointing.**

Angles

The Angles section in the Smart Guides dialog box let you pick what angles display guides when you drag an object. You can choose from seven presets or create Custom Angles of your own.

Snapping Tolerance

The Snapping Tolerance enables you to choose how close you have to have an object to another object before the first object automatically "snaps" to the second object. You set the Snapping Tolerance in points, and the lower the number, the closer you have to move the objects to each other.

Slices

The Show Slice Numbers option will make slice numbers visible in the upper left corner of each slice. These numbers represent the order that the slices appear. You can also set the Line Color using a preset color or by selecting the Other option to choose a custom color.

Hyphenation Preferences

The Hyphenation options dialog box contains options for customizing the way Illustrator hyphenates words. At the top of the dialog box is a pop-up menu that lists various languages. Select the default language. At the bottom of the dialog box is a list of Exceptions. You can add to the list of hyphenation exceptions by entering a word and clicking Add. These exceptions are words that you don't want Illustrator to hyphenate under any circumstances. Figure 15-11 illustrates the Hyphenation options screen of the Preferences dialog box.

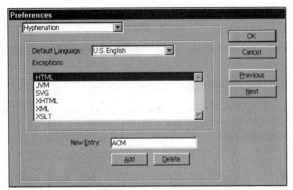

Figure 15-11: The Hyphenation screen of the Preferences dialog box

Tip   Acronyms are a good choice of words to place in the Exceptions list.

The Plug-ins & Scratch Disk Preferences

The next preference item in the Preference pop-up menu is a two-trick pony, the Plug-ins & Scratch Disks Preferences screen (see Figure 15-12). The first section in this dialog box enables you to specify a folder for plug-ins. The default is the Plug-Ins folder in the Adobe Illustrator folder. You can change this folder by clicking on the Choose button and selecting a new folder.

The second section in the Plug-in & Scratch Disk screen lets you define what drives to use as scratch disks — the place where Illustrator stores information when it runs out of RAM. Typically, you should assign the fastest, largest drive to be your primary scratch disk. The settings you choose won't take effect until you restart Illustrator.

The Files & Clipboard Preferences

The penultimate preference item in the Preference pop-up menu is the Files & Clipboard Preferences screen (see Figure 15-13). The first section in this screen enables you to specify when the links are updated. The options are to update links Automatically, which updates any linked images automatically whenever the linked resource is modified, and Manually, which can be done using the Links palette or the Ask When Modified option. The default is Ask When Modified. For Mac systems, an additional Append Extension option allows users to add an extension to the end of the file name.

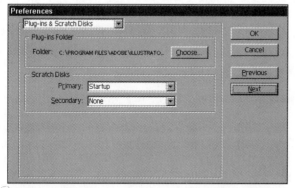

Figure 15-12: The Plug-ins & Scratch Disks screen of the Preferences dialog box

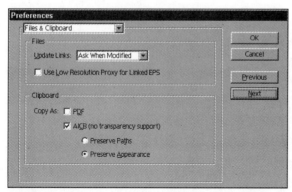

Figure 15-13: The Files & Clipboard screen of the Preferences dialog box

The Files section also contains an option to Use Low Resolution Proxy for Linked EPS. This option will display a low resolution copy for all linked raster images in an EPS file. This will help to ease the memory demands when manipulating the file and make it easier to make and view changes. If disabled, all linked raster images will be displayed and manipulated at full resolution.

The second section in the Files & Clipboard dialog box lets you specify how data is copied to the clipboard for transport to other applications. The checkbox options include PDF (Portable Document Format) and AICB, which stands for Adobe Illustrator Clipboard. The AICB option does not retain any transparency information when copied. For the AICB option, you can also designate to preserve the Appearance or Paths.

Note The PDF option can be used when copying content to a package that supports PDF objects, such as Adobe's InDesign. Other packages, such as Photoshop, accept AICB-pasted content.

Workgroup Preferences

The final screen of the Preferences dialog box, shown in Figure 15-14, is for the Workgroup settings. By enabling the workgroup features, you can have several designers collaborate on a single project. This is accomplished by saving the document to a WebDAV server. This server is on the internet and lets users check out a document and make changes. Once the document is checked back in, another user can check out the document and make additional changes.

Note You can only take advantage of the workgroup features of Illustrator if you connect to a WebDAV server. Information on WebDAV servers can be found at www.webdav.org.

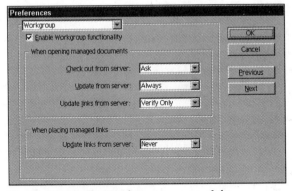

Figure 15-14: The Workgroup screen of the Preferences dialog box

The Workgroup screen in the Preferences dialog box can enable or disable workgroup functionality. You can also set how the handle check outs and updates. The options include having Illustrator ask every time a file is checked out, updated or updating links. Or you could set Illustrator to ignore or always allow these functions.

Cross-Reference The workgroup features are covered in more detail in Chapter 2, "Working with Illustrator Documents."

Adobe Online Preferences

With the Internet accessible to most users, Adobe has added a separate Preference dialog box, shown in Figure 15-15, for defining how often Illustrator is automatically updated. This dialog box can be opened using the Illustrator [Edit] ➪ Preferences ➪ Online Settings menu option. Using an Internet connection, you can set Illustrator to automatically download and install updates, Once a Day, Once a Week, Once a Month or Never. You also have the option of viewing the download progress.

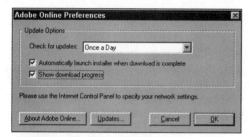

Figure 15-15: The Adobe Online Preferences dialog box

At the bottom of the Adobe Online Preferences dialog box are several buttons. The About Adobe Online button will open an info screen that displays the names of those individuals responsible for this brilliant feature. The Updates button will let you manually download and install any updates. This button can update the software at any time.

Note In order to connect to the Internet, you'll need to set up your connection options through your system settings.

If you have a dedicated line that is always connected to the Internet via a network, then the Once a Day setting may be fine, especially if you set the files to download and automatically install, but nondedicated computers can probably get by with refreshing Once a Week or Once a Month.

You can also open the Adobe Online Preferences using a button on the Adobe Online dialog box, shown in Figure 15-16, opened with the Help ➪ Adobe Online menu option. This dialog box also includes a button labeled Updates that will manually connect to Adobe Online and open the Adobe Product Updates dialog box.

Figure 15-16: The Adobe Online dialog box

The Adobe Product Updates dialog box, shown in Figure 15-17, will display all updates or just the new updates. You can select the files to update from the top pane of the dialog box and a description of the file will be displayed. Select the Download button to automatically download and install the selected files. At the bottom of the dialog box, you can choose the folder where the updates are installed.

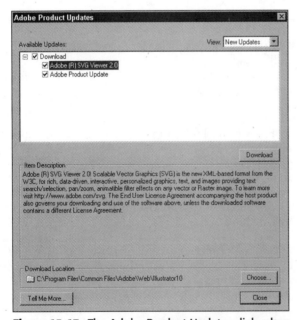

Figure 15-17: The Adobe Product Updates dialog box

Tip   If you want to download the updates, but update them at a later time, you can change the folder where the files will download to some other folder than the one that Illustrator is installed to.

The Help menu includes several options for getting information via a web browser. The Help ➪ Top Issues will display a list of the major technical support issues. By perusing this information you can find solutions to common problems. The Help ➪ Downloadables menu option will display a list of updates and files that can be downloaded. The Help ➪ Corporate News menu option will display Illustrator-specific news reported at Adobe. The Help ➪ Registration menu option will allow you to register Illustrator through the web. The Help ➪ Adobe Links menu includes links to various web pages that are good resources.

Placement and Toolbox Value Preferences

Most Illustrator users take many preferences for granted. If Illustrator didn't remember certain preferences, these users would be quite annoyed.

Palettes (including the toolbox) remain where they were when you last used Illustrator. Illustrator remembers their size and whether they were open. Values in the toolbox are still whatever you set them to last. For example, the options in the Paintbrush/Eyedropper dialog box remain the same between Illustrator sessions.

Keyboard Customization

Have you ever cursed Adobe for changing your favorite keyboard shortcut from version 6? Or, heaven forbid, would you like to make Illustrator's keyboard shortcuts the same as your desktop publishing package? The Edit menu now includes an option for Keyboard Shortcuts (⌘[Ctrl]+Shift+Option[Alt]+K). This menu option opens the Keyboard Shortcuts dialog box, shown in Figure 15-18, where you can select, alter, and update the current list of keyboard shortcuts.

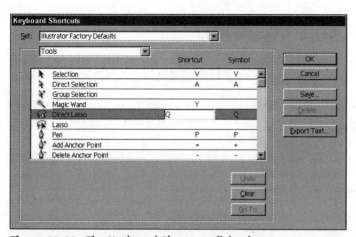

Figure 15-18: The Keyboard Shortcuts dialog box

Using the Set drop-down list at the top of the dialog box, you can create new sets of shortcuts. The Illustrator Factory Defaults is included as one of the sets that cannot be deleted and can be restored at any time using the dialog box.

Note   Another set of keyboard shortcuts that can be used are the shortcuts for Illustrator 6.

You can also select to alter the keyboard shortcuts for any tool and/or menu. To change a tool keyboard shortcut, do the following:

1. Open the Keyboard Shortcuts dialog box by selecting Edit ➪ Keyboard Shortcuts.

2. Select the tool that you wish to change and click it. The Shortcut key is highlighted.

3. Type in a new letter for the tool. If the selected letter is being used by another tool, then a warning dialog box appears.

4. Click the Symbol letter next to the Shortcut and change its value also.

5. After making changes to the current Shortcut set, click the Save button and enter a name for the new set.

6. Click the OK button to close the Keyboard Shortcuts dialog box and make the new set the default.

Note   Keyboard combinations that use the Option, Alt, Shift or Ctrl key cannot be used as a shortcut for the tools.

You can also export a list of the keyboard shortcuts to a text file. This is useful if you want to print a cheat-sheet of shortcuts to hang by your computer until you learn them all.

Things You Can't Customize

Unfortunately, you cannot customize a few items in Illustrator, and this can be annoying. The following are items that you cannot customize:

✦ Type information always defaults to 12-point Helvetica, Auto Leading, 100 percent Horizontal Scale, 0 Tracking, Flush Left, and Hyphenation Off. There is no easy way around this set of defaults.

✦ Layers for new documents are limited to one, which is colored light blue and called Layer 1.

✦ When you create new objects, they are always 0 percent Black Fill and a Black 1-point Stroke.

✦ The Selection tool is always the active tool.

Actions

The Actions palette (see Figure 15-19) was borrowed technology from Photoshop and was brought into Illustrator to ease mundane repetitive tasks. Actions are simply a series of Illustrator tasks that are recorded so they can be applied to other objects at a later time. The tasks of applying color, object transformations, and text functions are easily automated using the Actions palette. Illustrator comes with some prerecorded actions and you can create your own.

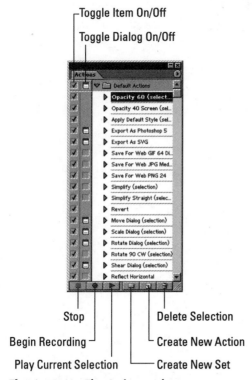

Figure 15-19: The Actions palette

Using a Default Action

The Default Actions are by far the easiest to use. Some Default Actions require a path or type while other Default Actions require nothing. Figure 15-20 shows the result of choosing a few of the Default Actions. To activate a Default Action, click the action to highlight it, and then press the Play button.

Figure 15-20: Isometric Cube, Round 3D button, Rectangle 3D button, Cast Shadow (type), Embossed (type), Marble (type), and Train Tracks (Stroke) are a few of the Default Actions.

Creating a New Action

If the numerous default actions aren't enough, you can create your own actions. To start recording a new action you need to create a new action. Click the Create New Action icon at the bottom of the Action palette or choose New Action from the pop-up menu. Hold down the Option [Alt] key to accept the defaults for the New Action dialog box to name the action and the action set. After entering a name (it's a good idea to give it a name that reflects what action it does), you hit the Record button and start doing your action. After you are done, you can move the order or delete parts of your action.

Creating a New Set

When you create a new action, it gets put in a folder with a set of actions. You can have multiple actions in a folder, or just one. A new action needs to be a part of a set (or in a folder). It can be an existing set or a new set. Think of actions as packages. To create a new set click the New Set icon at the bottom of the palette or select New Set from the pop-up menu.

Note

In Illustrator, not everything is recordable. As with anything, limits exist. If you attempt to record an action that is not recordable, Illustrator will warn you with a dialog box.

Duplicating and deleting an action

You can duplicate an action when you want to change something about an existing action and don't want to re-record the whole darn thing. To duplicate an action, first select an action in the Action palette, and then choose Duplicate from the pop-up menu. This makes a copy of the action. To change the name of the action, double-click the action to open the Action Options dialog box. You can change the name of an action this way, but not the name of the action set. Deleting an action is easy. Select the action you want to delete and drag it onto the trash icon at the bottom of the palette or use the pop-up menu item.

Starting and stopping recording

To start recording, do one of the following:

✦ Create a new action set and action.

✦ Select an existing action and click the Begin Recording icon at the bottom of the palette.

✦ Activate an action and select Start Recording in the pop-up menu.

To stop recording, do one of the following:

✦ Click the Stop Playing/Recording icon button.

✦ Select Stop Recording in the pop-up menu.

Inserting a menu item

If you have either duplicated an action, or want to add to an action, you may want to insert an item into the action. To insert a menu item, activate an action, start recording, and select Insert Menu Item from the pop-up menu. This enables you to record most menu items: File, Edit, Object, Type, Filter, and guide-related Views. You don't have to use this to record a menu item.

Inserting a stop

Insert Stop enables you to stop the playback of an action at a point where you may want to customize the action when you replay it. During your recording select Insert Stop in the pop-up menu. You can have some fun with this one because you are creating your own dialog box. Put in a message just for fun. Always let the user continue if he or she wants. This is great for using Actions to partially do the creation, but stops so you can customize it as you wish.

Action options

The Action options let you name or rename the action, move it to a set, assign a Function Key, or assign a Color to the Action. The Function key is a cool feature that lets you assign an "F" key number to an action so you can just hit the F+*number* and your action starts.

Playback options

The Playback options let you customize your actions even further. You can accelerate, step through, or pause your Actions, as follows:

✦ **Accelerated.** Plays the action all at once, quickly. This is great for monotonous, repetitive actions such as renaming figures or adding a tag line.

✦ **Step by step.** Plays the action one step at a time. This lets you decide whether you want to perform a step or add in-between steps.

✦ **Pause for.** Stops at each step for the specified time. This is a good choice if you want to closely see how something was recorded and would like to stop the recording at a certain spot.

Inserting a selected path

You cannot record the Pen tool or the Pencil tool, but you can record a path. First, draw the path. While the path is selected, start recording. Choose Insert Select Path from the pop-up menu, and then stop recording. You have just placed a path in your action.

Selecting an object

If you want to select an object to use later in your recording, you need to name and select an object or path first. The following steps describe this procedure:

1. Select the object or path.

2. Choose Show Note from the Attributes palette pop-up menu.

3. Enter the name you want to give the object in the bottom field and click the Actions palette to record the new setting.

4. When you need to select the object or path, choose Select Object in the pop-up menu, type in the name you gave it in the Attributes palette, and click OK. The object or path is now selected.

Clearing, resetting, loading, replacing, and saving actions

Whew, even after creating a bunch of cool actions, you want more options. You can clear, reset, load, replace, and save actions. Now you can create, delete, load sets, and save to your heart's content. The following describes what each option does:

✦ **Clear Action.** Deletes all the action sets in the Action palette.

✦ **Reset Action.** Resets the palette to the Default Actions.

✦ **Load New or Replace Action.** Lets you navigate to a folder that contains the action sets and select one. You can find a ton of prerecorded actions and action sets on the application CD-ROM.

✦ **Save Action.** Once you have recorded an action you need to save it in the same way you save a file if you want to use it the next time you launch Illustrator. Choose Save Action in the pop-up menu and navigate to where you want to save your action set (maybe the Action Sets folder within the application folder?).

Note The Button mode lets you play an action by clicking the button. You can only play — not record — in this mode.

Summary

If you're more comfortable with Photoshop than with Illustrator, then the features for handling raster-based images will make you feel like home within Illustrator. In this chapter, you learned that

✦ You can change two different preference areas in Illustrator: Preferences and the startup file.

✦ By changing the Adobe Illustrator Startup file, you can change the default colors, patterns, gradients, and zoom level of each new document created in Illustrator.

✦ You can change many preferences in Illustrator in the General panel of the Preferences dialog box.

✦ The Constrain Angle option controls the angle at which objects are drawn and moved when the Shift key is pressed.

✦ The Auto Trace option controls the behavior of the Auto Trace Tool.

✦ The General Units option determines how all measurements are controlled in Illustrator.

✦ Other Preference dialog box panels include settings for Grids and Guides, Type, Smart Guides, Plug-ins, and the Clipboard.

✦ Using the Adobe Online Web site, you can set the application to automatically update itself.

✦ You can customize keyboard shortcuts.

✦ The Actions palette provides a way to record Illustrator sequences for future playback.

✦   ✦   ✦

Outputting Illustrator

Part IV describes the ways to get stuff out of Illustrator. Once you have great-looking artwork, you have many options for outputting the final results. Artwork can leave to go to the print world, or go on an all-expenses paid trip to the Web.

Understanding Printing, Separations, and Trapping

You can print Illustrator documents in two ways: as a composite, which is a single printout that contains all the colors and tints used; and as a series of color separations, a printout for each color. Color separations are necessary for illustrations that are printed on a printing press.

Using PostScript to Print Clearly

Until the mid-1980s, computer graphics were, well, crusty. Blocky. Jagged. Rough. If we saw graphics that were done on computers in 1981 and printed to a black-and-white printer, we'd laugh so hard we couldn't breathe, stopping only when we realized that we were about to pass out. Of course, in 1981, the world went gaga over the capabilities of computers and computer graphics. Those same pictures were much admired, and the average person, in general, was vastly amazed. (The average designer, on the other hand, shuddered and prayed that this whole computer thing wouldn't catch on. . . .)

In the mid-1980s, several systems were developed to improve the printing process, and the one standout was PostScript from Adobe Systems. Apple licensed PostScript from Adobe for use on its first LaserWriter, and a star was born. Installed on every laser printer from that point on were two things from Adobe: the PostScript page description language, and the Adobe base 13 fonts, which included Times, Helvetica, Courier, and Symbol.

PostScript became fundamental to Apple Macintosh computers and laser printers and thus became the standard. To use PostScript, Apple had to pay licensing fees to Adobe for every laser printer it sold. Fonts were PostScript, and if there ever was a standard in graphics, the closest thing to it was PostScript (commonly called *EPS*, for Encapsulated PostScript).

Today, the majority of fonts for both Macintosh and Windows systems used for desktop publishing are still PostScript fonts, and almost all graphics and all desktop-publishing software can read PostScript in some form.

Seeing how PostScript works

A typical graphic object in painting software is based on a certain number of pixels in a specific color. Typically, if you make that graphic larger, the pixels get larger, giving a rough, jagged effect to the art (see Figure 16-1). To prevent these *jaggies*, you can make sure that the image has enough dots-per-inch so that when it is enlarged, the dots remain too small to appear jagged. Another alternative is to define graphics by mathematical equations instead of by dots. That's where PostScript comes in handy.

Figure 16-1: A bitmap image at normal size (left) and enlarged to 300 percent (right)

PostScript is a mathematical solution to the problem of how to achieve high-resolution images. Areas, or *shapes*, are defined, and then these shapes are either *filled* or *stroked* with a percentage of color. The shapes are made up of *paths*, and the paths are defined by a number of points along each one (*Anchor Points*), and controls off those points (*control handles*, sometimes called *curve handles* or *direction points*), which control the shape of the curve. Figure 16-2 shows a PostScript outline around a bitmapped image, and the enlarged outline filled with black.

Figure 16-2: A PostScript outline surrounds the original bitmapped image.

Because the Anchor Points and control handles have real locations on a page, mathematical processes can be used to create the shapes based on these points. The mathematical equations for Bézier curves are quite detailed—at least for someone who fears math.

PostScript is not just math, though. It is actually a programming language and, more specifically, a *page description language*. Like Basic, Pascal, and C, PostScript is made of lines of code that are used to describe artwork.

Fortunately, the average user never has to use PostScript code; instead, he or she uses a simplified interface, such as Illustrator. Software that has the capability to save files in PostScript or to print to a PostScript printer writes this PostScript code for you. Printers that are equipped with PostScript then take that PostScript code and convert it to dots on a printed page.

Applying PostScript to create cool art

That most applications can handle EPS files, and that many printers can print PostScript are facts of great benefit to users, but the strength of PostScript is not really based on its widespread use.

If you create a one-inch circle in Photoshop (a pixel-based circle, not a vector one since Photoshop can not handle vector objects) or any other pixel-based drawing software, and then enlarge that same circle in any application, the circle begins to lose detail. A 300-dpi circle at twice its original size becomes 150 dpi. This makes those jagged edges more apparent than ever.

On the other hand, if you create a one-inch circle in Illustrator you can enlarge it to *any size possible* without losing one iota of resolution. The Illustrator circle stays perfectly smooth, even enlarged to 200 percent, because the circle's resolution depends on the laser printer or imagesetter that prints it. This means that a perfect one-inch circle has the potential to be a perfect two-foot circle (providing you can find a printer or imagesetter that can print a two-foot by two-foot diameter circle).

But scaling objects is only the beginning. You can distort, stretch, rotate, skew, and flip objects created in Illustrator to your heart's content, and still the object will print to the resolution of the output device (see Figure 16-3).

Figure 16-3: The original PostScript mouse, named "Theme," appears in the upper-left corner. The other mice are, appropriately, variations on a Theme.

Here's an example: You are doing some work for a company wants its tiny logo to fill up a three-foot wide poster. If you use conventional methods, the edges will become fuzzy and gross-looking, pretty much unacceptable to your client. Your other "conventional" option would be to redraw the logo at a larger size, or to manually trace the blown-up version, a time-consuming proposition either way.

The solution is to scan the logo, trace it in either Adobe Streamline or with the Pen tool, and build your design around it. Afterward, you can output the illustration on a printer that can handle a poster of that size. In the end you get no loss of quality; instead, the enlarged version from Illustrator will often look better than the scanned original.

Prior to Printing

Before you start the printing process, a number of items may need to be changed or adjusted. For instance, you may need to change the page size and orientation, or set how certain colors separate. This section deals with the issues you should be aware of before you press ⌘+P [Ctrl+P] to send your file to the printer.

Document Setup

Choosing File ➪ Document Setup (⌘+Shift+P [Ctrl+Alt+P]) enables you to set the initial page size of an illustration via the artboard. The Document Setup dialog box displays a wealth of options that determine how your illustration is printed. These options are split into three different screens — Artboard (shown in Figure 16-4), Printing & Exporting, and Transparency. You can select the screen using the drop-down list at the top of the dialog box, or you can move between the different screens using the Previous and Next buttons to the right.

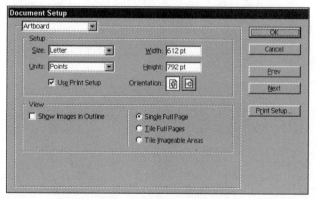

Figure 16-4: The Artboard screen of the Document Setup dialog box

If the Use Page Setup box is checked, then the artboard size is relative to the size of the page that is selected in the Page Setup dialog box. If the artboard is smaller than the printable page, then anything entirely outside the edges of the artboard is cropped when you print the illustration from Illustrator. Any objects that are partially on the artboard prints. Anything outside the artboard prints when you print the illustration from another application. The Page Setup command and dialog box are referred to as "Print Setup" in previous versions of Illustrator for Windows.

Rather than awkwardly repeating "Page Setup/Print Setup" throughout this chapter, we stick with "Page Setup." The Document Setup dialog box also includes a button that lets you open the Page Setup dialog box.

Another option in the Document Setup dialog box is the Show Images in Outline option, which enables you to choose whether patterns will preview and print. Unchecking this box prevents patterns from printing when you print from Illustrator.

The Page Tiling options also affect the way that pages appear when a document is printed:

✦ If you choose Single Full Page, only one page prints.

✦ If you choose Tile Full Pages, only full pages (as defined in the Page Setup dialog box) that appear on the artboard print. If no full pages can fit in the artboard, everything in the artboard prints.

✦ If you choose Tile Imageable Areas, a grid appears on the artboard. Any block of the grid that has a piece of the illustration prints. When choosing this option, you can specify in the Print dialog box which pages should be printed.

Page Setup (Macintosh)

The Page Setup dialog box, shown in Figure 16-5, is used for specifying printing options when printing a composite image.

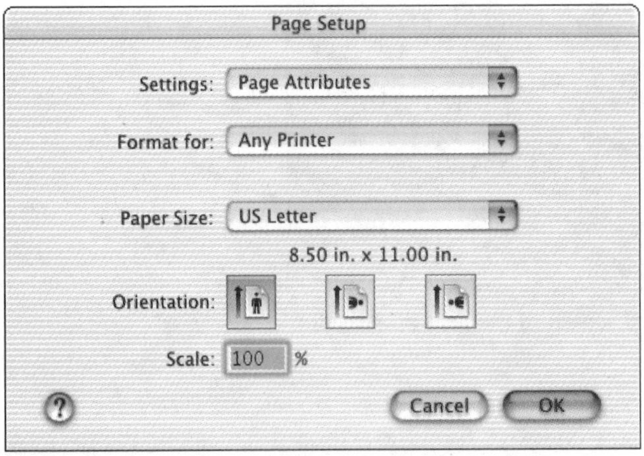

Figure 16-5: The Page Setup dialog box with Page Attributes selected

The printing options on this dialog box are Page Attributes and PostScript Options. The Page Attributes options are as follows:

✦ **Format for.** In this pop-up menu, you choose which printer you want to print to.

✦ **Paper.** In this pop-up menu are many different paper and envelope sizes and positions depending on the capabilities of your printer. You can choose any paper size, including one that your printer does not have the capacity to use The size that you choose shows up on the document as a dotted-line boundary when you select the Tile Full Pages or Single Full Pages option in the Document Setup dialog box. Another dotted-line boundary, inside the page-size boundary, is the *printable area*. The printable area is also displayed when you select the Tile Imageable Areas option in the Document Setup dialog box.

✦ **Orientation.** This option determines the direction of the image on the printed page — whether it is printed in portrait orientation (longest side vertical) or landscape orientation (longest side horizontal). Mac systems offer two different landscape orientations depending on how the page is rotated.

✦ **Scale.** This option sets the percentage of enlargement or reduction of the original document when it is printed. Reducing or enlarging affects the way that the dotted-line page boundaries and imageable-areas dotted lines appear in the document. A value above 100 percent makes the page smaller, while a value less than 100 percent makes the page and its boundaries larger. This feature is helpful when you want to print everything that's on a large artboard. If you select a reduced size in the Page Setup dialog box, the dotted lines in the document reflect the reduced size.

The Settings popup menu also includes options to set PostScript Options and to display a Summary of the page, as shown in Figure 16-6.

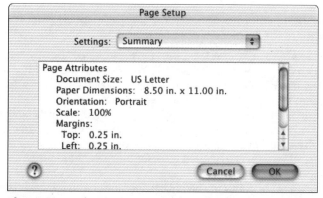

Figure 16-6: The Settings popup menu displays a Summary of a page.

The options in the PostScript Options dialog box are as follows:

✦ **Flip Horizontal.** This option prints the document as a mirror image of itself, flipped horizontally. You can use it with the Invert Image option to print negatives from Illustrator.

✦ **Flip Vertical.** This option prints the document as a mirror image of itself, flipped vertically. You can also use this option with the Invert Image option to print negatives from Illustrator. Using the Flip Horizontal and Flip Vertical options together rotates the document 180 degrees.

✦ **Invert Image.** This option prints a negative image of the illustration, where all white areas are black and all black areas are white.

✦ **Substitute Fonts.** Illustrator has built-in workarounds for font problems, and supposedly this checkbox is irrelevant to Illustrator users. For other programs, this option replaces any bitmapped fonts with corresponding fonts that are installed on the printer, which usually means that if you have Geneva, New York, and Monaco installed in bitmapped format only, Helvetica, Times, and Courier take their places. Any other bitmapped font is usually replaced with Courier. In general, if you don't have the PostScript printer font or the font in TrueType format, you shouldn't use that font with Adobe Illustrator, and you shouldn't check this box.

✦ **Smooth Text.** When Substitute Fonts is not checked and an illustration has a bitmapped font in it, Smooth Text makes the bitmapped font look slightly better. It still looks coarse, but it will look less coarse than just the plain bitmapped font.

✦ **Smooth Graphics.** Smooth Graphics does the same thing that Smooth Text does, but it does it to graphics. Because this feature works only with PICT and Paint images, which you cannot print in Illustrator, you should not check this option.

✦ **Precision Bitmap Alignment.** This option resamples bitmapped graphics so that they print better at the resolution of your printer.

✦ **Unlimited Downloadable Fonts in a Document.** Checking this box interferes with Illustrator's own downloading mechanism. You shouldn't check it when printing from Illustrator. When printing from other programs, this option does more than enable you to use many fonts. Checking Unlimited Downloadable Fonts in programs other than Illustrator makes the RAM (Random Access Memory) in the laser printer adjustable. As part of the document comes in and is processed, the information that was used to process that part of the document and the fonts that were needed to print it are flushed out of memory. The next section and its needed fonts are then loaded. This method takes longer than loading all of the fonts in the entire document at once and then processing the document, but it prevents out-of-memory printing errors when printing from programs such as QuarkXPress.

Print Setup (Windows)

The Print Setup dialog box (accessed by clicking the Print Setup button in the Document Setup dialog box) contains Print Setup options that are specific to your printer. The Print Setup dialog box is shown in Figure 16-7. Clicking the Properties button displays a plethora of options for customizing page size and other print properties.

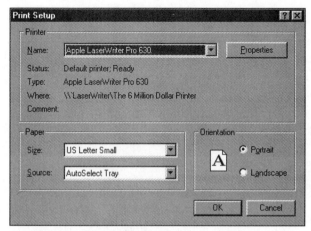

Figure 16-7: The Windows Print Setup dialog box

Printing composites

A composite printout looks very much like the image that appears on the screen when you preview the document (choose View ➪ Preview or press ⌘+Y [Ctrl+Y]). If you have a color printer, the image appears in color; otherwise, the colors are replaced by gray tints (see the next section, "Gray Colors").

Note   Objects that are hidden or that exist in layers that are currently hidden do not print. Objects that exist in layers that have the printing option unchecked in the Layers Option dialog box also do not print.

Choosing File ➪ Print (⌘+P [Ctrl+P]) opens the Print dialog box (Figures 16-8 and 16-9 show the Mac version; Figure 16-10 shows the Windows version), in which you may choose which pages to print, how many of each to print, and several other options. If you click the Cancel button (⌘+. (period) [Ctrl+. (period)]), the dialog box disappears, and no pages are printed. To print, click the Print button or press Return or Enter.

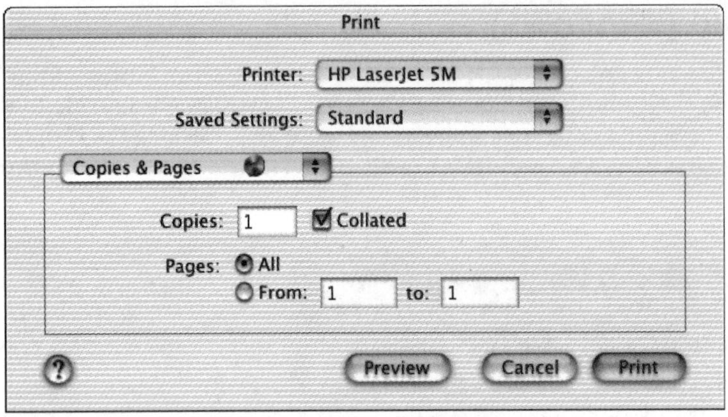

Figure 16-8: The Macintosh General Print dialog box

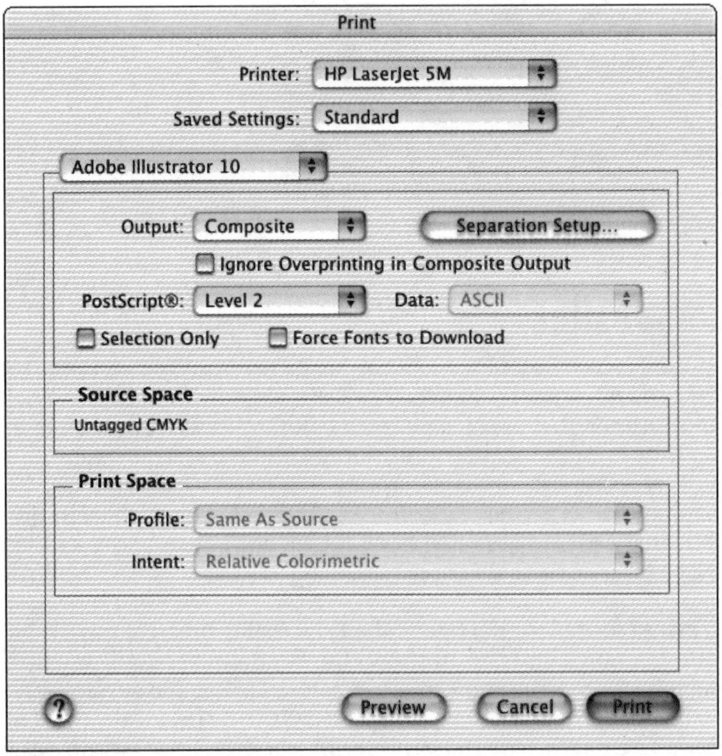

Figure 16-9: The Macintosh Illustrator Print dialog box

The Macintosh Illustrator Print dialog box (shown in Figure 16-9) and the Windows Print dialog box (shown in Figure 16-10) contain these options:

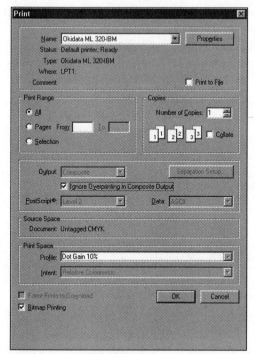

Figure 16-10: The Windows Print dialog box

The Macintosh General Print dialog box (shown in Figure 16-8) and the Windows Print dialog box (shown in Figure 16-10) contain these options:

✦ **Copies.** The number that you enter here determines how many copies of each page prints. All copies of a single page are printed at one time, so if you enter 4 when you are printing a four-page document, you get four copies of page 1, then four copies of page 2, and so on.

✦ **Pages (Print Range in Windows).** If you check the All button, all the pages that have artwork on them print. If you enter numbers in the From and To fields, only the pages that those numbers refer to prints.

✦ **Paper Source (Mac only).** If Paper Cassette (the default) is selected, all pages print on paper from the printer's cassette. If Manual Feed is selected, then the pages print on paper from the manual feed tray.

✦ **Destination (Mac only).** Choosing Printer prints the document to the laser printer as usual. Choosing File prints the document to a PostScript or PDF file on the hard disk drive that you can download to a laser printer at a future time by using a utility such as Acrobat Reader, Font Downloader or LaserWriter Font Utility. A PostScript file can also be used with Acrobat Distiller (Windows or Mac) or Adobe ScreenReady.

✦ **Output.** This option determines if the illustration is printed as a composite or divided into individual color separations.

✦ **Ignore Overprinting in Composite Output.** Any overprint settings found in the Attributes palette will not be appear in the composite.

✦ **PostScript.** This pop-up menu enables you to specify the PostScript interpreter (Level 1, Level 2, or PostScript 3) that is included in your Laser Printer.

Tip   Selecting Level 1 may eliminate various PostScript errors when printing to an older printer.

✦ **Data.** Keep this option on Binary, unless you have a very old printer that only understands PostScript data in ASCII format.

✦ **Source Space.** The Source Space displays the Color Model saved with the source artwork.

✦ **Print Space.** The Print Space can be set differently than the Source Space and can include a Profile and an Intent Color Model.

✦ **Selection Only (Mac only).** This handy little option lets you print only selected objects instead of the entire document.

✦ **Force Fonts to Download.** When this option is checked, the document's fonts download to the printer before printing.

✦ **Bitmap Printing (Windows only).** This option will send objects to a non-PostScript printer as a bitmap image, thereby reducing the chance for printer errors to halt the print job.

✦ **Separation Setup.** This button opens the Separation Setup dialog box, discussed in detail later in this chapter.

If you select the Imaging Options choice from the popup menu/drop-down list at the top of the dialog box, the Imaging Options dialog box appears.

The options in this dialog box vary depending on your printer driver and printer choice. The basic options are:

✦ **Cover Page.** If you choose First Page or Last Page, a separate sheet, which contains information about the name of the computer, the name of the file, the number of pages, and the dates, prints. This feature is useful for making each print job easily identifiable when several people share a laser printer.

✦ **Error Handling.** This option prints a detailed report when a PostScript error occurs.

Tip   Always select Print Detailed Report. When an illustration does not print, a sheet of paper prints with the error message on it.

✦ **Other Options.** The options in the lower section are specific to your printer. For instance, the printer information shown in the dialog box in Figure 16-8 is for a HP Laserjet 5M. Some of the other possible options are the resolution (300 or 600), and whether FinePrint and Photograde are turned on.

Tip   *Always* save before you print. Severe problems, when they happen, usually occur when you are printing. Don't let your unsaved document fall victim to one of those severe problems.

Gray colors

When you print a full-color illustration to a black-and-white printer, Illustrator substitutes gray values for colors. This way, the program creates the illusion that each color has a separate, distinct gray value.

Of course, each color can't have its own unique gray value, so the colors have to overlap at some point. Illustrator converts each of the process colors into specific gray values when it prints to a black-and-white printer.

Magenta is the darkest process color, ranging from 0 to 73 percent gray. Therefore, at 100 percent magenta, it prints at 73 percent gray. Cyan is second darkest, ranging from 0 to 57 percent gray. Yellow is extremely light, ranging from 0 percent to only 11 percent gray. Figure 16-11 shows a comparison of the four process colors at various settings and their printed results. The four bars show different values, indicated above the bars, for each process color. Within each bar is the percent of black that prints when you are printing that color at that percentage to a black-and-white printer.

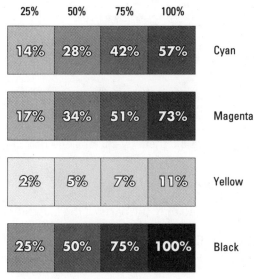

Figure 16-11: How colors appear when printed on a black-and-white laser printer

Different printers may produce different tints of gray. Lower-resolution printers, such as 300-dpi (dots per inch) laser printers, do not create an accurate gray tint because they use dots that are too large to create accurate tint patterns.

Separation Setup

After you choose File ➪ Separation Setup, the Separations Setup dialog box appears (shown in Figure 16-12). The left side shows how the illustration is aligned on the page and which elements print with the illustration. The right side contains all the options for how the illustration is to print on the page.

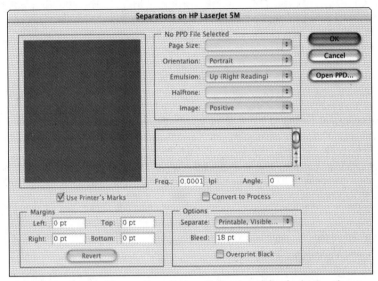

Figure 16-12: The Separations Setup dialog box (displaying options for a HP Laserjet 5M)

The picture on the left side initially shows the illustration on a portrait-oriented page, even if landscape was selected in Illustrator. The various marks shown on the page are the defaults. You can move or rearrange them by clicking and dragging.

The Bounding Box and Bleed

A Bounding Box surrounds the illustration, and only the parts of the illustration that are within this box print. Anything outside of the box is cropped. When you first open the Separation Setup dialog box, the Bounding Box is the size of the illustration. This box is as wide and as tall as is necessary to include all the printable objects in the illustration.

When you resize the Bounding Box manually (by clicking the edges or corners and dragging), the numbers in the Bounding Box text fields change because the four text fields correspond to the location of each edge of the Bounding Box. You also can resize the Bounding Box by typing new values in the Bounding Box text fields. The Bounding Box instantly reflects changes that you make in these text fields.

Tip   You can move the illustration within the Bounding Box by placing the cursor within the Bounding Box and clicking and dragging. As you move the illustration out of the Bounding Box, the illustration is cropped at its edges.

The Bleed text field near the bottom center of the Separation Setup dialog box determines how much of the illustration can be outside of the Bounding Box and still print. The default for bleed is 18 points, regardless of the size of the Bounding Box. To change the bleed, enter a distance in points in the Bleed text field. As you type the numbers, the bleed changes dynamically.

Bleed is useful when you want an illustration to go right up to the edge of the page. You need to account for bleed when you create an image in Illustrator so that the image is the correct size with the correct amount of bleed.

Changing printer information

To change the *PostScript Printer Description* (PPD), click the Open PPD button in the upper-right corner of the Separation Setup dialog box. The "Please choose a PPD file" window appears.

Select the PPD file that is compatible with your printer and click the Open button. Adobe Illustrator Installer automatically places the PPD folder in the Utilities folder.

Note   PPDs were created with specific printers in mind. Unpredictable and undesirable results occur when you use a PPD for a different printer than it is intended for. If you don't have a PPD for your printer and must use a substitute, always test the substitute PPD before relying on it to perform correctly.

If your printer's PPD is not included with Illustrator, contact the dealer from whom you purchased the printer and ask for it. If you bought the printer by mail order or from a retail store, the dealer probably does not have a PPD for you and may not even know what a PPD is. In this case, contact the printer manufacturer directly. Another place to find PPDs from manufacturers is at online services such as America Online. Adobe does not have PPDs for printers other than the ones supplied with the software.

Tip   If you have two or more printers in your workplace, chances are that from time to time you will change the PPD file in the Separation Setup dialog box. To make this task easier, open the PPD folder on the hard drive, select all the PPD files that you don't use, and drag them to the trash. Having a shorter list to choose from makes finding the right PPD much easier and frees up space on the hard drive. If you get a new printer later and need a different PPD, you can get it from the Illustrator floppy disk or CD-ROM.

When you choose a different PPD file, the information in the main panel changes to reflect the new selection. Certain default settings in the pop-up menus are activated at this time. You can change the settings at any time, but most of them revert to the defaults if you choose a new PPD.

Changing page size

The Page Size pop-up menu lists the available page sizes for the printer on which PPD is selected, not the printer selected in the Chooser on your Mac or your default Windows printer. For laser printers, few page and envelope sizes are supported. For imagesetters, many sizes are supported, and an Other option enables you to specify the size of the page that you want to print on.

When you choose Other in the Page Size pop-up menu, you see the Other dialog box. The default measurements in the box are the smallest size area within which the current illustration can fit. Enter the width and height of the desired page in their respective boxes. Use the Offset option to move the illustration a certain distance from the right edge of the page, and save media by using the Transverse option to turn the image sideways on the paper or film on which it is printing.

Imagesetters print on rolls of paper or film. Depending on the width of the roll, you may want to print the image sideways. For example, on a Linotronic 180 or 230 imagesetter, paper and film rolls are commonly 12 inches wide. For letter-size pages, you should check the Transverse option to print the letter-size page with the short end along the length of the roll. For a tabloid page (11×17 inches), do not check the Transverse option because you want the long edge (17 inches) of the page to be printed along the length of the roll. If you check Transverse for a tabloid-size document, 5 of the 17 inches is cropped because the roll is not wide enough. As always, when trying something new with printing, run a test page or two before sending a large job.

Note   The page size that you select in the Page Size pop-up menu determines the size of the page on the left side of the main panel. The measurements next to the name of the page size are not the page measurements; instead, they are the measurements of the imageable area for that page size. The imageable-area dimensions are always less than the dimensions of the page so that the margin marks can fit on the page with the illustration.

Changing the orientation

The Orientation setting controls how the illustration is placed on the page. You have two choices from the pop-up menu: Portrait and Landscape.

Selecting Portrait prints the illustration with its sides along the longest sides of the page. Selecting Landscape prints the illustration with its top and bottom sides along the longest sides of the page.

Usually, the orientation reflects the general shape of the illustration. If the illustration is taller than it is wide, you usually choose Portrait orientation. If the illustration is wider than it is tall, you usually choose Landscape orientation.

Note It doesn't matter to Illustrator whether the illustration fits on the page in one or both of these orientations. If you can't see all four edges of the Bounding Box, chances are the illustration will be cropped. Orientation is quite different from Transverse in the Other Page Size dialog box. Orientation changes the orientation of the illustration on the page, but Transverse changes the way that the page is put on the paper. A seemingly small difference, but a distinct and important one to understand.

Figure 16-13 shows an illustration that is placed on a page in both Portrait and Landscape orientations, with and without the Transverse option selected.

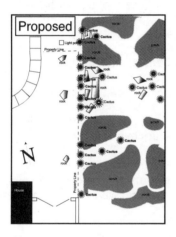

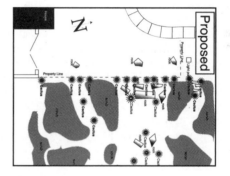

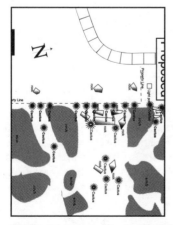

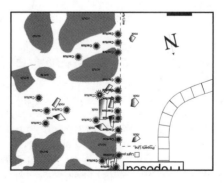

Figure 16-13: An illustration placed on a page in Portrait orientation (upper left), Landscape orientation (lower left), Portrait with Transverse checked (upper right), and Landscape with Transverse checked (lower right)

Understanding emulsion

Hang out around strippers (at a commercial printing company . . . get your mind out of the gutter), and you hear them constantly talk about "emulsion up" and "emulsion down." What they are referring to is the black stuff on film. If you have a piece of film from a printer lying around, look at it near a light. One side is shinier than the other side. The shinier side is without emulsion. When you are burning plates for presses, the emulsion side (dull side) should always be toward the plate.

In the Separation Setup dialog box, you use the Emulsion option to control which side the emulsion goes on. If you are printing negatives on film, choose Down (right reading) from the Emulsion pop-up menu. To see what the separations look like when printed on paper, choose Up (right reading). Always consult your commercial printer for the correct way to output film.

Tip

Although "wrong reading" isn't an option in the Separation Setup dialog box, you can reverse an illustration by choosing the opposite emulsion setting. In other words, Down (right reading) is also Up (wrong reading), and Up (right reading) is also Down (wrong reading). When you image film for offset printing, you want the film emulsion down, right reading. If you turn that same film over you will have emulsion up, wrong reading, and therefore the opposite is also true.

Reversing text creates the kind of secret code illustrations that you can send to your friends. The only way to understand the illustrations is by viewing them in a mirror. This technique works best with text, of course, and we wouldn't expect to fool really smart people with this type of code.

Thinking of the emulsion as the toner in a laser printer may help you understand this concept better. If the toner is on the top of the paper, and you can read it normally, the emulsion is Up, right reading. If the toner is on the bottom of the paper, and you can read the illustration only when you place the paper in front of a light, the emulsion is Down, right reading. Thinking along these lines was helpful back when we were new to the printing industry, and it should help you as well.

Setting up the halftone screen

The halftone screen setting is a great mystery to the graphic designer who is not in the know. A too-low halftone screen setting renders an illustration terribly, making text and pictures unclear and fuzzy, sometimes even showing the dots that create the tints in the illustration. But a too-high halftone screen setting causes blends and gradations to show banding, and some areas or the entire illustration may look posterized, where the color details are missing. The halftone setting can be too high for a particular press, resulting in smeared results.

Cross-Reference

Chapter 11, "Using Path Blends, Compound Paths, and Masks," discusses blends, gradations, and how to avoid banding.

Understanding halftone line screens

The most common mistake that graphic designers make is confusing dots per inch (dpi) with *lines per inch* (lpi). Lines per inch is another way of saying line screen or halftone line screen.

The number of dots per inch of the output device controls what the potential lines per inch settings are. The higher the dpi, the higher the lpi can be, but the higher the lpi, the lower the possible number of grays.

In bitmap graphics software such as Photoshop, the dpi of the image is also important. In Illustrator, objects that you create are based on locations of points rather than on dots per inch. Trust us, dealing with an image's dpi is no picnic, and the fact that Illustrator can bypass this specification entirely is a great boon. Of course, if you have placed or imported pixel-based images in your file, you haven't learned anything. . . .

Line screens are made up of a combination of halftone cells. Each halftone cell has a certain number of dots within it that can be turned on and off. Usually the dots are turned on and off in a round pattern to create a halftone dot.

As an example, consider a common dpi/lpi ratio, that of a 300-dpi laser printer with a 60-line screen. Each halftone dot is made up of a 5×5 halftone cell (300/60 = 5). The number of pixels within each cell is 25. Figure 16-14 shows 5×5 halftone cells at different percentages.

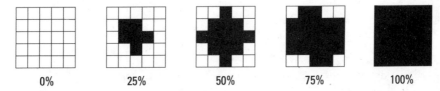

| 0% | 25% | 50% | 75% | 100% |

Figure 16-14: 5×5 halftone cells at different percentages

At a 25 percent tint, 25 percent of the dots are black. In a halftone cell of 25 dots, 6.25 dots would be black. Because you cannot print a quarter of a dot with this method, 6 dots are black.

Because the halftone cell has 25 pixels, only 26 levels of gray are available when you are using a 300-dpi laser printer with a 60-lpi screen (1 level for each of the 25 pixels plus 1 level for no pixels on at all yields 26). To get more grays, you need to lower the line screen.

Lower line screens seem rougher than higher line screens. The cutoff point for line screens is about 105; anything higher is considered a fine line screen, and anything lower is a coarse line screen.

A 300-dpi laser printer prints 90,000 dots for every square inch (300 × 300 = 90,000). Figure 16-15 shows one square inch enlarged 500 percent so you can see the different dot patterns in a small gradient.

Figure 16-15: Halftone gradients

In deciding on a halftone screen, you need to consider many things. The most important is the type of paper or media on which the image will be printed and the press on which it will be printed. Different types of paper will absorb ink at different rates. If you choose the wrong type of paper, then the printing run could be ruined because the ink isn't able to bond well with the paper.

Common settings for different types of print jobs are: newsprint and photocopiers, 85 lpi; standard magazines, 133 lpi; better quality magazines, 150 lpi; and high-quality book images, 150 or 175 lpi.

Adding custom line screens

In the Separation Setup dialog box, you can specify the line screen only by selecting one of the choices in the Halftone pop-up menu. This restriction can be very limiting, but you can get around it by seriously tinkering, as described in the following steps.

1. Make a copy of the PPD file that you want to add halftone screens to and add a suffix, such as new, to its name (for example, Laserwriter.new). Open the copy with SimpleText, Notepad, or other word processing program.

2. Scroll down to a section that looks similar to what you see in Figure 16-16. Depending on the PPD chosen, the halftone screen numbers may be different from the ones shown in the figure. Select the entire section and copy it. Press the left arrow once and paste.

```
*%  For  60  lpi / 300 dpi  ===================================

*ColorSepScreenAngle ProcessBlack.60lpi.300dpi/60 lpi / 300 dpi: "45"
*ColorSepScreenAngle CustomColor.60lpi.300dpi/60 lpi / 300 dpi: "45"
*ColorSepScreenAngle ProcessCyan.60lpi.300dpi/60 lpi / 300 dpi: "15"
*ColorSepScreenAngle ProcessMagenta.60lpi.300dpi/60 lpi / 300 dpi: "75"
*ColorSepScreenAngle ProcessYellow.60lpi.300dpi/60 lpi / 300 dpi: "0"

*ColorSepScreenFreq ProcessBlack.60lpi.300dpi/60 lpi / 300 dpi: "60"
*ColorSepScreenFreq CustomColor.60lpi.300dpi/60 lpi / 300 dpi: "60"
*ColorSepScreenFreq ProcessCyan.60lpi.300dpi/60 lpi / 300 dpi: "60"
*ColorSepScreenFreq ProcessMagenta.60lpi.300dpi/60 lpi / 300 dpi: "60"
*ColorSepScreenFreq ProcessYellow.60lpi.300dpi/60 lpi / 300 dpi: "60"
```

Figure 16-16: The line screen values that can be changed in a text editor

3. In the copy, change the numbers highlighted in Figure 16-16 to whatever line screen you choose. Paste the copy and repeat this step for every new halftone screen that you want to include in the PPD file.

4. Save the changes.

5. Open the new PPD in the Separation Setup dialog box. If all went well, new pop-up menu items reflect your recent changes.

The final thing to consider when you are choosing a halftone screen is the type of media on which the illustration will be output from an imagesetter. If the output is on paper, the halftone screen needs to be lower than if the output is on film.

Changing from positive to negative to positive

You use the Image pop-up menu to switch between printing positive and negative images. Usually, you use a negative image for printing film negatives and a positive image for printing on paper and for film positives. The default for this setting, regardless of the printer chosen or PPD selected, is Negative.

Working with different colors

In the middle-right section of the Separation Setup dialog box, a color list window displays where you can select different colors and set them to print or not print, and set Custom Colors to process separately.

The list of colors contains only the colors that are used in that particular illustration. At the top of the list of separation colors are the four process colors in italic, or spot colors that contain those process colors, if they are used in the illustration. Below the process colors is a list of all the spot colors in the document.

Tip   If the illustration has any guides in it, their colors are reflected in the color list window. From looking at the preview of the illustration in the Separation Setup dialog box, you can't easily determine that these blank separations will print. The best thing to do is release all guides and delete them.

By default, all process colors are set to print, and all spot colors are set to convert to process colors. Clicking the Convert to Process checkbox at the bottom of the Separation Setup dialog box toggles between converting everything (checked) and spot colors (unchecked).

Each color in the list has its own frequency and angle. Don't change the angle or frequency for process colors because Separator has automatically created the best values for the process colors at the halftone screen you've specified. Instead, make sure that any spot colors that may be printing have different angles from each other so that no patterns develop from them.

As soon as you type new values or check different options using the color list, the changes are applied.

Separations

To print with the settings you've selected, click OK in the Separation Setup dialog box, and then choose File ➪ Print (or press ⌘+P [Ctrl+P]). This displays the Print dialog box. On a Mac, choose Adobe Illustrator from the pop-up menu and change the Output pop-up to Separate. In Windows, change the Output option to Separations. The separations you've specified will print.

The Printing Process and Saving $$ with Your Computer

Having an idea of the printing process of a job from start to finish can help you understand some of the choices that you need to make when you are printing out of Separator. Of course, the following is a generalization, and all printers work a little differently.

First, the printer gathers all of the materials for the print job. These materials may include artwork, logos, photos, and copy, which are usually supplied electronically. The materials may go to different places, depending on what equipment the printer has. A typical commercial printer has limited prepress equipment in-house.

Color artwork and color photos are sent to a color separation house that specializes in creating film separations from full-color originals. The cost for each piece of artwork ranges depending on the quality desired and the quantity.

Text may be sent to a typesetting firm and set, but is frequently set in-house. Traditionally, black-and-white artwork and text are pasted on to pasteboards, proofed, and then shot with a camera. A stripper takes the resulting film to a light table where any seams in the film are opaqued out. However, most printers deal nowadays with electronic files that contain all the image information.

Film from the separation house is stripped into the film from the artwork and type. This particular step is the most time-consuming and adds substantially to the prepress portion of the labor bill.

At this point, proofs are created. Printers use many different proofing methods, but the least expensive and most basic is the *blueline*, so called for the blue color of the text and artwork that appears on the sheets.

After the blueline is approved (or *if*, to be more precise), each piece of film is used to create a printing press plate for each color.

The plates are applied to presses, and the number of copies specified by the customer is run. Printers usually print overruns to account for errors in printing and bindery.

After the ink on the printed paper dries, the copies are cut along crop marks, bound (such as for books), and, if needed, folded along fold marks. Depending on the type of product, the printed pieces may be bound, folded, and cut in any order.

The final piece is boxed and shipped to the client.

If you do everything you can with your system, you can save substantial amounts of money in all of the prepress areas. Do as many of the following as possible to save money and avoid problems:

✦ Do as much as you can electronically—this is one rule you should live by.

✦ Have someone else proof your work before you output it to film. Objectivity for your own work decreases proportionately in relation to the time you spend working on it. Your subconscious doesn't want to find mistakes.

Continued

Continued

✦ Get a separation house to scan photos and traditionally created artwork. Have the separation house provide you with the files on disk. Sure, you can buy an inexpensive flatbed desktop scanner, but color pictures from them can look like mush next to scans from a drum scanner at a separation house.

✦ Assemble all your artwork, type, and photos in a package such as QuarkXPress, FrameMaker, or PageMaker.

✦ Have all film negatives output by a reputable service bureau. If your job contains a large amount of color artwork or photos, or if you need the artwork and color photos to be of the best possible quality, take everything back to the color separation house to have your job output at a better quality than most imagesetters can produce.

Printing Color Separations

Color separations are necessary to print a color version of an illustration if it contains two or more colors on offset printing presses. Each separation creates a plate that is affixed to a round drum on a printing press. Ink that is the same color as that separation is applied to the plate, which is pressed against a sheet of paper. Because the ink adheres only to the printing areas of the plate, an image is produced on paper. Some printing presses have many different drums and can print a four-color job in one run. Other printing presses have only one or two drums, so the paper has to pass through the press four or two times, respectively, to print a four-color job.

The two types of color separation are process color separation and spot color separation. Each type has its own advantages and drawbacks, and any print job can be produced using one or a combination of these modes.

Tip   You should always determine which type of separation you want *before* you begin to create a job electronically.

Spot color separation

Jobs that are printed with spot colors are often referred to as two-color or three-color jobs when two or three colors are used. Although you can use any number of colors, most spot color jobs contain only a few colors.

Spot color printing is most useful when you are using two or three distinct colors in a job. For example, if we needed only black and green to create a certain illustration, we would use only black and a green custom color for all of the objects in the illustration.

Three main reasons exist for using spot color separation rather than process color separation:

✦ It's cheaper. Spot color printing requires a smaller press with fewer drums. For process color separation, you usually need to use a press with four drums or run the job through a smaller press two or four times.

✦ Spot colors are cleaner, brighter, and smoother than the same colors that you create as process colors. To get a green process color, for example, you need to mix both cyan and yellow on paper. Using one spot color results in a perfectly solid area of color.

✦ You cannot duplicate certain spot colors, especially fluorescent and metallic colors, with process colors.

Illustrator creates spot colors whenever you specify a spot color in a swatch. If you use six different spot colors and Black, you can print out seven different spot color separations.

Spot colors do have their limitations and disadvantages. The primary limitation of using only spot colors is that the number of colors is restricted to the number of color separations that you want to produce. Remember that the cost of a print job is directly related to the number of different colored inks in the job.

The cutoff point for using spot colors is usually three colors. When you use four spot colors, you limit yourself to four distinct colors and use as many colors as a process color job that can have an almost infinite number of colors. Sometimes people use more than three spot colors to keep colors distinct and clear. Spot color jobs of six colors are not unusual. Each of the six colors is bright, vibrant, and distinct from its neighbors, whereas different process colors seem to fade into one another.

Note Spot colors are often incorrectly referred to as Pantone colors. Pantone is a brand name for a color matching system. You can select Pantone colors as custom colors and use them in Illustrator, and you can print them as either spot colors or as process colors.

Process color separation

Process color separation, also known as four-color separation, creates almost any color by combining cyan, magenta, yellow, and black inks. By using various combinations of different tints of each of these colors, you can reproduce many of the colors (more than 16 million) that the human eye can see.

Process printing uses a subtractive process. You start with bright white paper, and darken the paper with various inks. Cyan, magenta, and yellow are the subtractive primaries, and black is added to create true black printing, which the primaries together don't do very well.

Using process color separation is advisable when

✦ The illustration includes color photographs.

✦ The illustration contains more than three different colors.

How many colors?

Everyone always says that you can create as many colors as you could ever want when you are using process colors. Maybe.

In Illustrator, you can specify colors up to $\frac{1}{100}$ percent accuracy. As a result, 10,000 different shades are available for each of the four process colors. So, theoretically, $10,000^4$, or 10,000,000,000,000,000, different colors should be available, which is 10 quadrillion or 10 million billion. Any way you look at it, you have a heck of a lot of color possibilities.

Unfortunately, most imagesetters and laser printers can produce only 256 different shades for each color. This limitation of the equipment (not PostScript) drops the number of available colors to 256^4, or 4,294,967,296, which is about 4.3 billion colors—only 4 millionths of the colors that Illustrator can create.

This limitation is fortunate for us however, because it is estimated that we can detect a maximum of 100 different levels of gray, probably less. As a result, we can view only 100^4, or 100,000,000, different colors.

We run into a problem when we preview illustrations, however. An RGB monitor (used on computers) can display up to 16.7 million colors, theoretically, if each Red, Green, and Blue pixel can be varied by 256 different intensities. Based on your configuration, some Macintoshes and Windows machines may be set to only 32,768 colors with their onboard video, and some (especially if your kids use your computer to play games) may be limited to 256. You need to set your video cards to display the 16.7 million colors that monitors can produce.

Another problem is that about 30 percent of the colors that you can view on an RGB monitor can't be reproduced by using cyan, magenta, yellow, and black inks on white paper. You can't create these unprintable colors in Illustrator, but you can create them in most other drawing and graphics software packages. These colors are for onscreen viewing pleasure only.

The secret to process color separation is that the four colors that make up all the different colors are themselves not visible. Each color is printed as a pattern of tiny dots, angled differently from the other three colors. The angles of each color are very important. If the angles are off even slightly, a noticeable, distorted pattern that is commonly known as a *moiré* emerges. This pattern often shows up in desktop scanned images of offset prints.

The colors are printed in a specific order — usually cyan, magenta, yellow, and black. Although the debate continues about the best order in which to print the four colors, black is always printed last.

To see the dots for each color, use a magnifying device to look closely at something that is preprinted and in full color. Even easier, look at the Sunday comics, which have bigger dots than most other printed pieces. The different color dots in the Sunday comics are quite visible, and their only colors are cyan, magenta, yellow, and black.

The size of the dots that produce each of these separations is also important. The smaller the dots, the smoother the colors appear. Large dots (such as those in the Sunday comics) can actually take away from the illusion of a certain unified color because the different color dots are visible.

For more information on the common dot sizes and on the relation of dot size to the quality of the illustration, see the section "Setting up the halftone screen," earlier in this chapter.

Figure 16-17 shows how process colors are combined to create new colors. In the figure, the first four rows show very large dots. The top three rows are cyan, magenta, and yellow. The fourth row is all four process colors combined, and the bottom row shows how the illustration looks when you print it.

Process color printing is best for photographs because photographs originate from a continuous tone that is made on photographic paper from film, instead of dots on a printing press.

In Illustrator, you can convert spot (or custom) colors to process colors before printing. To convert custom colors to process colors before printing, select any objects that have a specific custom color and tint and click the Process Color icon that appears in the rightmost column in the Swatches palette when the view is set to Name view. You can specify Name view in the Swatches palette pop-up menu. The color is converted to its process color counterpart, and all selected objects are filled with the new process color combination.

After you click the Process Color icon, if the selected objects become filled with White and the triangles for each process color are at zero percent, you have selected objects that contain different colors or tints. Undo the change immediately.

To make sure that you select only objects that have the same color, select one of the objects and choose Select ⇨ Same ⇨ Fill Color. Objects that have different strokes or objects with different tints of the same color are not selected.

You can convert custom colors to process colors in the Separation dialog box (see the "Working with different colors" section, earlier in this chapter) and in many page layout and graphics programs.

Figure 16-17: The top three rows display cyan, magenta, and yellow; the fourth row displays their combination; and the fifth row displays the colors as they will print (shown here in black-and-white only).

Combining both spot and process color separations

You can couple spot colors with process colors in Illustrator simply by creating both process and named spot colors in a document.

Usually, you add spot colors to process colors for these reasons:

✦ **You are using a company logo that has a specific color.** By printing that color as a spot color, you make it stand out from the other coloring. In addition, color is more accurate when it comes from a specific ink rather than from a process color combination. Often, the logo is a Pantone color that doesn't reproduce true to form when you use process color separation.

✦ **You need a color that you can't create by using process colors.** Such colors are most often metallic or fluorescent, but they can be any number of Pantone colors or other colors that you can't match with process colors.

✦ **You need a varnish for certain areas of an illustration.** A varnish is a glazed type of ink that results in a shiny area wherever you use the varnish. You commonly use varnishes on titles, logos, book covers, over photographs, and any piece that needs a sheen finish or protection of the colors.

✦ **You need a light color over a large area.** The dots that make up process colors are most noticeable in light colors, but by using a spot color to cover the area with a solid sheet of ink that has no dots, you make the area smoother and enhance it visually.

In some circumstances, you need to use a spot color as a spot color and also use it as a process color. Normally, you can't do both, but the following steps describe one way to get around this problem:

1. If the color doesn't exist as a swatch, create a swatch for the color.

2. In the Swatch Options (double-click the swatch), set the pop-up menu to Spot Color and click OK.

3. Duplicate the swatch by dragging it on top of the New Swatch icon (the little piece of paper).

4. In the Swatch Options for the duplicated swatch, set the pop-up menu to Process Color and click OK.

Note You can tell which swatch is which by looking at the lower-right corner of the swatches; the spot color swatch has a white triangle with a "spot" in it, the process swatch is solid.

Printing from Other Applications

Many other software programs, particularly page layout software programs, incorporate color-separation capabilities. These programs usually enable you to import Illustrator files that have been saved as Illustrator EPS files.

When you produce color separations from other software, make sure that any custom colors that are in the Illustrator illustration are present and accessible in the document in which the illustration is placed. Usually, you can set the custom colors to process separately or to spot separately.

Note You cannot change the colors of an imported Illustrator EPS document in a page layout program, so be sure that the colors are correct for the illustration while it is in Illustrator.

Learning Printing from the Experts

If you have never visited a printing company, make a point to visit one and take a tour. Most printing companies have staff members who are more than willing to explain their equipment and various printing processes. In a 30-minute tour with a knowledgeable guide, you can learn enough to save yourself hours of work, money, and misunderstandings.

When you are talking to a printing rep, find out what type of media they want your work on. Printing companies commonly use imagesetters that can output the job for you, and some companies even perform this service at no charge or for a significant discount if you have the job printed there.

Imagesetters are similar to laser printers, except that they produce images with a very high dpi, from 1,273 to 3,600, and sometimes higher. Imagesetters can print directly to RC (resin-coated) paper or to film negatives (or positives). The paper or film runs through the imagesetter, and then runs through a developing process for the images and text to appear.

Most printing company salespeople are fluent to a minor degree in desktop publishing-speak, although few know the difference between TIFF and EPS. They can tell you when to give them negs (film negatives) and paper, and which service bureau to use if they don't have an imagesetter in-house. Many can tell you which software their clients prefer and which software packages create problems, and they can give you tips that can help you get your project through the process without problems.

A service bureau is a company that has on its premises an imagesetter, and whose function is to provide the general community of desktop publishers with imagesetter output at a cost per page. Service bureaus often have color output capabilities, and offer disk-conversion and other services that are sometimes needed by desktop publishers.

Better yet, do what one of your authors did: Work at a printing company for a short period. The first job Ted Alspach had out of college, working in the prepress department of a four-color commercial printer, taught him more than he learned in four years of school. The experience instilled in him some of the most important basic skills for graphics design that he still uses and needs every day. Ever wonder why your printer gets so grumpy when you say your negs won't be available until two days past the promised date? Working at a printing company gives you an understanding of job scheduling — an art of prophecy and voodoo that gives ulcers to printing company managers and supervisors.

The more you know about printing and your printer, the better your print job turns out, and the fewer hassles you have to deal with.

Trapping

Trapping is one of the most important but least understood issues in printing. In the past, desktop publishing has been noted for its inefficiency in trapping, but QuarkXPress and a few after-the-fact trapping software packages, such as Luminus TrapWise and Island Trapper, have gradually improved the trapping capabilities of electronic publishing.

Note Illustrator, while it does incorporate a trapping filter, is not a trap-happy piece of software. For detailed illustrations, it usually isn't worth your time to set the trapping inside Illustrator; instead, you'll want to have your printer do the work for you.

Understanding what trapping does

Traps solve alignment problems when color separations are produced. The most common problem that occurs from misalignment is the appearance of white space between different colors.

Note The thought of trapping scares many graphic designers — not just because they don't know how to do it, but also because they aren't sure what trapping is and what purpose it serves. Understanding the concept of trapping is the hard part; trapping objects is easy (though somewhat tedious in Illustrator).

Figure 16-18 shows a spot color illustration with four colors. The top row shows each of the individual colors. The first illustration in the second row shows how the illustration prints if all the separations are aligned perfectly. The second illustration in the second row shows what happens when the colors are misaligned. The third illustration in the second row shows how the illustration looks when trapped, with black indicating where two colors overprint each other.

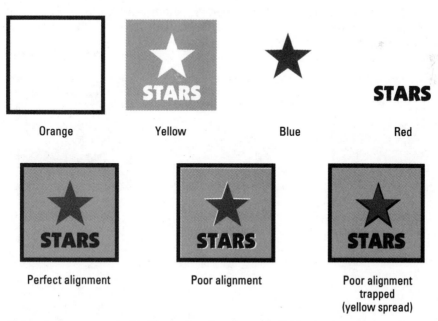

Figure 16-18: A spot color illustration that shows individual colors (top) and aligned, misaligned, and trapped composites (bottom)

This example shows extreme misalignment and excessive trapping; we designed it just as a black-and-white illustration for this book. Ordinarily, the overprinting colors may appear a tiny bit darker, but they do not show as black; we used black so that you can see what parts of the illustration overlap when trapping is used. The trapping in this case is more than sufficient to cover any of the white gaps in the second illustration.

Trapping is created by spreading or choking certain colors that touch each other in an illustration. To spread a color, enlarge an object's color so that it takes up more space around the edges of the background area. To choke a color, expand the color of the background until it overlaps the edges of an object.

The major difference between a spread and a choke has to do with which object is considered the background and which object is the foreground. The foreground object is the object that traps. If the foreground object is spread, the color of the foreground object is spread until it overlaps the background by a certain amount. If the foreground object is choked, the color of the background around the foreground object is expanded until it overlaps the foreground object by a certain amount.

 Tip   To determine whether to use a choke or a spread on an object, compare the lightness and darkness of the foreground and background objects. The general rule of thumb is that lighter colors expand or contract into darker colors.

Figure 16-19 shows the original misaligned illustration and two ways of fixing it with trapping. The middle star has been spread by 1 point, and the third star has been choked by 1 point.

Original   Blue (star shape)
1-pt spread   Blue (star shape)
1-pt choke

Figure 16-19: The original illustration (left), fixing the star by spreading it 1 point (middle), and fixing the star by choking it 1 point (right)

Why color separations do not properly align and require trapping

The three reasons why color separations don't align properly are that the negatives are not the same size, the plates on the press are not aligned perfectly when printing, or the gods have decided that a piece is too perfect and needs gaps between abutting colors. Trapping is required because it is a solution for covering gaps that occur when color separations do not properly align.

Negatives can be different sizes for several reasons. When the film was output to an imagesetter, the film may have been too near the beginning or the end of a roll, or separations in the same job may have been printed from different rolls. The pull on the rollers, while fairly precise on all but top-of-the-line imagesetters, where it should be perfect, can pull more film through when less resistance occurs (at the end of a roll of film), or less film when more resistance occurs (at the beginning of a roll of film). The temperature of the film may be different if a new roll is put on in the middle of a job, causing the film to shrink (if it is cold) or expand (if it is warm).

The temperature of the processor may have risen or fallen a degree or two while the film was being processed. Again, cooler temperatures in the chemical bays and in the air dryer as the film exits the process impact the size of the film.

Film negatives usually don't change drastically in size, but they can vary up to a few points on an 11-inch page. That distance is huge when a page has several abutting colors throughout. The change in a roll of film is usually along the length of the roll, not along the width. The quality of the film is another factor that determines how much the film stretches or shrinks.

Most strippers are aware of how temperature affects the size of negatives. A common stripper trick is to walk outside with a freshly processed negative during the colder months to shrink a negative that may have enlarged slightly during processing.

Check with your service bureau staff to see how long they warm up the processor before sending jobs through it. If the answer is less than an hour, the chemicals will not be at a consistent temperature, and negatives that are sent through too early certainly change in size. Another question to ask is how often they change their chemicals and check the density of their imagesetter. Once a week is acceptable for a good-quality service bureau, but the best ones change chemicals and check density once a day.

The plates on a press can be misaligned by either an inexperienced press operator or a faulty press. An experienced press operator knows the press and what to do to get color plates to align properly. A faulty press is one where plates move during printing or are not positioned correctly. An experienced press operator can determine how to compensate for a faulty press.

No press is perfect, but some of the high-end presses are pretty darn close. Even on those presses, the likelihood that a job with colors that abut one another can print perfectly is not very great.

If a job doesn't have some sort of trapping in it, it probably will not print perfectly, no matter how good the negatives, press, and press operator are.

How much trap?

The amount of trap that you need in an illustration depends on many things, but the deciding factor is what your commercial printer tells you is the right amount.

The most important thing to consider is the quality of the press on which the job will run. Of course, only the printer knows which press this is, so talking to the printer about trapping is imperative.

Other factors to consider include the colors of ink and types of stock used in the job. Certain inks soak into different stocks differently and vice versa.

Traps range from $\frac{2}{1,000}$ of an inch to $\frac{6}{1,000}$ of an inch. Most traditional printers refer to traps in thousandths of inches, but Illustrator likes values in points. Figure 16-20 is a chart with traps in increments of $\frac{1}{1,000}$, from $\frac{1}{1,000}$ of an inch to $\frac{10}{1,000}$ of an inch, and gives their point measurements. The trapped area is represented by black to be more visible in this example.

Remember that the greater the trap, the less chance that any white gaps appear, but the trap may actually be visible. Visible traps of certain color pairs can look almost as bad as white space.

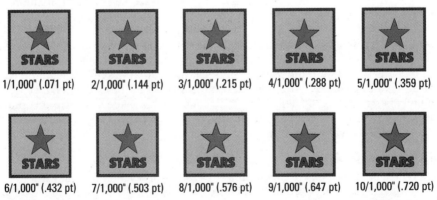

1/1,000" (.071 pt)   2/1,000" (.144 pt)   3/1,000" (.215 pt)   4/1,000" (.288 pt)   5/1,000" (.359 pt)

6/1,000" (.432 pt)   7/1,000" (.503 pt)   8/1,000" (.576 pt)   9/1,000" (.647 pt)   10/1,000" (.720 pt)

Figure 16-20: Different trap amounts

Trapping Illustrator files manually

In Illustrator, you accomplish manual (nonfilter) trapping by selecting a path's Stroke or Fill and setting it to overprint another path's Stroke or Fill. The amount that the two paths' Fills or Strokes overlap and overprint is the amount of trap that is used.

The most basic way to create a trap on an object is by giving it a Stroke that is either the Fill color of the object (to create a spread) or the Fill color of the background (to create a choke).

Tip Be sure to make the width of any Stroke that you use for trapping twice as wide as the intended trap, because only half of the Stroke (one side of the path) actually overprints a different color. In some circumstances, fixing a Stroke that is not wide enough initially can be difficult.

Follow these steps to manually trap an object:

1. Select one path of a pair of overlapping or abutting paths. If possible, select the lighter of the two paths.

2. Give the selected path a Stroke of the same color that the Fill is. Change the weight to the amount of trap you'd like to use. For this example, so it can be easily seen in this book, we've used a 3-point trap.

3. Set the overlapping Stroke to overprint. These steps are shown in Figure 16-21.

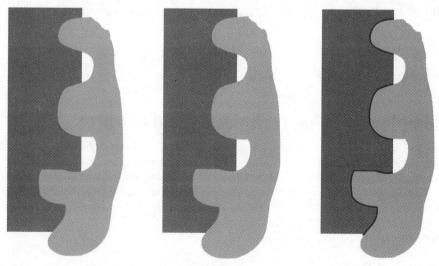

Figure 16-21: Steps for manual trapping

Trapping with Trap

You can also use the Trap feature in Illustrator to create traps on objects. This example uses the same paths from Figure 16-20 to show how Trap works.

1. Select all pieces of art that overlap or abut.

2. Choose Trap from the Pathfinder palette. (You find the Trap button when you choose Options from the Pathfinder pop-up menu.) The Pathfinder Trap dialog box appears. Enter the width in the Width/Height text field (see Figure 16-22).

3. Click OK and trapping is instantly applied to the object (well, if the artwork is complex it won't be instant . . .).

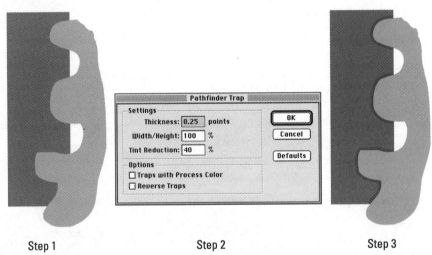

Step 1   Step 2   Step 3

Figure 16-22: Steps for trapping with Trap

Complex trapping techniques in Illustrator

The preceding trap illustrations are extremely simplified examples of trapping methods in Illustrator. In reality, objects never seem to be a solid color, and if they are, they are never on a solid background. In addition, most illustrations contain multiple overlapping objects that have their own special trapping needs.

When Trapping Yourself Isn't Worth It

Before you spend the long amounts of time that complex trapping entails and modify your illustration beyond recognition (at least in Outline mode), you may want to reconsider whether you should do the trapping yourself.

If you estimate that trapping your job will require several hours of work, the chances of doing it correctly dwindle significantly. If the illustration includes many crisscrossing blends and gradations or multiple-placed images, you may not have the patience to get through the entire process with your sanity intact.

If you determine that you cannot do the trapping yourself, you can have it done with Luminus TrapWise or Island Trapper, or you can have a service bureau with special output devices create trapping automatically. These services undoubtedly cost more than doing the trapping yourself, but they get the job done right, which is the important thing.

We consider trapping to be complex when we can't just go around selecting paths and applying trap quickly. Complex trapping involves several different techniques:

✦ **Create a separate layer for trapping objects.** By keeping trapping on its own layer, you make myriad options available that are not available if the trapping is intermixed with the rest of the artwork. Place the new layer above the other layers. Lock all the layers but the trapping layer so that the original artwork is not modified. You can turn trapping on and off by hiding the entire layer or turning off the Print option in the Layers Options dialog box.

✦ **Use the round joins and ends options in the Stroke portion of the Paint Style palette for all trapping Strokes.** Round joins and ends are much less conspicuous than the harsh corners and 90-degree angles of other joins and ends, and they blend smoothly into other objects.

✦ **Trap gradations by stroking them with paths that are filled with overprinting gradients.** You cannot Fill Strokes with gradients, but you can Fill paths with gradients. You can make any Stroke into a path by selecting it and choosing Outline from the Pathfinder palette. After you have transformed the Stroke into a path, Fill it with the gradient and check the Overprint Fill box (in the Attributes palette) for that path.

Note   Whenever we start a heavy-duty trapping project, we always work on a copy of the original illustration. Wrecking the original artwork is just too easy to do when you add trapping.

Summary

From this chapter, you've learned that printing involves so much more than selecting the Print option from a menu. Whether you're using separations or trappings, you now know how to handle complex printing jobs. In this chapter, you learned

✦ PostScript is a printing language used to represent vector-based images.

✦ The Document and Print Setup dialog boxes let you set the conditions for the printing of a document such as the size of the document and the output resolution.

✦ Print separations from Illustrator.

✦ Work with spot and process colors and halftone screens.

✦ Choose whether to print a composite or separations from the Print dialog box.

✦ Determine separation information in the Separation Setup dialog box.

✦ With Separation Setup, specify which colors print, and at what angle and frequency they print.

✦ Prevent potential white space that appears when an illustration isn't perfectly aligned with trapping.

✦   ✦   ✦

Using Illustrator to Generate Web Graphics

In the new century, the denizens of the Web are starting to clamor for vector-based Web graphics. Adobe is at the forefront of the effort to make vector-based graphics available on the Web and has endowed Illustrator with some impressive features for creating pixel- and vector-based Web graphics. In addition to the Acrobat PDF (Portable Document Format) format, Illustrator can export vector-based graphics using the SVG and Flash formats.

Before Illustrator 7, Illustrator had little to offer in the way of Web graphics. Sure, people would use it to set type because Photoshop 1 through 4 had such terrible type capabilities, but overall Illustrator was mostly left out in the cold.

Oddly enough, that didn't seem to stop Illustrator users from using Illustrator to create Web graphics.

But now, Illustrator is endowed with a large number of features for creating graphics for the Web, including these features:

✦ RGB Color Mode support

✦ GIF89A export capability

✦ JPEG export capability

✦ PNG export capability

✦ Flash (SWF) export capability

✦ SVG export capability

✦ SVG Filter effects

✦ URL assignment to objects

✦ Image map creation

✦ Web graphic optimization

✦ Pixel Preview mode

✦ Save for Web window

✦ Add JavaScript interactivity

✦ PDF 3.0 support

✦ Web-safe color palette

✦ Image slicing

✦ Data-driven graphics

This chapter covers these features in depth and provides some handy tips on Web-page creation.

How Illustrator Fits into the Web

With the Web-based features added to Illustrator, it is apparent that Adobe has finally started to take the Web seriously. Creating Web graphics can be frustrating for designers because they are severely limited in the size that they can use. Large graphics (like that perfect logo you created) need to be resized to where the type-face ends up looking like a system font.

Colors can be an issue also. To get consistent color across browsers on several different operating systems, you must use a Web-safe color palette. This limits the designer to a mere 216 unique colors and makes gradients look terrible. We have more colors in our favorite sweaters than that.

Note The value of 216 comes from the 256 possible colors available in an 8-bit palette such as those used for GIF images minus 40 unique system colors that the various operating systems use.

To get around the colors problem, designers can save their Web graphics as a JPEG image, but this format has lossy compression and the compressed image can end up distorted and blocky—kind of like looking at your graphics on a TV with bad reception through a frosted glass window using eyeglasses that are the wrong prescription.

Note The terms *lossy* and *lossless* refer to the type of compression that is used to reduce the size of the image file. Lossy compression reduces the file size by removing image information such as unneeded colors or details. Lossless compression doesn't remove any image information, but compresses the image by looking for sections of similar color that repeat within the image. An image compressed losslessly can be converted again to its original state. A lossy compressed image cannot.

Another common hassle is software hopping. Web images created in Illustrator need to be copied and taken to Photoshop to get their palette shifted and size set. Then the image is copied again to browser software such as GoLive before being transferred to the Web. This is like taking a cross-country flight with half a dozen layovers. Yes, you arrive at your final destination, but it is not a very pleasant way to travel.

Enough singing the Web-designer blues; the good news is that Adobe has heard the moans and groans and decided to do something about it. Illustrator 9 marked a sharp turn into the Web market by endowing Illustrator with the tools necessary to create and deliver Web graphics and now Illustrator 10 builds on these successes. Many of these features are borrowed from Photoshop, so the designer can now use either Illustrator or Photoshop without having to rely on the other and either software package can take its work directly into GoLive.

But wait, there's more. The Web itself is changing the way it works with graphics. Web users are getting tired of waiting for graphics to download and are demanding faster connections, which are improving every day. But another way to address the problem of slow downloads is to use graphics that have a smaller file size. Vector images, because they are mathematically defined, are a fraction of the size of their pixel-based relatives.

Two new vector-based formats have appeared and are beginning to be used widely. These formats enable rich vector-based graphics to be viewed and even animated in a Web browser. The first format, developed by Macromedia, is the Flash format. This is a proprietary format requiring a browser plug-in. The second is an industry open standard named SVG. The great news is that Illustrator supports both of these formats.

Working in Raster View

Although vector-based graphics are just starting to become prevalent on the Web, the majority of Web graphics are still pixel-based. Illustrator includes several features that make working with pixel-based graphics easier.

One way you can work with pixel-based images is by using the Pixel Preview feature under the View menu. This view mode lets you see exactly how the pixel-based graphic will look before you save the image.

Cross-Reference   Chapter 14, "Working with Pixels," covers how to use the Pixel Preview feature.

The Color Mode feature lets you select the document Color Mode to be either CMYK or RGB. Using the RGB Color Mode is most effective when creating pixel-based Web graphics. You can select the color mode to use anytime you create a new document. The current color mode is identified in the title bar of the current document.

Using the Web-safe Color palette

Illustrator can work with Web-safe colors. If you're publishing graphics on the Web that use the GIF format, you'll want to use Web-safe colors. These colors are guaranteed to be consistently represented regardless of the browser or the system that is being used to view the graphics.

Note   It is possible to use a color that is not included within the Web-safe Color palette, but doing so might result in the hue being off on certain systems or the graphics being dithered, which can cause the graphic to display incorrectly.

These colors are all contained in a special Swatches palette that contains Webspecific colors. Using this palette, you can create illustrations that use only the 216 cross-platform colors commonly used for GIF images on the Web. You can access this palette (shown in Figure 17-1) by choosing Window ⇨ Swatch Libraries ⇨ Web.

Figure 17-1: The Web
Swatches palette

If you'll be using the Web Swatches palette, be aware that using blends, gradients, color filters, and the Pathfinder function can dramatically change the colors in your document, creating potential dithering situations. If at all possible, stick to the solid colors found within the palette or use the Web Shift button to shift the color to the nearest Web-safe color.

Viewing hexadecimal color values

You can also select the Web-safe RGB color model, shown in Figure 17-2, from the pop-up menu in the Color palette. This color model enables you to only pick colors from the Web-safe palette. It also represents the color values as hexadecimal values. These values can be inserted directly into an HTML page.

If you move the mouse over the top of the colors within the Web palette, the hexadecimal value for the color is displayed if the Web-safe RGB color mode is selected. These hexadecimal values can be used within an HTML document to set Web page colors.

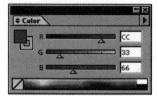

Figure 17-2: The Web-safe RGB color model in the Color palette

Shifting to a Web-safe color

If you're creating Web graphics and you wish to use Web-safe colors, the Color palette includes a helpful icon called the Out of Web Color Warning icon, which will shift the current color to the closest Web-safe color. This icon, as shown in Figure 17-3, looks like a small cube. When a Web-safe color is selected, the Web Shift cube icon will not be displayed.

Out of Web Color Warning

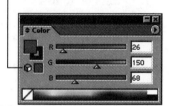

Figure 17-3: The Color palette includes a Web Shift button.

Note   The Color palette may also include an Out of Gamut Warning icon directly below the Out of Web Color Warning icon that identifies any color that is out of the accepted gamut range.

DPI settings

One of the most convenient aspects of working with Web graphics is that you don't need to guess the dpi settings. The maximum resolution that is possible for computer monitors is 72 dpi. This is the magic number. All Web graphics can be saved at this setting to ensure the best possible resolution. And now for the caveat—if the Web graphic is ever going to be printed, then you might want to worry about a higher resolution setting, but because the Web is all about small file sizes, reducing the dpi setting to 72 will keep the file size to a minimum.

The dpi resolution can be set in the Printing & Export panel of the Document Setup dialog box. You can open this dialog box using the File ⇨ Document Setup command.

Saving Pixel Images for the Web

Three different formats exist for saving pixel images that can be used on the Web — GIF, JPEG, and PNG. Each of these formats has its advantages and disadvantages, some of which are as follows:

✦ The **GIF** image format is perhaps the most popular and common graphic format used on the Web. This format includes a 256-color palette and features such as single color transparency, interlacing, and animation capability. GIF images also include automatic lossless compression.

✦ The **JPEG** image format is also used quite heavily on the Web. It supports 24-bit color (16.7 million separate colors) and features such as progressive enhancement, which enables the image to be displayed as it downloads. JPEG images can be compressed using a lossy compression algorithm. This algorithm can reduce the original file size by as much as 1/10 the size of the original image in some cases, but it does this by removing image information. Exporting to the JPEG format enables you to set the amount of compression to use.

✦ The **PNG** image format is fairly new and offers 36-bit color including alpha channel support. This format is gaining in popularity, but isn't supported on older browsers. The PNG format offers lossless compression. This format also comes in two flavors — PNG-8, which supports 256 colors and PNG-24, which supports a full 16.7 million colors.

The Save for Web dialog window can also be used to save images to the SWF and SVG vector formats. These formats will be covered in the "Saving Vector Images for the Web" section below.

All three of these formats are available in Illustrator, but you will not find them as File Types in the Export dialog box. Illustrator has moved these Web formats to a dialog window that can be opened using the File ⇨ Save for Web menu option. All you need to do is to open this dialog box and you'll see why we called it a dialog window.

The Save for Web dialog

The Save for Web dialog window, shown in Figure 17-4, includes its own set of tools that work within the dialog window. These tools, conveniently located to the left of the dialog window include the Hand (H), Slice Select (K), Zoom (Z), and Eyedropper (I) tools. The Hand tool lets you scroll about the displayed image by dragging with the mouse. The Zoom tool will zoom in on the area that is clicked. You can zoom out by holding down the Option [Alt] key while clicking. The Slice Select tool will let you divide the image into slices. Slices are convenient because each slice can have its own format. Slices are covered in more detail later in the chapter. The Eyedropper tool will let you select colors within the image. The current selected color is displayed in the color swatch directly below the Eyedropper tool. At the bottom of the tools is the Toggle Slices Visibility (Q) button. This button will make any slices within the image visible.

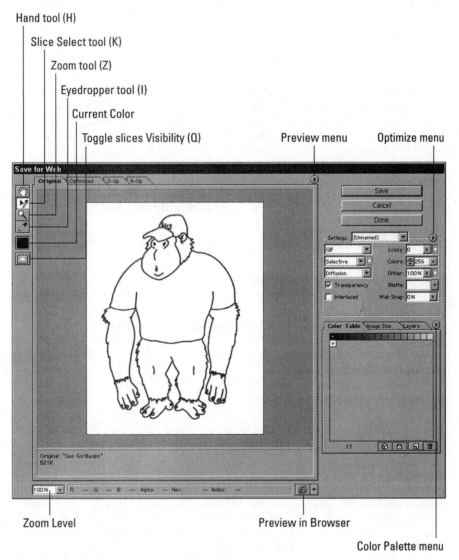

Figure 17-4: The Save for Web dialog window

Four tabs also appear at the top of the window that let you switch between the Original image, an Optimized version of the image, and 2 or 4 side by side comparison views of the image. At the top right corner of the image display is an icon that opens the Preview menu. Using this menu you can toggle options to dither the display and the download rate to use to compute the download time. Download rate options range from 9.6 Kbps to 2.0 Mbps.

Directly below the image display is some text that lists the file's name and size. For optimized images, the download speed (computed using the Download rate set in the Preview Menu) and image settings are also listed. At the bottom of the dialog window is a popup menu/drop-down list that can change the zoom amount. This zoom list also includes an option to fit the image on the screen.

Along the bottom of the dialog window are several text fields. The R, G, B, Alpha, Hex and Index values are listed and will change as you move over colors in the image with the Eyedropper tool. To the right of these values is a button for viewing the image in a browser. This button includes a popup menu/drop-down list for setting the test browser.

On the top right of the dialog window are the Save, Cancel and Done buttons. The Save button will present a file dialog box where you can save the image, the Cancel button will close the dialog window and the Done button will save the current settings in the dialog window and close it.

To the right of the dialog window are a number of different settings. The popup menu/drop-down list under the Done button can be used to save a grouping of settings. This list includes many preset options such as GIF 128 Dithered, GIF Web Palette, JPEG Medium and PNG-8 128 Dithered. You can add and delete setting configurations to the menu/list using the Save Settings and Delete Settings options in the pop-up menu. File settings are saved as files with an ins extension in the Presets/Save for Web Settings/Optimize folder. Below the Settings popup menu/drop-down list to the right is another popup menu/drop-down list that will let you select the image format. Options include GIF, JPEG, PNG-8, PNG-24, SWF and SVG. The other settings will change depending on the image format that is selected. These settings will be covered in the sections to follow.

Below the settings are three tabbed panels — Color Table, Image Size and Layers. These tabbed panels will also change as the different formats are selected.

The Color Table panel will display all the colors used with paletted images such as the GIF and PNG-8 formats. Selecting a color in the Color Table panel will let you change that color within the image. You can select multiple colors in a row by holding down the Shift key while clicking on the first and last color or multiple individual colors using the ⌘ [Ctrl] key. Using the icons at the bottom of the panel, you can select colors to be snapped to the Web-Safe palette, locked, added (using the Eyedropper tool) or deleted. Locked colors will not be drop as the image is optimized. At the bottom left of the panel is a number that identifies the unique colors used in the image.

Tip   All colors in the Color Table that are included in the Web-safe palette will have a small white square in the center of the color swatch and locked colors will have a small white square in the lower right corner.

The Image Size panel includes the Width and Height dimensions of the image. It also includes a Percent value for quickly enlarging or reducing the size of the image. The panel also includes options to Constrain Proportions, Anti-Alias and Clip to Artboard. You can change the size of the image by entering new size dimensions in the Width, Height or Percent fields.

The Layers panel includes an option to Export as CSS Layers. If this option is enabled, you can define whether each layer in the file as Visible, Hidden or Do Not Export. Exporting as layers enables animation frames to be saved in different layers.

Saving to the GIF format

The GIF format is the closest to a standard that the World Wide Web has. One of the best things about GIF files is their flexibility. GIF files are used as plain images, images with transparency, image maps, and as animations. Their biggest drawback—the limited number of colors usable—is also a giant strength. The GIF format can be selected from the Save for Web dialog window. When this format is selected, settings for palette type, dither type, lossy compression amount, number of colors, dither amount, matte color, and amount of Web Snap become active. You can also select to enable transparency and interlacing.

The GIF format compresses images using the LZW Compression algorithm. This algorithm works by keeping a count of adjacent pixels that are the same color, so it works very well for images that have large areas of consistent color. It wouldn't work well for images that contain gradients or noisy areas. To save the image using the GIF format, select the GIF option in the top drop-down list to the left in the right section of the dialog window. To see the amount of compression that is possible, click the Optimized tab in the Save for Web dialog window. Figure 17-5 shows the image with this tab selected. Notice how the graphic has been rasterized and is now displayed as a pixel image. You should also notice that the file size (shown underneath the image preview) has been reduced from 521K to 8.599K. The settings for this image are also displayed below the image to the right.

Note   The licensing (or actually issues that have arisen due to licensing) of the LZW Compression algorithm (by Unisys who holds the patent) has been instrumental in the development of the PNG format, which doesn't rely on licensing and patents.

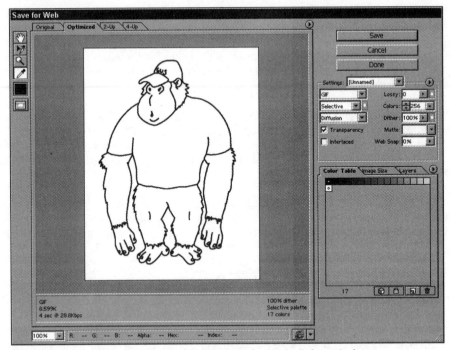

Figure 17-5: The Optimized panel in the Save for Web dialog window

With the GIF format selected, several setting fields will appear to the right of the image display. These settings will control the quality and eventual size of the file. The GIF format can be reduced using the Lossy setting. This setting looks for pixels within the image that can be removed. The higher the setting, the more aggressively pixels are removed. You can always check the results of removing pixels by comparing the optimized image with the original image.

Another way to reduce the file size of a GIF image is to reduce the number of colors included in the graphic. The Color Table panel shows the palette of colors used with the graphic. Using this panel, you can delete colors or shift colors to Web-safe colors. You can also specify the Web Snap value to shift colors to the Web-safe color palette. The higher the Web Snap setting, the more colors get shifted. Illustrator shifts the lesser-used colors first and shifts the colors that are used most often as the Web Snap setting is increased.

Directly below the format popup menu/drop-down list is a popup menu/drop-down list of the color reduction methods to use. The options include many of the common Photoshop methods such as Perceptual, Selective, Adaptive, Web, Black & White, Grayscale, Mac OS and Windows. There is also a Custom option for loading a custom palette. Once a method is selected you can specify the number of colors in the settings to the right. The Auto option will save the maximum number of the colors for the selected color reduction method.

You can also use the Colors popup menu/drop-down list to specify the number of colors to include in the graphic. A full palette uses 256 separate colors. This setting can be moved to as low as two colors. One color wouldn't make much sense, but it would result in a very small file size.

Below the palette popup menu/drop-down list is a list of dithering options. Dithering is the process of making an image appear to have more colors than it really does by placing patterns of given colors close to one another. For example, an image with only red and blue colors can approximate the color purple using a pattern of red and blue pixels. Options include different dithering methods including Diffusion, Pattern and Noise. There is also an option to have no dithering. For each dither method, you can set the amount of dithering using the Dither setting.

GIF images can be set to be transparent by enabling the Transparency setting. This will make only one color (defined by the color specified in the Matte setting) invisible. Typically you can use the background color (such as white) transparent, but this will make all white pixels within the image invisible. You can also enable the Interlaced option to enable the image to appear line by line as it is downloaded.

Figure 17-6 shows the Save for Web window with the 4-Up panel selected. The original image is shown in the upper-left corner. The other three optimized versions have been set to three different dither, color and lossy settings.

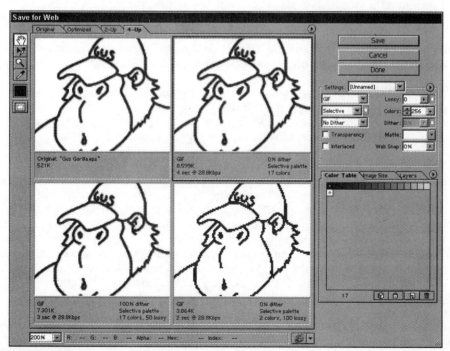

Figure 17-6: The Save for Web window displays the original image and three optimized versions of a GIF image.

Saving to the JPEG format

The JPEG (Joint Photographic Experts Group) format has been the most popular high compression standard for pixel-based images by far. It enables images to be compressed to as little as one percent of their original size. Of course, this extreme compression comes at a price — loss of detail. Using the higher compression settings may create blotches on images that look pretty terrible, but you can escape these problems if you select the right type of image or if you limit the amount of compression.

Tip   Images that include a lot of detail like the flowers shown in the next figure will compress very well, but the JPEG format will struggle with large flat areas of solid color and sharp lines like the cartoon shown in the previous figure.

When working with JPEG images, you will need to fight the quality versus file size battle. Illustrator offers a weapon to help you win this battle. Using the 2-Up and 4-Up tabs in the Save for Web dialog window, you can look at two or four different versions of the image simultaneously. This lets you home in on the quality of figure that you want to see. You can change the settings for any view by selecting the view and making a change.

Figure 17-7 shows four versions of a JPEG image. To save using the JPEG format, drag the format popup menu/drop-down list on the right to the JPEG option. The 2-Up and 4-Up tabs can display the image using different formats and settings. For this figure, the upper left image is the original image and the other three panes show the image as a JPEG image with different Quality levels. Notice how the quality of the image degrades as the file size decreases. We've also opened the Image Size panel because the Color Table doesn't apply to JPEG images.

For the JPEG format, a quality setting popup menu/drop-down list will appear directly below the format drop-down list. The options include Low, Medium, High and Maximum, which equate to Quality settings of 10, 30, 60 and 80 respectively. The Quality value can be set to any value between 0 and 100.

The JPEG format supports several unique options. The Optimized checkbox is a separate control that works independently of the Quality setting. If the Optimized checkbox is selected, then Illustrator more aggressively tries to reduce the file size while maintaining the settings. Other options include Progressive, which is like Interlacing and will make the image appear slowly as it is downloaded; and Matte, which enables you to select a single color that will be transparent in the final image. The Blur setting can be used to apply a Gaussian Blur to the image. It can be set between 0 and 2. Finally, the ICC Profile option will save the designated ICC profile with the image. Some browsers can use this information to color correct the image.

Caution   As when exporting to any bitmapped format, make sure you don't give the file being exported the same name as the Illustrator file. If you give it the same name, the exported file overwrites the Illustrator file, which makes the Illustrator file uneditable.

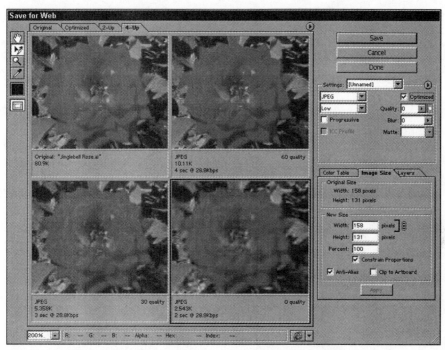

Figure 17-7: The 4-Up panel in the Save for Web dialog window

You can also save images in the JPEG format using the File ➪ Export menu option. This will open a dialog box that includes many of the same settings that are found in the Save for Web dialog window.

Saving to the PNG format

PNG (Portable Network Graphics) is a newer Web format and seems primed to take over from JPEG and many GIF (Graphics Interchange Format) uses, as it keeps file sizes small without losing any data. Files can be saved in up to 36-bit color (including alpha transparency) for maximum quality. The PNG format also supports transparency and interlacing. Illustrator can save images using a 256 color PNG format called PNG-8 and a 24-bit version called PNG-24. The major browsers are beginning to support this image format.

The PNG-8 format has many of the same options as the GIF format including Color Reduction method, number of colors, Diffusion method, Transparency, Interlacing, Dither amount, Matte color and Web Snap amount. The PNG-24 format includes options for Transparency, Interlacing and a Matte color. The amount of compression is automatically applied at its maximum amount without losing any image data.

Optimizing Web graphics

Optimizing Web graphics means making the images as small as possible. You have a number of ways to reduce the file size of a graphic depending on the file format. Smaller file sizes download more quickly when a user views a Web page in a browser. The trick is to reduce the file size without adversely affecting the quality of the graphic.

Although most optimizations take place by tweaking individual settings associated with the various formats, you can also optimize an image automatically using the Optimize to File Size menu option in the Optimize menu. This menu option will open the Optimize To File Size dialog box, shown in Figure 17-8. Using this dialog box, you can specify the desired file size. If you select the Auto Select GIF/JPEG option and specify a Desired File Size, then Illustrator automatically reduces the setting for the selected format to get as close as it can to the desired file size.

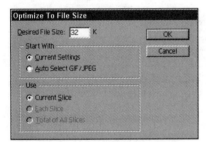

Figure 17-8: The Optimize To File Size dialog box will automatically optimize your image.

Viewing Web graphics in a browser

The final test for Web graphics is to view them in a browser. The Save for Web dialog window includes a button along its bottom edge that opens the current image with the current settings in the designated browser. You can select a different browser by clicking the arrow to the right of the button and selecting Other from the pop-up menu.

Figure 17-9 shows a Web graphic image being previewed in Microsoft's Internet Explorer browser. The browser preview also includes a tag listing the image name, dimensions, file size, settings, and the HTML code needed to place the image in a browser.

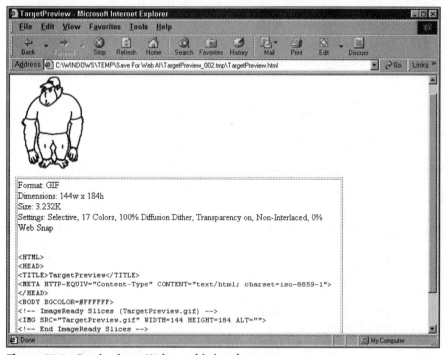

Figure 17-9: Previewing a Web graphic in a browser

Using Output Settings

Using the Edit Output Settings option in the pop-up menu, you can customize how the HTML that is generated looks. This menu option will open the Output Settings dialog box, shown in Figure 17-10. This dialog box will let you save and load custom output settings with the Load and Save buttons. Custom output settings are saved as a file with the .iros extension. The dialog box actually consists of four different panels — HTML, Background, Saving Files and Slices. You can move between these panels using the popup menu/drop-down list at the top of the dialog box.

In the HTML panel, you can specify whether tags and attributes are all uppercase, lowercase, or initial capped. You can also specify how Indents and Line Endings are handled. Slices can be represented as Cascading Style Sheets or as Tables. You can also set the position of image maps.

The Background panel will save the image as a background or as an image. If the image is saved as an HTML image, you can select a different image to use as the HTML background. This background image will be used when you view the image in a browser. Or you could specify a solid color matte instead of a background image.

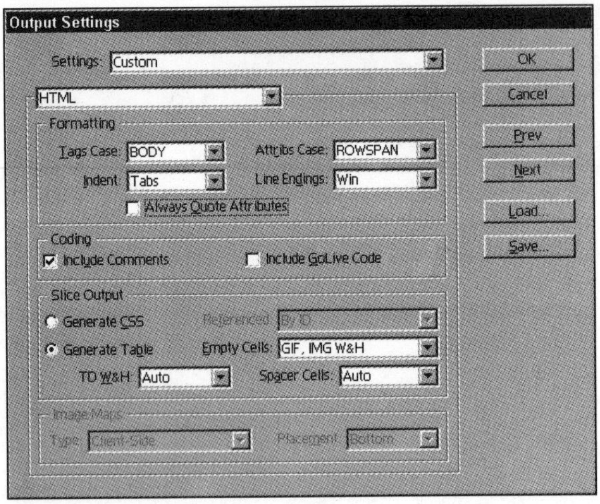

Figure 17-10: The HTML panel of the Output Settings
dialog box

The Saving Files panel, shown in Figure 17-11, lets you cobble together several identifying pieces of information into a file name such as slice name, trigger name, rollover state and more. You can also use this panel to specify the folder where the files are saved. This panel also lets you save the file for compatibility on other platforms. For example, if you create an image on a Mac, then Windows and Unix are options and Mac is disabled.

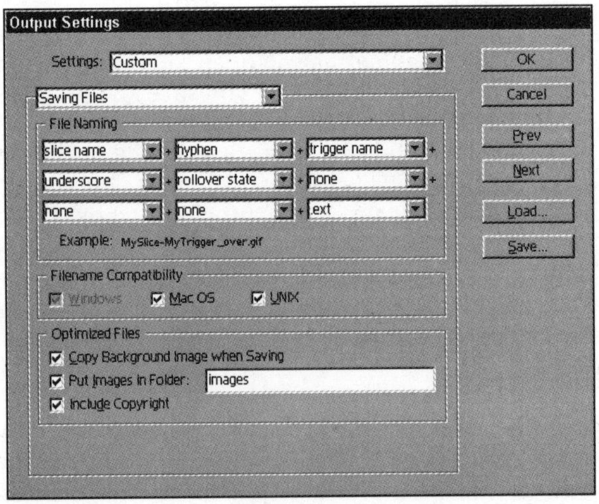

Figure 17-11: The Saving Files panel of the Output
Settings dialog box

The Slices panel also includes several popup menus/drop-down lists that you can use to build slice names similar to the file name apparatus in the Saving Files panel.

Saving Vector Images for the Web

Illustrator is a professional-level tool used to create professional quality images. Publishing images on the World Wide Web with its small file sizes, limited colors, and over-optimized graphics is far beneath such an important and distinguished product as Illustrator.

Well, welcome to the new century, where the Web produces some major money, employs legions of graphic designers, and enables artists to publish their art to millions of viewers instantaneously. For many of these designers and artists, Illustrator is still the tool of choice and Illustrator has adapted to meet the needs of these creative individuals by offering new features that make producing Web graphics easier.

But, Illustrator isn't the only software that is changing. The browsers are also expanding their features, including support for vector-based images. Vector-based images are resolution-independent, so they can be resized to any size. They are also mathematically defined, so their file sizes are greatly smaller than their raster-based counterparts. These advantages make vector-based images uniquely qualified to work well on the Web.

Illustrator supports two different vector-based formats — Flash (SWF) and Scalable Vector Graphics (SVG). For the Flash format, SWF stands for ShockWave Format. The Save for Web dialog window can be used to export these formats also.

New Feature Support for the SWF and SVG formats within the Save for Web dialog window is new to Illustrator 10.

Exporting to the Flash format

Flash is a vector-based format that can be viewed in a browser on the Web using a plug-in. Flash files are typically created using the Flash software created by Macromedia. These files can include interactivity, animation and even sound. Illustrator can also save artwork to this format by selecting the SWF option in the format drop-down list in the Save for Web dialog window or with the File ➪ Export menu option.

When the SWF option is selected in the Save for Web dialog window, you have an option to convert the AI File to an SWF File or to convert the Layers to an SWF File. For animation sequences that are saved in different layers, the second option allows the animation to be exported. The Read Only setting prevents the file from being edited outside of Illustrator. The Curve Quality setting controls the quality of the exported Bézier curves; the higher the value, the better the quality of the curves and the larger the file size. If you're exporting as an animation, you can set the Frame Rate for the frames. The Loop setting will cause the frames to be shown over and over.

Selecting the File ➪ Export command opens the Export dialog box. From the Export dialog box, you will need to select the Macromedia Flash (SWF) Format popup menu [File Type drop down list], type a name, and click OK. This opens the Macromedia Flash (SWF) Format Options dialog box, as shown in Figure 17-12.

Figure 17-12: The Macromedia Flash (SWF) Format Options dialog box

You can export Illustrator files as a single SWF file, as an animation where each layer becomes a separate frame, or where each layer becomes a separate file. If you're exporting as an animation, you can set the Frame Rate for the frames. The Macromedia Flash (SWF) Format Options dialog box also includes settings to Auto-create Symbols, save as Read Only, to Clip to Artboard Size, and to set the Curve Quality. The Auto-Create Symbols settings add the Illustrator objects to the Flash Symbol Library where they can be edited within the Flash program. The Clip to Artboard Size setting clips all the objects outside of the artboard when exporting. The Macromedia Flash (SWF) Format Options dialog box also includes a section where you can specify how the raster images within the document are handled. These images can be compressed using a lossless or lossy method. The lossy method uses the JPEG format where you can control the JPEG quality using a standard baseline or an optimized baseline. You can also set the resolution of the exported raster images.

Some incompatibilities exist between the Flash and Illustrator formats that could cause some trouble when exporting. Keep the following in mind:

✦ You should always flatten any transparency effects before exporting to the Flash format.

✦ Any gradients or gradient meshes that have more than eight color stops will be translated as raster images instead of vector objects.

✦ Flash only supports rounded caps on paths. Any square or beveled caps are converted to rounded caps during export.

✦ Convert all text to paths before exporting to the Flash format.

Exporting layers as an animation

Using layers, you can export animations to the Flash format. The trick is to place the objects used in each frame on a separate layer and then to export these layers to the Flash format as frames. To create a Flash animation, follow these steps:

1. Select the Star tool and drag within the artboard to create a star shape.

2. Duplicate the star shape and use the Twirl tool to create another modified shape.

3. Select both objects and choose the Object ➪ Blend ➪ Make command to blend between both shapes. Figure 17-13 shows the blend.

Figure 17-13: Blending between two shapes provides the frames for the Flash animation.

4. Open the Layer palette and select the Release to Layers (Sequence) option from the pop-up menu. This action places each object on a separate layer.

5. Select File ➪ Export. Name the file and select Macromedia Flash as the File Type. In the Macromedia Flash (SWF) Format Options dialog box, select the AI Layers to SWF Frames option in the Export As popup menu/drop-down list and click OK.

When the exported file is opened within a browser that has the Flash plug-in installed, the layers will be animated within the browser, as shown in Figure 17-14.

Note If you cannot view the Flash file in the browser, then you probably need to download and install the Flash plug-in, easily available on the Macromedia site at www.macromedia.com.

Figure 17-14: One frame of an exported Flash file viewed in a browser

Tip You can also use Illustrator in a roundabout way to create GIF animations. If you export each frame as a separate layer to Photoshop, you can then use Photoshop to create an animated GIF file.

Exporting to the SVG format

The SVG format stands for Scalable Vector Graphics. It has a many advantages over the Flash vector format. The SVG format is an open standard format, which means it has broad industry support and isn't owned and controlled by a single company. The format was created by an alliance of companies including Adobe, Apple, Corel, HP, IBM, Macromedia, Microsoft, Netscape, Quark, Sun, Xerox, and others.

Some of the key advantages that the SVG file format has over other Web graphic formats include the following:

✦ **Small file size.** Because vector graphics are mathematically defined, the format doesn't need to remember the color of every pixel within the image. This results in dramatically smaller file sizes, which download more quickly over the Web.

✦ **Resolution independence.** The SVG format isn't declaring war on its parent country and claiming its independence, but it is claiming independence from any specified resolution. This means that you can zoom in on an SVG file until the details are huge and they will maintain their shape. No jaggies here.

✦ **Embedded fonts.** When saving an SVG file, you can specify to embed the fonts within the file. This setting increases the file size, but the text remains as text and it can be edited without having to erase or delete the text. This makes the text open to spell checkers and quick updates.

✦ **24-bit color.** SVG files, like JPEG, can display over 16 million colors. This means that gradients are possible without banding. You can even use color profiles.

✦ **Cascading Style Sheets support.** Because the SVG format is saved as XML documents, you can embed Cascading Style Sheets (CSS) within the files. This enables you to define a single comprehensive and consistent style for all the images on your site that can be linked to all the SVG files. If you need to change the entire site, you simply change the master style sheet and ba-bing, you're done.

✦ **Interactivity.** JavaScript statements can be included within the SVG file also. You can use these statements to programmatically interact and control the various graphical elements according to the interactions of the user. For instance, you can have objects be highlighted as the user moves the mouse cursor over the top of them.

To export the completed document to the SVG format, select File ➪ Save for Web to open the Save for Web dialog window and select the SVG format from the format popup menu/drop-down list on the right. This will make several options available. One of these is the option to export files as Compressed SVG files. The other options for the SVG format include defining how the fonts are treated, whether fonts and raster images are embedded or linked, the number of decimal places, the encoding method and where the Cascading Style Sheet definitions are located.

SVG images are actually XML documents. XML stands for eXtensible Markup Language. XML documents include tags that describe the type of elements that are contained within the document. These documents can be pulled into programs that interpret the XML tags and display or otherwise manipulate the document elements.

SVG documents also support Cascading Style Sheets. This enables document creators to define specific styles and specify where they are used. Figure 17-15 shows a sample SVG document opened within Windows Notepad. If you are familiar with HTML or XML, the tags and attributes should look familiar. Notice also that the JavaScript statements and the link to an external JavaScript file that were entered into the SVG Interactivity palette are included within this document.

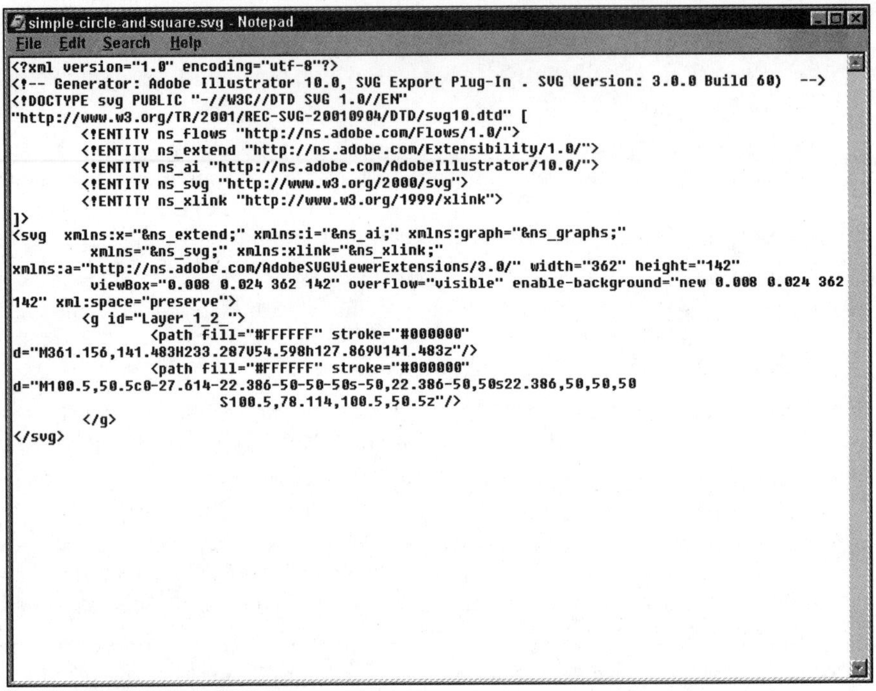


```
<?xml version="1.0" encoding="utf-8"?>
<!-- Generator: Adobe Illustrator 10.0, SVG Export Plug-In . SVG Version: 3.0.0 Build 60)  -->
<!DOCTYPE svg PUBLIC "-//W3C//DTD SVG 1.0//EN"
"http://www.w3.org/TR/2001/REC-SVG-20010904/DTD/svg10.dtd" [
	<!ENTITY ns_flows "http://ns.adobe.com/Flows/1.0/">
	<!ENTITY ns_extend "http://ns.adobe.com/Extensibility/1.0/">
	<!ENTITY ns_ai "http://ns.adobe.com/AdobeIllustrator/10.0/">
	<!ENTITY ns_svg "http://www.w3.org/2000/svg">
	<!ENTITY ns_xlink "http://www.w3.org/1999/xlink">
]>
<svg  xmlns:x="&ns_extend;" xmlns:i="&ns_ai;" xmlns:graph="&ns_graphs;"
	 xmlns="&ns_svg;" xmlns:xlink="&ns_xlink;"
xmlns:a="http://ns.adobe.com/AdobeSVGViewerExtensions/3.0/" width="362" height="142"
	 viewBox="0.008 0.024 362 142" overflow="visible" enable-background="new 0.008 0.024 362
142" xml:space="preserve">
	<g id="Layer_1_2_">
		<path fill="#FFFFFF" stroke="#000000"
d="M361.156,141.483H233.287V54.598h127.869V141.483z"/>
		<path fill="#FFFFFF" stroke="#000000"
d="M100.5,50.5c0-27.614-22.386-50-50-50s-50,22.386-50,50s22.386,50,50,50
			S100.5,78.114,100.5,50.5z"/>
	</g>
</svg>
```

Figure 17-15: A sample SVG document opened in Windows Notepad

The main Web browsers available do not currently support SVG files, but an SVG Viewer is installed automatically as part of the installation. This viewer will be embedded within the browser as a plug-in. Once installed, you will be able to view SVG files within the browser.

Adding JavaScript interactivity to an SVG file

When working with documents that you intend to export as SVG files, you can add interactivity to the objects using the JavaScript language. JavaScript can coexist with HTML within a Web page file and be used to make graphical elements respond to user actions. For example, you can specify that one graphic be replaced with another whenever the user moves the mouse over the top of the graphic. The reactions, called events, can be specified in Illustrator using the SVG Interactivity palette. This palette is shown in Figure 17-16.

You can choose events from the top popup menu/drop-down list. Figure 17-17 shows the complete list of available events.

ASK TOULOUSE: Why Not SVG?

Hawkeye: I can't wait to convert all my Web graphics to the SVG format.

Toulouse: You might want to think twice before doing that.

Hawkeye: Why?! Seeing that list of advantages is enough for me.

Toulouse: Well, you need to make sure that the browser you'll be using supports the SVG format.

Hawkeye: How can I check that?

Toulouse: Just open an SVG image in the browser. If you can see it, then the browser supports the format.

Hawkeye: What if it doesn't?

Toulouse: Then you can include a link to the Adobe site where people can download a viewer that they will need to view SVG graphics.

Hawkeye: Does the viewer need to be installed?

Toulouse: Yes, but that's easy to do.

Figure 17-16: The SVG Interactivity palette

To add an event to the selected object, choose one of the events from the drop-down list in the SVG Interactivity palette and type the JavaScript code to execute in the space provided. Then press the Enter key or click the Add Event and Function icon at the bottom of the palette or choose the Add Event option from the pop-up menu. The event and its JavaScript code will appear in the panel window. You can delete an event by selecting the event and clicking the Delete icon.

Figure 17-17: The complete list of available events

If you have JavaScript code contained in a separate file, you can link to that file by clicking the Link JavaScript Files icon at the bottom of the palette. This opens the JavaScript Files dialog box, as shown in Figure 17-18. This dialog box lets you add a link to an external JavaScript file. The link is shown in the dialog box. The link is also placed within the SVG file.

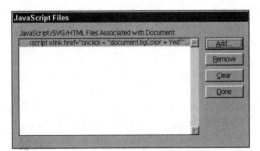

Figure 17-18: The JavaScript Files dialog box

Using SVG Effects

One of the neatest aspects of the SVG format is that it isn't limited to what the file is saved as. Because the file is an XML-based file, you can revisit it at any time and modify it as needed. An example of this is how Illustrator can apply SVG filters to the file. Illustrator includes several default SVG filters that are applied as effects using the Effect ⇨ SVG Filters ⇨ Apply SVG Filters menu option. This will open a dialog box, shown in Figure 17-19, where you can manage the available SVG filters.

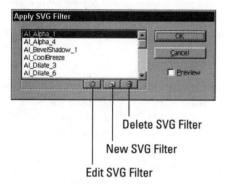

Figure 17-19: The Apply SVG Filter
dialog box

The icons at the bottom of the Apply SVG Filter dialog box will let you edit, add or delete the selected filter. If you click on the Edit SVG Filter icon, another dialog box will appear that displays the actual XML file, like the one shown in Figure 17-20. This dialog box is a text editor that you can use to edit the file to alter the filter. The Update Preview will update the look of the selected object that uses this filter.

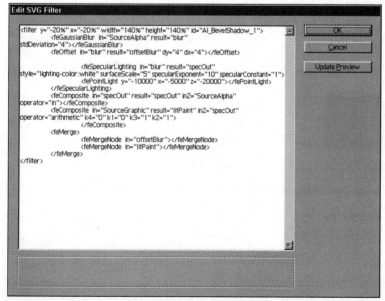

Figure 17-20: The Edit SVG Filter dialog box with the Bevel Shadow filter.

Caution   When applying an SVG filter, make sure that it is the last effect that is applied the object or the effect will be rasterized. You can check this by looking in the Appearance palette, the last effect will be at the very bottom of the list.

Choosing Effect ⇨ SVG Filter ⇨ Import SVG Filter will open a file dialog where you can select an SVG file containing an XML filter to be imported. There are many default SVG Filters included in Illustrator that make effects such as drop shadows possible.

Alpha

The Alpha filter adds some transparent turbulence to the object. This filter comes in two versions—Alpha 1 and Alpha 4, which differ in how complex the turbulence is. You can edit this value in the Edit SVG Filter dialog box by changing the numOctaves value. Figure 17-21 shows a simple rectangle filled with a pattern and the Alpha 1 (middle) and Alpha 4 (right) filters applied.

Figure 17-21: A patterned rectangle in its original form (left) and with the Alpha 1 (middle) and Alpha 4 (right) filters applied.

Bevel Shadow

The Bevel Shadow filter adds a soft beveled shadow to the lower right of the object. You can change the direction of the shadow by editing the X and Y values in the filter. Figure 17-22 shows the rectangle with the Bevel Shadow applied.

Figure 17-22: The Bevel Shadow SVG Filter applied to a rectangle and the Cool Breeze SVG filter applied to a straight line.

Cool Breeze

The Cool Breeze filter will thicken straight lines and add small disturbances to its edge and highlight the edge in blue. Figure 17-22 also shows the Cool Breeze filter applied to a straight line.

Caution   Be warned that this filter is more computationally expensive than most of the other filters and will take longer to be applied.

Dilate

The Dilate filter will increase the fill size of the object consistently around the outline of the object. This filter also comes in two varieties — Dilate 3 and Dilate 6, which will increase the object by 3 or 6 pixels. By applying this filter several times, you can gradually increase the size of your object. Figure 17-23 shows the Dilate filter.

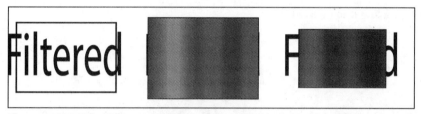

Figure 17-23: The Dilate 6 SVG filter was applied twice to the middle rectangle and the Erode 6 SVG filter was applied twice to the right rectangle.

Erode

The Erode filter will decrease the fill size of the object consistently around the outline of the object. This filter also comes in two varieties — Erode 3 and Erode 6, which will increase the object by 3 or 6 pixels. This filter is the opposite of the Dilate filter and can also be applied multiple times to reduce the size of the object. Figure 17-23 shows the Erode filter applied to the right rectangle.

Gaussian Blur

The Gaussian Blur filter will blur the object along its edges using the Gaussian algorithm. This is similar to the other Blur filters and effects. There are two versions of this filter — Gaussian Blur 4 and Gaussian Blur 7. The difference is in the amount of blur that is applied.

Pixel Play

The Pixel Play will display the paths in the object as highly pixelated lines. It will also fill in the object with a color. There are two varieties of this filter — Pixel Play 1 and Pixel Play 2. The difference depends on the size of the pixels. Figure 17-24 shows this filter applied to a path.

Shadow

The Shadow filters adds a hard shadow to the lower right of the object. There are two default Shadow SVG filters — Shadow 1 and Shadow 2. The later spreads the shadow further than the former. Figure 17-25 shows these filters applied to a simple logo.

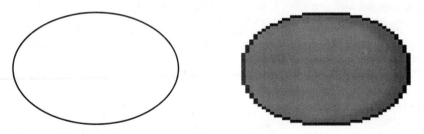

Figure 17-24: The Pixel Play SVG filter will pixelate a path to show how it is viewed on a low-resolution monitor.

Figure 17-25: The Shadow 1 SVG filter was applied to the middle logo and the Shadow 2 SVG filter was applied to the right logo.

Note   Notice how the Shadow filters have rasterized the logo in the previous figure. Some SVG filters will display the objects as a raster image. This is only for display in the Illustrator and the actual file when saved as an SVG file will appear correctly as a vector image in the browser.

Static

The Static filter will replace the fill color with transparent static interference. This filter is shown on the left of Figure 17-26.

Figure 17-26: The Static SVG filter was applied to the left rectangle, the Turbulence 3 SVG filter was applied to the middle rectangle, and the Woodgrain SVG filter was applied to the right rectangle.

Turbulence

The Turbulence filter adds transparent turbulent effects to the object. There are two Turbulence filters — Turbulence 3 and Turbulence 5. The Turbulence 3 filter is shown in the middle of Figure 17-26.

Woodgrain

The Woodgrain filter changes the fill color to be a woodgrain colored effect. This filter is shown on the right of Figure 17-26.

Exporting to the PDF Format

Another possible image format that can be viewed on the Web is the Portable Document Format (PDF). This format can only be viewed by browsers that have the Acrobat Reader plug-in installed. This plug-in is readily available and can be downloaded from the Adobe Web site (www.adobe.com). The PDF format is very similar to the PostScript format used by printers. One of the key benefits is that the text within PDF documents can be searched. PDF files can also contain hyperlinks.

You can find the PDF format as one of the default formats available under the Save As dialog box in the Format popup menu [File Type drop-down list].

You can use Illustrator to edit PDF files. To edit a PDF file, open the file in Illustrator. Illustrator identifies the separate pages in the PDF file and enables you to view a thumbnail of each page and select the page to edit. Once the edits are made, you can save the file as a PDF file again.

Cross-Reference You can find more information about saving to the PDF format in Chapter 2, "Working with Illustrator Documents."

Creating Images for the Web

Illustrator has several additional miscellaneous features that you can use to help build Web-page graphics. These features include using Illustrator to create image maps that include links to other Web pages. Another common use of Illustrator is to create graphical headings for Web pages.

Creating image maps

Image maps are Web page images that include hotspot areas that are linked to other Web pages. Using the Attributes palette, you can designate a selected object to be an image map. Hotspots can be drawn on top of objects that are designated to be image maps and these hotspots can be linked to a Uniform Resource Locators (URLs) such as `http://` and `ftp://` addresses.

You can attach a URL to an object by following these steps.

1. Select the path or group of objects you wish to attach the URL to.

2. Display the Attributes palette by choosing Window ➪ Show Attributes or by pressing F11.

3. If the URL field is not visible, choose Show All from the Attributes pop-up menu. You can access the pop-up menu by clicking the arrow icon near the upper-right corner of the palette. The Attributes palette should look like the one shown in Figure 17-27.

Figure 17-27: The Attributes palette

4. Type the complete URL for the selected object, such as `http://www.animabets.com`.

5. Press Return. The object now has that URL assigned to it.

Note   Each time you type in a new URL in the URL field, it is added to the URL pop-up menu (accessed by clicking to the right of the URL field). The Palette Options menu item (in the Attributes pop-up menu) lets you set the maximum number of URLs in the pop-up menu — up to 30 of them.

If an image map is saved using the GIF format, then the hotspots become active when viewed in a browser. Hotspots can be either rectangular or polygonal. Polygonal hotspots follow the outline of the object and rectangular hotspots create a Bounding Box around the object. You can check image map hotspots by clicking the Browser button in the Attributes palette.

The following steps show you how to save an image map file as a GIF image:

1. Assign pieces of artwork in your document to appropriate URLs.

2. Choose File ➪ Save for Web.

3. In the Save for Web dialog box, choose the GIF format and click OK.

4. In the Save As dialog box, select the Save HTML File option to generate an HTML file that will use the image map.

5. Click OK.

Creating Web page headings with Illustrator

A major strength of the GIF format is its capability to make the background color transparent. In addition, the GIF format can be set up to use a minimum number of colors, which keeps file sizes amazingly small. Transparency and minimizing the number of colors in an image can be done in the Save for Web dialog window.

However, what the GIF format is ideal for is creating headlines for Web pages. To get a page to look really good, fonts are needed. Unfortunately, specifying a font via HTML only works in certain browsers and then only if the specified font is installed on the system that is viewing the Web page. Of course (as always), the best alternative is the PDF format; however, if you want a font on an HTML page, you'll probably end up creating a GIF file, which is something that Illustrator really excels at. What's more, instead of just using a font, you can do all sorts of other things that HTML coders can only dream of.

Follow these steps to create a snazzy GIF heading:

1. Type your heading in Illustrator.

2. Choose the Character attributes (font, tracking, and so forth) for the heading.

3. Change the size of the heading to the size you want the text to appear on your Web site. It's usually best to view the document at 100 percent.

4. Choose the Paint Style for the type. If you wish to use a gradient or pattern instead of a solid color fill, select the type and choose Type ⇨ Create Outlines (⌘+Shift+O [Ctrl+Shift+O]) first. One of the advantages of using Illustrator for Web headings is that you can go back to the original Illustrator document, make changes, and then re-export the document for Web use.

5. To create a drop shadow (which can really make your text stand out), select the text and choose Effect ⇨ Stylize ⇨ Drop Shadow. The Drop Shadow dialog box appears. Select the setting you want to use and click OK.

6. Save the document as an Illustrator file (for example, Heading.ai).

7. Export the document with a different name as a GIF file (Heading.gif) in the same folder as your HTML page. In the Save for Web dialog window, choose Exact from the Palette pop-up menu (which uses only the colors in the heading), and select both the Interlace (which enables the heading to increase in resolution as it is downloaded to the browser) and Transparent options. Checking the Transparent option lets you place the heading on any background, even a tiled pattern.

Tips for Heading Design in Illustrator

Take advantage of Illustrator's powerful kerning and tracking capabilities. You can quickly kern between two letters by placing your cursor between the two letters and then pressing ⌘+Shift+[on the Mac [Ctrl+Shift+[in Windows] to remove space, or ⌘-Shift+] on the Mac [Ctrl+Shift+] in Windows] to add space between the letters. For tracking, select the range of characters to track and use the same key commands.

If you have fonts in Adobe's Expert collection (such as Adobe Garamond), you can use small caps in your heading, which always look classy.

If you are using a gradient or a pattern as a fill, try to use a heavy sans serif font.

Only check the Anti-Alias option in the Image Size panel of the Save for Web dialog window if you'll be using the same background color on your Web page as the one in your document. Two things happen when you check this box: The file size (due to the increased number of colors) increases dramatically, and the edges along the transparency border look "dissolved."

If horizontally scaling, try to avoid using fonts with big serifs, as they can often be stretched out of proportion.

Using the heading in a Web page (text-based editors)

Here are the steps to follow to use your new Web heading in a Web page:

1. Wherever you would like the Heading to be, type

```
<IMG SRC="Heading.gif">
```

2. Save your page and view it in your Web browser. If you rename or move the image, you'll need to type the correct path/file name into the IMG SRC code.

One of the benefits of creating a heading in Illustrator is that you can update it at any time by opening the Illustrator file that contains the heading, editing the text (if it isn't outlines), and then doing an export to replace the GIF file with an updated version.

The GIF file shown in Figure 17-28 is only 3,072 bytes, which means it should download to a 28.8 Kbps modem in one or two seconds. You can help make Web pages containing GIF file headings load more quickly by specifying the image size in the source code. For instance, the image created in this example is 519×39 pixels, so add this code:

```
<IMG SRC="Heading.gif" Width=519 Height=39>
```

Now the rest of the page loads first, and the heading will fill in afterward.

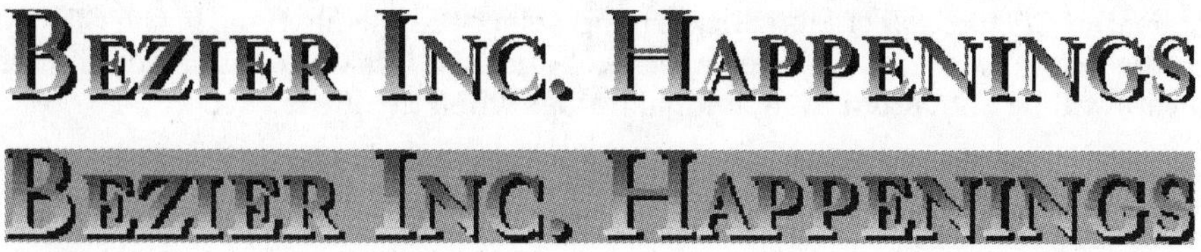

BEZIER INC. HAPPENINGS

BEZIER INC. HAPPENINGS

Figure 17-28: The original Illustrator image (top) and the GIF version of the image (bottom)

Heading effects

Of course, using Illustrator to create such basic headings seems like a waste of all the great typographical power in Illustrator, so here are a few ideas to really spruce up those headings:

✦ **Path Type on Curved Paths.** Why use straight, boring type when you can use funky curved type? Why, indeed! Create a wavy line and click it with the Path Type tool. Of course, path type is still completely editable.

✦ **Three-dimensional Type with Vector Effects.** Use Corel's Vector Effects with Illustrator to create three-dimensional type for headings. You must turn text into outlines before doing this, which means you'll lose the capability to edit the text in the future.

✦ **Place an Image in the Text.** Use the type as a mask and mask a placed image. The image can be a photograph, a pattern, or anything else you want to mask with the text.

Building an animated GIF

Animated GIF files that move around in the browser can be built using Illustrator, but you'll need some help from Illustrator's kid brother, Photoshop. Photoshop includes the export capabilities for animated GIF images.

The trick is this. Build the frames and keep them on separate layers in Illustrator. You can use the Release to Layers option in the Layers palette's pop-up menu to split blends and other combinations of objects into different layers. Once you've got each frame on a separate layer, save the document as a Photoshop file using the File ➪ Export command.

In the Export dialog box, select Photoshop in the Format popup menu [Save as Type drop-down list], give the file a name, and click the OK button. This makes the Photoshop Options dialog box appear. In this dialog box, shown in Figure 17-29, select the Screen Resolution option and the Write Layers and Write Nested Layers options.

Next, open the saved file in Photoshop. If you look in the Layers palette, you should see that all the objects were maintained on separate layers. To save the file as an animated GIF file, select File ➪ Export and select the GIF file type. In the GIF Options dialog box is an option to Save Layers as Frames. If this option is selected, then the layers will be converted to individual frames when the file is saved.

You can view the resulting GIF file in a browser to see the results.

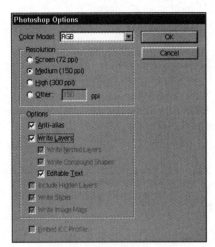

Figure 17-29: The Photoshop Options dialog box

Creating Image Slices

Imagine that you've created the perfect Web site layout that includes text, photographs, animations and everything and you're ready to place it on the Web. But, when you approach the developers, they throw a fit because you've combined the photographs (which should be saved as JPEGs) with text headers (which should be saved as GIF images). They end up throwing the finished files back at you in disgust. Confused and frustrated, you begin the tedious process of cutting up your design knowing that it won't look as good because the developers will mess up the spacing and kerning.

The answer to this painful situation is slices. A slice is simply a section of the artwork that is designated to be separate from the rest of the document. These slices can be saved using different formats and compression settings.

There are several different ways to create slices. If you select an object or objects and choose the Object ➪ Slice ➪ Make menu option, the artwork will make the selected objects a single slice and will automatically divide the rest of the artwork into slices. You can also select the Object ➪ Slice ➪ Create from Selection or the Object ➪ Slice ➪ Create from Guides menu options to make slices. The final way to divide the artwork into slices is by dragging with the Slice Select tool (Shift+K).

If you make a mistake while slicing some artwork, you can remove the slices using the Object ➪ Slice ➪ Release menu option.

Slicing a Web page

Figure 17-30 shows the front page of a simple article intended for a Web page. This page includes a placed JPEG photograph as well as text and some simple shapes. If this layout were saved as an AI file, its size would be 740 KB, much too large for the Web. From the Save for Web dialog window, the optimized file saved as a GIF image would weigh in at 49.1 KB, still pretty heavy for the Web, but much better and you'd lose most of the colors that make up the photograph.

Figure 17-30: A simple Web page spread before being sliced.

The JPEG format would fix the lost colors in the photograph, but would weigh in at 63.6 KB. The PNG-8 and PNG-24 options don't help our cause resulting in file sizes that are 39 KB and 134.2 KB. If we switch to the vector side, the SWF format yields a 108 KB file and the SVG format yields a 198 KB file.

This image is clearly an example that can benefit from image slicing. Before you begin chopping this image up into unnecessary slices, you should examine it closely looking for places where it makes sense to slice. You should look for sections that will require different Web formats. For the given image, the photograph in the center needs to be saved as a JPEG file and should be split away from the rest of the layout. The text that runs over the image also needs to be separated.

To split the centered photograph from the rest of the layout, simply select the image and then use the Object ➪ Slice ➪ Make menu option. This will slice the artwork into five slices as shown in Figure 17-31. Each slice is marked by a rectangular section with its slice name displayed in the upper left corner.

Figure 17-31: The Web page after slicing around the photograph.

The sliced layout works well, but the text that overlays the photograph needs also to be sliced. To slice this last section, use the Slice tool (Shift+K) and drag over the area that needs to be sliced. This will create an additional three slices to bring the total to eight as shown in Figure 17-32.

Figure 17-32: The Web page after additional slicing

Working with slices

Once artwork is sliced, you can select the slices by clicking on their border or on the slice icon that is displayed in the upper left corner. Multiple slices can be selected at once by holding down the Shift key while clicking on the slices. Selecting a slice will highlight its borders and make resize handles appear along its corners and edges. Dragging these handles will resize the slice and the slices around it will automatically be resized to accommodate the new size. You can also move the slice by dragging it like any other object.

If the slice is the same size as the object, it can be difficult to know if you're selecting the slice or the underlying object. To help with this problem, you can use the Slice Select tool, which is located under the Slice tool. With this tool, any can select slices by clicking on their edges. The Slice Select tool is also found in the Save for Web dialog window.

With a slice selected, several menu options in the Object ⇨ Slice menu become available. The Duplicate Slice menu option will duplicate the currently selected slice. If two or more slices are selected, the Combine Slice option is available. The Divide Slice option will let you divide the slice vertically or horizontally. The Slice Options option will open the Slice Options dialog box, shown in Figure 17-33. This dialog box includes two panels — Image, No Image and HTML Text. Using this dialog box, you can specify information about the image that is used by the browser such as the image name, its URL, an ALT tag, etc. The No Image panel can be used to enter text that will appear in the cell and its alignment. You can also specify a background color for the slice.

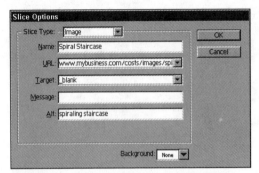

Figure 17-33: The Slice Options dialog box

Slices can be selected and aligned using the Align palette. If you want to lock or hide a slice, you can do so using the View ⇨ Lock Slices or View ⇨ Hide Slices.

Saving Slices

The Save for Web dialog window can be used to set which slice gets which settings. Selecting a slice requires that you select the Slice Select tool (K) and click on a slice. The slice will be highlighted and it will get the settings that you choose at the right. The Shift key can be used to select multiple slices. If two or more slices are selected, you can link them together using the Link Slices menu option in the Optimization menu. Linked slices will have a small icon that looks like an 8 in its upper left corner. Linked slices will share the same settings as their linked counterparts.

For example, Figure 17-34 shows the Web page layout with the first slice selected. This slice has been set to be saved as a GIF image with no dithering, 128-colors and a selective palette.

The Output Settings dialog box includes a panel that can be used to specify the naming structure for slice files. In the Save Optimized As file dialog box that appears when you click the Save button, you can select to save All Slices or just the Selected Slices. Once saved all the slices will appear as different files identified by the slice number. For the Web page shown previously, the total file size of the eight slices was a mere 22.3 KB.

Note   You can also export slices to Photoshop using the File ⇨ Export menu option.

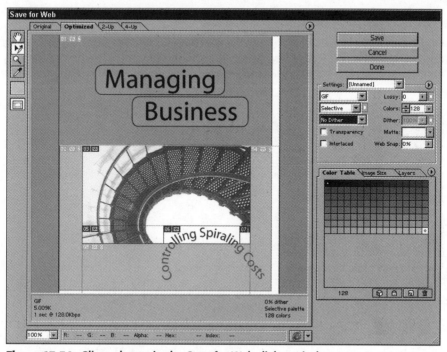

Figure 17-34: Slices shown in the Save for Web dialog window

Using Data-Driven Graphics

If you work for a medium- to large-sized company then more than likely you have a group in your corporation that call themselves developers. These individuals are really scary (actually I manage a group of developers and they aren't that bad at all if you can speak their language) and have dangerous weapons called applications and databases. With these weapons, the developers claim control over what they call mission critical processes. Well, the developers at Adobe have decided that these weapons can be used by creative geniuses also and they have made it possible for Illustrator to use Data-Driven Graphics.

The idea behind Data-Driven Graphics is that you load a database with the information that will change regularly, you can then create a script that will replace this information with the current information in a layout. The result is a template that can be loaded and reloaded with ever changing text, image, graph data, etc. This is especially useful if you use Illustrator to create Web page layouts.

Using the Variables palette

Objects that are stored in the database and that change are referred to as variables and are stored in the Variables palette. A variable is simply a name that the object is referred to within the script. The Variables palette is shown in Figure 17-35.

Figure 17-35: The Variables palette

To add a new variable to the palette, you can click on the New Variable icon button at the bottom of the palette or select the New Variable menu option in the palette menu. This will add a new unbound variable to the palette named Variable1. If you double click on the variable row, the Variable Options dialog box will open. This dialog box, shown in Figure 17-36, will let you change the name of the variable and its Type. Possible types include: No Type, Graph Data, Linked File, Text String and Visibility. To the right of each variable name is an icon that indicates the variable type. These icons are grayed out until the variable is bound to an object in the document.

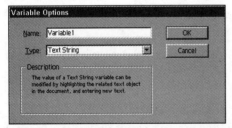

Figure 17-36: The Variable Options dialog box lets you name the variable and set its type.

Selecting a variable in the Variables palette will let you bind it to the selected document object if you click on the Make Object Dynamic or Make Visibility Dynamic icon buttons (or use the menu options in the palette menu). Objects can only be bound to variables of the same type, i.e. text variables with text objects. However, visibility can be set for any object. You can also automatically create a variable for the selected object using the Make Object Dynamic and Make Visibility Dynamic menu options (and icon buttons). If the selected object is a text string, a graph or a linked file, then the object can be made dynamic and the type will be set automatically based on the object. Variables can be unbound with the Unbind Variable icon button or menu.

To prevent editing variables, you can click on the Lock icon button to the right of the palette. This will prevent all variables from being edited and/or deleted. If variables aren't locked, they can be deleted with the palette menu or the Delete Variable icon button.

Once you have all the variables setup and at least one of them bound, you can create a Data Set. A Data Set is simply a collection of variables that are grouped together for easy reference. Data Sets are created using the Capture Data Set button in the upper left corner of the palette. Each Data Set can be named and you can move through the available Data Sets with the arrow buttons. These Data Sets can be made portable by saving them as a Variable Library. You can save the variables as an XML file using the Save Variable Library menu option. Saved XML files can be reloaded using the Load Variable Library menu option.

Working with Templates

To change the objects that are bound to variables, you simply need to edit the objects like you would normally using Illustrator. For edit dynamic text objects, simply select the Text tool and double click on the text object and type the new text. Linked images can be replaced using the File ⇨ Place menu option. Graphs can be edited by updating the graph data and Visibility can be altered using the Layers palette.

To save a template so it can be used by other Adobe products such as GoLive and AlterCast (Adobe's product for creating iterative artwork), you'll need to save the document as an SVG file. During the Saving process, click on the Advanced button and select the Include Extended Syntax for Variable Data option. This will save all the variables so they can be referenced by the other Adobe products.

Using Scripts

Scripting is a way of programmatically taking control of Illustrator. Using scripts, you can add basic functions that don't require full-blown plug-in development using a programming language. Scripts can be written using JavaScript, VBScript, or AppleScript. To execute a script within Illustrator, simply select the File ⇨ Scripts ⇨ Browse menu option. This will open a file dialog where you can locate the script that you wish to execute.

To get you started, Illustrator includes several default scripts. These scripts are located in the `Illustrator 10\Presets\Scripts` folder and can be opened into a text editor. The default scripts will do the following:

✦ **Add Watermark.** This script adds a simple watermark to the document. By editing the script file, you can change the watermark text from 'DRAFT" to whatever.

✦ **Apply Style to Text Selection.** This script will apply the current style to the selected text object.

✦ **Change Sizes of Text Selection.** This script will randomly change the sizes of the letters in the selected text string.

✦ **Export Docs As Flash.** This script will export the current document as a Flash file.

✦ **Save Docs As PDF.** This script will save the file as a PDF file.

Summary

It took some time before Illustrator became a full-fledged Web graphics creation tool, but with its current array of features, it has easily made up lost ground. In this chapter, you learned

✦ The Web is beginning to support vector-based graphics such as Flash and SVG with the help of specialized plug-ins.

✦ Illustrator documents can be rasterized in order to be saved as a raster-based Web format.

✦ The JPEG format is valuable because it supports an unlimited number of colors in any image.

✦ The Save for Web dialog window offers many controls for optimizing and exporting graphics to Web-friendly formats.

✦ GIF images, while limited to 256 colors, provide transparency, image map capabilities, and interlacing.

✦ Assign URLs to objects (or several objects at once) by selecting them and using the Attributes palette.

✦ PDF exporting is another alternative for displaying graphics on the Web.

✦ SVG filters can be applied to add effects to SVG objects.

✦ Web graphics can be optimized by changing the settings in the Save for Web window.

✦ You can create animated GIF images by saving layers to the Photoshop format and using Photoshop to export the layers as frames.

✦ Slices can be used to divide artwork into separate sections, each of which has its own format and settings.

✦ Data-Driven Graphics can be enabled by binding variables to objects.

✦ Scripts can be used to control simpler aspects of Illustrator.

✦　　✦　　✦

What's New in Illustrator 10

APPENDIX

A

✦ ✦ ✦ ✦

In This Appendix

New features

New tools

✦ ✦ ✦ ✦

Adobe has once again come up with an amazing upgrade worthy of shelling out the bucks to update Illustrator to Version 10. Many user requests have been answered to add some bold new features to an already strong package. This appendix summarizes the major new features of Illustrator 10.

New Features

Although this release of Illustrator includes many advancements, improvements and changes, this appendix lists just the major new features. As you begin to use Illustrator 10, you will find many subtle changes, some of which will take some getting used to.

The changes to this version address several new ways that Illustrator is being used such as for creating Web graphics. Changes such as slices take Illustrator into new territory. Other major categories of improvements offer new ways to do old tricks such as with the Liquify tools.

Dynamic Data-Driven Graphics

Using Dynamic Data-Driven Graphics enables designers to use templates and variables to define a page layout. The variables are placed as stand-ins for the graphics that are to appear there. These graphics can be held in a database and can be swapped out for new graphics at any time without having to open and work with the document. The logic behind the Dynamic Data-Driven Graphics can be written using AppleScript, JavaScript or Microsoft's Visual Basic and can link to any ODBC-compliant database. The variables used for the Dynamic Data-Driven Graphics are defined in the new Variables palette. These variables can represent images, text, graphs or drawn objects.

Once a layout template is created and the variables are enabled, a developer can write a script to retrieve the correct objects from a database. The single template can then be used to produce multiple unique layouts without additional help from the designer or the developer. Dynamic Data-Driven Graphics are especially valuable for creating web sites that need to be frequently updated.

Chapter 17, "Using Illustrator to Generate Web Graphics," covers creating and working with Dynamic Data-Driven Graphics.

Slicing

The slicing features in Illustrator 10 enable a designer to split graphics intended for a web page into several different sections. Each section (or slice) can have its own interactivity, such as a mouse rollover, applied to it. Each slice can also be saved in its own format. This will result in an overall web page that will load quicker into a web browser. For example, a photograph in the center of the page layout can be sliced and saved as a JPEG file while the surrounding text and graphics can be saved as quick-loading GIF images. These defined formats remain even if changes are made to the artwork. The various slices can be saved as HTML, GIF, JPEG, PNG, SVG and Flash (SWF). Different slices can even have different compression settings. You can also set the order in which slices appear. Slices can be set using an object, a group or a layer. Each slice can have different Cascading Style Sheet (CSS) definitions.

Illustrator includes several tools to slice a graphic layout. Object-based slices will change size automatically as the artwork is resized. Surrounding slices will be repositioned as an object-based slice is moved. Using the Slice and Slice Selection tools, you can manually decide where images are split. This gives you precise control over how the objects in your document are sliced. The slices are recognized in the Save for Web dialog box.

Any slices created in Illustrator will remain intact when opened in Adobe Photoshop, Image Ready or GoLive.

Chapter 17, "Using Illustrator to Generate Web Graphics," offers details and insights into using Illustrator's slicing features.

Symbols

Just like saving a Pattern or a Style, graphics can be saved as Symbols and reused over and over again. Each re-used instance of a symbol is simply referenced from the original symbol. Using symbols will keep the file size down (which makes them ideal for the web and for animations) because Illustrator only needs to remember the original symbol and the information about all its instances. As the original symbol is updated, all instances of the symbol are automatically updated. Symbols can also be stored in a library, which can be made available to other designers.

Symbols are stored in the new Symbols palette and can be dragged and dropped from the palette onto the current document or they can be sprayed about the document using the Symbol Sprayer tool. All sprayed symbols are grouped together and treated as a single object. A group of symbols can be interactively altered in many different ways using the Symbolism tools. These tools include a Shifter, Scruncher, Sizer, Spinner, Stainer, Screener and a Styler (all of which creatively start with the letter, S). These tools will change the size, orientation, color and style of the symbols by dragging the respective tool over the symbol group.

Improved SVG and SWF Support

As the Scalable Vector Graphics (SVG) format improves, these changes are supported in Illustrator. The SVG Interactivity palette includes many events. SVG files can now be imported into Illustrator. This is significant because it enables a developer to add some code to the file, which will be maintained as the designer works on the file. Illustrator also includes support for live SVG effects such as drop shadow and distortions. Under the Effect menu, you can also find an option that makes importing and editing of SVG Filters possible.

Illustrator's support for the Flash (SWF) format has also been increased. You can now create Flash animations directly from Illustrator using the Save for Web dialog box. Illustrator will even create the referencing HTML for you. Files that are exported to Flash that use Symbols will export the symbols as Flash symbols. This means that the Flash format will re-use instances of the symbols like Illustrator does without adding to the file size.

Live Distortion features

Illustrator 10 includes more ways than ever to bend, twist, twirl and scrunch objects and the kicker is that all these effects are live and allow you to edit the base object even after the distortion effect is applied. Under the Effect menu, you'll find a new submenu of Warp Effects. The complete set of Warp effects includes:

- ✦ Arc
- ✦ Arc Lower
- ✦ Arc Upper
- ✦ Arch
- ✦ Bulge
- ✦ Fish
- ✦ Fisheye
- ✦ Flag

+ Inflate

+ Rise

+ Shell Lower

+ Shell Upper

+ Squeeze

+ Twist

+ Wave

Another new way to distort objects is with envelopes. Envelopes allow any path to be assigned as an envelope that another object conforms to. These distortion envelopes can be used to fit objects within an envelope. For example, text can be placed into an envelope that is shaped like a train and the text will mold to the shape. Illustrator also includes a specialized type of envelope called an Envelope Mesh, which imposes a mesh grid over an object. The underlying object will be changed as the mesh grid points are changed.

Other very handy distortion tools are the Liquify tools. These tools let you distort artwork by dragging a brush over the artwork. The Liquify tools include Warp, Twirl, Pucker, Bloat, Scallop, Crystallize, and Wrinkle. The brush for each of these tools can be altered to provide you with the exact amount of detail that you need.

New Tools

The toolbox includes several new and helpful tools, including a new Line Segment tool, which can be used to draw straight lines quickly and easily. In addition to this tool is the Arc tool and two new grid tools — Rectangular Grid and Polar Grid. Dragging with the Rectangular Grid tool will create a grid of cells. The dividers that make up these grids can be skewed logarithmically.

The Flare tool can be used to add quick flares to artwork. These flares include primary and secondary highlights with transparent highlights.

The Magic Wand tool makes it easy to select all the objects in the document with similar fill color, strokes, transparency and/or style.

Workgroup Management

In the File menu, you will find the Manage Workgroup menu option. This option will let you coordinate in a workgroup who has which file. This will enable a workgroup to collaborate on a single document without stepping on each other's toes. Documents are saved on WebDAV servers where users can check the documents out to work on them and then check them back in once their task is complete.

Better Integration with Other Adobe Products

The integration between the various Adobe products has tightened the overall product line. Layers, masks and transparency are maintained between Illustrator and Photoshop. Illustrator files can be dropped directly into InDesign. Images dropped into GoLive from Illustrator can be edited by simply double clicking on them in GoLive. Illustrator also includes support for Adobe's AlterCast, a dynamic image server. Scripts can be shared between Illustrator and LiveMotion.

Other Features

Many other minor features make Illustrator 10 a delight to work with. This section outlines these minor improvements:

✦ The Select menu has received a promotion and now appears between the Type and Filter menus.

✦ The Pathfinder palette has been overhauled with the new features taken from Photoshop 6. Compound shapes can now be edited after the Pathfinder has been applied.

✦ Artwork can be viewed before being flattened with the Flattener Preview.

✦ Illustrator includes native support for Mac OS X.

✦   ✦   ✦

APPENDIX

B

◆ ◆ ◆ ◆

In This Appendix

Commands

Functions

Shortcuts

◆ ◆ ◆ ◆

Shortcuts in Illustrator 10

Illustrator has more keyboard commands, functions, and shortcuts than ever before. The tables in this appendix give you a quick reference to the commands, functions, and shortcuts for both Macintosh and Windows (as in the rest of the book, the Windows commands are in square brackets).

Caution Macintosh users should check to make sure their function keys aren't assigned to complete any system tasks. In Macintosh's Keyboard Control panel, you can set the function keys to be passed through in order to avoid any conflicts. This isn't the default value.

Menu Commands

Table B-1	
The File Menu	
Command	**Shortcut**
New	⌘ [Ctrl]+N
Open	⌘ [Ctrl]+O
Revert	F12
Close	⌘ [Ctrl]+W
Save	⌘ [Ctrl]+S
Save As	⌘ [Ctrl]+Shift+S
Save a Copy	⌘ [Ctrl]+Option [Alt]+S
Save for Web	⌘ [Ctrl]+Shift+Option [Alt]+S

Continued

Table B-1 (continued)

Command	Shortcut
Document Setup	⌘ [Ctrl]+Option [Alt]+P
Page [Print] Setup	⌘ [Ctrl]+Shift+P
Print [Print]	⌘ [Ctrl]+P
Quit [Exit] Illustrator	⌘ [Ctrl]+Q

Table B-2
The Edit Menu

Command	Shortcut
Undo	⌘ [Ctrl]+Z
Redo	⌘ [Ctrl]+Shift+Z
Cut	⌘ [Ctrl]+X
Copy	⌘ [Ctrl]+C
Paste	⌘ [Ctrl]+V
Paste in Front	⌘ [Ctrl]+F
Paste in Back	⌘ [Ctrl]+B
Clear	Delete
Keyboard Shortcuts	⌘ [Ctrl]+Shift+Option [Alt]+K
General Preferences	⌘ [Ctrl]+K (under the Illustrator menu for Mac OS X)

Table B-3
The Object Menu

Command	Shortcut
Transform ⇨ Transform Again	⌘ [Ctrl]+D
Transform ⇨ Move	⌘ [Ctrl]+Shift+M
Transform ⇨ Transform Each	⌘ [Ctrl]+Shift+Option [Alt]+D
Bring to Front	⌘ [Ctrl]+Shift+]

Command	Shortcut
Bring Forward	⌘ [Ctrl]+]
Send Backward	⌘ [Ctrl]+[
Send to Back	⌘ [Ctrl]+Shift+[
Group	⌘ [Ctrl]+G
Ungroup	⌘ [Ctrl]+Shift+G
Lock ⇨ Selection	⌘ [Ctrl]+2
Unlock All	⌘ [Ctrl]+Option [Alt]+2
Hide ⇨ Selection	⌘ [Ctrl]+3
Show All	⌘ [Ctrl]+Option [Alt]+3
Path ⇨ Join	⌘ [Ctrl]+J
Path ⇨ Average	⌘ [Ctrl]+Option [Alt]+J
Blend ⇨ Make	⌘ [Ctrl]+Option [Alt]+B
Blend ⇨ Release	⌘ [Ctrl]+Option [Alt]+Shift+B
Envelope Distort ⇨ Make with Warp	⌘ [Ctrl]+Option [Alt]+W
Envelope Distort ⇨ Make with Mesh	⌘ [Ctrl]+Option [Alt]+M
Envelope Distort ⇨ Make with Top Object	⌘ [Ctrl]+Option [Alt]+C
Envelope Distort ⇨ Edit Contents	⌘ [Ctrl]+Shift+V
Clipping Mask ⇨ Make	⌘ [Ctrl]+7
Clipping Mask ⇨ Release	⌘ [Ctrl]+Option [Alt]+7
Compound Path ⇨ Make	⌘ [Ctrl]+8
Compound Path ⇨ Release	⌘ [Ctrl]+Option [Alt]+8

Table B-4
The Type Menu

Command	Shortcut
Font	⌘ [Ctrl]+Option [Alt]+Shift+M
Create Outlines	⌘ [Ctrl]+Shift+O

Table B-5
The Select Menu

Command	Shortcut
Select All	⌘ [Ctrl]+A
Deselect All	⌘ [Ctrl]+Shift+A
Reselect	⌘ [Ctrl]+6
Next Object Above	⌘ [Ctrl]+Option [Alt]+]
Next Object Below	⌘ [Ctrl]+Option [Alt]+[

Table B-6
The Filter Menu

Command	Shortcut
Apply Last Filter	⌘ [Ctrl]+E
Last Filter	⌘ [Ctrl]+Option [Alt]+E

Table B-7
The Effect Menu

Command	Shortcut
Apply Last Filter	⌘ [Ctrl]+Shift+E
Last Filter Dialog Box	⌘ [Ctrl]+Shift+Option [Alt]+E

Table B-8
The View Menu

Command	Shortcut
Outline/Preview	⌘ [Ctrl]+Y (toggle)
Overprint Preview	⌘ [Ctrl]+Shift+Option [Alt]+Y
Pixel Preview	⌘ [Ctrl]+Option [Alt]+Y
Zoom In	⌘ [Ctrl]++ (plus sign)

Command	Shortcut
Zoom Out	⌘ [Ctrl]+−
Fit in Window	⌘ [Ctrl]+0 (zero) Double-click Hand tool
Actual Size (100%)	⌘ [Ctrl]+1 Double-click Zoom tool
Hide Edges	⌘ [Ctrl]+H (toggle)
Hide Template	⌘ [Ctrl]+Shift+W (toggle)
Show/Hide Rulers	⌘ [Ctrl]+R (toggle)
Show/Hide Bounding Box	⌘ [Ctrl]+Shift+B (toggle)
Show/Hide Transparency Grid	⌘ [Ctrl]+Shift+D (toggle)
Guides ⇨ Show/Hide Guides	⌘ [Ctrl]+; (toggle)
Guides ⇨ Lock Guides	⌘ [Ctrl]+Option [Alt]+;
Guides ⇨ Make Guides	⌘ [Ctrl]+5
Guides ⇨ Release Guides	⌘ [Ctrl]+Option [Alt]+5
Smart Guides	⌘ [Ctrl]+U
Show/Hide Grid	⌘ [Ctrl]+"(toggle)
Snap to Grid [Pixel]	⌘ [Ctrl]+Shift+"
Snap to Point	⌘ [Ctrl]+Option [Alt]+"

Table B-9
The Window Menu

Command	Shortcut
Show/Hide Align	Shift+F7 (toggle)
Show/Hide Appearance	Shift+F6 (toggle)
Show/Hide Attributes	F11 (toggle)
Show/Hide Brushes	F5 (toggle)
Show/Hide Color	F6 (toggle)
Show/Hide Gradient	F9 (toggle)
Show/Hide Info	F8 (toggle)
Show/Hide Layers	F7 (toggle)

Continued

Table B-9 *(continued)*	
Command	**Shortcut**
Show/Hide Pathfinder	Shift+F9 (toggle)
Show/Hide Stroke	F10 (toggle)
Show/Hide Styles	Shift+F5 (toggle)
Show/Hide Symbols	Shift+F11 (toggle)
Show/Hide Transform	Shift+F8 (toggle)
Show/Hide Transparency	⌘ Shift+F10 (toggle)
Show/Hide Character Palette	⌘ [Ctrl]+T (toggle)
Show/Hide Paragraph Palette	⌘ [Ctrl]+M (toggle)
Tab Ruler Palette	⌘ [Ctrl]+Shift+T

Table B-10 **The Help Menu**	
Command	**Shortcut**
Illustrator Help	F1 (Windows only)

Toolbox Commands

Table B-11 **Tool Selection**	
Function	**Shortcut**
Select the next pop-up tool	Drag to the right and release on desired tool Option [Alt]+click on a tool
Open tool dialog box	Double click on the tool
Hide toolbox and palettes	Tab

Table B-12
Selection Tools

Tool	Shortcut
Selection tool	V
	Ctrl+Tab with Direct Selection tool, and then hold ⌘ [Ctrl]
	⌘ [Ctrl] with all other tools if Selection tool was the last tool used
Direct Selection tool	A (Mac and Windows)
	Ctrl+Tab with Selection tool, and then hold ⌘ [Ctrl]+Option [Alt] with Group Selection tool
	⌘ [Ctrl] with all other tools if Direct Selection tool was the last tool used
Group Selection tool	Option [Alt] with Direct Selection tool
	⌘ [Ctrl]+Option [Alt] with all other tools if Direct Selection tool was the last tool used
Magic Wand tool	Y
Direct Select Lasso tool	Q

Function	Procedure
Select one point	Click with Direct Selection tool
Select one segment	Click with Direct Selection tool
Select one path	Click with Group Selection tool
Select next group up	Click selected path again with Group Selection tool
Select top-level group	Click with Selection tool
Select additional	Shift+click
Select specific points	Drag with Direct Selection tool
Select specific paths	Drag with Selection tool
Deselect selected	Shift+click selected
Move selection	Drag
Duplicate selection	Option [Alt]+drag
Constrain to 45° movement	Shift+drag
Duplicate and constrain	Option [Alt]+Shift+drag
Proportionately resize object	Shift+drag Bounding Box handle

Continued

Table B-12 *(continued)*

Function	Procedure
Resize from center	Option [Alt]+drag Bounding Box handle
Resize proportionately from center	Option [Alt]+Shift+drag Bounding Box handle
Select all	⌘ [Ctrl]+A
Deselect all	⌘ [Ctrl]+Shift+A
Select all objects with similar Fill, Stroke, Opacity and/or Blending Mode	Click with Magic Wand tool
Add similar colored and stroked objects to current selection	Shift+Magic Wand tool
Subtract similar colored and stroked objects from the current selection	Option [Alt]+Magic Wand tool
Set Magic Wand options	Double click on Magic Wand tool to open the Magic Wand palette

Table B-13
Path Tools

Tool	Shortcut
Pen tool	P
Add Anchor Point tool	+ (actual the key is the equals (=) sign, not the Shift+=; the plus sign on the numeric keyboard doesn't work for this)
	Option [Alt]+Delete Anchor Point tool
	Option [Alt]+Scissors tool
Delete Anchor Point tool	–
	Option [Alt]+Add Anchor Point tool
Convert Anchor Point tool	Shift+C
	Option [Alt]+Pen tool
Pencil tool	N
Smooth tool	Option [Alt]+ Pencil tool
	Option [Alt]+ Erase tool
	Option [Alt]+ Paintbrush tool

Tool	Shortcut
Paintbrush tool	B
Scissors tool	C

Function	Procedure
Create a straight corner point	Click with Pen tool
Create a smooth point	Drag with Pen tool
Continue existing open path	Click+drag with Pen tool on end point of existing path
Close open path	While drawing, click+drag with Pen tool on the initial end point
	Click+drag with Pen tool on each end point in succession
	Select path and join (⌘ [Ctrl]+J)
Constrain new point to 45 degrees from last point	Shift+drag with Pen tool
Constrain control handles to 45 degrees	Shift while dragging handle with Pen tool
Create a path	Click+drag a succession of points with Pen tool
Add anchor points to existing path	Click with the Pen tool on path
Delete anchor points from existing path	Shift+click with Pen tool on an anchor point
Convert anchor point to smooth point existing point	Drag with Convert Direction Point tool on
Convert smooth point to corner point	Click with Convert Direction Point tool on smooth point
Convert smooth corner to combination corner	Drag one handle with Direct Selection tool back into the anchor point
Convert smooth corner to curved corner	Drag one handle with Convert Direction Point tool
Draw freestyle paths	Drag with Pencil tool
View Paintbrush options	Double-click Paintbrush tool in toolbox
Reshape a path	Select points with Direct Selection, and then drag with Reshape tool
Split path	Click with Scissors tool
Slice multiple paths	Drag with Knife tool
Constrain Knife slice to straight lines	Option[Alt]+drag with Knife tool
Constrain Knife slice to 45°	Shift+Option[Alt]+drag with Knife tool

Table B-14 **Type Tools**	
Tool	**Shortcut**
Type tool	T
	Shift+Vertical Type tool
Area Type tool	Option [Alt]+Path Type tool
	Shift+Vertical Area Type tool
	Option [Alt]+Shift Vertical Path Type tool
Path Type tool	Option [Alt]+Area Type tool
	Shift+Vertical Path Type tool
	Option [Alt]+Shift+Vertical Area Type tool
Vertical Type tool	Shift+Type tool
Vertical Area Type tool	Option [Alt]+Vertical Path Type tool
	Shift+Area Type tool
	Option [Alt]+Shift+Area Type tool
Vertical Path Type tool	Option [Alt]+Vertical Area Type tool
	Shift+Path Type tool
	Option [Alt]+Shift +Area Type tool
Function	**Procedure**
Create point type	Click with Type tool
Create rectangle type	Drag with Type tool
Place path type on a closed path	Click path with Path Type tool
	Option [Alt]+click path with Type tool
	Option [Alt]+click path with Area Type tool
Place path type on an open path	Click path with Path Type tool
	Click path with Type tool
	Option [Alt]+click path with Area Type tool
Place area type on a closed path	Click path with Area Type tool
	Click path with Type tool
	Option[Alt]+click path with Path Type tool
Place area type on an open path	Click path with Area Type tool
	Option [Alt]+click path with Type tool
	Option [Alt]+click path with Path Type tool

Function	Procedure
Change vertical type to horizontal type	Choose Type ➪ Type Orientation ➪ Horizontal
Change horizontal type to vertical type	Choose Type ➪ Type Orientation ➪ Vertical
Select entire text block	Click text block with Selection tool
Select one character	Drag across character with any Type tool
Select one word	Double-click word with any Type tool
Select one paragraph	Triple-click paragraph with any Type tool
Select all text in text block	Click in text block with any Type tool, and then press ⌘ [Ctrl]+A
Flip type on a path	Double-click the I-bar with any selection tool or just drag it to the opposite side

Table B-15
Line Tools

Tool	Shortcut
Line Segment tool	\

Function	Procedure
Create line segments using numbers	Click with the Line Segment tool
Draw a line segment	Drag with Line Segment tool
Constrain line segments to 45 degrees	Shift+drag with Line Segment tool
Create line segment from midpoint using numbers	Option [Alt]+click with Line Segment tool
Draw line segment from midpoint	Option [Alt]+drag with Line Segment tool
Move line segment while drawing	Spacebar+drag with Line Segment tool
Create multiple line segments	~+drag with Line Segment tool
Create arc segments using numbers	Click with the Arc tool
Draw an arc segment	Drag with Arc tool
Constrain arc segments to circular sections	Shift+drag with Arc tool
Create arc segment from the center	Option [Alt]+click with Arc tool

Continued

Table B-15 (continued)

Function	Procedure
Draw arc segment from the center	Option [Alt]+drag with Arc tool
Move arc segment while drawing	Spacebar+drag with Arc tool
Create multiple arc segments	~+drag with Arc tool
Toggle arc between concave and convex	X+drag with Arc tool
Toggle between open and closed arcs	C+drag with Arc tool
Flip the arc	F+drag with Arc tool
Increase arc slope	↑+drag with Arc tool
Decrease arc slope	↓+drag with Arc tool
Create spiral using numbers	Click with Spiral tool
Draw spiral	Drag with Spiral tool
Constrain spiral angle	Shift+drag with Spiral tool
Move spiral while drawing	Spacebar+drag with Spiral tool
Create multiple spirals	~+drag with Spiral tool
Decrease spiral decay	⌘ [Ctrl]+drag with Spiral tool
Increase spiral length and size	Option [Alt]+drag with Spiral tool (toggle)
Increase spiral length	↑+drag with Spiral tool
Decrease spiral length	↓+drag with Spiral tool
Create a rectangular grid using numbers	Click with the Rectangular Grid tool
Draw an rectangular grid	Drag with Rectangular Grid tool
Constrain rectangular grid to a square	Shift+drag with Rectangular Grid tool
Create a square rectangular grid	Option [Alt]+click with Rectangular Grid tool
Draw rectangular grid from the center	Option [Alt]+drag with Rectangular Grid tool
Move rectangular grid while drawing	Spacebar+drag with Rectangular Grid tool
Create multiple rectangular grid	~+drag with Rectangular Grid tool
Skew horizontal dividers to the left	X+drag with Rectangular Grid tool
Skew horizontal dividers to the right	C+drag with Rectangular Grid tool
Skew vertical dividers to the top of the rectangular grid	F+drag with Rectangular Grid tool
Skew vertical dividers to the bottom of the rectangular grid	V+drag with Rectangular Grid tool
Increase vertical dividers	↑+drag with Rectangular Grid tool

Function	Procedure
Decrease vertical dividers	↓+drag with Rectangular Grid tool
Increase horizontal dividers	→+drag with Rectangular Grid tool
Decrease horizontal dividers	←+drag with Rectangular Grid tool
Create a polar grid using numbers	Click with the Polar Grid tool
Draw an polar grid	Drag with Polar Grid tool
Constrain polar grid to a circle	Shift+drag with Polar Grid tool
Create a circular polar grid	Option [Alt]+click with Polar Grid tool
Draw polar grid from the center	Option [Alt]+drag with Polar Grid tool
Move polar grid while drawing	Spacebar+drag with Polar Grid tool
Create multiple polar grid	~+drag with Polar Grid tool
Skew concentric dividers inward	X+drag with Polar Grid tool
Skew concentric dividers outward	C+drag with Polar Grid tool
Skew radial dividers counterclockwise	F+drag with Polar Grid tool
Skew radial dividers clockwise	V+drag with Polar Grid tool
Increase concentric dividers	↑+drag with Polar Grid tool
Decrease concentric dividers	↓+drag with Polar Grid tool
Increase radial dividers	→+drag with Polar Grid tool
Decrease radial dividers	←+drag with Polar Grid tool

Table B-16
Shape Tools

Tool	Shortcut
Rectangle tool	M
Ellipse tool	L

Function	Procedure
Create rectangle using numbers	Click with Rectangle tool or Rounded Rectangle tool
Draw rectangle	Drag with Rectangle tool
Draw square	Shift+drag with Rectangle tool
Create centered rectangle using numbers	Option [Alt]+click with Rectangle tool

Continued

Table B-16 *(continued)*

Function	Procedure
Draw centered rectangle	Option [Alt]+drag with Rectangle tool
Draw square from center	Option [Alt]+Shift+drag with Rectangle tool
Move rectangle while drawing	Spacebar+drag with Rectangle tool
Create multiple rectangles	~+drag with Rectangle tool
Create rounded rectangle using numbers	Click with Rounded Rectangle tool
Draw rounded rectangle	Drag with Rounded Rectangle tool
Draw square with rounded corners	Shift+drag with Rounded Rectangle tool
Create centered rounded rectangle	Option [Alt]+click with Rounded Rectangle tool
Draw centered rounded rectangle	Option [Alt]+drag with Rounded Rectangle tool
Draw square from center with rounded corners	Option [Alt]+Shift+drag with Rounded Rectangle tool
Move rounded rectangle while drawing	Spacebar+drag with Rounded Rectangle tool
Create multiple rounded rectangles	~+drag with Rounded Rectangle tool
Create ellipse using numbers	Click with Ellipse tool
Draw ellipse	Drag with Ellipse tool
Draw circle	Shift+drag with Ellipse tool
Create centered ellipse using numbers	Option [Alt]+click with Ellipse tool
Draw centered ellipse	Option [Alt]+drag with Ellipse tool
Move ellipse while drawing	Spacebar+drag with Ellipse tool
Create multiple ellipses	~+drag with Ellipse tool
Create polygon using numbers	Click with Polygon tool
Draw polygon	Drag with Polygon tool
Constrain polygon angle	Shift+drag with Polygon tool
Create centered polygon using numbers	Option [Alt]+click with Polygon tool
Draw centered polygon	Option [Alt]+drag with Polygon tool
Increase polygon sides	↑+drag with Polygon tool
Decrease polygon sides	↓+drag with Polygon tool
Move polygon while drawing	Spacebar+drag with Polygon tool
Create multiple polygons	~+drag with Polygon tool
Create star using numbers	Click with Star tool
Draw star	Drag with Star tool

Function	Procedure
Constrain star angle	Shift+drag with Star tool
Draw even-shouldered star	Option [Alt]+drag with Star tool
Move outer points only	⌘ [Ctrl]+drag with Star tool
Increase star points	↑+drag with Star tool
Decrease star points	↓+drag with Star tool
Move star while drawing	Spacebar+drag with Star tool
Create multiple stars	~+drag with Star tool

Table B-17
Transformation Tools

Tool	Shortcut
Rotate tool	R
Reflect tool	O
Scale tool	S
Free Transform tool	E

Function	Procedure
Moving objects	Drag with the Selection or Free Transform tool
Constrain movements along 45 degree axis	Shift+drag with the Selection or Free Transform tool
Rotate using numbers	Option [Alt]+click with Rotate tool
Rotate from center of selection with numbers	Double-click with Rotate tool
Free Rotate (live)	Click with Rotate to set Origin, and then drag with Rotate tool
Free Rotate around selection center	Drag with Rotate tool
Constrain rotation to 45 degrees	Shift+drag with Rotate tool
Rotate a copy	Option [Alt]+drag with Rotate tool
Rotate pattern only	~+drag with Rotate tool
Scale using numbers	Option [Alt]+click with Scale tool
Scale from center of selection with numbers	Double-click with Scale tool

Continued

Table B-17 *(continued)*

Function	Procedure
Free Scale (live)	Click with Scale to set Origin, and then drag with Scale tool
Free Scale around selection center	Drag with Scale tool
Constrain scaling to 45 degrees	Shift+drag with Scale tool
Scale a copy	Option [Alt]+drag with Scale tool
Scale pattern only	~+drag with Scale tool
Reflect using numbers	Option [Alt]+click with Reflect tool
Reflect from center of selection with numbers	Double-click with Reflect tool
Free Reflect (live)	Click with Reflect to set Origin, and then drag with Reflect tool
Free Reflect around selection center	Drag with Reflect tool
Constrain reflecting angle to 45 degrees	Shift+drag with Reflect tool
Reflect a Copy	Option [Alt]+drag with Reflect tool
Reflect Pattern only	~+drag with Reflect tool
Shear using numbers	Option [Alt]+click with Shear tool
Shear from Center of Selection with numbers	Double-click with Shear tool
Free Shear (live) with Shear	Click with Shear to set Origin, and then drag
Free Shear around selection center	Drag with Shear
Constrain shearing to 45 degrees	Shift+drag with Shear tool
Shear a copy	Option [Alt]+drag with Shear tool
Shear pattern only	~+drag with Shear tool

Table B-18
Distortion Tools

Tool	Shortcut
Warp tool	Shift+R

Function	Procedure
Twirl using numbers	Option [Alt]+click with Rotate tool
Free Twirl (live)	Drag with Twirl tool

Function	Procedure
Reshape distortion brush	Option [Alt]+drag with Warp, Twirl, Pucker, Bloat, Scallop, Crystallize or Wrinkle tool
Constrain brush to horizontal or vertical movement	Shift+drag with Warp , Twirl, Pucker, Bloat, Scallop, Crystallize or Wrinkle tool
Set distortion options	Double click on the selected distortion tool

Table B-19
Symbol Tools

Tool	Shortcut
Symbol Sprayer tool	Shift+S

Function	Procedure
Add a single symbol	Click+Symbol Sprayer tool
Add multiple symbols	Drag+Symbol Sprayer tool
Remove symbols from set	Option [Alt]+ Symbol Sprayer tool
Move the symbols in a set	Drag with the Symbol Shifter tool
Change the stacking order of the symbols	Option [Alt]+ Symbol Shifter tool
Scrunch the symbols closer together	Drag with the Symbol Scruncher tool
Move the symbols farther apart	Option [Alt]+ Symbol Scruncher tool
Increase the symbol size	Drag with the Symbol Sizer tool
Decrease the symbol size	Option [Alt]+ Symbol Sizer tool
Rotate the symbols	Drag with the Symbol Spinner tool
Increase the symbol's transparency	Drag with the Symbol Screener tool
Decrease the symbol's transparency	Option [Alt]+ Symbol Screener tool
Change the symbol's color	Drag with the Symbol Stainer tool
Restore the symbol's original color	Option [Alt]+ Symbol Stainer tool
Apply a style to the symbol	Drag with the Symbol Styler tool
Remove the style from a symbol	Option [Alt]+ Symbol Styler tool

Table B-20
Graph Tools

Tool	Shortcut
Column Graph tool	J

Function	Procedure
Create a Graph sized by numbers	Click with any Graph tool
Create a Graph sized by dragging	Drag with any Graph tool
Create a square or circular graph	Shift+drag with any Graph tool
Create a Graph from the center	Option [Alt]+drag with any Graph tool

Table B-21
Paint Tools

Tool	Shortcut
Gradient tool	G
Gradient Mesh tool	U
Paint Bucket tool	K
	Option[Alt]+Eyedropper tool
Eyedropper tool	I
	Option [Alt]+Paint Bucket tool

Function	Procedure
Change Linear Gradient direction and/or length	Drag with Gradient tool
Constrain Gradient Direction to 45° angles	Shift+drag with Gradient tool
Change Radial Gradient size and/or location	Drag with Gradient tool
Change Radial Gradient origin point	Click with Gradient tool
Sample color to Color palette	Click with Eyedropper tool
Sample Screen color to Color palette	Shift+click with Eyedropper tool
Change Paint Style of selected objects	Double-click with Eyedropper tool on an object with the desired style
Paint unselected objects	Click objects with the Paint Bucket tool
Measure a distance	Click the start and end location with the Measure tool
Measure a distance by 45° angles	Shift+click the start and end location with the Measure tool

Table B-22
Blend, Auto Trace and Slice Tools

Tool	Shortcut
Blend tool	W
Slice tool	Shift+K

Function	Procedure
Blend between two paths	Click corresponding selected points on each path with Blend tool
Set Blend options	Double click on the Blend tool
Auto Trace Images	Click area to be traced with Auto Trace tool
Divide artwork into slices	Drag+Slice tool
Constrain slice to a square	Option [Alt]+drag with the Slice tool
Slice selected objects	Drag+Slice Selected tool

Table B-23
Viewing Tools

Tool	Shortcut
Hand tool	H
	Spacebar (when not entering text)
Zoom tool	Z
	⌘ [Ctrl]+spacebar
Zoom Out tool	⌘ [Ctrl]+Option[Alt]+spacebar
	Option [Alt]+Zoom tool

Function	Procedure
Reposition the page	Drag with the Hand tool
Fit the page within the document window	Double click on the Hand tool
Moving page boundaries	Drag with the Page tool
Reset page boundaries	Double click on the Page tool
Zoom in	Click with the Zoom tool
	⌘ [Ctrl]++ (plus sign)

Continued

Table B-23 *(continued)*	
Function	**Procedure**
Zoom out	Option [Alt]+click with the Zoom tool
	⌘ [Ctrl]+- (hyphen)
Zoom in to a specific area	Drag with the Zoom tool
Move the Zoom Marquee while drawing	Spacebar while dragging with the Zoom tool
Draw the Zoom Marquee from its center	Ctrl+drag with the Zoom tool

Type Commands

Table B-24 **Type Shortcuts**	
Action	**Shortcut**
Copy type on a path	Option [Alt]+drag the I-bar using any selection tool. (This shortcut actually creates two paths as well as two text stories.)
Flip type on a path	Double-click the I-bar with any selection tool or just drag it to the opposite side of the path
Move insertion point to next character	→ (right arrow)
Move insertion point to previous character	← (left arrow)
Move insertion point to next line	↓ (down arrow)
Move insertion point to previous line	↑ (up arrow)
Move insertion point to next word	⌘ [Ctrl]+→
Move insertion point to previous word	⌘ [Ctrl]+←
Move insertion point to next paragraph	⌘ [Ctrl]+↓
Move insertion point to previous paragraph	⌘ [Ctrl]+↑
Select (by highlighting) all type in story	⌘ [Ctrl]+A when the insertion point is in the story
Select all type in document	⌘ [Ctrl]+A when any tool but the Type tools are selected
Select next character	Shift+→

Action	Shortcut
Select previous character	Shift+←
Select next line	Shift+↓
Select previous line	Shift+↑
Select next word	⌘ [Ctrl]+Shift+→
Select previous word	⌘ [Ctrl]+Shift+←
Select next paragraph	⌘ [Ctrl]+Shift+↓
Select previous paragraph	⌘ [Ctrl]+Shift+↑
Select word	Double-click word
Select paragraph	Triple-click paragraph
Deselect all type	⌘ [Ctrl]+Shift+A
Duplicate column outline and flow text	Option [Alt]+drag column outline with Direct Selection tool
Insert discretionary hyphen	⌘ [Ctrl]+Shift+- (hyphen)
Insert line break	Press Return [Enter] (on keypad)

Table B-25
Paragraph Formatting

Action	Shortcut
Display Paragraph palette	⌘ [Ctrl]+Shift+M
Align paragraph flush left	⌘ [Ctrl]+Shift+L
Align paragraph flush right	⌘ [Ctrl]+Shift+R
Align paragraph flush center	⌘ [Ctrl]+Shift+C
Align paragraph justified	⌘ [Ctrl]+Shift+J
Align paragraph force justified	⌘ [Ctrl]+Shift+F
Display Tab Ruler palette	⌘ [Ctrl]+Shift+T
Align Tab palette to selected paragraph	Click Tab palette size box
Cycle through tab stops	Option [Alt]+click tab stop
Move multiple tab stops	Shift+drag tab stops
Cycle tab measurements	Click

Table B-26
Character Formatting

Action	Shortcut
Display Character palette	⌘ [Ctrl]+T
Highlight font	⌘[Ctrl]+Option [Alt]+Shift+M
Increase type size	⌘ [Ctrl]+Shift+>
Decrease type size	⌘ [Ctrl]+Shift+<
Increase type to next size on menu	⌘ [Ctrl]+Option [Alt]+>
Decrease type to next size on menu	⌘ [Ctrl]+Option [Alt]+<
Highlight size	none
Set leading to Solid (same as pt. size)	Double-click Leading symbol in Character palette
Highlight leading	none
Increase Baseline Shift (Raise)*	Option [Alt]+Shift+↑
Decrease Baseline Shift (Lower)*	Option [Alt]+Shift+↓
Increase Baseline Shift (Raise) ×5*	⌘ [Ctrl]+Option [Alt]+Shift+↑
Decrease Baseline Shift (Lower) ×5*	⌘ [Ctrl]+Option [Alt]+Shift+↓
Reset Baseline Shift to 0	none
Highlight Baseline Shift	none
Kern/Track closer*	Option [Alt]+←
Kern/Track apart*	Option [Alt]+→
Kern/Track closer ×5*	⌘ [Ctrl]+Option [Alt]+←
Kern/Track apart ×5*	⌘ [Ctrl]+Option [Alt]+→
Reset Kerning/Tracking to 0	⌘ [Ctrl]+Shift+Q
Highlight Kerning/Tracking	⌘ [Ctrl]+Option [Alt]+K
Reset Horizontal Scale to 100%	⌘ [Ctrl]+Shift+X

* Value/amount set in Preferences

Color Commands

Table B-27
Color Palette

Action	Shortcut
Show/Hide Color palette	F6 (toggle)
	⌘ [Ctrl]+I (toggle)
Revert to default colors	D (White Fill, Black Stroke; Mac and Windows)
Toggle focus between Fill and Stroke	X
Choose current color in Color palette	, (comma)
Change paint to None	/
Apply to inactive Fill/Stroke (Fill when Stroke is active, Stroke when Fill is active)	Option [Alt]+click in color ramp on Color palette
Apply color to unselected object	Drag color swatch from Color palette to object
Apply color to selected object	Click swatch in Color palette
Copy Paint Style to unselected objects	Click unselected objects with Paint Bucket
Copy Paint Style from any (source) object to all selected objects	Click source object with Eyedropper
Tint process color	Shift+drag any Color palette slider
Cycle through Color modes	Shift+click Color Ramp (Grayscale, CMYK, RGB; Mac and Windows)

Table B-28
Swatches Palette

Action	Shortcut
Show/Hide Swatches palette	F5 (toggle)
Toggle focus between Fill and Stroke	X
Add swatch	Click the New Swatch icon
	Drag from Color or Gradient palette into swatches

Continued

Table B-28 *(continued)*
Swatches Palette

Action	Shortcut
Replace swatch palette into swatches	Option [Alt]+drag from Color or Gradient
Duplicate swatch icon in Swatches palette	Option [Alt]+drag swatch onto New Swatch
Delete swatch	Drag to Trash icon in Swatches palette
	Click Trash icon with swatches selected
Select contiguous swatches	Shift+click first and last swatches
Select noncontiguous swatches	⌘ [Ctrl]+click each swatch
Switch keyboard focus to Swatches palette (for selecting swatches by name as they are typed)	⌘ [Ctrl]+Option [Alt]+click in Swatches palette
Apply color to unselected object	Drag color swatch from Swatches palette to object
Apply color to selected object	Click swatch in Swatches palette

Table B-29
Gradient Palette

Action	Shortcut
Choose current gradient in Gradient palette	. (period)
Show/Hide Gradient palette	F9 (toggle)
Apply swatch to selected color stop on gradient palette	Option [Alt]+click swatch
Add new color stop	Click below gradient ramp
Duplicate color stop	Option [Alt]+drag color stop
Swap color stops	Option[Alt]+drag color stop on top of another
"Suck" color for color stop with Eyedropper	Shift+click with Eyedropper
Reset Gradient to default Black, White	⌘ [Ctrl]+click in Gradient swatch
Apply color to unselected object	Drag color swatch from Gradient palette to object
Apply color to selected object	Click swatch in Gradient palette

Table B-30
Stroke Palette

Action	Shortcut
Show/Hide Stroke palette	F10 (toggle)
Increase/decrease Stroke weight	Highlight Stroke field, use up or down arrows, press Return[Enter] when finished
Increase/decrease Miter amount	Highlight Miter field, use up or down arrows, press Return [Enter] when finished

Other Palettes

Table B-31
Miscellaneous Palette Commands

Action	Shortcut
Collapse/display Palette	Click box in upper-right corner
Cycle through Palette views	Double-click palette tab
Apply settings	Return [Enter]
Apply settings while keeping last text field highlighted	Shift+Return [Enter]
Highlight next text field	Tab
Highlight Previous Text field	Shift+Tab
Highlight any text field	Click label or double-click current value
Increase value by base increment	Highlight field, ↑
Decrease value by base increment	Highlight field, ↓
Increase value by large increment	Highlight field, Shift+↑
Decrease value by large increment	Highlight field, Shift+↓
Combine palettes	Drag palette tab within other palette
Dock palette	Drag palette tab to bottom of other palette
Separate palette	Drag palette tab from current palette

Table B-32
Transform Palette

Action	Shortcut
Show/Hide Transform palette	none
Copy object while transforming	Option [Alt]+Return [Enter]
Scale proportionately	⌘ [Ctrl]+Return [Enter]
Copy object while scaling proportionately	⌘ [Ctrl]+Option [Alt]+Return [Enter]

Table B-33
Layers Palette

Action	Shortcut
Show/Hide Layers palette	F7
New layer	Click New Layer icon
New layer with Options dialog box	Option [Alt]+click New Layer icon
New layer above active layer	⌘ [Ctrl]+Option [Alt]+click New Layer icon
New layer below active layer	⌘ [Ctrl]+click New Layer icon
Duplicate layer(s)	Drag layer(s) to New Layer icon
Change layer order	Drag layers up or down within Layer list
Select all objects on a layer	Option [Alt]+click that layer
Select all objects on several layers	Shift+Option [Alt]+click each layer
Select contiguous layers	Shift+click layers
Select noncontiguous layers	⌘ [Ctrl]+click layers
Move objects to a different layer	Drag colored square to a different layer
Copy objects to a different layer	Option [Alt]+drag color square to a different layer
Hide/Show layer	Click Eyeball icon
View layer while hiding others	Option [Alt]+click Eyeball icon
View layer in Artwork mode	⌘ [Ctrl]+click Eyeball icon
View layer in Preview while others are artwork	⌘ [Ctrl]+Option [Alt]+click Eyeball icon
Lock/Unlock layer	Click Pencil icon
Unlock layer while locking others	Option [Alt]+click Pencil icon

Action	Shortcut
Delete layer	Drag layer to Trash icon
	Select layer and click Trash icon
Delete layer without warning	Option [Alt]+drag layer to Trash icon
	Select layer and Option [Alt]+click trash icon

Miscellaneous Commands

Table B-34 Viewing Shortcuts	
Action	Shortcut
Zoom in	⌘ [Ctrl]++ (plus sign)
	Click with Zoom tool
Zoom out	⌘ [Ctrl]+- (hyphen)
	Option [Alt]+click with Zoom tool
Fit document in Window	⌘ [Ctrl]+0
	Double-click Hand tool
View at actual size (100%)	⌘ [Ctrl]+1
	Double-click Zoom tool
Artwork/Preview mode	⌘ [Ctrl]+Y (toggle)
Preview Selection mode	⌘ [Ctrl]+P+Option [Alt]+Y
Custom View recall	⌘ [Ctrl]+Option [Alt]+Shift+1 through ⌘ [Ctrl]+Option [Alt]+Shift+0
Show/Hide edges	⌘ [Ctrl]+H (toggle)
Show/Hide guides	⌘ [Ctrl]+;
Show/Hide grid	⌘ [Ctrl]+'
Show/Hide rulers	⌘ [Ctrl]+R
Hide selected objects	⌘ [Ctrl]+3
Hide unselected objects	⌘ [Ctrl]+Option [Alt]+3
Show all hidden objects	⌘ [Ctrl]+Shift+3

Continued

Table B-34 *(continued)*

Action	Shortcut
Window mode (normal)	F (when in Full Screen mode in Mac or Windows)
Full Screen mode with menu	F (when in Window mode in Mac or Windows)
Full Screen mode (no menus)	F (when in Full Screen mode with menu in Mac or Windows)

Table B-35
Miscellaneous Commands

Action	Shortcut
Nudge selection*	Arrow keys
See special Status Line categories	Option [Alt]+click status bar (lower-left corner)
Cycle through units	⌘+Ctrl+U (Mac only)
Display Illustrator debug screen	⌘+Option+Ctrl+0 (zero; Mac only)
View anagrams of credits	Option [Alt]+click Illustrator click toolbox
Speed up credits in About box	Option [Alt]
Display context-sensitive menus	Ctrl+click [Right-click]
Highlight last active text field	⌘ [Ctrl]+~ (tilde)

* Value/amount set in Preferences

Generic Dialog Box Commands

Table B-36
Generic Dialog Box Commands

Action	Shortcut
Cancel	Esc
OK (or dark bordered button)	Return [Enter]
Highlight next text field	Tab
Highlight previous text field	Shift+Tab
Highlight any text field	Click label or double-click current value

✦   ✦   ✦

Resources

This appendix lists resources for related products, services, and other information that Illustrator users may find useful. All phone numbers, addresses, and version numbers are subject to change without notice, of course.

Getting answers and information from Adobe

When you can't find an answer to a problem or want to know whether a way exists to do some tedious task more efficiently, call the Adobe Tech Support line.

The main problem with most software support these days is the "not our fault" answer. (Whatever problem or question you have, it isn't the software company's fault.) You don't find this attitude at Adobe. Most of the support staff are polite and they will help even the most befuddled user along, as well as give additional tips and techniques. The main problem with Adobe Tech Support is the difficulty in reaching a human being. When you call, you get routed through a series of questions ("If you are having trouble designing a hang glider with Adobe Illustrator, press 465.") that hardly ever seem to pertain to your particular problem. After a grueling telephone touch-pad question-and-answer session, you are put on hold while some tech people argue about who has to answer the call (and other tech people place bets on how long it will be before you hang up). Actually, we're kidding about this; we're sure they jump from one call to the next without pausing to catch a breath. Adobe now has a special support line that you pay a premium for, which the tech people are the first to answer, and most of them pick up within the first movement of the classical music you're forced to listen to.

If you don't need an answer right away, you can fax Adobe (check the Adobe Web site at www.adobe.com or your Illustrator documentation for the correct phone number). You should get a response within one business day either by phone or return fax. Faxing is great because you can send along your illustration so that the tech people can actually look at it.

Online Resources

Many resources online offer news, support, training, tips, and tricks. Knowing where these sites are can help you find what you are looking for and can be a great help to both beginner and advanced Illustrator users.

 Tip   This resource appendix only scratches the surface of the available resources. To find more resources, try doing a search on Google.com or some other search engine. Be warned that searching for Illustrator will show you sites for individuals that are illustrators by profession. Searching for Adobe Illustrator will limit the occurrence of general illustrators.

About.com

The Graphics Software section of the About.com site includes several valuable Illustrator resource sections including tutorials, plug-ins, and templates. You can find this site by going to `www.about.com` and searching for Illustrator.

Adobe.com

One of the first and best places to start is with Adobe's own Web site. You can find Illustrator specific information at `www.adobe.com/products/illustrator/main.html`. The Adobe site includes files that you can download, including a tryout version of Illustrator 10, a gallery of Illustrator art, reviews, news, and product information sections that describe in detail all the new features found in Illustrator 10. The site also includes a support and training section, which can help you troubleshoot and fine-tune your software.

Designs by Mark

The Designs by Mark Web site is at `www.designsbymark.com`. This site only has a small handful of Illustrator tips that are suitable for beginners. The site also includes tips for other packages such as Photoshop and Flash.

DesktopPublishing.com

The DesktopPublishing.com site includes many graphic and design sections. It also includes an Illustrator message board, which you can find at `http://desktoppublishing.com/illustrator/illustratortalk.html`. The site only has a limited selection of tutorials.

Illustrator-Resources.com

The www.illustrator-resources.com site has a number of separate sections covering Illustrator, InDesign, Photoshop, Freehand, CorelDraw, and other products. The Illustrator section includes links to tutorials, brush and plug-in collections, and inspirational sites.

Illustrator Training

The site at www.illustratortraining.com includes links to many different Illustrator resources including a large list of downloadable PDF tutorial files. Many of these resources are contained on other sites. It also includes links to the Q and A sections from *Adobe Magazine* found on the Adobe site.

Inside Illustrator

Inside Illustrator is a monthly journal created by elementk. They post much of their content online at www.elementkjournals.com/iai. The journal includes articles and tips. The site also offers a pay-per-view archive.

Mike's Sketchpad

You can find Mike's Sketchpad at www.sketchpad.net. This site provides a good quick overview of drawing packages such as Illustrator. This information is useful for beginner users.

Illustrator newsgroups

You can also find a wealth of information or ask questions of other users through the Illustrator newsgroup. The group can be found at alt.graphics.illustrator. Another more general newsgroup for design professional is alt.design.graphics.

Plug-in Resources

Many of the main plug-in manufacturers can also be found online. This section lists a few of the more popular plug-in resources. The Adobe site keeps an up-to-date list of available plug-ins at www.adobe.com/store/plugins/illustrator/main.html.

Avenza

Avenza has produced a product called MAPublisher that can use Geographical Information System (GIS) data and create high-resolution maps. The Web site at www.avenza.com has all the information you will need.

Corel

Corel has obtained the rights and will be distributing the KPT Vector Effects plug-ins created by MetaCreations. You can find information on these plug-ins at http:// newgraphics.corel.com/products/kptvectoreffects.html. This package of plug-ins includes 3D Transform, Shatterbox, Shadowland, Sketch, Warp, Neon, Flare, Emboss, and others.

CValley

CValley's FilterIt plug-in for Illustrator adds many new real-time effects to Illustrator including Emboss, Tiling, Explosion, Reflections, and Galaxy. You can get details from the company Web site at www.cvalley.com.

Hot Door

You know you're doing good if the plug-ins you've developed show up in the next version of the software. Hot Door has created some great Illustrator plug-ins including Transparency for Illustrator 8 and CADtools, which adds CAD functionality to Illustrator. Information on the Hot Door plug-ins is waiting for you at www.hotdoor.com.

Illom

Illom Development has a product named Toolbox 1 that includes features to help improve the productivity of Illustrator. Information on this product is online at www.illom.se.

Sapphire Innovations

Sapphire Innovations has created two plug-in sets for Illustrator. These two sets contain Sapphire Pack, which includes advanced options for working with multiple paths to create spirals, grids, stars, pie slices, and more. The second set of plug-ins, called Layers, work specifically with layers for creating layered animations and color effects. The Web site at www.sapphire-innovations.com has information on these plug-ins.

Vertigo

Vertigo creates several plug-ins for Illustrator including PopArt, Dizzy, and 3D Words. These plug-ins can add depth to flat shapes, converting them into 3D objects. Find information on these plug-ins at www.vertigo3d.com.

Virtual Mirror

Vector Studio, an advanced set of new features for Illustrator, is available from Virtual Mirror. Vector Studio includes features for working with glass, creating gradient textures, using morph brushes, and editing with an envelope mesh. Virtual Mirror also produces other plug-ins such as TextureWorks and LiveAction. Information on these products is a click away at www.virtualmirror.com.

Zaxwerks

Zaxwerks' product, 3D Invigorator, is designed to create 3D objects within Illustrator. You can get information on this product at www.zaxwerks.com.

✦   ✦   ✦

Installing Illustrator 10

The installation of Illustrator is pretty straightforward. If you've installed any software recently on your Macintosh or Windows system, you're already familiar with the installation process. This appendix provides some additional information you may find helpful when installing Illustrator. The first section deals with installing Illustrator for Macintosh, and the second section addresses installing Illustrator for Windows.

System Requirements for Macintosh

To run Adobe Illustrator 10 on a Macintosh, your computer system needs to meet certain requirements. Of these, the CPU and RAM are the most important.

The minimum system requirements for Illustrator 10 for Macintosh are

- ✦ A PowerPC G3, G4 or G4 dual processor
- ✦ MacOS versions 9.1, 9.2, or Mac OS X version 10.1
- ✦ CD-ROM drive
- ✦ 128MB of RAM installed
- ✦ 180MB of free hard-disk space for installation
- ✦ Video card supporting a resolution of 800×600

Illustrator 10 needs a minimum of 128MB of memory to run efficiently. What this means is that your system should have *at the very least* 64MB of RAM total. A good way to check how much RAM you have available for Illustrator is to restart your system. After the desktop appears, go to the Apple in the upper-left corner and pull down About This Mac. This will tell you the total amount of RAM installed on your computer.

Installing Illustrator 10 for Macintosh

Follow these steps to install Illustrator on your Mac:

1. Remove all extensions except the ones needed to run your CD-ROM drive (for OS 9, use a startup manager to facilitate this). For OS X, you need to have the Classic interface installed.

2. Insert and open the Illustrator installation CD-ROM and double-click the Install Me icon.

3. The Adobe Welcome screen is displayed. Click the Next button and select the Adobe Illustrator 10 installation button. It will ask for the serial number during installation.

   Illustrator installs itself in a matter of minutes. It's actually faster and easier to install Illustrator this way and then remove items you don't want than to go through and do a Custom Install of Illustrator.

Note For OS 9, Illustrator installs ATM 4 into your System Folder, requiring you to restart after installation.

4. OS 10 will not require that you reboot. You can now run Illustrator.

Take a moment to register your copy of Illustrator. This is a good thing to do, as it provides Adobe with your contact information regarding special deals and upgrades.

System Requirements for Windows

To run Illustrator 10 on a PC, your computer system needs to meet certain requirements. Of these, the CPU, installed RAM, and operating system are the most important.

The minimum system requirements for Illustrator 10 for Windows are

+ Intel Pentium II, III or IV processor
+ Microsoft Windows 98, Windows ME, Windows 2000, or Windows XP operating system

Note If using Windows 2000, make sure that Service Pack 2 is installed. Also note that Illustrator will work under Windows 95, but it is not supported by Adobe.

+ CD-ROM drive
+ 128MB of RAM installed
+ 180MB of free hard-disk space for installation
+ Video card supporting a resolution of 800×600

Adobe, however, recommends

✦ Pentium III or greater processor

✦ High-resolution 24-bit video display card

✦ 256MB or more of RAM installed

Personally, we recommend a 1.2 GHz or better Pentium. Anything slower starts to slow Illustrator down. Also, if you are using lots of placed bitmap images (or raster-izing at high resolution within Illustrator), you'll want to have more RAM on hand. For slower systems, you should use Outline mode extensively.

Installing Illustrator 10 for Windows

Follow these steps to install Illustrator in Windows:

1. Insert the Adobe Illustrator 10 CD-ROM. Autoplay causes the Welcome screen to appear automatically. If Autoplay doesn't start, double-click the Setup icon. Click the Next button to get to the Installation screen. With the Installation button highlighted, click the Adobe Illustrator 10 button.

   The Install Wizard prepares the installation (this takes a while on slower sys-tems). One of the first steps of the installation Wizard is to select the country. This sets the language of the licensing agreement, which will be displayed.

2. If you agree with the licensing agreement, click the Accept button to accept it.

   After accepting the agreement, you will have the choice to install a Typical, Compact, or Custom setup. Selecting Typical installs the main features. Additional features will need to be reinstalled later if needed. The Compact option only installs those files needed to run the program using a minimum amount of hard drive space. The Custom option lets you specifically select which items to include in your installation. Item categories include the Illustrator 10 application, Illustrator Plug-ins, File Format Plug-ins, Photoshop Filters and Effects, and Brush Libraries. If you select a category and click the Change button, then you can select additional specific categories. Using the Custom option you can install only the components that you need.

3. Select the installation options you prefer, and then press the Next button.

4. Enter your name, title, and serial number, and continue pressing Next until Illustrator has installed.

5. Once the installation is complete, the Installation Wizard asks if you want to restart your computer.

Note   As part of the installation, an SVG Viewer is installed as a plug-in for your default Web browser. This viewer lets you view SVG files within your browser.

After installation, Illustrator provides a method for you to register at that time. This is a good thing to do, as it provides Adobe with your contact information regarding special deals and upgrades.

After the installation is complete, double-click the Illustrator 10 icon (or choose Illustrator 10 from the Start ⇨ Programs menu) to run Illustrator.

Summary

Before you can run the software, you'll need to install the software. Adobe provides a simple procedure to do this. It is also important to make sure your computer meets or exceeds the minimum system requirements.

✦   ✦   ✦

Index

Symbols and Numerics

Continued

Continued

Continued

Continued

Continued

Continued

Continued